The United States Constitution

The United States Constitution
Law, Policy, and Society

Laura E. Little
James G. Schmidt Professor of Law
Temple University School of Law

To contact Customer Service, e-mail customer.service@aspenpublishing.com, call 1-800-950-5259, or mail correspondence to:

Aspen Publishing
Attn: Order Department
1 Wall Street
Burlington, MA 01803

Cover image: iStock.com/La Cassette Bleue

Printed in the United States of America.

1 2 3 4 5 6 7 8 9 0

ISBN 978-1-5438-5757-3

Library of Congress Cataloging-in-Publication Data
Names: Little, Laura E., 1957-author.
Title: The United States Constitution : law, policy, and society / Laura E.
    Little, James G. Schmidt Professor of Law, Temple University School of Law.
Description: 1e. | Burlington : Aspen Publishing, 2024. | Includes
    bibliographical references and index. | Summary: "This book lays out an
    overview of broad Constitutional issues and provides deeper analysis and
    discussions of the Constitutional controversies that affect Americans
    today"—Provided by publisher.
Identifiers: LCCN 2023048242 (print) | LCCN 2023048243 (ebook) | ISBN
    9781543857573 (hardcover) | ISBN 9781543857580 (epub)
Subjects: LCSH: United States. Constitution. | Constitutional law—United
    States. | Judicial power—United States. | Legislative power—United
    States. | Executive power—United States.
Classification: LCC KF4550.L573 2024 (print) | LCC KF4550 (ebook) | DDC
    342.73—dc23/eng/20231016
LC record available at https://lccn.loc.gov/2023048242
LC ebook record available at https://lccn.loc.gov/2023048243

About Aspen Publishing

Aspen Publishing is a leading provider of educational content and digital learning solutions to law schools in the U.S. and around the world. Aspen provides best-in-class solutions for legal education through authoritative textbooks, written by renowned authors, and breakthrough products such as Connected eBooks, Connected Quizzing, and PracticePerfect.

The Aspen Casebook Series (famously known among law faculty and students as the "red and black" casebooks) encompasses hundreds of highly regarded textbooks in more than eighty disciplines, from large enrollment courses, such as Torts and Contracts to emerging electives such as Sustainability and the Law of Policing. Study aids such as the *Examples & Explanations* and the *Emanuel Law Outlines* series, both highly popular collections, help law students master complex subject matter.

Major products, programs, and initiatives include:

- **Connected eBooks** are enhanced digital textbooks and study aids that come with a suite of online content and learning tools designed to maximize student success. Designed in collaboration with hundreds of faculty and students, the Connected eBook is a significant leap forward in the legal education learning tools available to students.
- **Connected Quizzing** is an easy-to-use formative assessment tool that tests law students' understanding and provides timely feedback to improve learning outcomes. Delivered through CasebookConnect.com, the learning platform already used by students to access their Aspen casebooks, Connected Quizzing is simple to implement and integrates seamlessly with law school course curricula.
- **PracticePerfect** is a visually engaging, interactive study aid to explain commonly encountered legal doctrines through easy-to-understand animated videos, illustrative examples, and numerous practice questions. Developed by a team of experts, PracticePerfect is the ideal study companion for today's law students.
- The **Aspen Learning Library** enables law schools to provide their students with access to the most popular study aids on the market across all of their courses. Available through an annual subscription, the online library consists of study aids in e-book, audio, and video formats with full text search, note-taking, and highlighting capabilities.
- Aspen's **Digital Bookshelf** is an institutional-level online education bookshelf, consolidating everything students and professors need to ensure success. This program ensures that every student has access to affordable course materials from day one.
- **Leading Edge** is a community centered on thinking differently about legal education and putting those thoughts into actionable strategies. At the core of the program is the Leading Edge Conference, an annual gathering of legal education thought leaders looking to pool ideas and identify promising directions of exploration.

To my wonderful family and to all the Constitutional Law students who have taught me over the years.

Summary of Contents

Contents		*xi*
Preface		*xvii*
Acknowledgments		*xix*
Credits		*xxi*
About the Author		*xxv*

1	Introduction	1

PART A — Structure of Government
Federalism and the Federal Government · 31

2	Federalism: Sharing of State and Federal Power	33
3	Powers of the Federal Courts	51
4	Powers of Congress	89
5	Powers of the President	129

PART B — Individual Rights · 179

6	The First Amendment: Basic Freedom of Communication Principles	181
7	The First Amendment: Selected Topics in Humor, Hate Speech, and Religion	239
8	The Second Amendment: The Right to Bear Arms	313
9	Introduction to the Fourteenth Amendment	347
10	Racial Discrimination	357
11	Women's Equality Rights	405

Introduction to Chapters
12, 13, and 14   435

12	Reproductive Rights	437
13	Sexual Freedoms	491
14	Marriage	517
	Epilogue	547

The Text of the U.S. Constitution   549

Chronological Tables of
U.S. Supreme Court Justices   567

Brief Biographies of Selected U.S. Supreme Court Justices   571

Glossary   583

Table of Cases   593

Index   595

Contents

Preface   xvii
Acknowledgments   xix
Credits   xxi
About the Author   xxv

Chapter 1: Introduction   1

A. The History of the Constitution's Creation   1
B. Basics of Understanding Current Constitutional Law as Interpreted
    by the U.S. Supreme Court   5
    1. Composition and Operation of the U.S. Supreme Court   5
        a. Composition of the Court   5
        b. How a Case Gets to the Court   8
        c. Tracing a Case Through the U.S. Supreme Court   10
    2. Basics of Reading a U.S. Supreme Court Opinion   16
        a. How to Interpret an Opinion   18
    3. Approaches to Constitutional Interpretation   22

Structure of Government
Federalism and the Federal Government

PART A

Chapter 2: Federalism: Sharing of State and Federal Power   33

A. Constitutional Roots of Federalism   33
B. United States Constitution Article VI   34
    Bond v. United States   41

Chapter 3: Powers of the Federal Courts   51

A. Basics of Article III   51
B. Judicial Review   54
    Marbury v. Madison   57
C. Justiciability   64
    1. Standing: Regulating Who Can Bring a Lawsuit   67
        Elk Grove Unified School District v. Newdow   68
    2. The Doctrines Restricting When a Court Can Adjudicate a Case   73
        a. Ripeness   74
        b. Mootness   74
    3. Political Question Doctrine: Regulating What May
        Be the Subject of a Lawsuit   76
        Rucho v. Common Cause   79

Chapter 4: Powers of Congress   89

A. Basics of Article I   89
B. Commerce Power   91
    Wickard v. Filburn   93
    United States v. Lopez   99
    United States v. Morrison   114
C. Taxing and Spending Power   121
    South Dakota v. Dole   122
D. Tying Congress's Power Together   126

Chapter 5: Powers of the President   129

A. Introduction to Article II   129
B. Models of Executive Power   130
    Youngstown Sheet & Tube Co. v. Sawyer   130
C. Foreign Affairs   143
    Zivotofsky v. Kerry   144
    Korematsu v. United States   155
    Hamdi v. Rumsfeld   163

Individual Rights

Chapter 6: The First Amendment: Basic Freedom of Communication Principles 181

A. Freedom of Expression Values: Explication and Critique 182
B. Content-Based and Content-Neutral Regulations 185
  1. Identifying Content-Based Regulations 186
  2. Content-Neutral Restrictions: Time, Place, and Manner
    Restrictions 187
C. The Importance of Political Debate and Protest Versus the Need
  to Protect Public Safety 188
  1. Speech That Incites Violence 188
    Brandenburg v. Ohio 190
  2. Symbolic Speech 194
    United States v. O'Brien 196
    Texas v. Johnson 201
  3. Freedom of the Press 208
    New York Times Co. v. Sullivan 210
D. School Interests in Imparting Moral Values and Substantive
  Knowledge Versus Encouraging Creative Thinking, Personal
  Autonomy, and Free Expression for Students 216
    Tinker v. Des Moines Independent Community School District 216
    Morse v. Frederick 220
    Mahanoy Area School District v. B.L. 224
E. The Public Forum Doctrine 230
  1. Traditional Public Forums 232
  2. Designated Public Forums 233
  3. Limited Public Forums 233
  4. Nonpublic Forums 234

Chapter 7: The First Amendment: Selected Topics in Humor, Hate Speech, and Religion 239

A. The Benefits of Humor and Entertainment Versus Protecting Against
  Corruption of Societal Fabric and the Pain of Individual Offense 239
  1. Courts Become Comedy Critics When Regulating Humor 240
    Hustler Magazine v. Falwell 241

Vereinigung Bildender Künstler (VBK) v. Austria   249
  Matal v. Tam   259
 2. Muzzling the Stand-up Comedian   267
  Federal Communications Commission v. Pacifica Foundation   268
 3. Other Ways the Law Regulates Humor   275
B. Free Expression Rights to Express Hate and Other Offense
Versus Human Dignity   277
 R.A.V. v. St. Paul   278
 Virginia v. Black   285
 Elonis v. United States   292
C. The Religion Clauses   301
 Kennedy v. Bremerton   303

Chapter 8: The Second Amendment: The Right to Bear Arms   313

District of Columbia v. Heller   315
New York State Rifle & Pistol Association, Inc. v. Bruen   332

Chapter 9: Introduction to the Fourteenth Amendment   347

A. Background and Components of the Amendment   347
 1. The Slaughterhouse Cases   348
B. The State Action Requirement   352

Chapter 10: Racial Discrimination   357

A. The Status of Slaves or Former Slaves as Citizens   357
 Dred Scott v. Sanford   359
B. Separation of the Races   364
 Plessy v. Ferguson   366
 Brown v. Board of Education   371
C. Affirmative Action   385
D. Voting Rights   387
 Shelby County, Alabama v. Holder   388

Chapter 11: Women's Equality Rights   405

A. Development of Recognition of Women's Rights   405
    1. Early Years   405
        Bradwell v. People of the State of Illinois   407
    2. The Nineteenth Amendment   417
B. Intermediate Scrutiny   422
        United States v. Virginia   423
C. The Equal Rights Amendment   431

Introduction to Chapters 12, 13, and 14

Chapter 12: Reproductive Rights   437

Griswold v. Connecticut   438
Roe v. Wade   452
Dobbs v. Jackson Women's Health Organization   464

Chapter 13: Sexual Freedoms   491

Bowers v. Hardwick   492
Romer et al. v. Evans et al.   497
Lawrence et al. v. Texas   504

Chapter 14: Marriage   517

Loving v. Virginia   518
Obergefell v. Hodges   527

Epilogue   547

xvi Contents

The Text of the U.S. Constitution   549

Chronological Tables of U.S. Supreme Court Justices   567

Brief Biographies of Selected U.S. Supreme Court Justices   571

Glossary   583

Table of Cases   593

Index   595

Preface

Constitutional law is the perfect vehicle for exploring the dynamics of government, the relationship between citizens and government, the status of the United States in the rest of the world, and the unique interaction between the Constitution and culture. In other words, constitutional law provides great raw material for engaging curious minds trying to figure out how the big wheels turn.

This book covers classic topics and themes of constitutional knowledge such as federalism, individual rights, and separation of powers. That said, it does so through the means of topics central to the lives of U.S. citizens today. Examples of these current topics include the following:

- Do existing interpretations of the Constitution's freedom of expression principles adequately handle regulation by privately owned entities such as X (formerly Twitter) and Facebook concerning offensive or false speech?
- Hate speech is one of the most troublesome problems of human civilization. How does the U.S. Constitution handle this issue? Does it do a good job? How does the case law in the United States compare with that of other countries?
- How do U.S. Supreme Court cases reinforce existing racial, class, and gender stratifications? Are there decisions that challenged and attempted to change the existing hierarchy? If so, were the decisions successful in doing so? To what extent do individual decisions reproduce and reinforce superior power of one group over another?
- How do Supreme Court cases regulate popular culture? How does popular culture influence Supreme Court cases?
- What on earth does a Supreme Court case with weird facts from 1803 (*Marbury v. Madison*) have to do with whether a state can regulate your BB gun or whether a high school can tell students what they can post on Instagram off campus and after school hours?
- Has the Constitution helped or hindered the struggle in the United States to overcome the vestiges of slavery?

A Constitutional Law course is to legal understanding what an Anatomy and Physiology course is to medical understanding. Both disciplines are octopus-like, encompassing an ungainly swath of human existence. This book does not encompass all constitutional law. After setting the stage with materials on the operation of the U.S. Supreme Court and instructing on techniques for accurate reading of Supreme Court decisions, the book presents a curated selection of key topics, each organized around a central theme.

The major topics include:

1. The role of each branch of government and the separation of powers.
2. The relationship between the state and federal governments.
3. The special protection afforded to freedom of communication.
4. The U.S. Supreme Court's approach to regulating other rights important to U.S. citizens: the right to bear arms, reproductive freedom, racial discrimination, LGBTQIA+ rights, and women's rights.

As you make your way through these diverse topics, look for shared angles with cases in other chapters. Questions you might ask in each context include: (1) How does the historical context for a case explain the result of the case? (2) Do neutral constitutional principles exist or does the discussion of constitutional rules simply serve to mask hidden agendas? (3) How do the rules that are articulated in different contexts resemble each other? Questions such as these not only help to tie the various topics together, but they also bring out the deeper meaning in the cases. In that way, you can avoid feeling enmeshed in a complex jumble of rules. You might even find fun in the material.

To give you a preview, the book features quirky historical cases, protests on topics that are likely to touch your heart, popular culture references, and unsavory case facts. Each of the major cases in the book is carefully edited and presented under the heading "From the Bench." Background on these cases and behind-the-scenes details appear in sections marked "Behind the Curtain." These "Behind the Curtain" features share in-depth descriptions of intrigue that occurred in the background of the case and shed light on the influences explaining the case's qualities. Your professor may choose to use the "Questions for Discussion" for in-class exchanges, but even if these questions are not used in class, they point you to the core meaning of the case. To provide further understanding, hypotheticals flagged with the question "What's Your Learned Opinion?" offer factual scenarios inviting you to take the rules of law and reasoning of a major case and apply them in a new context. Evaluating these factual scenarios will not only help you remember the case, but will illustrate the strength, parameters, and ambiguities of the case. Finally, each chapter ends with review questions enabling you to test your knowledge of the chapter's details.

Read on. Hope that you enjoy the ride!

Acknowledgments

I am grateful for the able assistance of many talented Temple Law students: Joe Salaman, Lilli Friedman, Zachary Bailey, Daisy Mase, Joseph Campbell, Aaron Freedman, Samantha Rodgers, Emily Zeidman, Darren Jay Kaplan, Jr., Catherine Baldwin, Chelsea Sissom, Amelia Hardy, Andrew Rosen, Amanda Januszewski, and Mayce Van. I am very lucky to have you all in my corner. I also benefitted from the knowledge and careful guidance of my editor, Nicholas T. Lasoff.

Portions of the freedom of communication and religion clauses discussions in Chapters 6 and 7 were adapted from my previous work reflected in Laura E. Little, *First Amendment Examples and Explanations* (Aspen 2021). Portions of Chapter 7 were also adapted from my studies of the intersection of law and humor, such as reflected in Laura Little, *Guilty Pleasures: Comedy and Law in America* (Oxford 2019).

Credits

Images

"BONG HiTs 4 JESUS" banner on display at the First Amendment Museum in Augusta, Maine. Photograph. Wikimedia Commons.

"Silent Sentinels" picketing at the White House gate, January 1917. Photograph. Library of Congress.

"School Segregation Banned." Headline. The Topeka State Journal. Courtesy of the Kansas Historical Society

Chief Justice William Rehnquist. Photograph. World History Archive/Alamy Stock Photo.

Display of handguns. Photograph. Wikimedia Commons. Licensed under CC BY-SA 4.0, https://creativecommons.org/licenses/by-sa/4.0/deed.en.

Fred T. Korematsu. Photograph. Courtesy of the family of Fred T. Korematsu/ Wikimedia Commons. Licensed under CC BY-SA 2.0, https://creativecommons .org/licenses/by-sa/2.0/deed.en.

Gun-free school zone sign. Photograph. undefined undefined/iStock Photo.

Heed Their Rising Voices, 1960. Advertisement. The New York Times. National Archives.

Hogs in the Slaughterhouse. Illustration. Courtesy of The Historic New Orleans Collection.

Hustler Magazine parody featuring an unauthorized use of Jerry Falwell's publicity photograph. Copyright © 1983 Hustler Magazine, Inc.

Klansmen in robes with burning cross, January 1958. Photograph. Courtesy of the State Archives of North Carolina.

A Peep into the Antifederal Club, 1793. Historical Society of Pennsylvania.

Richard and Mildred Loving. Photograph. AP Photo.

Richard Hodges, Former Director of the Ohio Health Department. Photograph. Courtesy of Richard Hodges.

The Slants. Photograph. Reprinted with permission from Simon Tam.

Supervised shooting of handgun. Photograph. Wikimedia Commons.

Supreme Court Conference Room, ca. 1975. Photograph. Collection of the Supreme Court of the United States.

Ames, Ezra. *Gouverneur Morris*, 1817. Avery Library, New York. Wikimedia Commons.

Barnes, Elvert. James Obergefell and Attorney Al Gerhardstein at the 2015 Marriage Equality Decision Day Rally. Photograph. Wikimedia Commons. Licensed under CC BY-SA 2.0, https://creativecommons.org/licenses/ by-sa/2.0/deed.en.

Charles, William. *The Present State of Our Country*, 1806-1820. C. W. McAlpin Collection. The New York Public Library.

Draft card burning. Photograph. Keystone Press/Alamy Stock Photo.

Gay, Eric. A woman stands among 15 crosses that stand on a hill above Columbine High School in Littleton, Colorado. Photograph. AP Photo/Eric Gay.

Inman, Henry. *Chief Justice John Marshall*, 1832. Virginia State Library, Richmond, Virginia.

Jenkins, R. Michael. Ruth Bader Ginsburg at her confirmation hearing in 1993. Photograph. Library of Congress.

Kaster, Carolyn. Menachem Zivotofsky and his father Ari Zivotofsky, 2017. Photograph. AP Photo/Carolyn Kaster.

Lange, Dorothea. First-graders, some of Japanese ancestry, at the Weill public school, San Francisco, pledging allegiance to the United States flag, 1942. Photograph. Library of Congress.

Masker, Stephen. Justice Scalia Testifying Before the House Judiciary Committee. Photograph. Wikimedia Commons.

McCoy, Shane T. Detainees at Camp X-Ray at Guantanamo Bay, Cuba. Photograph. Wikimedia Commons.

McLaughlin, H. Lockwood. Cadets in training. Photograph. Copyright © 2022 Virginia Military Institute.

Mehta, Kunal. Pro-abortion protesters in Foley Square, New York City, May 2022. Wikimedia Commons. Licensed under CC BY-SA 4.0, https://creativecommons .org/licenses/by-sa/4.0/deed.en.

Nicastro, Brent. Michael Newdow. Photograph. Courtesy of Brent Nicastro.

O'Halloran, Thomas J. Thurgood Marshall. Photograph. U.S. News & World Report Magazine. Library of Congress.

Peale, Rembrandt. *Thomas Jefferson*, 1801. White House Historical Association/ Wikimedia Commons.

Rattanataipob, Sumruay. The earth's penumbra during a lunar eclipse. Photograph. Sumruay Rattanataipob/Shutterstock.

Schultze, Louis. Portrait of Dred Scott. Courtesy of the Missouri Historical Society, via Wikimedia Commons.

Shankbone, David. Derrick Bell. Photograph. Wikimedia Commons. License under CC BY-SA 3.0, https://creativecommons.org/licenses/by-sa/3.0/.

Seidenstein, Joel. Attorney William Kunstler with Defendant Gregory Lee Johnson Circa 1989. Wikimedia Commons. Licensed under CC-BY-SA-3.0, https://creativecommons.org/licenses/by-sa/3.0/.

Spurgeon, Mary Lou Filbrun. Roscoe C. Filburn and his wheat. Photograph.

Strovato, Michael. Tyron Garner and John Geddes Lawrence. Photograph. AP Photo/Michael Stravato.

Tisdale, Elkanah. Original cartoon of "The Gerry-Mander," 1812. Originally published in the Boston Centinel. Wikimedia Commons.

Trumbull, John. *Alexander Hamilton*, 1806. National Portrait Gallery, Washington D.C. Wikimedia Commons.

The Federal Pillars, 1788. Library of Congress.

Texts

About the Author

A longtime member of the Temple Law School faculty, Professor Laura E. Little specializes in constitutional law, First Amendment law, conflict of laws, and federal courts. She teaches, lectures, and consults internationally on these subjects and is routinely engaged in training judges as well as speeches at academic and judicial conferences. She is the author of numerous books and articles, including a sole-authored casebook, *Conflict of Laws* (2d ed. Aspen Publishing, 2018); two treatises: *Federal Courts* and *First Amendment*, both in Aspen Publishing's *Examples and Explanations* series; and *Guilty Pleasures: Law and Comedy in America* (Oxford 2019). Among her many awards for teaching and scholarship are several law school awards, a regional Lindback Award for teaching excellence, and Temple's highest award for teaching, the University Great Teacher Award. In 2014, the American Law Institute appointed Professor Little to serve as Associate Reporter, Restatement (Third) of Conflict of Laws.

Before entering academia, Professor Little practiced law in Philadelphia, where she litigated commercial cases and represented the print media in First Amendment cases. Prior to her law practice, Professor Little served as a law clerk to Chief Justice William H. Rehnquist, Supreme Court of the United States (October Term 1986) and Judge James Hunter, III of the U.S. Court of Appeals for the Third Circuit (1985–1986). Professor Little has several times taught in Temple's programs in Tokyo, Japan, and Rome, Italy. She has served as a visiting professor at the University of Sydney (Australia), and University College of Cork (Ireland). She has lectured frequently throughout China. Professor Little's scholarship has a strong interdisciplinary character, integrating law, social science, and humanities. She has traveled extensively throughout the world lecturing on law and humor and has written several studies on how legal doctrines regulate various forms of comedy.

Introduction

A. The History of the Constitution's Creation

The historical outlines of the U.S. Constitution's creation have a key role in fashioning the contours of the current U.S. constitutional process. One could start describing that history as early as June 1215, when King John signed the Magna Carta, declaring that the sovereign was not above the law and enunciating the basic liberties of "free men." For present purposes, however, a student of U.S. Constitutional history might reasonably start centuries later, in 1776, with the Declaration of Independence—followed two years later by the Articles of Confederation—and yet another three years later, when all 13 of the original colonies ratified the Articles.

The Articles of Confederation created a central government for the 13 colonies but omitted many governmental powers. For example, the Articles did not include the power to declare war, borrow or coin money, impose taxes, appoint a commander in chief, enter into a treaty, and perhaps equally important, regulate commerce among the states. As a consequence of this latter omission, the states enacted tariffs that obstructed commerce with sister states, thereby Balkanizing the country. Each of these omitted powers inspired a group of men (yes, men) to convene in 1787 and draft a new constitution establishing the central government of the Union. (The men who attended the convention are often called delegates or Framers of the Constitution.) To this day, the absence of key provisions in the Articles of Confederation substantially informs how the U.S. Supreme Court interprets parts of our modern-day Constitution, especially those governmental powers included in our Constitution but omitted from the Articles of Confederation.

Because the drafting convention resulted in our current Constitution, judges and scholars place deep significance on the record of the debates at the convention. One will see snippets of these records invoked by opinion writers for the

U.S. Supreme Court for more than 200 years of opinions. The key votes and maneuvers during the convention appear in the official journal of the Constitutional Convention. Additionally, a prominent delegate, James Madison, individually took diligent and copious notes. Madison's notes are often quoted in scholarship, parties' filings, and formal opinions. As with any collective body, the personal intentions of the 55 delegates who actually attended, drafted, and voted on the document were likely varied according to the delegates' individual knowledge and preferences. Each individual had his own view, his own goals, and his own intent. That reality, however, does not stop us from relying on the written record. As you read the edited versions of the Supreme Court opinions in this book, consider the following question: Are the Justices "cherry-picking" only those parts of constitutional history supporting their individual positions?

Several key parts of the convention's debates deserve highlighting. First, the so-called Virginia Plan called for the horizontal separation of powers (separation among legislative, executive, and judiciary). The plan fortified this concept with the notion of checks and balances, the core premise being that authority must be divided so that no governmental branch has the sole power to accomplish important actions. Instead, the judgment and approval of another branch stand as necessary components of accomplishing that action. Little disagreement over the separation of powers and the checks and balances system appears in the convention records. From the record, the consensus easily coalesced on the Constitution's main structure beginning with three articles, each addressing a different branch: Article 1 (the legislature), Article II (the executive), and Article III (the judiciary).

Also apparently subject to little disagreement was the vision of a bicameral legislature: two houses of Congress. Disagreement readily emerged, however, around the details of representation in these houses. This issue reflected a clash between states with small populations and states with large populations. If all states participated in both houses of Congress on the basis of population, the small states perceived they would be at a grave disadvantage. A compromise emerged: The "people" (represented by population) would directly elect the representatives in the lower house (the House of Representatives). For the upper house (the Senate), however, two senators would represent each state, irrespective of population. No bill could pass unless a majority of the Senate and the House of Representatives voted to approve the bill.

A related division among the represented states, a division that caused North–South tensions, related to race: Should slaves be counted as part of the population? Ultimately, the delegates reached a compromise on this point: only three-fifths of the slaves should be counted for the purpose of apportionment. So as not to name the elephant in the room, however, slaves were not called slaves, but "other persons" instead. Importantly, the result of the Three-Fifths Clause was that the slave-owning South was overrepresented in the House and therefore in the Electoral College. The Electoral College is discussed in more detail later.

Other compromises on slavery that appear in the Constitution drive home the original sin on which our country was founded. For example, the Constitution states in Article I, §9, cl. 1 (again using euphemistic language) that the importation and migration of slaves should be allowed, and a tax or duty may be imposed on importation, so long as the sum was not exorbitant. Here is the language:

> The Migration or Importation of Such Persons as any of the States now existing shall think proper to admit, shall not be prohibited by the Congress prior to the Year one thousand eight hundred and eight, but a Tax or duty may be imposed on such Importation, not exceeding ten dollars for each Person.

Finally on the issue of slavery is the Fugitive Slave Clause (Art. IV, §2, cl. 3), which the framers inserted in the Constitution to discourage those who were inclined to provide safe havens for runaways. This clause states that "no person held to service or labor" would be released from bondage in the event they escaped to a free state.

Another important debate concerned the power of the federal judiciary. Consensus ultimately formed around the idea that the judiciary should include a supreme court, independent of the other branches. Disagreement, however, surrounded the question of whether the national judicial system should include lower courts. One group of delegates believed that lower federal courts were needed to enforce federal laws; another group feared that lower federal courts would usurp state court power. Again, a compromise resolved this clash. The Framers punted to the legislature: Article III, §1 states that "the judicial power of the United States" may include "such inferior Courts as the Congress may from time to time ordain and establish."

Finally, the convention delegates strongly debated the method of selecting the President. Given the division between small and large states, disagreement took hold over whether a direct election by the people should select the President. The compromise on this issue created the electoral college system, under which each state enjoyed a number of electors equal to the number of members for the state represented in the U.S. House of Representatives and U.S. Senate. Delegates justified this system on the belief that the electors would be better informed on issues than the mass of voters themselves.

The constitutional design included two types of separation of powers: separation among the branches of the federal government (which was also reflected in state governments) as well as separation between the state governments and the federal government (see Figure 1.1). This latter separation was in part important for navigating issues of slavery as well as the tension between small and large states. Horizontal separation of powers refers to the separation among the branches of a single sovereign entity (such as the federal government or a state government, individually). Vertical separation of powers refers to the separation between two sovereign powers (such as the separation of governmental powers over U.S. citizens divided between the federal government and the state governments). This dual vision of separation of powers is often deemed an important innovation of the U.S. experiment and is frequently attributed to Benjamin Franklin.

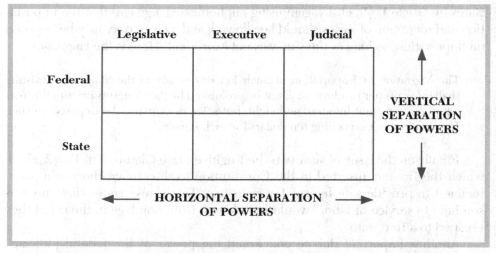

Figure 1.1   Our Federalist System

QUESTION FOR DISCUSSION

1.1   The creation of a vertical separation of powers and a horizontal separation of powers sounds complicated. Is this complication justified? What exactly might the Framers have been worried about when they created two systems of power separation?

A final point of contention worth highlighting concerned whether the Constitution should enunciate specific individual civil liberties. Delegate Alexander Hamilton advocated against including language protecting individuals against government. Hamilton argued that government had no power to infringe civil liberties and that a document establishing the powers of government need not enunciate what powers the government may not have. To do otherwise might suggest that the only restraints on government were those mentioned.

The text of the original Constitution shows that Hamilton's view prevailed, but not for long: The nation soon adopted a bill of rights—in the form of the first ten amendments to the Constitution—in 1791.

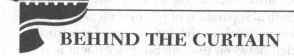

BEHIND THE CURTAIN

During the convention, Thomas Jefferson served as a trade commissioner, and eventually foreign minister, in Paris, representing American interests. When he heard news about the convention, he made plain his agreement with the necessity of a stronger federal government, but expressed distress that the delegates were conducting the proceedings in secrecy. Writing to John Adams in August 1787, Jefferson regretted that the convention would set "so abominable a precedent as that of tying up the tongues of their members." As a foreshadowing of the First Amendment and current precedent interpreting that amendment, Jefferson mourned that the delegates' secrecy policy showed "ignorance of the value of public discussions." Nonetheless, he celebrated the choice of delegates, describing them as "an assembly of demigods."

Thomas Jefferson's official presidential portrait by Rembrandt Peale (1801). *White House Collection/White House Historical Association.*

B. Basics of Understanding Current Constitutional Law as Interpreted by the U.S. Supreme Court

1. Composition and Operation of the U.S. Supreme Court

The first crucial elements for understanding the basics of current constitutional law are details surrounding the Supreme Court's membership and operating systems.

a. Composition of the Court

The Constitution does not designate the number of justices to serve on the Supreme Court. The number has fluctuated over the years but has stayed at nine since 1869. The Constitution does prescribe, however, that the President nominate U.S. Supreme Court Justices, who must then be confirmed by the Senate.

The job of a Supreme Court Justice is generally a treasured prize for the recipient: A Justice gets an appointment for life; the job is regarded as the apex of the legal profession; Justices enjoy high rank within the protocol of hierarchy and respect; they can make an important mark on the great body of the law; and they get a place in history. To whom do they owe this honor? First and foremost, the honor goes to the President who picked them out of the sea of qualified candidates. Is it any wonder that Justices are often identified in newspaper reports on cases as an appointee of a particular president—even years after their appointment? Why would that be a significant way to describe a Justice? Could it be because a U.S. Supreme Court appointment is the type of benefit for which one's parents and teachers make clear the social or moral duty of expressing gratitude toward the person who bestowed the benefit? Could it be that Presidents thought they were "getting something" that could work to their personal, political, or ideological advantage when they made the nomination?

To the extent that a Justice feels compelled by morality, duty, or social graces to show gratitude, the compulsion is in tension with a judge's duty of impartiality. This duty of impartiality requires a judge to decide cases without prejudice, bias, or predisposition toward a particular party. Thus is the possible dissonance at work in the minds of our Justices (and other federal judges). One would expect (hope?) that the tension dissipates over time—particularly after the appointing President fades outside of daily U.S. news.

Another factor potentially influencing Supreme Court Justices is their experience at their confirmation hearing before the Senate. In many cases, confirmation hearings are relatively uncontentious. The hearings are nonetheless important, especially now that they are televised. Consider the confirmation hearing for Justice Elena Kagan, which sparked controversy, but nonetheless seemed to sail through to success. She impressed many in the U.S. public as someone with grace, self-possession, and a sense of humor. For example, when Senator Lindsay Graham asked how she spent Christmas Day, Kagan quipped, "Senator, like most Jews, I was probably at a Chinese restaurant."[1] Perhaps her relatively smooth confirmation experience provided an auspicious start to Justice Kagan's Supreme Court career. Nonetheless, Senator Graham repeated his religious belief probe during his first salvo to Judge Ketanji Brown Jackson during her confirmation hearings:

> *Graham:* "What faith are you . . . ?
> *Brown Jackson:* . . . "nondenominational Protestant."
> *Graham:* "Could you fairly judge a Catholic?"[2]

As this last example reveals, the hearings can be quite bruising—insulting even. For example, Justice Clarence Thomas described his confirmation hearing as a "high-tech lynching" and Justice Brett Kavanaugh made the following statement at the end of his confirmation hearing:

> This whole two-week effort has been a calculated and orchestrated political hit, fueled with apparent pent-up anger about President Trump and the 2016 election. Fear that has been unfairly stoked about my judicial record. Revenge on behalf of the Clintons. And millions of dollars in money from outside left-wing opposition groups.
>
> This is a circus. The consequences will extend long past my nomination. The consequences will be with us for decades. This grotesque and coordinated character assassination will dissuade competent and good people of all political persuasions from serving our country.

And as we all know, in the United States political system of the early 2000s, what goes around comes around.[3]

Observers found the last phrase of this quote quite chilling, perhaps suggesting that Kavanaugh might use his lifetime appointment and judicial perch to exact revenge for what he perceived as grossly unfair treatment during the confirmation hearing. As you read through the cases in this book, see if you can find any evidence of this.

These last two examples show the Supreme Court confirmation process as highly politicized. One wonders whether the Framers anticipated these highly charged political disputes when they divided the appointment power between the President and the Senate. Again, one finds it difficult to perceive the intent of the corpus of drafters. Deep partisan differences existed at the time of our nation's founding, however, so one must assume that the Framers anticipated the possibility of bitter clashes.

Of course, it is hard to gauge whether bitterness and grudges resulting from confirmation battles influence Justices' individual decision making. Received wisdom has it that whatever resentment exists fades over time, the realities of independence and life tenure free a Justice from unpleasant confirmation memories.

As a result of life tenure, a Justice may stay on the bench for many years. By contrast, the occupants of other branches of government change more rapidly, often in response to changes in political preferences and whims of citizens who elect the President and members of Congress. One consequence is that the Supreme Court can often reflect a quite different ideological or political orientation than the rest of the country and the democratically elected occupants of the other parts of the federal government. One wonders whether the Framers designed for this dynamic (perhaps as a component of the separation of powers system) or whether it is an unanticipated byproduct of the system's design.

The appendix of this book shows the membership of the Supreme Court over time, which is unsurprisingly made up of an overwhelming majority of White men. With growing demographic diversity in the United States as well as the growing representation of minorities in the legal profession, one starts to observe increasing demographic diversity on the Supreme Court—particularly with respect to women justices. One element of diversity (or lack thereof) that is often too sensitive for many to mention is religious faith. The U.S. Supreme Court decides many cases that touch on religious beliefs. On occasion—as mentioned earlier—the question of religion does come up in confirmation hearings, but it is not explicitly probed as a component of judicial decision making.

QUESTION FOR DISCUSSION

Should this observation about the issue of diversity be a factor in calling for more candid discussion in the selection of nominees?

Out of respect, commentators and others often shy away from discussing the actual religious affiliation of nominees. Is that prudent? Is there something to be said to ensure that the Court reflects membership in a variety of religions? Does the current Supreme Court reflect religious diversity? If not, does that suggest something is missing from the goal of ensuring fair decisions of the Supreme Court? An individual's upbringing in the Catholic faith might suggest a sensitivity and understanding of its doctrines and the prejudice one might encounter in society. But is that individual equally able to appreciate the doctrines and prejudice encountered by a member of the Sikh religion or a follower of Islam?

b. How a Case Gets to the Court

After a dispute arises between two or more parties that cannot be solved outside of the legal realm, one party (the plaintiff or plaintiffs) will file a complaint against another party (the defendant or defendants). The plaintiff files the complaint in a state or federal trial court, depending on the nature of the case and the plaintiff's preference. A complaint details the plaintiff's claims against the defendant and asks the trial court to resolve these issues. After the case is resolved in the trial court, the losing party may appeal to an appellate court. After the appellate court (or courts) rules on the case, the case may again be appealed with the possibility of making it to the U.S. Supreme Court.

The U.S. Supreme Court controls the cases it will decide, picking and choosing among cases coming from courts around the country. Unlike most other courts, the Supreme Court has a lot of control over what it does. In more technical terms, the Supreme Court is the master of its own docket. (A docket is the list of cases parties have filed with a court.) But there is one significant limitation to the Supreme Court's power to influence the law: The Court cannot just identify a legal issue it wants to decide. Justices must wait for an issue to come to the Court in the context of a case—a real dispute between real parties. In other words, the Court has a passive role—at least to the extent that it must wait for a live controversy between two or more entities to come, rather than identify a social or political issue that it would like to resolve.

QUESTION FOR DISCUSSION

1.3 It may be wise for the U.S. Supreme Court's workload to be confined to real controversies. After all, the Justices are nine human beings with limited energy—their efforts should be confined to contested problems. But is it necessary that their power be confined to controversies between real entities (whether those entities be humans or organizations) who are in the throes of active disputes with each other? Some social, political, or economic issues are deeply divisive among the public. Should the Court be able to reach out to decide some of *those* issues — even when actual disputants do not present themselves?

The title of a case, called a caption, names the parties before the court. The original caption in the trial court usually is the last name of each party. In most courts, the plaintiff's last name is listed first and the defendant's last name is listed second (e.g., *Gideon v. Wainwright*). If the case is brought by or against the government, the government is listed in the caption as a party (*United States v. Jones*; *Miranda v. Arizona*). In criminal cases, the government will always be a party and the person or entity the government is charging is called the defendant. After an appeal is filed, the terminology may change a little. The party that lost in the lower court and is now appealing that decision is known as the appellant or petitioner. The party that won in the prior proceeding is known as the appellee or respondent.

Cases can come to the U.S. Supreme Court from both state and federal courts. Figure 1.2 presents a graph of the two avenues to the Supreme Court.

In the U.S. Supreme Court, the party that lost in the lower court (the appellant or petitioner) will have its name first on the caption. You can remember this as "loser on top" in the captions of U.S. Supreme Court cases. For example, in *United States v. Jones*, the U.S. government lost in the court below the Supreme Court and brought the case to the Supreme Court, asking for intervention.

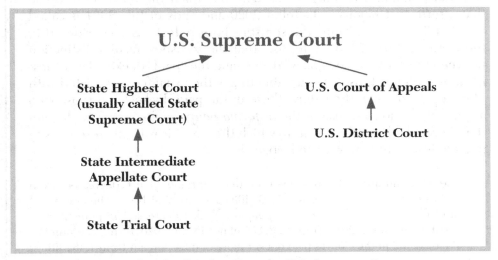

Figure 1.2 State and Federal Pathways to the U.S. Supreme Court

c. Tracing a Case Through the U.S. Supreme Court

When a petition for review is filed in the Clerk's Office of the Supreme Court of the United States, the office places the petition on the docket unless the filing shows a grave defect. (The docket is simply the list of cases calling for some action before a court.) Almost all cases come to the U.S. Supreme Court through a route that grants the Supreme Court significant choice about whether to grant review or accept review. This route involves filing a petition asking the Court to issue what is called a writ of certiorari. When the Court evaluates the petition, it has full discretion whether or not to issue the writ. A tiny portion of the cases come to the Court by appeal as of right—the Court must take these cases unless in fact the cases do not fall into the Court's mandatory jurisdiction, which obliges the Court to review them. One remarkable observation is how few cases the Court actually hears in full—when viewed in light of the cases that the litigants want them to hear. In other words, the Court agrees to review in detail only a tiny handful of cases that are presented to it.

BEHIND THE CURTAIN

Here's a deeper look at the small fraction of the filed cases asking for review that the U.S. Supreme Court actually takes. Notably, the number of cases for which the Supreme Court has granted review and reached a final decision has diminished considerably over the last several decades. Consider these statistics released from the report of the Chief Justice of the United States for the year 2021. Note that the Supreme Court terms are named according to the date on which the term started—so that a term that begins in October 2020 and ends in July 2021 is called October Term 2020. Thus, the statistics here reflect cases considered in the October Term 2020. Note, too, that the statistics make a distinction between the *"in forma pauperis"* docket and the "paid" docket. These designations refer to those who are able to pay the usual fees associated with filing a petition with the Court (those in the paid docket) and those who are unable to do so (those in the *in forma pauperis* docket). The distinction therefore shows the extent to which the Court is using its resources to provide justice to impoverished citizens:

> The total number of cases filed in the Supreme Court decreased from 5,411 filings in the 2019 Term to 5,307 filings in the 2020 Term. The number of cases filed in the Court's *in forma pauperis* docket decreased 12 percent from 3,930 filings in the 2019 Term to 3,477 filings in the 2020 Term. The number of cases filed in the Court's paid docket increased 24 percent from 1,481 filings

in the 2019 Term to 1,830 filings in the 2020 Term. During the 2020 Term, 72 cases were argued and 69 were disposed of in 55 signed opinions, compared to 73 cases argued and 69 disposed of in 53 signed opinions in the 2019 Term. The Court also issued three per curiam decisions in argued cases during the 2020 Term.[4]

In Figure 1.3, adapted from the statistics provided in the 2021 Report of the Chief Justice of the United States, *2021 Year End Report on the Federal Judiciary*, note that the number of cases granted and argued (in gray) is minuscule compared to the number of cases for which litigants actually requested a writ of certiorari (in blue).

Once a petition for review reaches the Clerk's office of the U.S. Supreme Court, the clerk places the petition on the list of cases to be reviewed unless a grave defect in the filing, or the power to review the case, are evident. The clerk's office then sends the petition, and any response to the petition from parties opposing the petition, to individual Justices. The Justices (or most likely their law clerks) review the paperwork to determine whether the Court should hear the case. What do they consider? In particular, they focus on the legal issue in the case, which the petitioner advances as the "Question Presented." Here are some factors that bear on whether a case is "certworthy," that is, the type of case on which the Justices want to expend energy and resources:

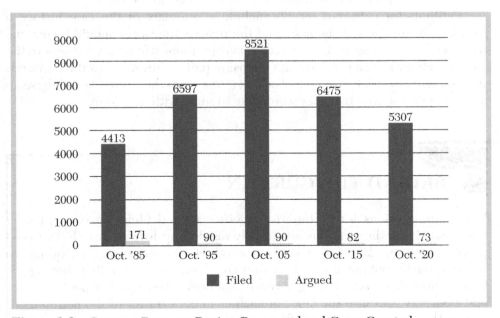

Figure 1.3   Contrast Between Review Requested and Cases Granted

- Is this a legal issue over which lower courts are confused and perhaps have come to differing resolutions? Is there a particular need to have the issue resolved with one voice—that is, the voice of the Supreme Court?
- Does this issue strike at the core of what makes our constitutional system operate fairly and effectively?
- Does the issue pertain to prior U.S. Supreme Court precedent, a common unwritten federal practice, or a federal statute or rule, which contains ambiguities that frequently cause confusion for parties and the lower courts?
- Does this issue have ramifications beyond this case? Could it have a significant effect on our economy, the day-to-day operation of any aspect of government (including the operation of lower federal courts), the course of litigation in many cases, or the health and safety of citizens?
- Has this issue so recently emerged in litigation that justice may benefit from waiting until the lower courts get a chance to consider the issue in different contexts?

If the decision in a lower court is simply incorrect or if the resolution of the case is bound to its particular facts, the case is not likely to be considered worthy of granting a writ of certiorari. In addition, if the circumstances of the case include a complication—such as the strong possibility that the challenged statute will be repealed, or that circumstances will be such that the issue will no longer have ramifications in the lives of citizens—the Justices might conclude that the case is not a proper vehicle for resolving the question presented, even if that question presented will call for the Supreme Court's attention in the future.

Petitions for certiorari usually include a summary of the case history, a summary of the facts of the case, and the reasons the Court should review the decision. Other filings that often accompany petitions when they are sent to the Justices' chambers can include the opposing parties' response to the certiorari petition and any briefs from *amici curiae* ("friends of the Court," which have an argument on the case that they would like to share with the Court).

BEHIND THE CURTAIN

When the petitions for certiorari and other related filings reach a Justice's chambers, the petitions are usually divided up for the law clerks to process, with one law clerk taking responsibility for one case. (Individual Justices usually, but not always, have four law clerks). Most chambers belong to a collaborative effort among several chambers called the cert pool. The cert pool serves to save the labor of each chamber's review of the petition. Within the pool, only one clerk from one chamber reviews the petition and prepares a memorandum. The memorandum summarizes the facts of the case, the prior history of the case in lower courts (also called the procedural posture), and existing law on the question(s) presented. Most importantly, it also includes an initial recommendation as to whether the Court should review the case. The memorandum is circulated to other chambers participating in the cert pool, where at least one clerk in the participating chamber reviews the memorandum and usually passes on the memorandum and comments to the individual Justice as well. For those chambers not participating in the cert pool, either the Justice or one of the law clerks in the chamber reviews each petition. These individuals will occasionally search out information on what the cert pool is saying about whether the case is certworthy to judge whether it is worth it to fight to have the Court accept review of a particular case.

To give perspective on this process, note that law clerks for Supreme Court Justices are usually just two years out of law school, in the ballpark of 24 years old with no legal practice experience. Consider the significant influence of these individuals on whether the Court ultimately reviews the merits of a case. Is this a good system?

Whether by cert pool memo or otherwise, all chambers ultimately decide whether or not a particular case is worthy of full review by the entire U.S. Supreme Court. Each chamber sends a list of the cases to the Chief Justice that the Justice would like to discuss at a conference among all nine Justices. At the conference, all cases on the "discuss list" are considered. For each case discussed at the conference, the Justices proceed to vote around a conference table (usually in descending order of seniority) on whether to take the case. If four Justices vote to grant the writ of certiorari, the case will come before the full Court and the Court Clerk's Office will issue a public order, notifying the parties of the review grant and the briefing schedule.

Importantly, this process allows for a minority of the Justices (four out of nine) to control the agenda for the Court, the agenda being the cases for which the Court hears their merits and provides a vehicle for announcing the "law of the land." Ironically, however, the success of four Justices in getting the Court to hear the case does not at all guarantee that these Justices will ultimately "win" on the merits. To set law that indisputably serves as precedent for other cases, five votes among the nine Justices are needed. Thus, it takes four Justices to set the agenda of cases, but five Justices to set precedent. In other words, a Justice can fight hard to get some colleagues to agree to take a case, only to lose in achieving a desired bottom-line result on the merits of the case. In that situation, a Justice can be said to win the battle, but lose the war. Accordingly, Justices must be strategic about the cases for which they urge a certiorari grant.

Supreme Court conference room circa 1975. *Collection of the Supreme Court of the United States.*

QUESTION FOR DISCUSSION

1.4   What do you think of a system that allows a minority of the Court to set the agenda for the Court (by requiring only four votes to decide that a case should be heard), but also requires a majority of the Court to change the actual result in the case and possibly provide a ruling that changes an important rule of law? Does it serve fairness and an open opportunity for airing different points of view? Or is it merely inefficient?

After a writ of certiorari is issued and the parties receive the briefing sched-ule, the Clerk's Office sets the case on the oral argument calendar. If the issue in the case is one that immediately concerns other entities in society—such as nonprofit public interest organizations, trade associations, and State Attorneys General—then those entities might file a petition to participate as amicus cur-iae. (These petitions are almost always granted and briefs *amicus curiae* setting forth arguments follow.) Sometimes, the Solicitor General of the United States may file an amicus brief—either on their own motion or at the request of the Justices. The Solicitor General is a high-ranking member of the President's executive department who represents the United States in all cases before the U.S. Supreme Court. The Solicitor General's Office contains top appellate attorneys. The U.S. Supreme Court Justices value their legal reasoning, legal research, and mode of presentation.

At oral argument, the parties usually have 30 minutes to present their argu-ments. (Sometimes the Court invites the Solicitor General to send someone for that task as well.) Oral arguments can be intimidating for advocates, as the Justices sometimes use the oral advocate as a vehicle or tool for showing other Justices the merits of a particular point of view.

The Justices meet at a conference soon after oral argument to take a tentative vote on how the case should be decided. Options generally are:

- Affirm: validate the lower court's decision
- Reverse: undo the lower court's decision
- Vacate: nullify the lower court's decision
- Remand: send the case back to the lower court for further proceedings in light of the Supreme Court's opinion
- Dismiss the writ of certiorari as improvidently granted: find something about the case that rendered it a bad idea for the Justices to hear the issue or the case when it was granted or at the time it was heard.

Once the conference vote is taken, opinion-writing assignments follow. In this role, the Chief Justice enjoys the greatest power of that position. If the Chief Justice is in the majority, the Chief Justice assigns the Justice to write the majority opinion and the senior Justice in the minority assigns the dissent. If the Chief Justice is in the minority of those who voted on a disposition of the case, the most senior Justice in the majority gets the assignment power for the majority and the Chief Justice assigns the dissent. The assignment power is significant, as a justice could be launched into historical fame with the assignment of a particular case and the direction of the law often results from the tenor of the writing in a lead opinion.

Majority and dissenting opinions are sometimes started at the same time, although dissenting opinions are usually reactive. That is, in large part, they respond to the bottom line and reasoning of the majority opinion. Thus, draft dissenting opinions are not generally circulated to the entire Court until the draft majority opinion is circulated. Sometimes a Justice will join a majority opinion, concurring opinion, or at least the ultimate resolution of a case (i.e., affirm, reverse, or vacate)—but nonetheless want to express a unique viewpoint or caveat. To follow this impulse, concurring opinions are written. Although the case reports are sometimes ambiguous, some opinions are marked "concurring in the judgment," and other opinions are marked "concurring in the opinion of Justice XYZ." An opinion concurring in the judgment agrees only with the bottom line of the majority of the Justices, the majority's view of the case's ultimate outcome in terms of who wins and who loses. An opinion concurring in the opinion of another Justice agrees with the reasoning of the opinion (why one side wins and the other loses) but has reasoning or caveats to add. Finally, as is often the case, if a dissenting Justice has two cents (or more!) to add to explain a dissenting vote from the majority's disposition of the case, the Justice writes their own dissent to supplement the lead dissent or writes a separate dissent altogether.

And then there's a troublesome development: With increasing frequency over the last 25 years, no majority opinion emerges from the Justices. Nearly always, a majority of Justices will vote on the ultimate resolution of a case. With increasing frequency, however, that majority will not agree on the reasons for this ultimate resolution. In other words, the Justices agree on the outcome but they do not agree on the reasoning that led to the outcome. In that event, the lead opinion (often assigned by the Chief Justice) will not set forth the majority reasoning, nor will any other opinion in the case. In these instances, the opinions are often written in harsh tones.

Why is this troublesome? The controlling interpretation of the meaning of the U.S. Constitution comes only from a majority opinion of the U.S. Supreme Court. If no majority opinion happens, legal guidance suffers. In these situations, the best that lawyers, judges, and law-abiding citizens can do is first to identify whether an opinion is joined by the plurality of the Justices. A plurality of votes is the number cast for a particular opinion that receives more than any other opinion (but does not receive a majority of votes). A plurality of votes is the largest proportion among all votes cast. A plurality opinion does not contain the same gravitas as a majority opinion, but can often carry similar weight, particularly if concurring opinions express views in the same ballpark of analysis that with some effort can be reconciled in part with the plurality. More on this issue in the next section of this chapter.

Once all opinions have been circulated and written and all opinions have reacted to each other (barbs and all), the decision is announced, first with a (usually) short announcement geared to the tourists in the Supreme Court courtroom gallery on the opinion-announcing day, and then by releasing the full text of the opinions online. Figure 1.4 provides a summary of the handling of a Supreme Court case. After the announcement, the press darts out of the gallery to read the actual opinions and write up a synopsis for the public.

2. Basics of Reading a U.S. Supreme Court Opinion

The U.S. Constitution lays out a carefully crafted skeleton of the U.S. government and the individual rights enjoyed by our citizens. Yet a sophisticated understanding of constitutional law requires careful reading of U.S. Supreme Court opinions from a number of perspectives. Indeed, most of constitutional law comes from Supreme Court opinions, not the actual text of the Constitution.

This book encourages you to develop an eye toward understanding how these opinions might be perceived by nonlawyers: the public and the press. You will also analyze the cases as legal thinkers do. To wrap your mind around both angles, you also need to know some basics about the U.S. litigation process.

In reading the cases using the lens of the lay public and the press, you should identify the social message taken from the case. So, for example, when you read a case called *Brown v. Board of Education*, you might understand that people took it to mean that Black and White children had to go to school together. Or

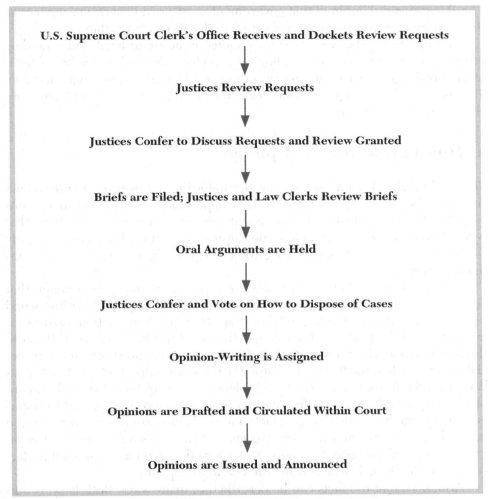

U.S. Supreme Court Clerk's Office Receives and Dockets Review Requests

Justices Review Requests

Justices Confer to Discuss Requests and Review Granted

Briefs are Filed; Justices and Law Clerks Review Briefs

Oral Arguments are Held

Justices Confer and Vote on How to Dispose of Cases

Opinion-Writing is Assigned

Opinions are Drafted and Circulated Within Court

Opinions are Issued and Announced

Figure 1.4   Summary of Processing U.S. Supreme Court Cases

you might read a case called *Roe v. Wade* and appreciate that people understood the case to protect a person's right to have an abortion if the person chooses to do so. For the purposes of popular understanding, these "rough and ready" understandings are important for a full appreciation of how Supreme Court opinions actually govern the nation.

To truly appreciate the link between law and U.S. society, though, you will also need to read cases as a trained legal thinker. From this perspective, you will see that the U.S. Supreme Court in *Brown v. Board of Education* focused its ruling on the state law practice of requiring segregated schools and that the Court held that states could not constitutionally do so. The *Brown* Court did not decide that states had to provide integrated schools. Rather, the *Brown* Court prohibited states from requiring segregated schools. Likewise, the Court in *Roe v. Wade* held that states may not impose absolute prohibitions on abortion.

The *Roe* Court did not hold that government must provide abortion services or that government may not restrict abortion under some circumstances.

The eyeglasses that you wear for gaining an accurate legal understanding of the cases require focused reading on actual words used and a bit of technical knowledge about what goes into writing a U.S. Supreme Court decision. The technical knowledge necessary for you to read a U.S. Supreme Court case "like a lawyer" appears next.

a. How to Interpret an Opinion

You might find it helpful to focus on the following big picture of an opinion's sections when seeking to understand its importance. In addition to sections mapping the big picture, opinions might also contain extra information that is less important to understanding the Supreme Court's ruling. Try to identify the following takeaways and avoid getting distracted by interesting, but superfluous, information.

A lead opinion (whether a plurality, a majority, or simply the opinion that comes first) will begin with presenting the facts, which explain what happened between the parties that prompted them to go to court. Some facts are so important that if they did not occur the ruling of the Court would be different. Because these facts are legally decisive, they are most important and should receive special attention when reading a case. Other facts are less important and function as background information for the case or details that help fill out the full picture of what happened and why. Often you need to use your own judgment to distinguish between the result-changing facts and the background facts. Facts assume particular importance when comparing current cases to similar cases that came before, so-called precedential cases. Make sure that you have a general understanding of the facts before reading the rest of the opinion.

Also, note that the facts can be described in many ways. Both lawyers and judges capitalize on this. Opposing parties will attempt to frame their facts more narrowly or more broadly in an effort to argue that their facts do or do not conform to the facts of a particular precedential case. When the Justices write their opinions, the reader can often tell which version of the facts the opinion writer embraced and how that spin on the facts influenced the ultimate decision in the case.

The question presented in a case is the particular question providing the Court's focal point. The issue identifies the precise legal inquiry that the parties are requesting the Court to resolve. Although a case might contain several legal issues, not every issue makes it before the U.S. Supreme Court on appeal. The Supreme Court is supposed to answer only the issues presented to it. This rule is generally followed, but sometimes the Court will go beyond the current issues presented for decision and decide questions outside the scope of what was requested. On the other hand, sometimes the Supreme Court will avoid resolving certain issues.

Before answering the legal issue presented for decision, a U.S. Supreme Court opinion will sometimes describe the prior decisions it has handed down on the same or similar topics. Under the theory of precedent—otherwise known as stare decisis—a court should generally follow prior decisions in resolving a current dispute. The doctrine of stare decisis mandates that previous rulings must be followed by lower courts when the Supreme Court has already decided on a substantially similar issue. Therefore, when the Supreme Court has established a legal principle for resolving certain disputes, stare decisis instructs that cases with substantially similar facts must be decided the same way as the precedential case(s) direct. Sometimes the Court will establish its own "test," or framework, for viewing a certain category of cases. This test is a framework used in future cases to determine how the particular case corresponds to the earlier cases.

Do not expect the Justices to adhere to this doctrine of stare decisis in all cases. Sometimes the Justices decide to ignore stare decisis, either by turning a blind eye to prior decisions or by expressly overruling them. The Supreme Court is criticized for doing so, but those actions make Constitutional Law study interesting. As you read through the opinions in this text, consider whether you believe the Court acted legitimately, thoughtfully, and honorably when it overruled a prior case.

Once a U.S. Supreme Court opinion explains prior cases, the opinion usually turns to applying the law from the cited cases to the particular dispute before the Court. Sometimes the Court will find that the current facts apply directly to the prior law in a way that is so substantially similar that the same outcome is required as the Supreme Court had reached in the earlier case. Other times, the Court will distinguish the facts of this case from the facts of prior cases, so that the Court can come to an entirely different decision than in the earlier case. The idea here is that just as an alike case should be decided similarly, dissimilar cases can be decided dissimilarly.

As part of its discussion of prior law, the Supreme Court explains the rationale for its ruling. Sometimes the Supreme Court uses simple logic. Other times the Supreme Court talks about public policy, explaining how the decision leads to the best result for society as a whole. The Supreme Court could look to legislation to determine public policy goals. Other times the Supreme Court will base its rationale on the function of the judiciary in society and government. Often, the Supreme Court chooses to cite what it believes is the original intent of the Framers of the Constitution. The Court might defer certain decisions to the legislative or executive branches and simply uphold what that body of government believes to be correct. Finally, the Court may rely on morality, justice, general fairness, or social science to rationalize its decision.

In reading decisions, deep understanding requires appreciating the lives of those affected by the decision. With that being said, you will relieve yourself from much confusion and stress if you accept that some judicial opinions are ambiguous and vague. Sometimes the Justices do this intentionally: They are smart enough to understand that they cannot predict the future and cannot anticipate all effects of their rulings. Other times they understand that they cannot get other Justices to agree with the opinion unless they avoid a strong stance, at least on some parts of the opinion. The Justices are nine human beings who must seek a compromise. Sometimes compromise is born of ambiguity: Future certainty is compromised for present peace. For these reasons, the Justices sometimes keep things "fuzzy" so that society and government can figure out how their decision affects specific parts of life as life unfolds.

To understand the true effect and meaning of a case, one must distinguish between the holding and the dicta. The holding is often the most important part of a case. A holding is the U.S. Supreme Court's conclusion or resolution of the legal issue. The holding expresses exactly how the Court decides the question presented in light of the facts of the case. Technically, the holding is what binds lower federal courts, state courts, other state and federal authorities, and private citizens. The U.S. Supreme Court often uses language that flags the holding: At the end of opinions, you will sometimes note telling language at the beginning of sentences, most often with opening phrases such as "we hold," "we decide," and "we conclude." These are sentences that the Justices tool over and sometimes negotiate over. Pay attention to these sentences.

Dicta are statements or remarks in a judicial opinion that are not necessary to resolve the issue or to reach the holding. These statements are not holdings. These statements are also not necessarily binding. In the view of some, these statements are merely background comments. The main difference between dicta and holdings is that dicta do not control subsequent attempts to resolve a similar set of facts. Dicta are technically merely "persuasive," but statements qualified as dicta are sometimes still used in later cases as quite important or even authoritative. They are certainly suggestive of what is present on the Justices' minds when opining on a particular issue.

The end of an opinion will contain a disposition, which states the U.S. Supreme Court's action on each issue. These actions could include statements that the judgment in the case will affirm, reverse, vacate, remand, or some combination of these dispositions. Look for this final paragraph as you read a case. In fact, you might find it useful to read this paragraph as you begin reading the case. It could enhance your understanding of why an opinion appears to be going in a certain direction.

Affirm. *When the Court affirms a decision, it is upholding the ruling of the lower court. This means that the Court concludes that the lower court was correct in its ruling, and, sometimes, even endorses the lower court's reasoning. Generally, no further litigation on the issue decided can occur in the case.*

Reverse. *When a decision is reversed, the Court is overturning the decision of the lower court and ruling for the other side. Depending on the details of the case, further litigation in the lower courts may be possible.*

Vacate and Further Proceedings. *When a decision is vacated, the Supreme Court is eliminating any legal effect of the lower court's ruling. Reverse and vacate actions are often coupled with an action for remand, which is when the Supreme Court sends the case back to the lower court for further proceedings. This further action could include a retrial, additional investigation between the parties on a particular issue, presentation of supplementary evidence at a hearing—or simply asking the lower court to evaluate how the newly announced law applies to the facts of the case.*

Opinions of the Court. *Opinions marked "Opinions of the Court," also known as majority opinions, serve as the controlling opinion in a particular case. This type of opinion occurs when more than half of the justices join the opinion. The holding of the majority opinion will apply as precedent for subsequent cases.*

Concurring and Dissenting Opinions. *Concurring and dissenting opinions allow Justices who do not wholly agree with the majority opinion to express either slightly or drastically different views of the case. Sometimes a Justice will agree with the ruling of the Supreme Court but believe that the ruling is correct for a different or additional reason than expressed in the majority opinion. In these instances, the Justice will write a concurring opinion describing what he or she believes to be the correct rationale for the Supreme Court's holding. As described above, this is often listed as an opinion concurring in the judgment (both may determine who wins and who loses). If the opinion is listed as concurring in another Justice's opinion, this means that the concurring Justice agrees with the rationale given in that other opinion but has further comments to add. Opinions concurring in another Justice's opinion can be useful for identifying what reasoning represents the thinking of the majority of the Court, a factor important for identifying the reasoning the majority believes should control future similar cases.*

In some instances, a Justice will refuse to join a majority or concurring opinion because the Justice disagrees with how at least some members of the rest of the Supreme Court resolved the dispute. A dissenting opinion usually explains why the dissenting Justice does not join the majority opinion and does not agree with the disposition of the case. Dissenting opinions are not binding precedent, but they might be used when later arguing for limiting or overruling an earlier case. These opinions sometimes foreshadow changes in the law and overruling precedent. Sometimes, though, dissenting opinions are viewed as mere whining—explanations for why a Justice is upset for not getting his or her way for the precise disposition of the case.

On some occasions, no majority opinion will be achieved because there is no opinion in which more than half of the Justices joined. On those occasions, a majority of Justices almost always agree with the bottom line of what to do with the case (the disposition of the lower court's judgment), but no majority agrees with the precise reasons for the result. In these instances, one needs to identify the opinions for which the greatest number (although not the majority) of Justices agree.

In a common occurrence, the Justices write three opinions: one opinion that four Justices join, a concurring opinion in which two Justices join, and a dissenting opinion in which three Justices join. The 4-Justice opinion is called a plurality opinion—if in fact no other opinion is written that is joined by four Justices (this rarely happens). Considering the votes of all nine Justices, this is the opinion that got the most votes—even though it is not a majority of them. For that reason, the plurality opinion has a strong influence. Yet because it does not have the vote of a majority of the Justices, it is not technically controlling on the nation's corpus of law and does not technically enjoy the force of binding precedent. If one puts together the bottom line of the plurality opinion (affirm, reverse, or vacate the lower court's decision) with the bottom line of the concurring opinion, one can find the majority's disposition of the case. Sometimes this is obvious from the last section of the lead opinion, which can be confined to a disposition of the case and designated as "joined" by the Court—meaning the majority of the Justices on the Court.[5]

On some occasions, future courts look to concurring opinions as providing the rule to follow, at least in those instances when one could hypothesize that the plurality of the Court would agree with what the concurring opinion says, but also would go further. One might describe this situation as one in which the concurring opinion expresses the "lowest common denominator" of agreement among a majority of the Justices.

QUESTION FOR DISCUSSION

1.5 Plurality opinions can be confusing and can muddle the understanding of lawyers, judges, and general citizens. Should Congress pass a law that prohibits the Court from deciding cases without a majority opinion? How would that law be enforced? Would the system be wise? Would it jeopardize the system of judicial independence?

3. Approaches to Constitutional Interpretation

The U.S. Constitution speaks in general terms: Commerce Among the States! Necessary and Proper! Faithfully Execute the Law of the United States! Due Process of Law! Vague language, no? You likely get the idea.

For good reasons, the Framers—and those who wrote amendments to our Constitution—did not use self-defining language. Why good reasons? Mostly because a constitution is best used to layout a spectrum of values, with emphasis on those values that should guide governance: No one can wholly foresee the future, but clearly enunciated values can aid in marking an appropriate path. Some parts of our Constitution turned into what can be described as truths about human nature: One realistic, but sad notion that motivated our constitutional scheme is that those who seek prominence in our government are generally motivated by personal ambition. This is an important insight into our separation of powers system. That system includes a separation of powers among the branches of the federal government (horizontal separation of powers) as well as the separation of power between the state and the federal government (vertical separation of powers). One of two of the U.S. Constitution's founders, James Madison or Alexander Hamilton, in their jointly written *Federalist Papers*, thought of separation of powers this way: Those in government (politicians) are ambitious. This can stand as an obstacle to an honest government. Accordingly, in structuring government, Madison or Hamilton opined that "ambition must be made to counteract ambition."[6] This is one of the dominant truths with which to interpret our Constitution. This truth (and other platitudes one finds in the *Federalist Papers*), though, does not shed clear light on broad, ambiguous constitutional phrases discussed in the chapters that follow, such as Congress's power to pass laws that are "necessary and proper" and the President's power to "take Care that the Laws be faithfully executed." The general observations in the *Federalist Papers* provide a useful beginning to understanding the meaning of the Constitution, but the justices (and scholars) need other guidance for interpretation purposes.

For interpretation debate, perhaps the biggest divide that comes up in cases and scholarship is a debate between originalism and nonoriginalism. Originalism starts from the idea that our Constitution has clear implicit or stated norms that must be enforced. The interpretation of this approach varies. One view holds that one can find constitutional guidance only from the text of the document, or from the meaning of the text that common sense suggests was obviously intended. According to this view, because our Constitution says nothing about the right to privacy, one cannot find any constitutional protection for the decision on whether to beget a child (when the issue concerns birth control or abortion). Likewise, one cannot find constitutional protection for a police officer's decision to do a pat-down search of a man in a hoodie even without probable cause to believe a crime has been committed (or will be committed).

Several permutations of originalism or close cousins of originalism exist. For example, most originalists believe that understandings of words used in the Constitution—as reflected in dictionaries contemporaneous with drafting a particular constitutional provision—are safe sources for interpreting constitutional meaning. Moving slightly away from the most orthodox view, some originalists believe that ratification debates in the states, as well as laws handed down relatively soon after a constitutional provision was drafted, show important insights into intent.

Some originalists accommodate contemporary questions that emerge as a consequence of changes in society by defining original intent on a more general level. Take, for example, the Due Process Clause of the Fifth Amendment, which restrains how the federal government treats citizens. One would be hard pressed to argue that those who drafted and ratified that amendment uniformly believed that this language ensured that non-White, nonmale citizens enjoyed equal protection under the laws. A moderate originalist, though, might say that equality among citizens is at the root of Fifth Amendment due process. Under their reformed view, now that—in the era after the Civil War—our country has recognized full citizen rights for nonmale folks and people of color, one can reasonably interpret the Fifth Amendment's reference to due process of law to encompass equal rights for *all* citizens of the United States.

BEHIND THE CURTAIN

Justice Antonin Scalia served on the U.S. Supreme Court from 1986 to 2016. He is generally associated with the role of intellectual anchor for the originalism in constitutional interpretation. Justice Amy Coney Barrett cites him as a beacon for her judicial and constitutional philosophy. Justice Scalia made an interesting comment when asked about his beliefs. His answer is relevant to whether he believes cases such as *Brown v. Board of Education* were correctly decided. As you will see later in this book, *Brown* held that state-financed pub-

Justice Scalia testifying before the House Judiciary Committee's Commercial and Administrative Law Subcommittee on Capitol Hill, May 20, 2010. *Stephen Masker/Wikimedia Commons.*

lic schools that were segregated according to race were inherently unequal and thus a violation of the Equal Protection Clause of the Fourteenth Amendment (which governs the relationship between state governments and state citizens). The problem with this holding for originalists is that, at the time the Fourteenth Amendment was written, in the wake of the Civil War, the state governments in the United States did not provide any guaranteed public primary or secondary education for anyone. This suggests, of course, that those who wrote and ratified the amendment did not have any consciousness that the amendment would apply to primary or secondary education—much less whether that education should be provided to everyone regardless of race, color, or creed. Does that mean that originalists condemn *Brown v. Board of Education*, commonly thought of as a foundation of modern constitutional law, even though it is regarded as a "sacred cow" when it comes to U.S. constitutional jurisprudence?

When asked whether he agreed with the long-held case holdings (of which *Brown v. Board of Education* would be a candidate), Justice Scalia replied that he generally does not believe in undoing old laws: "I'm an originalist and a textualist, not a nut."[7] Question: What does that mean for his view of *Brown*? Answer: Justice Scalia said in one interview that he would have voted with the majority in *Brown*, holding that separate education for different races cannot be equal in public education under the Fourteenth Amendment.[8]

Nonoriginalism is much more diffuse than originalism and takes many forms. Why? Because it does not focus on what controls interpretation, but rather highlights what does not control interpretation.[9] Interpretative ideas associated with nonoriginalism generally focus either on (1) how to construe the actual language of the Constitution in light of current society; (2) how dominant forces in society influence the way government actors apply and interpret the Constitution; or (3) approaches that include elements of both (1) and (2).

A prominent example of the first category is the idea that one should view the Constitution as a living document when interpreting its language. Particularly associated with Justice William Brennan (who served on the Court from 1986 to 2016), this "living Constitution" approach follows the view that the Framers envisioned that the meaning of the U.S. Constitution would change and grow as society evolves. A related interpretative approach — known as the popular Constitution theory — recognizes that the Constitution is designed simply to govern the citizens and thus means only so much as it is understood in popular understanding. In other words, ordinary citizens — not courts or constitutional scholars — are the most authoritative source of constitutional meaning. The views of citizens must be canvased to pin down contemporary constitutional meaning.

A second approach to constitutional interpretation focuses on critical theories describing long-lasting forces in society that influence how constitutional law develops. A general theory, critical legal theory, views legal analysis, including constitutional law interpretation, as motivated by a desire to maintain society's status quo (including reproducing society's existing hierarchies). According to most critical legal theory thinkers, this motivation to maintain the status quo results in maintaining existing bias against marginalized groups, rather than fostering evenhanded laws.

A related theory is critical race theory (sometimes called CRT). According to the NAACP Legal Defense Fund, critical race theory can be defined as follows:

> Critical Race Theory recognizes that racism is more than the result of individual bias and prejudice. It is embedded in laws, policies and institutions that uphold and reproduce racial inequalities. According to CRT, societal issues like Black Americans'

higher mortality rate, outsized exposure to police violence, the school-to-prison pipeline, denial of affordable housing, and the rates of the death of Black women in childbirth are not unrelated anomalies.[10]

Using concepts and frameworks from critical race theory, a wide variety of critical theories have developed to analyze the relationship between the law and specific marginalized groups, such as Asian critical legal studies (AsianCrit), Latinx critical studies (LatCrit), disability critical race studies (DisCrit), and more. For example, AsianCrit makes use of concepts from CRT and other fields to put forth a legal framework that accounts for the unique "racial ambiguity" and "positioning in American racial hierarchy" of South Asian Americans.[11]

BEHIND THE CURTAIN

The person generally identified as the man behind critical race theory is Derrick Bell, a lawyer, scholar, and civil rights activist who lived from 1930 to 2011. Serving as a law professor at a number of universities, including Harvard and New York University, Bell had a straight-forward message: Identifying opportunities for change in racially discriminatory institutions must begin with an analysis of structural, insti-tutional reasons for racism that are embedded in our society. Bell died in 2011, but his ideas have had an enormous impact. Later in this vol-ume, you can read Bell's rewriting of the majority opinion in *Brown v. Board of Education* — in which he argues that law should address the institutional roots of segregation, rather than simply make the broad statement that sep-arate does not mean equal.

Derrick Bell photographed by David Shankbone in 2007. *Wikimedia Commons.*

Another important branch of critical interpretations of the Constitution comes from feminist jurisprudence. Like critical race theory, feminist jurispru-dence observes that constitutional interpretation over the years has marginalized women, reinforcing the notion that females are servers, mothers, reproducers, weak warriors, and the like. Feminist jurisprudence has different branches and approaches. For example, some subscribe to the philosophy that the rights and privileges of both males and females should be the same. Others urge that females and males have inherent differences, which should be accounted for in connection with constitutional interpretation. Still others believe that the binary characterization of gender (males and females) is, itself, oppressive and discriminatory. Later in this volume, you will have the opportunity to read a "rewrite" of a classic opinion that touches on gender from a feminist jurisprudence thinker.

Beyond the distinction between originalism and nonoriginalism, other categorizations of interpretive approaches to the Constitution exist. One prominent view on constitutional interpretation approaches was developed by Philip Bobbitt, who identified six modalities of constitutional argument: historical, textual, structural, doctrinal, prudential, and ethical.[12] The historical approach bases interpretation on what the authors of the Constitution intended, using evidence from the document's drafting and ratification debates. Next, the textual argument focuses solely on the meaning of the words in the document "as they would be interpreted by the average contemporary 'man on the street.'" The structural argument uses principles about the relationship between the institutions established by the Constitution to guide interpretation. Similarly, the doctrinal argument follows principles established by precedent: Those principles combine to constitute doctrine, that is, the various rules of constitutional law. The prudential modality directs interpretation according to cost-benefit analysis. Finally, the ethical argument invokes principles discerned from the Constitution about morality to guide interpretation.

This summary of various theories of constitutional interpretation, visualized in Figure 1.5, is far from exhaustive, but it provides a taste of the various debates that rage among deep thinkers and scholars about how to confront the meaning of the broad and vague language of the Constitution.

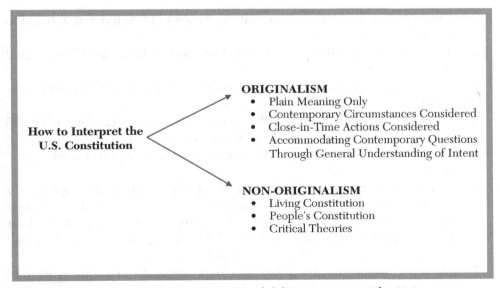

Figure 1.5   Summary of a Prominent Model for Interpreting the U.S. Constitution

QUESTIONS FOR DISCUSSION

1.6 Which theory of interpretation do you think is most valid? Is it appropriate for a court to use more than one theory?

1.7 As you make your way through the materials in this book, consider the following. In a book written at the end of his career on the Supreme Court in 2022, Justice Stephen Breyer took the position that Supreme Court Justices are focused on law, not politics. He insisted that "politics in [the] elemental sense is not present at the Court."[13] He further asserted that "'political' is the wrong word to describe even the more controversial court decisions."[14] Do you agree with this statement? Doesn't it depend on how you define politics? How would you define it?

The next chapter covers material closely yoked to the issues highlighted above. After dealing with the notion of federalism, we turn first to the following question: Who is the final authoritative interpreter of the Constitution? Spoiler alert: The federal judiciary has claimed that title for itself. Read on and evaluate whether you agree that the judiciary deserves that crown.

QUESTIONS FOR REVIEW

1. What were some of the reasons that the Articles of Confederation failed to create a workable union?
2. What is an example of how the written Constitution formalized "the original sin" of slavery?
3. What were the arguments for and against having a powerful federal judiciary?
4. How did the delegates justify the electoral college system, and what did they decide about how it should be constituted?
5. What is the difference between horizontal separation of powers and vertical separation of powers?
6. As a matter of tradition, the location of a party's name in the caption of a U.S. Supreme Court opinion depends on what happened in the court that heard the case immediately before the U.S. Supreme Court decided to hear the case. When a party's name is listed first (or "on top"), what does that show about the result in the court immediately below?
7. List the reasons why the Supreme Court might deem a case worthy of granting the writ of certiorari.
8. What are the unique powers of the Chief Justice of the United States?

9. Define a plurality opinion.
10. What is the difference between an opinion concurring in the judgment and an opinion concurring in the opinion written by another Justice? How does the precedential effect of these types of opinions differ?
11. What are dicta?
12. How would you define the method of constitutional interpretation known as critical race theory?

ENDNOTES

1. The Nomination of Elena Kagan to be an Associate Justice of the Supreme Court of the United States Hearing Before the Committee on the Judiciary, United States Senate One Hundred Eleventh Congress Second Session June 28-30 and July 1, 2010, Serial No. J-111-98.
2. *Graham Gets Combative with Jackson: "What Faith Are You, by the Way?"* The Hill (March 22, 2022), https://thehill.com/homenews/senate/599208-graham-gets-combative-with-jackson-what-faith-are-you-by-the-way?rl=1 (last accessed March 23, 2022).
3. Brett Kavanaugh, testimony before the Senate Judiciary Committee, September 27, 2018.
4. *2021 Year-End Report on the Federal Judiciary*, 7, https://www.supremecourt.gov/publicinfo/year-end/2021year-endreport.pdf (last accessed June 6, 2022).
5. All this is slightly complicated in those instances when a Justice needs to decline to participate because of a personal conflict of interest (such as when a relative is participating in the case). The rules in those instances are basically the same: The opinion with the most votes of the active members of the Court is treated as the plurality opinion.
6. *Federalist* 51, "The Structure of the Government Must Furnish the Proper Checks and Balances between the Different Departments."
7. Interview by Nina Totenberg, *Justice Scalia, the Great Dissenter, Opens Up*, (2008), https://www.npr.org/templates/story/story.php?storyId=89986017 (accessed March 16, 2022).
8. *What Would Scalia Do?*, ABA Journal, https://www.abajournal.com/news/article/the_brown_v._board_of_education_question_what_would_scalia_do (accessed March 26, 2022).
9. Erwin Chemerinsky, *Constitutional Law* 22 (6th ed. 2019).
10. NAACP Legal Defense Fund, "Critical Race Theory: Frequently Asked Questions," https://www.naacpldf.org/critical-race-theory-faq/?gclid=EAIaIQobChMIlbacnMbK9gIV0sizCh3b0woCEAAYASAAEgLmxvD_BwE (accessed March 16, 2022).
11. Vinay Harpalani, *DesiCrit: Theorizing the Racial Ambiguity of South Asian Americans*, 69 N.Y.U. Annual Survey of Am. L. 77, 179 (2013).
12. Philip Bobbitt, *Constitutional Interpretation* 12-13 (1991).
13. Stephen Breyer, *The Authority of the Court and the Peril of Politics* 52 (2021).
14. *Id.* at 51-52.

Structure of Government

Federalism and the Federal Government

This part of the book reckons with a big task. It confronts issues of power by sorting out the question "Who's got the power?" in several contexts. We begin with the concept of federalism, which is an overarching, distinctive feature of our Constitution.

Federalism takes the unique view that our country will enjoy a separation of powers between the different branches of the state and federal government (vertical separation of powers) and the state and federal government as sovereign entities. What does this mean about power? Primarily, it means that the U.S. Constitution and the federal government—which is the centerpiece of this book and the centerpiece of some (but not all) of the U.S. mindset—do not hold all the power. Complicating matters, federalism also accommodates the view that within each sovereign entity, the powers of the legislature, judiciary, and executive are separate (horizontal separation of powers). The matter defining federalism, however, is the vertical separation of powers.

Much of federalism, of course, concerns the scope of state power. Part of this scope is in the hands of states and is off limits for the federal government to define. But the balance between state and federal power is very much a matter of federal constitutional law. Moreover, equally—if not more important—components of our constitutional structure of government are the various powers of the federal judiciary, legislature, and executive. Following a look at federalism under the Constitution in Chapter 2, the remainder of the chapters in this part take a close look at the powers of these three federal compartments.

Federalism
Sharing of State and Federal Power

A. Constitutional Roots of Federalism

As explained in Chapter 1, the Framers devised a power-sharing system whereby the control of the lives of U.S. citizens is divided between the state and federal governments. During the constitutional debates, the Framers clashed over how strong the federal government should be. Some Framers urged that the states should enjoy the bulk of governmental power, whereas others were concerned about the local parochialism that led to the disfunction under the Articles of Confederation. After the failed attempt at a unified nation under the Articles of Confederation, the Framers of our Constitution knew that they must provide for a strong union with strong compartments (judiciary, executive, and legislature). Through their own personal power struggles over the issue with each other, the Framers sought a compromise.

On one hand, the Framers drafted the Constitution in such a way as to make clear that the federal government had limited power. If the Constitution did not grant the federal government specific power, it could not exercise power. This resulted in leaving most specific powers of governance to state governments.

In contrast to the notion of limited powers, the Framers granted the federal government an "ace in the hole" over human governance with the states—the Supremacy Clause, which states:

> This Constitution, and the Laws of the United States which shall be made in Pursuance thereof; and all Treaties made, or which shall be made, under the Authority of the United States, shall be the supreme Law of the Land; and the Judges in every State shall be bound thereby, any Thing in the Constitution or Laws of any state to the Contrary notwithstanding.

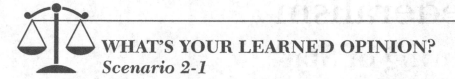

WHAT'S YOUR LEARNED OPINION?
Scenario 2-1

Assume that you are house-sitting for a family who will be away from their home for one week. You are wondering what food in the house you are welcome to consume. Assume further that your host has left you one of the following notes. Consider how the two notes differ in what they authorize you to consume.

Note 1: Please feel free to consume everything in the house except for alcoholic beverages.

Note 2: Please feel free to use the spices and pasta in the cabinet. Please also feel free to finish the milk and the orange juice in the refrigerator.

Which note gives you limited power to consume? Which note gives you broad, general power to consume?

B. United States Constitution Article VI

These two approaches to the federal government in the Constitution, limited powers and the Supremacy Clause, do not contravene each other, but the matter is tricky. The two approaches present contrasting views of the scope of federal power, with the limited power notion being restrictive and the Supremacy Clause establishing dominance. Read together, the two approaches are designed to ensure that the federal government does not displace state prerogatives (relating to limited powers), but also make sure that when the federal government acts within the parameters of its given power, the states must comply with the federal government's edicts (relating to the Supremacy Clause).

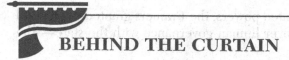

BEHIND THE CURTAIN

In today's world, one still discerns political and cultural tensions among different parts of the country. Nonetheless, with the advent of easy transportation and electronic communication, the country has become more connected and perhaps slightly more homogenized. One thesis about the tension between state and federal sovereignty is that it derives from intense animosity among the colonies and ultimately the states of the United

States. Is this tension overblown? Did it ever really exist on an intensely hostile level? One historical clue comes from the will of a prominent figure in Revolutionary America, Lewis Morris. A leading colonist from New York, Lewis Morris apparently looked with great disdain on Connecticut and perhaps all of the northern colonies. In his will, he stated the following:

Portrait of Gouverneur Morris (1752–1816), a Framer of the U.S. Constitution, by Ezra Ames. *Avery Library via Wikimedia Commons.*

> It is my wish that my son may have the best education that is to be had in England or America. But my express will and direction are, that he never be sent for that purpose to the Connecticut colonies, lest he imbibe in his youth, that low craft and cunning, so incidental to the people of that country, which is so interwoven in their constitutions, that their acts cannot disguise it from the world; many of them, under the sanctified garb of religion, have endeavored to impose themselves on the world of honest men.

Modern principles of law would likely not provide any legal enforcement mechanism for Lewis's words. The words are nonetheless suggestive of the disdain that the citizen of one colony held for the citizen of an adjacent colony. Although this is but one example, it does suggest that the Framers were reacting to existing sentiments among the colonies when they created mechanisms for negotiating intergovernmental prejudice. One stark example of this is the provision in Article III for federal courts (deemed a neutral arbiter of cases) to hear cases between citizens from different states. Postscript: Lewis's son, Gouverneur Morris, did not attend higher education in Connecticut (presumably that would be Yale), but instead attended what is now Columbia University and went on to be one of the Framers of the U.S. Constitution.

QUESTION FOR DISCUSSION

2.1   Consider the benefit of having states versus the benefit of having a uniform federal union. What thoughts do you have on this question? If we have a firm handle on the benefits of each, perhaps we can start to make intelligent judgments about how our nation might balance the two. That is the essence of federalism. Please make a list of these benefits.

Various government powers do not fall neatly into discrete buckets: a state government bucket and a federal government bucket. Instead, a particular social issue will likely fall into both buckets. Take, for example, the legality of home-grown marijuana intended for medicinal use. On one hand, home-grown marijuana is almost exclusively a commodity for in-state use only, because the question of whether marijuana sale and use are lawful when intended for medical treatment implicates the power of a state government over ensuring the health and welfare of its citizens. On the other hand, even home-grown marijuana is a commodity traded on a commercial market. The U.S. government has power over matters that could affect interstate commerce. The regulation of home-grown marijuana affects interstate commerce and therefore concurrently falls within the U.S. government's power.[1]

The technical name for this state of affairs is jurisdictional concurrency. Jurisdiction in this instance is a synonym for power, and "concurrency" here, essentially, means "at the same time." You can view a depiction of this concept in Figure 1.1, which appeared in Chapter 1.

QUESTION FOR DISCUSSION

2.2 In deciding how to divide power between two governmental units, is jurisdictional concurrency a good idea? What are the positive consequences? Negative consequences?

The struggle between state and federal power and the debate between proper roles for state and federal governance continues today. Some Supreme Court Justices and constitutional scholars take a generous view of the scope of federal power, emphasizing the Supremacy Clause and the failure of the Articles of Confederation. Other Supreme Court Justices and scholars take a dim view of expansive federal power, emphasizing the dominance of state prerogatives as reflected by the limited nature of the Constitution's grants of power to the branches of the federal government. This latter group often finds support for their position in the Tenth Amendment to the Constitution:

The powers not delegated to the United States by the Constitution, nor prohibited by it to the States, are reserved to the States respectively, or to the people.

One of the most intriguing qualities of constitutional law appears in the debates about federalism. Although not always the case, one often sees a matchup between preferences on state or federal power and ideological preferences on social issues. One often sees a strong connection between preference for state power and conservative social policy on one hand and preference for federal power and liberal social policy on the other hand (Figure 2.1). On a superficial

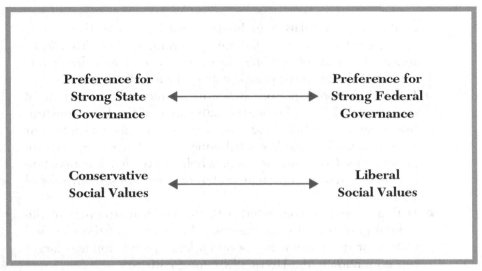

Figure 2.1   Connection Between Government Models and Social Values

level, the connection is not obvious between the preferable size of the entity to control an issue (either a state or the whole of the federal union depending on your preference) and the moral and ideological concerns underlying a social issue.

What might qualify as social values? Issues that implicate religious faith, sexual orientation, public school curriculum, and reproductive freedoms are representative. Anything else?

QUESTION FOR DISCUSSION

2.3   As you read through the various cases in this book, pay attention to the union of these preferences and consider whether you can identify a connection between the two sets of governmental and social values. The questions below present possible modes of inquiry. At this stage of your understanding, you might not have any definitive answer—or like many constitutional scholars, you might never have a definitive answer. Nonetheless, please keep these questions in mind as you navigate the various issues in this book. Perhaps by the end of the book, you will have a clearer view of which factors might be most pertinent to explaining the yoking of preference for governmental structure vis-à-vis preference of certain social values. Here are the questions:

- Is the connection pure happenstance (just an arbitrary coincidence)?
- Is there a geographic reason? May one say—given its capital in the mid-Atlantic United States and given the strong representation

of the large population of liberal coastal states in the federal government—that the federal government has historically reflected a more liberal attitude toward social issues than many small-population, conservative state governments?

- Is there a historical reason? Resentment among different areas of our country dates to before the ratification of the U.S. Constitution. One can see that these resentments remained well after our nation's founding, likely contributing to our Civil War, and still linger today. Do these resentments help to explain the connection between a state government preference and conservative social values?

- Is there a reason connected with the political structure of the federal government—for example, the realities of the electoral college or the relationship between large population and larger representation in the House of Representatives?

- Is there an analytical connection between the features of a smaller government and conservative social values? Smaller governmental units tend to provide more direct representation, reflecting more intimate knowledge of the realities of living in a particular area. Smaller governments are arguably more attuned to libertarian preferences. Is there any reason that this quality might have a greater kinship with conservative social values rather than liberal social values?

- Is the connection tied to religion? Some pockets of the country are more religiously observant than others. Some have a predominance of particular faiths. Different faiths can have different attitudes toward various social values. Can you connect these observations with preferences for state power that might be more effective in protecting particular tenets of religious faith than the federal government?

You will encounter federalism issues throughout this course. Indeed, few cases present struggles with the concept in a vacuum. Most cases confront the federalism issue in the context of construing another provision of the U.S. Constitution, a state law, a federal statute or regulation, or in debates about the best form of government to serve democracy.

The following case wrestles with federalism within the context of a federal prosecution under a criminal statute. Background on three concepts is especially important for understanding the case. First is a description of the power held by states. As noted above, states hold all power of governance unless the federal government has exercised power that is granted to it in the Constitution—in

Two Americans pulling on the pillars of democracy and federalism as George Washington looks on from heaven. Engraving by William Charles. *New York Public Library.*

which event the federal government "wins" under the Supremacy Clause. Otherwise, states maintain governance control over matters related to the health and welfare of citizens. As a term of art, this is called the state's police power—a power that extends far beyond law enforcement protection.

Another (second) important concept mentioned in the case is the Necessary and Proper Clause. This is a clause in the Constitution that provides the U.S. Congress an enormous advantage. The clause expands federal powers that are explicitly described and granted to Congress. You might think of it as an elastic band that stretches Congress's explicit authority. The Necessary and Proper Clause appears after a long list of powers listed in Article I of the Constitution. The Clause states that

> Congress shall have the power . . . [t]o make all Laws which shall be necessary and proper for carrying into Execution the foregoing Powers, and all other Powers vested by this Constitution in the Government of United States, or in any Department or Officer thereof.

As interpreted by the U.S. Supreme Court, this clause grants Congress broad authority: It allows Congress to pass laws that are deemed appropriate to ensure that the powers granted to any department or officer of the federal government are given meaning.

QUESTION FOR DISCUSSION

2.4   Assume that Congress concluded that it needs to regulate the local roads in a state to ensure effective transportation among military bases in the state. Congress justifies this action by pointing to its power over the "land and naval forces" enumerated in Article I, §8, together with the Necessary and Proper Clause. Assume that the state pushes back on this assertion of power over local roads, citing the concept that the federal government is one of limited powers. Does this suggest that the Necessary and Proper Clause and the concept of limited powers are mutually inconsistent? Or does it only illustrate that the two concepts are in tension with one another?

Given the authority made possible by the Necessary and Proper Clause, the question then becomes this: What specific limits on Congress exist? One answer is that the Constitution and its amendments prohibit particular types of laws, such as laws that make an action criminal after the action has occurred (so-called ex post facto laws) or laws that improperly suppress freedom of speech under the First Amendment. The following case takes up the federalism limitation on the scope of congressional power. The federalism limitation is trickier than limitations such as the prohibition against ex post facto laws or suppression of free speech because the limitation is implicit in the Constitution. Without explicit language, the federalism limitations are harder to pin down.

A final (third) key concept for understanding *Bond* is the presumption in favor of the constitutionality of congressional enactments. This presumption arises out of principles of separation of powers and deference to the democratic process of electing those who serve in Congress. The presumption instructs federal courts to err on the side of upholding the constitutional validity of a statute when the court encounters ambiguity in the statutory language, rather than interpret the ambiguity as support for the conclusion that the statute is unconstitutional. Checking against federal court power vis-à-vis legislative power, the presumption requires federal courts to presume that Congress acted within its constitutionally granted power unless the court identifies clear intent to the contrary. In this way, the presumption is intended to ensure that Congress "gets its way" whenever possible—but also to ensure that the federal courts give due deference to the powers of Congress.

FROM THE BENCH

BOND v. UNITED STATES
572 U.S. 84 (2014)

Chief Justice ROBERTS delivered the opinion of the Court.

. . . The question presented by this case is whether the Implementation Act also reaches a purely local crime: an amateur attempt by a jilted wife to injure her husband's lover, which ended up causing only a minor thumb burn readily treated by rinsing with water. Because our constitutional structure leaves local criminal activity primarily to the States, we have generally declined to read federal law as intruding on that responsibility, unless Congress has clearly indicated that the law should have such reach. The Chemical Weapons Convention Implementation Act contains no such clear indication, and we accordingly conclude that it does not cover the unremarkable local offense at issue here.

I

A

In 1997, the President of the United States, upon the advice and consent of the Senate, ratified the Convention on the Prohibition of the Development, Production, Stockpiling, and Use of Chemical Weapons and on Their Destruction. The nations that ratified the Convention (State Parties) had bold aspirations for it: "general and complete disarmament under strict and effective international control, including the prohibition and elimination of all types of weapons of mass destruction." This purpose traces its origin to World War I, when "[o]ver a million casualties, up to 100,000 of them fatal, are estimated to have been caused by chemicals . . . , a large part following the introduction of mustard gas in 1917." The atrocities of that war led the community of nations to adopt the 1925 Geneva Protocol, which prohibited the use of chemicals as a method of warfare . . .

Congress gave the Convention domestic effect in 1998 when it passed the Chemical Weapons Convention Implementation Act. The Act closely tracks the text of the treaty: It forbids any person knowingly "to develop, produce, otherwise acquire, transfer directly or indirectly, receive, stockpile, retain, own, possess, or use, or threaten to use, any chemical weapon." It defines "chemical

FROM THE BENCH

weapon" in relevant part as "[a] toxic chemical and its precursors, except where intended for a purpose not prohibited under this chapter as long as the type and quantity is consistent with such a purpose." "Toxic chemical," in turn, is defined in general as "any chemical which through its chemical action on life processes can cause death, temporary incapacitation or permanent harm to humans or animals. The term includes all such chemicals, regardless of their origin or of their method of production, and regardless of whether they are produced in facilities, in munitions or elsewhere." Finally, "purposes not prohibited by this chapter" is defined as "[a]ny peaceful purpose related to an industrial, agricultural, research, medical, or pharmaceutical activity or other activity," and other specific purposes. A person who violates section 229 may be subject to severe punishment: imprisonment "for any term of years," or if a victim's death results, the death penalty or imprisonment "for life."

B

Petitioner Carol Anne Bond is a microbiologist from Lansdale, Pennsylvania. In 2006, Bond's closest friend, Myrlinda Haynes, announced that she was pregnant. When Bond discovered that her husband was the child's father, she sought revenge against Haynes. Bond stole . . . an arsenic-based compound from her employer, a chemical manufacturer. She also ordered a vial of . . . chemicals commonly used in printing photographs or cleaning laboratory equipment on Amazon.com. Both chemicals are toxic to humans and, in high enough doses, potentially lethal. It is undisputed, however, that Bond did not intend to kill Haynes. She instead hoped that Haynes would touch the chemicals and develop an uncomfortable rash.

Between November 2006 and June 2007, Bond went to Haynes's home on at least 24 occasions and spread the chemicals on her car door, mailbox, and doorknob. These attempted assaults were almost entirely unsuccessful. The chemicals that Bond used are easy to see, and Haynes was able to avoid them all but once. On that occasion, Haynes suffered a minor chemical burn on her thumb, which she treated by rinsing with water. Haynes repeatedly called the local police to report the suspicious substances, but they took no action. When Haynes found powder on her mailbox, she called the police again, who told her to call the post office. Haynes did so, and postal inspectors placed surveillance cameras around her home. The cameras caught Bond opening Haynes's mailbox, stealing an envelope, and stuffing potassium dichromate inside the muffler of Haynes's car.

Federal prosecutors naturally charged Bond with two counts of mail theft, in violation of 18 U.S.C. §1708. More surprising, they also charged her with two counts of possessing and using a chemical weapon, in violation of section 229(a). Bond moved to dismiss the chemical weapon counts on the ground that section 229 exceeded Congress's enumerated powers and invaded powers reserved to the States by the Tenth Amendment. The District Court denied Bond's motion. She then entered a conditional guilty plea that reserved her right to appeal. The District Court sentenced Bond to six years in federal prison plus five years of supervised release, and ordered her to pay a $2,000 fine and $9,902.79 in restitution.

[After extensive proceedings, the Court of Appeals for the Third Circuit rejected Bonds' challenge and allowed the guilty plea to stand. The government then brought the case to the U.S. Supreme Court.]

On remand, Bond renewed her constitutional argument. She also argued that section 229 does not reach her conduct because the statute's exception for the use of chemicals for "peaceful purposes" should be understood in contradistinction to the "warlike" activities that the Convention was primarily designed to prohibit. Bond argued that her conduct, though reprehensible, was not at all "warlike." The Court of Appeals rejected this argument. . . . The Third Circuit also rejected Bond's constitutional challenge to her conviction, holding that section 229 was "necessary and proper to carry the Convention into effect. . . ."

II

In our federal system, the National Government possesses only limited powers; the States and the people retain the remainder. The States have broad authority to enact legislation for the public good—what we have often called a "police power." The Federal Government, by contrast, has no such authority and "can exercise only the powers granted to it," including the power to make "all Laws which shall be necessary and proper for carrying into Execution" the enumerated powers. For nearly two centuries it has been "clear" that, lacking police power, "Congress cannot punish felonies generally." A criminal act committed wholly within a State "cannot be made an offence against the United States, unless it has some relation to the execution of a power of Congress, or to some matter within the jurisdiction of the United States."

The Government frequently defends federal criminal legislation on the ground that the legislation is authorized pursuant to Congress's power to regulate interstate commerce. In this case, however, the Court of Appeals held that the Government had explicitly disavowed that argument before the District Court. As a result, in this Court the parties have devoted significant effort to arguing whether section 229, as applied to Bond's offense, is a necessary and proper means of executing the National Government's power to make treaties. . . . Notwithstanding this debate, it is "a well-established principle governing the prudent exercise of this Court's jurisdiction that normally the Court will not decide a constitutional question if there is some other ground upon which to dispose of the case." Bond argues that section 229 does not cover her conduct. So we consider that argument first.

III

Section 229 exists to implement the Convention, so we begin with that international agreement. As explained, the Convention's drafters intended for it to be a comprehensive ban on chemical weapons. But even with its broadly worded definitions, we have doubts that a treaty about *chemical weapons* has anything to do with Bond's conduct. The Convention, a product of years of worldwide study, analysis, and multinational negotiation, arose in response to war crimes and acts of terrorism. There is no reason to think the sovereign nations that ratified the Convention were interested in anything like Bond's common law assault.

Even if the treaty does reach that far, nothing prevents Congress from implementing the Convention in the same manner it legislates with respect to innumerable other matters—observing the Constitution's division of responsibility between sovereigns and leaving the prosecution of purely local crimes to the States. The Convention, after all, is agnostic between enforcement at the state versus federal level: It provides that "[e]ach State Party shall, *in accordance with its constitutional processes*, adopt the necessary measures to implement its obligations under this Convention."

Fortunately, we have no need to interpret the scope of the Convention in this case. Bond was prosecuted under section 229, and the statute—unlike the Convention—must be read consistent with principles of federalism inherent in our constitutional structure.

A

In the Government's view, the conclusion that Bond "knowingly" "use[d]" a "chemical weapon" in violation of section 229(a) is simple: The chemicals that Bond placed on Haynes's home and car are "toxic chemical[s]" as defined by the statute, and Bond's attempt to assault Haynes was not a "peaceful purpose." The problem with this interpretation is that it would "dramatically intrude[] upon traditional state criminal jurisdiction," and we avoid reading statutes to have such reach in the absence of a clear indication that they do.

Part of a fair reading of a statutory text is recognizing that "Congress legislates against the backdrop" of certain unexpressed presumptions. . . . So even though section 229, read on its face, would cover a chemical weapons crime if committed by a U.S. citizen in Australia, we would not apply the statute to such conduct absent a plain statement from Congress. The notion that some things "go without saying" applies to legislation just as it does to everyday life.

Among the background principles of construction that our cases have recognized are those grounded in the relationship between the Federal Government and the States under our Constitution. . . . Closely related to these principles is the well-established principle that "'it is incumbent upon the federal courts to be certain of Congress' intent before finding that federal law overrides'" the "usual constitutional balance of federal and state powers. . . ." We have applied this background principle when construing federal statutes that touched on several areas of traditional state responsibility . . .

. . . [It] is appropriate to refer to basic principles of federalism embodied in the Constitution to resolve ambiguity in a federal statute. In this case, the ambiguity derives from the improbably broad reach of the key statutory definition given the term—"chemical weapon"—being defined; the deeply serious consequences of adopting such a boundless reading; and the lack of any apparent need to do so in light of the context from which the statute arose—a treaty about chemical warfare and terrorism. We conclude that, in this curious case, we can insist on a clear indication that Congress meant to reach purely local crimes, before interpreting the statute's expansive language in a way that intrudes on the police power of the States.

B

We do not find any such clear indication in section 229. "Chemical weapon" is the key term that defines the statute's reach, and it is defined extremely broadly. But that general definition does not constitute a clear statement that Congress meant the statute to reach local criminal conduct.

In fact, a fair reading of section 229 suggests that it does not have as expansive a scope as might at first appear. To begin, as a matter of natural meaning, an educated user of English would not describe Bond's crime as involving a "chemical weapon." . . . The substances that Bond used bear little resemblance to the deadly toxins that are "of particular danger to the objectives of the Convention." More to the point, the use of something as a "weapon" typically connotes "[a]n instrument of offensive or defensive combat," or "[a]n instrument of attack or defense in combat, as a gun, missile, or sword." But no speaker in natural parlance would describe Bond's feud-driven act of spreading irritating chemicals on Haynes's doorknob and mailbox as "combat." . . . Bond's crime is worlds apart from such hypotheticals, and covering it would give the statute a reach exceeding the ordinary meaning of the words Congress wrote.

In settling on a fair reading of a statute, it is not unusual to consider the ordinary meaning of a defined term, particularly when there is dissonance between that ordinary meaning and the reach of the definition. In *Johnson v. United States*, for example, we considered the statutory term "'violent felony,'" which the Armed Career Criminal Act defined in relevant part as an offense that "'has as an element the use . . . of physical force against the person of another.'" Although "physical force against . . . another" might have meant *any* force, however slight, we thought it "clear that in the context of a statutory definition of '*violent* felony,' the phrase 'physical force' means *violent* force—that is, force capable of causing physical pain or injury to another person." The ordinary meaning of "chemical weapon" plays a similar limiting role here . . .

FROM THE BENCH

The Government's reading of section 229 would "'alter sensitive federal-state relationships,'" convert an astonishing amount of "traditionally local criminal conduct" into "a matter for federal enforcement," and "involve a substantial extension of federal police resources." It would transform the statute from one whose core concerns are acts of war, assassination, and terrorism into a massive federal anti-poisoning regime that reaches the simplest of assaults. . . .

In fact, with the exception of this unusual case, the Federal Government itself has not looked to section 229 to reach purely local crimes. The Government has identified only a handful of prosecutions that have been brought under this section. Most of those involved either terrorist plots or the possession of extremely dangerous substances with the potential to cause severe harm to many people. . . .

This case is unusual, and our analysis is appropriately limited. Our disagreement with our colleagues reduces to whether section 229 is "utterly clear." We think it is not, given that the definition of "chemical weapon" in a particular case can reach beyond any normal notion of such a weapon, that the context from which the statute arose demonstrates a much more limited prohibition was intended, and that the most sweeping reading of the statute would fundamentally upset the Constitution's balance between national and local power. This exceptional convergence of factors gives us serious reason to doubt the Government's expansive reading of section 229, and calls for us to interpret the statute more narrowly.

In sum, the global need to prevent chemical warfare does not require the Federal Government to reach into the kitchen cupboard, or to treat a local assault with a chemical irritant as the deployment of a chemical weapon. There is no reason to suppose that Congress—in implementing the Convention on Chemical Weapons—thought otherwise.

· · ·

The Convention provides for implementation by each ratifying nation "in accordance with its constitutional processes." As James Madison explained, the constitutional process in our "compound republic" keeps power "divided between two distinct governments." If section 229 reached Bond's conduct, it would mark a dramatic departure from that constitutional structure and a serious reallocation of criminal law enforcement authority between the Federal Government and the States. Absent a clear statement of that purpose, we will not presume Congress to have authorized such a stark intrusion into traditional state authority.

The judgment of the Court of Appeals is reversed, and the case is remanded for further proceedings consistent with this opinion.

It is so ordered.

Justice SCALIA, with whom Justice THOMAS joins, and with whom Justice ALITO joins as to Part I, concurring in the judgment.

Somewhere in Norristown, Pennsylvania, a husband's paramour suffered a minor thumb burn at the hands of a betrayed wife. The United States Congress—"everywhere extending the sphere of its activity, and drawing all power into its impetuous vortex"—has made a federal case out of it. What are we to do?

It is the responsibility of "the legislature, not the Court, . . . to define a crime, and ordain its punishment." And it is "emphatically the province and duty of the judicial department to say what the law [including the Constitution] is." Today, the Court shirks its job and performs Congress'. As sweeping and unsettling as the Chemical Weapons Convention Implementation Act of 1998 may be, it is clear beyond doubt that it covers what Bond did; and we have no authority to amend it. So we are forced to decide—there is no way around it—whether the Act's application to what Bond did was constitutional. . . . I would hold that it was not, and for that reason would reverse the judgment of the Court of Appeals for the Third Circuit.

I. The Statutory Question

A. *Unavoidable Meaning of the Text*

The meaning of the Act is plain. No person may knowingly "develop, produce, otherwise acquire, transfer directly or indirectly, receive, stockpile, retain, own, possess, or use, or threaten to use, any chemical weapon." A "chemical weapon" is "[a] toxic chemical and its precursors, except where intended for a purpose not prohibited under this chapter as long as the type and quantity is consistent with such a purpose." A "toxic chemical" is "any chemical which through its chemical action on life processes can cause death, temporary incapacitation or permanent harm to humans or animals. The term includes all such chemicals, regardless of their origin or of their method of production, and regardless of whether they are produced in facilities, in munitions or elsewhere." A "purpose not prohibited" is "[a]ny peaceful purpose related to an industrial, agricultural, research, medical, or pharmaceutical activity or other activity."

Applying those provisions to this case is hardly complicated. Bond possessed and used "chemical[s] which through [their] chemical action on life processes can cause death, temporary incapacitation or permanent harm." Thus, she possessed "toxic chemicals." And, because they were not possessed or used only for a "purpose not prohibited," they were "chemical weapons." Ergo, Bond violated the Act. . . . The Court does not think the interpretive exercise so simple. But that is only because its result-driven antitextualism befogs what is evident . . .

QUESTIONS FOR DISCUSSION

2.5 Chief Justice Roberts writing for the majority and Justice Scalia in concurrence in the judgment in *Bond* came to different conclusions about the proper interpretation of the Chemical Weapons Convention Implementation Act. Both justices took account of the presumption in favor of the constitutionality in making their decision. Who had the more reasonable argument? Is Justice Scalia correct in concluding that the "unavoidable meaning" of the Act yields the conclusion that Congress violated federalism principles?

2.6 Joined by Justices Thomas and Alito, Justice Scalia "concurred in the judgment" that was reached by Chief Justice Roberts's majority. In other words, Justice Scalia reached the same bottom line as Chief Justice Roberts: reversing the decision of the lower courts upholding the prosecution of Carol Anne Bond under the Chemical Weapons Convention Implementation Act. Justice Scalia and Chief Justice Roberts purported to take dramatically different approaches to interpreting Congress's intended meaning. How is it then that they reached the same bottom line? Were their approaches really that different?

The *Bond* decision serves as a useful vehicle for introducing the concept of federalism. The decision, however, is also remarkable for its reflection relating to some of the powers among all branches of the federal government. A review of the various powers implicated in *Bond* provides a useful introduction to the rest of this part, which surveys the powers of the judiciary, legislative, and executive branches of the federal government.

The Treaty-making Power of the Senate and the President

The treaty at issue in *Bond*, known as the Convention on the Prohibition of the Development, Production, Stockpiling, and Use of Chemical Weapons and on Their Destruction, was the product of both the executive and legislative branches of the federal government. President Clinton worked with other nations to create the Convention and then sought the consent of the Senate to ensure that the Convention became a treaty of the United States.[2] This process is outlined in Article II, §2 of the U.S. Constitution: "The President shall have Power, by and with the Advice and Consent of the Senate, to make Treaties, provided two thirds of the Senators concur."

Congress's Power to Ensure That Treaties Are Executed

If the House of Representatives and the Senate pass a statute that implements the provisions of a treaty, these departments ensure that the provisions of the treaty constitute law of the United States and federal courts will enforce the law. The statute at issue in *Bond* (the Chemical Weapons Convention Implementation Act) was just such a piece of legislation. By passing that Act, Congress ensured that the federal courts would enforce (as deemed appropriate) the provisions of the treaty as translated through the provisions of the Act.

The Expansion of Congress's Power Through the Necessary and Proper Clause

As described earlier, the Necessary and Proper Clause is enormously important to expanding Congress's explicit detailed powers that are listed in Article I, §8 of the Constitution. As such, the clause was important for evaluating whether Congress has overstepped its constitutionally granted powers. In later chapters, you will read about how the terms "necessary and proper" enjoy an expansive reading.

Executive Power in the Form of Prosecutorial Decision Making

The first federal executive entity to investigate Carol Anne Bond's case was the U.S. Postal Inspector, who had power over the case by virtue of the presence of the chemical substance on the postal box. The Postal Inspector then brought the case to another federal executive entity: prosecutors at the U.S. Attorney's Office for the Eastern District of Pennsylvania. After hearing the facts of the crime, the prosecutors brainstormed about which federal criminal statute best fit the crime and settled on the Chemical Weapons Convention Implementation Act. They decided to proceed with the prosecution, bringing charges against Carol Anne Bond for using the toxic chemical substance on Haynes's mailbox in violation of the Act. After negotiations, Bond agreed to plead guilty. The prosecutors drafted a plea agreement, which a federal judge accepted after a "colloquy" (dialogue) with the defendant to ensure she understood the consequences of pleading guilty. Once the federal judge accepted the plea agreement, the guilty plea took on the status of a federal conviction.

Judicial Power to Review Acts of Congress for Compliance with the U.S. Constitution

Although not mentioned in the *Bond* opinion, one should note that it was federal courts that possessed the role of evaluating whether the Chemical Weapons Convention Implementation Act—as applied to the *Bond* facts—was constitutional in light of federalism principles. Embracing that task without question in the case, the U.S. Supreme Court majority joined Chief Justice Roberts's decision to employ the presumption in favor of constitutionality to construe the Act so as to avoid invalidating it as applied to the case. Importantly, however, the Court *could* have found the Act unconstitutional as applied to *Bond* and the facts of the case—as Justice Scalia argued. This prerogative to declare an act of Congress unconstitutional is called the power of judicial review—the topic that headlines Chapter 3.

QUESTIONS FOR REVIEW

1. How does the difference between vertical separation of powers and horizontal separation of powers relate to the scope of Congress's power?
2. Under the constitutional scheme, which jurisdiction has the most expansive power: the federal government or the state government? What is the basis for your answer? How does the Supremacy Clause influence your answer?
3. What is the presumption of constitutionality and what influence did it have in the disposition of the *Bond* case?
4. Chief Justice Roberts and Justice Scalia reached the same result in disposing of *Bond* (reversing the lower court). They did, however, use different reasoning to get to that conclusion. Describe the differences in their reasoning.
5. What are the arguments in favor of jurisdictional concurrency? What are the arguments against it?
6. The *Bond* decision implicates many different powers of the three branches of the federal government. Name those powers.

ENDNOTES

1. *See Gonzales v. Raich*, 545 U.S. 1 (2005).
2. The word "convention" is generally regarded as synonymous with "treaty." Conventions or treaties are also sometimes referred to as "agreements" as well.

Powers of the Federal Courts

3

A. Basics of Article III

Before starting to read this chapter, you will find it helpful to peruse Article III as it appears in the U.S. Constitution, reproduced at the end of this book. In reviewing Article III, you should first note that it purports to define "the federal judicial power" of the United States. This is another name for the federal courts.

Interestingly, Article III creates only one court: the U.S. Supreme Court. The Article does refer to "such inferior Courts as the Congress may from time to time ordain and establish." This is an elegant way of saying that the Framers punted on whether the federal government should contain lower federal courts. Some Framers believed that lower federal courts were advisable to ensure that federal law is accurately interpreted, honored, and enforced. Others were worried that lower federal courts would usurp primary power over the day-to-day affairs of citizens that had been vested in state government. James Madison devised a compromise that appears in Article III: Let Congress decide. Thus, we have the above-quoted language regarding "such inferior Courts that Congress may from time to time. . . ." Congress worked with dispatch and created lower federal courts in the Judiciary Act of 1789, passed soon after the Constitution was fully ratified.

Most of Article III lays out a job description for federal courts. Most prominent is the restriction of what a federal court can do: It can resolve only "cases" or "controversies." In other words, federal courts are confined to resolving problems that litigants bring to them. This limitation influences the way that federal courts dispose of legal and policy issues. Although the U.S. Supreme Court occasionally outlines a general strategy for resolving specific types of cases, the Court usually restricts its reasoning to the facts of individual cases. Confined to this restriction, the federal courts are passive: They simply lay back and wait for specifically defined issues to be brought to them by litigants who have disputes. In nearly every case, it is the litigants, not the courts, that define the issues.

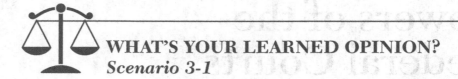

WHAT'S YOUR LEARNED OPINION?
Scenario 3-1

In July 1793, then-Secretary of State Thomas Jefferson addressed a letter to the U.S. Supreme Court outlining difficult questions of federal law that the executive branch confronted. The questions depended on "their solution on the constructions of our treaties, on the laws of nature and nations, and on the laws of the land." Jefferson explained the questions concerned matters of foreign affairs that arose under circumstances in which they would not make their way into the courts of the United States. On behalf of President George Washington, Jefferson, therefore, beseeched the Supreme Court Justices to provide their advice on the resolution of a series of abstract questions that either had already arisen or would likely soon occur. Washington's cabinet thereafter developed a series of questions for the Justices to answer.[1]

Given the language of the Constitution regarding the power of federal courts, what would be the proper answer to this request?

Article III, §2 precisely outlines the nature of the cases or controversies that federal courts can hear. This list is exclusive and is confined to nine types of cases: If a particular type of case is not listed, federal courts do not have the power to decide the case. Unlike Congress, the federal courts do not enjoy a corollary to the Necessary and Proper Clause. The different cases listed fall into two general categories. The most common category of cases is the category that authorizes federal courts to interpret and enforce the federal government's power. This includes cases that arise under the U.S. Constitution, treaties, and other U.S laws. It also includes disputes in which the United States is a party and those that concern the U.S. government's interest in matters relating to federal policy, as well as admiralty and maritime. The second class of cases is those that cast federal courts as umpires in the federal system, negotiating and resolving disputes between different states, citizens from different states, and the like.

WHAT'S YOUR LEARNED OPINION?
Scenario 3-2

Finbarr imports a brand of whiskey made in Ireland named Celtic Gold. In promoting his brand from 2020 to 2022, Finbarr made public statements that a competing brand, Green Isle Mother's Milk, cannot be viewed as Irish because a substantial part of the processing for the product occurs in Scotland. The manufacturer of Green Isle Mother's Milk informed Finbarr that his statements were damaging its business profits and threatened to sue him under federal laws. Finbarr negotiated an agreement under which the Green Isle Mother's Milk producers agreed not to sue Finbarr for "statements made before 2023 regarding the source of the Green Isle beverage" if Finbarr promised not to make any further public statements about Green Isle Mother's Milk.

One year passed, and Finbarr resumed work on his advertising campaign promoting Celtic Gold. Finbarr concluded that his best approach would be to emphasize the true Irish identity of his product and to point out the non-Irish connections of his competitors. Just to be careful, Finbarr decided he should file a declaratory judgment action in federal court, asking the court to declare that he could lawfully make these planned public statements about his competitors.

A declaratory judgment action is a type of lawsuit that asks the court to render a decision on the correct resolution under the law of a potential conflict between two or more parties. Green Isle Mother's Milk moved to dismiss the declaratory judgment action, arguing that such action is improper because no case or controversy exists between the parties. Should the federal court accept this argument?

BEHIND THE CURTAIN

During the debates in New York over whether to ratify the Constitution, Alexander Hamilton, writing in *The Federalist*, No. 78, argued:

> Whoever attentively considers the different departments of power must perceive, that in a government in which they are separated from each other, the judiciary, from the nature of its functions, will always be the least dangerous to the political rights of the constitution: because it will be least in a capacity to annoy or injure them. The executive not only dispenses the honors, but holds the sword of the community. The legislature not only commands the purse, but prescribes the rules by which the duties and rights of every citizen are to be regulated. The judiciary, on the contrary, has no influence over either the sword or the purse; no direction either of

A posthumous portrait of Alexander Hamilton by John Trumbull. *National Portrait Gallery.*

the strength or of the wealth of the society; and can take no active resolution whatever. It may truly be said to have neither Force nor Will, but merely judgment; and must ultimately depend upon the aid of the executive arm even for the efficacy of its judgments.

These words deserve attention as you go through the course. Questions to consider in light of these statements and future materials include:

- Did the recognition of judicial review in *Marbury v. Madison* reduce the accuracy of these words?
- Do U.S. Supreme Court decisions rendered in the Commerce Clause, taxing and spending power, and executive power areas cast doubt on Hamilton's statement that the judiciary lacks any influence over "either the sword or the purse"?
- Is it true that the efficacy of dramatic decisions such as *Brown v. Board of Education*—which announced legal principles requiring integration of public schools—depended "upon the aid of the executive arm even for the efficacy of [the Supreme Court's] judgments"?
- On matters such as the right to privacy—which informed birth control and abortion disputes—can one say that the judiciary exerted no control over "the rules by which the duties and rights of every citizen are to be regulated"?

B. Judicial Review

The initial decade of the U.S. Supreme Court's history brought few tasks to the Court. A variety of reasons for this exist: Facilities and support personnel were lacking (no chambers and few employees), traditions and customs were absent, and little institutional recognition or identity existed. Given this weak status, the Court decided few significant cases, but questions about the scope of the Court's power to overturn government actions that were contrary to the fundamental principles animating the U.S. government became more prevalent in the general legal and governmental culture.

This background is important because the Constitution says absolutely nothing about the power of judicial review, a term used to describe the ability of a court to declare the acts of another branch of government to be invalid as inconsistent with the Constitution. In laying out the job description for those giving life to the "federal judicial power," the Constitution speaks only of protections for independence (life tenure and protection from salary diminution) and cases and controversies.

In the period immediately following the ratification of the Constitution, judges, politicians, and thought leaders expressed conflicting opinions about whether it was proper for the federal judiciary to have the final say on the meaning of the Constitution. For example, Justice Chase, writing in *Calder v. Bull*, 3 Dall. (3 U.S.) 199 (1796), wrote that the U.S. Supreme Court had the power to overturn laws that violate fundamental principles, including the Constitution's mission of "establish(ing) justice . . . promot(ing) the general welfare, secur[ing] the blessings of liberty and protect(ing) their person and property from violence." By contrast, Thomas Jefferson took a different tack, maintaining that each department of the federal government is "independent of the others and has an equal right to decide for itself what is the meaning of the Constitution." He went on to argue that each of the three branches of the federal government "has equally the right to decide for itself what is its duty under the Constitution, without regard to what the others may have decided for themselves under a similar question."[2]

QUESTION FOR DISCUSSION

3.1 What do you think of Jefferson's argument? Does it have some weight, given that Article III is explicit in limiting the power of the judiciary and says nothing about the power of judicial review? Remember to evaluate his argument again once you learn more about how the Constitution treats the powers of the legislature and the executive. In the meantime, compare his arguments to those of Chief Justice John Marshall in *Marbury v. Madison*.

Scholars often refer to *Marbury v. Madison* as the most important decision in all of U.S. constitutional history. Perhaps that it is an overstatement: Consider that proposition as you make your way through this book and see if you agree. In any event, the opinion is crucial in that it cemented the federal judiciary's job of being the final word on whether the actions of the federal legislature and the federal executive are constitutional.

Marbury arose out of a quirky turn of events arising from the fiercely contested 1800 presidential election (with shenanigans that rivaled—if not exceeded—the controversies surrounding presidential elections in more recent years). The leading contenders in that election were John Adams (incumbent), Thomas Jefferson, and Aaron Burr. Jefferson and Burr tied in the Electoral College (although Jefferson received the popular-vote majority). Adams was out of the race.

Jefferson was ultimately named the winner. This heightened the controversy because Adams was a Federalist (known during that time for preferring a strong national power) and Jefferson was a Nationalist (known during that time

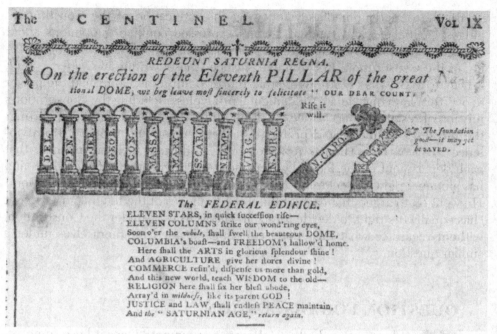

The CENTINEL   Vol IX

REDEUNT SATURNIA REGNA.
On the erection of the Eleventh PILLAR of the great National DOME, we beg leave most sincerely to felicitate "OUR DEAR COUNTRY."

Rise it will.

The foundation good—it may yet be SAVED.

The FEDERAL EDIFICE.

ELEVEN STARS, in quick succession rise—
ELEVEN COLUMNS strike our wond'ring eyes,
Soon o'er the whole, shall swell the beauteous DOME,
COLUMBIA's boast—and FREEDOM's hallow'd home.
Here shall the ARTS in glorious splendour shine!
And AGRICULTURE give her stores divine!
COMMERCE refin'd, dispense us more than gold,
And this new world, teach WISDOM to the old—
RELIGION here shall fix her blest abode,
Array'd in mildness, like its parent GOD!
JUSTICE and LAW, shall endless PEACE maintain,
And the " SATURNIAN AGE," return again,

This woodcut from 1788 shows columns representing the states supporting the "Federal Edifice." A hand extends from a cloud to position the column representing North Carolina under "The Great National Dome." To the right, Rhode Island remains to be placed. The Massachusetts Centinel, *August 2, 1788/Library of Congress.*

as concerned about maintaining strong state governments). In the last days of Adams's term, Federalists were intent on buttressing Federalist power. To that end, Adams named a Federalist, John Marshall, as Chief Justice of the United States. Marshall was also Secretary of State at the time. Immediately before Adams's term ended, the Federalist Congress adopted the Organic Act of the District of Columbia, authorizing the President to appoint 42 new justices of the peace.

As Secretary of State, Marshall signed the commissions appointing these justices of the peace to their position and solicited his brother to deliver them on the day before Jefferson's inauguration. A few individuals, however, did not receive their commission in time. Once Jefferson took office, he instructed his own Secretary of State, James Madison, to withhold the undelivered commissions. William Marbury was one of the individuals who did not receive a commission. He filed suit in the U.S. Supreme Court, seeking a writ of mandamus to compel Madison to deliver the commission. A writ of mandamus is an order issued by a court to an official requiring the official to perform a duty within the scope of the official's job.

"A Peep into the Antifederal Club." A Federalist cartoon of 1793 ridiculing the Jeffersonian anti-Federalists as an unruly mob opposed to government and in concert with the devil. Jefferson himself is shown at center right, standing on the table and orating. *Historical Society of Pennsylvania.*

FROM THE BENCH

MARBURY v. MADISON
5 U.S. (1 Cranch) 137 (1803)

Opinion of the court.

In the order in which the court has viewed this subject, the following questions have been considered and decided.

1st. Has the applicant a right to the commission he demands?

2dly. If he has a right, and that right has been violated, do the laws of his country afford him a remedy?

3dly. If they do afford him a remedy, is it a *mandamus* issuing from this court?

The first object of inquiry is,

1st. Has the applicant a right to the commission he demands?

His right originates in an act of congress passed in February 1801, concerning the district of Columbia . . .

It is . . . decidedly the opinion of the court, that when a commission has been signed by the President, the appointment is made; and that the commission is complete, when the seal of the United States has been affixed to it by the secretary of state . . .

Mr. Marbury, then, since his commission was signed by the President, and sealed by the secretary of state, was appointed; and as the law creating the office, gave the officer a right to hold for five years, independent of the executive, the appointment was not revocable; but vested in the officer legal rights, which are protected by the laws of this country.

To withhold his commission, therefore, is an act deemed by the court not warranted by law, but violative of a vested legal right.

This brings us to the second inquiry; which is,

2dly. If he has a right, and that right has been violated, do the laws of this country afford him a remedy?

The very essence of civil liberty certainly consists in the right of every individual to claim the protection of the laws, whenever he receives an injury . . .

Is it in the nature of the transaction? Is the act of delivering or withholding a commission to be considered as a mere political act, belonging to the executive department alone, for the performance of which, entire confidence is placed by our constitution in the supreme executive; and for any misconduct respecting which, the injured individual has no remedy.

[The Court ruled that the President and his close officers are entitled to immunity from review by the judiciary when performing certain "discretionary" functions, but that these individuals are not immune from review when performing nondiscretionary, "ministerial" functions. In this particular situation, the Court determined that the delivery of the commission was ministerial and thus subject to review.]

It remains to be inquired whether,

3dly. He is entitled to the remedy for which he applies. This depends on,

1st. The nature of the writ applied for, and,

2dly. The power of this court.

1st. The nature of the writ. [The Court here explained that the remedy that Marbury asked for—a writ of mandamus—had been used to make government officers take action that the law required them to take.]

. . . This, then, is a plain case for a mandamus, either to deliver the commission, or a copy of it from the record; and it only remains to be inquired,

Whether it can issue from this court.

The act to establish the judicial courts of the United States authorizes the supreme court "to issue writs of mandamus, in cases warranted by the principles and usages of law, to any courts appointed, or persons holding office, under the authority of the United States."

The secretary of state, being a person holding an office under the authority of the United States, is precisely within the letter of the description; and if this court is not authorized to issue a writ of mandamus to such an officer, it must be because the law is unconstitutional, and therefore absolutely incapable of conferring the authority, and assigning the duties which its words purport to confer and assign.

The constitution vests the whole judicial power of the United States in one supreme court, and such inferior courts as congress shall, from time to time, ordain and establish. This power is expressly extended to all cases arising under the laws of the United States; and consequently, in some form, may be exercised over the present case; because the right claimed is given by a law of the United States.

In the distribution of this power, it is declared that "the supreme court shall have original jurisdiction in all cases affecting ambassadors, other public ministers and consuls, and those in which a state shall be a party. In all other cases, the supreme court shall have appellate jurisdiction."

It has been insisted, at the bar, that as the original grant of jurisdiction, to the supreme and inferior courts is general, and the clause, assigning original jurisdiction to the supreme court, contains no negative or restrictive words; the power remains to the legislature, to assign original jurisdiction to that court in other cases than those specified in the article which has been recited; provided those cases belong to the judicial power of the United States.

If it had been intended to leave it in the discretion of the legislature to apportion the judicial power between the supreme and inferior courts according to the will of that body, it would certainly have been useless to have proceeded further than to have defined the judicial power, and the tribunals in which it should be vested. The subsequent part of the section is mere surplusage, is entirely without meaning, if such is to be the construction. If congress remains at liberty to give this court appellate jurisdiction, where the constitution has declared their jurisdiction shall be original; and original jurisdiction where the constitution has declared it shall be appellate; the distribution of jurisdiction, made in the constitution, is form without substance.

Affirmative words are often, in their operation, negative of other objects than those affirmed; and in this case, a negative or exclusive sense must be given to them or they have no operation at all.

It cannot be presumed that any clause in the constitution is intended to be without effect; and therefore, such a construction is inadmissible unless the words require it . . .

When an instrument organizing fundamentally a judicial system, divides it into one supreme, and so many inferior courts as the legislature may ordain and establish; then enumerates its powers, and proceeds so far to distribute them, as to define the jurisdiction of the supreme court by declaring the cases in which it shall take original jurisdiction, and that in others it shall take appellate jurisdiction; the plain import of the words seems to be, that in one class of cases its

FROM THE BENCH

jurisdiction is original, and not appellate; in the other, it is appellate, and not original. If any other construction would render the clause inoperative, that is an additional reason for rejecting such other construction, and for adhering to their obvious meaning.

To enable this court then to issue a mandamus, it must be shewn [*sic*] to be an exercise of appellate jurisdiction, or to be necessary to enable them to exercise appellate jurisdiction . . .

It is the essential criterion of appellate jurisdiction, that it revises and corrects the proceedings in a cause already instituted, and does not create that cause. Although, therefore, a mandamus may be directed to courts, yet to issue such a writ to an officer for the delivery of a paper, is in effect the same as to sustain an original action for that paper, and therefore seems not to belong to appellate, but to original jurisdiction. Neither is it necessary in such a case as this, to enable the court to exercise its appellate jurisdiction.

The authority, therefore, given to the supreme court, by the act establishing the judicial courts of the United States, to issue writs of mandamus to public officers, appears not to be warranted by the constitution; and it becomes necessary to enquire whether a jurisdiction, so conferred, can be exercised.

The question, whether an act, repugnant to the constitution, can become the law of the land, is a question deeply interesting to the United States; but, happily, not of an intricacy proportioned to its interest. It seems only necessary to recognize certain principles, supposed to have been long and well established, to decide it.

That the people have an original right to establish, for their future government, such principles as, in their opinion, shall most conduce to their own happiness, is the basis, on which the whole American fabric has been erected. The exercise of this original right is a very great exertion; nor can it, nor ought it to be frequently repeated. The principles, therefore, so established, are deemed fundamental. And as the authority, from which they proceed, is supreme, and can seldom act, they are designed to be permanent.

This original and supreme will organizes the government, and assigns, to different departments, their respective powers. It may either stop here; or establish certain limits not to be transcended by those departments.

The government of the United States is of the latter description. The powers of the legislature are defined, and limited; and that those limits may not be mistaken, or forgotten, the constitution is written. To what purpose are powers limited, and to what purpose is that limitation committed to writing, if these limits may, at any time, be passed by those intended to be restrained? The distinction, between a government with limited and unlimited powers, is abolished, if those limits do not confine the persons on whom they are imposed, and if acts prohibited and acts allowed, are of equal obligation. It is a proposition too plain to be contested, that the constitution controls any legislative act repugnant to it; or, that the legislature may alter the constitution by an ordinary act.

Between these alternatives there is no middle ground. The constitution is either a superior, paramount law, unchangeable by ordinary means, or it is on a level with ordinary legislative acts, and like other acts, is alterable when the legislature shall please to alter it. . . .

Certainly all those who have framed written constitutions contemplate them as forming the fundamental and paramount law of the nation, and consequently the theory of every such government must be, that an act of the legislature, repugnant to the constitution, is void.

This theory is essentially attached to a written constitution, and is consequently to be considered, by this court, as one of the fundamental principles of our society. It is not therefore to be lost sight of in the further consideration of this subject.

If an act of the legislature, repugnant to the constitution, is void, does it, notwithstanding its invalidity, bind the courts, and oblige them to give it effect? Or, in other words, though it be not law, does it constitute a rule as operative as if it was a law? This would be to overthrow in fact what was established in theory; and would seem, at first view, an absurdity too gross to be insisted on. It shall, however, receive a more attentive consideration.

It is emphatically the province and duty of the judicial department to say what the law is. Those who apply the rule to particular cases, must of necessity expound and interpret that rule. If two laws conflict with each other, the courts must decide on the operation of each.

So if a law be in opposition to the constitution; if both the law and the constitution apply to a particular case, so that the court must either decide that case conformably to the law, disregarding the constitution; or conformably to the constitution, disregarding the law; the court must determine which of these conflicting rules governs the case. This is of the very essence of judicial duty. . . .

The judicial power of the United States is extended to all cases arising under the constitution.

Could it be the intention of those who gave this power, to say that, in using it, the constitution should not be looked into? That a case arising under the constitution should be decided without examining the instrument under which it arises?

This is too extravagant to be maintained.

In some cases then, the constitution must be looked into by the judges. And if they can open it at all, what part of it are they forbidden to read, or to obey?

There are many other parts of the constitution which serve to illustrate this subject.

It is declared that "no tax or duty shall be laid on articles exported from any state." Suppose a duty on the export of cotton, of tobacco, or of flour; and a suit instituted to recover it. Ought judgment to be rendered in such a case? ought the judges to close their eyes on the constitution, and only see the law.

The constitution declares that "no bill of attainder or *ex post facto* law shall be passed."

FROM THE BENCH

If, however, such a bill should be passed and a person should be prosecuted under it; must the court condemn to death those victims whom the constitution endeavors to preserve? "No person," says the constitution, "shall be convicted of treason unless on the testimony of two witnesses to the same overt act, or on confession in open court."

Here the language of the constitution is addressed especially to the courts. It prescribes, directly for them, a rule of evidence not to be departed from. If the legislature should change that rule, and declare *one* witness, or a confession *out of* court, sufficient for conviction, must the constitutional principle yield to the legislative act?

From these, and many other selections which might be made, it is apparent, that the framers of the constitution contemplated that instrument, as a rule for the government of *courts*, as well as of the legislature.

Why otherwise does it direct the judges to take an oath to support it? This oath certainly applies, in an especial manner, to their conduct in their official character. How immoral to impose it on them, if they were to be used as the instruments, and the knowing instruments, for violating what they swear to support?

The oath of office, too, imposed by the legislature, is completely demonstrative of the legislative opinion on this subject. It is in these words, "I do solemnly swear that I will administer justice without respect to persons, and do equal right to the poor and to the rich; and that I will faithfully and impartially discharge all the duties incumbent on me as according to the best of my abilities and understanding, agreeably to *the constitution*, and laws of the United States."

Why does a judge swear to discharge his duties agreeably to the constitution of the United States, if that constitution forms no rule for his government? if it is closed upon him, and cannot be inspected by him?

If such be the real state of things, this is worse than solemn mockery. To prescribe, or to take this oath, becomes equally a crime.

It is also not entirely unworthy of observation, that in declaring what shall be the *supreme* law of the land, the *constitution* itself is first mentioned; and not the laws of the United States generally, but those only which shall be made in *pursuance* of the constitution, have that rank.

Thus, the particular phraseology of the constitution of the United States confirms and strengthens the principle, supposed to be essential to all written constitutions, that a law repugnant to the constitution is void; and that *courts*, as well as other departments, are bound by that instrument.

The rule must be discharged.

Scholars herald the brilliance of Marshall's rhetorical tactics in *Marbury v. Madison*. One even might say that he gave the impression of giving away the fight on behalf of the Federalists,[3] but ultimately lost a battle in the short run but won the war in the long run. How did this occur? Given the politics of the time, most agree that Marshall would have been unwise to grant Marbury's request for mandamus, as the chances were excellent that Jefferson would disregard the decision and a constitutional crisis might have resulted. (This fact alone tells much about the diminished power of the Supreme Court at the time of the founding of our nation. After Marshall jump-started the Supreme Court's power with the *Marbury v. Madison* decision, the Court's influence, respect, and prestige have grown.)

Other political realities of the time also suggest the wisdom of not picking a fight with the Jefferson administration, which could have retaliated by taking such actions as trying to impeach Federalist justices. Thus, Marshall handed Jefferson a bottom-line win. It was a short-term win, though, when viewed in light of Marshall's decision to take the occasion to solidify the concept of judicial review, which is essential to the power of the federal judiciary and, at this point in history, is generally regarded as nonnegotiable.

BEHIND THE CURTAIN

Chief Justice Marshall was not our first Chief Justice, but most would agree that he was our most influential during this early era. In addition to *Marbury v. Madison*, you will see that Marshall wrote two other influential Federalist opinions ensuring a strong position for the U.S. Congress, *McCulloch v. Maryland* and *Gibbons v. Ogden*, which you will encounter later in this book. In both *Marbury* and *McCulloch*, Marshall issued a complex, blockbuster opinion within days of oral argument. Students of the Supreme Court have always wondered whether he had a defined agenda and had already thought through what he wanted to say. Or . . . had he written the opinions well before the time he issued them?

The official portrait of Chief Justice John Marshall by Henry Inman hangs in the Virginia State Library, Richmond, Virginia. *Virginia State Library, Richmond, Virginia.*

In considering Marshall's role in deciding *Marbury*, note the importance of his earlier involvement in the facts of the case. Marshall was intimately involved as Secretary of State in processing the commissions that were at the root of the case. Indeed, his brother was even involved as the delivery person. Yet then he sat in judgment of whether or not the commission was valid, whether Marbury had a right that deserved a remedy, and the like. Under today's ethical rules, this would have been dubious. Under today's ethical rules, a judge should not participate in a case in which the judge has an actual conflict of interest or even the appearance of a conflict of interest. Additionally, a judge should not participate in a case in which the judge might become a witness to the facts.

Whatever one says about his actions, motives, or ethics, Chief Justice Marshall clearly did a lot to secure a strong federal government and the prestige of the U.S. Supreme Court. He had a long tenure (1801–1835) and adroitly used the circumstances of a young republic to make his mark. Remarkably, however, the U.S. Supreme Court did not actually use the power of judicial review until more than 50 years after *Marbury v. Madison*, when it handed down the much-reviled decision in *Dred Scott v. Sanford*, discussed in Part B of this volume. Why? Possible reasons are that the country was generally less litigious in the era after *Marbury* than it is now and no legal theory existed for bringing constitutional civil rights suits against the use of state power against citizens. Before 1925, the Supreme Court did not even start to apply the protections of the Bill of Rights to state governments. Under the allocation of power and duties of state and federal governments, state governments are in the primary position to interact with citizens on the details of everyday life (e.g., garbage collection, public education, police protection, health regulation, and the like). These are major ways in which state governments have an opportunity to violate what are now identified as individual liberties of citizens. But before the Bill of Rights protections covered state governmental action, no federal opportunity existed for pursuing a state governmental violation of civil rights guaranteed under the first ten amendments of the Constitution. This matter is covered more fully in Part B of this volume.

C. Justiciability

Although the case and controversy requirement for federal courts sounds like a wooden, technical concept, it turns out to have great significance for the process of constitutional litigation. Formally, the requirement works to constrain the policy-making power of federal courts. Federal courts may not reach out, identify a social problem, and try to come up with ways to fix the problem. As illustrated by the interaction between the first Chief Justice, John Jay, and Thomas Jefferson (alluded to in Scenario 3-1 above), the requirement also keeps federal courts out of important issues confronting other branches of the federal government that have not yet risen to the level of a lawsuit.

The federal courts refer to the collection of principles that enable this type of maneuvering as justiciability doctrines. Technically, a court can decide that a case is "justiciable" if it presents the type of lawsuit that is capable of judicial resolution. According to Supreme Court descriptions, a case is justiciable if it possesses a current disagreement between the parties of the character that courts have the tools to resolve. As explained immediately below, the U.S. Supreme Court has refined four doctrines that define whether a case satisfies the requirement for the case to have attributes ensuring that courts can ably resolve the controversy in the case within the confines of the Constitution's grant of power to federal courts.

As defined, this justiciability requirement sounds like it restricts what a court can do. The requirement is not completely a negative constraint on federal court power, though. As a practical matter, the federal courts might discover that the case or controversy requirement provides them with a potent weapon for picking and choosing which hot-button issues they are willing to confront and which they want to duck. Whatever its true motives may be, when the Supreme Court recognizes that a particular structure of lawsuit is not justiciable, it effectively ensures that lawsuits that resemble that structure are dead at the threshold of federal litigation. This can effectively stunt the growth of constitutional principles and ensures a particular result in the suit. Thus, in evaluating the wisdom of the justiciability doctrines, please take note of how the doctrines constrain courts from actively deciding a constitutional issue, but also empower the courts to pick only those issues they desire to confront head-on, avoid those they do not want to reckon with, and passively leave in place potentially objectionable governmental policies that federal litigation cannot change.

The federal courts have carried over this concern with getting into conflicts where they might not belong when they are asked to evaluate attempts to bring a lawsuit under circumstances that are politically charged. Accordingly, they have used their judicial review power to infer four separate justiciability doctrines from the case and controversy requirement. If the federal court finds a justiciability problem with the case, the court will not even look into the real controversy in the case (called the merits of the case).

The courts describe these doctrines as having a jurisdictional component. This means that the federal court actually lacks the power to hear a particular case if the requirements of the justiciability doctrines are not met. If the court finds that it lacks power over the case, the court will dismiss the case without looking into the merits. For at least one justiciability doctrine—the standing doctrine—federal courts have also developed prudential standards that might counsel the court not to reach the merits of a case, even though it concludes that it technically has the power to hear the merits.

Here is a rundown of the four justiciability doctrines. One way to think of the doctrines is to focus on how each doctrine interacts with the qualities in a case.

The Standing Doctrine: Focuses on **Who** is bringing a lawsuit, asking whether the parties are truly adverse and whether the parties to the suit have a true stake in the outcome.

The Ripeness Doctrine: Focuses on **When** the lawsuit is brought, asking whether the suit is brought too early.

The Mootness Doctrine: Focuses on **When** as well, but looks to see if the lawsuit is brought too late.

The Political Question Doctrine: Focuses on **What** characterizes the topic of the lawsuit.

Thus, the justiciability doctrines boil down to *who* brings a lawsuit, the timing of *when* the lawsuit was brought and remains pending, and the subject matter of *what* the lawsuit is about. Because all the justiciability doctrines can have the effect of eliminating litigation at the "courthouse door" and derive from the case and controversy requirement, they often operate interchangeably. For all of the doctrines except the political question doctrine, one can use the following "rough and ready" concept: It takes two to have a fight. Both sides of the lawsuit must take some active part in the dispute. On occasion when the court or a party invokes the political question doctrine, one of the two parties does not take active part in the suit. For example, there have been situations when a presidential administration does not agree with a policy that an earlier presidential administration has put in place. If a lawsuit was filed before the subsequent presidential administration came into office, that administration might wish to keep the case in the courts for strategic or political reasons. In that situation, the two parties are not truly adversary. Consider how this concept that a lawsuit must present an adversary battle might play out in the context of Scenario 3-3.

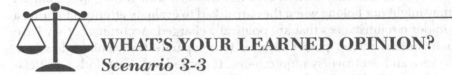

WHAT'S YOUR LEARNED OPINION?
Scenario 3-3

The town of Political Repression passed an ordinance saying that residents in the town may not have a visible political campaign sign on their property—whether it be outside the house or displayed in a window. Maria is offended by the ordinance and wants to challenge it. Consider the following circumstances in evaluating whether there is a justiciability problem with Maria's federal lawsuit in each instance.

1. Assume that Maria does not live in the town of Political Repression, but nonetheless wants to challenge the ordinance as a violation of the First Amendment.
2. Assume that Maria does not have any present intention of putting a sign on her lawn but thinks she might want to do so in a future election.
3. Assume that Maria files a federal court lawsuit and immediately thereafter the town of Political Repression repeals the ordinance.

In each instance, can you identify the most likely justiciability problem? Do these examples help you see the similarity among the doctrines? In other words, do you see the possibility that one can place a justiciability label on one scenario, and without much effort place another justiciability label on the same scenario?

Scenario 3-4

Alberto is unemployed. He lives off his investments and pays for his expenses, including local personal property tax, from his securities holdings. He heard that the local government in his township just passed a tax on wage income. Alberto has no plans to work for wages in the future: He is content with his current lifestyle and does not want the hassle and structure of working at a paying job. He is nonetheless deeply offended by the legislation and files a suit challenging it. He fashions his claim as a challenge under the U.S. Constitution. Does Alberto have standing to bring this suit?

1. Standing: Regulating Who Can Bring a Lawsuit

Federal courts can adjudicate only cases brought by litigants who have standing. The standing doctrine seeks to confine judicial energy to those cases in which a plaintiff—the person who brought the suit—(1) has suffered personal injury that (2) is traceable to the conduct of the defendant (the person being sued), and (3) is capable of being redressed by the federal court. The standing doctrine has proved the most versatile and most extensively used of all the justiciability doctrines. Consider Scenario 3-5.

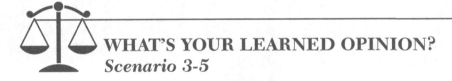

WHAT'S YOUR LEARNED OPINION?
Scenario 3-5

A university professor, Professor Concerned Cheryl, was watching the morning news on television and saw a story about an event that troubled her. The story reported that two officers of a major city's police department had pulled over an individual driving a car, Danny Driver, for having a burned-out tail-light. The officers then gruffly and rudely subjected Danny to a search of his body. When Danny protested orally to the search, the officers began beating him with their nightsticks. Danny suffered significant injuries and needed medical treatment.

    After watching this news story, Professor Cheryl conducted extensive factual research and concluded that the beating is a typical occurrence in the city. She believes that the courts can assist in bringing an end to this injustice. She has therefore brought a federal court suit, alleging that the U.S. Constitution is offended by this police brutality. The suit requests that the federal court (1) require the police department to pay damages for Danny's injury, (2) issue an order declaring the recorded conduct illegal under the U.S. Constitution, and (3) issue an order requiring the police department to order its officers to cease engaging in such a brutal manner in the future.

Consider this scenario from two angles: (1) Looking at the matter from a general policy level, do you see any reasons why Professor Concerned Cheryl should not be able to pursue this lawsuit? (2) Looking at the legal requirements (listed above) for establishing standing (to ensure the Court has power to hear the lawsuit), do you see any requirements that Concerned Cheryl might not be able to establish?

As mentioned above, the standing doctrine has two components: Article III standing (which is tied directly to the case and controversy requirement and the court's power) and prudential standing (which reflects cautious, institutional limits that federal courts have created to implement decision-making policies). The notion behind prudential standing is that—even though a federal court has the power to hear a lawsuit because the case and controversy requirement is satisfied—wisdom counsels that it is not a good idea for the court to get involved in the dispute. The prudential component of the standing doctrine has had a checkered history. Some Supreme Court cases have disfavored it. The opinion below shows how the doctrine can be used to put together a reason unique to a particular case.

FROM THE BENCH

ELK GROVE UNIFIED SCHOOL DISTRICT v. NEWDOW
542 U.S. 1 (2004)

Justice STEVENS delivered the opinion of the Court.

Elk Grove Unified School District has a policy that requires students to recite the pledge of allegiance at the beginning of the school day. In 1954 Congress passed a law ("1954 Act") that added the words "under God" to the pledge. Michael A. Newdow's daughter is a student in the school district.

Michael Newdow, an atheist, claimed the 1954 Act and the school district policy interfered with his right to direct his daughter's religious education. Newdow alleged that he has standing to sue on his own behalf and on behalf of his daughter as "next friend."

After instituting proceedings, it came to light that while Newdow shared "physical custody" of his daughter, Sandra Banning (the mother) claimed "exclusive legal custody . . . including the sole right to represent [the daughter's] legal interests and make all decision[s] about her education" and welfare. Banning stated that her daughter did not object to reciting the pledge and that it was her belief that it was not in her child's interest to be a party to Newdow's lawsuit.

After further proceedings, the [U.S. Court of Appeals] noted that Newdow no longer claimed to represent his daughter, but unanimously concluded that "the grant of sole legal custody to Banning" did not deprive Newdow, "as a noncustodial parent, of Article III standing to object to unconstitutional government action affecting his child."

. . . In every federal case, the party bringing the suit must establish standing to prosecute the action. "In essence, the question of standing is whether the litigant is entitled to have the court decide the merits of the dispute or of particular issues." The standing requirement is born partly of " 'an idea, which is more than an intuition but less than a rigorous and explicit theory, about the constitutional and prudential limits to the powers of an unelected, unrepresentative judiciary in our kind of government.' "

The command to guard jealously and exercise rarely our power to make constitutional pronouncements requires the strictest adherence when matters of great national significance are at stake. Even in cases concededly within our jurisdiction under Article III, we abide by "a series of rules under which [we have] avoided passing upon a large part of all the constitutional questions pressed upon [us] for decision." Always we must balance "the heavy obligation to exercise jurisdiction," against the "deeply rooted" commitment "not to pass on questions of constitutionality" unless the adjudication of the constitutional issue is necessary.

Consistent with these principles, our standing jurisprudence contains two strands: Article III standing, which enforces the Constitution's case-or-controversy requirement, and prudential standing, which embodies "judicially self-imposed limits on the exercise of federal jurisdiction." The Article III limitations are familiar: The plaintiff must show that the conduct of which he complains has caused him to suffer an "injury in fact" that a favorable judgment will redress. Although we have not exhaustively defined the prudential dimensions of the standing doctrine, we have explained that prudential standing encompasses "the general prohibition on a litigant's raising another person's legal rights, the rule barring adjudication of generalized grievances more appropriately addressed in the representative branches, and the requirement that a plaintiff's complaint falls within the zone of interests protected by the law invoked." . . . "Without such limitations—closely related to Art. III concerns but essentially matters of judicial self-governance—the courts would be called upon to decide abstract questions of wide public significance even though other governmental institutions may be more competent to address the questions and even though judicial intervention may be unnecessary to protect individual rights."

One of the principal areas in which this Court has customarily declined to intervene is the realm of domestic relations. Long ago we observed that "[t]he whole subject of the domestic relations of husband and wife, parent and child, belongs to the laws of the States and not to the laws of the United States." So strong is our deference to state law in this area that we have recognized a "domestic relations exception" that "divests the federal courts power to issue divorce, alimony, and child custody decrees. We have also acknowledged that it might be appropriate for the federal courts to decline to hear a case involving "elements of the domestic relationship," even when divorce, alimony, or child custody is not strictly at issue:

> This would be so when a case presents 'difficult questions of state law bearing on policy problems of substantial public import whose importance transcends the result in the case then at bar.' Such might well be the case if a federal suit were filed prior to effectuation of a divorce, alimony, or child custody decree, and the suit depended on a determination of the status of the parties.

Thus, while rare instances arise in which it is necessary to answer a substantial federal question that transcends or exists apart from the family law issue, in general, it is appropriate for the federal courts to leave delicate issues of domestic relations to the state courts.

. . . [The California State] Superior Court announced that the parents have "joint legal custody," but that Banning "makes the final decisions if the two . . . disagree." Newdow contends that despite Banning's final authority, he retains "an unrestricted right to inculcate in his daughter—free from governmental interference—the atheistic beliefs he finds persuasive." The difficulty with that argument is that Newdow's rights, as in many cases touching upon family relations, cannot be viewed in isolation. This case concerns not merely Newdow's interest in inculcating his child with his views on religion, but also the rights of the child's mother as a parent generally and under the Superior Court order specifically. And most important, it implicates the interests of a young child who finds herself at the center of a highly public debate over her custody, the propriety of a widespread national ritual, and the meaning of our Constitution.

The interests of the affected persons, in this case, are in many respects antagonistic. Of course, legal disharmony in family relations is not uncommon, and in many instances, that disharmony poses no bar to federal-court adjudication of proper federal questions. What makes this case different is that Newdow's standing derives entirely from his relationship with his daughter, but he lacks the right to litigate as her next friend. [In this case] the interests of this parent and this child are not parallel and, indeed, are potentially in conflict.

Newdow's parental status is defined by California's domestic relations law. Our custom on questions of state law ordinarily is to defer to the interpretation of the Court of Appeals for the Circuit in which the State is located. In this case, the Court of Appeals, which possesses greater familiarity with California law, concluded that state law vests in Newdow a cognizable right to influence his daughter's religious upbringing. The court based its ruling on two intermediate state appellate cases holding that "while the custodial parent undoubtedly has the right to make ultimate decisions concerning the child's religious upbringing, a court will not enjoin the noncustodial parent from discussing religion with the child or involving the child in his or her religious activities in the absence of a showing that the child will be thereby harmed." Animated by a conception of "family privacy" that includes "not simply a policy of minimum state intervention but also a presumption of parental autonomy," the state cases create a zone of private authority within which each parent, whether custodial or noncustodial, remains free to impart to the child his or her religious perspective.

Nothing that either Banning or the School Board has done, however, impairs Newdow's right to instruct his daughter in his religious views. He wishes to forestall his daughter's exposure to religious ideas that her mother, who wields a form of veto power, endorses, and to use his parental status to challenge the influences to which his daughter may be exposed in school when he and Banning disagree. The California cases simply do not stand for the proposition that Newdow has a right to dictate to others what they may and may not say to his child respecting religion.

In our view, it is improper for the federal courts to entertain a claim by a plaintiff whose standing to sue is founded on family law rights that are in dispute when prosecution of the lawsuit may have an adverse effect on the person who is the source of the plaintiff's claimed standing. When hard questions of domestic relations are sure to affect the outcome, the prudent course is for the federal court to stay its hand rather than reach out to resolve a weighty question of federal constitutional law. There is a vast difference between Newdow's right to communicate with his child—which both California law and the First Amendment recognize—and his claimed right to shield his daughter from influences to which she is exposed in school despite the terms of the custody order. We conclude that, having been deprived under California law of the right to sue as next friend, Newdow lacks prudential standing to bring this suit in federal court. The judgment of the Court of Appeals is reversed.

Chief Justice REHNQUIST, with whom Justice O'CONNOR joins, and with whom Justice THOMAS joins in relevant Part.

Surely, under California case law and the current custody order, respondent may not tell Banning what she may say to their child respecting religion, and respondent does not seek to. Just as surely, respondent cannot name his daughter as a party to a lawsuit against Banning's wishes. But his claim is

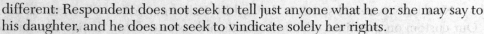

different: Respondent does not seek to tell just anyone what he or she may say to his daughter, and he does not seek to vindicate solely her rights.

Respondent asserts that the School District's Pledge ceremony infringes his right under California law to expose his daughter to his religious views. While she is intimately associated with the source of respondent's standing (the father-daughter relationship and respondent's rights thereunder), the daughter *is not the source* of respondent's standing; instead it is their relationship that provides respondent his standing, which is clear once respondent's interest is properly described.

QUESTION FOR DISCUSSION

3.2   Can you identify the different elements of the prudential standing concept developed in *Newdow*? What are the chances that the concept will fit the facts of future cases? Would it be accurate to say that the concept developed in *Newdow* is the analogue to "an excursion ticket for one train, one day only?"

Note the effect of the Supreme Court's decision: The Court did not touch the question of whether the First Amendment controlled whether an atheistic belief is worthy of protection from government control. The Court thus left in place the ability of the government to require school children to say that they belonged to a nation "under God." One might accuse the Court of being motivated to pursue that bottom-line result when it chose to find that prudence counseled preventing Newdow from continuing to pursue his constitutional challenge. We might speculate about the majority's motivations, but we should remember that we will likely never know for sure.

While critical thinking skills encourage scratching the surface of stated reasons for a decision, caution suggests placing too much weight on our hunches regarding true motivations. For example, it could simply be the case that a majority of the *Newdow* Court could not agree on the precise way to resolve the constitutional challenge and thought it unwise to leave the law in disarray on the First Amendment protection for atheism question. Following this theory on what was *really* going on in the case, the *Newdow* majority might have come to the consensus that a prudential standing resolution was an appropriate way of avoiding that disarray.

BEHIND THE CURTAIN

Here are some interesting facts about *Newdow:*

Michael Newdow. *Brent Nicastro.*

- If your case reached the Supreme Court, would you personally argue in front of the nine Justices? Newdow did, speaking directly after the Solicitor General of the United States. (The Solicitor General is a high-ranking member of the executive department of the U.S. government and is responsible for arguing all cases that reach the Court that implicate the interests of the United States.) By any account, Newdow did a pretty good job with his oral advocacy. (You can listen at https://www.oyez.org/cases/2003/02-1624; he begins at [26:10] and speaks for 30 minutes.) Newdow is an attorney, a full-time emergency room physician, and the founder of his own institution dedicated to atheist beliefs.
- During oral argument in the *Newdow* case, Chief Justice Rehnquist stated that the fact that nobody in Congress voted against the inclusion of the words "under God" shows that the practice is not divisive. Newdow responded, "only because no atheist can get elected to public office." Newdow's response garnered applause from the audience. The Chief Justice chastised the audience stating, "The courtroom will be cleared if there's any more clapping."
- Several years after the decision, Newdow sued Chief Justice John Roberts, challenging the practice of the Chief Justice reciting the words "so help me God" when swearing in the President. Newdow asked for an injunction preventing the Chief Justice from saying those words during Barack Obama's inauguration. The federal district court refused to grant the injunction, and, on appeal, the Circuit Court of Appeals found that Michael Newdow "lack[ed] standing to challenge" the practice.

2. The Doctrines Restricting When a Court Can Adjudicate a Case

A federal court can resolve a case only at the right time, neither too early (before the parties are truly adversaries or before harm is imminent) nor too late (when the parties no longer have a disagreement for which the federal court can find a remedy). Claims entering a court too early—before the nature of any controversy is known—trigger the ripeness doctrine. The mootness doctrine applies when the parties' controversy has disappeared, usually by virtue of some event that occurs before a plaintiff files a lawsuit or during the pendency of the lawsuit.

a. Ripeness

The ripeness doctrine prevents courts from adjudicating matters deemed premature because the injury is speculative and might never occur. To determine whether a case is ripe for judicial review, courts consider two factors: (1) "the hardship to the parties of withholding court consideration," and (2) "the fitness of the issues for judicial decision." *Abbott Labs. v. Gardner*, 387 U.S. 136, 149 (1967). Courts often conclude that the hardship consideration is satisfied if an individual is faced with the choice between subjecting herself to punishment and forgoing activities she believes are lawful. The fitness factor generally concerns whether the parties can develop a factual record enabling a court to evaluate the consequences of a legal ruling.

A typical circumstance when a court might grapple with whether or not a case is ripe for review is a constitutional challenge to a criminal statute that government authorities have not yet enforced. Under those circumstances, it could be unfair to ask an individual to violate the terms of a law and subject herself to punishment before she can test the constitutionality of the law. On the other hand, the case might be unripe because it is unclear how the prosecutor will use the law, and what, if any, precise type of conduct prosecutors will target for punishment under the law. The case law in this area comes to different conclusions, depending on whether the case includes specific facts tipping the scales toward finding the case sufficiently concrete and ripe for judicial resolution. For predicting which way a court might rule on the ripeness question, remember the "rough and ready" test: It takes two to have a fight. In other words, are both sides truly fighting over whether the law should be enforced? Does the plaintiff really want to engage in conduct that will violate the law? Are prosecutors really planning to enforce the law?

b. Mootness

Unlike cases that might not yet be ripe for review, the mootness doctrine may apply in cases with a well-developed record documenting a true controversy. Mootness ensures that a court hears a case only so long as it remains alive throughout the litigation process: A court may no longer hear a case when the parties cease to be adversaries. A case could present a live controversy throughout a substantial amount of time and litigation effort, yet become moot upon the occurrence of an event. When an event takes away a real controversy between the parties, the federal court loses its power to continue exercising authority over the case. Thus, the mootness doctrine prevents unnecessary federal court decisions, limits federal judges' authority, and saves judicial effort for those cases when the litigants actually have a concrete stake in the outcome.

Yet events can apparently "moot" a case after the parties and the court system have spent considerable resources. In four circumstances when this happens, the mootness doctrine includes at least four exceptions:

- A controversy may survive even if a litigant's main "injury" can no longer be avoided—as long as the consequences of the injury remain. For example, a defendant's challenge to her criminal conviction does not become moot after she finishes serving her sentence, because she may continue to suffer the consequences of a criminal record after she is released from prison.
- The second exception arises from class actions. (A class action arises when many people have been injured by something a defendant has done. In class actions, one or more individuals collectively represent the group.) In class actions, courts are exempted from the mootness doctrine once a class becomes "certified" as valid by the court. The reason for this exception stems from practical problems associated with the representative structure of class actions.
- The third exception allows federal courts to consider certain types of cases that technically do not contain a current controversy. In these cases, the actual controversy between the parties may be moot, but the controversy is capable of repetition. Yet, without this exception, the controversy would also likely evade review because the controversy will be moot any time the case gets to court again. For this exception to apply, the plaintiff must likely suffer the same injury again, and the injury must be inherently limited in duration such that it will likely disappear before federal litigation is complete. Consider pregnancy. Indeed, *Roe v. Wade*, 410 U.S. 113 (1973), is a classic example of this exception: Pregnancy is inherently limited in duration, and a state official's actions in preventing a fertile person from obtaining an abortion of an unwanted pregnancy is an alleged injury the fertile person is likely to suffer again.
- The fourth exception arises in situations where the defendant voluntarily stops engaging in the conduct at the root of the lawsuit. Those who are sued might be tempted to feign abandonment of the challenged conduct. To avoid giving these defendants the ability to control whether a federal court can continue to hear the suit, the Supreme Court has established that a defendant's promise to cease offending behavior will not ordinarily moot a controversy. Only if "it is absolutely clear the allegedly wrongful behavior could not reasonably be expected to recur" will a defendant be able to moot a case. *Friends of the Earth, Inc. v. Laidlaw Envtl. Servs., Inc.*, 528 U.S. 167, 189 (2000).

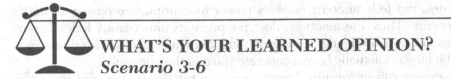

WHAT'S YOUR LEARNED OPINION?
Scenario 3-6

Thomas is an immigrant to the United States who has little realistic chance of obtaining citizenship. He is addicted to illegal drugs and was arrested for possessing a controlled substance. Federal authorities detained Thomas in accordance with a federal statute allowing the detention of a person who is removable from the United States for a crime involving a controlled substance. After two weeks in detention, Thomas filed a federal court action against the federal authorities, challenging the legality of his detention under the U.S. Constitution and seeking an order requiring his release. While the trial court was evaluating whether his detention complied with the Constitution, Thomas was released from custody, but remained in the United States. The defendant argued that the case was moot. Should the federal trial court dismiss the case as moot?

3. Political Question Doctrine: Regulating What May Be the Subject of a Lawsuit

The political question doctrine prohibits federal courts from deciding matters deemed best resolved by the politically accountable branches of the federal government: Congress and the President. This justiciability doctrine contemplates that courts will undertake a case-specific inquiry into whether a dispute turns on a nonjusticiable political question. The U.S. Supreme Court often lists six factors for a federal court to analyze in deciding whether a question is too political for judicial resolution: (1) "a textually demonstrable constitutional commitment of the issue to a coordinate political department"; (2) "a lack of judicially discoverable and manageable standards for resolving it"; (3) "the impossibility of deciding without an initial policy determination of a kind clearly for nonjudicial discretion"; (4) "the impossibility of a court's undertaking independent resolution without expressing lack of the respect due to coordinate branches of government"; (5) "an unusual need for unquestioning adherence to a political decision already made"; and (6) "the potentiality of embarrassment from multifarious pronouncements by various departments on one question." *Baker v. Carr*, 369 U.S. 186, 217 (1962).

The Supreme Court, however, has not consistently relied on all these factors in confronting political question issues. The Court most frequently emphasizes the first of these *Baker v. Carr* factors: "a textually demonstrable constitutional commitment of the issue to a coordinate political department." The Court has never definitively stated that any particular combination of the six factors is decisive. In fact, federal court decisions on the political question doctrine have been notoriously difficult to predict. That said, courts often invoke the doctrine when U.S. foreign affairs are implicated in the case. We will read an example of such a case in Chapter 5 in connection with the powers of the President, *Zivotofsky v. Kerry*, 576 U.S. 1 (2015). In the meantime, consider Scenario 3-7.

WHAT'S YOUR LEARNED OPINION?
Scenario 3-7

Assume that before 2019, there existed a country known as the United Republic of Whitebread (URW). In 2017, officials from the URW rented offices in New York City to open a consulate there. The consulate represented the official interests of the URW in the United States, granting visas, performing customs functions, and answering questions from the public about travel, study, and work in the URW. URW officials signed a ten-year lease for these New York City offices. In 2019, however, the URW ceased to exist, breaking into two separate sovereignties, and the consulate personnel vacated the rented offices. Nevertheless, the landlord sued the two successor sovereignties, alleging that they succeeded the interests of the URW and, therefore, were liable for the rent owed for the remainder of the lease term. Is this case justiciable?

Scholars and other commentators often note that the federal courts invoke the political question doctrine inconsistently to manipulate a result on the merits of a particular dispute. This can make potential political question problems tricky to resolve. Nonetheless, in evaluating fact patterns for possible application of the doctrine, one can find guidance by considering the types of matters that the Supreme Court has found the political question doctrine should govern: cases concerning the ratification of treaties, conduct of war, qualifications of ambassadors, enforcement of the Constitution's "republican form of government clause," internal governance of Congress, and adequacy of National Guard training. In addition, one should be careful to avoid the conclusion that a case presents a nonjusticiable political question simply because it touches on a politically charged topic. The fact that a dispute might have "significant political overtones does not automatically" trigger the doctrine. *INS v. Chadha*, 462 U.S. 919, 942-993 (1983). Consider whether the following case dealing with gerrymandering follows that pattern. Before we turn to the case itself, however, the following background on gerrymandering is helpful for understanding the importance and ramifications of the issue.

Introduction to Gerrymandering

Have you ever voted in a government election? If not, why? Maybe you think your vote doesn't matter? Your vote does matter, but it might matter a little less following the Supreme Court's *Rucho v. Common Cause* decision, set forth below. The case concerns how members of the House of Representatives are elected. If you live in the United States, you have a single representative in the House of Representatives, and that representative is determined by the geographic district in which you live. Of course, any district has to have a border, and that border might run right down the middle of your street. If you move outside the district, you get a different representative.

Every ten years, a census is taken, and districts are redrawn according to the new census data. But who does this redrawing? The Constitution assigns the

The original political cartoon by Elkanah Tisdale (1771-1835) that led to the coining of the term "gerrymander." The Boston Centinel, *1812, Wikimedia Commons.*

power to prescribe the "Times, Places and Manner of holding Elections" to state legislatures while giving Congress the power to "alter such Regulations." Art. I, §4, cl. 1. Do you see a conflict with that? Should Congress members decide how to organize the districts that vote for them (or not)? What if the National Football League routinely asked the winning Super Bowl champions from one season to write the rules for the next season? Wouldn't you expect that team to use their advantage to make the rules even more favorable for them? That is precisely what legislatures have done using a process known as gerrymandering.

The process of gerrymandering often creates voting districts with unlikely—sometimes even bizarre—shapes. Historians suggest that the term derives from a Massachusetts politician, Governor Gerry, who signed a bill creating a voting district north of Boston in the shape of a salamander. Although the term is felicitous, the result of the practice is serious. Voting map drawers who engage in gerrymandering create a map that "packs and cracks" voters into certain districts, thereby influencing the effect those voters will have on the election. Partisan gerrymandering uses this process to elect members of a particular party. For example, let us assume we have 100 voters (50 Republicans/50 Democrats) split into five districts. What would you do if you belonged to one of those parties and were tasked with drawing the map? You could "pack" opposing party voters together into one district (20 to 0) and "crack" the rest into the remaining four (7 to 13, or 8 to 12), thereby spreading out any influence these latter votes would have. In doing so, your party would receive 80 percent of the representatives with only 50 percent of the vote.

Does this sound fair? You probably answered "no," and if you did, you might have put your finger on the problem. What is fair? Can you define a test to determine fairness? Even if you can, certainly most maps will not be perfect, so how much imperfection or political bias should we allow? Should the U.S. Constitution have a role to play in monitoring whether extreme unfairness is at play with partisan gerrymandering? That is the crux of the *Rucho* case.

FROM THE BENCH

RUCHO v. COMMON CAUSE
139 S. Ct. 2484 (2019)

Chief Justice ROBERTS delivered the opinion of the Court.

Voters and other plaintiffs in North Carolina and Maryland challenged their States' congressional districting maps as unconstitutional partisan gerrymanders.

FROM THE BENCH

The North Carolina plaintiffs complained that the State's districting plan discriminated against Democrats; the Maryland plaintiffs complained that their State's plan discriminated against Republicans. The plaintiffs alleged that the gerrymandering violated the First Amendment, the Equal Protection Clause of the Fourteenth Amendment, the Elections Clause, and Article I, §2, of the Constitution. The District Courts in both cases ruled in favor of the plaintiffs, and the defendants appealed directly to this Court.

These cases require us to consider once again whether claims of excessive partisanship in districting are "justiciable"—that is, properly suited for resolution by the federal courts. This Court has not previously struck down a districting plan as an unconstitutional partisan gerrymander, and has struggled without success over the past several decades to discern judicially manageable standards for deciding such claims. The districting plans at issue here are highly partisan, by any measure. The question is whether the courts below appropriately exercised judicial power when they found them unconstitutional as well.

I.

The first case involves a challenge to the congressional redistricting plan enacted by the Republican-controlled North Carolina General Assembly in 2016. The Republican legislators leading the redistricting effort instructed their mapmaker to use political data to draw a map that would produce a congressional delegation of ten Republicans and three Democrats. As one of the two Republicans chairing the redistricting committee stated, "I think electing Republicans is better than electing Democrats. So I drew this map to help foster what I think is better for the country." The General Assembly . . . approved the 2016 Plan by a party-line vote.

. . . [In the second case] the Maryland Legislature—dominated by Democrats—undertook to redraw the lines of that State's eight congressional districts. The Governor at the time, Democrat Martin O'Malley, led the process. He appointed a redistricting committee to help redraw the map, and asked Congressman Steny Hoyer, who has described himself as a "serial gerrymanderer," to advise the committee. The Governor later testified that his aim was to "use the redistricting process to change the overall composition of Maryland's congressional delegation to 7 Democrats and 1 Republican by flipping" one district.

II.

. . . The question here is whether there is an "appropriate role for the Federal Judiciary" in remedying the problem of partisan gerrymandering—whether such claims are claims of *legal* right, resolvable according to *legal* principles, or political questions that must find their resolution elsewhere.

Partisan gerrymandering is nothing new. Nor is frustration with it. The practice was known in the Colonies prior to Independence, and the Framers were familiar with it at the time of the drafting and ratification of the Constitution. During the very first congressional elections, George Washington and his Federalist allies accused Patrick Henry of trying to gerrymander Virginia's districts against their candidates—in particular James Madison, who ultimately prevailed over fellow future President James Monroe. . . .

. . . To hold that legislators cannot take partisan interests into account when drawing district lines would essentially countermand the Framers' decision to entrust districting to political entities. The "central problem" is not determining whether a jurisdiction has engaged in partisan gerrymandering. It is "determining when political gerrymandering has gone too far."

III.

In considering whether partisan gerrymandering claims are justiciable, . . . Any standard for resolving such claims must be grounded in a "limited and precise rationale" and be "clear, manageable, and politically neutral." An important reason for those careful constraints is that, as a Justice with extensive experience in state and local politics put it, "[t]he opportunity to control the drawing of electoral boundaries through the legislative process of apportionment is a critical and traditional part of politics in the United States." An expansive standard requiring "the correction of all election district lines drawn for partisan reasons would commit federal and state courts to unprecedented intervention in the American political process."

. . . If federal courts are to "inject [themselves] into the most heated partisan issues" by adjudicating partisan gerrymandering claims, they must be armed with a standard that can reliably differentiate unconstitutional from "constitutional political gerrymandering."

Partisan gerrymandering claims rest on an instinct that groups with a certain level of political support should enjoy a commensurate level of political power and influence. Explicitly or implicitly, a districting map is alleged to be unconstitutional because it makes it too difficult for one party to translate statewide support into seats in the legislature. But such a claim is based on a "norm that does not exist" in our electoral system—"statewide elections for representatives along party lines."

Partisan gerrymandering claims invariably sound in a desire for proportional representation. As Justice O'Connor put it, such claims are based on "a conviction that the greater the departure from proportionality, the more suspect an apportionment plan becomes." . . . "Our cases, however, clearly foreclose any claim that the Constitution requires proportional representation or that legislatures in reapportioning must draw district lines to come as near as possible to allocating seats to the contending parties in proportion to what their anticipated statewide vote will be."

FROM THE BENCH

. . . The initial difficulty in settling on a "clear, manageable and politically neutral" test for fairness is that it is not even clear what fairness looks like in this context. There is a large measure of "unfairness" in any winner-take-all system. Fairness may mean a greater number of competitive districts. Such a claim seeks to undo packing and cracking so that supporters of the disadvantaged party have a better shot at electing their preferred candidates. But making as many districts as possible more competitive could be a recipe for disaster for the disadvantaged party. As Justice White has pointed out, "[i]f all or most of the districts are competitive . . . even a narrow statewide preference for either party would produce an overwhelming majority for the winning party in the state legislature."

On the other hand, perhaps the ultimate objective of a "fairer" share of seats in the congressional delegation is most readily achieved by yielding to the gravitational pull of proportionality and engaging in cracking and packing, to ensure each party its "appropriate" share of "safe" seats. Such an approach, however, comes at the expense of competitive districts and of individuals in districts allocated to the opposing party.

Or perhaps fairness should be measured by adherence to "traditional" districting criteria, such as maintaining political subdivisions, keeping communities of interest together, and protecting incumbents. But protecting incumbents, for example, enshrines a particular partisan distribution. And the "natural political geography" of a State—such as the fact that urban electoral districts are often dominated by one political party—can itself lead to inherently packed districts.

Deciding among just these different visions of fairness (you can imagine many others) poses basic questions that are political, not legal. There are no legal standards discernible in the Constitution for making such judgments, let alone limited and precise standards that are clear, manageable, and politically neutral. Any judicial decision on what is "fair" in this context would be an "unmoored determination" of the sort characteristic of a political question beyond the competence of the federal courts.

. . . Nor do our racial gerrymandering cases provide an appropriate standard for assessing partisan gerrymandering. "[N]othing in our case law compels the conclusion that racial and political gerrymanders are subject to precisely the same constitutional scrutiny. In fact, our country's long and persistent history of racial discrimination in voting—as well as our Fourteenth Amendment jurisprudence, which always has reserved the strictest scrutiny for discrimination on the basis of race—would seem to compel the opposite conclusion." Unlike partisan gerrymandering claims, a racial gerrymandering claim does not ask for a fair share of political power and influence, with all the justiciability conundrums that entails. It asks instead for the elimination of a racial classification. A partisan gerrymandering claim cannot ask for the elimination of partisanship.

. . . Excessive partisanship in districting leads to results that reasonably seem unjust. But the fact that such gerrymandering is "incompatible with democratic principles," does not mean that the solution lies with the federal judiciary. We conclude that partisan gerrymandering claims present political questions beyond the reach of the federal courts. Federal judges have no license to reallocate political power between the two major political parties, with no plausible grant of authority in the Constitution, and no legal standards to limit and direct their decisions. "[J]udicial action must be governed by standard, by rule," and must be "principled, rational, and based upon reasoned distinctions" found in the Constitution or laws. Judicial review of partisan gerrymandering does not meet those basic requirements.

As noted, the Framers gave Congress the power to do something about partisan gerrymandering in the Elections Clause. The first bill introduced in the 116th Congress would require States to create 15-member independent commissions to draw congressional districts and would establish certain redistricting criteria, including protection for communities of interest, and ban partisan gerrymandering. [The Court gives examples of other proposed and unenacted bills to address the gerrymandering issue.]

We express no view on any of these pending proposals. We simply note that the avenue for reform established by the Framers, and used by Congress in the past, remains open.

■ ■ ■

No one can accuse this Court of having a crabbed view of the reach of its competence. But we have no commission to allocate political power and influence in the absence of a constitutional directive or legal standards to guide us in the exercise of such authority. "It is emphatically the province and duty of the judicial department to say what the law is." *Marbury v. Madison*, 5 U.S. 137 (1803). In this rare circumstance, that means our duty is to say "this is not law."

Justice KAGAN, with whom Justice GINSBURG, Justice BREYER, and Justice SOTOMAYOR join, dissenting.

For the first time ever, this Court refuses to remedy a constitutional violation because it thinks the task beyond judicial capabilities.

And not just any constitutional violation. The partisan gerrymanders in these cases deprived citizens of the most fundamental of their constitutional rights: the rights to participate equally in the political process, to join with others to advance political beliefs, and to choose their political representatives. In so doing, the partisan gerrymanders here debased and dishonored our democracy, turning upside-down the core American idea that all governmental power derives from the people. These gerrymanders enabled politicians to entrench themselves in office as against voters' preferences. They promoted partisanship above respect for the popular will. They encouraged a politics of polarization and dysfunction. If left unchecked, gerrymanders like the ones here may irreparably damage our system of government.

And checking them is *not* beyond the courts. The majority's abdication comes just when courts across the country, including those below, have coalesced

FROM THE BENCH

around manageable judicial standards to resolve partisan gerrymandering claims. Those standards satisfy the majority's own benchmarks. They do not require—indeed, they do not permit—courts to rely on their own ideas of electoral fairness, whether proportional representation or any other. And they limit courts to correcting only egregious gerrymanders, so judges do not become omnipresent players in the political process. But yes, the standards used here do allow—as well they should—judicial intervention in the worst-of-the-worst cases of democratic subversion, causing blatant constitutional harms. In other words, they allow courts to undo partisan gerrymanders of the kind we face today from North Carolina and Maryland. In giving such gerrymanders a pass from judicial review, the majority goes tragically wrong. . . .

. . . Is that how American democracy is supposed to work? I have yet to meet the person who thinks so.

"Governments," the Declaration of Independence states, "deriv[e] their just Powers from the Consent of the Governed." The Constitution begins: "We the People of the United States." The Gettysburg Address (almost) ends: "[G]overnment of the people, by the people, for the people." If there is a single idea that made our Nation (and that our Nation commended to the world), it is this one: The people are sovereign. The "power," James Madison wrote, "is in the people over the Government, and not in the Government over the people."

Free and fair and periodic elections are the key to that vision. The people get to choose their representatives. And then they get to decide, at regular intervals, whether to keep them. Madison again: "[R]epublican liberty" demands "not only, that all power should be derived from the people; but that those entrusted with it should be kept in dependence on the people." Members of the House of Representatives, in particular, are supposed to "recollect[ ] [that] dependence" every day. To retain an "intimate sympathy with the people," they must be "compelled to anticipate the moment" when their "exercise of [power] is to be reviewed." Election day—next year, and two years later, and two years after that—is what links the people to their representatives, and gives the people their sovereign power. That day is the foundation of democratic governance.

And partisan gerrymandering can make it meaningless. At its most extreme—as in North Carolina and Maryland—the practice amounts to "rigging elections." By drawing districts to maximize the power of some voters and minimize the power of others, a party in office at the right time can entrench itself there for a decade or more, no matter what the voters would prefer. Just ask the people of North Carolina and Maryland. The "core principle of republican government," this Court has recognized, is "that the voters should choose their representatives, not the other way around." Partisan gerrymandering turns it the other way around. By that mechanism, politicians can cherry-pick voters to ensure their reelection. And the power becomes, as Madison put it, "in the Government over the people." 4 Annals of Cong. 934.

The majority disputes none of this. I think it important to underscore that fact: The majority disputes none of what I have said (or will say) about how gerrymanders undermine democracy. Indeed, the majority concedes (really, how could it not?) that gerrymandering is "incompatible with democratic principles." And therefore what? That recognition would seem to demand a response. [They say] that political gerrymanders have always been with us. [However,] (as the majority rightly notes), racial and residential gerrymanders were also once with us, but the Court has done something about that fact.

. . . Partisan gerrymandering operates through vote dilution—the devaluation of one citizen's vote as compared to others. A mapmaker draws district lines to "pack" and "crack" voters likely to support the disfavored party. He packs supermajorities of those voters into a relatively few districts, in numbers far greater than needed for their preferred candidates to prevail. Then he cracks the rest across many more districts, spreading them so thin that their candidates will not be able to win. Whether the person is packed or cracked, his vote carries less weight—has less consequence—than it would under a neutrally drawn (non-partisan) map. In short, the mapmaker has made some votes count for less, because they are likely to go for the other party.

So the only way to understand the majority's opinion is as follows: In the face of grievous harm to democratic governance and flagrant infringements on individuals' rights—in the face of escalating partisan manipulation whose compatibility with this Nation's values and law no one defends—the majority declines to provide any remedy. For the first time in this Nation's history, the majority declares that it can do nothing about an acknowledged constitutional violation because it has searched high and low and cannot find a workable legal standard to apply.

. . . But in throwing up its hands, the majority misses something under its nose: What it says can't be done has been done. Over the past several years, federal courts across the country—including, but not exclusively, in the decisions below—have largely converged on a standard for adjudicating partisan gerrymandering claims (striking down both Democratic and Republican districting plans in the process). And that standard does what the majority says is impossible. The standard does not use any judge-made conception of electoral fairness—either proportional representation or any other; instead, it takes as its baseline a State's own criteria of fairness, apart from partisan gain. . . . This Court has long understood that it has a special responsibility to remedy violations of constitutional rights resulting from politicians' districting decisions. Over 50 years ago, we committed to providing judicial review in that sphere, recognizing as we established the one-person-one-vote rule that "our oath and our office require no less." Of course, our oath and our office require us to vindicate all constitutional rights. But the need for judicial review is at its most urgent in cases like these. "For here, politicians' incentives conflict with voters' interests, leaving citizens without any political remedy for their constitutional harms." Those harms arise because politicians want to stay in office. No one can look to them for effective relief. . . . Of all times to abandon the Court's duty to declare the law, this was not the one. The practices challenged in these cases imperil our system of government. Part of the Court's role in that system is to defend its foundations. None is more important than free and fair elections. With respect but deep sadness, I dissent.

Gerrymandering is an issue that has dogged federal courts for a long time. One wrinkle comes from the issue of racial gerrymandering. As with partisan gerrymandering, racial gerrymandering can take two forms: (1) "cracking," or breaking up a minority group into different districts to dilute the group's overall influence among many districts; and (2) "packing," or putting most members of minority groups in just a few districts to ensure that group's influence in the overall election result is minimized. Unlike partisan gerrymandering, courts cannot easily avoid enforcing the prohibitions against racial gerrymandering. These prohibitions come from Congress's Voting Rights Act as well as the clear purposes of the Fourteenth Amendment (dealing with equal protection of the laws) and the Fifteenth Amendment (dealing with voting rights based on race). In other words, in racial gerrymandering cases, the courts must reckon with either or both a constitutional and statutory question without invoking the political question doctrine.

WHAT'S YOUR LEARNED OPINION?
Scenario 3-8

In an earlier decision on gerrymandering, Justice Kagan pointed out that different racial groups tend to track certain partisan preferences—with some groups (usually non-White folks) favoring the Democratic party and some groups (usually White folks) favoring the Republican party. From this point of view, would it be accurate to say that partisan gerrymandering is a "cover" for illegal racial gerrymandering? If courts can regulate racial gerrymandering, why shouldn't they be able to regulate partisan gerrymandering?

BEHIND THE CURTAIN

As you read more opinions of the U.S. Supreme Court, you'll note that the Justices generally speak of their fellow Justices with respect in their written opinions. But sometimes the opinions get spiced up and break from the norm of congeniality. The opinions in *Rucho* showed some evidence of this "snark." Consider these examples from the majority and dissenting opinions in the case:

- "We appreciate that the dissent finds all the unanswerable questions annoying."
- "After dutifully reciting each case's facts, the majority leaves them forever behind."

- "To prove its point, the majority throws a bevy of question marks on the page. (I count nine in just two paragraphs.)"
- "But in throwing up its hands, the majority misses something under its nose."
- "But the courts below did not gaze into crystal balls, as the majority tries to suggest."
- "No worries, the majority says; it has another idea."

We also see this caustic tone appear in oral arguments. One of the remarkable things about oral arguments is that the Justices use the advocate to toy with, insult, or try to persuade a fellow Justice. (This is no doubt very scary for the lawyer arguing before the Court.) Consider this description of an interchange between Justices Kagan and Gorsuch at the oral argument for the *Rucho* case:

> Justice Gorsuch pushed counsel who was advocating against the constitutionality of the gerrymandering, causing her to become somewhat flustered.
>
> Justice Kagan interjected by giving the counselor a lifeline, cutting in to ask "why isn't the answer to Justices Gorsuch's question that . . ." and laying out an answer.
>
> The lawyer accepted Justice Kagan's answer.
>
> Justice Gorsuch retorted "counsel . . . you've wisely adopted a very fine answer, given for you."

Can you blame the oral advocate for adopting Justice Kagan's suggestion? Would you reject the assistance of a Supreme Court Justice during an oral argument before the nine Justices?

Although these jabs might be somewhat entertaining, think about the lesson they provide for everyday discourse. One might think, "If an esteemed Justice of the U.S. Supreme Court can be sarcastic and belittling, why shouldn't I do so?" Alternatively, is this all part of robust debate that should be tolerated and celebrated as keen intellectual jousting that will ultimately get us closer to the truth as we struggle with constitutional questions?

In providing an overview of the Constitution's system of federal courts, we saw that the Constitution has been interpreted to include important power for federal courts, particularly the power of judicial review. But we also saw specific limitations on court power, exemplified by the justiciability doctrines and the precise list of cases that appear in Article III, §2. In the next chapter, you will see that the Constitution is more generous in granting powers to Congress.

QUESTIONS FOR REVIEW

1. What courts did Article III of the Constitution create? What legal instrument created the lower federal courts?

2. What general categories of disputes does Article III state that federal courts can hear?

3. Thomas Jefferson expressed the view that each branch of the federal government has the power to determine the meaning of the federal Constitution. Did that view carry the day? If not, what is the source of the contrary point of view?

4. Name the four justiciability doctrines and describe their general focus and attributes.

5. Why did the Court in *Elk Grove Unified School District v. Newdow* conclude that Michael Newdow lacked standing to bring the case?

6. What are the exceptions to the mootness doctrine?

7. Describe gerrymandering. What is the difference between gerrymandering by cracking and gerrymandering by packing? Why did the Court in *Rucho v. Common Cause* determine that the gerrymandering challenge in that case was nonjusticiable under the political question doctrine?

ENDNOTES

1. *See Editorial Note: The Referral of Neutrality Questions to the Supreme Court*, Founders Online, National Archives, https://founders.archives.gov/documents/Jefferson/01-26-02-0465-0001. [Original source: *The Papers of Thomas Jefferson, vol. 26, 11 May-31 August 1793*, ed. John Catanzariti. Princeton, NJ: Princeton University Press, 1995, 524-526.]

2. Alexander Bickel, *The Supreme Court and the Idea of Progress* (1970).

3. In today's language, a "Federalist" is generally regarded as an individual who prefers a strong state government over the federal government. At the time of the Framers, however, the term for such a person would be an anti-Federalist. For the Framers, a Federalist was someone who placed importance on a strong *federal* government.

Powers of Congress

A. Basics of Article I

As mentioned earlier in this volume, Congress's powers are limited to the 18 points listed in Article I, §8 of the U.S. Constitution. That said, Congress enjoys two expansions on the precise terms of the listed powers. One expansion comes from an early interpretation of Congress's powers, known as the doctrine of implied powers. The expansion derives from the notion that expressly stated powers also authorize use of inferred powers that make full the promise of the express powers. The second expansion comes from the Necessary and Proper Clause, which states that Congress has the power to enact laws that are necessary and proper for ensuring that Congress's specifically listed powers are effective. This clause was described in Chapter 2 in connection with *Bond v. United States.* The clause appears at the end of the powers of Congress listed in Article I, §8, and states that Congress shall have "the power . . . [t]o make all Laws which shall be necessary and proper for carrying into Execution the foregoing Powers, and all other Powers vested by this Constitution in the Government of United States, or in any Department or Officer thereof."

Unsurprisingly, this expansive doctrine of implied powers and the expansive reading of the Necessary and Proper Clause were announced by the same author of the opinion announcing the broad powers of the federal courts, Chief Justice Marshall.

Marshall announced the definitive view of these two concepts in *McCulloch v. Maryland*, 17 U.S (4 Wheat.) 316 (1819). As he had done for the federal judiciary, Marshall used the case to enunciate a broad scope of federal powers of the U.S. Congress. The specifics of the case concerned whether Congress could create a national bank. Confronted with the fact that the Constitution lists many powers of Congress in Article I, §8, but did not list any reference to Congress having the power to create a bank, Marshall said the following:

A constitution, to contain an accurate detail of all the subdivisions of which its great powers will admit, and of all the means by which they may be carried into execution, would partake of the prolixity of a legal code, and could scarcely be embraced by the human mind. . . . [W]e must never forget that it is a *constitution* we are expounding.

17 U.S. at 407.

In other words, Marshall made clear that the Constitution's failure to mention a particular power should not negate Congress's control over that subject. Congress may use a power that is implied from the constitutionally mentioned power to carry out a specifically mentioned power, so long as that implied power is not prohibited by the Constitution. To argue to the contrary would suggest that the Framers had the unreasonable responsibility of anticipating and articulating every means that might be used to execute a specifically mentioned power.

Marshall was not finished, however, with this description of implied powers. Later in the opinion, he turned to an expansive reading of the Necessary and Proper Clause. Here's what he said:

Let the end be legitimate, let it be within the scope of the constitution, and all means which are appropriate, which are plainly adapted to that end, which are prohibited, but consist with the letter and spirit of the constitution, are constitutional.

Rejecting any suggestion that the purpose of the Necessary and Proper Clause was to limit Congress's power, Marshall explained that "necessary" means useful or desirable (and is not confined to means that are indispensable or essential to accomplishing a task). Such is the stuff of legal hairsplitting: No way could "necessary" mean "essential!"

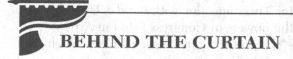

BEHIND THE CURTAIN

McCulloch v. Maryland arose from one of the many contentious episodes early in our nation's history—featuring a power struggle between the Federalists and the Anti-Federalists. The precise legal question posed in *McCulloch* was whether the State of Maryland could collect a tax from the Bank of the United States.

The controversy in the case actually began in 1790 when Congress and the executive branch disputed whether the United States had the power to create a national bank. The Secretary of the U.S. Treasury at the time, Alexander Hamilton, advocated for the bank's creation and was opposed by the then-Secretary of State, Thomas Jefferson. A debate in Congress ensued, with James Madison (then in the House of Representatives) siding with Jefferson. Meanwhile, however, Hamilton had convinced President George Washington to support the bank and the Federalists (who controlled

Congress at the time) successfully ensured that the Bank of the United States came into existence.

The bank's charter expired in 1811 by operation of the federal statute that authorized the bank, but Congress re-created the bank in 1816 to address economic problems caused by the War of 1812. The bank did not cure these economic problems but succeeded in alienating the states by calling in loans owed by the states. Maryland was one of the states in opposition, passing a law that required any banks not chartered in the state (such as the Bank of the United States) to pay a tax to the state.

When the Bank of the United States refused to pay the tax, representatives of the State of Maryland sued to recover the tax. The defendant, McCulloch, was the cashier for the Baltimore branch of the Bank of the United States.

B. Commerce Power

By far the most used—and thus likely the most important—power of Congress is the commerce power. As described in Article I, §8, "Congress shall have the power . . . [t]o regulate Commerce with foreign Nations, and among the several States, and with the Indian Tribe. . . ." Commerce Clause cases are particularly interesting in how they have waxed and waned over the years. In response to political and economic attitudes and challenges throughout U.S. history, the rules emerging from the Commerce Clause cases have vacillated between expanding federal power and restricting federal power over interstate commerce. One could spend an entire semester studying Commerce Clause cases and evaluating how they reflect the political and economic history of the United States. Nonetheless, the following brief history of the beginning of Commerce Clause jurisprudence is sufficient for our purposes.

The classic starting point in discussing the Commerce Clause is yet another Chief Justice Marshall opinion—*Gibbons v. Ogden*, 22 U.S. (9 Wheat.) 1 (1824). *Gibbons* arose from a dispute regarding the constitutionality of a federal law that authorized licenses to "vessels in the coasting trade." The *Gibbons* Court upheld the federal law, concluding that it was authorized under the Commerce Clause. In doing so, the Court determined the following:

Commerce. *Commerce includes more than traffic. It includes intercourse—that is, all phases of business, including navigation.*

Among the States. *When the Constitution speaks of commerce "among the states," it means "intermingled with," not simply something that stops at* *boundary lines. This, according to the* Gibbons *Court, includes intrastate activity if that activity had an effect on intrastate activities.*

Effect of State Sovereignty. *The Court rejected the notion that state sovereignty restrained the reach of the Commerce Clause. In fact, the Court stated that the commerce power "is complete in itself, may be exercised to its utmost and acknowledges no limitations."* Id. *at 196-197.*

In subsequent decisions, the Supreme Court has not always faithfully followed these interpretations. One can easily trace the Court's narrow and broad definitions of the Commerce Clause in tandem with economic theories such as society's embrace of laissez-faire economic theory, economic realities such as the Great Depression, and varying societal trends on whether the government should implement social welfare regulation. Despite these subtleties, the *Gibbons* Court's straightforward breakdown of the issues—the definition of "commerce" and "among the states" as well as the role of state sovereignty in reigning in commerce power—continues to set the agenda for debate.

When the Great Depression began in 1929, many members of government balked at the notion of government tinkering with the operation of government. On election in 1933, President Franklin Roosevelt initiated a series of legislative initiatives designed to jump-start the nation's economy. Enacted based on the Commerce Clause, Roosevelt's so-called New Deal approach to economic management met with hostility in the U.S. Supreme Court. The Court's anti–New Deal opinions led President Roosevelt to propose an infamous court-packing plan, under which Roosevelt would nominate an additional justice for each sitting justice who reached the age of 70, up to a total of 15 justices.

While the court-packing discussion continued, the Court changed its commerce power approach. The turning point came with *West Coast v. Parrish*, 300 U.S. 379 (1937), when a 5-4 majority of the Court upheld a minimum wage law for women. This change is credited to the decision of Justice Owen Roberts to change his vote on Commerce Clause issues, a change referred to as "a switch in time that saved nine." In other words, once Roosevelt's initiatives cleared Supreme Court scrutiny, the court-packing debate faded.

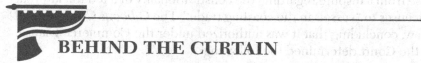

BEHIND THE CURTAIN

The more things change, the more they stay the same. Indeed, the court-packing notion came up again during the confirmation hearings of Justices Amy Coney Barrett and Ketanji Brown Jackson. During those hearings, some Congress members called for "packing the Court" by appointing more Justices to the Supreme Court than the traditional nine. (Nothing in the Constitution mandates the size of the Supreme Court.) Indeed, the proposed Judiciary Act of 2021 called for adding four seats, taking the size of the Supreme Court to 13 Justices. The purpose of this legislation, brought by Democrats, was to prevent what they saw as a conservative majority from overwhelming control of the Court. At the time of Justice Brown Jackson's appointment, six of the nine Justices were appointed by Republican presidents, and an expansion would take that six-Justice supermajority to less than a bare majority (i.e., six of thirteen). The proposed Act never became law.

The following case is representative of the shift toward a broad interpretation of congressional commerce power—in service of attempts to support the U.S. economy. The issue in the case is, on the surface, rather mundane. At bottom, the Court was faced with the issue of whether the appellee, farmer Roscoe Filburn, had to pay a penalty on wheat he grew to feed his cows and his family. The federal government had put a cap on the amount of wheat a person could grow, and Filburn had exceeded that limit. Under the statute passed by Congress, Filburn was required to pay the penalty. Filburn argued that Congress had no power to regulate what he grew on his own farm to meet his needs.

Unless you are a farmer, you might think this case has little bearing on your life. You would be wrong. In finding that farmer Filburn had to pay up, the Court defined the Constitution's Commerce Clause broadly and effectively enlarged Congress's power to regulate various aspects of your life that might not even appear to reach outside the state where you live. The deeper question in the case that the Court had to resolve was whether the language of the Commerce Clause, which speaks of commerce "among the several states," could be interpreted to reach activity that took place entirely in a single state.

FROM THE BENCH

WICKARD v. FILBURN
317 U.S. 111 (1942)

Justice JACKSON delivered the opinion of the Court.

The appellee for many years past has owned and operated a small farm in Montgomery County, Ohio, maintaining a herd of dairy cattle, selling milk, raising poultry, and selling poultry and eggs. It has been his practice to raise a small acreage of winter wheat, sown in the Fall and harvested in the following July;

FROM THE BENCH

Roscoe C. Filburn and his wheat. *Mary Lou Filburn Spurgeon.*

to sell a portion of the crop; to feed part to poultry and livestock on the farm, some of which is sold; to use some in making flour for home consumption; and to keep the rest for the following seeding. The intended disposition of the crop here involved has not been expressly stated.

In July of 1940, pursuant to the Agricultural Adjustment Act of 1938 there were established for the appellee's 1941 crop a wheat acreage allotment of 11.1 acres and a normal yield of 20.1 bushels of wheat an acre. He was given notice of such allotment in July of 1940, before the Fall planting of his 1941 crop of wheat, and again in July of 1941, before it was harvested. He sowed, however, 23 acres, and harvested from his 11.9 acres of excess acreage 239 bushels, which under the terms of the Act as amended on May 26, 1941, constituted farm marketing excess, subject to a penalty of 49 cents a bushel, or $117.11 in all.

The general scheme of the Agricultural Adjustment Act of 1938 as related to wheat is to control the volume moving in interstate and foreign commerce in order to avoid surpluses and shortages and the consequent abnormally low or high wheat prices and obstructions to commerce. Within prescribed limits and by prescribed standards the Secretary of Agriculture is directed to ascertain and proclaim each year a national acreage allotment for the next crop of wheat, which is then apportioned to the states and their counties, and is eventually broken up into allotments for individual farms.

It is urged that under the Commerce Clause of the Constitution, Article I, §8, clause 3, Congress does not possess the power it has in this instance sought to exercise. The question would merit little consideration since our decision in *United States v. Darby*, sustaining the federal power to regulate production of goods for commerce, except for the fact that this Act extends federal regulation to production not intended in any part for commerce but wholly for consumption on the farm. Penalties do not depend upon whether any part of the wheat, either within or without the quota, is sold or intended to be sold.

Appellee says that this is a regulation of production and consumption of wheat. Such activities are, he urges, beyond the reach of Congressional power under the Commerce Clause, since they are local in character, and their effects upon interstate commerce are at most "indirect."

We believe that a review of the course of decision under the Commerce Clause will make plain, however, that questions of the power of Congress are not to be decided by reference to any formula which would give controlling force to nomenclature such as "production" and "indirect" and foreclose consideration of the actual effects of the activity in question upon interstate commerce.

Once an economic measure of the reach of the power granted to Congress in the Commerce Clause is accepted, questions of federal power cannot be decided simply by finding the activity in question to be "production," nor can consideration of its economic effects be foreclosed by calling them "indirect." The commerce power is not confined in its exercise to the regulation of commerce among the states. It extends to those activities intrastate which so affect interstate commerce, or the exertion of the power of Congress over it, as to make regulation of them appropriate means to the attainment of a legitimate end.

Whether the subject of the regulation in question was "production," "consumption," or "marketing" is, therefore, not material for purposes of deciding the question of federal power before us. Even if appellee's activity be local and though it may not be regarded as commerce, it may still, whatever its nature, be reached by Congress if it exerts a substantial economic effect on interstate commerce, and this irrespective of whether such effect is what might at some earlier time have been defined as "direct" or "indirect."

The parties have stipulated a summary of the economics of the wheat industry. Commerce among the states in wheat is large and important. Although wheat is raised in every state but one, production in most states is not equal to consumption. Sixteen states on average have had a surplus of wheat above their own requirements for feed, seed, and food. Thirty-two states and the District of Columbia, where production has been below consumption, have looked to these surplus-producing states for their supply as well as for wheat for export and carry-over.

The effect of consumption of home-grown wheat on interstate commerce is due to the fact that it constitutes the most variable factor in the disappearance of the wheat crop. Consumption on the farm where grown appears to vary in an amount greater than 20 per cent of average production. The total amount of wheat consumed as food varies but relatively little, and use as seed is relatively constant.

The maintenance by government regulation of a price for wheat undoubtedly can be accomplished as effectively by sustaining or increasing the demand as by limiting the supply. The effect of the statute before us is to restrict the amount which may be produced for market and the extent as well to which one may forestall resort to the market by producing to meet his own needs. That appellee's own contribution to the demand for wheat may be trivial by itself is not enough to remove him from the scope of federal regulation where, as here, his contribution, taken together with that of many others similarly situated, is far from trivial.

It is well established by decisions of this Court that the power to regulate commerce includes the power to regulate the prices at which commodities in that commerce are dealt in and practices affecting such prices. One of the primary purposes of the Act in question was to increase the market price of wheat, and to that end to limit the volume thereof that could affect the market. It can hardly be denied that a factor of such volume and variability as home-consumed wheat would have a substantial influence on price and market conditions. This may arise because being in marketable condition such wheat overhangs the market and, if induced by rising prices, tends to flow into the market and check price increases. But if we assume that it is never marketed, it supplies a need of the man who grew it which would otherwise be reflected by purchases in the open market. Home-grown wheat in this sense competes with wheat in commerce. The stimulation of commerce is a use of the regulatory function quite as definitely as prohibitions or restrictions thereon. This record leaves us in no doubt that Congress may properly have considered that wheat consumed on the farm where grown, if wholly outside the scheme of regulation, would have a substantial effect in defeating and obstructing its purpose to stimulate trade therein at increased prices.

QUESTIONS FOR DISCUSSION

4.1 Remember the two basic limitations placed on the Commerce Clause: The activity regulated must concern more than one state. In addition, many cases suggest that the activity must be commercial. Indeed, the Court in its 1824 decision in *Gibbons v. Ogden* stated, "[i]t is not intended to say that [the Commerce Clause] comprehends that commerce, which is completely internal, which is carried on between man and man in a State, or between different parts of the same State, and which does not extend to or affect other States. Such a power would be inconvenient and is certainly unnecessary." Do you believe *Wickard* is consistent with these requirements? Under *Wickard*, Congress can regulate activity that has "a substantial economic effect on interstate commerce," even if the activity itself is not commercial and is entirely intrastate. Is this an absurd ruling given the text of the clause? Is this an example of the court working backward to legally justify the decision the Justices wanted? Why would the court need to do this? Is it because they are applying a document from 1787, interpreted in 1824, to a situation arising in 1942 when the country was still in the throes of a depression? If so, is this legitimate decision making?

4.2 Lin-Manuel Miranda's musical *Hamilton* featured the infamous rivalry between founding fathers Alexander Hamilton and Thomas Jefferson. Both men had very different understandings of the federal government's role in relation to the governments of the several states: Hamilton advocated for broad federal power, and Jefferson favored limited federal power. Another Framer of the Constitution featured in *Hamilton* (James Madison) sided with Jefferson's view and described the federal government's powers as "few and defined." So, under this view of the defined powers in Article I, §8, Congress may do all of the things enumerated there, but nothing more. If this were taken as indisputable truth, *Hamilton* would have been a less exciting play, and constitutional law would be a much more manageable topic. Yet the debate between preference for state versus federal power persists today. Which of the founding fathers would have been more likely to support the *Wickard* decision?

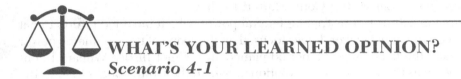

WHAT'S YOUR LEARNED OPINION?
Scenario 4-1

A restaurant owner in Tuscaloosa, Alabama, decided that he hates Auburn University (also located in Alabama) so much that his restaurant instituted a total ban on serving all Auburn graduates. U.S. Senator Tommy Tuberville, the former Auburn football head coach, learns of the restaurant and gets a law passed that makes it illegal to turn away any patron based on the college they graduated from. The restaurant owner challenges the law and can show that every patron of his establishment and every person banned is a resident of Alabama. Is the restaurant owner likely to win his challenge?

Scenario 4-2

As you will see in Chapter 12, the U.S. Supreme Court has overruled its earlier decision, *Roe v. Wade*, which recognized a constitutional protection for the right of a woman to terminate a pregnancy in the first and second trimesters. Under a clause in Article IV of the Constitution—the Supremacy Clause—*Roe v. Wade* restricted what state governments could do in regulating abortion. That, however, does not answer how *Roe* affected Congress's power.

May the federal Congress properly create a statutory protection for a woman's right to abortion? In other words, is protecting a person's right to choose abortion a valid exercise of legislative power? For present purposes, discuss whether preserving a person's right to choose to terminate a pregnancy is a valid exercise of Congress's Commerce Clause power.

From 1937 through the 1980s, the U.S. Supreme Court adopted an expansive view of Congress's commerce power and refused to constrain that power using other parts of the Constitution, such as the Tenth Amendment. During that period, the Court found no federal laws unconstitutional for exceeding the scope of Congress's commerce power. In the 1990s, the Supreme Court changed course, started to take a more limited view of the Commerce Clause, and started to elevate the importance of other parts of the Constitution pertaining to the importance of state prerogatives, including the Tenth Amendment.

Chief Justice William Rehnquist. *World History Archive/ Alamy Stock Photo.*

Beginning with the decision in the next case, *United States v. Lopez*, the Court started to show much greater interest in restricting federal power, which included efforts to cut back on congressional power. *Lopez* focused on the scope of the commerce power and marked the beginning of a period named after Chief Justice William Rehnquist, known as the Rehnquist Revolution, in which the Court sought to limit the reach of federal power.

As is often the case with constitutional decisions, the historical backdrop for a decision is important for appreciating its reasoning and scope. Although *Lopez* clearly arose from a concern about the increase in federal power as a general matter, the decision also arose from Congress's reaction to increased gun violence in the United States. Consider this backdrop as well as events subsequent to the *Lopez* decision.

On April 20, 1999, two students entered Columbine High School in Colorado and killed 12 students and a teacher. Since the Columbine massacre, similar events have become commonplace in the United States. Inevitably, as is frequently the case after such events, calls have been made for Congress to step in to regulate gun ownership. To determine the available remedies, attention turned to what Congress has the power to regulate.

Foreseeing a problem with guns and schools ten years before the Columbine massacre, Congress passed the Gun-Free School Zones Act of 1990, which restricted the presence of guns near schools. In the case you are about to read, the Supreme Court invalidated the law as outside the power of Congress. The statute might not have prevented any of the mass shootings that have taken place, but the case informs what actions Congress has available to address the current epidemic of mass shootings.

Here are the specifics: In *Lopez v. United States*, the Court was asked whether the Gun-Free School Zones Act of 1990 was a valid exercise of Congress's Commerce Clause power. The Act, in relevant part, banned the possession of a firearm within 1,000 feet of any school. Importantly, the Act did not attempt to regulate the purchase of the gun. Doesn't it seem strange to use interstate commerce to regulate this noncommercial activity that likely occurred entirely within the borders of a single state? Remember the cumulative effect test in *Wickard*. In invalidating the Gun-Free School Zones Act, the

A woman stands among 15 crosses that stand on a hill above Columbine High School in Littleton, Colorado. *AP Photo/Eric Gay.*

Court effectively announced the end of an era of Supreme Court Commerce Clause jurisprudence. Curiously, however, *Lopez* did not invalidate the holding of *Wickard*, which remains a viable vestige from an earlier era.

At the time that *Lopez* was decided, the Supreme Court had not yet concluded that the Constitution created an individual right to possess guns. One wonders, however, whether Chief Justice Rehnquist was able to garner enough votes from other conservative Justices to create a majority opinion because some of the Justices were keen on increasing constitutional protection for private gun ownership and possession.

FROM THE BENCH

UNITED STATES v. LOPEZ
514 U.S. 549 (1995)

Chief Justice Rehnquist delivered the opinion of the Court.

In the Gun-Free School Zones Act of 1990, Congress made it a federal offense "for any individual knowingly to possess a firearm at a place that the individual knows, or has reasonable cause to believe, is a school zone." The Act neither regulates a commercial activity nor contains a requirement that the possession be connected in any way to interstate commerce. We hold that the Act exceeds the authority of Congress "to regulate Commerce . . . among the several States. . . ."

On March 10, 1992, respondent, who was then a 12th-grade student, arrived at Edison High School in San Antonio, Texas, carrying a concealed .38 caliber handgun and five bullets. Acting upon an anonymous tip, school authorities confronted respondent, who admitted that he was carrying the weapon. He was arrested and charged under Texas law with firearm possession on school premises. The next day, the state charges were dismissed after federal agents charged respondent by complaint with violating the Gun-Free School Zones Act of 1990.

Respondent moved to dismiss his federal indictment on the ground that [the Gun-Free School Zones Act] "is unconstitutional as it is beyond the power of Congress to legislate control over our public schools." The District Court conducted a bench trial, found him guilty of violating [the Gun-Free School Zones Act], and sentenced him to six months' imprisonment and two years' supervised release.

We start with first principles. The Constitution creates a Federal Government of enumerated powers. As James Madison wrote, "the powers delegated by the proposed Constitution to the federal government are few and defined. Those which are to remain in the State governments are numerous and indefinite." This constitutionally mandated division of authority "was adopted by the Framers to ensure protection of our fundamental liberties." "Just as the separation and independence of the coordinate branches of the Federal Government serve to prevent the accumulation of excessive power in any one branch, a healthy balance of power between the States and the Federal Government will reduce the risk of tyranny and abuse from either front."

The Constitution delegates to Congress the power "to regulate Commerce with foreign Nations, and among the several States, and with the Indian Tribes." [The Court then reviews its prior cases interpreting the Commerce Clause.]

Wickard ushered in an era of Commerce Clause jurisprudence that greatly expanded the previously defined authority of Congress under that Clause. In part, this was a recognition of the great changes that had occurred in the way business was carried on in this country. Enterprises that had once been local or at most regional in nature had become national in scope. But the doctrinal change also reflected a view that earlier Commerce Clause cases artificially had constrained the authority of Congress to regulate interstate commerce. But even these modern-era precedents which have expanded congressional power under the Commerce Clause confirm that this power is subject to outer limits. [This Court has] warned that the scope of the interstate commerce power "must be considered in the light of our dual system of government and may not be extended so as to embrace effects upon interstate commerce so indirect and remote that to embrace them, in view of our complex society, would effectually obliterate the distinction between what is national and what is local and create a completely centralized government."

Consistent with this structure, we have identified three broad categories of activity that Congress may regulate under its commerce power. First, Congress may regulate the use of the channels of interstate commerce. Second, Congress is empowered to regulate and protect the instrumentalities of interstate commerce, or persons or things in interstate commerce, even though the threat may come only from intrastate activities. Finally, Congress' commerce authority includes the power to regulate those activities that substantially affect interstate commerce.

Within this final category, admittedly, our case law has not been clear whether an activity must "affect" or "substantially affect" interstate commerce in order to be within Congress' power to regulate it under the Commerce Clause. We conclude, consistent with the great weight of our case law, that the proper test requires an analysis of whether the regulated activity "substantially affects" interstate commerce.

We now turn to consider the power of Congress, in the light of this framework, to enact [the Gun-Free School Zones Act]. The first two categories of authority may be quickly disposed of: [the Act] is not a regulation of the use of the channels of interstate commerce, nor is it an attempt to prohibit the interstate transportation of a commodity through the channels of commerce; nor can [the Act] be justified as a regulation by which Congress has sought to protect an instrumentality of interstate commerce or a thing in interstate commerce. Thus, if [the Gun-Free School Zones Act] is to be sustained, it must be under the third category as a regulation of an activity that substantially affects interstate commerce.

First, we have upheld a wide variety of congressional Acts regulating intrastate economic activity where we have concluded that the activity substantially affected interstate commerce. Even *Wickard*, which is perhaps the most far-reaching example of Commerce Clause authority over intrastate activity, involved economic activity in a way that the possession of a gun in a school zone does not. The [statute in *Wickard*] was designed to regulate the volume of wheat moving in interstate and foreign commerce in order to avoid surpluses and shortages, and concomitant fluctuation in wheat prices, which had previously obtained.

[The Gun-Free School Zones Act] is a criminal statute that by its terms has nothing to do with "commerce" or any sort of economic enterprise, however broadly one might define those terms. [The Act] is not an essential part of a larger regulation of economic activity, in which the regulatory scheme could be undercut unless the intrastate activity were regulated. It cannot, therefore, be sustained under our cases upholding regulations of activities that arise out of or are connected with a commercial transaction, which viewed in the aggregate, substantially affects interstate commerce.

Gun-free school zone sign in Atlantic City, New Jersey. *Christian Ouellet/iStock Photo.*

Second, [the Act] contains no jurisdictional element which would ensure, through case-by-case inquiry, that the firearm possession in question affects interstate commerce. For example, in *United States v. Bass*, the Court interpreted former 18 U.S.C. §1202(a), which made it a crime for a felon to "receive, posses[s], or transport in commerce or affecting commerce . . . any firearm." The Court interpreted the possession component of §1202(a) to require an additional nexus to interstate commerce both because the statute was ambiguous and because "unless Congress conveys its purpose clearly, it will not be deemed to have significantly changed the federal-state balance." Unlike the statute in Bass, [the Gun-Free School Zones Act] has no express jurisdictional element which might limit its reach to a discrete set of firearm possessions that additionally have an explicit connection with or effect on interstate commerce.

Although as part of our independent evaluation of constitutionality under the Commerce Clause we of course consider legislative findings, and indeed even congressional committee findings, regarding effect on interstate commerce, the Government concedes that "neither the statute nor its legislative history contain[s] express congressional findings regarding the effects upon interstate commerce of gun possession in a school zone." We agree with the Government that Congress normally is not required to make formal findings as to the substantial burdens that an activity has on interstate commerce. But to the extent that congressional findings would enable us to evaluate the legislative judgment that the activity in question substantially affected interstate commerce, even though no such substantial effect was visible to the naked eye, they are lacking here.

The Government's essential contention is that we may determine here that [the Gun-Free School Zones Act] is valid because possession of a firearm in a local school zone does indeed substantially affect interstate commerce. The Government argues that possession of a firearm in a school zone may result in violent crime and that violent crime can be expected to affect the functioning of the national economy in two ways. First, the costs of violent crime are substantial, and, through the mechanism of insurance, those costs are spread throughout the population. Second, violent crime reduces the willingness of individuals to travel to areas within the country that are perceived to be unsafe. The Government also argues that the presence of guns in schools poses a substantial threat to the educational process by threatening the learning environment. A handicapped educational process, in turn, will result in a less productive citizenry. That, in turn, would have an adverse effect on the Nation's economic well-being. As a result, the Government argues that Congress could rationally have concluded that [the Gun-Free School Zones Act] substantially affects interstate commerce.

We pause to consider the implications of the Government's arguments. The Government admits, under its "costs of crime" reasoning, that Congress could regulate not only all violent crime, but all activities that might lead to violent crime, regardless of how tenuously they relate to interstate commerce. Similarly, under the Government's "national productivity" reasoning, Congress could regulate any activity that it found was related to the economic productivity of individual citizens: family law (including marriage, divorce, and child custody), for example. Under the theories that the Government presents in support of [the Gun-Free School Zones Act], it is difficult to perceive any limitation on federal power, even in areas such as criminal law enforcement or education where States historically have been sovereign. Thus, if we were to accept the Government's arguments, we are hard-pressed to posit any activity by an individual that Congress is without power to regulate.

Although Justice Breyer argues that acceptance of the Government's rationales would not authorize a general federal police power, he is unable to identify any activity that the States may regulate but Congress may not. For instance, if Congress can, pursuant to its Commerce Clause power, regulate activities that adversely affect the learning environment, then it also can regulate the educational process directly. Congress could determine that a school's curriculum has a "significant" effect on the extent of classroom learning. As a result, Congress could mandate a federal curriculum for local elementary and secondary schools because what is taught in local schools has a significant "effect on classroom learning," and that, in turn, has a substantial effect on interstate commerce. Justice Breyer's rationale lacks any real limits because, depending on the level of generality, any activity can be looked upon as commercial.

Admittedly, a determination whether an intrastate activity is commercial or noncommercial may in some cases result in legal uncertainty. But, so long as Congress' authority is limited to those powers enumerated in the Constitution, and so long as those enumerated powers are interpreted as having judicially enforceable outer limits, congressional legislation under the Commerce Clause always will engender "legal uncertainty."

"The [federal] government is acknowledged by all to be one of enumerated powers. The principle, that it can exercise only the powers granted to it . . . is now universally admitted. But the question respecting the extent of the powers actually granted, is perpetually arising, and will probably continue to arise, as long as our system shall exist."

Congress has operated within this framework of legal uncertainty ever since this Court determined that it was the Judiciary's duty "to say what the law is." *Marbury v. Madison*, 5 U.S. Any possible benefit from eliminating this "legal uncertainty" would be at the expense of the Constitution's system of enumerated powers.

These are not precise formulations, and in the nature of things they cannot be. But we think they point the way to a correct decision of this case. The possession of a gun in a local school zone is in no sense an economic activity that might, through repetition elsewhere, substantially affect any sort of interstate commerce. Respondent was a local student at a local school; there is no indication

FROM THE BENCH

that he had recently moved in interstate commerce, and there is no requirement that his possession of the firearm have any concrete tie to interstate commerce.

To uphold the Government's contentions here, we would have to pile inference upon inference in a manner that would bid fair to convert congressional authority under the Commerce Clause to a general police power of the sort retained by the States. Admittedly, some of our prior cases have taken long steps down that road, giving great deference to congressional action. The broad language in these opinions has suggested the possibility of additional expansion, but we decline here to proceed any further. To do so would require us to conclude that the Constitution's enumeration of powers does not presuppose something not enumerated and that there never will be a distinction between what is truly national and what is truly local. This we are unwilling to do.

Justice KENNEDY, with whom Justice O'CONNOR joins, concurring.

The history of the judicial struggle to interpret the Commerce Clause during the transition from the economic system the Founders knew to the single, national market still emergent in our own era counsels great restraint before the Court determines that the Clause is insufficient to support an exercise of the national power. That history gives me some pause about today's decision, but I join the Court's opinion with these observations on what I conceive to be its necessary though limited holding.

The history of our Commerce Clause decisions contains at least two lessons of relevance to this case. The first is the imprecision of content-based boundaries used without more to define the limits of the Commerce Clause. The second is that the Court as an institution and the legal system as a whole have an immense stake in the stability of our Commerce Clause jurisprudence as it has evolved to this point. Stare decisis operates with great force in counseling us not to call in question the essential principles now in place respecting the congressional power to regulate transactions of a commercial nature. That fundamental restraint on our power forecloses us from reverting to an understanding of commerce that would serve only an 18th-century economy, dependent then upon production and trading practices that had changed but little over the preceding centuries; it also mandates against returning to the time when congressional authority to regulate undoubted commercial activities was limited by a judicial determination that those matters had an insufficient connection to an interstate system. Congress can regulate in the commercial sphere on the assumption that we have a single market and a unified purpose to build a stable national economy.

Though on the surface the idea may seem counter-intuitive, it was the insight of the Framers that freedom was enhanced by the creation of two governments, not one. "The different governments will control each other, at the same time that each will be controlled by itself." (James Madison). If, as Madison expected, the Federal and State Governments are to control each other, and hold each other in check by competing for the affections of the people those citizens must have some means of knowing which of the two governments to hold accountable for the failure to perform a given function. Were the Federal Government to take over the regulation of entire areas of traditional state concern, areas having nothing to do with the regulation of commercial activities, the boundaries between the spheres of federal and state authority would blur and political responsibility would become illusory.

For these reasons, it would be mistaken and mischievous for the political branches to forget that the sworn obligation to preserve and protect the Constitution in maintaining the federal balance is their own in the first and primary instance. At the same time, the absence of structural mechanisms to require those officials to undertake this principled task, and the momentary political convenience often attendant upon their failure to do so, argue against a complete renunciation of the judicial role. Although it is the obligation of all officers of the Government to respect the constitutional design, the federal balance is too essential a part of our constitutional structure and plays too vital a role in securing freedom for us to admit inability to intervene when one or the other level of Government has tipped the scales too far.

The statute before us upsets the federal balance to a degree that renders it an unconstitutional assertion of the commerce power, and our intervention is required. As the Chief Justice explains, unlike the earlier cases to come before the Court here neither the actors nor their conduct have a commercial character, and neither the purposes nor the design of the statute have an evident commercial nexus. The statute makes the simple possession of a gun within 1,000 feet of the grounds of the school a criminal offense. In a sense any conduct in this interdependent world of ours has an ultimate commercial origin or consequence, but we have not yet said the commerce power may reach so far. If Congress attempts that extension, then at the least we must inquire whether the exercise of national power seeks to intrude upon an area of traditional state concern.

An interference of these dimensions occurs here, for it is well established that education is a traditional concern of the States. The proximity to schools, including of course schools owned and operated by the States or their subdivisions, is the very premise for making the conduct criminal. In these circumstances, we have a particular duty to ensure that the federal-state balance is not destroyed.

While it is doubtful that any State, or indeed any reasonable person, would argue that it is wise policy to allow students to carry guns on school premises, considerable disagreement exists about how best to accomplish that goal. In this circumstance, the theory and utility of our federalism are revealed, for the States may perform their role as laboratories for experimentation to devise various solutions where the best solution is far from clear.

If a State or municipality determines that harsh criminal sanctions are necessary and wise to deter students from carrying guns on school premises, the reserved powers of the States are sufficient to enact those measures. Indeed, over 40 States already have criminal laws outlawing the possession of firearms on or near school grounds.

Other, more practicable means to rid the schools of guns may be thought by the citizens of some States to be preferable for the safety and welfare of the schools those States are charged with maintaining. These might include inducements to inform on violators where the information leads to arrests or confiscation of the guns, programs to encourage the voluntary surrender of guns with some provision for amnesty, penalties imposed on parents or guardians for failure to supervise the child, laws providing for suspension or expulsion of gun-toting students, or programs for expulsion with assignment to special facilities.

The statute now before us forecloses the States from experimenting and exercising their own judgment in an area to which States lay claim by right of history and expertise, and it does so by regulating an activity beyond the realm of commerce in the ordinary and usual sense of that term. The tendency of this statute to displace state regulation in areas of traditional state concern is evident from its territorial operation. There are over 100,000 elementary and secondary schools in the United States. Each of these now has an invisible federal zone extending 1,000 feet beyond the (often irregular) boundaries of the school property. In some communities no doubt it would be difficult to navigate without infringing on those zones. Yet throughout these areas, school officials would find their own programs for the prohibition of guns in danger of displacement by the federal authority unless the State chooses to enact a parallel rule.

Absent a stronger connection or identification with commercial concerns that are central to the Commerce Clause, that interference contradicts the federal balance the Framers designed and that this Court is obliged to enforce.

Justice THOMAS, concurring.

Although I join the majority, I write separately to observe that our case law has drifted far from the original understanding of the Commerce Clause. In a future case, we ought to temper our Commerce Clause jurisprudence in a manner that both makes sense of our more recent case law and is more faithful to the original understanding of that Clause.

While the principal dissent concedes that there are limits to federal power, the sweeping nature of our current test enables the dissent to argue that Congress can regulate gun possession. But it seems to me that the power to regulate "commerce" can by no means encompass authority over mere gun possession, any more than it empowers the Federal Government to regulate marriage, littering, or cruelty to animals, throughout the 50 States. Our Constitution quite properly leaves such matters to the individual States, notwithstanding these activities' effects on interstate commerce. Any interpretation of the Commerce Clause that even suggests that Congress could regulate such matters is in need of reexamination.

In an appropriate case, I believe that we must further reconsider our "substantial effects" test with an eye toward constructing a standard that reflects the text and history of the Commerce Clause without totally rejecting our more recent Commerce Clause jurisprudence.

At the time the original Constitution was ratified, "commerce" consisted of selling, buying, and bartering, as well as transporting for these purposes. As one would expect, the term "commerce" was used in contradistinction to productive activities such as manufacturing and agriculture. [I]nterjecting a modern sense of commerce into the Constitution generates significant textual and structural problems. For example, one cannot replace "commerce" with a different type of enterprise, such as manufacturing. When a manufacturer produces a car, assembly cannot take place "with a foreign nation" or "with the Indian Tribes."

The Constitution not only uses the word "commerce" in a narrower sense than our case law might suggest, it also does not support the proposition that Congress has authority over all activities that "substantially affect" interstate commerce. The Commerce Clause does not state that Congress may "regulate matters that substantially affect commerce with foreign Nations, and among the several States, and with the Indian Tribes."

Indeed, if a "substantial effects" test can be appended to the Commerce Clause, why not to every other power of the Federal Government? There is no reason for singling out the Commerce Clause for special treatment. Accordingly, Congress could regulate all matters that "substantially affect" the Army and Navy, bankruptcies, tax collection, expenditures, and so on. In that case, the Clauses of §8 all mutually overlap, something we can assume the Founding Fathers never intended.

I am aware of no cases prior to the New Deal that characterized the power flowing from the Commerce Clause as sweepingly as does our substantial effects test.

As recently as 1936, the Court continued to insist that the Commerce Clause did not reach the wholly internal business of the States. These cases all establish a simple point: From the time of the ratification of the Constitution to the mid-1930's, it was widely understood that the Constitution granted Congress only limited powers, notwithstanding the Commerce Clause. Moreover, there was no question that activities wholly separated from business, such as gun possession, were beyond the reach of the commerce power. If anything, the "wrong turn" was the Court's dramatic departure in the 1930's from a century and a half of precedent.

Apart from its recent vintage and its corresponding lack of any grounding in the original understanding of the Constitution, the substantial effects test suffers from the further flaw that it appears to grant Congress a police power over the Nation. The substantial effects test suffers from this flaw, in part, because of its "aggregation principle." Under so-called "class of activities" statutes, Congress can regulate whole categories of activities that are not themselves either "interstate" or "commerce." In applying the effects test, we ask whether the class of activities as a whole substantially affects interstate commerce, not whether any specific activity within the class has such effects when considered in isolation.

FROM THE BENCH

The aggregation principle is clever, but has no stopping point. Suppose all would agree that gun possession within 1,000 feet of a school does not substantially affect commerce, but that possession of weapons generally (knives, brass knuckles, nunchakus, etc.) does. Under our substantial effects doctrine, even though Congress cannot single out gun possession, it can prohibit weapon possession generally. But one always can draw the circle broadly enough to cover an activity that, when taken in isolation, would not have substantial effects on commerce. Under our jurisprudence, if Congress passed an omnibus "substantially affects interstate commerce" statute, purporting to regulate every aspect of human existence, the Act apparently would be constitutional. Even though particular sections may govern only trivial activities, the statute in the aggregate regulates matters that substantially affect commerce.

If we wish to be true to a Constitution that does not cede a police power to the Federal Government, our Commerce Clause's boundaries simply cannot be "defined" as being "'commensurate with the national needs'" or self-consciously intended to let the Federal Government "'defend itself against economic forces that Congress decrees inimical or destructive of the national economy'" [quoting Breyer's Dissent]. Such a formulation of federal power is no test at all: It is a blank check.

At an appropriate juncture, I think we must modify our Commerce Clause jurisprudence. Today, it is easy enough to say that the Clause certainly does not empower Congress to ban gun possession within 1,000 feet of a school.

Justice SOUTER, dissenting.

The practice of deferring to rationally based legislative judgments "is a paradigm of judicial restraint." In judicial review under the Commerce Clause, it reflects our respect for the institutional competence of the Congress on a subject expressly assigned to it by the Constitution and our appreciation of the legitimacy that comes from Congress's political accountability in dealing with matters open to a wide range of possible choices. A look at history's sequence will serve to show how today's decision tugs the Court off course, leading it to suggest opportunities for further developments that would be at odds with the rule of restraint to which the Court still wisely states adherence.

Justice BREYER, with whom Justice STEVENS, Justice SOUTER, and Justice GINSBERG join, dissenting.

The issue in this case is whether the Commerce Clause authorizes Congress to enact a statute that makes it a crime to possess a gun in, or near, a school. In my view, the statute falls well within the scope of the commerce power as this Court has understood that power over the last half century.

In reaching this conclusion, I apply three basic principles of Commerce Clause interpretation. First, the power to "regulate Commerce . . . among the several States," encompasses the power to regulate local activities insofar as they significantly affect interstate commerce.

Second, in determining whether a local activity will likely have a significant effect upon interstate commerce, a court must consider, not the effect of an individual act (a single instance of gun possession), but rather the cumulative effect of all similar instances (i.e., the effect of all guns possessed in or near schools).

Third, the Constitution requires us to judge the connection between a regulated activity and interstate commerce, not directly, but at one remove. Courts must give Congress a degree of leeway in determining the existence of a significant factual connection between the regulated activity and interstate commerce—both because the Constitution delegates the commerce power directly to Congress and because the determination requires an empirical judgment of a kind that a legislature is more likely than a court to make with accuracy. The traditional words "rational basis" capture this leeway. Thus, the specific question before us, as the Court recognizes, is not whether the "regulated activity sufficiently affected interstate commerce," but, rather, whether Congress could have had "a rational basis" for so concluding.

Applying these principles to the case at hand, we must ask whether Congress could have had a rational basis for finding a significant (or substantial) connection between gun-related school violence and interstate commerce. Or, to put the question in the language of the explicit finding that Congress made when it amended this law in 1994: Could Congress rationally have found that "violent crime in school zones," through its effect on the "quality of education," significantly (or substantially) affects "interstate" or "foreign commerce"? As long as one views the commerce connection, not as a "technical legal conception," but as "a practical one," the answer to this question must be yes. Numerous reports and studies—generated both inside and outside government—make clear that Congress could reasonably have found the empirical connection that its law, implicitly or explicitly, asserts.

For one thing, reports, hearings, and other readily available literature make clear that the problem of guns in and around schools is widespread and extremely serious. These materials report, for example, that four percent of American high school students (and six percent of inner-city high school students) carry a gun to school at least occasionally; that 12 percent of urban high school students have had guns fired at them, 20 percent of those students have been threatened with guns, and that, in any 6-month period, several hundred thousand schoolchildren are victims of violent crimes in or near their schools. And, they report that this widespread violence in schools throughout the Nation significantly interferes with the quality of education in those schools. Based on reports such as these, Congress obviously could have thought that guns and learning are mutually exclusive. Congress could therefore have found a substantial educational problem—teachers unable to teach, students unable to learn—and concluded that guns near schools contribute substantially to the size and scope of that problem.

Having found that guns in schools significantly undermine the quality of education in our Nation's classrooms, Congress could also have found, given the effect of education upon interstate and foreign commerce, that gun-related violence in and around schools is a commercial, as well as a human, problem. Education, although far more than a matter of economics, has long been inextricably intertwined with the Nation's economy.

[T]here is evidence that, today more than ever, many firms base their location decisions upon the presence, or absence, of a work force with a basic education. Congress has written that "the occurrence of violent crime in school zones" has brought about a "decline in the quality of education" that "has an adverse impact on interstate commerce and the foreign commerce of the United States." The violence-related facts, the educational facts, and the economic facts, taken together, make this conclusion rational. And, because under our case law, the sufficiency of the constitutionally necessary Commerce Clause link between a crime of violence and interstate commerce turns simply upon size or degree, those same facts make the statute constitutional.

In sum, to find this legislation within the scope of the Commerce Clause would permit "Congress . . . to act in terms of economic . . . realities." It would interpret the Clause as this Court has traditionally interpreted it. Upholding this legislation would do no more than simply recognize that Congress had a "rational basis" for finding a significant connection between guns in or near schools and (through their effect on education) the interstate and foreign commerce they threaten.

BEHIND THE CURTAIN

In 2022, Justice Breyer stepped down after more than 27 years on the Supreme Court. At the time of the *Lopez* case, he was the most junior member of the Court, a position he would hold for more than ten years, longer than any Justice since 1823. As a form of light hazing, the most junior member is tasked with answering the conference door during closed Court meetings (to roll in a tea cart and similar chores) and running the Court's cafeteria committee, a task Justice Ginsburg described as a "truly disheartening assignment."

Although regarded as a brilliant legal thinker, Justice Breyer was known for his sometimes off-the-wall statements on the bench. In response to the U.S. lawyer arguing for the rational basis test to be used in a particular case, Justice Breyer retorted by quoting Ben Franklin, stating, "It's so wonderful

to be a rational animal, that there is a reason for everything that one does."
This retort is particularly ironic given that Justice Breyer repeatedly advocated for the Court to use a rational basis approach to evaluating a statute,
just as he did in *Lopez*. Perhaps even more outlandish, Justice Breyer made
the following exclamation during oral arguments in a case evaluating the
constitutionality of a student strip search: "In my experience when I was 8 or
10 or 12 years old, you know, we did take our clothes off once a day. . . . We
changed for gym, OK? And in my experience, too, people did sometimes
stick things in my underwear."

The Court in *Lopez* summarized more than 200 years of Commerce Clause
jurisprudence and added essential precedent. According to the Court, the Commerce Clause authorizes legislation pertaining to three categories of things:
(1) channels of interstate commerce, (2) instrumentalities of interstate commerce, and (3) activities that substantially affect interstate commerce. All of the
Commerce Clause cases in this book, including *Lopez*, fall within the third category, which is the most complicated. The former two categories are relatively
straightforward. Channels of interstate commerce include places where interstate commerce occurs, including roadways, waterways, and airways. The second
category, instrumentalities, consists of the items that carry interstate commerce,
such as railroads, vehicles, ships, and airplanes. Importantly, the Commerce
Clause gives Congress the power to regulate these areas even when the activity
is entirely intrastate. For both categories, federal regulation is just a matter of
practical utility. Imagine the issues that would arise if each state was responsible
for controlling its own airspace (channel). A plane traveling from Los Angeles to
New York City would fly over at least ten different states and be subject to different authorities and standards in each one. In terms of instrumentalities, consider
the rather mundane issue of mudflaps on trucks. If each state had a drastically
different required size for mudflaps, truck drivers would have to pull over and
switch their mudflaps every time they crossed a border. Allowing federal regulation in this area ensures conformity. In fact, when a state implements such an
onerous requirement, the state regulation can itself be deemed to violate the
intent of the Commerce Clause. When the Commerce Clause regulates in this
way, it is called the Dormant Commerce Clause.

The third category, activities that substantially affect interstate commerce,
is the one most often the subject of litigation. The *Lopez* Court identified three
ways in which an activity meets the substantial effects test, although the Court
was not clear on whether all three ways must be established:

■ First, Congress includes an element of any claim or criminal offense
outlined in a statute that is substantially connected to interstate commerce. This is called a jurisdictional element in the statute, referring

to the connection with interstate commerce as establishing the power of the federal government to regulate. If including such an element ensures the statute is valid, would Congress ever not have such a provision? One answer is that by adding this element, Congress narrows the statute's reach and makes it harder to prove that the statute violates the Constitution. In the case of *Lopez*, a jurisdictional element would have saved the statute but likely would have also prevented the law from applying to Lopez himself: Lopez's activity might not have had a connection with interstate commerce. Still, jurisdictional elements have become ubiquitous in the law, especially after the *Lopez* decision. An example is found in the federal hate crime law. Without understanding the context, laypeople sometimes consider crossing a state border to commit a crime as more morally blameworthy. If two people plan to carry out a hate crime during a PRIDE festival in Philadelphia, does it matter that person traveled from Camden, New Jersey, and the other from Pittsburgh, Pennsylvania? Arguably both are just as morally culpable. Nonetheless, the Camden resident may be prosecuted by both Pennsylvania's authorities and the federal government, whereas the Pittsburgh resident is under the exclusive jurisdiction of the Commonwealth of Pennsylvania. What justifies this difference? If the federal government acts, it must rely on a grant of power in the Constitution.

■ Second, Congress justifies using Commerce Clause power with legislative findings. As the *Lopez* majority put it, "congressional findings would enable [a court] to evaluate the legislative judgment that the activity in question substantially affected interstate commerce." That said, legislative findings of a substantial effect on interstate commerce do not necessarily alleviate the concern that the Commerce Clause will extend to almost every aspect of U.S. life without limiting principles. In other words, legislative finding alone will not necessarily be enough to justify rejecting a constitutional challenge to an act of Congress.

■ Finally, the activity regulated should substantially affect interstate commerce. The Court did not articulate a clear standard here, but generally explained that the activity must have a clear substantial link to interstate commerce to fall within this category. The Court cited *Wickard*, suggesting a person growing their own wheat could affect interstate commerce by decreasing the demand for the wheat on the market and, in so doing, affecting the market. On the other hand, a person carrying a gun to school is less likely to be considered a cause of economic effects, such as inspiring a shortage of educated workers.

QUESTION FOR DISCUSSION

4.3   Justice Breyer claimed that deference should be given to Congress to define the commerce power partly because "the determination requires an empirical judgment of a kind that a legislature is more likely than a court to make with accuracy." What did he mean by that?

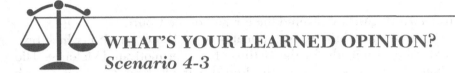

WHAT'S YOUR LEARNED OPINION?
Scenario 4-3

Congress becomes concerned that companies harvest personal data and sell it to third parties. In response, it passes a law that no company can transfer personal data to any other company. Congress does not include a jurisdictional element in the statute, nor does it present any formal findings that sharing personal information substantially affects interstate commerce. Ben's Sub Shop has been tracking customer purchases (which were considered personal data under the new act) and sends the information to their distributor in exchange for discounts on purchases. Although giving a discount is not identical to "selling," assume that authorities maintain that Ben's Sub Shop violates the terms of the federal law. Is the law constitutional as applied to Ben's if the distributor is based in the same state as Ben's? Would it matter if the distributor uses the data only to prepare for Ben's Sub Shop's next order?

In the wake of the Court's *Lopez* decision, dozens of federalism challenges arose across the country against a wide range of federal laws. In 2000, led again by Chief Justice Rehnquist, the Court considered the constitutionality of certain provisions of the Violence Against Women Act (VAWA) in the case below, *United States v. Morrison*. VAWA became law in 1994 and provided $1.6 billion to investigate and prosecute violent crimes against women. VAWA also created a cause of action for women to sue their abusers in federal court. Congress did this believing that state governments often failed to protect women from violent abuse. In justifying the Act, Congress created an extensive legislative record showing that gender-based violence deters women's travel interstate, restricts women's choice of jobs and their ability to carry out their jobs, increases medical costs, and reduces national productivity. Unlike the *Lopez* statute, the history of Congress's consideration of VAWA reflects extensive congressional findings regarding the impact of the regulated behavior on interstate commerce.

FROM THE BENCH

UNITED STATES v. MORRISON
529 U.S. 598 (2000)

Chief Justice REHNQUIST delivered the opinion of the Court.

[W]e consider [here] the constitutionality of 42 U.S.C. §13981, which provides a federal civil remedy for the victims of gender-motivated violence. The United States Court of Appeals for the Fourth Circuit, sitting en banc, struck down §13981 because it concluded that Congress lacked constitutional authority to enact the section's civil remedy. [W]e affirm.

Petitioner Christy Brzonkala enrolled at Virginia Polytechnic Institute (Virginia Tech) in the fall of 1994. In September of that year, Brzonkala met respondents Antonio Morrison and James Crawford, who were both students at Virginia Tech and members of its varsity football team. Brzonkala alleges that, within 30 minutes of meeting Morrison and Crawford, they assaulted and repeatedly raped her. After the attack, Morrison allegedly told Brzonkala, "You better not have any . . . diseases." In the months following the rape, Morrison also allegedly announced in the dormitory's dining room that he "liked to get girls drunk and. . . ." The omitted portions, quoted verbatim in the briefs on file with this Court, consist of boasting, debased remarks about what Morrison would do to women, vulgar remarks that cannot fail to shock and offend.

Brzonkala alleges that this attack caused her to become severely emotionally disturbed and depressed. She sought assistance from a university psychiatrist, who prescribed antidepressant medication. Shortly after the rape Brzonkala stopped attending classes and withdrew from the university.

In early 1995, Brzonkala filed a complaint against respondents under Virginia Tech's Sexual Assault Policy. During the school-conducted hearing on her complaint, Morrison admitted having sexual contact with her despite the fact that she had twice told him "no." After the hearing, Virginia Tech's Judicial Committee found insufficient evidence to punish Crawford, but found Morrison guilty of sexual assault and sentenced him to immediate suspension for two semesters.

Virginia Tech's dean of students upheld the judicial committee's sentence. However, in July 1995, Virginia Tech informed Brzonkala that Morrison intended to initiate a court challenge to his conviction under the Sexual Assault Policy. University officials told her that a second hearing would be necessary to remedy the school's error in prosecuting her complaint under that policy, which had not been widely circulated to students. [T]he Judicial Committee again found Morrison guilty and sentenced him to an identical 2-semester suspension. This time, however, the description of Morrison's offense was, without explanation, changed from "sexual assault" to "using abusive language."

Morrison appealed his second conviction through the university's administrative system. On August 21, 1995, Virginia Tech's senior vice president and provost set aside Morrison's punishment. Virginia Tech did not inform Brzonkala of this decision. After learning from a newspaper that Morrison would be returning to Virginia Tech for the fall 1995 semester, she dropped out of the university.

In December 1995, Brzonkala sued Morrison, Crawford, and Virginia Tech in the United States District Court for the Western District of Virginia. Her complaint alleged that Morrison's and Crawford's attack violated §13981. Section 13981 was part of the Violence Against Women Act of 1994. It states that "persons within the United States shall have the right to be free from crimes of violence motivated by gender." To enforce that right, subsection (c) declares:

"A person . . . who commits a crime of violence motivated by gender and thus deprives another of the right declared in subsection (b) of this section shall be liable to the party injured, in an action for the recovery of compensatory and punitive damages, injunctive and declaratory relief, and such other relief as a court may deem appropriate."

Due respect for the decisions of a coordinate branch of Government demands that we invalidate a congressional enactment only upon a plain showing that Congress has exceeded its constitutional bounds. With this presumption of constitutionality in mind, we turn to the question whether §13981 falls within Congress' power under Article I, §8, of the Constitution. Brzonkala and the United States rely upon the third clause of the Article, which gives Congress power "to regulate Commerce with foreign Nations, and among the several States, and with the Indian Tribes." As we discussed at length in *Lopez*, our interpretation of the Commerce Clause has changed as our Nation has developed. [Since *Wickard*] Congress has had considerably greater latitude in regulating conduct and transactions under the Commerce Clause than our previous case law permitted.

Lopez emphasized, however, that even under our modern, expansive interpretation of the Commerce Clause, Congress' regulatory authority is not without effective bounds.

As we observed in *Lopez*, modern Commerce Clause jurisprudence has "identified three broad categories of activity that Congress may regulate under its commerce power." "First, Congress may regulate the use of the channels of interstate commerce." "Second, Congress is empowered to regulate and protect the instrumentalities of interstate commerce, or persons or things in interstate commerce, even though the threat may come only from intrastate activities." "Finally, Congress' commerce authority includes the power to regulate those activities having a substantial relation to interstate commerce, . . . i.e., those activities that substantially affect interstate commerce."

Petitioners do not contend that these cases fall within either of the first two of these categories of Commerce Clause regulation. They seek to sustain §13981 as a regulation of activity that substantially affects interstate commerce. Given

§13981's focus on gender-motivated violence wherever it occurs (rather than violence directed at the instrumentalities of interstate commerce, interstate markets, or things or persons in interstate commerce), we agree that this is the proper inquiry.

Lopez's review of Commerce Clause case law demonstrates that in those cases where we have sustained federal regulation of intrastate activity based upon the activity's substantial effects on interstate commerce, the activity in question has been some sort of economic endeavor.

Lopez rested in part on the fact that the link between gun possession and a substantial effect on interstate commerce was attenuated. We rejected [the arguments in *Lopez*] because they would permit Congress to "regulate not only all violent crime, but all activities that might lead to violent crime, regardless of how tenuously they relate to interstate commerce."

With these principles underlying our Commerce Clause jurisprudence as reference points, the proper resolution of the present cases is clear. Gender-motivated crimes of violence are not, in any sense of the phrase, economic activity. While we need not adopt a categorical rule against aggregating the effects of any noneconomic activity in order to decide these cases, thus far in our Nation's history our cases have upheld Commerce Clause regulation of intrastate activity only where that activity is economic in nature.

Like the Gun-Free School Zones Act at issue in *Lopez*, §13981 contains no jurisdictional element establishing that the federal cause of action is in pursuance of Congress' power to regulate interstate commerce. Although *Lopez* makes clear that such a jurisdictional element would lend support to the argument that §13981 is sufficiently tied to interstate commerce, Congress elected to cast §13981's remedy over a wider, and more purely intrastate, body of violent crime.

In contrast with the lack of congressional findings that we faced in *Lopez*, §13981 is supported by numerous findings regarding the serious impact that gender-motivated violence has on victims and their families. But the existence of congressional findings is not sufficient, by itself, to sustain the constitutionality of Commerce Clause legislation. As we stated in *Lopez*, " 'Simply because Congress may conclude that a particular activity substantially affects interstate commerce does not necessarily make it so.' " Rather, " 'whether particular operations affect interstate commerce sufficiently to come under the constitutional power of Congress to regulate them is ultimately a judicial rather than a legislative question, and can be settled finally only by this Court.' "

Congress found that gender-motivated violence affects interstate commerce "by deterring potential victims from traveling interstate, from engaging in employment in interstate business, and from transacting with business, and in places involved in interstate commerce; . . . by diminishing national productivity, increasing medical and other costs, and decreasing the supply of and the demand for interstate products."

Given these findings and petitioners' arguments, the concern that we expressed in *Lopez* that Congress might use the Commerce Clause to completely obliterate the Constitution's distinction between national and local authority seems well founded. If accepted, petitioners' reasoning would allow Congress to regulate any crime as long as the nationwide, aggregated impact of that crime has substantial effects on employment, production, transit, or consumption. Indeed, if Congress may regulate gender-motivated violence, it would be able to regulate murder or any other type of violence since gender-motivated violence, as a subset of all violent crime, is certain to have lesser economic impacts than the larger class of which it is a part.

Petitioners' reasoning, moreover, will not limit Congress to regulating violence but may, as we suggested in *Lopez*, be applied equally as well to family law and other areas of traditional state regulation since the aggregate effect of marriage, divorce, and childrearing on the national economy is undoubtedly significant.

We accordingly reject the argument that Congress may regulate noneconomic, violent criminal conduct based solely on that conduct's aggregate effect on interstate commerce. The Constitution requires a distinction between what is truly national and what is truly local. In recognizing this fact we preserve one of the few principles that has been consistent since the Clause was adopted.

Justice SOUTER, with whom Justice STEVENS, Justice GINSBURG, and Justice BREYER join, dissenting.

Our cases, which remain at least nominally undisturbed, stand for the following propositions. Congress has the power to legislate with regard to activity that, in the aggregate, has a substantial effect on interstate commerce. The fact of such a substantial effect is not an issue for the courts in the first instance, but for the Congress, whose institutional capacity for gathering evidence and taking testimony far exceeds ours. By passing legislation, Congress indicates its conclusion, whether explicitly or not, that facts support its exercise of the commerce power. The business of the courts is to review the congressional assessment, not for soundness but simply for the rationality of concluding that a jurisdictional basis exists in fact. Any explicit findings that Congress chooses to make, though not dispositive of the question of rationality, may advance judicial review by identifying factual authority on which Congress relied.

One obvious difference from *United States v. Lopez*, is the mountain of data assembled by Congress, here showing the effects of violence against women on interstate commerce. Passage of the Act in 1994 was preceded by four years of hearings.

Based on the data, Congress found that "crimes of violence motivated by gender have a substantial adverse effect on interstate commerce, by deterring potential victims from traveling interstate, from engaging in employment in interstate business, and from transacting with business, and in places involved, in interstate commerce . . . [,] by diminishing national productivity, increasing medical and other costs, and decreasing the supply of and the demand for interstate products. . . ."

Congress thereby explicitly stated the predicate for the exercise of its Commerce Clause power. Is its conclusion irrational in view of the data amassed? True, the methodology of particular studies may be challenged, and some of the figures arrived at may be disputed. But the sufficiency of the evidence before Congress to provide a rational basis for the finding cannot seriously be questioned.

Indeed, the legislative record here is far more voluminous than the record compiled by Congress and found sufficient in two prior cases upholding Title II of the Civil Rights Act of 1964 against Commerce Clause challenges.

In *Wickard*, we upheld the application of the Agricultural Adjustment Act to the planting and consumption of homegrown wheat. The effect on interstate commerce in that case followed from the possibility that wheat grown at home for personal consumption could relieve its grower of any need to purchase wheat in the market. The Commerce Clause predicate was simply the effect of the production of wheat for home consumption on supply and demand in interstate commerce. Supply and demand for goods in interstate commerce will also be affected by the deaths of 2,000 to 4,000 women annually at the hands of domestic abusers, and by the reduction in the work force by the 100,000 or more rape victims who lose their jobs each year or are forced to quit. Violence against women may be found to affect interstate commerce and affect it substantially.

The premise that the enumeration of powers implies that other powers are withheld is sound; the conclusion that some particular categories of subject matter are therefore presumptively beyond the reach of the commerce power is, however, a non sequitur. From the fact that Art. I, §8, cl. 3 grants an authority limited to regulating commerce, it follows only that Congress may claim no authority under that section to address any subject that does not affect commerce. It does not at all follow that an activity affecting commerce nonetheless falls outside the commerce power, depending on the specific character of the activity, or the authority of a State to regulate it along with Congress. My disagreement with the majority is not, however, confined to logic, for history has shown that categorical exclusions have proven as unworkable in practice as they are unsupportable in theory. Why is the majority tempted to reject the lesson so painfully learned in 1937?

If we now ask why the formalistic economic/noneconomic distinction might matter today, after its rejection in *Wickard*, the answer is not that the majority fails to see causal connections in an integrated economic world. The answer is that in the minds of the majority there is a new animating theory that makes categorical formalism seem useful again. Just as the old formalism had value in the service of an economic conception, the new one is useful in serving a conception of federalism. It is the instrument by which assertions of national power are to be limited in favor of preserving a supposedly discernible, proper sphere of state autonomy to legislate or refrain from legislating as the individual States see fit. The legitimacy of the Court's current emphasis on the noncommercial nature of regulated activity, then, does not turn on any logic serving the text of the Commerce Clause or on the realism of the majority's view of the national economy.

BEHIND THE CURTAIN

As illustrated in *Lopez* and *Morrison*, challenging the constitutionality of a law is sometimes a winning strategy, but if that is the strategy you choose to pursue, you should prepare for a fight. When Morrison challenged the Violence Against Women Act, he went from defending against his accuser (Christy Brzonkala) to defending against the U.S. government. In oral argument, the United States was represented by the Solicitor General, a highly skilled advocate who had argued in front of the Supreme Court 19 separate times. Additionally, the U.S. government has deep pockets and defending a case up to the Supreme Court is not cheap. Although Morrison won the case, the publicity continued to follow him. Despite professional football aspirations, he was not able to find a job outside retail. Christy Brzonkala did not return to college following the case and instead worked as a waitress. She sued Virginia Tech for its mishandling of the situation. The university agreed to pay $75,000 but did not admit any wrongdoing. The question arises whether this was sufficient to remedy the harm she suffered. Although compensatory damages are meant to "make a person whole," money simply cannot fully rectify some wrongs.

QUESTIONS FOR DISCUSSION

4.4 Everyone can likely agree that holding sexual abusers liable for their abuse is a laudable goal. Yet, most of the Supreme Court struck down a law that did just that. How can this be the correct outcome? To quote Justice Scalia, "if you're going to take the position that the Federal Government is a Government of limited powers, it means a limitation on doing good things, as well as limitations on doing bad things—you swallow it." Do you agree with Scalia? If not, then would you ask the Court to make a judgment call on what are good things and what are bad things? The Court is comprised of nine unelected individuals who serve for life. Do you trust them to serve as the country's conscience, deciding which laws are morally acceptable and which are not? What if the Court renders a decision you disagree with? Unlike your representatives in Congress or the President, you cannot vote them out of their position. Who should you blame if you are upset about Ms. Brzonkala's treatment when she tried to seek a remedy in federal court?

4.5   Congress did not put a jurisdictional element into the Violence Against Women Act. Why not? Had a jurisdictional element been in place, would the Court have upheld VAWA and held that Morrison could be liable for his actions?

4.6   "The fight for 20" has been a social movement calling for the establishment of a $20 per hour minimum wage. If Congress were to pass said law, would it survive a constitutional challenge on the grounds that it is a valid exercise of commerce authority?

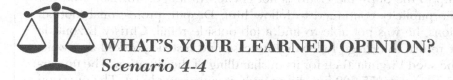

WHAT'S YOUR LEARNED OPINION?
Scenario 4-4

The Green New Deal was legislation proposed to create public policy reform addressing climate change and growing economic inequality; the name was a takeoff on President Franklin Roosevelt's New Deal legislation. Part of the Green New Deal proposed to bring carbon emissions to net neutrality. As part of this goal, could Congress constitutionally use its Commerce Clause power to ban the sale of coal-powered stoves after extensive legislative findings that coal is the most carbon-inefficient type of fuel and it heavily pollutes the environment?

Scenario 4-5

In Scenario 4-2 (appearing after the *Wickard* case), you considered whether Commerce Clause authority could be used to justify abortion regulation. After reading *Lopez* and *Morrison*, has your answer changed? What if Congress added a jurisdictional element to its abortion statute?

Following the *Morrison* decision, the composition of the U.S. Supreme Court became slightly more inclined to read Congress's commerce power more expansively. This became clear in the Court's decision in *Gonzales v. Raich*, 545 U.S. 1 (2005). In *Raich*, the Court did not revisit its holdings in *Lopez* and *Morrison*, both providing a rigorous test for determining whether Congress can regulate noneconomic activities under the theory that the activities had a substantial effect on commerce. Rather, *Raich* stands for the proposition that the appropriate test for evaluating the constitutionality of a statute regulating an economic activity is the easy-to-satisfy rational basis test—at least when a constitutional challenge to the statute is limited to the application of the statute to the particular facts of the case. The Court defined economic activity as production, distribution, and consumption of commodities. Moreover, *Raich* concluded that a statute is authorized by the Commerce Clause even in the context of wholly intrastate economic activity so long as Congress had a rational basis for concluding that the cumulative effect of that activity had a substantial effect on interstate activity.

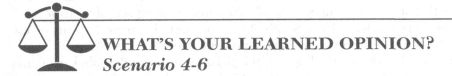

WHAT'S YOUR LEARNED OPINION?
Scenario 4-6

The Controlled Substances Act makes it a federal crime to possess marijuana. Jeremy High decides to grow marijuana on his own property. He produces no more than he smokes. He lives in Philadelphia, where marijuana is decriminalized, and as such, neither local nor state law enforcement decide to prosecute him. Federal law enforcement gets involved and arrests Jeremy for violation of the Controlled Substances Act. In his defense, Jeremy claims that (1) his activity is not commerce because he never sold anything and therefore had no effect on interstate commerce (much less a substantial one), (2) his activity could not possibly have a substantial effect on commerce because marijuana is illegal, and therefore no interstate market exists to feel an effect, and (3) the Controlled Substances Act contains neither a jurisdictional element nor formal legislative findings and is therefore invalid under *Lopez* and *Morrison*. Which of these defenses, if any, is likely to be effective?

C. Taxing and Spending Power

Aside from the Commerce Clause in Article I, §8, the taxing and spending power in that same section of the Constitution is another important source of congressional power. Specifically, Article I, §8, cl. 1 states that "The Congress shall have Power To lay and collect Taxes, Duties, Imposts and Excises, to pay the Debts and provide for the common Defense and general Welfare of the United States; but all Duties, Imposts and Excises shall be uniform throughout the United States."

Like many constitutionally vested powers, the spending power has its limits. First, Congress may exercise this power only in the pursuit of the "general welfare" of the United States. Second, if Congress were to condition a state's receipt of federal funds, it must do so unambiguously, as to enable a state to choose to comply or not comply with this condition "knowingly." Third, conditions on the receipt of federal funds should be reasonably related to the particular federal interest in the project or program that Congress attaches to the funds. Finally, other constitutional provisions may bar a particular conditional grant of federal funds. For example, the condition must not run afoul of the Tenth Amendment because it is "coercive," giving the state no option but to adopt the condition.

The next case concerns the question of whether Congress has authorized a condition on the receipt of federal funds that violates any of these three limitations. The case, *South Dakota v. Dole*, concerns a 1984 congressional act that provides that states must follow a legal minimum drinking age of 21 to receive federal highway funds. In 1984, South Dakota permitted persons 19 years of age or older to purchase beer containing 3.2 percent alcohol.

Because this federal spending power legislation concerned alcohol, concerns arose about the Constitution's Twenty-First Amendment. The Twenty-First Amendment repealed the Eighteenth Amendment, which had prohibited alcohol in the United States. Section 2 of the Twenty-First Amendment prohibits the transportation, use, or possession of alcohol in any state that is in violation of that state's laws. In other words, after the Twenty-First Amendment, states controlled laws and regulation regarding alcohol. This provision also comports with the Tenth Amendment, which states, "The powers not delegated to the United States by the Congress, nor prohibited by it to the States, are reserved to the States respectively, or to the people." Thus, the federal law in *Dole* implicated both the Tenth and the Twenty-First Amendments.

FROM THE BENCH

SOUTH DAKOTA v. DOLE
483 U.S. 203 (1987)

Chief Justice REHNQUIST delivered the opinion of the Court.

Petitioner South Dakota permits persons 19 years of age or older to purchase beer containing up to 3.2% alcohol. In 1984, Congress enacted 23 U.S.C.

§158, which directs the Secretary of Transportation to withhold a percentage of federal highway funds otherwise allocable from States "in which the purchase or public possession . . . of any alcoholic beverage by a person who is less than twenty-one years of age is lawful." The State sued in United States District Court seeking a declaratory judgment that §158 violates the constitutional limitations on congressional exercise of the spending power and violates the Twenty-first Amendment to the United States Constitution. The Court of Appeals for the Eighth Circuit affirmed.

The Constitution empowers Congress to "lay and collect Taxes, Duties, Imposts, and Excises, to pay the Debts and provide for the common Defence and general Welfare of the United States." Incident to this power, Congress may attach conditions on the receipt of federal funds, and has repeatedly employed the power "to further broad policy objectives by conditioning receipt of federal moneys upon compliance by the recipient with federal statutory and administrative directives."

[Although a broad power], the spending power is of course not unlimited, but is instead subject to several general restrictions articulated in our cases. The first of these limitations is derived from the language of the Constitution itself: the exercise of the spending power must be in pursuit of "the general welfare." In considering whether a particular expenditure is intended to serve general public purposes, courts should defer substantially to the judgment of Congress. Second, we have required that, if Congress desires to condition the States' receipt of federal funds, it "must do so unambiguously . . . , enabl[ing] the States to exercise their choice knowingly, cognizant of the consequences of their participation." Third, our cases have suggested (without significant elaboration) that conditions on federal grants might be illegitimate if they are unrelated "to the federal interest in particular national projects or programs." Finally, we have noted that other constitutional provisions may provide an independent bar to the conditional grant of federal funds.

South Dakota does not seriously claim that §158 is inconsistent with any of the first three restrictions mentioned above. We can readily conclude that the provision is designed to serve the general welfare. Congress found that the differing drinking ages in the States created particular incentives for young persons to combine their desire to drink with their ability to drive, and that this interstate problem required a national solution. The means it chose to address this dangerous situation were reasonably calculated to advance the general welfare. The conditions upon which States receive the funds, moreover, could not be more clearly stated by Congress. Indeed, the condition imposed by Congress is directly related to one of the main purposes for which highway funds are expended—safe interstate travel.

We have also held that a perceived Tenth Amendment limitation on congressional regulation of state affairs did not concomitantly limit the range of conditions legitimately placed on federal grants. Our decisions have recognized that, in some circumstances, the financial inducement offered by Congress might be so coercive as to pass the point at which "pressure turns into compulsion." Here, however, Congress has directed only that a State desiring to establish a minimum drinking age lower than 21 lose a relatively small percentage of certain federal highway funds. Petitioner contends that the coercive nature of this program is evident from the degree of success it has achieved. We cannot conclude, however, that a conditional grant of federal money of this sort is unconstitutional simply by reason of its success in achieving the congressional objective.

When we consider, for a moment, that all South Dakota would lose if she adheres to her chosen course as to a suitable minimum drinking age is 5% of the funds otherwise obtainable under specified highway grant programs, the argument as to coercion is shown to be more rhetoric than fact.

Justice BRENNAN, dissenting.

I agree with Justice O'Connor that regulation of the minimum age of purchasers of liquor falls squarely within the ambit of those powers reserved to the States by the Twenty-first Amendment. Since States possess this constitutional power, Congress cannot condition a federal grant in a manner that abridges this right. The Amendment, itself, strikes the proper balance between federal and state authority. I therefore dissent.

Justice O'CONNOR, dissenting.

The Court today upholds the National Minimum Drinking Age Amendment, as a valid exercise of the spending power conferred by Article I, §8. But §158 is not a condition on spending reasonably related to the expenditure of federal funds, and cannot be justified on that ground. Rather, it is an attempt to regulate the sale of liquor, an attempt that lies outside Congress' power to regulate commerce because it falls within the ambit of §2 of the Twenty-first Amendment. . . . [In addition], establishment of a minimum drinking age of 21 is not sufficiently related to interstate highway construction to justify so conditioning funds appropriated for that purpose.

QUESTIONS FOR DISCUSSION

4.7   In arguing the case, South Dakota asserted that "[t]he power to regulate liquor, pursuant to the Twenty-first Amendment, is entitled to greater protection than a power merely reserved pursuant to the Tenth Amendment." Why would this be true? Consider the relevant language of the two amendments:

- Tenth Amendment: "The powers not delegated to the United States, nor prohibited by it to the States, are reserved to the people."
- Twenty-First Amendment: "The transportation or importation into any State, Territory, or possession of the United States for delivery or use therein of intoxicating liquors, in violation of the laws thereof, is hereby prohibited."
- Does the difference in language of the two amendments help to justify South Dakota's arguments?

4.8   Many empirical studies support the wisdom of the federal government's position on controlling driving by 19- and 20-year-olds, including findings that this restriction promotes temperance later in life. In addition, according to President Ronald Reagan, by 1984, nearly every state that had raised the drinking age to 21 had produced a significant drop in teenage driving fatalities. Finally, confirmed statistics showed that drunk driving fatalities declined 50 percent from 1982 to 2018.

Do these apparent facts support the federal government's claim (and the Supreme Court's decision) that the condition imposed on the states in *South Dakota v. Dole* satisfies the requirements for a valid exercise of the spending power?

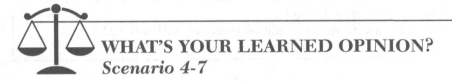

WHAT'S YOUR LEARNED OPINION?
Scenario 4-7

Assume that Congress has passed the Inclusive School Lunch Act of 2022. This act instructs the U.S. Department of Agriculture to withhold 5 percent of federal school lunch funding for state schools that do not "investigate allegations of discrimination based on gender identity, or update their non-discrimination policies and signage to include prohibitions against discrimination based on gender identity." Assume further that Congress has stated that the purpose of the act is "in line with their efforts to promote nutrition security, which is the consistent access to safe, healthy, affordable food essential to optimal health and well-being." Congress also states that "nutrition security places an emphasis on advancing equity to ensure all Americans have access to nutritious foods that promote health and well-being regardless of race, ethnicity identity, or background."

Is this condition constitutionally permissible under *Dole*? In evaluating this question, assume that a state not meeting these conditions would not be in violation of a constitutional provision or other congressional act.

Scenario 4-8

Assume that Congress has made it a legislative focus to combat corruption by elected officials, appointed officials, and civil service employees throughout state and federal governments. Many Congress members say their constituents are concerned about financial impropriety and personal financial gain. Congress therefore passes a bill, the Clean Government Act, that bars federal and state employees from engaging in any political activity, either during working or nonworking hours. This prohibition applies whether or not the political activity relates to the employee's official responsibilities at work. The Act conditions receipt of federal highway funds by the jurisdiction where the employee works on compliance by all employees with the Act's prohibition on political activity.

The California State Highway Commission (CSHC) has received federal funding to finance road and infrastructure projects for decades. An official at the CSHC is the head secretary of a political party in California. A reviewing body responsible for enforcing the Clean Government Act determines that this official's position in the political party violates the Act, and requests that the employee resign his secretaryship or be terminated from his position at the CSHC. If compliance with the Clean Government Act is not met, the reviewing body recommends that the federal highway funds be withheld from California. This funding amounts to 20 percent of California's entire infrastructure construction budget.

Is the federal government's condition constitutional under *Dole*?

D. Tying Congress's Power Together

As you have seen, the Commerce Clause and the Taxing and Spending Clause are two major sources of Congress's power. As you will later see in connection with the individual rights protections of the Fourteenth Amendment, Section 5 of the Fourteenth Amendment gives Congress additional power to enforce the protective provisions of the amendment. The Commerce Clause and Spending Clause cases discussed above make clear that Congress does not exercise its powers in a vacuum: Even if a congressional action is authorized by these clauses, other parts of the Constitution might constrain that action. Candidates for constraint on the taxing and spending power as well as the commerce power include the individual rights protections in the Bill of Rights as well as the Tenth Amendment protection for state prerogatives.

Problems arise with the Tenth Amendment under quite varied circumstances. As illustrated in the *Dole* case, one trigger for Tenth Amendment concerns is whether the congressional statute is coercive. Generally, a federal spending clause statute is coercive if the state has no choice but to accept a federal condition. One case in which the U.S. Supreme Court found a condition coercive, *National Federation of Independent Business v. Sebelius*, concerned the 2010 Affordable Care Act (sometimes referred to as Obamacare), which sought to cure problems with health care in the United States. One part of this law sought to have states increase coverage for low-income individuals under Medicaid. In this part of the law, Congress conditioned the provision of federal funding for Medicaid on a state's agreement to agree to expand the Medicaid program. Because federal funding accounted for a large percentage of some states' budgets, a majority of the Supreme Court analogized this condition to "a gun to the head" of the states, which relied heavily on this federal funding. Indeed, the Court noted that Medicaid spending accounted "for over 20% if the average state's budget, with federal funds covering 50 to 83% of those costs."

In other cases, the U.S. Supreme Court has found a Tenth Amendment violation when the federal government has commandeered part of the state administrative apparatus in service of federal goals, such as requiring state law enforcement to administer gun control legislation. The Court has also found the federal government to have violated the Tenth Amendment when it forced state law-making bodies to create laws that implement federal standards. In such instances, the Court reasoned, the voting public could be confused about which elected officials (state or federal) are responsible for possibly onerous legal requirements.

The constitutional authorization for congressional power is easier to satisfy when Congress exercises its taxing and spending power than when it exercises its commerce power. The Taxing and Spending Clause jurisprudence provides for fewer restrictions and less rigorous judicial review than the Commerce Clause jurisprudence. Congress acts appropriately when relying on more than one of its powers in the context of one legislative initiative. Indeed, Congress often does so, such as in the *Morrison* case discussed earlier in this chapter and the Affordable Care Act, which was partially invalidated by the Court in *National Federation of Independent Business v. Sebelius*, 567 U.S. 519 (2012).

You will note from this chapter that the Constitution uses a list of specific powers when describing what Congress may do. Although this list is long, one would think that list works to confine Congress's powers to those powers enumerated. The specificity of the powers enumerated does impose some control on Congress, but case law has expanded these enumerated powers, particularly by virtue of the doctrine of implied powers and the Necessary and Proper Clause, discussed earlier in this chapter. In the next chapter, you will see that the Constitution does not use that approach when describing the power of the President of the United States. Instead, the constitutional language is broad and vague.

As you read through the material in the next chapter, evaluate how this broad approach influences the scope of the President's power. Does this approach render the President's power greater than the power of the other two branches of the federal government?

QUESTIONS FOR REVIEW

1. What is the doctrine of implied powers?
2. How has the Necessary and Proper Clause been interpreted?
3. What did the farmer wheat case—*Wickard v. Filburn*—add to Commerce Clause jurisprudence?
4. Why was the Gun-Free School Zones Act struck down as unconstitutional in *United States v. Lopez*?
5. What is the test for evaluating whether the Commerce Clause authorizes a congressional statute regulating noneconomic activity that does not constitute a channel or instrumentality of commerce?
6. How is an economic activity defined for the purpose of Commerce Clause jurisprudence?
7. What is the test for evaluating whether the Commerce Clause authorizes a congressional statute regulating economic activity?
8. What are the three requirements for upholding a statute that Congress passed pursuant to the taxing and spending power?
9. List some potential reasons why a congressional statute could run afoul of the Tenth Amendment.

Powers of the President

A. Introduction to Article II

The Constitution's Framers chose an approach to describing the powers of the President that contrasts starkly to their approaches for Congress and the federal courts. For Congress's powers, the Framers chose specific limiting language: "All legislative Powers herein granted shall be vested in a Congress of the United States." As discussed in Chapter 4, these specifically listed powers were enlarged by the doctrine of implied powers and the Necessary and Proper Clause of Article I, §8. The federal judiciary, however, did not have the advantage of these two expanding concepts. Rather, Article III, §2 lists nine classes of cases that the federal courts may hear and no more. By contrast, the Framers described the President's role in the U.S. government in broad, sweeping terms: "The executive power shall be vested in a President of the United States of America."

To be sure, some parts of Article II do mention more targeted powers, but the words chosen are nonetheless broad. For example, the President is described as the "Commander in Chief," with no description of what that role entails. Similarly, Article II grants the President to authority to "receive Ambassadors and other public Ministers," and perhaps most ambiguous of all, the President must "take Care that the Laws be faithfully executed."

All of these broad and ambiguous power grants have given rise to litigation over the years. Even more important, they have given rise to a debate about the President: Does the President have inherent power—that is, should the President be presumed to have a broad collection of powers necessary to adequately govern the nation, but not mentioned in the text of the Constitution? This inherent-powers issue has given rise to centuries of partisan debates. One camp, which relies on the views of James Madison, has found the inherent-powers concept inimical to the Framers' deep concern of avoiding the power consolidation emblematic of a tyrannical monarchy as well as the basic concept that the Constitution creates a federal government of *limited* power only. The other camp, which finds support in Alexander Hamilton's arguments, point to the contrast of the sweeping Article II language with the more specific power grants in Article I and Article III.

B. Models of Executive Power

The perennial debate about whether the President enjoys inherent power has given rise to various theories or models of executive power. The case that follows, *Youngstown Sheet & Tube v. Sawyer*, is perhaps the most authoritative exploration of the matter. *Youngstown* is regarded as the foundational exposition on the President's power and completes a triad of cases laying out general principles on the role of the three branches of government: In other words, *Youngstown* is to the federal executive branch as *Marbury v. Madison* (Chapter 3) is to the federal judiciary and *McCulloch v. Maryland* (Chapter 4) is to the federal legislature. Unfortunately, however, the Justices wrote seven separate opinions in *Youngstown*, each giving unique interpretations of whether the President has the power to act without an express constitutional or legislative grant of power to do so. The case does, however, include a majority opinion that provides a preliminary beacon on how to handle inherent power questions.

FROM THE BENCH

YOUNGSTOWN SHEET & TUBE CO. v. SAWYER
343 U.S. 579 (1952)

Mr. Justice BLACK delivered the opinion of the Court.

We are asked to decide whether the President was acting within his constitutional power when he issued an order directing the Secretary of Commerce to take possession of and operate most of the Nation's steel mills. The mill owners argue that the President's order amounts to lawmaking, a legislative function which the Constitution has expressly confided to the Congress and not to the President. The Government's position is that the order was made on findings of the President that his action was necessary to avert a national catastrophe which would inevitably result from a stoppage of steel production, and that in meeting this grave emergency the President was acting within the aggregate of his constitutional powers as the Nation's Chief Executive and the Commander in Chief of the Armed Forces of the United States. The issue emerges here from the following series of events:

In the latter part of 1951, a dispute arose between the steel companies and their employees over terms and conditions that should be included in new collective bargaining agreements. Long-continued conferences failed to resolve the dispute. On December 18, 1951, the employees' representative, United Steelworkers of America, C.I.O., gave notice of an intention to strike when the existing bargaining agreements expired on December 31. The Federal Mediation and Conciliation Service then intervened in an effort to get labor and management to agree. This failing, the President on December 22, 1951, referred the dispute to the Federal Wage Stabilization Board to investigate and make recommendations for fair and equitable terms of settlement. This Board's report resulted in no settlement. On April 4, 1952, the Union gave notice of a nationwide strike called to begin at 12:01 A.M. April 9. The indispensability of steel as a component of substantially all weapons and other war materials led the President to believe that the proposed work stoppage would immediately jeopardize our national defense and that governmental seizure of the steel mills was necessary in order to assure the continued availability of steel. Reciting these considerations for his action, the President, a few hours before the strike was to begin, issued Executive Order 10340. The order directed the Secretary of Commerce to take possession of most of the steel mills and keep them running. The Secretary immediately issued his own possessory orders, calling upon the presidents of the various seized companies to serve as operating managers for the United States. They were directed to carry on their activities in accordance with regulations and directions of the Secretary. The next morning the President sent a message to Congress reporting his action. Twelve days later he sent a second message. Congress has taken no action.

Obeying the Secretary's orders under protest, the companies brought proceedings against him in the District Court. Their complaints charged that the seizure was not authorized by an act of Congress or by any constitutional provisions.

The President's power, if any, to issue the order must stem either from an act of Congress or from the Constitution itself. There is no statute that expressly authorizes the President to take possession of property as he did here. Nor is there any act of Congress to which our attention has been directed from which such a power can fairly be implied. Indeed, we do not understand the Government to rely on statutory authorization for this seizure. There are two statutes which do authorize the President to take both personal and real property under certain conditions. However, the Government admits that these conditions were not met and that the President's order was not rooted in either of the statutes.

Moreover, the use of the seizure technique to solve labor disputes in order to prevent work stoppages was not only unauthorized by any congressional enactment; prior to this controversy, Congress had refused to adopt that method of

FROM THE BENCH

settling labor disputes. When the Taft-Hartley Act was under consideration in 1947, Congress rejected an amendment which would have authorized such governmental seizures in cases of emergency. Apparently, it was thought that the technique of seizure, like that of compulsory arbitration, would interfere with the process of collective bargaining. Consequently, the plan Congress adopted in that Act did not provide for seizure under any circumstances. Instead, the plan sought to bring about settlements by use of the customary devices of mediation, conciliation, investigation by boards of inquiry, and public reports. In some instances temporary injunctions were authorized to provide cooling-off periods. All this failing, unions were left free to strike after a secret vote by employees as to whether they wished to accept their employers' final settlement offer.

It is clear that if the President had authority to issue the order he did, it must be found in some provisions of the Constitution. And it is not claimed that express constitutional language grants this power to the President. The contention is that presidential power should be implied from the aggregate of his powers under the Constitution. Particular reliance is placed on provisions in Article II which say that "the executive Power shall be vested in a President . . ."; that "he shall take Care that the Laws be faithfully executed"; and that he "shall be Commander in Chief of the Army and Navy of the United States."

The order cannot properly be sustained as an exercise of the President's military power as Commander in Chief of the Armed Forces. The Government attempts to do so by citing a number of cases upholding broad powers in military commanders engaged in day-to-day fighting in a theater of war. Such cases need not concern us here. Even though "theater of war" be an expanding concept, we cannot with faithfulness to our constitutional system hold that the Commander in Chief of the Armed Forces has the ultimate power as such to take possession of private property in order to keep labor disputes from stopping production. This is a job for the Nation's lawmakers, not for its military authorities.

Nor can the seizure order be sustained because of the several constitutional provisions that grant executive power to the President. In the framework of our Constitution, the President's power to see that the laws are faithfully executed refutes the idea that he is to be a lawmaker. The Constitution limits his functions in the lawmaking process to the recommending of laws he thinks wise and the vetoing of laws he thinks bad. And the Constitution is neither silent nor equivocal about who shall make laws which the President is to execute.

The Founders of this Nation entrusted the lawmaking power to the Congress alone in both good and bad times. It would do no good to recall the historical events, the fears of power and the hopes for freedom that lay behind their choice. Such a review would but confirm our holding that this seizure order cannot stand.

Mr. Justice FRANKFURTER, concurring.

We must therefore put to one side consideration of what powers the President would have had if there had been no legislation whatever bearing on the authority asserted by the seizure, or if the seizure had been only for a short, explicitly temporary period, to be terminated automatically unless Congressional approval were given. These and other questions, like or unlike, are not now here. I would exceed my authority were I to say anything about them.

The question before the Court comes in this setting. Congress has frequently—at least 16 times since 1916—specifically provided for executive seizure of production, transportation, communications, or storage facilities. In every case it has qualified this grant of power with limitations and safeguards. The power to seize has uniformly been given only for a limited period or for a defined emergency, or has been repealed after a short period. Its exercise has been restricted to particular circumstances such as "time of war or when war is imminent," the needs of "public safety" or of "national security or defense," or "urgent and impending need." The period of governmental operation has been limited, as, for instance, to "sixty days after the restoration of productive efficiency." Congress also has not left to implication that just compensation be paid: it has usually legislated in detail regarding enforcement of this litigation-breeding general requirement.

Congress in 1947 was again called upon to consider whether governmental seizure should be used to avoid serious industrial shutdowns. Congress decided against conferring such power generally and in advance, without special congressional enactment to meet each particular need. Under the urgency of telephone and coal strikes in the winter of 1946, Congress addressed itself to the problems raised by "national emergency" strikes and lockouts. The termination of wartime seizure powers on December 31, 1946, brought these matters to the attention of Congress with vivid impact. A proposal that the President be given powers to seize plants to avert a shutdown where the "health or safety" of the nation was endangered, was thoroughly canvassed by Congress and rejected. No room for doubt remains that the proponents as well as the opponents of the bill which became the Labor Management Relations Act of 1947 clearly understood that as a result of that legislation the only recourse for preventing a shutdown in any basic industry, after failure of mediation, was Congress. Authorization for seizure as an available remedy for potential dangers was unequivocally put aside. An amendment presented in the House providing that where necessary "to preserve and protect the public health and security" the President might seize any industry in which there is an impending curtailment of production, was voted down after debate, by a vote of more than three to one.

[N]othing can be plainer than that Congress made a conscious choice of policy in a field full of perplexity and peculiarly within legislative responsibility for choice. In formulating legislation for dealing with industrial conflicts, Congress could not more clearly and emphatically have withheld authority than it did in 1947. Perhaps as much so as is true of any piece of modern legislation, Congress acted with full consciousness of what it was doing and in the light of much recent history. Previous seizure legislation had subjected the powers granted to the President to restrictions of varying degrees of stringency. Instead of giving him even limited powers, Congress in 1947 deemed it wise to require the President, upon failure of attempts to reach a voluntary settlement, to report to Congress if he deemed the power of seizure a needed shot for his locker. The President could not ignore the specific limitations of prior seizure statutes. No more could he act in disregard of the limitation put upon seizure by the 1947 Act.

It cannot be contended that the President would have had power to issue this order had Congress explicitly negated such authority in formal legislation. Congress has expressed its will to withhold this power from the President as though it had said so in so many words.

Deeply embedded traditional ways of conducting government cannot supplant the Constitution or legislation, but they give meaning to the words of a text or supply them. It is an inadmissibly narrow conception of American constitutional law to confine it to the words of the Constitution and to disregard the gloss which life has written upon them. In short, a systematic, unbroken, executive practice, long pursued to the knowledge of the Congress and never before questioned, engaged in by Presidents who have also sworn to uphold the Constitution, making as it were such exercise of power part of the structure of our government, may be treated as a gloss on "executive Power" vested in the President by §1 of Art. II. Down to the World War II period, then, the record is barren of instances comparable to the one before us.

A scheme of government like ours no doubt at times feels the lack of power to act with complete, all-embracing, swiftly moving authority. No doubt a government with distributed authority, subject to be challenged in the courts of law, at least long enough to consider and adjudicate the challenge, labors under restrictions from which other governments are free. It has not been our tradition to envy such governments. In any event our government was designed to have such restrictions. The price was deemed not too high in view of the safeguards which these restrictions afford.

Mr. Justice DOUGLAS, concurring.

There can be no doubt that the emergency which caused the President to seize these steel plants was one that bore heavily on the country. But the emergency did not create power; it merely marked an occasion when power should be exercised. And the fact that it was necessary that measures be taken to keep steel in production does not mean that the President, rather than the Congress, had the constitutional authority to act. The Congress, as well as the President, is trustee of the national welfare. The President can act more quickly than the Congress. The President with the armed services at his disposal can move with force as well as with speed. All executive power—from the reign of ancient kings to the rule of modern dictators—has the outward appearance of efficiency.

Legislative power, by contrast, is slower to exercise. There must be delay while the ponderous machinery of committees, hearings, and debates is put into motion. That takes time; and while the Congress slowly moves into action, the emergency may take its toll in wages, consumer goods, war production, the standard of living of the people, and perhaps even lives. Legislative action may indeed often be cumbersome, time-consuming, and apparently inefficient. But as Mr. Justice Brandeis stated in his dissent in *Myers v. United States*:

> The doctrine of the separation of powers was adopted by the Convention of 1787 not to promote efficiency but to preclude the exercise of arbitrary power. The purpose was not to avoid friction, but, by means of the inevitable friction incident to the distribution of the governmental powers among three departments, to save the people from autocracy.

We therefore cannot decide this case by determining which branch of government can deal most expeditiously with the present crisis. The answer must depend on the allocation of powers under the Constitution. That in turn requires an analysis of the conditions giving rise to the seizure and of the seizure itself.

The legislative nature of the action taken by the President seems to me to be clear. When the United States takes over an industrial plant to settle a labor controversy, it is condemning property. The seizure of the plant is a taking in the constitutional sense. A permanent taking would amount to the nationalization of the industry. A temporary taking falls short of that goal. But though the seizure is only for a week or a month, the condemnation is complete and the United States must pay compensation for the temporary possession.

The President has no power to raise revenues. That power is in the Congress by Article I, Section 8 of the Constitution. The President might seize and the Congress by subsequent action might ratify the seizure. But until and unless Congress acted, no condemnation would be lawful. The branch of government that has the power to pay compensation for a seizure is the only one able to authorize a seizure or make lawful one that the President had effected. That seems to me to be the necessary result of the condemnation provision in the Fifth Amendment. It squares with the theory of checks and balances expounded by Mr. Justice BLACK in the opinion of the Court in which I Join.

Mr. Justice JACKSON, concurring in the judgment and opinion of the Court.

That comprehensive and undefined presidential powers hold both practical advantages and grave dangers for the country will impress anyone who has served as legal adviser to a President in time of transition and public anxiety. A judge, like an executive adviser, may be surprised at the poverty of really useful and unambiguous authority applicable to concrete problems of executive power as they actually present themselves. Just what our forefathers did envision, or would have envisioned had they foreseen modern conditions, must be divined from materials almost as enigmatic as the dreams Joseph was called upon to interpret for Pharaoh. A century and a half of partisan debate and scholarly speculation yields no net result but only supplies more or less apt quotations from respected sources on each side of any question. They largely cancel each other.

And court decisions are indecisive because of the judicial practice of dealing with the largest questions in the most narrow way.

We may well begin by a somewhat over-simplified grouping of practical situations in which a President may doubt, or others may challenge, his powers, and by distinguishing roughly the legal consequences of this factor of relativity.

1. When the President acts pursuant to an express or implied authorization of Congress, his authority is at its maximum, for it includes all that he possesses in his own right plus all that Congress can delegate. In these circumstances, and in these only, may he be said (for what it may be worth), to personify the federal sovereignty. If his act is held unconstitutional under these circumstances, it usually means that the Federal Government as an undivided whole lacks power. A seizure executed by the President pursuant to an Act of Congress would be supported by the strongest of presumptions and the widest latitude of judicial interpretation, and the burden of persuasion would rest heavily upon any who might attack it.

2. When the President acts in absence of either a congressional grant or denial of authority, he can only rely upon his own independent powers, but there is a zone of twilight in which he and Congress may have concurrent authority, or in which its distribution is uncertain. Therefore, congressional inertia, indifference or quiescence may sometimes, at least as a practical matter, enable, if not invite, measures on independent presidential responsibility. In this area, any actual test of power is likely to depend on the imperatives of events and contemporary imponderables rather than on abstract theories of law.

3. When the President takes measures incompatible with the expressed or implied will of Congress, his power is at its lowest ebb, for then he can rely only upon his own constitutional powers minus any constitutional powers of Congress over the matter. Courts can sustain exclusive Presidential control in such a case only by disabling the Congress from acting upon the subject. Presidential claim to a power at once so conclusive and preclusive must be scrutinized with caution, for what is at stake is the equilibrium established by our constitutional system.

Into which of these classifications does this executive seizure of the steel industry fit? It is eliminated from the first by admission, for it is conceded that no congressional authorization exists for this seizure. That takes away also the support of the many precedents and declarations which were made in relation, and must be confined, to this category.

Can it then be defended under flexible tests available to the second category? It seems clearly eliminated from that class because Congress has not left seizure of private property an open field but has covered it by three statutory policies inconsistent with this seizure.

This leaves the current seizure to be justified only by the severe tests under the third grouping, where it can be supported only by any remainder of executive power after subtraction of such powers as Congress may have over the subject. In short, we can sustain the President only by holding that seizure of such strike-bound industries is within his domain and beyond control by Congress. Thus, this Court's first review of such seizures occurs under circumstances which leave Presidential power most vulnerable to attack and in the least favorable of possible constitutional postures.

The clause on which the Government next relies is that "The President shall be Commander in Chief of the Army and Navy of the United States. . . ." These cryptic words have given rise to some of the most persistent controversies in our constitutional history. Assuming that we are in a war de facto, whether it is or is not a war de jure, does that empower the Commander-in-Chief to seize industries he thinks necessary to supply our army? The Constitution expressly places in Congress power "to raise and support Armies" and "to provide and maintain a Navy." This certainly lays upon Congress primary responsibility for supplying the armed forces. Congress alone controls the raising of revenues and their appropriation and may determine in what manner and by what means they shall be spent for military and naval procurement. I suppose no one would doubt that Congress can take over war supply as a Government enterprise. On the other hand, if Congress sees fit to rely on free private enterprise collectively bargaining with free labor for support and maintenance of our armed forces can the Executive because of lawful disagreements incidental to that process, seize the facility for operation upon Government-imposed terms?

There are indications that the Constitution did not contemplate that the title Commander-in-Chief of the Army and Navy will constitute him also Commander-in-Chief of the country, its industries and its inhabitants. He has no monopoly of "war powers," whatever they are. While Congress cannot deprive the President of the command of the army and navy, only Congress can provide him an army or navy to command. That military powers of the Commander-in-Chief were not to supersede representative government of internal affairs seems obvious from the Constitution and from elementary American history.

The executive action we have here originates in the individual will of the President and represents an exercise of authority without law. No one, perhaps not even the President, knows the limits of the power he may seek to exert in this instance and the parties affected cannot learn the limit of their rights. We do not know today what powers over labor or property would be claimed to flow from Government possession if we should legalize it, what rights to compensation would be claimed or recognized, or on what contingency it would end. With all its defects, delays and inconveniences, men have discovered no technique for long preserving free government except that the Executive be under the law, and that the law be made by parliamentary deliberations. Such institutions may be destined to pass away. But it is the duty of the Court to be last, not first, to give them up.

Mr. Chief Justice VINSON, with whom Mr. Justice REED and Mr. Justice MINTON join, dissenting.

The President of the United States directed the Secretary of Commerce to take temporary possession of the Nation's steel mills during the existing emergency because "a work stoppage would immediately jeopardize and imperil our national defense and the defense of those joined with us in resisting aggression, and would add to the continuing danger of our soldiers, sailors and airmen engaged in combat in the field."

In passing upon the question of Presidential powers in this case, we must first consider the context in which those powers were exercised. Those who suggest that this is a case involving extraordinary powers should be mindful that these are extraordinary times. A world not yet recovered from the devastation of World War II has been forced to face the threat of another and more terrifying global conflict.

In 1950, when the United Nations called upon member nations "to render every assistance" to repel aggression in Korea, the United States furnished its vigorous support. For almost two full years, our armed forces have been fighting in Korea, suffering casualties of over 108,000 men. Hostilities have not abated. The "determination of the United Nations to continue its action in Korea to meet the aggression" has been reaffirmed. Congressional support of the action in Korea has been manifested by provisions for increased military manpower and equipment and for economic stabilization, as hereinafter described. Alert to our responsibilities, which coincide with our own self preservation through mutual security, Congress has enacted a large body of implementing legislation. As an illustration of the magnitude of the over-all program, Congress has appropriated $130 billion for our own defense and for military assistance to our allies since the June, 1950, attack in Korea.

The President has the duty to execute the foregoing legislative programs. Their successful execution depends upon continued production of steel and stabilized prices for steel. Accordingly, when the collective bargaining agreements between the Nation's steel producers and their employees, represented by the United Steel Workers, were due to expire on December 31, 1951, and a strike shutting down the entire basic steel industry was threatened, the President acted to avert a complete shutdown of steel production.

One is not here called upon even to consider the possibility of executive seizure of a farm, a corner grocery store or even a single industrial plant. Such considerations arise only when one ignores the central fact of this case—that the Nation's entire basic steel production would have shut down completely if there had been no Government seizure. Even ignoring for the moment whatever confidential information the President may possess as "the Nation's organ for foreign affairs," the uncontroverted affidavits in this record amply support the finding that "a work stoppage would immediately jeopardize and imperil our national defense."

Plaintiffs do not remotely suggest any basis for rejecting the President's finding that any stoppage of steel production would immediately place the Nation in peril. At the time of seizure there was not, and there is not now, the slightest evidence to justify the belief that any strike will be of short duration. The Union and the steel companies may well engage in a lengthy struggle. Plaintiff's counsel tells us that "sooner or later" the mills will operate again. That may satisfy the steel companies and, perhaps, the Union. But our soldiers and our allies will hardly be cheered with the assurance that the ammunition upon which their lives depend will be forthcoming—"sooner or later," or, in other words, "too little and too late." Accordingly, if the President has any power under the Constitution to meet a critical situation in the absence of express statutory authorization, there is no basis whatever for criticizing the exercise of such power in this case.

A review of executive action demonstrates that our Presidents have on many occasions exhibited the leadership contemplated by the Framers when they made the President Commander in Chief, and imposed upon him the trust to "take Care that the Laws be faithfully executed." With or without explicit statutory authorization, Presidents have at such times dealt with national emergencies by acting promptly and resolutely to enforce legislative programs, at least to save those programs until Congress could act. Congress and the courts have responded to such executive initiative with consistent approval.

Focusing now on the situation confronting the President on the night of April 8, 1952, we cannot but conclude that the President was performing his duty under the Constitution to "take Care that the Laws be faithfully executed"—a duty described by President Benjamin Harrison as "the central idea of the office." The President reported to Congress the morning after the seizure that he acted because a work stoppage in steel production would immediately imperil the safety of the Nation by preventing execution of the legislative programs for procurement of military equipment. And, while a shutdown could be averted by granting the price concessions requested by plaintiffs, granting such concessions would disrupt the price stabilization program also enacted by Congress. Rather than fail to execute either legislative program, the President acted to execute both.

Much of the argument in this case has been directed at straw men. We do not now have before us the case of a President acting solely on the basis of his own notions of the public welfare. Nor is there any question of unlimited executive power in this case. The President himself closed the door to any such claim when he sent his Message to Congress stating his purpose to abide by any action of Congress, whether approving or disapproving his seizure action. Here, the President immediately made sure that Congress was fully informed of the temporary action he had taken only to preserve the legislative programs from destruction until Congress could act.

Faced with the duty of executing the defense programs which Congress had enacted and the disastrous effects that any stoppage in steel production would have on those programs, the President acted to preserve those programs by seizing the steel mills. There is no question that the possession was other than temporary in character and subject to congressional direction—either

FROM THE BENCH

approving, disapproving or regulating the manner in which the mills were to be administered and returned to the owners. The President immediately informed Congress of his action and clearly stated his intention to abide by the legislative will. No basis for claims of arbitrary action, unlimited powers or dictatorial usurpation of congressional power appears from the facts of this case. On the contrary, judicial, legislative and executive precedents throughout our history demonstrate that in this case the President acted in full conformity with his duties under the Constitution.

BEHIND THE CURTAIN

Truman's decision to seize the steel companies was quite controversial—something the President no doubt anticipated. Interestingly, it later came to light that the President had consulted with the Chief Justice of the United States, Chief Justice Vinson, who advised President Truman that the Constitution supported the seizure.[1]

The seizure of the steel mills made big headlines. *Metro Washington Labor Council AFL-CIO.*

Given the separation of powers in our constitutional system, President Truman made an unusual move. In the early days of the republic, the Supreme Court made clear to the executive branch that the judiciary only resolves actual cases and controversies; it does not render advisory opinions even at the President's request. Of course, Chief Justice Vinson turned out to be overly optimistic about his ability to garner enough of his colleagues' votes to support his position.

Further evidence of the controversial nature of the seizure can be seen in the spirit and tone of the briefs on behalf of and in support of the steel companies. Consider this "parade of horribles" argument in the steel companies' brief:

> *If arbitrary executive action to force a wage increase is lawful today, then arbitrary executive action to force a wage decrease, or longer hours, or anything else, will be equally lawful tomorrow; and the constitutional rights of all citizens — not of these plaintiffs alone — will be gravely endangered.*

Also of interest is a friend of the Court brief filed in support of the steel companies and against the President by three unions: the Brotherhood of Locomotive Engineers, Brotherhood of Locomotive Firemen and Enginemen, and Order of Railway Conductors. This brief responded to the President's claim to be forced to act in light of purported Congressional inertia.

> *However, the Government is so insistent that the President must have some power to deal with emergencies, at least until Congress can act, that we believe we would be remiss in our duties, were we to fail to point out that here Congress has acted.*

QUESTIONS FOR DISCUSSION

5.1 Note how the various Justices relied on broadly worded constitutional clauses describing the President's power to support their contrary positions on the merits of the case. Does this lead you to form a judgment about the wisdom of the Framers of the Constitution choosing to use broad, rather than specific, language? Do the conflicting interpretations cancel each other out or are you persuaded by the accuracy of one of the two interpretations?

5.2 Justice Frankfurter pointed out that Congress had earlier considered whether to authorize government seizure of industrial assets during labor-management strife. According to Justice Frankfurter, Congress had rejected that option. What is the significance of Congress's earlier decision in the context of the *Youngstown* case?

5.3 One way that legal scholars have distilled the various opinions in the case is by identifying four separate models of presidential authority that emerged:[2]

- **No inherent power.** The President possesses no inherent power and may act only when a statute or the Constitution provides authority.
- **Residual inherent power.** The President possesses inherent power when and only when the President's actions do not interfere with another branch performing its duties or do not usurp another branch's power. Under this theory, the judiciary is often credited with the dominant and final determination on whether the President's actions interfere with another branch.
- **Legislative dominance.** The President possesses inherent power so long as the President's actions do not violate the Constitution or statute. Congress may take away the President's power in this situation by acting—in which case the President must honor Congress's will.
- **Broad inherent power.** The President possesses inherent power unless the President's actions would violate the Constitution. Some interpretations of this theory credit only the President with the judgment of whether an action falls into this category in the event the President concludes that the action is in the greatest public interest.[3]

Given these theories, one might be surprised to learn that Justice Jackson's separate approach in his concurring opinion is actually the theory that has become most influential. (It sometimes happens in constitutional law that a concept espoused in a concurring opinion carries the day.) What are the components of Justice Jackson's approach? Which of the four models described above is most similar to Jackson's approach?

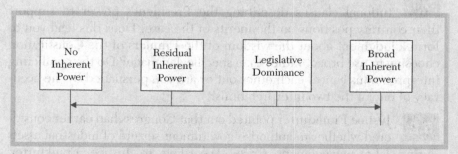

Figure 5.1   Various Theories of Inherent Power Arising from *Youngstown Sheet & Tube Co. v. Sawyer*

WHAT'S YOUR LEARNED OPINION?
Scenario 5-1

Assume all the facts from *Youngstown Sheet & Tube Co. v. Sawyer*, but instead of Congress "tak[ing] no action" on President Truman's order when he notified them of it, Congress decided to ratify the order. Would the Court have ruled the steel seizure constitutional in this instance?

Scenario 5-2

Assume a pandemic gripped the world for two years, but is finally slowing down: Vaccination rates are rising, hospitalizations are down, and spirits are lifting. After a meeting with his top advisors, the U.S. President wants to deliver a final blow to the virus by issuing an executive order requiring all individuals to wear facemasks for three weeks, which he believes will isolate and eliminate the virus. Up to this point, the President has acted pursuant to a congressional statute, the Virus Act, two years before, which was passed by an overwhelming congressional majority. The act provides broad authority to the President and administrative agencies to "take such measures as the President determines necessary to combat and defeat the virus." Buried within the bill, however, is a mask mandate provision, which reads "the issuance of a mask mandate is to be reserved to the Governors of the respective States as they are better equipped to know the unique conditions of their States."

Evaluate the constitutionality of the President's executive order in terms of the scope of the President's power under Article II of the United States Constitution. Assume that other advisors are evaluating the Tenth Amendment and individual rights issues raised by the order, so you do not need to be concerned about those issues.

C. Foreign Affairs

The inherent powers issue rears its head in all questions regarding the scope of the President's authority. Yet the issue is particularly prominent when issues regarding the President's powers over foreign affairs arise. Indeed, several Justices over the years have expressed the position that limitations on the President's inherent powers exist only in the context of internal or domestic matters.

According to this view, the heightened importance of matters of national security and the stature of the United States on the world stage justify giving the President wide discretion in matters of foreign policy, to ensure the strength of the nation is buttressed by consistent policy expressed by one voice, and to allow swift, decisive action in the case of an emergency. Legal thinkers who push back on this approach emphasize that the Framers intended that all branches of the federal government enjoy only limited power. Furthermore, they argue, the specific grants of power pertaining to foreign affairs—such as the treaty-making power, the war powers, and the power to appoint ambassadors—would not be necessary if the President possessed unfettered control over these matters.

The following case raises these questions in the context of a tug of war between the executive branch and Congress over whether the United States should diplomatically recognize the state of Israel. As you read the opinion, evaluate which view of the President's inherent authority in the area carried the day in the opinion of the Court.

FROM THE BENCH

ZIVOTOFSKY v. KERRY
576 U.S. 1059 (2015)

Justice KENNEDY delivered the opinion of the Court.

A delicate subject lies in the background of this case. That subject is Jerusalem. Questions touching upon the history of the ancient city and its present legal and international status are among the most difficult and complex in international affairs. In our constitutional system these matters are committed to the Legislature and the Executive, not the Judiciary. As a result, in this opinion the Court does no more, and must do no more, than note the existence of international debate and tensions respecting Jerusalem. Those matters are for Congress and the President to discuss and consider as they seek to shape the Nation's foreign policies.

The Court addresses two questions to resolve the interbranch dispute now before it. First, it must determine whether the President has the exclusive power to grant formal recognition to a foreign sovereign. Second, if he has that power, the Court must determine whether Congress can command the President and his Secretary of State to issue a formal statement that contradicts the earlier recognition. The statement in question here is a congressional mandate that allows a United States citizen born in Jerusalem to direct the President and Secretary of State, when issuing his passport, to state that his place of birth is "Israel."

I

A

Jerusalem's political standing has long been, and remains, one of the most sensitive issues in American foreign policy, and indeed it is one of the most delicate issues in current international affairs. In 1948, President Truman formally recognized Israel in a signed statement of "recognition." That statement did not recognize Israeli sovereignty over Jerusalem. Over the last 60 years, various actors have sought to assert full or partial sovereignty over the city, including Israel, Jordan, and the Palestinians. Yet, in contrast to a consistent policy of formal recognition of Israel, neither President Truman nor any later United States President has issued an official statement or declaration acknowledging any country's sovereignty over Jerusalem. Instead, the Executive Branch has maintained that "'the status of Jerusalem . . . should be decided not unilaterally but in consultation with all concerned.'"

The President's position on Jerusalem is reflected in State Department policy regarding passports and consular reports of birth abroad. Understanding that passports will be construed as reflections of American policy, the State Department's Foreign Affairs Manual instructs its employees, in general, to record the place of birth on a passport as the "country [having] present sovereignty over the actual area of birth." Because the United States does not recognize any country as having sovereignty over Jerusalem, the FAM instructs employees to record the place of birth for citizens born there as "Jerusalem."

In 2002, Congress passed the Act at issue here, the Foreign Relations Authorization Act, Fiscal Year 2003. Section 214 of the Act is titled "United States Policy with Respect to Jerusalem as the Capital of Israel." The subsection that lies at the heart of this case, §214(d) [hereinafter Passport Provision], addresses passports. That subsection seeks to override the FAM by allowing citizens born in Jerusalem to list their place of birth as "Israel." Titled "Record of Place of Birth as Israel for Passport Purposes," the Passport Provision states "[f]or purposes of the registration of birth, certification of nationality, or issuance of a passport of a United States citizen born in the city of Jerusalem, the Secretary shall, upon the request of the citizen or the citizen's legal guardian, record the place of birth as Israel."

II

In considering claims of Presidential power this Court refers to Justice Jackson's familiar tripartite framework from *Youngstown Sheet & Tube Co. v.*

FROM THE BENCH

Sawyer (1952) (concurring opinion). The framework divides exercises of Presidential power into three categories: First, when "the President acts pursuant to an express or implied authorization of Congress, his authority is at its maximum, for it includes all that he possesses in his own right plus all that Congress can delegate." Second, "in absence of either a congressional grant or denial of authority" there is a "zone of twilight in which he and Congress may have concurrent authority," and where "congressional inertia, indifference or quiescence may" invite the exercise of executive power. Finally, when "the President takes measures incompatible with the expressed or implied will of Congress . . . he can rely only upon his own constitutional powers minus any constitutional powers of Congress over the matter." To succeed in this third category, the President's asserted power must be both "exclusive" and "conclusive" on the issue.

In this case the Secretary contends that the Passport Provision infringes on the President's exclusive recognition power by "requiring the President to contradict his recognition position regarding Jerusalem in official communications with foreign sovereigns." In so doing the Secretary acknowledges the President's power is "at its lowest ebb." Because the President's refusal to implement the Passport Provision falls into Justice Jackson's third category, his claim must be "scrutinized with caution," and he may rely solely on powers the Constitution grants to him alone.

To determine whether the President possesses the exclusive power of recognition the Court examines the Constitution's text and structure, as well as precedent and history bearing on the question.

A

Recognition is a "formal acknowledgement" that a particular "entity possesses the qualifications for statehood" or "that a particular regime is the effective government of a state." It may also involve the determination of a state's territorial bounds. Recognition is often effected by an express "written or oral declaration." It may also be implied—for example, by concluding a bilateral treaty or by sending or receiving diplomatic agents.

Legal consequences follow formal recognition. Recognized sovereigns may sue in United States courts, and may benefit from sovereign immunity when they are sued. The actions of a recognized sovereign committed within its own territory also receive deference in domestic courts under the act of state doctrine. Recognition at international law, furthermore, is a precondition of regular diplomatic relations. Recognition is thus "useful, even necessary," to the existence of a state.

Despite the importance of the recognition power in foreign relations, the Constitution does not use the term "recognition," either in Article II or elsewhere. The Secretary asserts that the President exercises the recognition power based on the Reception Clause, which directs that the President "shall receive

Ambassadors and other public Ministers." Art. II, §3. As Zivotofsky notes, the Reception Clause received little attention at the Constitutional Convention. In fact, during the ratification debates, Alexander Hamilton claimed that the power to receive ambassadors was "more a matter of dignity than of authority," a ministerial duty largely "without consequence." The Federalist No. 69, p. 420 (C. Rossiter ed. 1961).

At the time of the founding, however, prominent international scholars suggested that receiving an ambassador was tantamount to recognizing the sovereignty of the sending state. It is a logical and proper inference, then, that a Clause directing the President alone to receive ambassadors would be understood to acknowledge his power to recognize other nations. As a result, the Reception Clause provides support, although not the sole authority, for the President's power to recognize other nations.

The inference that the President exercises the recognition power is further supported by his additional Article II powers. It is for the President, "by and with the Advice and Consent of the Senate," to "make Treaties, provided two thirds of the Senators present concur." Art. II, §2, cl. 2. In addition, "he shall nominate, and by and with the Advice and Consent of the Senate, shall appoint Ambassadors" as well as "other public Ministers and Consuls."

As a matter of constitutional structure, these additional powers give the President control over recognition decisions. At international law, recognition may be effected by different means, but each means is dependent upon Presidential power. In addition to receiving an ambassador, recognition may occur on "the conclusion of a bilateral treaty," or the "formal initiation of diplomatic relations," including the dispatch of an ambassador. The President has the sole power to negotiate treaties, and the Senate may not conclude or ratify a treaty without Presidential action. The President, too, nominates the Nation's ambassadors and dispatches other diplomatic agents. Congress may not send an ambassador without his involvement. Beyond that, the President himself has the power to open diplomatic channels simply by engaging in direct diplomacy with foreign heads of state and their ministers. The Constitution thus assigns the President means to effect recognition on his own initiative. Congress, by contrast, has no constitutional power that would enable it to initiate diplomatic relations with a foreign nation.

The text and structure of the Constitution grant the President the power to recognize foreign nations and governments. The question then becomes whether that power is exclusive. The various ways in which the President may unilaterally effect recognition — and the lack of any similar power vested in Congress — suggest that it is. So, too, do functional considerations. Put simply, the Nation must have a single policy regarding which governments are legitimate in the eyes of the United States and which are not. Foreign countries need to know, before entering into diplomatic relations or commerce with the United States, whether their ambassadors will be received; whether their officials will be immune from suit in federal court; and whether they may initiate lawsuits here to vindicate their rights. These assurances cannot be equivocal.

FROM THE BENCH

Recognition is a topic on which the Nation must "'speak . . . with one voice.'" That voice must be the President's. Between the two political branches, only the Executive has the characteristic of unity at all times. And with unity comes the ability to exercise, to a greater degree, "[d]ecision, activity, secrecy, and dispatch." The Federalist No. 70, p. 424 (A. Hamilton). The President is capable, in ways Congress is not, of engaging in the delicate and often secret diplomatic contacts that may lead to a decision on recognition. These qualities explain why the Framers listed the traditional avenues of recognition—receiving ambassadors, making treaties, and sending ambassadors—as among the President's Article II powers.

B

No single precedent resolves the question whether the President has exclusive recognition authority and, if so, how far that power extends. In part that is because, until today, the political branches have resolved their disputes over questions of recognition. The relevant cases, though providing important instruction, address the division of recognition power between the Federal Government and the States, or between the courts and the political branches, not between the President and Congress. As the parties acknowledge, some isolated statements in those cases lend support to the position that Congress has a role in the recognition process. In the end, however, a fair reading of the cases shows that the President's role in the recognition process is both central and exclusive.

C

Having examined the Constitution's text and this Court's precedent, it is appropriate to turn to accepted understandings and practice. In separation-of-powers cases this Court has often "put significant weight upon historical practice." Here, history is not all on one side, but on balance it provides strong support for the conclusion that the recognition power is the President's alone. As Zivotofsky argues, certain historical incidents can be interpreted to support the position that recognition is a shared power. But the weight of historical evidence supports the opposite view, which is that the formal determination of recognition is a power to be exercised only by the President.

III

As the power to recognize foreign states resides in the President alone, the question becomes whether the Passport Provision infringes on the Executive's consistent decision to withhold recognition with respect to Jerusalem.

The Passport Provision requires that, in a passport or consular report of birth abroad, "the Secretary shall, upon the request of the citizen or the citizen's legal guardian, record the place of birth as Israel" for a "United States citizen born in the city of Jerusalem." That is, the Passport Provision requires the President, through the Secretary, to identify citizens born in Jerusalem who so request as being born in Israel. But according to the President, those citizens were not born in Israel. As a matter of United States policy, neither Israel nor any other country is acknowledged as having sovereignty over Jerusalem. In this way, the Passport Provision "directly contradicts" the "carefully calibrated and longstanding Executive branch policy of neutrality toward Jerusalem."

If the power over recognition is to mean anything, it must mean that the President not only makes the initial, formal recognition determination but also that he may maintain that determination in his and his agent's statements. This conclusion is a matter of both common sense and necessity. If Congress could command the President to state a recognition position inconsistent with his own, Congress could override the President's recognition determination. Under international law, recognition may be effected by "written or oral declaration of the recognizing state." In addition an act of recognition must "leave no doubt as to the intention to grant it." Thus, if Congress could alter the President's statements on matters of recognition or force him to contradict them, Congress in effect would exercise the recognition power.

As Justice Jackson wrote in *Youngstown*, when a Presidential power is "exclusive," it "disabl[es] the Congress from acting upon the subject." Here, the subject is quite narrow: The Executive's exclusive power extends no further than his

After President Trump recognized Jerusalem as Israel's capital in 2017, Menachem Zivotofsky (shown here with his father Ari in 2014) eventually received a U.S. passport in 2020 with Israel designated as his birthplace. *AP Photo/Carolyn Kaster.*

formal recognition determination. But as to that determination, Congress may not enact a law that directly contradicts it. This is not to say Congress may not express its disagreement with the President in myriad ways. For example, it may enact an embargo, decline to confirm an ambassador, or even declare war. But none of these acts would alter the President's recognition decision.

If Congress may not pass a law, speaking in its own voice, that effects formal recognition, then it follows that it may not force the President himself to contradict his earlier statement. That congressional command would not only prevent the Nation from speaking with one voice but also prevent the Executive itself from doing so in conducting foreign relations.

Although the statement required by the Passport Provision would not itself constitute a formal act of recognition, it is a mandate that the Executive contradict his prior recognition determination in an official document issued by the Secretary of State. As a result, it is unconstitutional. This is all the more clear in light of the longstanding treatment of a passport's place-of-birth section as an official executive statement implicating recognition.

From the face of the Passport Provision, from the legislative history, and from its reception, it is clear that Congress wanted to express its displeasure with the President's policy by, among other things, commanding the Executive to contradict his own, earlier stated position on Jerusalem. This Congress may not do.

It is true, as Zivotofsky notes, that Congress has substantial authority over passports. The Court does not question the power of Congress to enact passport legislation of wide scope. In holding the Passport Provision invalid the Court does not question the substantial powers of Congress over foreign affairs in general or passports in particular. This case is confined solely to the exclusive power of the President to control recognition determinations, including formal statements by the Executive Branch acknowledging the legitimacy of a state or government and its territorial bounds. Congress cannot command the President to contradict an earlier recognition determination in the issuance of passports.

Chief Justice ROBERTS, with whom Justice ALITO joins, dissenting.

Today's decision is a first: Never before has this Court accepted a President's direct defiance of an Act of Congress in the field of foreign affairs. We have instead stressed that the President's power reaches "its lowest ebb" when he contravenes the express will of Congress, "for what is at stake is the equilibrium established by our constitutional system." *Youngstown Sheet & Tube Co. v. Sawyer* (1952) (Jackson, J., concurring).

In this case, the President claims the exclusive and preclusive power to recognize foreign sovereigns. The Court devotes much of its analysis to accepting the Executive's contention. I have serious doubts about that position. The majority places great weight on the Reception Clause, which directs that the Executive "shall receive Ambassadors and other public Ministers." But that provision, framed as an obligation rather than an authorization, appears alongside the *duties* imposed on the President by Article II, Section 3, not the *powers* granted to

FROM THE BENCH

him by Article II, Section 2. Indeed, the People ratified the Constitution with Alexander Hamilton's assurance that executive reception of ambassadors "is more a matter of dignity than of authority" and "will be without consequence in the administration of the government." In short, at the time of the founding, "there was no reason to view the reception clause as a source of discretionary authority for the president." Adler, The President's Recognition Power: Ministerial or Discretionary?

The majority's other asserted textual bases are even more tenuous. The President does have power to make treaties and appoint ambassadors. Art. II, §2. But those authorities are *shared* with Congress, so they hardly support an inference that the recognition power is *exclusive*.

Precedent and history lend no more weight to the Court's position. The majority cites dicta suggesting an exclusive executive recognition power, but acknowledges contrary dicta suggesting that the power is shared. When the best you can muster is conflicting dicta, precedent can hardly be said to support your side.

As for history, the majority admits that it too points in both directions. Some Presidents have claimed an exclusive recognition power, but others have expressed uncertainty about whether such preclusive authority exists. Those in the skeptical camp include Andrew Jackson and Abraham Lincoln, leaders not generally known for their cramped conceptions of Presidential power. Congress has also asserted its authority over recognition determinations at numerous points in history. The majority therefore falls short of demonstrating that "Congress has accepted" the President's exclusive recognition power. In any event, we have held that congressional acquiescence is only "pertinent" when the President acts in the absence of express congressional authorization, not when he asserts power to disregard a statute, as the Executive does here.

In sum, although the President has authority over recognition, I am not convinced that the Constitution provides the "conclusive and preclusive" power required to justify defiance of an express legislative mandate.

But even if the President does have exclusive recognition power, he still cannot prevail in this case, because the statute at issue *does not implicate recognition*. The relevant provision, the Passport Provision, simply gives an American citizen born in Jerusalem the option to designate his place of birth as Israel "[f]or purposes of" passports and other documents. The State Department itself has explained that "identification"—not recognition—"is the principal reason that U.S. passports require 'place of birth.'" Congress has not disputed the Executive's assurances that the Passport Provision does not alter the longstanding United States position on Jerusalem. And the annals of diplomatic history record no examples of official recognition accomplished via optional passport designation.

The majority acknowledges both that the "Executive's exclusive power extends no further than his formal recognition determination" and that the Passport Provision does "not itself constitute a formal act of recognition." Taken together, these statements come close to a confession of error. The majority attempts to reconcile its position by reconceiving the Passport Provision as a "mandate that the Executive contradict his prior recognition determination in an official document issued by the Secretary of State." But as just noted, neither Congress nor the Executive Branch regards the Passport Provision as a recognition determination, so it is hard to see how the statute could contradict any such determination.

. . .

In the final analysis, the Constitution may well deny Congress power to recognize—the power to make an international commitment accepting a foreign entity as a state, a regime as its government, a place as a part of its territory, and so on. But whatever else the Passport Provision may do, it plainly does not make (or require the President to make) a commitment accepting Israel's sovereignty over Jerusalem.

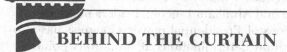

BEHIND THE CURTAIN

Remember the political question doctrine (Chapter 3), a principle of judiciability covering whether a federal court should hear a case that touches on sensitive political matters. Instances when the Court invokes the doctrine to avoid the merits of a case are often criticized as wimpy and wrong. On the other hand, the Court is also criticized for not invoking the doctrine when its precedents suggest that it should, the theory being that the Court ignores the doctrine when it is eager to throw its weight in on a particular issue.

Zivotofsky v. Kerry arguably fell into the latter category. The U.S. Supreme Court has invoked the doctrine when it has been called to speak on matters of foreign affairs, when the Court judges that it is important in a particular instance that the "nation speaks with one voice." For example, in *Goldwater v. Carter* (1979), the Court used the political question doctrine to dismiss a Senate complaint against President Jimmy Carter's unilateral abrogation of a defense treaty with Taiwan. The *Zivotofsky* majority avoided this result, however, by characterizing the legal issue in the case as simply involving a private individual's right under a federal statute. In framing the case in this way, the Court was able to view the case as no more than an individual rights dispute implicating the constitutionality of a statute—a matter that federal courts routinely handle.

QUESTIONS FOR DISCUSSION

5.4   Compare the majority and the dissent in light of the various approaches from the *Youngstown* case. Which approach does the majority best reflect? Which approach does the dissent best reflect?

5.5   During oral argument in the case, Justice Kagan made the following comment on the congressional statute at issue in the case: "This is a very selective vanity plate law, if we might call it that." What do you think she meant by that?

5.6   Subsequent to the *Zivotofsky* opinion and after Donald Trump was elected President, Trump unilaterally decided to recognize Jerusalem as Israel's capital and to move the U.S. embassy there. Did President Trump's decision implicate the same issues at play in *Zivotofsky*? If so, did the *Zivotofsky* decision support Trump's action?

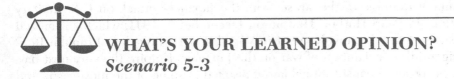

WHAT'S YOUR LEARNED OPINION?
Scenario 5-3

Assume that in recent years, opposition movements within Russia have gradually accrued political domestic support, so much so that Democracy Russia, a popular democratic movement, won seats all over the country in a recent election at the municipal and federal levels. Democracy Russia then made the bold decision to proclaim St. Petersburg the capital of a new democratic Russia. The constitutional government in Moscow was furious. The U.S. Congress seeks to aid Democracy Russia. Congress passes legislation (overriding the U.S. President's veto) recognizing St. Petersburg as the capital of Russia. Upset at what he considers Congress's interference in a diplomatic problem, the President orders the State Department to ignore the law as an unconstitutional infringement on executive prerogative. Congress filed suit in federal court to enforce the law. You have been instructed to ignore a potential political question issue with this situation, but have been asked to opine on whether Congress is acting consistently with the Constitution. Frame your response.

Scenario 5-4

Now assume that Congress is upset after losing in court on the St. Petersburg recognition issue. In response, Congress decides it is best to both cooperate with the President and assist Democracy Russia. Although the President displayed visible anger over the recognition fight, he is no ally of the current Russian government. In fact, the President's national security team is developing plans to funnel weapons to the Democracy Russia insurgents in hopes that they prevail in securing a democratic Russia. Congress agrees to assist in this endeavor by passing legislation that delegates to the President the discretion to approve or deny the sale of arms to Democracy Russia. Because of this decision, certain arms shipments from private manufacturers to entities other than Democracy Russia will be prohibited, causing a furor among the negatively affected arms dealers.

Arms R Us is a private gun manufacturer whose arms shipments to Russia are prohibited as a result of the new legislation. They have retained you for advice on whether to challenge the delegation by Congress of power to the President regarding arms shipments. What do you think?

The question of the President's latitude in acting without congressional authorization appears often in events that implicate the President's war powers. A prominent example of this arose from the Japanese attack on U.S. military installations in Pearl Harbor, Hawaii, on December 7, 1941, which galvanized public support for U.S. involvement in World War II: President Franklin Roosevelt signed the declaration of war on the Japanese Empire the very next day. For the purposes of constitutional law, it also led to some of the most castigated decisions in the history of the Supreme Court. In response to purported national security concerns, President Roosevelt issued Executive Order 9066, the legal basis for several facially anti-Japanese U.S. policies. In *Hirabayashi v. United States* (1943), the U.S. Supreme Court upheld a curfew order that applied only to Japanese Americans in areas designated by the military authorities. Despite the facially discriminatory nature of the curfew, the Court reasoned that "[t]he challenged orders were defense measures for the avowed purpose of safeguarding the military area in question." The case that follows, *Korematsu v. United States* (1944), upheld the President's decision to force Japanese Americans into internment camps.

In addition to documenting an important part of the history of the United States, *Korematsu* is credited with announcing the necessity of using strict judicial scrutiny to evaluate government action that has the effect of discriminating based on race. Ironically, the Court developed this standard in the context of Japanese Americans, rather than African Americans, a group for which the standard of scrutiny has been most often deployed. In addition, the case represents one of the few instances when the Court concluded that the government action satisfied strict scrutiny. Indeed, it is usually the case that strict scrutiny is "strict in theory, but fatal in fact."[4] In other words, a court's decision to use strict scrutiny to evaluate government action is effectively a decision to declare the action unconstitutional.

First graders, some of Japanese ancestry, at the Weill public school, San Francisco, pledging allegiance to the United States flag, 1942. *Dorothea Lange/Library of Congress.*

FROM THE BENCH

KOREMATSU v. UNITED STATES
323 U.S. 214 (1944)

Mr. Justice BLACK delivered the opinion of the Court.

The petitioner, an American citizen of Japanese descent, was convicted in a federal district court for remaining in San Leandro, California, a "Military Area," contrary to Civilian Exclusion Order No. 34 of the Commanding General of the Western Command, U.S. Army, which directed that after May 9, 1942, all persons of Japanese ancestry should be excluded from that area. No question was raised as to petitioner's loyalty to the United States.

It should be noted, to begin with, that all legal restrictions which curtail the civil rights of a single racial group are immediately suspect. That is not to say that all such restrictions are unconstitutional. It is to say that courts must subject them to the most rigid scrutiny. Pressing public necessity may sometimes justify the existence of such restrictions; racial antagonism never can.

FROM THE BENCH

One of the series of orders and proclamations, a curfew order, which like the exclusion order here was promulgated pursuant to Executive Order 9066, subjected all persons of Japanese ancestry in prescribed West Coast military areas to remain in their residences from 8 p.m. to 6 a.m. As is the case with the exclusion order here, that prior curfew order was designed as a "protection against espionage and against sabotage." In *Kiyoshi Hirabayashi v. United States* (1943), we sustained a conviction obtained for violation of the curfew order. The Hirabayashi conviction and this one thus rest on the same 1942 Congressional Act and the same basic executive and military orders, all of which orders were aimed at the twin dangers of espionage and sabotage.

In the light of the principles we announced in the *Hirabayashi* case, we are unable to conclude that it was beyond the war power of Congress and the Executive to exclude those of Japanese ancestry from the West Coast war area at the time they did. True, exclusion from the area in which one's home is located is a far greater deprivation than constant confinement to the home from 8 p.m. to 6 a.m. Nothing short of apprehension by the proper military authorities of the gravest imminent danger to the public safety can constitutionally justify either. But exclusion from a threatened area, no less than curfew, has a definite and close relationship to the prevention of espionage and sabotage. The military authorities, charged with the primary responsibility of defending our shores, concluded that curfew provided inadequate protection and ordered exclusion. They did so, as pointed out in our *Hirabayashi* opinion, in accordance with Congressional authority to the military to say who should, and who should not, remain in the threatened areas.

Like curfew, exclusion of those of Japanese origin was deemed necessary because of the presence of an unascertained number of disloyal members of the group, most of whom we have no doubt were loyal to this country. It was because we could not reject the finding of the military authorities that it was impossible to bring about an immediate segregation of the disloyal from the loyal that we sustained the validity of the curfew order as applying to the whole group. In the instant case, temporary exclusion of the entire group was rested by the military on the same ground. The judgment that exclusion of the whole group was for the same reason a military imperative answers the contention that the exclusion was in the nature of group punishment based on antagonism to those of Japanese origin. That there were members of the group who retained loyalties to Japan has been confirmed by investigations made subsequent to the exclusion. Approximately five thousand American citizens of Japanese ancestry refused to swear unqualified allegiance to the United States and to renounce allegiance to the Japanese Emperor, and several thousand evacuees requested repatriation to Japan.

We uphold the exclusion order as of the time it was made and when the petitioner violated it. In doing so, we are not unmindful of the hardships imposed by it upon a large group of American citizens. But hardships are part of war, and war is an aggregation of hardships. All citizens alike, both in and out of uniform, feel the impact of war in greater or lesser measure. Citizenship has its responsibilities as well as its privileges, and in time of war the burden is always heavier. Compulsory exclusion of large groups of citizens from their homes, except under circumstances of direst emergency and peril, is inconsistent with our basic governmental institutions. But when under conditions of modern warfare our shores are threatened by hostile forces, the power to protect must be commensurate with the threatened danger.

To cast this case into outlines of racial prejudice, without reference to the real military dangers which were presented, merely confuses the issue. Korematsu was not excluded from the Military Area because of hostility to him or his race. He was excluded because we are at war with the Japanese Empire, because the properly constituted military authorities feared an invasion of our West Coast and felt constrained to take proper security measures, because they decided that the military urgency of the situation demanded that all citizens of Japanese ancestry be segregated from the West Coast temporarily, and finally, because Congress, reposing its confidence in this time of war in our military leaders—as inevitably it must—determined that they should have the power to do just this. There was evidence of disloyalty on the part of some, the military authorities considered that the need for action was great, and time was short. We cannot—by availing ourselves of the calm perspective of hindsight—now say that at that time these actions were unjustified.

Mr. Justice MURPHY, dissenting.

This exclusion of "all persons of Japanese ancestry, both alien and non-alien," from the Pacific Coast area on a plea of military necessity in the absence of martial law ought not to be approved. Such exclusion goes over "the very brink of constitutional power" and falls into the ugly abyss of racism.

In dealing with matters relating to the prosecution and progress of a war, we must accord great respect and consideration to the judgments of the military authorities who are on the scene and who have full knowledge of the military facts. The scope of their discretion must, as a matter of necessity and common sense, be wide. And their judgments ought not to be overruled lightly by those whose training and duties ill-equip them to deal intelligently with matters so vital to the physical security of the nation.

At the same time, however, it is essential that there be definite limits to military discretion, especially where martial law has not been declared. Individuals must not be left impoverished of their constitutional rights on a plea of military necessity that has neither substance nor support. Thus, like other claims conflicting with the asserted constitutional rights of the individual, the military claim must subject itself to the judicial process of having its reasonableness determined and its conflicts with other interests reconciled. "What are the allowable limits of military discretion, and whether or not they have been overstepped in a particular case, are judicial questions."

The judicial test of whether the Government, on a plea of military necessity, can validly deprive an individual of any of his constitutional rights is whether the

FROM THE BENCH

deprivation is reasonably related to a public danger that is so "immediate, imminent, and impending" as not to admit of delay and not to permit the intervention of ordinary constitutional processes to alleviate the danger. Civilian Exclusion Order No. 34, banishing from a prescribed area of the Pacific Coast "all persons of Japanese ancestry, both alien and non-alien," clearly does not meet that test. Being an obvious racial discrimination, the order deprives all those within its scope of the equal protection of the laws as guaranteed by the Fifth Amendment. It further deprives these individuals of their constitutional rights to live and work where they will, to establish a home where they choose and to move about freely. In excommunicating them without benefit of hearings, this order also deprives them of all their constitutional rights to procedural due process. Yet no reasonable relation to an "immediate, imminent, and impending" public danger is evident to support this racial restriction which is one of the most sweeping and complete deprivations of constitutional rights in the history of this nation in the absence of martial law. [T]he exclusion order necessarily must rely for its reasonableness upon the assumption that all persons of Japanese ancestry may have a dangerous tendency to commit sabotage and espionage and to aid our Japanese enemy in other ways. It is difficult to believe that reason, logic or experience could be marshalled in support of such an assumption.

That this forced exclusion was the result in good measure of this erroneous assumption of racial guilt rather than bona fide military necessity is evidenced by the Commanding General's Final Report on the evacuation from the Pacific Coast area. In it he refers to all individuals of Japanese descent as "subversive," as belonging to "an enemy race" whose "racial strains are undiluted," and as constituting "over 112,000 potential enemies . . . . at large today" along the Pacific Coast. In support of this blanket condemnation of all persons of Japanese descent, however, no reliable evidence is cited to show that such individuals were generally disloyal, or had generally so conducted themselves in this area as to constitute a special menace to defense installations or war industries, or had otherwise by their behavior furnished reasonable ground for their exclusion as a group.

The main reasons relied upon by those responsible for the forced evacuation, therefore, do not prove a reasonable relation between the group characteristics of Japanese Americans and the dangers of invasion, sabotage and espionage. The reasons appear, instead, to be largely an accumulation of much of the misinformation, half-truths and insinuations that for years have been directed against Japanese Americans by people with racial and economic prejudices — the same people who have been among the foremost advocates of the evacuation. A military judgment based upon such racial and sociological considerations is not entitled to the great weight ordinarily given the judgments based upon strictly military considerations. Especially is this so when every charge relative to race, religion, culture, geographical location, and legal and economic status has been substantially discredited by independent studies made by experts in these matters.

The military necessity which is essential to the validity of the evacuation order thus resolves itself into a few intimations that certain individuals actively aided the enemy, from which it is inferred that the entire group of Japanese Americans could not be trusted to be or remain loyal to the United States. Moreover, this inference, which is at the very heart of the evacuation orders, has been used in support of the abhorrent and despicable treatment of minority groups by the dictatorial tyrannies which this nation is now pledged to destroy. To give constitutional sanction to that inference in this case, however well-intentioned may have been the military command on the Pacific Coast, is to adopt one of the cruelest of the rationales used by our enemies to destroy the dignity of the individual and to encourage and open the door to discriminatory actions against other minority groups in the passions of tomorrow. No adequate reason is given for the failure to treat these Japanese Americans on an individual basis by holding investigations and hearings to separate the loyal from the disloyal, as was done in the case of persons of German and Italian ancestry.

Moreover, there was no adequate proof that the Federal Bureau of Investigation and the military and naval intelligence services did not have the espionage and sabotage situation well in hand during this long period. Nor is there any denial of the fact that not one person of Japanese ancestry was accused or convicted of espionage or sabotage after Pearl Harbor while they were still free. It seems incredible that under these circumstances it would have been impossible to hold loyalty hearings for the mere 112,000 persons involved—or at least for the 70,000 American citizens—especially when a large part of this number represented children and elderly men and women. Any inconvenience that may have accompanied an attempt to conform to procedural due process cannot be said to justify violations of constitutional rights of individuals.

During a period of six months, the 112 alien tribunals or hearing boards set up by the British Government shortly after the outbreak of the present war summoned and examined approximately 74,000 German and Austrian aliens. These tribunals determined whether each individual enemy alien was a real enemy of the Allies or only a "friendly enemy." About 64,000 were freed from internment and from any special restrictions, and only 2,000 were interned.

I dissent, therefore, from this legalization of racism. Racial discrimination in any form and in any degree has no justifiable part whatever in our democratic way of life. It is unattractive in any setting but it is utterly revolting among a free people who have embraced the principles set forth in the Constitution of the United States. All residents of this nation are kin in some way by blood or culture to a foreign land. Yet they are primarily and necessarily a part of the new and distinct civilization of the United States. They must accordingly be treated at all times as the heirs of the American experiment and as entitled to all the rights and freedoms guaranteed by the Constitution.

FROM THE BENCH

Mr. Justice JACKSON, dissenting.

Korematsu was born on our soil, of parents born in Japan. The Constitution makes him a citizen of the United States by nativity and a citizen of California by residence. No claim is made that he is not loyal to this country. There is no suggestion that apart from the matter involved here he is not law-abiding and well disposed. Korematsu, however, has been convicted of an act not commonly a crime. It consists merely of being present in the state whereof he is a citizen, near the place where he was born, and where all his life he has lived.

Even more unusual is the series of military orders which made this conduct a crime. They forbid such a one to remain, and they also forbid him to leave. They were so drawn that the only way Korematsu could avoid violation was to give himself up to the military authority. This meant submission to custody, examination, and transportation out of the territory, to be followed by indeterminate confinement in detention camps.

A citizen's presence in the locality, however, was made a crime only if his parents were of Japanese birth. Had Korematsu been one of four—the others being, say, a German alien enemy, an Italian alien enemy, and a citizen of American-born ancestors, convicted of treason but out on parole—only Korematsu's presence would have violated the order. The difference between their innocence and his crime would result, not from anything he did, said, or thought, different than they, but only in that he was born of different racial stock.

My duties as a justice as I see them do not require me to make a military judgment as to whether General DeWitt's evacuation and detention program was a reasonable military necessity. I do not suggest that the courts should have attempted to interfere with the Army in carrying out its task. But I do not think they may be asked to execute a military expedient that has no place in law under the Constitution. I would reverse the judgment and discharge the prisoner.

BEHIND THE CURTAIN

A U.S. citizen and the son of Japanese immigrants, Fred Korematsu was a 23-year-old welder at Bay Area shipyards at the time of the internment order. He chose not to accompany his parents to the location where Japanese Americans were designated to be sent by the order. He chose instead to stay behind in Oakland, California, with his Italian American girlfriend. Later he fled Oakland, and had plastic surgery on his eyes to avoid recognition. He was ultimately arrested, however, in May 1942, thus providing the basis for the *Korematsu* case.

Korematsu married after the war, returned to the Bay Area, and found work as a draftsman. One would think that his community might have celebrated his bravery in standing up to the internment order, but he was shunned instead. He therefore kept a low profile and remained quiet about his history. In fact, his daughter tells the story of reading in junior high school about a man named Korematsu who defied the internment order. She came home that evening and asked her father if she was related to that man.

Toward the end of his life, Korematsu received the Presidential Medal of Freedom in 1998 from President Bill Clinton. It was not until 2018, however, that the Supreme Court explicitly disavowed the *Korematsu* decision, stating "The forceable relocation of U.S. citizens to concentration camps, solely and explicitly on the basis of race, is objectively unlawful and outside the scope of presidential authority . . . *Korematsu* was gravely wrong the day it was decided, has been overruled in the court of history, and—to be clear—'has no place in law under the Constitution.'" *Trump v. Hawaii*, 138 S. Ct. 2392 (2018). *Trump v. Hawaii* is the Supreme Court case upholding President Trump's executive order suspending the entry into the United States of nationals from seven Muslim-majority countries—the so-called Muslim ban.

After World War II, Fred Korematsu became an activist and worked to advance racial equity, social justice, and human rights. *Image courtesy of the family of Fred T. Korematsu.*

QUESTIONS FOR DISCUSSION

5.7   Fred Korematsu's brief before the U.S. Supreme Court ended with the following rhetorical question:

> Is war power to be regarded as a shallow excuse to hide the fact of dictatorship? Are Congress, the Courts and the Nation so impotent they are to be deemed parts of the tail to a military commander's kite either in war or in peace?

What was Korematsu trying to suggest? Did the Supreme Court fall prey to the "shallow excuse" to which Korematsu referred?

5.8 In part of his *Korematsu* dissent, Justice Murphy noted that during a period of six months at the beginning of World War II, the British Government set up "112 alien tribunals or hearing boards . . . examined approximately 74,000 German and Austrian aliens [to determine] whether each individual enemy alien was a real enemy of the Allies." He further reported that "[a]bout 64,000 were freed from internment and from any special restrictions, and only 2,000 were interned." What point was Justice Murphy trying to make by highlighting these facts?

5.9 The majority in *Korematsu* stated:

It should be noted, to begin with, that all legal restrictions which curtail the civil rights of a single racial group are immediately suspect. That is not to say that all such restrictions are unconstitutional. It is to say that courts must subject them to the most rigid scrutiny.

This is the language that identifies *Korematsu* as the beginning of strict scrutiny for racially discriminatory laws. Do you agree that the *Korematsu* Court actually applied the strictest level of judicial scrutiny? If not, would you describe the majority's evaluation of the executive order in the case as deferential?

Like the attack on Pearl Harbor, the terrorist attacks of September 11, 2001 (9/11) resulted in a robust, yet divisive, executive response. Indeed, times of national emergency and crisis are a reliable, predictable source of division over the scope of presidential power. Those who support broad and inherent executive power posit that Article II's vagueness envisioned such power to confront national security issues assertively. Conversely, critics reject such a position, instead advocating a circumscribed executive to avoid unchecked power and tyranny. Following the 9/11 attacks on the United States, the President's decision to detain individuals as enemy combatants and the use of military tribunals to try suspected terrorists emerged as two prominent executive power issues. This controversy gave rise to a power struggle—what one might even call a cat-and-mouse game—among Congress, President George W. Bush, and the U.S. Supreme Court.

The case that follows, *Hamdi v. Rumsfeld* (2004), was one of the first among several cases that came to the Court concerning the detention of terror suspects on a U.S. military base in Guantanamo Bay, Cuba, and the use of military tribunals there. The *Hamdi* Court determined that a U.S. citizen captured in a foreign country and detained as an enemy combatant is entitled to due process, including notice of suspected charges, a factual hearing, and an opportunity to be heard.

FROM THE BENCH

HAMDI v. RUMSFELD
542 U.S. 507 (2004)

Justice O'CONNOR announced the judgment of the Court and delivered an opinion, in which The Chief Justice, Justice KENNEDY, and Justice BREYER join.

At this difficult time in our Nation's history, we are called upon to consider the legality of the Government's detention of a United States citizen on United States soil as an "enemy combatant" and to address the process that is constitutionally owed to one who seeks to challenge his classification as such. The United States Court of Appeals for the Fourth Circuit held that petitioner's detention was legally authorized and that he was entitled to no further opportunity to challenge his enemy-combatant label. We now vacate and remand. We hold that although Congress authorized the detention of combatants in the narrow circumstances alleged here, due process demands that a citizen held in the United States as an enemy combatant be given a meaningful opportunity to contest the factual basis for that detention before a neutral decisionmaker.

I

On September 11, 2001, the al Qaeda terrorist network used hijacked commercial airliners to attack prominent targets in the United States. Approximately 3,000 people were killed in those attacks. One week later, in response to these "acts of treacherous violence," Congress passed a resolution authorizing the President to "use all necessary and appropriate force against those nations, organizations, or persons he determines planned, authorized, committed, or aided the terrorist attacks" or "harbored such organizations or persons, in order to prevent any future acts of international terrorism against the United States by such nations, organizations or persons." Soon thereafter, the President ordered United States Armed Forces to Afghanistan, with a mission to subdue al Qaeda and quell the Taliban regime that was known to support it.

This case arises out of the detention of a man whom the Government alleges took up arms with the Taliban during this conflict. His name is Yaser Esam Hamdi. Born an American citizen in Louisiana in 1980, Hamdi moved with his family to Saudi Arabia as a child. By 2001, the parties agree, he resided in Afghanistan. At some point that year, he was seized by members of the Northern Alliance, a coalition of military groups opposed to the Taliban government,

Detainees in orange jumpsuits sit in a holding area under the watchful eyes of military police at Camp X-Ray at Naval Base Guantanamo Bay, Cuba. *Shane T. McCoy/Wikimedia Commons.*

and eventually was turned over to the United States military. The Government asserts that it initially detained and interrogated Hamdi in Afghanistan before transferring him to the United States Naval Base in Guantanamo Bay in January 2002. In April 2002, upon learning that Hamdi is an American citizen, authorities transferred him to a naval brig in Norfolk, Virginia, where he remained until a recent transfer to a brig in Charleston, South Carolina. The Government contends that Hamdi is an "enemy combatant," and that this status justifies holding him in the United States indefinitely—without formal charges or proceedings—unless and until it makes the determination that access to counsel or further process is warranted.

II

The threshold question before us is whether the Executive has the authority to detain citizens who qualify as "enemy combatants." There is some debate as to the proper scope of this term, and the Government has never provided any court with the full criteria that it uses in classifying individuals as such. It has made clear, however, that, for purposes of this case, the "enemy combatant" that it is seeking to detain is an individual who, it alleges, was "'part of or supporting forces hostile to the United States or coalition partners'" in Afghanistan and who "'engaged in an armed conflict against the United States'" there. We therefore answer only the narrow question before us: whether the detention of citizens falling within that definition is authorized.

The Government maintains that no explicit congressional authorization is required, because the Executive possesses plenary authority to detain pursuant to Article II of the Constitution. We do not reach the question whether Article II provides such authority, however, because we agree with the Government's alternative position, that Congress has in fact authorized Hamdi's detention.

Our analysis on that point, set forth below, substantially overlaps with our analysis of Hamdi's principal argument for the illegality of his detention. He posits that his detention is forbidden by 18 U.S.C. §4001(a). Section 4001(a) states that "[n]o citizen shall be imprisoned or otherwise detained by the United States except pursuant to an Act of Congress." Congress passed §4001(a) in 1971 as part of a bill to repeal the Emergency Detention Act of 1950, which provided procedures for executive detention, during times of emergency, of individuals deemed likely to engage in espionage or sabotage. Congress was particularly concerned about the possibility that the Act could be used to reprise the Japanese internment camps of World War II. The Government again presses two alternative positions. First, it argues that §4001(a) . . . applies only to "the control of civilian prisons and related detentions," not to military detentions. Second, it maintains that §4001(a) is satisfied, because Hamdi is being detained "pursuant to an Act of Congress"—the [Authorization for Use of Military Force]. Again, because we conclude that the Government's second assertion is correct, we do not address the first. In other words, for the reasons that follow, we conclude that the AUMF is explicit congressional authorization for the detention of individuals in the narrow category we describe (assuming, without deciding, that such authorization is required), and that the AUMF satisfied §4001(a)'s requirement that a detention be "pursuant to an Act of Congress" (assuming, without deciding, that §4001(a) applies to military detentions).

The AUMF authorizes the President to use "all necessary and appropriate force" against "nations, organizations, or persons" associated with the September 11, 2001, terrorist attacks. There can be no doubt that individuals who fought against the United States in Afghanistan as part of the Taliban, an organization known to have supported the al Qaeda terrorist network responsible for those attacks, are individuals Congress sought to target in passing the AUMF. We conclude that detention of individuals falling into the limited category we are considering, for the duration of the particular conflict in which they were captured, is so fundamental and accepted an incident to war as to be an exercise of the "necessary and appropriate force" Congress has authorized the President to use.

The capture and detention of lawful combatants and the capture, detention, and trial of unlawful combatants, by "universal agreement and practice," are "important incident[s] of war." *Ex parte Quirin*. The purpose of detention is to prevent captured individuals from returning to the field of battle and taking up arms once again. [I]t is of no moment that the AUMF does not use specific language of detention. Because detention to prevent a combatant's return to the battlefield is a fundamental incident of waging war, in permitting the use of "necessary and appropriate force," Congress has clearly and unmistakably authorized detention in the narrow circumstances considered here.

Hamdi contends that the AUMF does not authorize indefinite or perpetual detention. Certainly, we agree that indefinite detention for the purpose of interrogation is not authorized. Further, we understand Congress' grant of authority for the use of "necessary and appropriate force" to include the authority to detain for the duration of the relevant conflict, and our understanding is based on long-standing law-of-war principles. If the practical circumstances of a given conflict are entirely unlike those of the conflicts that informed the development of the law of war, that understanding may unravel. But that is not the situation we face as of this date. Active combat operations against Taliban fighters apparently are ongoing in Afghanistan. The United States may detain, for the duration of these hostilities, individuals legitimately determined to be Taliban combatants who "engaged in an armed conflict against the United States." If the record establishes that United States troops are still involved in active combat in Afghanistan, those detentions are part of the exercise of "necessary and appropriate force," and therefore are authorized by the AUMF.

Ex parte Milligan (1866), does not undermine our holding about the Government's authority to seize enemy combatants, as we define that term today. In that case, the Court made repeated reference to the fact that its inquiry into whether the military tribunal had jurisdiction to try and punish Milligan turned in large part on the fact that Milligan was not a prisoner of war, but a resident of Indiana arrested while at home there. That fact was central to its conclusion. Had Milligan been captured while he was assisting Confederate soldiers by carrying a rifle against Union troops on a Confederate battlefield, the holding of the Court might well have been different. The Court's repeated explanations that Milligan was not a prisoner of war suggest that had these different circumstances been present he could have been detained under military authority for the duration of the conflict, whether or not he was a citizen.

III

Even in cases in which the detention of enemy combatants is legally authorized, there remains the question of what process is constitutionally due to a citizen who disputes his enemy-combatant status. Hamdi argues that he is owed a meaningful and timely hearing and that "extra-judicial detention [that] begins and ends with the submission of an affidavit based on third-hand hearsay" does not comport with the Fifth and Fourteenth Amendments. The Government counters that any more process than was provided below would be both unworkable and "constitutionally intolerable." Our resolution of this dispute requires a careful examination both of the writ of habeas corpus, which Hamdi now seeks to employ as a mechanism of judicial review, and of the Due Process Clause, which informs the procedural contours of that mechanism in this instance.

A

Though they reach radically different conclusions on the process that ought to attend the present proceeding, the parties begin on common ground. All agree that, absent suspension, the writ of habeas corpus remains available to every individual detained within the United States. Only in the rarest of circumstances has Congress seen fit to suspend the writ. All agree suspension of the writ has not occurred here. Thus, it is undisputed that Hamdi was properly before an Article III court to challenge his detention.

B

First, the Government urges the adoption of the Fourth Circuit's holding below—that because it is "undisputed" that Hamdi's seizure took place in a combat zone, the habeas determination can be made purely as a matter of law, with no further hearing or factfinding necessary. This argument is easily rejected. As the dissenters from the denial of rehearing en banc noted, the circumstances surrounding Hamdi's seizure cannot in any way be characterized as "undisputed," as "those circumstances are neither conceded in fact, nor susceptible to concession in law, because Hamdi has not been permitted to speak for himself or even through counsel as to those circumstances." Further, the "facts" that constitute the alleged concession are insufficient to support Hamdi's detention. Under the definition of enemy combatant that we accept today as falling within the scope of Congress' authorization, Hamdi would need to be "part of or supporting forces hostile to the United States or coalition partners" and "engaged in an armed conflict against the United States" to justify his detention in the United States for the duration of the relevant conflict. The habeas petition states only that "[w]hen seized by the United States Government, Mr. Hamdi resided in Afghanistan." An assertion that one *resided* in a country in which combat operations are taking place is not a concession that one was "*captured* in a zone of active combat operations in a foreign theater of war," and certainly is not a concession that one was "part of or supporting forces hostile to the United States or coalition partners" and "engaged in an armed conflict against the United States." Accordingly, we reject any argument that Hamdi has made concessions that eliminate any right to further process.

C

The Government's second argument requires closer consideration. This is the argument that further factual exploration is unwarranted and inappropriate in light of the extraordinary constitutional interests at stake. Under the Government's most extreme rendition of this argument, "[r]espect for separation of powers and the limited institutional capabilities of courts in matters of military decision-making in connection with an ongoing conflict" ought to eliminate entirely any individual process, restricting the courts to investigating only whether legal authorization exists for the broader detention scheme. At most, the Government argues, courts should review its determination that a citizen is an enemy combatant under a very deferential "some evidence" standard. Under this review, a court would assume the accuracy of the Government's articulated basis for Hamdi's detention, as set forth in the Mobbs Declaration, and assess only whether that articulated basis was a legitimate one.

In response, Hamdi emphasizes that this Court consistently has recognized that an individual challenging his detention may not be held at the will of the Executive without recourse to some proceeding before a neutral tribunal to determine whether the Executive's asserted justifications for that detention have basis in fact and warrant in law.

Both of these positions highlight legitimate concerns. And both emphasize the tension that often exists between the autonomy that the Government asserts is necessary in order to pursue effectively a particular goal and the process that a citizen contends he is due before he is deprived of a constitutional right. The ordinary mechanism that we use for balancing such serious competing interests, and for determining the procedures that are necessary to ensure that a citizen is not "deprived of life, liberty, or property, without due process of law," is the test that we articulated in *Mathews v. Eldridge* (1976). *Mathews* dictates that the process due in any given instance is determined by weighing "the private interest that will be affected by the official action" against the Government's asserted interest, "including the function involved" and the burdens the Government would face in providing greater process. The *Mathews* calculus then contemplates a judicious balancing of these concerns, through an analysis of "the risk of an erroneous deprivation" of the private interest if the process were reduced and the "probable value, if any, of additional or substitute safeguards." We take each of these steps in turn.

1

It is beyond question that substantial interests lie on both sides of the scale in this case. Hamdi's "private interest . . . affected by the official action," is the most elemental of liberty interests—the interest in being free from physical detention by one's own government. Nor is the weight on this side of the *Mathews* scale offset by the circumstances of war or the accusation of treasonous behavior, for "[i]t is clear that commitment for *any* purpose constitutes a significant deprivation of liberty that requires due process protection," and at this stage in the *Mathews* calculus, we consider the interest of the *erroneously* detained individual. Indeed, as *amicus* briefs from media and relief organizations emphasize, the risk of erroneous deprivation of a citizen's liberty in the absence of sufficient process here is very real. Moreover, as critical as the Government's interest may be in detaining those who actually pose an immediate threat to the national security of the United States during ongoing international conflict, history and common sense teach us that an unchecked system of detention carries the potential to become a means for oppression and abuse of others who do not present that sort of threat. We reaffirm today the fundamental nature of a citizen's right to be free from involuntary confinement by his own government without due process of law, and we weigh the opposing governmental interests against the curtailment of liberty that such confinement entails.

2

On the other side of the scale are the weighty and sensitive governmental interests in ensuring that those who have in fact fought with the enemy during a war do not return to battle against the United States. As discussed above, the law of war and the realities of combat may render such detentions both necessary and appropriate, and our due process analysis need not blink at those realities. Without doubt, our Constitution recognizes that core strategic matters of warmaking belong in the hands of those who are best positioned and most politically accountable for making them.

The Government also argues at some length that its interests in reducing the process available to alleged enemy combatants are heightened by the practical difficulties that would accompany a system of trial-like process. In its view, military officers who are engaged in the serious work of waging battle would be unnecessarily and dangerously distracted by litigation half a world away, and discovery into military operations would both intrude on the sensitive secrets of national defense and result in a futile search for evidence buried under the rubble of war. To the extent that these burdens are triggered by heightened procedures, they are properly taken into account in our due process analysis.

3

Striking the proper constitutional balance here is of great importance to the Nation during this period of ongoing combat. But it is equally vital that our calculus not give short shrift to the values that this country holds dear or to the privilege that is American citizenship. It is during our most challenging and uncertain moments that our Nation's commitment to due process is most severely tested; and it is in those times that we must preserve our commitment at home to the principles for which we fight abroad.

We therefore hold that a citizen-detainee seeking to challenge his classification as an enemy combatant must receive notice of the factual basis for his classification, and a fair opportunity to rebut the Government's factual assertions before a neutral decisionmaker. These essential constitutional promises may not be eroded.

FROM THE BENCH

At the same time, the exigencies of the circumstances may demand that, aside from these core elements, enemy combatant proceedings may be tailored to alleviate their uncommon potential to burden the Executive at a time of ongoing military conflict. . . . Thus, once the Government puts forth credible evidence that the habeas petitioner meets the enemy-combatant criteria, the onus could shift to the petitioner to rebut that evidence with more persuasive evidence that he falls outside the criteria. A burden-shifting scheme of this sort would meet the goal of ensuring that the errant tourist, embedded journalist, or local aid worker has a chance to prove military error while giving due regard to the Executive once it has put forth meaningful support for its conclusion that the detainee is in fact an enemy combatant. In the words of [our landmark due process case *Mathews v. Eldridge*], process of this sort would sufficiently address the "risk of erroneous deprivation" of a detainee's liberty interest while eliminating certain procedures that have questionable additional value in light of the burden on the Government.

We think it unlikely that this basic process will have the dire impact on the central functions of warmaking that the Government forecasts. The parties agree that initial captures on the battlefield need not receive the process we have discussed here; that process is due only when the determination is made to *continue* to hold those who have been seized.

D

In so holding, we necessarily reject the Government's assertion that separation of powers principles mandate a heavily circumscribed role for the courts in such circumstances. Indeed, the position that the courts must forgo any examination of the individual case and focus exclusively on the legality of the broader detention scheme cannot be mandated by any reasonable view of separation of powers, as this approach serves only to *condense* power into a single branch of government. We have long since made clear that a state of war is not a blank check for the President when it comes to the rights of the Nation's citizens. Whatever power the United States Constitution envisions for the Executive in its exchanges with other nations or with enemy organizations in times of conflict, it most assuredly envisions a role for all three branches when individual liberties are at stake. Thus, while we do not question that our due process assessment must pay keen attention to the particular burdens faced by the Executive in the context of military action, it would turn our system of checks and balances on its head to suggest that a citizen could not make his way to court with a challenge to the factual basis for his detention by his government, simply because the Executive opposes making available such a challenge. Absent suspension of the writ by Congress, a citizen detained as an enemy combatant is entitled to this process.

Because we conclude that due process demands some system for a citizen detainee to refute his classification, the proposed "some evidence" standard is inadequate. Any process in which the Executive's factual assertions go wholly unchallenged or are simply presumed correct without any opportunity for the alleged combatant to demonstrate otherwise falls constitutionally short.

Justice SOUTER, with whom Justice GINSBURG joins, concurring in part, dissenting in part, and concurring in the judgment.

The plurality . . . accept[s] the Government's position that if Hamdi's designation as an enemy combatant is correct, his detention (at least as to some period) is authorized by an Act of Congress as required by §4001(a), that is, by the Authorization for Use of Military Force. Here, I disagree and respectfully dissent. The Government has failed to demonstrate that the Force Resolution authorizes the detention complained of here even on the facts the Government claims. If the Government raises nothing further than the record now shows, the Non-Detention Act entitles Hamdi to be released.

II

The threshold issue is how broadly or narrowly to read the Non-Detention Act, the tone of which is severe: "No citizen shall be imprisoned or otherwise detained by the United States except pursuant to an Act of Congress." Should the severity of the Act be relieved when the Government's stated factual justification for incommunicado detention is a war on terrorism, so that the Government may be said to act "pursuant" to congressional terms that fall short of explicit authority to imprison individuals? With one possible though important qualification, the answer has to be no. For a number of reasons, the prohibition within §4001(a) has to be read broadly to accord the statute a long reach and to impose a burden of justification on the Government.

First, the circumstances in which the Act was adopted point the way to this interpretation. The provision superseded a cold-war statute, the Emergency Detention Act of 1950, which had authorized the Attorney General, in time of emergency, to detain anyone reasonably thought likely to engage in espionage or sabotage. That statute was repealed in 1971 out of fear that it could authorize a repetition of the World War II internment of citizens of Japanese ancestry; Congress meant to preclude another episode like the one described in *Korematsu v. United States* (1944).

The fact that Congress intended to guard against a repetition of the World War II internments when it repealed the 1950 statute and gave us §4001(a) provides a powerful reason to think that §4001(a) was meant to require clear congressional authorization before any citizen can be placed in a cell. Congress's understanding of the need for clear authority before citizens are kept detained is itself therefore clear, and §4001(a) must be read to have teeth in its demand for congressional authorization.

Finally, even if history had spared us the cautionary example of the internments in World War II, . . . there would be a compelling reason to read §4001(a) to demand manifest authority to detain before detention is authorized. The defining character of American constitutional government is its constant tension between security and liberty, serving both by partial helpings of each. . . .

III

Since the Government has given no reason either to deflect the application of §4001(a) or to hold it to be satisfied, I need to go no further; the Government hints of a constitutional challenge to the statute, but it presents none here. I will, however, stray across the line between statutory and constitutional territory just far enough to note the weakness of the Government's mixed claim of inherent, extrastatutory authority under a combination of Article II of the Constitution and the usages of war. It is in fact in this connection that the Government developed its argument that the exercise of war powers justifies the detention, and what I have just said about its inadequacy applies here as well. Beyond that, it is instructive to recall Justice Jackson's observation that the President is not Commander in Chief of the country, only of the military. *Youngstown Sheet & Tube Co. v. Sawyer* (1952) (concurring opinion) (Presidential authority is "at its lowest ebb" where the President acts contrary to congressional will).

There may be room for one qualification to Justice Jackson's statement, however: in a moment of genuine emergency, when the Government must act with no time for deliberation, the Executive may be able to detain a citizen if there is reason to fear he is an imminent threat to the safety of the Nation and its people (though I doubt there is any want of statutory authority). This case, however, does not present that question, because an emergency power of necessity must at least be limited by the emergency; Hamdi has been locked up for over two years.

Whether insisting on the careful scrutiny of emergency claims or on a vigorous reading of §4001(a), we are heirs to a tradition given voice 800 years ago by Magna Carta, which, on the barons' insistence, confined executive power by "the law of the land."

IV

Because I find Hamdi's detention forbidden by §4001(a) and unauthorized by the Force Resolution, I would not reach any questions of what process he may be due in litigating disputed issues in a proceeding under the habeas statute or prior to the habeas enquiry itself. For me, it suffices that the Government has failed to justify holding him in the absence of a further Act of Congress, criminal charges, a showing that the detention conforms to the laws of war, or a demonstration that §4001(a) is unconstitutional.

Justice SCALIA, with whom Justice STEVENS joins, dissenting.

Petitioner, a presumed American citizen, has been imprisoned without charge or hearing in the Norfolk and Charleston Naval Brigs for more than two years, on the allegation that he is an enemy combatant who bore arms against his country for the Taliban. His father claims to the contrary, that he is an inexperienced aid worker caught in the wrong place at the wrong time. This case brings into conflict the competing demands of national security and our citizens' constitutional right to personal liberty. Although I share the Court's evident unease as it seeks to reconcile the two, I do not agree with its resolution.

Where the Government accuses a citizen of waging war against it, our constitutional tradition has been to prosecute him in federal court for treason or some other crime. Where the exigencies of war prevent that, the Constitution's Suspension Clause, Art. I, §9, cl. 2, allows Congress to relax the usual protections temporarily. Absent suspension, however, the Executive's assertion of military exigency has not been thought sufficient to permit detention without charge. No one contends that the congressional Authorization for Use of Military Force, on which the Government relies to justify its actions here, is an implementation of the Suspension Clause. Accordingly, I would reverse the decision below.

The very core of liberty secured by our Anglo-Saxon system of separated powers has been freedom from indefinite imprisonment at the will of the Executive. The allegations here, of course, are no ordinary accusations of criminal activity. Yaser Esam Hamdi has been imprisoned because the Government believes he participated in the waging of war against the United States. The relevant question, then, is whether there is a different, special procedure for imprisonment of a citizen accused of wrongdoing *by aiding the enemy in wartime.*

Justice O'Connor, writing for a plurality of this Court, asserts that captured enemy combatants (other than those suspected of war crimes) have traditionally been detained until the cessation of hostilities and then released. That is probably an accurate description of wartime practice with respect to enemy *aliens*. The tradition with respect to American citizens, however, has been quite different. Citizens aiding the enemy have been treated as traitors subject to the criminal process. . . .

QUESTIONS FOR DISCUSSION

5.10   Consider the plurality opinion of Justice O'Connor in light of the various models of executive authority articulated in the *Youngstown Sheet & Tube* case at the beginning of this chapter. Did the plurality opinion explicitly adopt one of the models? If so, which one? If not, did the analysis in the opinion appear to favor any of the models?

5.11   The United States had many options in deciding how to handle those individuals (many of whom were noncitizens), who were apprehended outside the United States and suspected of assisting with the 9/11 terrorist attacks. Just a few of those options included (1) kill the suspects immediately upon apprehension; (2) try the suspects in domestic criminal courts within the United States; (3) request that the United Nations convene an international criminal tribunal to try the suspects for international crimes; and (4) detain the suspects indefinitely outside the territorial limits of the United States in a place such as Guantanamo Bay, Cuba, where the United States has significant control and provide the suspects with a truncated hearing to evaluate whether they are enemies of the United States dedicated to fighting U.S. authority. What are the pros and cons of each of these alternatives?

5.12   The definition of an enemy combatant is not firmly established. Generally, however, an enemy combatant is deemed to be a person who does not belong to the organized military of a country officially at war with the United States, who has joined others to fight against the interests of the United States. Enemy combatants are usually apprehended in foreign areas where violent actions in opposition to the United States are occurring. Can you think of any persons who may be present in these hostile areas who are not there with any intention to take violent action against the interests of the United States?

5.13   Note that the military's decision to transfer Hamdi from Guantanamo to a brig on a Navy ship happened after Hamdi's status as a U.S. citizen came to light. In his dissent, Justice Scalia reasoned that Hamdi's citizenship radically changed the appropriate constitutional analysis. Why does it make a difference if a detainee is a citizen or a noncitizen?

WHAT'S YOUR LEARNED OPINION?
Scenario 5-5

In response to a surprise military attack on U.S. soil, Congress passes the Victory at All Costs Act. Specifically, the Act authorizes the President "to use any and all force against responsible parties." After significant intelligence gathering, the United States determines that agents of the Russian state are responsible for the attack. Immediately, the President orders the Defense Department to blueprint military operations to initiate a war with Russia. Several weeks after the invasion of Russia, pro-American allied

Russians capture John Doe, a U.S. citizen allegedly fighting for the Russian government. John Doe is first detained by U.S military authorities in Russia, then he is transferred to an offshore location near the United States. After a military hearing, John Doe is classified as an "enemy combatant," but after officials learn of his citizenship, he is transferred to a federal facility in Pennsylvania. John Doe is being held indefinitely as an enemy combatant with no formal charges and no access to counsel. He wishes to challenge his detention. He is finally permitted to speak to counsel and you take on his case. What arguments would you make in challenging John Doe's detention?

Scenario 5-6

Since the 9/11 terrorist attacks, the President has relied on the Authorization for the Use of Military Force (AUMF) to apprehend those responsible. The AUMF authorizes the President to "use all necessary and appropriate force against those nations, organizations, or persons he determines planned, authorized, committed, or aided the terrorist attacks." After exhaustive intelligence gathering, the United States concludes that al Qaeda is responsible for the attack. Over the next decade, the United States has successfully defeated al Qaeda. As a result, al Qaeda disbanded, but the remaining survivors vow revenge on the United States. In response, they have formed a new militant outfit called ISIS. In 2016, President Obama was informed of this new terrorist group. He determined that ISIS was a residual operation of al Qaeda, with an emphasis on individual members who in fact planned and aided the 9/11 terrorist attacks. Since this determination, President Obama and his successors have relied on the AUMF to launch drone strikes at ISIS strongholds every year since 2016.

The year is now 2021. The Senate Foreign Affairs Committee is concerned about the increasing militarization of ISIS, but they do not support the drone strike strategy. In response, the Committee has assembled a strategy group to recommend policies more in line with their views. Specifically, they intend to challenge the President's invocation of the AUMF as an unconstitutional use of presidential power. What are the arguments on both sides of the question?

This chapter has showcased diverse controversies about the President's power and has illustrated the different ways in which the broad and vague language of the Constitution either expanded or restricted the authority of the President in diverse contexts. These last several chapters conclude this volume's focus on the structure of the U.S. federalist system. The next part of the book presents a change in orientation and focuses on the tools that individual citizens possess to protect themselves from overbearing government control. That said, when you proceed through the next part, please look for ways that the federal government's structure influences how individual rights are either protected or infringed.

QUESTIONS FOR REVIEW

1. The language regarding executive power differs from the language about legislative and judicial power in the U.S. Constitution. Describe how the executive power language is different.
2. Describe the events that gave rise to the dispute in *Youngstown Sheet & Tube Co. v. Sawyer*. What action did the President take that precipitated the controversy?
3. Explain the meaning of inherent presidential power.
4. Describe Justice Jackson's approach to outlining the various elements of presidential power.
5. Some of the Justices who wrote opinions in *Youngstown Sheet & Tube Co. v. Sawyer* emphasized Congress's approach to the particular presidential action at issue in the case. Describe how they used that congressional action in their analysis.
6. What was the factual background that gave rise to the dispute in *Zivotofsky v. Kerry*?
7. Which of the various presidential power models best describes the majority opinion by Justice Kennedy in *Zivotofsky v. Kerry*?
8. Is the following statement true or false: The power of the President to recognize another sovereign is explicitly mentioned in the Constitution. If the answer is true, what are the precise words in the Constitution? If the answer is false, what constitutional language would support the conclusion that the President has that power?
9. In the area of foreign affairs, including war powers issues, the U.S. Supreme Court appears more willing to recognize broad (sometimes even exclusive) presidential powers. Explain why you believe that is the case.
10. Describe the relationship between *Korematsu v. United States* and the current practice under federal constitutional law of using strict judicial scrutiny to evaluate government action that discriminates based on race.
11. Explain the difference between how the United States handled the internment of Japanese Americans during World War II and how Britain handled internment of Italians and Austrians who lived in Britain during World War II.
12. In his dissent in *Korematsu*, did Justice Jackson express that the presidential and military decision to intern Japanese Americans deserved any judicial deference? If so, describe Justice Jackson's view of the contours of that deference.

13. How are the circumstances that gave rise to *Korematsu v. United States* similar to the circumstances that gave rise to *Hamdi v. Rumsfeld*?
14. What was the congressional action that the plurality in *Hamdi* believed gave authorization to the president to detain enemy combatants and subject them to military tribunals?
15. For the purposes of the constitutional issues in the case, did it matter that the petitioner in the case, Yaser Esam Hamdi, was a citizen of the United States? If so, why?

ENDNOTES

1. Stuart Taylor, Jr., *Advice by Chief Justice to Truman Is Depicted*, The New York Times (August 24, 1982), A17, https://www.nytimes.com/1982/08/24/us/advice-by-chief-justice-to-truman-is-depicted .html (last accessed June 19, 2023).
2. Erwin Chemerinsky, *Constitutional Law: Principles and Policies* 365-370 (6th ed. 2019).
3. Credit goes to Erwin Chemerinsky for his contribution to framing these descriptions.
4. Gerald Gunther, *The Supreme Court, 1971 Term-Forward: In Search of Evolving Doctrine on a Changing Court: A Model for a Newer Equal Protection*, 86 Harv. L. Rev. 1, 8 (1972).

Individual Rights

The individual civil rights of citizens of the United States are rooted in the first ten amendments to the Constitution, known as the Bill of Rights. Although the Framers initially reached a relative consensus that enunciation of these rights in the Constitution was unnecessary or unwise, proceedings to ratify the Constitution within the states raised strong sentiments in favor of naming basic liberties that protect citizens from government interference. Indeed, the absence of a Bill of Rights in the original Constitution posed a potential obstacle to its ratification by the states. In response, James Madison, who had originally argued that a Bill of Rights was unnecessary and perhaps even harmful, changed his mind and drafted a list of rights. These eventually became the first ten amendments to the Constitution in 1791. Of particular note is the Ninth Amendment, which embodies the Framers' concern that listing some rights in the Constitution might produce a negative inference that other rights did not enjoy protection under our system of government. Responding to this concern, the Ninth Amendment states, "[t]the enumeration in the Constitution, of certain rights, shall not be construed to deny or disparage others retained by the people."

A frequently misunderstood question about Bill of Rights mandates concerns the entities that these mandates restrict. Most important, they do not generally restrain private behavior. So, for example, if another human being tells you to shut your mouth and you protest that the person is violating your free speech rights, that is a correct statement only if the person is affiliated with the government and is acting in their governmental capacity. Someone acting as a private individual trying to muzzle you does not present a First Amendment violation. This is called the "state action" requirement. (Note, however, that exceptions to the state action requirement that have cropped up over the years will be mentioned later in this chapter.)

Originally, the protections of the Bill of Rights restricted only the federal government. This limited application, however, changed after the Civil War when the Fourteenth Amendment became part of the Constitution in 1868. The Fourteenth Amendment states in part that no state shall "deprive any person of life, liberty, or property, without due process of law."

In a series of decisions handed down at the beginning of the twentieth century, the Supreme Court began to incorporate the Bill of Rights protections into the "liberty" component of the Due Process Clause and to apply them to restrict state governments. Today, the most important Bill of Rights protections have been applied to the states, but some of the protections—such as the right to a grand jury indictment before being accused of a crime and the right not to be forced to quarter soldiers in one's home—apply only to the federal government and have not been incorporated.

This book does not cover all of the Bill of Rights in detail. Instead, we take a deep dive into the most prominent ones in today's United States to display how the provisions touch everyday lives and affect culture and society. Topics covered are the First Amendment (including both freedom of communication and matters pertaining to religion), the Second Amendment, portions of the Fourth and Fifth Amendments, and equal protection and due process rights guaranteed by the Fourteenth Amendment. This latter group of rights covers a large swath of contemporary issues, ranging from race discrimination and women's equality rights to rights regarding reproduction, sexuality, and marriage. The remainder of this book covers each of these matters—each presented in separate chapters.

The First Amendment
Basic Freedom of Communication Principles

As with many parts of the U.S. Constitution, the language of the First Amendment does not mean precisely what it says. Nor does it have the impact that it suggests. Here's the precise language:

> Congress shall make no law respecting an establishment of religion, or prohibiting the free exercise thereof, or abridging the freedom of speech, or of the press; or the right of the people peaceably to assemble, and to petition the Government for a redress of grievances.

To explain how this language does not mean what it says, consider the following. First, the language does not just control Congress, but binds all of government. Also, the amendment speaks in absolutes, suggesting that it precludes all governmental limits on citizens' activities. Yet the amendment does not limit all activities. Instead, the doctrines developed to give effect to the amendment are nuanced and qualified, belying the simplicity of its words.

The brevity of the First Amendment is also misleading (its words represent only a small fraction of the Constitution's text). Possessing remarkably brief admonitions, the First Amendment has nonetheless had an impressive impact on government, culture, society, and everyday life. The length of this part of the chapter stands as a testament to the complexity of First Amendment case law.

The words mentioning "speech, or of the press" also suggest that the First Amendment applies only to oral or printed communication, but the amendment also applies to nonverbal, symbolic expressions such as flag burning. Finally, the First Amendment's text suggests that all speech is of equal value, deserving equal protection. Yet a dominant theme in First Amendment case law highlights the importance of political speech, which in the Supreme Court's opinion serves as an essential handmaiden to effective democratic self-government. By contrast, other forms of speech receive no protection, as is the case with obscenity, speech that causes violence, and deceptive commercial speech.

Likewise, the vagueness of the words in the amendment regarding speech can also create problems. Further questions arise because the First Amendment also contains two clauses pertaining to religion: One clause guarantees freedom of religion and the other clause prohibits government's establishment of religion. How do you define "religion"? Freedom of religion? What on earth does "establishment of religion" mean?

Given the highly charged nature of both speech and religion protections, the First Amendment has in the past become a victim of the U.S. Supreme Court's inclination to duck difficult issues, to politicize issues, and to foster polarization among the justices. The doctrines have been unstable and contradictory. As with many areas of constitutional law that have received attention from many different members of the Supreme Court over the years, the body of First Amendment law is made up of parallel strands that are redundant, inconsistent, or inexplicably diverse. A particular fact pattern logically may be resolved using several of the competing strands, but the Court has never clarified why it chooses one strand rather than another in the various cases it decides. Many reasons suggest themselves, but two of the most likely explanations are (1) the personal preference of the Justice who writes the lead opinion, and (2) a reaction to how the advocates pitch a particular case. One must remember that the U.S. litigation and decision-making systems are driven by the litigants who bring their case or controversy to the courts for resolution. That is the essence of the adversary system of litigation in the United States. Accordingly, courts — even the Supreme Court — often defer to how the litigants frame the legal issues in a case. In many cases, the Supreme Court frames its arguments with the same characterization and slant as the arguments in the parties' briefs.

As frustrating and baffling as these qualities might be, study of the First Amendment holds many rewards. Its centrality to our system of government and our definition as a people renders it extraordinarily important. Indeed, its place at the beginning of the Bill of Rights is no mistake. In addition, the present composition of the Supreme Court suggests a renewed interest among a majority of the Justices in creating new First Amendment doctrine, particularly in the area of religion. For some, this might be welcome and for others this could be cause for great concern, but for all this should be a matter of intense interest.

This chapter addresses only basic freedom of expression concerns. (Needless to say, that topic alone is sufficient to fill a library of books.) Chapter 7 covers more specialized freedom of communication issues: limits on hate speech and the benefits of humor. For organizational reasons, Chapter 7 also surveys issues related to religion.

A. Freedom of Expression Values: Explication and Critique

With all of the complexities among First Amendment cases, you will likely encounter difficulties making a judgment about how to analyze a First Amendment freedom of expression issue. Being mindful of the values behind First Amendment rulings helps to guide general understanding of the stakes at play in cases and provide guides for navigating compelling arguments on opposite sides of an issue. As you read through the freedom of communication subjects presented in the volume, you will find it helpful to (1) watch how courts use the values in developing rationales for decisions, and (2) evaluate whether the rationales are valid or are only a misplaced crutch to give the justices a tiebreaker to resolve a difficult case.

Perhaps the most frequently urged value for protecting freedom of communication is the need to promote effective democratic government. To ensure that citizens knowledgeably participate in elections and other aspects of government, they must educate themselves. As the theory goes, proper education requires access to an extensive information store, which becomes available only when communication of ideas is free-flowing. Moreover, citizens' ability to monitor official action and criticize government is an important check on government corruption. Run by human beings with self-preservation and promotion instincts, government cannot be expected to censor its critics evenhandedly with its supporters.

This view of freedom of communication focuses on what good the freedom can achieve. (One might describe that as an instrumental view: We cherish the amendment because of what it can make possible.) One can also take the position, though, that freedom of communication is more than a means to an end; it is an end in itself. In what ways might that be true? One might say that free expression is an essential part of human dignity and the basic human impulse to express oneself. Aligned with the concept of individual dignity is the theory that free communication fosters the value of self-realization—a state of being in which individuals can explore ways to ensure their own well-being and the well-being of others. One can argue that the result is personal growth, self-sufficiency, and autonomy. This angle on the First Amendment could be described as "nonconsequential," as it focuses on properties intrinsic to the free expression, rather than its consequences.

A related communication value is truth-seeking. Without a vigorous marketplace of ideas, the argument goes, individuals cannot fully understand all possible points of view. Nor can we fully know what ideas are false and how to counter these false ideas. Only through free debate, speech, and counterspeech can pernicious ideas be fully identified and understood. Under this theory, a vigorous marketplace of ideas arises only with aggressive speech protection.

One can observe that the self-realization and truth-seeking values justify protecting a broader range of speech than would be protected if the only focus of free speech principles were to ensure a functioning democracy. Focus on democratic values leads to particular concerns with protecting speech on political matters. By contrast, focus on self-realization and truth-seeking not only concerns political speech, but also emphasizes communicating about other phenomena such as science and art—without regard to whether these phenomena include a political message or not.

Finally, some argue that freedom of communication promotes an important value in society: tolerance. This argument starts with the premise that we do not have the First Amendment to protect speech that we favor. Such speech does not need protection from censorship. Rather, the First Amendment's main function is to protect unfavored speech.

Starting from the premise that the First Amendment is designed primarily to protect unpopular, scandalous, or hateful ideas, one can argue that incidents that call for First Amendment protection force self-restraint among the government and general population, encouraging them to develop their capacity to control negative reactions to unpleasant speech. According to the tolerance theory, protecting unpopular speech is an act of tolerance, and such tolerance models and encourages more tolerance. The end result, this theory maintains, is that citizens learn to better navigate a conflict-infused society, and difficult line-drawing that might suppress valuable speech is avoided.

Several critiques of developing a First Amendment approach based on these values focus on contemporary social and technical realities. Critics of relying on the self-government value note that its asserted importance assumes that individual citizens have the capacity, time, and interest to make independent personal decisions. That assumption, the argument maintains, ignores many voters' tendency to turn off their critical faculties, and even become alienated, in the face of mass media, social media, and big government. Some argue that theories based on the self-government value overemphasize speech on political topics, ignoring other categories of speech such as speech about philosophy, literature, and the arts that also contribute to thoughtful engagement about how government can contribute to a rich culture and meaning to human life.

In a similar vein, critics attack the premise that a marketplace of ideas promotes the truth-seeking value. The marketplace of ideas theory necessarily assumes that those who consume communications are critically thinking, rational decision makers. This assumption ignores that humans in modern life are busy and possibly too distracted to make concerted informed judgments about all important issues. The assumption also does not note that humans rely on emotions and instincts in making decisions. Skeptics maintain that sophisticated or wealthy opinion leaders can dominate and manipulate the media. When added to the inclination of today's citizens to consume one-sided social media, and (sometimes) the message of demagogues, the notion of a robust and honest exchange of speech and counterspeech is illusory.

The argument continues that, even assuming that truth can ultimately emerge from a robust exchange of ideas in contemporary society, the process of debate is time-consuming. This luxury of time is not always available, particularly in the context of elections, social unrest, and immediate threats to safety. Disparity in financing enhances this problem: Wealthy communicators (e.g., corporations and powerful, affluent citizens) have easier access to avenues for propagating their message than lone, impoverished individuals. Finally, there are those who challenge the underlying notion that objective truth even exists, thus viewing as fool-hardy the notion that the truth-seeking value provides a useful guide for navigating free speech challenges.

Those who challenge reliance on the self-realization value in the free speech context largely emphasize the value of other modes of promoting self-determination and self-realization. Alternative avenues for expression, such as music creation or refinement of athletic skill, could equally contribute to these goals. Yet the heightened constitutional protection that speech enjoys is usually not extended to these activities and thus, one can argue, receives protection that is not matched for its benefits.

A common response to the value of promoting tolerance acknowledges that it reflects the honorable goal of shaping society's intellectual character for the better. Is it true, though, that allowing disparaging speech simply allows it to flourish, a result that does not actually promote tolerance.

QUESTION FOR DISCUSSION

6.1   What is your opinion of each of the justifications for protecting freedom of expression? Which is most persuasive to you? Which do you find least persuasive? What are your criticisms of each? For example, consider the goal of promoting tolerance. Is there truly a strong causal link between tolerating hateful, ugly speech and tolerating diversity and difference among members of society? If we permit a surge in hateful expression, does that prevent or encourage other hateful expression?

B. Content-Based and Content-Neutral Regulations

When evaluating a restriction on speech, courts often start with an evaluation of whether the restriction is triggered by the substance or subject matter of the message conveyed. For example, if the content of the speech restricted is a criticism of government, courts tend to closely analyze the nature of the restriction and its purpose. Regulations that focus on a message's substance or subject matter are called content-based restrictions. The First Amendment principles governing these restrictions are surveyed immediately below. A content-neutral speech regulation is one that is unrelated to the speech's content. Although several types of regulations are content-neutral, the most common examples are time, place, and manner restrictions, discussed at the end of this section.

1. Identifying Content-Based Regulations

The courts are particularly suspicious of content-based restrictions because they are a form of censorship and carry the appearance that the government is attempting to take particular subject matters out of the marketplace of ideas. Accordingly, once a court labels a restriction as content based, the court will carefully evaluate the restriction with strict scrutiny. Strict scrutiny is a form of judicial review. When a court applies strict scrutiny to a restriction, the restriction is constitutional only if it serves a compelling interest and is narrowly tailored to serve that interest. That is, the restriction must sweep no further than necessary, acting as the least restrictive means of furthering that interest.

Most common examples of content-based restrictions are those that are aimed at a particular subject and those with restrictions resulting from the speaker's identity. A particularly suspicious content-based restriction is one that is also viewpoint based; that is, a restriction targeted at one side of a debate. So, for example, assume that a public university banned all speakers on campus who discussed current events. This appears to be a content-based restriction. If the ban were more fine-tuned, targeting only speakers who criticize the President, then the restriction would be viewpoint based as well. Courts generally apply strict scrutiny to viewpoint-based restrictions with particular vigor. A viewpoint-based restriction not only targets a particular subject matter, but it shows hostility to one perspective on that subject. One might think of the restriction as censorship on steroids.

Here's another example: Assume City #1 bans all marches down the city's main artery during rush hour. The city explains that it instituted the ban to avoid disrupting traffic during particularly congested times of day. City #2 bans all marches down the city's main artery in support of the Black Lives Matter movement. City #2 argues that the ban's purpose is to avoid disrupting traffic and that Black Lives Matter marches can become highly disruptive. Both cities maintain that their bans are not content based.

Only City #1 is correct. Its ban makes no reference to the subject of the march and it proffers an explanation for the ban that applies to all marches at a particular time. For that reason, content-neutral justifications warrant the ban. In arguing that the ban is constitutional, City #1 can also point out that the ban is limited to particular times of day. Accordingly, alternative times exist when a march can occur on a main artery.

City #2's ban focuses on marches concerning a specific subject and is therefore content based. City #2's explanation for the ban might be relevant to evaluating whether the ban can satisfy strict scrutiny but does not qualify for making the ban content neutral. In arguing that the ban is unconstitutional, challengers might also point out that the ban sweeps throughout the day, leaving no time when Black Lives Matter marches on the main arteries may take place.

This example presents a relatively easy case for distinguishing between content-neutral and content-based restrictions. Determining how to characterize a restriction, however, is not always simple. In *Reed v. Town of Gilbert*, the Court described the framework for determining whether a government's regulation of speech is a content-based law that "target[s] speech based on its communicative content," or a content-neutral "time, place, or manner" restriction. 576 U.S. 155 (2015). The *Reed* Court described the content-based test as a "commonsense" determination: A government regulation of speech is content based if "on its face [it] draws distinctions based on the message a speaker conveys." In the "second step" of the *Reed* test, a facially neutral regulation will also be classified as content based if it "cannot be justified without reference to the content of the regulated speech" or if it "was adopted by the government because of disagreement with the message [the speech] conveys." *Reed* added, however, that the government's motive for passing the regulation is not relevant. In the *Reed* Court's words, "A law that is content based on its face is subject to strict scrutiny regardless of the government's benign motive, content-neutral justification, or lack of 'animus toward the ideas contained' in the regulated speech." *Id.* at 2228. In other words, a law that is content based on its face will not be viewed as content neutral even if the government did not wish to censor any particular message.

2. Content-Neutral Restrictions: Time, Place, and Manner Restrictions

The government can regulate speech indirectly by imposing limits that are not concerned with the content of speech, but affect the circumstances under which expression takes place. These restrictions are content neutral. If the restriction is content neutral, the restriction is still subject to First Amendment concerns. Although courts take a more relaxed approach to content-neutral regulations than content-based regulations that are generally subject to strict scrutiny, courts still subject content-neutral restrictions to intermediate scrutiny. That is, they find that a government regulation can be constitutional if the regulation:

1. Is narrowly tailored to serve a significant government interest;
2. Is justified without reference to the content of the regulated speech; and
3. Leaves open ample alternative avenues for communication of the information.

"Time, place, and manner restrictions" are the most common category of content-neutral restrictions. These types of restrictions are often used by the government to regulate the use of government property for speech purposes.

Time, place, and manner restrictions are, by nature, content neutral because they are not focused on the identity or the subject or message of the speech. Rather, these restrictions focus on the circumstances under which the speech is delivered. Yet because time, place, and manner restrictions can have the effect of limiting expression and restricting the audience for expression, the law carefully evaluates whether the restrictions are appropriately limited and are truly intended to regulate only based on the time, place, and manner in which the communication occurs. To be constitutional, the regulation must also be narrowly tailored to serve a significant state interest and must leave open ample alternative channels for communication. (It should be noted, however, that the government need not satisfy these constitutional time, place, and manner requirements when the government is the speaker restricted by the time, place, and manner rules. In other words, government is free to restrict itself however it wants.)

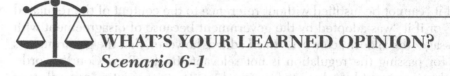

WHAT'S YOUR LEARNED OPINION?
Scenario 6-1

The state fair committee in a U.S. state instituted a rule requiring anyone seeking to distribute or sell "merchandise" (including printed material) to obtain a license and perform activities in a fixed location. Under the rule, representatives of the organization could stroll the fairgrounds and orally reach out to patrons, but all sales, fund solicitation, and distribution had to occur at a fixed, designated location on the fairgrounds. The state fair committee decided that the rule was necessary to avoid impeding pedestrian traffic flow through the most congested areas of the fairgrounds. Representatives of a religious organization challenged the rule as an unconstitutional restriction. Are they correct that the restriction is unconstitutional?

C. The Importance of Political Debate and Protest Versus the Need to Protect Public Safety

1. Speech That Incites Violence

The question of how much society may suppress speech inciting others to engage in illegal activities presents two important policy questions requiring a delicate balance for societies that cherish civil peace, an opportunity to express unpopular views, and a robust democracy:

1. How important is maintaining social control?
2. Does this concern with social control outweigh the value of free expression?

These two concerns oppose each other and require balancing. This evaluation process can be difficult because the content of speech intended to incite illegal action frequently includes highly valued speech pertaining to politics. Making matters even more charged, protesters know that they can heighten their political message by advocating violations of law.

The Supreme Court has grappled with several different approaches to dealing with this difficult balance. The various standards used to evaluate threatened illegal activities are unique to this context and differ from the more general intermediate and strict scrutiny standards used in other contexts. An early, famous approach asked whether speech posed "a clear and present danger" of creating violence. *Schenck v. United States*, 249 U.S. 47, 52 (1919). The words "clear" and "present" suggest focus on probability that harm will occur as well as on whether the harm is likely to occur soon. The *Schenck* Court added to the test, stating that questions of proximity and degree are also important. In so stating, the Court was apparently referring to whether the danger is grave and whether it is also close in time and space.

Varying this inquiry in subsequent periods of U.S. history, the Court often emphasized concern with radical illegality and loosened the First Amendment restrictions (and endorsed restrictive regulations) in apparent reaction to concerns about national security. Although the clear and present danger standard might appear difficult for authorities to satisfy, courts did not necessarily apply the standard with rigor. For example, the U.S. Supreme Court upheld convictions in the early twentieth century under the federal Espionage Act of individuals' antiwar advocacy that was unlikely to have significant effect. Instead, the Court merely focused on the *tendency* of the advocacy to cause harm. *Frohwerk v. United States*, 249 U.S. 204 (1919); *Debs v. United States*, 249 U.S. 211 (1919).

At other points in history, the Court eased its concern with advocacy of harm and tightened up protections for speech. In *Schenck*, Justice Holmes hedged on regulation of speech advocating potential violence: "If the act (speaking, or circulating a paper), its tendency and the intent with which it is done are the same, we perceive no ground for saying that success alone warrants making the act a crime."[1] But Justice Holmes evolved in his thinking. Dissenting in *Abrams v. United States*, 250 U.S. 616 (1919), Justice Holmes shrouded his clear-and-present-danger approach with a speech-protecting veneer. He stated that even though the desire to suppress dissenting opinions is an understandable human inclination,

> . . . we should be eternally vigilant against attempts to check the expression of opinions that we loathe and believe to be fraught with death, unless they so imminently threaten immediate interference with the lawful and pressing purposes of the law that an immediate check is required to save the country.[2]

It took some time, however, before the majority of the U.S. Supreme Court embraced this view of avoiding the temptation to regulate incitement to violence. The Court moved even further toward restricting dissenting speech in *Gitlow v. New York*, 268 U.S. 652 (1925). In upholding a prosecution for advocating the overthrow of government by force and violence, the Supreme Court announced a highly deferential test: Did the legislature act reasonably in enacting the statute? (The "reasonableness" test represents one of the most hands-off, reverential approaches that a court can take in reviewing a legislative enactment.)

Applying this test in *Gitlow*, the Court determined that the legislature could reasonably authorize punishment for "threatened danger in its incipiency."[3] Unlike Justice Holmes's *Gitlow* dissent, this language allows punishment for advocacy well before words inspire immediate grave danger.

Swinging back to a more speech-protective approach, Justice Brandeis rejected *Gitlow's* reasonableness approach in *Whitney v. California*, 274 U.S. 357 (1927). Rejecting *Gitlow's* deferential "reasonableness" approach to legislatures, Justice Brandeis stated that repression of speech should occur only when grave danger is near:

> Whenever the fundamental rights of free speech and assembly are alleged to have been invaded, it must remain open to a defendant to present the issue whether there actually did exist at the time a clear danger, whether the danger, if any, was imminent, and whether the evil apprehended was one so substantial as to justify the stringent restriction interposed by the Legislature. The legislative declaration, like the fact that the statute was passed and was sustained by the highest court of the State, creates merely a rebuttable presumption that these conditions have been satisfied.

Id. at 378-379.

Justice Brandeis's position failed to persuade the Court majority in the next major decision in this area, *Dennis v. United States*, 341 U.S. 494 (1951). Writing at the time of strong anti-Communist fervor in the McCarthy era, the Supreme Court held that the "inflammable nature of world conditions" justified finding that the existence of a conspiracy—without a showing of imminence and the like—was alone sufficient to justify suppression.

Tracking the ebbs and flows of the advocacy of illegality case law, heightened concern with potentially dangerous speech often coincided with international and internal threats to the United States. In 1969, the U.S. Supreme Court settled on what appears to be an equilibrium—the currently prevailing general test for evaluating the constitutionality of speech that incites illegality. This approach seems to hold in First Amendment jurisprudence. Favoring speech protection over social control, the Court announced the test in *Brandenburg v. Ohio*, 395 U.S. 444 (1969).

FROM THE BENCH

BRANDENBURG v. OHIO
395 U.S. 444 (1969)

Per Curiam.

[Charles Brandenburg], a leader of a Ku Klux Klan group, was convicted under the Ohio Criminal Syndicalism statute for "advocat[ing] . . . the duty, necessity, or propriety of crime, sabotage, violence, or unlawful methods of terrorism as a means of accomplishing industrial or political reform" and for "voluntarily assembl[ing] with any society, group, or assemblage of persons formed to teach or advocate the doctrines of criminal syndicalism." He was fined $1,000 and sentenced to one-to-10 years' imprisonment. The appellant challenged the constitutionality of the criminal syndicalism statute under the First and Fourteenth Amendments to the United States Constitution, but the intermediate appellate court of Ohio affirmed his conviction without opinion. The Supreme Court of Ohio dismissed his appeal, *sua sponte*, "for the reason that no substantial constitutional question exists herein." . . . We reverse.

The record shows that a man, identified at trial as the appellant, telephoned an announcer-reporter on the staff of a Cincinnati television station and invited him to come to a Ku Klux Klan "rally" to be held at a farm in Hamilton County. With the cooperation of the organizers, the reporter and a cameraman attended the meeting and filmed the events. Portions of the films were later broadcast on the local station and on a national network.

The prosecution's case rested on the films and on testimony identifying the appellant as the person who communicated with the reporter and who spoke at the rally. The State also introduced into evidence several articles appearing in the film, including a pistol, a rifle, a shotgun, ammunition, a Bible, and a red hood worn by the speaker in the films.

One film showed 12 hooded figures, some of whom carried firearms. They were gathered around a large wooden cross, which they burned. No one was present other than the participants and the newsmen who made the film. Most of the words uttered during the scene were incomprehensible when the film was projected, but scattered phrases could be understood that were derogatory of Negroes and, in one instance, of Jews. Another scene on the same film showed the appellant, in Klan regalia, making a speech. [Here is a portion of the speech]:

> This is an organizers' meeting. We have had quite a few members here today which are—we have hundreds, hundreds of members throughout the State of Ohio. I can quote from a newspaper clipping from the Columbus, Ohio Dispatch, five weeks ago Sunday morning. The Klan has more members in the State of Ohio than does any other organization. We're not a revengent (sic) organization, but if our President, our Congress, our Supreme Court, continues to suppress the white, Caucasian race, it's possible that there might have to be some revengeance (sic) taken.
>
> We are marching on Congress July the Fourth, four hundred thousand strong. From there we are dividing into two groups, one group to march on St. Augustine, Florida, the other group to march into Mississippi. Thank you.

The second film showed six hooded figures one of whom, later identified as the appellant, repeated a speech very similar to that recorded on the first film. The reference to the possibility of "revengeance" was omitted, and one sentence was added: "Personally, I believe the nigger should be returned to Africa, the

Jew returned to Israel." Though some of the figures in the films carried weapons, the speaker did not.

In 1927, this Court sustained the constitutionality of California's Criminal Syndicalism Act, the text of which is quite similar to that of the laws of Ohio. *Whitney v. California*, 274 U.S. 357 (1927) . . . *Whitney* has been thoroughly discredited by later decisions [such as] *Dennis v. United States*, 341 U.S. 494, at 507 (1951).

These later decisions have fashioned the principle that the constitutional guarantees of free speech and free press do not permit a State to forbid or proscribe advocacy of the use of force or of law violation except where such advocacy is directed to inciting or producing imminent lawless action and is likely to incite or produce such action. As we said in *Noto v. United States*, 367 U.S. 290, 297-298 (1961), "the mere abstract teaching . . . of the moral propriety or even moral necessity for a resort to force and violence, is not the same as preparing a group for violent action and steeling it to such action." A statute which fails to draw this distinction impermissibly intrudes upon the freedoms guaranteed by the First and Fourteenth Amendments. It sweeps within its condemnation speech which our Constitution has immunized from governmental control.

Measured by this test, Ohio's Criminal Syndicalism Act cannot be sustained. The Act punishes persons who "advocate or teach the duty, necessity, or propriety" of violence "as a means of accomplishing industrial or political reform"; or who publish or circulate or display any book or paper containing such advocacy; or who "justify" the commission of violent acts "with intent to exemplify, spread or advocate the propriety of the doctrines of criminal syndicalism"; or who "voluntarily assemble" with a group formed "to teach or advocate the doctrines of criminal syndicalism."

Accordingly, we are here confronted with a statute which, by its own words and as applied, purports to punish mere advocacy and to forbid, on pain of criminal punishment, assembly with others merely to advocate the described type of action. Such a statute falls within the condemnation of the First and Fourteenth Amendments.

Reversed.

QUESTIONS FOR DISCUSSION

6.2 The history of the case law in this area suggests that one way to ensure a prohibition against speech that incites violence is to focus on four qualities: urging violence that is (1) close in time, (2) probable to occur, (3) capable of serious harm, and (4) uttered with intent. Is there any part of the opinion of *Brandenburg* that captures these elements?

6.3 Why would the Supreme Court include proof of intent to incite violence in the *Brandenburg* test? Is requiring proof of intent somehow more protective of free expression than exposing a speaker to legal consequences for just making a mistake, albeit an unreasonable mistake (e.g., acting negligently)?

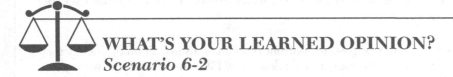

WHAT'S YOUR LEARNED OPINION?
Scenario 6-2

Protesters attended a campaign rally to show their disagreement with the candidate who was speaking at the rally. As the candidate spoke, the protesters loudly ridiculed the candidate's speech. On six occasions during his speech, the candidate responded to the commotion, pointing to the protesters and saying, "I am asking the crowd to do whatever you can to get 'em out of here without delay." Law enforcement authorities eventually ushered the protesters out of the rally. Members of the audience pushed, shoved, and assaulted the protesters as law enforcement escorted them out of the room. Several of the protesters suffered significant injuries from the crowd. The protesters want the candidate punished for unlawful incitement to inflict violence. Would the *Brandenburg* test be satisfied if charges were brought?

Scenario 6-3

A high school student, David, was an avid player of the video game called High School Football, which features the killing of members of a football team by a student using six guns during a high school game. David showed up at a live high school football game with six guns and shot players on the field in the same way and with the same shot angles, language, and flourish as the shooter used in the video game. David's parents filed suit against the company that produced and maintained the High School Football video games, which the parents alleged glorified violence for their son and provided a model for his crime. Is the *Brandenburg* test satisfied by these facts?

Scenario 6-4

On January 6, 2021, then President Donald Trump gave a speech to a large group of people outside of the White House. During the speech, he was behind what appeared to be bulletproof clear protection—presumably erected at government expense. The White House was visible in the background, and he was flanked by U.S. flags. After the speech, many in the crowd marched up Pennsylvania Avenue and committed violent acts at the U.S. Capitol. Deaths and several severe injuries to law enforcement resulted. The following are excerpts from former President Trump's speech. Is it your judgment that his words satisfy the *Brandenburg* test—such that he cannot claim First Amendment protection for his words? Here are some excerpts from his speech:

> Now, it is up to Congress to confront this egregious assault on our democracy. And after this, we're going to walk down, and I'll be there with you, we're going to walk down, we're going to walk down. . . . Because you'll never take back our country with weakness. You have to show strength and you have to be strong. We have come to demand that Congress do the right thing and only count the electors who have been lawfully slated, lawfully slated. . . . The Republicans have to get tougher. You're not going to have a Republican Party if you don't get tougher. . . . I know that everyone here will soon be marching over to the Capitol building to peacefully and patriotically make your voices heard. . . .
>
> And we fight. We fight like hell. And if you don't fight like hell, you're not going to have a country anymore. . . . Our exciting adventures and boldest endeavors have not yet begun. My fellow Americans, for our movement, for our children, and for our beloved country . . . And I say this despite all that's happened. The best is yet to come. . . .
>
> So we're going to, we're going to walk down Pennsylvania Avenue. I love Pennsylvania Avenue. And we're going to the Capitol, and we're going to try and give. . . . The Democrats are hopeless—they never vote for anything. Not even one vote. But we're going to try and give our Republicans, the weak ones because the strong ones don't need any of our help. We're going to try and give them the kind of pride and boldness that they need to take back our country. . . . So let's walk down Pennsylvania Avenue.[4]

2. Symbolic Speech

When one thinks of the world at the time the states ratified the First Amendment, one thinks of citizens expressing controversial views in angry speeches in public squares, reputation-piercing newspaper articles appearing in old-timey type, and sharply accusatory pamphlets. Nevertheless, at that time (and even earlier), citizens also used symbols and nonverbal forms of expression. Since then, norms have changed and new technology—together with creative spirit—have introduced new ways to express messages nonverbally. Perhaps as a result of these changes, courts and litigants have started to pay close attention to nonverbal speech. Over time, perhaps as a consequence of changing norms and a growing orientation in favor of filing lawsuits, Ku Klux Klan members wearing white hoods and burning crosses have become a frequent source of litigation. This type of symbolic speech is covered in the next chapter in connection with hate speech regulation materials.

First Amendment case law easily accommodated the notion that "speech" does not necessarily include words but can also embrace conduct alone. As with any legal concept, however, this development presented a definitional challenge: What type of conduct counts as protected speech? Panhandling in the park without words? Allowing a dog to defecate on a hated neighbor's lawn as part of a feud? Assassinating a public figure? Case law on this definitional problem tends to focus on two questions: (1) Does the conduct express a message? (2) Does the conduct cause clear public harm or personal injury that can be prohibited by law even if it had no communicative content?

The Vietnam War prompted many types of protests, including the burning of draft cards. *Keystone Press/Alamy Stock Photo.*

The 1960s, in particular, featured protests using symbols to drive home an idea: Examples include armbands, bra burning, desecration of effigies, and large message-bearing inflatable balloons. These acts had clear expressive content and did not usually threaten injury to others. Of particular challenge to the U.S. citizenry and establishment, however, were symbolic expressions that ridiculed public patriotism and the government's authority to conduct wars. The next two cases marked key developments in this area, illustrating the Supreme Court's current approach to the vexing issues such as draft card burning and flag burning.

FROM THE BENCH

UNITED STATES v. O'BRIEN
391 U.S. 367 (1968)

Mr. Chief Justice WARREN delivered the opinion of the Court.

On the morning of March 31, 1966, David Paul O'Brien and three companions burned their Selective Service registration certificates [i.e., "draft cards"] on the steps of the South Boston Courthouse. A sizable crowd, including several agents of the Federal Bureau of Investigation, witnessed the event. Immediately after the burning, members of the crowd began attacking O'Brien and his companions. An FBI agent ushered O'Brien to safety inside the courthouse. After he was advised of his right to counsel and to silence, O'Brien stated to FBI agents that he had burned his registration certificate because of his beliefs, knowing that he was violating federal law.

O'Brien was indicted, tried, convicted, and sentenced for burning his draft card. He did not contest the fact that he had burned the card. He stated in argument to the jury that he burned the card publicly to influence others to adopt his anti-war beliefs, as he put it, "so that other people would reevaluate their positions with Selective Service, with the armed forces, and reevaluate their place in the culture of today, to hopefully consider my position."

The indictment upon which he was tried charged that he "willfully and knowingly did mutilate, destroy, and change by burning . . . [his draft card] in violation of Universal Military Training and Service Act of 1948." We hold that the 1965 Amendment is constitutional both as enacted and applied.

I

When a male reaches the age of 18, he is required by the 1948 Act to register with a local draft board. Both the registration and classification certificates are small white cards, approximately 2 by 3 inches. The registration certificate specifies the name of the registrant, the date of registration, and the number and address of the local board with which he is registered. Also inscribed upon it are the date and place of the registrant's birth, his residence at registration, his physical description, his signature, and his Selective Service number. The Selective Service number itself indicates his State of registration, his local board, his year of birth, and his chronological position in the local board's classification record. Both the registration and classification certificates bear notices that the registrant must notify his local board in writing of every change in address, physical condition, and occupational, marital, family, dependency, and military status, and of any other fact which might change his classification.

. . . . Under the original 1948 Act, it was unlawful (1) to transfer a certificate to aid a person in making false identification; (2) to possess a certificate not duly issued with the intent of using it for false identification; (3) to forge, alter, "or in any manner" change a certificate or any notation validly inscribed thereon; (4) to photograph or make an imitation of a certificate for the purpose of false identification, and (5) to possess a counterfeited or altered certificate. In addition, as previously mentioned, regulations of the Selective Service System required registrants to keep both their registration and classification certificates in their personal possession at all times. . . . In 1965 Congress added [a provision] subjecting to criminal liability not only one who "forges, alters, or in any manner changes," but also one who "knowingly destroys, [or] knowingly mutilates" a certificate. [T]here is nothing necessarily expressive about such conduct. The Amendment does not distinguish between public and private destruction, and it does not punish only destruction engaged in for the purpose of expressing views.

II

O'Brien . . . argues that the 1965 Amendment is unconstitutional as applied to him because his act of burning his registration certificate was protected "symbolic speech" within the First Amendment. His argument is that the freedom of expression which the First Amendment guarantees includes all modes of "communication of ideas by conduct," and that his conduct is within this definition because he did it in "demonstration against the war and against the draft."

We cannot accept the view that an apparently limitless variety of conduct can be labeled "speech" whenever the person engaging in the conduct intends thereby to express an idea. However, even on the assumption that the alleged communicative element in O'Brien's conduct is sufficient to bring into play the First Amendment, it does not necessarily follow that the destruction of a registration certificate is constitutionally protected activity. This Court has held that, when "speech" and "nonspeech" elements are combined in the same course of conduct, a sufficiently important governmental interest in regulating the nonspeech element can justify incidental limitations on First Amendment freedoms. To characterize the quality of the governmental interest which must appear, the Court has employed a variety of descriptive terms: compelling; substantial; subordinating; paramount; cogent; strong. Whatever imprecision inheres in these terms, we think it clear that a government regulation is sufficiently justified if it is within the constitutional power of the Government; if it furthers an important or substantial governmental interest; if the governmental interest is unrelated to the suppression of free expression; and if the incidental restriction on First Amendment freedoms is no greater than is essential to the furtherance of that interest. We find that the 1965 Amendment to [the 1948] Act meets all of these requirements, and consequently that O'Brien can be constitutionally convicted for violating it.

The constitutional power of Congress to raise and support armies and to make all laws necessary and proper to that end is broad and sweeping. Pursuant to this power, Congress may establish a system of registration for individuals liable for training and service, and may require such individuals, within reason, to cooperate in the registration system. The issuance of certificates indicating the registration and eligibility classification of individuals is a legitimate and substantial administrative aid in the functioning of this system.

. . . Many of these purposes would be defeated by the certificates' destruction or mutilation. Among these are:

1. The registration certificate serves as proof that the individual described thereon has registered for the draft. The classification certificate shows the eligibility classification of a named but undescribed individual. Voluntarily displaying the two certificates is an easy and painless way for a young man to dispel a question as to whether he might be delinquent in his Selective Service obligations. Correspondingly, the availability of the certificates for such display relieves the Selective Service System of the administrative burden it would otherwise have in verifying the registration and classification of all suspected delinquents. Additionally, in a time of national crisis, reasonable availability to each registrant of the two small cards assures a rapid and uncomplicated means for determining his fitness for immediate induction.

2. The information supplied on the certificates facilitates communication between registrants and local boards, simplifying the system and benefiting all concerned.

3. Both certificates carry continual reminders that the registrant must notify his local board of any change of address, and other specified changes in his status. The smooth functioning of the system requires that local boards be continually

aware of the status and whereabouts of registrants, and the destruction of certificates deprives the system of a potentially useful notice device.

4. The regulatory scheme involving Selective Service certificates includes clearly valid prohibitions against the alteration, forgery, or similar deceptive misuse of certificates. The destruction or mutilation of certificates obviously increases the difficulty of detecting and tracing abuses such as these. Further, a mutilated certificate might itself be used for deceptive purposes.

The many functions performed by Selective Service certificates establish beyond doubt that Congress has a legitimate and substantial interest in preventing their wanton and unrestrained destruction and assuring their continuing availability by punishing people who knowingly and willfully destroy or mutilate them. And we are unpersuaded that the preexistence of the nonpossession regulations in any way negates this interest.

. . . In conclusion, we find that, because of the Government's substantial interest in assuring the continuing availability of issued Selective Service certificates, because the 1965 Amendment is an appropriately narrow means of protecting this interest and condemns only the independent noncommunicative impact of conduct within its reach, and because the noncommunicative impact of O'Brien's act of burning his registration certificate frustrated the Government's interest, a sufficient governmental interest has been shown to justify O'Brien's conviction.

QUESTIONS FOR DISCUSSION

6.4   One of the complicated qualities of rules surrounding the First Amendment is that its various doctrines offer similar, although slightly different, ways of evaluating whether an infringement on communication is constitutional. This is sometimes called a standard of review. A court applies this standard to determine whether something is constitutional. Can you identify the standard that the Supreme Court used for evaluating whether the infringement on symbolic speech in *O'Brien* was constitutional?

6.5   Are you convinced that the governmental interests listed in *O'Brien* are genuine and sufficient to justify the abridgment of First Amendment rights? If not, what would be the explanation for the Court's decision?

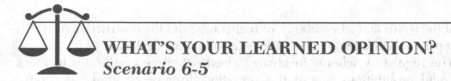

WHAT'S YOUR LEARNED OPINION?
Scenario 6-5

A number of people formed a group named Community for Creative Non-Violence (CCNV). They decided to set up camp and sleep overnight in a park in front of the White House to demonstrate how homeless people live. The National Park Service, which is in charge of managing the park, denied CCNV's request that demonstrators be permitted to sleep in the symbolic tents. The National Park Service maintained that the tent camp would threaten to damage the park and deter tourists from visiting near an important national symbol, The White House. CCNV claims that the park violated members' First Amendment rights by preventing them from using conduct as symbolic expression. Does CCNV have a winning First Amendment claim?

Scenario 6-6

Beginning in 2016, some players in U.S. professional sports chose to kneel instead of standing for the national anthem. They made clear that the reason for this conduct was to protest police brutality when police confront Black men. Do you believe kneeling during the national anthem should be considered protected expression? Do you see any other issues that may bear on whether this conduct is protected by the First Amendment or whether these players could be forced to stand? For example, does the identity of the entity prohibiting the conduct matter?

Flag desecration is often a form of expressive conduct. Yet this action is deeply offensive to many, and thus triggers strong sentiments and questions about whether it should be an exception to the usual First Amendment rules for expressive conduct. In *Street v. New York* (1969), the Supreme Court overturned the flag-burning conviction of a man, holding that an individual cannot be punished for speaking with contempt toward the flag. Similarly, in *Spence v. Washington* (1974), the Court ruled that a peace symbol taped to an American flag was protected under the First Amendment. The issue came to a head again in the 1980s, making its way to the Court in *Texas v. Johnson*.

The dispute in this case arose in 1984 when Johnson attended a political demonstration in Dallas, Texas, during the Republican National Convention with approximately 100 protesters. The purpose of the demonstration was to protest the Reagan administration and to shed light on the deadly consequences of nuclear war. During the protest, Johnson came into possession of an American flag. He subsequently doused the flag in kerosene and set it on fire. As the flag burned, the protestors chanted, "America, the red, white, and blue, we spit on you." Johnson was charged with and convicted of the "desecration of a venerated object" in violation of Texas law. He appealed, arguing that his conviction violated his First Amendment rights.

FROM THE BENCH

TEXAS v. JOHNSON
391 U.S. 397 (1989)

Justice Brennan delivered the opinion of the Court.

The First Amendment literally forbids the abridgment only of "speech," but we have long recognized that its protection does not end at the spoken or written word. Conduct can be labeled "speech" whenever the person engaging in the conduct intends thereby to express an idea. In deciding whether particular conduct possesses sufficient communicative elements to bring the First Amendment into play, we have asked whether "[a]n intent to convey a particularized message was present, and [whether] the likelihood was great that the message would be understood by those who viewed it."

That we have had little difficulty identifying an expressive element in conduct relating to flags should not be surprising. The very purpose of a national flag is to serve as a symbol of our country; it is, one might say, "the one visible manifestation of two hundred years of nationhood." We have not automatically concluded, however, that any action taken with respect to our flag is expressive. Instead, in characterizing such action for First Amendment purposes, we have considered the context in which it occurred.

Johnson burned an American flag as part—indeed, as the culmination—of a political demonstration that coincided with the convening of the Republican Party and its renomination of Ronald Reagan for President. The expressive, overtly political nature of this conduct was both intentional and overwhelmingly apparent.

The government generally has a freer hand in restricting expressive conduct than it has in restricting the written or spoken word. It may not, however, proscribe particular conduct *because* it has expressive elements.

We must first determine whether Johnson's burning of the flag constituted expressive conduct, permitting him to invoke the First Amendment in challenging his conviction. If his conduct was expressive, we next decide whether the State's regulation is related to the suppression of free expression. If the State's regulation is not related to expression, then the less stringent standard we announced in *United States v. O'Brien* for regulations of noncommunicative conduct controls. If it is [expressive], then we are outside of *O'Brien*'s test, and we must ask whether this interest justifies Johnson's conviction under a more demanding standard. A third possibility is that the State's asserted interest is simply not implicated on these facts, and, in that event, the interest drops out of the picture.

Thus, although we have recognized that, where " 'speech' and 'nonspeech' elements are combined in the same course of conduct, a sufficiently important governmental interest in regulating the nonspeech element can justify incidental limitations on First Amendment freedoms." We must decide whether Texas has asserted an interest in support of Johnson's conviction that is unrelated to the suppression of expression. The State offers two separate interests to justify this conviction: preventing breaches of the peace and preserving the flag as a symbol of nationhood and national unity. We hold that the first interest is not implicated on this record, and that the second is related to the suppression of expression.

Texas claims that its interest in preventing breaches of the peace justifies Johnson's conviction for flag desecration. However, no disturbance of the peace actually occurred or threatened to occur because of Johnson's burning of the flag. Although the State stresses the disruptive behavior of the protestors during their march toward City Hall, it admits that "no actual breach of the peace occurred at the time of the flag burning or in response to the flag burning." The only evidence offered by the State at trial to show the reaction to Johnson's actions was the testimony of several persons who had been seriously offended by the flag burning.

The State's position, therefore, amounts to a claim that an audience that takes serious offense at particular expression is necessarily likely to disturb the peace, and that the expression may be prohibited on this basis. Our precedents do not countenance such a presumption. On the contrary, they recognize that a principal "function of free speech under our system of government is to invite dispute. It may indeed best serve its high purpose when it induces a condition of unrest, creates dissatisfaction with conditions as they are, or even stirs people to anger."

Thus, we have not permitted the government to assume that every expression of a provocative idea will incite a riot, but have instead required careful consideration of the actual circumstances surrounding such expression, asking whether the expression "is directed to inciting or producing imminent lawless action and is likely to incite or produce such action." *Brandenburg v. Ohio* (1969). To accept Texas' arguments that it need only demonstrate "the potential for a breach of the peace," and that every flag burning necessarily possesses that potential, would be to eviscerate our holding in *Brandenburg*. This we decline to do.

We thus conclude that the State's interest in maintaining order is not implicated on these facts. The State need not worry that our holding will disable it from preserving the peace. We do not suggest that the First Amendment forbids a State to prevent "imminent lawless action."

. . . It remains to consider whether the State's interest in preserving the flag as a symbol of nationhood and national unity justifies Johnson's conviction. Texas argues that its interest in preserving the flag as a symbol of nationhood and national unity survives this close analysis. The State's claim is that it has an interest in preserving the flag as a symbol of nationhood and national unity, a symbol with a determinate range of meanings.

Moreover, Johnson was prosecuted because he knew that his politically charged expression would cause "serious offense." If he had burned the flag as a means of disposing of it because it was dirty or torn, he would not have been convicted of flag desecration under this Texas law: federal law designates burning as the preferred means of disposing of a flag "when it is in such condition that it is no longer a fitting emblem for display," and Texas has no quarrel with this means of disposal. The Texas law is thus not aimed at protecting the physical integrity of the flag in all circumstances, but is designed instead to protect it only against impairments that would cause serious offense to others.

. . . If there is a bedrock principle underlying the First Amendment, it is that the government may not prohibit the expression of an idea simply because society finds the idea itself offensive or disagreeable. We have not recognized an exception to this principle even where our flag has been involved.

In short, nothing in our precedents suggests that a State may foster its own view of the flag by prohibiting expressive conduct relating to it. To bring its argument outside our precedents, Texas attempts to convince us that, even if its interest in preserving the flag's symbolic role does not allow it to prohibit words or some expressive conduct critical of the flag, it does permit it to forbid the outright destruction of the flag. The State's argument cannot depend here on the distinction between written or spoken words and nonverbal conduct. That distinction, we have shown, is of no moment where the nonverbal conduct is expressive, as it is here, and where the regulation of that conduct is related to expression, as it is here.

Texas' focus on the precise nature of Johnson's expression, moreover, misses the point of our prior decisions: their enduring lesson, that the government may not prohibit expression simply because it disagrees with its message, is not dependent on the particular mode in which one chooses to express an idea. If we were to hold that a State may forbid flag burning wherever it is likely to endanger the flag's symbolic role, but allow it wherever burning a flag promotes that role—as where, for example, a person ceremoniously burns a dirty flag—we would be saying that when it comes to impairing the flag's physical integrity, the flag itself may be used as a symbol—as a substitute for the written or spoken word or a "short cut from mind to mind"—only in one direction. We would be permitting a State to "prescribe what shall be orthodox" by saying that one may burn the flag to convey one's attitude toward it and its referents only if one does not endanger the flag's representation of nationhood and national unity.

To conclude that the government may permit designated symbols to be used to communicate only a limited set of messages would be to enter territory having no discernible or defensible boundaries.

It is not the State's ends, but its means, to which we object. It cannot be gainsaid that there is a special place reserved for the flag in this Nation, and thus we do not doubt that the government has a legitimate interest in making efforts to "preserv[e] the national flag as an unalloyed symbol of our country." To say that the government has an interest in encouraging proper treatment of the flag, however, is not to say that it may criminally punish a person for burning a flag as a means of political protest.

We are fortified in today's conclusion by our conviction that forbidding criminal punishment for conduct such as Johnson's will not endanger the special role played by our flag or the feelings it inspires. We are tempted to say, in fact, that the flag's deservedly cherished place in our community will be strengthened, not weakened, by our holding today. Our decision is a reaffirmation of the principles of freedom and inclusiveness that the flag best reflects, and of the conviction that our toleration of criticism such as Johnson's is a sign and source of our strength. Indeed, one of the proudest images of our flag, the one immortalized in our own national anthem, is of the bombardment it survived at Fort McHenry. It is the Nation's resilience, not its rigidity, that Texas sees reflected in the flag—and it is that resilience that we reassert today.

Precisely because it is our flag that is involved, one's response to the flag-burner may exploit the uniquely persuasive power of the flag itself. We can imagine no more appropriate response to burning a flag than waving one's own, no better way to counter a flag burner's message than by saluting the flag that burns, no surer means of preserving the dignity even of the flag that burned than by—as one witness here did—according its remains a respectful burial. We do not consecrate the flag by punishing its desecration, for in doing so we dilute the freedom that this cherished emblem represents.

Chief Justice R̲E̲H̲N̲Q̲U̲I̲S̲T̲, with whom Justice W̲H̲I̲T̲E̲ and Justice O'C̲O̲N̲N̲O̲R̲ join, dissenting.

In holding this Texas statute unconstitutional, the Court ignores Justice Holmes' familiar aphorism that "a page of history is worth a volume of logic." For more than 200 years, the American flag has occupied a unique position as the symbol of our Nation, a uniqueness that justifies a governmental prohibition against flag burning in the way respondent Johnson did here.

The flag symbolizes the Nation in peace as well as in war. It signifies our national presence on battleships, airplanes, military installations, and public buildings from the United States Capitol to the thousands of county courthouses and city halls throughout the country. Two flags are prominently placed in our courtroom. Countless flags are placed by the graves of loved ones each year on what was first called Decoration Day, and is now called Memorial Day. The flag is traditionally placed on the casket of deceased members of the Armed Forces, and it is later given to the deceased's family. Congress has provided that the flag be flown at half-staff upon the death of the President, Vice President, and other government officials "as a mark of respect to their memory."

No other American symbol has been as universally honored as the flag. In 1931, Congress declared "The Star-Spangled Banner" to be our national anthem. In 1987, John Philip Sousa's "The Stars and Stripes Forever" was designated as the national march. Congress has also established "The Pledge of Allegiance to the Flag" and the manner of its deliverance.

The American flag, then, throughout more than 200 years of our history, has come to be the visible symbol embodying our Nation. It does not represent the views of any particular political party, and it does not represent any particular political philosophy. The flag is not simply another "idea" or "point of view" competing for recognition in the marketplace of ideas. Millions and millions of Americans regard it with an almost mystical reverence regardless of what sort of social, political, or philosophical beliefs they may have. I cannot agree that the First Amendment invalidates the Act of Congress, and the laws of 48 of the 50 States, which make criminal the public burning of the flag.

Here it may equally well be said that the public burning of the American flag by Johnson was no essential part of any exposition of ideas, and at the same time it had a tendency to incite a breach of the peace. Johnson was free to make any verbal denunciation of the flag that he wished; indeed, he was free to burn the flag in private. He could publicly burn other symbols of the Government or effigies of political leaders. He did lead a march through the streets of Dallas, and conducted a rally in front of the Dallas City Hall. He engaged in a "die-in" to protest nuclear weapons. He shouted out various slogans during the march, including: "Reagan, Mondale which will it be? Either one means World War III"; "Ronald Reagan, killer of the hour, Perfect example of U.S. power"; and "red, white and blue, we spit on you, you stand for plunder, you will go under." Brief for Respondent 3. For none of these acts was he arrested or prosecuted; it was only when he proceeded to burn publicly an American flag stolen from its rightful owner that he violated the Texas statute.

The Texas statute deprived Johnson of only one rather inarticulate symbolic form of protest—a form of protest that was profoundly offensive to many—and left him with a full panoply of other symbols and every conceivable form of verbal expression to express his deep disapproval of national policy. Thus, in no way can it be said that Texas is punishing him because his hearers—or any other group of people—were profoundly opposed to the message that he sought to convey. Such opposition is no proper basis for restricting speech or expression under the First Amendment. It was Johnson's use of this particular symbol, and not the idea that he sought to convey by it or by his many other expressions, for which he was punished.

FROM THE BENCH

Justice STEVENS, dissenting.

As the Court analyzes this case, it presents the question whether the State of Texas, or indeed the Federal Government, has the power to prohibit the public desecration of the American flag. The question is unique. In my judgment rules that apply to a host of other symbols, such as state flags, armbands, or various privately promoted emblems of political or commercial identity, are not necessarily controlling. Even if flag burning could be considered just another species of symbolic speech under the logical application of the rules that the Court has developed in its interpretation of the First Amendment in other contexts, this case has an intangible dimension that makes those rules inapplicable.

A country's flag is a symbol of more than "nationhood and national unity." It also signifies the ideas that characterize the society that has chosen that emblem as well as the special history that has animated the growth and power of those ideas. The fleurs-de-lis and the tricolor both symbolized "nationhood and national unity," but they had vastly different meanings. The message conveyed by some flags—the swastika, for example—may survive long after it has outlived its usefulness as a symbol of regimented unity in a particular nation.

So it is with the American flag. It is more than a proud symbol of the courage, the determination, and the gifts of nature that transformed 13 fledgling Colonies into a world power. It is a symbol of freedom, of equal opportunity, of religious tolerance, and of good will for other peoples who share our aspirations. The symbol carries its message to dissidents both at home and abroad who may have no interest at all in our national unity or survival.

The value of the flag as a symbol cannot be measured. Even so, I have no doubt that the interest in preserving that value for the future is both significant and legitimate. Conceivably that value will be enhanced by the Court's conclusion that our national commitment to free expression is so strong that even the United States as ultimate guarantor of that freedom is without power to prohibit the desecration of its unique symbol. But I am unpersuaded. The creation of a federal right to post bulletin boards and graffiti on the Washington Monument might enlarge the market for free expression, but at a cost I would not pay. Similarly, in my considered judgment, sanctioning the public desecration of the flag will tarnish its value—both for those who cherish the ideas for which it waves and for those who desire to don the robes of martyrdom by burning it. That tarnish is not justified by the trivial burden on free expression occasioned by requiring that an available, alternative mode of expression including uttering words critical of the flag, be employed.

The ideas of liberty and equality have been an irresistible force in motivating leaders like Patrick Henry, Susan B. Anthony, and Abraham Lincoln, schoolteachers like Nathan Hale and Booker T. Washington, the Philippine Scouts who fought at Bataan, and the soldiers who scaled the bluff at Omaha Beach. If those ideas are worth fighting for—and our history demonstrates that they are—it cannot be true that the flag that uniquely symbolizes their power is not itself worthy of protection from unnecessary desecration. I respectfully dissent.

QUESTIONS FOR DISCUSSION

6.6 Justice Stevens was known as a Court liberal. He was a Justice who could generally be relied on to vote in favor of whatever civil liberty was at issue in a case. Given this reputation, one would have expected him to vote in favor of Johnson's First Amendment rights. But he did not do that and instead dissented from the majority opinion. Of course, we cannot read his mind and—without further evidence—identify why he voted the way he did. But we can think about what—in his background, age, or life experience—motivated him to take this step that was unusual for him. After consulting the brief biographical description of him in the appendix, do you have any thoughts on this?

6.7 Note that each of the opinions reproduced above had little rigorous legal doctrine. Instead, each opinion is notable for various rhetorical devices that the Justices used to drive home the accuracy of their views. Can you identify any of those rhetorical devices?

BEHIND THE CURTAIN

Johnson was represented in his case before the Supreme Court by a famous civil rights lawyer, William Kunstler. Kunstler had represented many activists—some of whom were regarded as "radicals"—during the 1960s and 1970s. Some of his most famous clients included prison inmates who created dramatic unrest at Attica State Prison in New York. Kunstler had a reputation for a feisty, flamboyant temperament, a quality that came in handy as he represented African American citizens accused of murdering police officers, and the Chicago Seven, individuals accused of conspiring to

Attorney William Kunstler with defendant Gregory Lee Johnson circa 1989. *Seidenstein/Wikimedia Commons.*

incite riots in Chicago during the 1968 Democratic Convention. During the oral argument in *Texas v. Johnson*, Kunstler managed the following snipe at the Justices:

> By the way, talking about flags in front of the Supreme Court, when I came today, the flags were up in the rain, and under 36 U.S. Code, the leading provision there is [that] flags shall not be displayed in inclement weather.

3. Freedom of the Press

Along with its explicit protection of freedom of speech, the First Amendment also provides for freedom "of the press." One might wonder whether this means that the press should receive special constitutional protection. The U.S. Supreme Court has avoided proclaiming this in its decisions. To be sure, many of the general principles covered in this chapter help to serve press freedoms and to ensure that the press can do its job. These include special scrutiny of content-based regulation and prior restraints against speech. The Supreme Court has also developed specialized doctrines designed to protect the press. These primarily cover rules designed to facilitate media access to information and government institutions, including court filings and proceedings. The Court has also placed restrictions on a judge's decision to "gag" litigation participants from speaking to the press and to impose protective orders on the disclosure of information obtained as part of private litigation. In addition, the Court has provided nuanced rules governing publication of private facts about the lives of individuals, protection of confidential sources, and the public's access to different types of media and the press.

By far, the most famous of the Supreme Court's rulings in this area concerns the liability of the press for defamation. Generally speaking, a communication is defamatory if the statement made (1) tends to blacken the reputation of the plaintiff in the community, (2) is "of and concerning" the plaintiff, and (3) was published (made available to) to at least one party other than the plaintiff and the defendant. Until 1964, a plaintiff did not encounter a high bar in proving these elements, which required only that the press did not act reasonably in publishing something that was defamatory. In other words, a mere negligent mistake was sufficient to establish liability. Two forms of defamation exist: libel (written defamation) and slander (oral defamation).

On constitutional law issues, the Supreme Court has issued several "thunderbolt" cases: The 1964 decision in *New York Times Co. v. Sullivan* is certainly one. The decision was very much a creature of its times. Nonviolent protests such as those organized and led by Dr. Martin Luther King, Jr. during the civil rights era spread the movement across the country. Faced with evidence of injustice, the nation demanded change. The press played an integral role in telling the story of the protests and the struggles of the movement. However, in 1960, a case rose through the Alabama state courts that threatened the movement's forward momentum.

The case focused on an advertisement in the *New York Times* stating that nonviolent civil rights demonstrations against segregation in the South were encountering a "wave of terror" from officials there. The plaintiff in the case, L.B. Sullivan, was the public safety commissioner for Montgomery, Alabama. He was not named in the advertisement, but he claimed that its description of police conduct negatively reflected on him as the administrator of the Montgomery, Alabama, police. As such, the dispute was not only an outgrowth of the civil rights movement in the 1960s but was also evidence of efforts by southern

The New York Times.

NEW YORK, TUESDAY, MARCH 29, 1960.

*"The growing movement of peaceful mass
demonstrations by Negroes is something
new in the South, something understandable....
Let Congress heed their rising voices,
for they will be heard."*
—*New York Times editorial
Saturday, March 19, 1960*

Heed Their Rising Voices

As the whole world knows by now, thousands of Southern Negro students are engaged in widespread non-violent demonstrations in positive affirmation of the right to live in human dignity as guaranteed by the U. S. Constitution and the Bill of Rights. In their efforts to uphold these guarantees, they are being met by an unprecedented wave of terror by those who would deny and negate that document which the whole world looks upon as setting the pattern for modern freedom....

In Orangeburg, South Carolina, when 400 students peacefully sought to buy doughnuts and coffee at lunch counters in the business district, they were forcibly ejected, tear-gassed, soaked to the skin in freezing weather with fire hoses, arrested en masse and herded into an open barbed-wire stockade to stand for hours in the bitter cold.

In Montgomery, Alabama, after students sang "My Country, 'Tis of Thee" on the State Capitol steps, their leaders were expelled from school, and truckloads of police armed with shotguns and tear-gas ringed the Alabama State College Campus. When the entire student body protested to state authorities by refusing to re-register, their dining hall was padlocked in an attempt to starve them into submission.

In Tallahassee, Atlanta, Nashville, Savannah, Greensboro, Memphis, Richmond, Charlotte, and a host of other cities in the South, young American teenagers, in face of the entire weight of official state apparatus and police power, have boldly stepped forth as protagonists of democracy. Their courage and amazing restraint have inspired millions and given a new dignity to the cause of freedom.

Small wonder that the Southern violators of the Constitution fear this new, non-violent brand of freedom fighter . . . even as they fear the upswelling right-to-vote movement. Small wonder that they are determined to destroy the one man who, more than any other, symbolizes the new spirit now sweeping the South—the Rev. Dr. Martin Luther King, Jr., world-famous leader of the Montgomery Bus Protest. For it is his doctrine of non-violence which has inspired and guided the students in their widening wave of sit-ins; and it this same Dr. King who founded and is president of the Southern Christian Leadership Conference—the organization which is spearheading the surging right-to-vote movement. Under Dr. King's direction the Leadership Conference conducts Student Workshops and Seminars in the philosophy and technique of non-violent resistance.

Again and again the Southern violators have answered Dr. King's peaceful protests with intimidation and violence. They have bombed his home almost killing his wife and child. They have assaulted his person. They have arrested him seven times—for "speeding," "loitering" and similar "offenses." And now they have charged him with "perjury"—a felony under which they could imprison him for ten years. Obviously, their real purpose is to remove him physically as the leader to whom the students and millions

of others—look for guidance and support, and thereby to intimidate *all* leaders who may rise in the South. Their strategy is to behead this affirmative movement, and thus to demoralize Negro Americans and weaken their will to struggle. The defense of Martin Luther King, spiritual leader of the student sit-in movement, clearly, therefore, is an integral part of the total struggle for freedom in the South.

Decent-minded Americans cannot help but applaud the creative daring of the students and the quiet heroism of Dr. King. But this is one of those moments in the stormy history of Freedom when men and women of good will must do more than applaud the rising-to-glory of others. The America whose good name hangs in the balance before a watchful world, the America whose heritage of Liberty these Southern Upholders of the Constitution are defending, is our America as well as theirs...

We must heed their rising voices—yes—but we must add our own.

We must extend ourselves above and beyond moral support and render the material help so urgently needed by those who are taking the risks, facing jail, and even death in a glorious re-affirmation of our Constitution and its Bill of Rights.

We urge you to join hands with our fellow Americans in the South by supporting, with your dollars, this Combined Appeal for all three needs—the defense of Martin Luther King—the support of the embattled students—and the struggle for the right-to-vote.

Your Help Is Urgently Needed . . . NOW!!

Stella Adler
Raymond Pace Alexander
Shelly Appelton
Harry Van Arsdale
Harry Belafonte
Julie Belafonte
Dr. Algernon Black
Marc Blitzstein
William Bowe
William Branch
Marlon Brando
Mrs. Ralph Bunche
Diahann Carroll
Dr. Alan Knight Chalmers

Joseph Cohen
Richard Coe
Nat King Cole
Cheryl Crawford
Dorothy Dandridge
Ossie Davis
Sammy Davis, Jr.
Ruby Dee
Harry Duffy
Scotty Eckford
Dr. Philip Elliott
Dr. Harry Emerson Fosdick

Anthony Franciosa
Mathew Guinan
Lorraine Hansbury
Rev. Donald Harrington
Nat Hentoff
James Hicks
Mary Hinkson
Van Heflin
Langston Hughes
Morris Iushewitz
Mahalia Jackson
Paul Jennings
Mordecai Johnson
John Killens

Eartha Kitt
Rabbi Edward Klein
Hope Lange
John Lewis
Viveca Lindfors
David Livingston
William Michelson
Carl Murphy
Don Murray
John Murray
A. J. Muste
Frederick O'Neal
Peter Orlley
L. Joseph Overton

Albert P. Palmer
Clarence Pickett
Shad Polier
Sidney Poitier
Michael Potolow
A. Philip Randolph
John Raitt
Elmer Rice
Cleveland Robinson
Jackie Robinson
Mrs. Eleanor Roosevelt
Bayard Rustin
Robert Ryan
Maureen Stapleton

Frank Silvera
Louis Singer
Hope Stevens
David Sullivan
Julius Suni
George Tabori
Rev. Gardner C. Taylor
Norman Thomas
Kenneth Tynan
Charles White
Shelley Winters
Max Youngstein

We in the south who are struggling daily for dignity and freedom warmly endorse this appeal

Rev. Ralph D. Abernathy
(Montgomery, Ala.)

Rev. Fred L. Shuttlesworth
(Birmingham, Ala.)

Rev. Kelley Miller Smith
(Nashville, Tenn.)

Rev. W. A. Dennis
(Chattanooga, Tenn.)

Rev. C. K. Steele
(Tallahassee, Fla.)

Rev. Matthew D. McCollom
(Orangeburg, S. C.)

Rev. William Holmes Borders
(Atlanta, Ga.)

Rev. Douglas Moore
(Durham, N. C.)

Rev. Wyatt Tee Walker
(Petersburg, Va.)

Rev. Walter L. Hamilton
(Norfolk, Va.)

I. S. Levy
(Columbia, S. C.)

Rev. Martin Luther King, Sr.
(Atlanta, Ga.)

Rev. Henry C. Bunton
(Memphis, Tenn.)

Rev. S. S. Seay, Sr.
(Montgomery, Ala.)

Rev. Samuel W. Williams
(Atlanta, Ga.)

Rev. A. L. Davis
(New Orleans, La.)

Mrs. Katie E. Whickham
(New Orleans, La.)

Rev. W. H. Hall
(Hattiesburg, Miss.)

Rev. J. E. Lowery
(Mobile, Ala.)

Rev. T. J. Jemison
(Baton Rouge, La.)

COMMITTEE TO DEFEND MARTIN LUTHER KING AND THE STRUGGLE FOR FREEDOM IN THE SOUTH
312 West 125th Street, New York 27, N. Y. UNiversity 6-1700

Chairmen: A. Philip Randolph, Dr. Gardner C. Taylor; *Chairmen of Cultural Division:* Harry Belafonte, Sidney Poitier; *Treasurer:* Nat King Cole; *Executive Director:* Bayard Rustin; *Chairmen of Church Division:* Father George B. Ford, Rev. Harry Emerson Fosdick, Rev. Thomas Kilgore, Jr., Rabbi Edward E. Klein; *Chairmen of Labor Division:* Morris Iushewitz, Cleveland Robinson

Please mail this coupon TODAY!

**Committee To Defend Martin Luther King
and
The Struggle For Freedom In The South**
312 West 125th Street, New York 27, N. Y.
UNiversity 6-1700

I am enclosing my contribution of $........
for the work of the Committee.

(PLEASE PRINT)

Name ....

Address ....

City .... Zone ...... State ....

☐ I want to help   ☐ Please send further information

Please make checks payable to:
Committee To Defend Martin Luther King

This full-page advertisement, "Heed Their Rising Voices," appeared in the *New York Times*, March 29, 1960. *Courtesy of the National Archives (National Archives Identifier 2641477).*

officials to use state defamation law to discourage northern newspapers from covering attempts to quell civil rights demonstrations. Relying on Alabama libel law, the jury found in favor of Sullivan. The Alabama courts all upheld a damage award of $500,000—an extremely large sum for the time.

The state courts' decisions immediately had a ripple effect. Those in power began to use the threat of libel to stifle the civil rights movement. It was difficult for publications to report on any civil rights actions in the South because any error, no matter the intent, could hit the publication with a bankruptcy-inducing libel case.

The U.S. Supreme Court, however, reversed the large judgment that Sullivan had won as a public official, holding that the First Amendment requires proof of a heightened standard of care for a public official to successfully recover for defamation.

FROM THE BENCH

NEW YORK TIMES CO. v. SULLIVAN
376 U.S. 254 (1964)

Mr. Justice BRENNAN delivered the opinion of the Court.

We are required in this case to determine for the first time the extent to which the constitutional protections for speech and press limit a State's power to award damages in a libel action brought by a public official against critics of his official conduct.

Respondent L. B. Sullivan is one of the three elected Commissioners of the City of Montgomery, Alabama. He testified that he was "Commissioner of Public Affairs and the duties are supervision of the Police Department, Fire Department, Department of Cemetery and Department of Scales." He brought this civil libel action against the four individual petitioners, who are Negroes and Alabama clergymen, and against petitioner the New York Times Company, a New York corporation which publishes the New York Times, a daily newspaper. A jury in the Circuit Court of Montgomery County awarded him damages of $500,000, the full amount claimed, against all the petitioners, and the Supreme Court of Alabama affirmed.

Respondent's complaint alleged that he had been libeled by statements in a full-page advertisement that was carried in the New York Times on March 29, 1960. Entitled "Heed Their Rising Voices," the advertisement began by stating that "As the whole world knows by now, thousands of Southern Negro students are engaged in widespread non-violent demonstrations in positive affirmation of the right to live in human dignity as guaranteed by the U.S. Constitution and the Bill of Rights." It went on to charge that "in their efforts to uphold these guarantees, they are being met by an unprecedented wave of terror by those who would deny and negate that document which the whole world looks upon as setting the pattern for modern freedom." Succeeding paragraphs purported to illustrate the "wave of terror" by describing certain alleged events. The text concluded with an appeal for funds.

Of the 10 paragraphs of text in the advertisement, the third and a portion of the sixth were the basis of respondent's claim of libel. They read as follows:

Third paragraph:
"In Montgomery, Alabama, after students sang 'My Country, 'Tis of Thee' on the State Capitol steps, their leaders were expelled from school, and truckloads of police armed with shotguns and tear-gas ringed the Alabama State College Campus. When the entire student body protested to state authorities by refusing to re-register, their dining hall was padlocked in an attempt to starve them into submission."
Sixth paragraph:
"Again and again the Southern violators have answered Dr. King's peaceful protests with intimidation and violence. They have bombed his home almost killing his wife and child. They have assaulted his person. They have arrested him seven times—for 'speeding,' 'loitering' and similar 'offenses.'"

It is uncontroverted that some of the statements contained in the two paragraphs were not accurate descriptions of events which occurred in Montgomery. Although Negro students staged a demonstration on the State Capital steps, they sang the National Anthem and not "My Country, 'Tis of Thee." Although nine students were expelled by the State Board of Education, this was not for leading the demonstration at the Capitol, but for demanding service at a lunch counter in the Montgomery County Courthouse on another day. Not the entire student body, but most of it, had protested the expulsion, not by refusing to register, but by boycotting classes on a single day; virtually all the students did register for the ensuing semester. The campus dining hall was not padlocked on any occasion, and the only students who may have been barred from eating there were the few who had neither signed a preregistration application nor requested temporary meal tickets. Although the police were deployed near the campus in large numbers on three occasions, they did not at any time "ring" the campus, and they were not called to the campus in connection with the demonstration on the State Capitol steps, as the third paragraph implied. Dr. King had not been arrested seven times, but only four; and although he claimed to have been assaulted some years earlier in connection with his arrest for loitering outside a courtroom, one of the officers who made the arrest denied that there was such an assault. . . .

. . . We hold that the rule of law applied by the Alabama courts is constitutionally deficient for failure to provide the safeguards for freedom of speech and

FROM THE BENCH

of the press that are required by the First and Fourteenth Amendments in a libel action brought by a public official against critics of his official conduct. We further hold that under the proper safeguards the evidence presented in this case is constitutionally insufficient to support the judgment for respondent.

The question before us is whether this rule of liability, as applied to an action brought by a public official against critics of his official conduct, abridges the freedom of speech and of the press that is guaranteed by the First and Fourteenth Amendments. The general proposition that freedom of expression upon public questions is secured by the First Amendment has long been settled by our decisions. The constitutional safeguard, we have said, "was fashioned to assure unfettered interchange of ideas for the bringing about of political and social changes desired by the people." Thus we consider this case against the background of a profound national commitment to the principle that debate on public issues should be uninhibited, robust, and wide-open, and that it may well include vehement, caustic, and sometimes unpleasantly sharp attacks on government and public officials. The present advertisement, as an expression of grievance and protest on one of the major public issues of our time, would seem clearly to qualify for the constitutional protection. The question is whether it forfeits that protection by the falsity of some of its factual statements and by its alleged defamation of respondent.

Authoritative interpretations of the First Amendment guarantees have consistently refused to recognize an exception for any test of truth—whether administered by judges, juries, or administrative officials—and especially one that puts the burden of proving truth on the speaker. The constitutional protection does not turn upon "the truth, popularity, or social utility of the ideas and beliefs which are offered." As Madison said, "Some degree of abuse is inseparable from the proper use of everything; and in no instance is this more true than in that of the press." [E]rroneous statement is inevitable in free debate, and that it must be protected if the freedoms of expression are to have the "breathing space" that they "need . . . to survive." Criticism of their official conduct does not lose its constitutional protection merely because it is effective criticism and hence diminishes their official reputations.

If neither factual error nor defamatory content suffices to remove the constitutional shield from criticism of official conduct, the combination of the two elements is no less inadequate. This is the lesson to be drawn from the great controversy over the Sedition Act of 1798, which first crystallized a national awareness of the central meaning of the First Amendment. That statute made it a crime, punishable by a $5,000 fine and five years in prison, "if any person shall write, print, utter or publish . . . any false, scandalous and malicious writing or writings against the government of the United States, or either house of the Congress . . . , or the President . . . , with intent to defame . . . or to bring them, or either of them, into contempt or disrepute; or to excite against them, or either or any of them, the hatred of the good people of the United States." The Act allowed the defendant the defense of truth, and provided that the jury were to be judges both of the law and the facts. Despite these qualifications, the Act was vigorously condemned as unconstitutional in an attack joined in by Jefferson and Madison.

Although the Sedition Act was never tested in this Court, the attack upon its validity has carried the day in the court of history. Fines levied in its prosecution were repaid by Act of Congress on the ground that it was unconstitutional. Calhoun, reporting to the Senate on February 4, 1836, assumed that its invalidity was a matter "which no one now doubts." Jefferson, as President, pardoned those who had been convicted and sentenced under the Act and remitted their fines.

The state rule of law is not saved by its allowance of the defense of truth. A rule compelling the critic of official conduct to guarantee the truth of all his factual assertions—and to do so on pain of libel judgments virtually unlimited in amount—leads to a comparable "self-censorship." Allowance of the defense of truth, with the burden of proving it on the defendant, does not mean that only false speech will be deterred. Under such a rule, would-be critics of official conduct may be deterred from voicing their criticism, even though it is believed to be true and even though it is in fact true, because of doubt whether it can be proved in court or fear of the expense of having to do so. They tend to make only statements which "steer far wider of the unlawful zone." The rule thus dampens the vigor and limits the variety of public debate. It is inconsistent with the First and Fourteenth Amendments.

The constitutional guarantees require, we think, a federal rule that prohibits a public official from recovering damages for a defamatory falsehood relating to his official conduct unless he proves that the statement was made with "actual malice"—that is, with knowledge that it was false or with reckless disregard of whether it was false or not.

We hold today that the Constitution delimits a State's power to award damages for libel in actions brought by public officials against critics of their official conduct. Since this is such an action, the rule requiring proof of actual malice is applicable. [W]e consider that the proof presented to show actual malice lacks the convincing clarity which the constitutional standard demands, and hence that it would not constitutionally sustain the judgment for respondent under the proper rule of law. The case of the individual petitioners requires little discussion. Even assuming that they could constitutionally be found to have authorized the use of their names on the advertisement, there was no evidence whatever that they were aware of any erroneous statements or were in any way reckless in that regard. The judgment against them is thus without constitutional support. As to the Times, we similarly conclude that the facts do not support a finding of actual malice.

The judgment of the Supreme Court of Alabama is reversed and the case is remanded to that court for further proceedings not inconsistent with this opinion.

Reversed and remanded.

QUESTIONS FOR DISCUSSION

6.8 The principal effect of the *New York Times Co. v. Sullivan* case was to create a new standard of fault that a defamation plaintiff—who is a public official—must prove to recover damages. The *New York Times Co. v. Sullivan* standard of fault is more difficult to establish than the previous level of fault imposed in defamation cases: regular negligence. As explained above, a plaintiff can establish regular negligence simply by showing that the defendant made a mistake that a reasonable person exercising reasonable care would not make. In justifying this decision to make it more difficult for the public official plaintiff to win, the Court stated the following:

> [E]rroneous statement is inevitable in free debate, and that it must be protected if the freedoms of expression are to have the "breathing space" that they "need . . . to survive." . . . A rule compelling the critic of official conduct to guarantee the truth of all his factual assertions—and to do so on pain of libel judgments virtually unlimited in amount—leads to a comparable "self-censorship." Allowance of the defense of truth, with the burden of proving it on the defendant, does not mean that only false speech will be deterred. Under such a rule, would-be critics of official conduct may be deterred from voicing their criticism, even though it is believed to be true and even though it is in fact true, because of doubt whether it can be proved in court or fear of the expense of having to do so. They tend to make only statements which "steer far wider of the unlawful zone."

Explain what the Court was concerned about in making this statement.

6.9 Take note of the specific details of the standard of fault that the Court imposed on the public official in *New York Times Co. v. Sullivan*: making a statement with knowledge of its falsity or reckless disregard for its falsity. What was the Court trying to regulate with this standard? Specifically, what types of activity was the Court trying to protect and what types of activity was the Court trying to subject to liability?

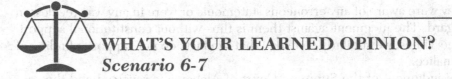

WHAT'S YOUR LEARNED OPINION?
Scenario 6-7

Irvin Thomas, a columnist for *The National Times*, published an article about Congressman Elijah Li, alleging that Li was having an affair with his tennis partner. Thomas did several interviews with confidential sources. Prior to publication, the column was read by other newspaper personnel for accuracy. Congressman Li claimed that the newspaper had previously failed to check the accuracy of the column and sued for libel. Is it likely that he would be successful in establishing his libel claim?

Scenario 6-8

An internationally renowned professor at a private university, Fatima Costa, collected petition signatures in support of a complete ban of fossil fuels. Professor Costa frequently injects herself into high-visibility disputes about public policy. The House Energy and Commerce Committee took an interest in the professor's efforts and held a hearing. In the hearing, the Committee requested that she provide them with the names of the individuals who had signed her petition. The professor refused to do so, fearing that there might be some repercussions for those who signed. The university radio show was critical of this professor in the past, running multiple negative pieces on her research and her teaching style. After the hearing, the show falsely reported that the professor had been cited for contempt of Congress. The professor sued the radio show for defamation. Does the actual malice standard apply to the professor's suit?

Showing its commitment to press freedoms in this corner of the law, the Supreme Court has handed down several cases parsing out aspects of this holding and expounded on the definitions of a "public official," "defamatory falsehood," and "actual malice." Since *Sullivan*, the Court has also expanded the rule and spirit of *Sullivan* to include public figures, limited-purpose public figures, and some private persons who speak on matters of public interest as well. According to the Court, private figures may also be considered public if they choose to "thrust themselves to the forefront of particular public controversies in order to influence the resolution of the issues involved." Finally, the Court has extended *Sullivan*—along with its refinements—into suits based on legal theories that are similar to, but different from, defamation. These theories include a claim for intentional infliction of emotional distress, which is the subject of the decision in *Hustler v. Falwell*, which is presented in connection with law and humor later in this chapter. Despite the general popularity and embrace of the *New York Times Co. v. Sullivan* rule, the rule has its detractors. Notably, Justice Clarence Thomas has stated that he believes that *New York Times Co. v. Sullivan* was wrongly decided, declaring that the decision was policy-driven, "masquerading as constitutional law."

D. School Interests in Imparting Moral Values and Substantive Knowledge Versus Encouraging Creative Thinking, Personal Autonomy, and Free Expression for Students

The question of First Amendment protection of expressive conduct takes on a unique twist in the context of young people and public secondary schools. Skilled teaching of teenagers requires ensuring uninterrupted efforts to educate students on substantive material including humanities, social sciences, math, and science, as well as the values of civility, discipline, and order. At the same time, the values of U.S. society also counsel toward promoting understanding and protecting constitutional concepts such as the value of free expression, particularly extending protection for creative thinking and expressing political opinions that bear on the operation of governmental matters. The following group of cases illustrate how the U.S. Supreme Court has navigated that tension.

The landmark case in this area, *Tinker v. Des Moines Independent Community School District*, follows. In 1965, five Des Moines public school students were suspended for wearing black armbands in protest of the Vietnam War. Following nationwide public protests, school officials claimed they were concerned about the volatile situation and needed to ban the armbands to maintain order and discipline without disruption.

FROM THE BENCH

TINKER v. DES MOINES INDEPENDENT COMMUNITY SCHOOL DISTRICT
393 U.S. 503 (1969)

Justice FORTAS delivered the opinion of the Court.

In December, 1965, a group of adults and students in Des Moines [Iowa] held a meeting at the Eckhardt home. The group decided to publicize their objections to the hostilities in Vietnam and demonstrate their support for a truce by wearing black armbands during the holiday season.

The principals of the Des Moines schools became aware of the plan to wear armbands. On December 14, 1965, they met and adopted a policy that any student wearing an armband to school would be asked to remove it, and, if he refused, he would be suspended until he returned without the armband.

On December 16, Mary Beth and Christopher [Tinker] wore black armbands to their schools. John Tinker wore his armband the next day. They were all sent home and suspended from school until they would come back without their armbands.

First Amendment rights, applied in light of the special characteristics of the school environment, are available to teachers and students. It can hardly be argued that neither students or teachers shed their constitutional rights to freedom of speech or expression at the schoolhouse gate. This has been the unmistakable holding of this Court for almost 50 years.

On the other hand, the Court has repeatedly emphasized the need for affirming the comprehensive authority of the States and of school officials, consistent with fundamental constitutional safeguards, to prescribe and control conduct in the schools. Our problem lies in the area where students in the exercise of First Amendment rights collide with the rules of the school authorities.

The problem posed by the present case does not relate to regulation of the length of skirts or the type of clothing, to hair style, or deportment. It does not concern aggressive, disruptive action or even group demonstrations. Our problem involves direct, primary First Amendment rights akin to "pure speech."

The school officials banned and sought to punish petitioners for a silent, passive expression of opinion, unaccompanied by any disorder or disturbance on the part of petitioners. There is here no evidence whatever of petitioners' interference, actual or nascent, with the schools' work or of collision with the rights of other students to be secure and to be let alone. Accordingly, this case does not concern speech or action that intrudes upon the work of the schools or the rights of other students. . . . In order for the State in the person of school officials to justify prohibition of a particular expression of opinion, it must be able to show that its action was caused by something more than a mere desire to avoid the discomfort and unpleasantness that always accompany an unpopular viewpoint.

Our independent examination of the record fails to yield evidence that the school authorities had reason to anticipate that the wearing of the armbands would substantially interfere with the work of the school or impinge upon the rights of other students. Even an official memorandum prepared after the suspension that listed the reasons for the ban on wearing the armbands made no reference to the anticipation of such disruption. On the contrary, the action of the school authorities appears to have been based upon an urgent wish to avoid the controversy which might result from the expression, even by the silent symbol of armbands, of opposition to this Nation's part in the conflagration in Vietnam.

It is also relevant that the school authorities did not purport to prohibit the wearing of all symbols of political or controversial significance. The record shows that students in some of the schools wore buttons relating to national political campaigns, and some even wore the Iron Cross, traditionally a symbol of Nazism. The order prohibiting the wearing of armbands did not extend to these. Instead, a particular symbol—black armbands worn to exhibit opposition to this Nation's involvement in Vietnam—was singled out for prohibition. Clearly, the prohibition of expression of one particular opinion, at least without evidence that it is necessary to avoid material and substantial interference with schoolwork or discipline, is not constitutionally permissible.

In our system, state-operated schools may not be enclaves of totalitarianism. School officials do not possess absolute authority over their students. Students in school, as well as out of school, are "persons" under our Constitution. They are possessed of fundamental rights which the State must respect, just as they themselves must respect their obligations to the State. In our system, students may not be regarded as closed-circuit recipients of only that which the State chooses to communicate. They may not be confined to the expression of those sentiments that are officially approved. In the absence of a specific showing of constitutionally valid reasons to regulate their speech, students are entitled to freedom of expression of their views.

QUESTIONS FOR DISCUSSION

6.10   In setting the balance between the educational mission of public schools and free expression values, the *Tinker* Court used the standard of "substantial interference with schoolwork and discipline." Is this an appropriate standard? Does it promise to promote consistency in decisions regarding when to censor student speech?

6.11   The *Tinker* Court pointed out that the school officials in that case had not banned students from wearing depictions of the Iron Cross, traditionally associated with Nazism. Why would that be significant in evaluating the constitutionality of the school officials' actions?

WHAT'S YOUR LEARNED OPINION?
Scenario 6-9

In response to a state law prohibiting teachers from discussing sexual orientation and gender identity in early elementary classrooms, high school students across the state organized walkouts where they chanted, "We say gay!," carried signs reading "Protect Trans Kids," and waved rainbow flags. One school district's officials warned students they would be disciplined for leaving class. Hundreds of students participated anyway. One student who was suspended for leaving class as part of this organized walkout claimed the suspension was a violation of her First Amendment right to free speech. How would the case come out under the *Tinker* standard?

The next major school expression case to come up after *Tinker* was *Bethel School District v. Fraser*, 478 U.S. 675 (1986), in which a student included sexual innuendos in a speech before a school assembly. After being punished, Fraser took the case to the Supreme Court, which held that school officials may constitutionally prohibit vulgar and lewd speech.

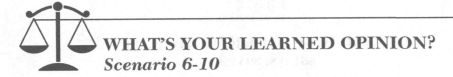

WHAT'S YOUR LEARNED OPINION?
Scenario 6-10

As part of a campaign to raise awareness for breast cancer, 14-year-old student Bria wore a bracelet reading "I love boobies! (KEEP A BREAST)!" to school every day for several weeks. There were no reports of the bracelets causing any school disruptions or inappropriate comments, but the principal eventually banned the bracelets, claiming the word "boobies" was vulgar and a violation of the school dress code. On the school's Breast Cancer Awareness Day, Bria wore her "I love boobies!" bracelet. When asked to remove it, she refused and was given in-school suspension for a day and a half and forbidden from attending the winter dance. Was this prohibition and punishment a violation of her First Amendment right to free speech under the *Tinker* and *Bethel School* standards?

Two years later, the Court decided *Hazelwood School District v. Kuhlmeier*, 484 U.S. 260 (1988). That case arose when a student newspaper planned to publish an article about three students' experiences with pregnancy as well as the impact of divorce on students. The school principal rejected the article and prevented it from being published. The Supreme Court upheld the principal's decision, ruling that the school had significant latitude in regulating the newspaper's content. The Court reasoned that where a school is in a position to support student speech affirmatively (such as sponsoring a student newspaper), the situation implicates "educators' authority over school-sponsored publications, theatrical productions, and other expressive activities that students, parents, and members of the public might reasonably perceive to bear on the imprimatur of the school."

The next case places the Court's approach to proper regulation of student speech within a slightly new context. Not only does the case concern arguably ironic, humorous student expression, but it also arose during a nonformal, out-of-classroom sponsored school event. You will note that the majority writes more in the spirit of *Hazelwood* than in the spirit of *Tinker*.

FROM THE BENCH

MORSE v. FREDERICK
551 U.S. 393 (2007)

Chief Justice ROBERTS delivered the opinion of the Court.

On January 24, 2002, the Olympic Torch Relay passed through Juneau, Alaska, on its way to the winter games in Salt Lake City, Utah. The torchbearers were to proceed along a street in front of Juneau-Douglas High School (JDHS) while school was in session. Deborah Morse, the school principal, decided to permit staff and students to participate in the Torch Relay as an approved social event or class trip. Students were allowed to leave class to observe the relay from either side of the street. Teachers and administrative officials monitored the students' actions. As the torchbearers and camera crews passed by, Frederick and his friends unfurled a 14-foot banner bearing the phrase: "BONG HiTS 4 JESUS." The large banner was easily readable by the students on the other side of the street. Principal Morse immediately crossed the street and demanded that the banner be taken down. Everyone but Frederick complied. Morse confiscated the banner and told Frederick to report to her office, where she suspended him for 10 days.

I

At the outset, we reject Frederick's argument that this is not a school speech case—as has every other authority to address the question. The event occurred during normal school hours. It was sanctioned by Principal Morse "as an approved social event or class trip," and the school district's rules expressly provide that pupils in "approved social events and class trips are subject to district rules for student conduct." Teachers and administrators were interspersed

As of 2022, the original "BONG HiTs 4 JESUS" banner is on display at the First Amendment Museum in Augusta, Maine. *Wikimedia Commons.*

among the students and charged with supervising them. The high school band and cheerleaders performed. Frederick, standing among other JDHS students across the street from the school, directed his banner toward the school, making it plainly visible to most students. Under these circumstances, we agree with the superintendent that Frederick cannot "stand in the midst of his fellow students, during school hours, at a school-sanctioned activity and claim he is not at school."

II

The message on Frederick's banner is cryptic. It is no doubt offensive to some, perhaps amusing to others. To still others, it probably means nothing at all. Frederick himself claimed "that the words were just nonsense meant to attract television cameras." But Principal Morse thought the banner would be interpreted by those viewing it as promoting illegal drug use, and that interpretation is plainly a reasonable one.

As Morse later explained in a declaration, when she saw the sign, she thought that "the reference to a 'bong hit' would be widely understood by high school students and others as referring to smoking marijuana." She further believed that "display of the banner would be construed by students, District personnel, parents and others witnessing the display of the banner, as advocating or promoting illegal drug use"—in violation of school policy.

We agree with Morse. At least two interpretations of the words on the banner demonstrate that the sign advocated the use of illegal drugs. First, the phrase could be interpreted as an imperative: "[Take] bong hits . . ."—a message

equivalent, as Morse explained in her declaration, to "smoke marijuana" or "use an illegal drug." Alternatively, the phrase could be viewed as celebrating drug use — "bong hits [are a good thing]," or "[we take] bong hits" — and we discern no meaningful distinction between celebrating illegal drug use in the midst of fellow students and outright advocacy or promotion.

[T]he dissent emphasizes] the importance of political speech and the need to foster "national debate about a serious issue," as if to suggest that the banner is political speech. But not even Frederick argues that the banner conveys any sort of political or religious message. [Thus,] this is plainly not a case about political debate over the criminalization of drug use or possession.

III

The question thus becomes whether a principal may, consistent with the First Amendment, restrict student speech at a school event, when that speech is reasonably viewed as promoting illegal drug use. We hold that she may.

In *Tinker*, this Court made clear that "First Amendment rights, applied in light of the special characteristics of the school environment, are available to teachers and students." Tinker held that student expression may not be suppressed unless school officials reasonably conclude that it will "materially and substantially disrupt the work and discipline of the school." The only interest the Court discerned underlying the school's actions was the "mere desire to avoid the discomfort and unpleasantness that always accompany an unpopular viewpoint," or "an urgent wish to avoid the controversy which might result from the expression."

[The Court recognizes] that deterring drug use by schoolchildren is an "important — indeed, perhaps compelling" interest. Drug abuse can cause severe and permanent damage to the health and well-being of young people. . . . Thousands of school boards throughout the country — including JDHS — have adopted policies aimed at effectuating this message. Student speech celebrating illegal drug use at a school event, in the presence of school administrators and teachers, thus poses a particular challenge for school officials working to protect those entrusted to their care from the dangers of drug abuse.

The "special characteristics of the school environment," *Tinker*, 393 U.S., at 506, and the governmental interest in stopping student drug abuse — reflected in the policies of Congress and myriad school boards, including JDHS — allow schools to restrict student expression that they reasonably regard as promoting illegal drug use. *Tinker* warned that schools may not prohibit student speech because of "undifferentiated fear or apprehension of disturbance" or "a mere desire to avoid the discomfort and unpleasantness that always accompany an unpopular viewpoint." The danger here is far more serious and palpable.

The concern here is not that Frederick's speech was offensive, but that it was reasonably viewed as promoting illegal drug use. The First Amendment does not require schools to tolerate at school events student expression that contributes to those dangers.

Justice STEVENS, with whom Justice SOUTER and Justice GINSBURG join, dissenting.

A significant fact barely mentioned by the Court sheds a revelatory light on the motives of both the students and the principal of Juneau-Douglas High School (JDHS). As Joseph Frederick repeatedly explained, he did not address the curious message—"BONG HiTS 4 JESUS"—to his fellow students. He just wanted to get the camera crews' attention. Moreover, concern about a nation-wide evaluation of the conduct of the JDHS student body would have justified the principal's decision to remove an attention-grabbing 14-foot banner, even if it had merely proclaimed "Glaciers Melt!"

I agree with the Court that the principal should not be held liable for pulling down Frederick's banner. I would hold, however, that the school's interest in protecting its students from exposure to speech "reasonably regarded as promoting illegal drug use," cannot justify disciplining Frederick for his attempt to make an ambiguous statement to a television audience simply because it contained an oblique reference to drugs. The First Amendment demands more, indeed, much more. . . .

Even in high school, a rule that permits only one point of view to be expressed is less likely to produce correct answers than the open discussion of countervailing views. In the national debate about a serious issue, it is the expression of the minority's viewpoint that most demands the protection of the First Amendment. Whatever the better policy may be, a full and frank discussion of the costs and benefits of the attempt to prohibit the use of marijuana is far wiser than suppression of speech because it is unpopular.

I respectfully dissent.

QUESTIONS FOR DISCUSSION

6.12　As you can discern from the trend reflected in the cases decided after *Tinker*, the Supreme Court has shown increased deference to school officials who choose to punish students for their speech. Is this deference appropriate or does it fail to adequately protect students' rights from arbitrary administrator actions?

6.13　Suppose Frederick and his friends unfurled a banner that read "LEGALIZE MARIJUANA." Would that change the majority's conclusion about the First Amendment issue?

Recall that before the following case was decided, the U.S. Supreme Court had established the following four categories of student speech that schools generally could regulate:

1. Indecent, lewd, or vulgar on-campus speech;
2. Speech promoting illegal drug use in school-related activities;
3. Speech that bears the imprimatur of the school or appears to be school sponsored; and
4. Speech that "materially disrupts classwork or involves substantial disorder or invasion of the rights of others." *Tinker v. Des Moines Indep. Sch. Dist.*, 393 US 503, 513 (1969).

The Court had not yet addressed the extent to which schools could regulate student speech when it occurred off campus. In the age of social media, the lines between on- and off-campus speech are more blurred than ever before. An online post can easily reach into and substantially affect the school environment. With the upswing of online bullying and harassment, moreover, schools developed a very strong interest in stepping in to protect students and the school's objectives. In *Mahanoy Area School District v. B. L.*, the Court attempted to provide guidelines for when schools may and may not reach into the home to regulate student off-campus speech.

As you read *Mahanoy*, recall *Tinker's* statement providing, "[C]onduct by [a] student, in class or out of it, which for any reason . . . materially disrupts classwork or involves substantial disorder or invasion of the rights of others is, of course, not immunized by the constitutional guarantee of freedom of speech." Does the Court's holding in *Mahanoy* logically follow from *Tinker*?

FROM THE BENCH

MAHANOY AREA SCHOOL DISTRICT v. B.L.
141 S. Ct. 2038 (2021)

Justice BREYER delivered the opinion of the Court.

I

A

[B.L., a high school student, tried out for the varsity cheerleading squad but did not make it. On the weekend, she and a friend were at a local convenience store. Upset, B.L. posted two photos to her Snapchat story that could be seen by 250 of her friends for 24 hours. The first was a picture of B.L. and a friend with their middle fingers raised, captioned "Fuck school fuck softball fuck cheer fuck everything." The second was blank with a caption that read "Love how me and [another student] get told we need a year of jv before we make varsity but tha[t] doesn't matter to anyone else?" An upside-down smiley face emoji was also in the caption. Other students and members of the cheerleading squad saw the images, and one showed the coach. Several students were "visibly upset" about the posts. They were discussed during an Algebra class. In response, the coaches suspended B.L. from cheerleading for the year.]

B

. . . Because B.L.'s speech took place off campus, the [Third Circuit] concluded that the *Tinker* standard did not apply and the school consequently could not discipline B.L. for engaging in a form of pure speech. . . .

C

The school district filed a petition for certiorari in this Court, asking us to decide "[w]hether [*Tinker*], which holds that public school officials may regulate speech that would materially and substantially disrupt the work and discipline of the school, applies to student speech that occurs off campus."

II

We have made clear that students do not "shed their constitutional rights to freedom of speech or expression," even "at the school house gate." But we have also made clear that courts must apply the First Amendment "in light of the special characteristics of the school environment." One such characteristic, which we have stressed, is the fact that schools at times stand *in loco parentis*, *i.e.*, in the place of parents.

This Court has previously outlined three specific categories of student speech that schools may regulate in certain circumstances: (1) "indecent," "lewd," or "vulgar" speech uttered during a school assembly on school grounds; (2) speech, uttered during a class trip, that promotes "illegal drug use"; and (3) speech that others may reasonably perceive as "bear[ing] the imprimatur of the school," such as that appearing in a school-sponsored newspaper. . . . Finally, in *Tinker*, we said schools have a special interest in regulating speech that "materially disrupts classwork or involves substantial disorder or invasion of the rights of others." These special characteristics call for special leeway when schools regulate speech that occurs under its supervision. . . . [W]e do not believe the special characteristics that give schools additional license to regulate student

FROM THE BENCH

speech always disappear when a school regulates speech that takes place off campus . . . . [For example, schools have an interest in regulating] serious or severe bullying or harassment targeting particular individuals; threats aimed at teachers or other students; the failure to follow rules concerning lessons, the writing of papers, the use of computers, or participation in other online school activities; and breaches of school security devices, including material maintained within school computers.

We are uncertain as to . . . how such a list [of exceptions] might vary, depending upon a student's age, the nature of the school's off-campus activity, or the impact upon the school itself. Thus, we do not now set forth a broad, highly general First Amendment rule stating just what counts as "off campus" speech. . . . We can, however, mention three features of off-campus speech that often, even if not always, distinguish schools' efforts to regulate that speech from their efforts to regulate on-campus speech. . . .

First, a school, in relation to off-campus speech, will rarely stand *in loco parentis*. The doctrine of *in loco parentis* treats school administrators as standing in the place of students' parents under circumstances where the children's actual parents cannot protect, guide, and discipline them. Geographically speaking, off-campus speech will normally fall within the zone of parental, rather than school-related, responsibility.

Second, from the student speaker's perspective, regulations of off-campus speech, when coupled with regulations of on-campus speech, include all the speech a student utters during the full 24-hour day. That means courts must be more skeptical of a school's efforts to regulate off-campus speech, for doing so may mean the student cannot engage in that kind of speech at all. When it comes to political or religious speech that occurs outside school or a school program or activity, the school will have a heavy burden to justify intervention.

Third, the school itself has an interest in protecting a student's unpopular expression, especially when the expression takes place off campus. America's public schools are the nurseries of democracy. Our representative democracy only works if we protect the "marketplace of ideas." This free exchange facilitates an informed public opinion, which, when transmitted to lawmakers, helps produce laws that reflect the People's will. That protection must include the protection of unpopular ideas, for popular ideas have less need for protection. Thus, schools have a strong interest in ensuring that future generations understand the workings in practice of the well-known aphorism, "I disapprove of what you say, but I will defend to the death your right to say it."

. . . Taken together, these three features of much off-campus speech mean that the leeway the First Amendment grants to schools in light of their special characteristics is diminished. We leave for future cases to decide where, when, and how these features mean the speaker's off-campus location will make the critical difference. This case can, however, provide one example.

III

Consider B.L.'s speech. Putting aside the vulgar language, the listener would hear criticism, of the team, the team's coaches, and the school—in a word or two, criticism of the rules of a community of which B.L. forms a part. This criticism did not involve features that would place it outside the First Amendment's ordinary protection. B.L.'s posts, while crude, did not amount to fighting words. And while B.L. used vulgarity, her speech was not obscene as this Court has understood that term. To the contrary, B.L. uttered the kind of pure speech to which, were she an adult, the First Amendment would provide strong protection.

Consider too when, where, and how B.L. spoke. Her posts appeared outside of school hours from a location outside the school. She did not identify the school in her posts or target any member of the school community with vulgar or abusive language. B.L. also transmitted her speech through a personal cellphone, to an audience consisting of her private circle of Snapchat friends. These features of her speech, while risking transmission to the school itself, nonetheless . . . diminish the school's interest in punishing B.L.'s utterance.

But what about the school's interest, here primarily an interest in prohibiting students from using vulgar language to criticize a school team or its coaches—at least when that criticism might well be transmitted to other students, team members, coaches, and faculty? We can break that general interest into three parts.

First, we consider the school's interest in teaching good manners and consequently in punishing the use of vulgar language aimed at part of the school community. The strength of this anti-vulgarity interest is weakened considerably by the fact that B.L. spoke outside the school on her own time.

B.L. spoke under circumstances where the school did not stand *in loco parentis*. And there is no reason to believe B.L.'s parents had delegated to school officials their own control of B.L.'s behavior at the Cocoa Hut. Moreover, the vulgarity in B.L.'s posts encompassed a message, an expression of B.L.'s irritation with, and criticism of, the school and cheerleading communities. Further, the school has presented no evidence of any general effort to prevent students from using vulgarity outside the classroom. Together, these facts convince us that the school's interest in teaching good manners is not sufficient, in this case, to overcome B.L.'s interest in free expression.

Second, the school argues that it was trying to prevent disruption, if not within the classroom, then within the bounds of a school-sponsored extracurricular activity. But we can find no evidence in the record of the sort of "substantial disruption" of a school activity or a threatened harm to the rights of others that might justify the school's action. Rather, the record shows that discussion of the matter took, at most, 5 to 10 minutes of an Algebra class "for just a couple of days" and that some members of the cheerleading team were "upset" about the content of B.L.'s Snapchats. . . . The alleged disturbance here does not meet *Tinker*'s demanding standard.

Third, the school presented some evidence that expresses (at least indirectly) a concern for team morale. One of the coaches testified that the school decided to suspend B.L., not because of any specific negative impact upon a particular member of the school community, but "based on the fact that there was negativity put out there that could impact students in the school." There is little else, however, that suggests any serious decline in team morale—to the point where it could create a substantial interference in, or disruption of, the school's efforts to maintain team cohesion. As we have previously said, simple "undifferentiated fear or apprehension . . . is not enough to overcome the right to freedom of expression."

It might be tempting to dismiss B.L.'s words as unworthy of the robust First Amendment protections discussed herein. But sometimes it is necessary to protect the superfluous in order to preserve the necessary.

■ ■ ■

[F]or the reasons expressed above, . . . we . . . agree that the school violated B.L.'s First Amendment rights. The judgment of the Third Circuit is therefore affirmed.

QUESTION FOR DISCUSSION

6.14   Briefs are pieces of persuasive writing submitted by each party to the Court detailing their arguments. Take a look at the beginning of the school's brief from this case. Does the emotional language confirm or change your opinion in any way?

School administrators entrusted with the operation of public schools "have a difficult job, and a vitally important one." . . . This case is about how schools address the bad days. A swollen-eyed student breaks down during English class; her teacher discovers that her classmates are calling her worthless on social media and urging her to kill herself. The science teacher goes on leave after his students create a fake email account that impersonates him and spews invective about other students, prompting outrage from parents. . . . Older students follow a disabled student home and describe sexual acts in such graphic terms that he cannot face returning to school.

Every day, schools face hard calls about how to address such off-campus speech, which requires balancing students' First Amendment rights with the "special needs" that "inhere in the public school context" (citation omitted). But the answer under the First Amendment should not be to force schools to ignore student speech that upends the campus environment simply because that speech originated off campus. . . .

In its ruling against the school, do you think the Court adequately addressed the concerns listed in the brief? What is the balance between "address[ing] the bad days" and students' First Amendment rights?

WHAT'S YOUR LEARNED OPINION?
Scenario 6-11

Alex, a rising high school freshman, is a member of the football team. The team, including the student athletes and coaches, have a chat group on social media. After he missed several practices, the coaches and Alex engaged in back-and-forth banter in the group, with the coaches trying to convince Alex to come to practice. One student wrote, "Bro just come to practice." The conversation took a turn for the worse, and the two students began threatening to fight each other. Alex finally said, "I'll grab a bottle and bash it on your face until I see your brain," followed by an image of him with a BB gun, although initially, the other group members believed it was a real gun. The messages and picture were shown to the school administrators, and Alex was suspended from the football team for the year. Alex claims that under *Mahanoy*, his off-campus speech on social media was protected. What would the court decide?

Scenario 6-12

Using a personal cell phone after school hours, high school student Cameron created a Facebook group titled S.A.S.H. She claimed it stood for "Students Against Sluts Herpes." Beneath the title was written, "No No Herpes. We don't want no herpes." One of the two dozen friends Cameron invited to join uploaded a picture of a third student Shay, where the friend had drawn red dots on her face to simulate herpes and a sign near her pelvis reading, "Warning: Enter at your own risk." On a second photograph of Shay another friend uploaded was captioned "portrait of a whore." Note that Cameron did not personally upload these pictures. Nonetheless, Cameron and the other members of the group commented on the photographs favorably, joining in on the "joke." When Shay learned of the group, she filed a complaint with the school and missed a day of school because she was uncomfortable being in a class with the students who were a part of this group.

Cameron was suspended for creating a "hate website" in violation of the school's Student Code of Conduct. Cameron alleged this suspension violates her First Amendment free speech rights. What should the court decide under the *Mahanoy* case?

E. The Public Forum Doctrine

The public forum doctrine started to develop when the U.S. Supreme Court recognized that government creates spaces designed to give citizens a place to communicate with each other. Since the 1930s, the U.S. Supreme Court has recognized that citizens may use government property for some types of speech under many circumstances. As declared in *Hague v. CIO*, 307 U.S. 496 (1939): "Wherever the title of streets and parks may rest, they have immemorially been held in trust for the use of the public and, time out of mind, have been used for purposes of assembly, communicating thoughts between citizens, and discussing public questions."

Like other parts of First Amendment law, public forum principles have become more complicated. After the *Hague v. CIO* case, the Supreme Court developed rules that demarcate the breadth of the constitutional protection for open public space for citizens to disseminate ideas and information. One theory offered for why these spaces are so important is that many citizens do not have the resources to gain private access — through media or otherwise — to the means to communicate with large numbers of citizens. Another important theory suggests that if governments had the unfettered ability to close public spaces to speakers, governments would be tempted to do so to shut down communication of ideas that the governments do not like. This type of content discrimination is, of course, inimical to basic freedom of speech principles.

As the U.S. Supreme Court has tooled the contours of its commitment to keeping public spaces open for communication, the Court has settled on four categories of government property relevant to analyzing public speech access questions. The degree of First Amendment restrictions on speech depends on how the property is categorized. The fifth category of location is private property, where no First Amendment restrictions apply:

Traditional Public Forums.   *Describing traditional public forums, the Supreme Court has stated that in areas "such as public streets and parks, 'any restriction based on the content of . . . speech must satisfy strict scrutiny, that is, the restriction must be narrowly tailored to serve a compelling government* *interest.'"* Christian Legal Soc'y Chapter of the Univ. of Cal. v. Martinez, *561 U.S. 661, 679 n.11 (2010).*

Designated Public Forums. *Designated public forums occur on government property that has traditionally been closed, but that the government has designated to be opened. An example of a designated public forum is a large conference room dedicated to judicial deliberations. This space was never intended to be a public space, but the government may decide to open the conference room to small community group meetings when the judiciary is not using the space. Speech restrictions in designated public forums are subject to strict scrutiny.*

Limited Public Forums. *Limited public forums occur on government property opened for "limited . . . use by certain groups or dedicated solely to the discussion of certain subjects. . . . [I]n such a forum, a government entity may impose restrictions on speech that are reasonable and viewpoint-neutral."* Christian Legal Soc'y Chapter of the Univ. of Cal. v. Martinez, *567 U.S. 661, 679 n.11 (2010). An example would be a government building designed to be open to the public, yet restricted to limited use, such as a city hall dedicated primarily to city offices that provide services for citizens. The public may use the services' offices and may use the hallways to access the offices and confer with others about their business with these offices. In such a place, however, the government may prevent the public from posting personal notices or artwork on the walls, so long as the government imposes that regulation in a neutral manner.*

Nonpublic Forums. *Nonpublic forums occur on government property that the government may properly close and has not opened. This includes public property that "is not by tradition or designation a forum for public communication. . . ."* Perry Educ. Ass'n v. Perry Local Educators' Ass'n, *460 U.S. 37, 46 (1983). The Supreme Court has said that the government may prohibit speech only if the prohibition is viewpoint neutral and reasonable. The area within the interior of a city bus between the seats and the bus roof can be a nonpublic forum, properly reserved for government safety notices about riding on the bus. If, however, the government begins to allow some nonpublic advertisements in this space, then the government must withhold permission for posting some advertisements only if it does so reasonably without discriminating against specific viewpoints.*

Private Property. *In a series of cases, the U.S. Supreme Court has ruled that private owners of property could exclude speakers from their property. Although the Court at first determined that privately owned shopping malls could be public forums, the Court changed its mind and determined that the First Amendment does not apply to privately owned malls.*

1. Traditional Public Forums

The standard for a government regulation of speech that occurs in an area designated as a public forum is well settled: The regulation must be content neutral unless it is narrowly tailored to serve a compelling interest. These constraints on government raise the stakes on deciding exactly what qualifies as a public forum.

Streets, sidewalks, and parks clearly fall into the "traditional public forum" category. The U.S. Supreme Court is reluctant to designate other locations as public forums. *See, e.g., International Society for Krishna Consciousness v. Lee*, 505 U.S. 672 (1992) (holding that airport terminals are not public forums); *Ark. Educ. Comm'n v. Forbes*, 523 U.S. 666 (1998) (determining that televised political debates are not a traditional public forum). Although this inclination not to recognize "new" forms of public forums simplifies the analysis, the question of when a park is a park, or a street a street, is not always simple. Under the prevailing approach, a court will not only consider a space's designation as a park, street, or sidewalk, but will also inquire into the government's pattern of allowing speech in the space, as well as the space's purpose and the compatibility of the speech in question with that purpose.

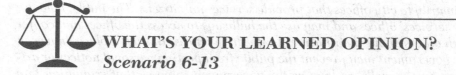

WHAT'S YOUR LEARNED OPINION?
Scenario 6-13

Seeking to spur economic revival in its downtown business district, a city converted a shopping street into a pedestrian shopping walkway. The city closed the street to vehicular traffic and installed several attractive art pieces. The project was successful, attracting investment, brick-and-mortar stores, street vendors, and street performers. Pedestrians used the plaza as a thoroughfare, but were often attracted to the stores, vendors, and performers.

A religious group sought to hand out leaflets on the walkway, but was denied a license to do so. The religious group then brought a First Amendment challenge, arguing that the walkway had become a traditional public forum. Is the religious group correct?

Scenario 6-14

A governor maintains a social media page where she posts updates about public events, state services, and her political stances. The format of the social media page provides a comments section where those who read the section can provide opinions. This section is interactive, allowing the governor to respond to comments and enter the exchange among members of the public.

After the governor made a post advocating for a restriction on political canvassing, a citizen posted hostile comments on the governor's social media page. Using the blocking mechanism of the social media site, the governor prevented the citizen from posting further comments.

According to the citizen, the governor's social media page is a public forum and the governor therefore violated the First Amendment rights of the citizen. The governor takes the position that her social media page contains only government speech (which First Amendment doctrine places outside the strictures of First Amendment restraints). For that reason, the governor states that the page cannot be characterized as a public forum. Does the governor have a valid argument?

2. Designated Public Forums

Occasionally, a government chooses to transform a place that the government could close to speech into a place to open to speakers. When that occurs, the place becomes a designated public forum. An example of a designated public forum might be a public elementary school cafeteria. In the interest of education and student safety, the government officials who run the school might have intended that the cafeteria be closed to the public entirely. The officials may decide, however, that it would be a service to the community to open up the space for community groups to meet during nonschool hours. Once the government creates a designated public forum, courts evaluating the First Amendment validity of designated public forum regulations will use the same strict scrutiny review as applied to traditional public forums.

It is difficult to distinguish a designated public forum concept from a limited public forum, described immediately below. A government creates a limited public forum in a similar way as a designated public forum: The government transforms a space formerly closed to speech into one open to speakers. One way to distinguish the two concepts is this: The government opens up designated public forums for most speakers, yet permits only specific speakers and topics in a limited public forum. Because the concept of a designated public forum is rarely used, the concept of a limited public forum is more relevant.

3. Limited Public Forums

A limited public forum is a place that government has opened for speech by a particular group or on a particular topic. Once the government opens the space within the confines of these constraints, the government need not allow all persons to speak there. Nor does the government need to allow speech on every subject. The government restrictions must, however, be "reasonable in light of the purpose served by the forum" and the government must not discriminate against any speech on the basis of viewpoint.

As with a traditional public forum, a government does not create a limited public forum by inaction. The government must evince an intent to open up a forum for speech for the location to take on the public forum designation. The government's intent must be viewed objectively. Moreover, the question of whether the government intended to create a limited public forum must be measured by reviewing not only the government's stated policy, but also the government's actions and the extent of the public's use of the space.

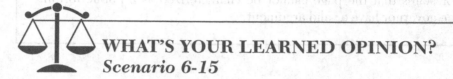

WHAT'S YOUR LEARNED OPINION?
Scenario 6-15

A public university installed bulletin boards on its campus: Some were inside academic buildings and others were outside and located along the main pedestrian thoroughfares on campus. At the time the bulletin boards were installed, any student was permitted to post informational flyers on the bulletin boards located inside the lobby of academic buildings. The university, however, restricted the outside bulletin boards along pedestrian thoroughfares by permitting only registered student organizations to post flyers there. The university's reason for this distinction was that outside bulletin board space on the campus was limited and could easily be viewed by the general public. For the purposes of practicality and to convey a professional, competent, and attractive public image, the university wished to keep the appearance of these outside bulletin board neat and to ensure that the notices posted were readable, in good taste, and current. For those reasons, the university restricted those who could post on the bulletin boards to groups that it could contact if necessary. (The university had a policy that registered student groups must inform the university of the contact information for the group's leaders at the beginning of each academic year.)

Does the First Amendment allow the university to deny those who are not part of registered student organizations access to posting flyers in the outside bulletin boards?

4. Nonpublic Forums

A nonpublic forum is a space that does not fit into the traditional public forum categories and one in which the government has expressed no intent to open the space up for expressive activities. The use of the word "forum" in the phrase is misleading because one does not usually associate a forum with something nonpublic. The term is phrased that way, however, as a term of art describing an alternative to the other permutations of the public forum concept. Within nonpublic forums, the government may regulate speech so long as their restrictions are viewpoint neutral and reasonable.

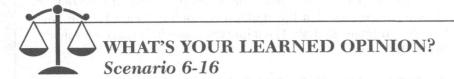

WHAT'S YOUR LEARNED OPINION?
Scenario 6-16

An advocacy group wished to have airplanes tow aerial banners above a public beach in a resort town. Pointing to a town ordinance prohibiting aerial banners in the area of beaches, the government entity that regulated the beach refused to allow the advocacy group permission to do so. The government entity explained that the restriction's purpose was to avoid the cost of monitoring the banners and to foster tourism by avoiding distraction from the pristine natural beauty of the area. The advocacy group argued that the airspace above a public beach had been traditionally regarded as a public forum. Is the advocacy group correct?

Scenario 6-17

Over many years, the City of New York followed the practice of featuring advertisements on both buses and subways. The transit system had come to rely on the advertisements as a significant source of income and the riding public had come to expect the buses and subways to be filled with advertisements of all kinds, including political ads, ads with religious themes, and the like. The transit system was in the practice of allowing ads so long as space was available to post them. The record shows that the system has not turned down any ads.

The city transit system, however, declined to carry an advertisement from a local magazine that said that the magazine was "Possibly the only good thing in New York Rudy hasn't taken credit for." The magazine took the position that the advertising space was a public forum and that the transit system's refusal to carry their advertisement amounted to content discrimination. The city transit system took the position that the advertising space on buses and subways was a nonpublic forum, emphasizing that the fundraising reasons behind the practice and the concern with offensive content qualified the restrictions as reasonable regulations of a nonpublic forum. Which side is correct?

Scenario 6-18

Recall Scenario 6-6. Beginning in 2016, some players in U.S. professional sports chose to kneel instead of standing for the national anthem. They made clear that the reason for this conduct was to protest police brutality when police confront Black men.

Assume that the players for a particular team that plays in a particular athletic stadium argue that that the stadium is a public forum for the purpose of First Amendment analysis. What questions would you ask to evaluate the validity of the claim?

The U.S. Supreme Court has created several analytical threads of general approaches to handle First Amendment problems: content-based versus content-neutral distinctions, principles of protecting political speech rights, symbolic speech, freedom of the press, special school interests, and the public forum doctrine. One dispute might fit into more than one of these analytical threads. One strategy is to decide on the approach you believe has the best fit; another strategy is to use several approaches to analyze and ultimately find the best solution for the dispute. As with much of law, no mandated approach exists. Hence one of the joys of legal reasoning: an opportunity for flexible thinking and creativity. The next chapter explores even more possibilities for freedom of communication analysis.

QUESTIONS FOR REVIEW

1. Does the First Amendment apply to government entities other than the U.S. Congress? If so, to which other entities does it apply?
2. What are the basic four values that the freedom of expression component of the First Amendment is designed to serve?
3. What is generally the level of judicial scrutiny that applies to evaluating a restriction on speech that regulates on the basis of content?
4. What is an example of a time, place, and manner restriction?
5. There are four elements for upholding the constitutionality of state law punishing an incitement to violence. What needs to be present to show the incitement-to-violence statute is constitutional?
6. What does the U.S. Supreme Court's decision in *United States v. O'Brien* explain that must be present for a government to prosecute expressive (nonverbal) speech without violating the First Amendment?
7. Why did the Court in *Texas v. Johnson* hold that the flag-burning prosecution was unconstitutional?

8. *New York Times Co. v. Sullivan* set forth a definition of actual malice. Describe the definition and what it means.

9. Describe the U.S. Supreme Court's approach to the First Amendment rights of high school students as well as the constitutional limits on school officials to control that speech. How does the Court's approach differ between expression that is connected with school-sponsored events and expression that occurs off-campus via social media?

10. Describe the differences among the concepts of a traditional public forum, a designated public forum, a limited public forum, a nonpublic forum, and private property.

ENDNOTES

1. *Schenk*, 249 U.S. at 52.
2. *Id.* at 630.
3. *Id.* at 669.
4. For the full speech, see https://www.npr.org/2021/02/10/966396848/read-trumps-jan-6-speech-a-key-part-of-impeachment-trial

The First Amendment

Selected Topics in Humor, Hate Speech, and Religion

7

The previous chapter provided an overview of basic First Amendment freedom of communication principles. Those principles touch many specific parts of life. Here are just a few parts of life affected by the First Amendment: pornography, advertisements, speech rights in government-controlled institutions such as the military and prisons, and the political contribution rights of corporations. This chapter takes a close look at two important and current freedom of communication topics: humor and hate speech. In addition, the chapter concludes with an introduction to the present state of the law concerning the religion clauses in the First Amendment.

A. The Benefits of Humor and Entertainment Versus Protecting Against Corruption of Societal Fabric and the Pain of Individual Offense

Humor is everywhere in human civilization. Law also tends to be everywhere in human civilization. It is no surprise then that the two—law and humor—intersect. One particularly salient quality of humor is that it tends to be "edgy" when it comes to social norms. To put it differently, humor often pushes the envelope of social acceptability. This quality adds much of the sizzle that ensures that humor is amusing, but this same quality also often ensures that humor can offend. Humor can run straight into an outright criminal prohibition or governmental regulation; for example, thou shalt not joke about killing the President or about blowing up an airport when going through airport security. It can also cause intense anger, fear, and emotional pain to private individuals, who are inspired to look to courts for resolution and remedy.

Then, of course, humor is a form of communication. Deep ideas are often embedded in its meaning. Hence any government regulation of humor implicates the First Amendment. In evaluating the propriety of government regulation and the breadth of First Amendment protection, one must start from the premise that humor can be quite attention-grabbing (and often good fun) and is therefore potent communication. Also informing the First Amendment questions are studies in a variety of disciplines—medicine, psychology, workplace management, and educational theory, to name a few—that document humor's beneficial effects. These include such valuable contributions to society as creating community, increasing efficiency, and serving as a safety valve for releasing anxiety.

Given the importance of humor in contemporary society, the relationship between law and humor is worthy of close attention. What follows is a cross-section of cases illustrating how courts have used U.S. constitutional law to navigate this task.

1. Courts Become Comedy Critics When Regulating Humor

As you will see later in this chapter, the U.S. Supreme Court in the pathbreaking case of *New York Times Co. v. Sullivan* held that, to protect speech, public officials may recover for damage to reputation only upon showing that the speaker acted with a higher degree of fault. Under this higher standard, a public official cannot recover damages for defamation unless he or she can prove through clear and convincing evidence that the defamatory statements were made with "actual malice." In this context, actual malice means that a news outlet or individual made a statement knowing that the statement was false or with reckless disregard for whether a statement was false. This higher standard makes it harder to succeed in a lawsuit and is based on the rationale that public officials operate at the center of the government, and therefore their decisions should be subject to monitoring by the citizens.

In a subsequent case, *Gertz v. Robert Welch, Inc.*, the Court explained how this higher standard applied to individuals considered "public figures" (as opposed to "public officials"). Public figures are those who have "assumed roles of especial prominence in the affairs of society," and generally fall into two categories: (1) those who occupy positions of strong power and influence, and (2) those who push themselves to the foreground of certain public controversies so that they may have some influence on these issues. The bottom line is that public figures invite attention and commentary by voluntarily enjoying public attention, thereby exposing themselves to a heightened risk of reputational harm.

The case that follows concerns a public figure, the television evangelical minister Reverend Jerry Falwell. The Supreme Court wrestled with the question of whether the heightened standard of proof (actual malice) should apply to a parody about a public official in a lawsuit. As the suit made its way through the courts, the only relevant claim was intentional infliction of emotional distress. Intentional infliction of emotional distress is a claim that is a type of privacy tort and a close cousin of defamation. The Court in the case that follows treated the two claims as closely analogous.

FROM THE BENCH

HUSTLER MAGAZINE v. FALWELL
458 U.S. 46 (1988)

Chief Justice REHNQUIST delivered the opinion of the Court.

Petitioner Hustler Magazine, Inc., is a magazine of nationwide circulation. Respondent Jerry Falwell, a nationally known minister who has been active as a commentator on politics and public affairs, sued petitioner and its publisher, petitioner Larry Flynt, to recover damages. . . . [In the district court, the jury found that Hustler Magazine was liable for intentional infliction of emotional distress and awarded damages of $100,000 in compensatory damages, as well as $50,000 in punitive damages]. The United States Supreme Court took the case to consider whether this award is consistent with the First and Fourteenth Amendments of the United States Constitution.

The inside front cover of the November 1983 issue of Hustler Magazine featured a "parody" of an advertisement for Campari Liqueur that contained the name and picture of respondent and was entitled "Jerry Falwell talks about his first time." This parody was modeled after actual Campari ads that included interviews with various celebrities about their "first times." Although it was apparent by the end of each interview that this meant the first time they sampled Campari, the ads clearly played on the sexual double entendre of the general subject of "first times." Copying the form and layout of these Campari ads, Hustler's editors chose respondent as the featured celebrity and drafted an alleged "interview" with him in which he states that his "first time" was during a drunken incestuous rendezvous with his mother in an outhouse. The Hustler parody portrays respondent and his mother as drunk and immoral, and suggests that respondent is a hypocrite who preaches only when he is drunk. In small print at the bottom of the page, the ad contains the disclaimer, "ad parody—not to be taken seriously." The magazine's table of contents also lists the ad as "Fiction; Ad and Personality Parody."

Reproduction of *Hustler's* parody.
Copyright © 1983 *Hustler Magazine, Inc.*

. . . This case presents us with a novel question involving First Amendment limitations upon a State's authority to protect its citizens from the intentional infliction of emotional distress. We must decide whether a public figure may recover damages for emotional harm caused by the publication of an ad parody offensive to him, and doubtless gross and repugnant in the eyes of most. Respondent would have us find that a State's interest in protecting public figures from emotional distress is sufficient to deny First Amendment protection to speech that is patently offensive and is intended to inflict emotional injury, even when that speech could not reasonably have been interpreted as stating actual facts about the public figure involved. This we decline to do.

At the heart of the First Amendment is the recognition of the fundamental importance of the free flow of ideas and opinions on matters of public interest and concern. "The freedom to speak one's mind is not only an aspect of individual liberty — and thus a good unto itself — but also is essential to the common quest for truth and the vitality of society as a whole." We have therefore been particularly vigilant to ensure that individual expressions of ideas remain free from governmentally imposed sanctions. The First Amendment recognizes no such thing as a "false" idea. As Justice Holmes wrote, "When men have realized that time has upset many fighting faiths, they may come to believe even more than they believe the very foundations of their own conduct that the ultimate good desired is better reached by free trade in ideas — that the best test of truth is the power of the thought to get itself accepted in the competition of the market. . . ."

The sort of robust political debate encouraged by the First Amendment to produce speech that is critical of those who hold public office or those public figures who are "intimately involved in the resolution of important public questions or, by reason of their fame, shape events in areas of concern to society at large." Justice Frankfurter put it succinctly in *Baumgartner v. United States* when he said that "one of the prerogatives of American citizenship is the right to criticize public men and measures." Such criticism, inevitably, will not always be reasoned or moderate; public figures as well as public officials will be subject to "vehement, caustic, and sometimes unpleasantly sharp attacks."

Of course, this does not mean that any speech about a public figure is immune from sanction in the form of damages. Since *New York Times Co. v. Sullivan, supra,* we have consistently ruled that a public figure may hold a speaker liable for the damage to reputation caused by publication of a defamatory falsehood, but only if the statement was made "with knowledge that it was false or with reckless disregard of whether it was false or not." False statements of fact are particularly valueless; they interfere with the truth-seeking function of the marketplace of ideas, and they cause damage to an individual's reputation that cannot easily be repaired by counterspeech, however persuasive or effective.

Respondent argues, however, that a different standard should apply in this case because here the State seeks to prevent not reputational damage, but the severe emotional distress suffered by the person who is the subject of an offensive publication.

Thus while such a bad motive may be deemed controlling for purposes of tort liability in other areas of the law, we think the First Amendment prohibits such a result in the area of public debate about public figures.

Were we to hold otherwise, there can be little doubt that political cartoonists and satirists would be subjected to damages awards without any showing that their work falsely defamed its subject. Webster's defines a caricature as "the deliberately distorted picturing or imitating of a person, literary style, etc. by exaggerating features or mannerisms for satirical effect." The appeal of the political cartoon or caricature is often based on exploration of unfortunate physical traits or politically embarrassing events—an exploration often calculated to injure the feelings of the subject of the portrayal. The art of the cartoonist is often not reasoned or evenhanded, but slashing and one-sided. . . .

Despite their sometimes caustic nature, from the early cartoon portraying George Washington as an ass down to the present day, graphic depictions and satirical cartoons have played a prominent role in public and political debate. Nast's castigation of the Tweed Ring . . . Lincoln's tall, gangling posture, Teddy Roosevelt's glasses and teeth, and Franklin D. Roosevelt's jutting jaw and cigarette holder have been memorialized by political cartoons with an effect that could not have been obtained by the photographer or the portrait artist. From the viewpoint of history it is clear that our political discourse would have been considerably poorer without them.

Respondent contends, however, that the caricature in question here was so "outrageous" as to distinguish it from more traditional political cartoons. There is no doubt that the caricature of respondent and his mother published in Hustler is at best a distant cousin of the political cartoons described above, and a rather poor relation at that. If it were possible by laying down a principled standard to separate the one from the other, public discourse would probably suffer little or no harm. But we doubt that there is any such standard, and we are quite sure that the pejorative description "outrageous" does not supply one. "Outrageousness" in the area of political and social discourse has an inherent subjectiveness about it which would allow a jury to impose liability on the basis of the jurors' tastes or views, or perhaps on the basis of their dislike of a particular expression. An "outrageousness" standard thus runs afoul of our longstanding refusal to allow damages to be awarded because the speech in question may have an adverse emotional impact on the audience.

Admittedly, these oft-repeated First Amendment principles, like other principles, are subject to limitations. We recognized in *Pacifica Foundation*, that speech that is "'vulgar,' 'offensive,' and 'shocking'" is "not entitled to absolute constitutional protection under all circumstances." In *Chaplinsky v. New Hampshire*, we held that a state could lawfully punish an individual for the use of insulting "'fighting' words—those which by their very utterance inflict injury or tend to incite an immediate breach of the peace." . . . But the sort of expression involved in this case does not seem to us to be governed by any exception to the general First Amendment principles stated above.

We conclude that public figures and public officials may not recover for the tort of intentional infliction of emotional distress by reason of publications such as the one here at issue without showing in addition that the publication contains a false statement of fact which was made with "actual malice," i.e., with knowledge that the statement was false or with reckless disregard as to whether or not it was true. This is not merely a "blind application" of the *New York Times* standard, it reflects our considered judgment that such a standard is necessary to give adequate "breathing space" to the freedoms protected by the First Amendment.

Here it is clear that respondent Falwell is a "public figure" for purposes of First Amendment law.[5] The jury found against respondent on his libel claim when it decided that the Hustler ad parody could not "reasonably be understood as describing actual facts about [respondent] or actual events in which [he] participated." The Court of Appeals interpreted the jury's finding to be that the ad parody "was not reasonably believable," and in accordance with our custom we accept this finding. Respondent is thus relegated to his claim for damages awarded by the jury for the intentional infliction of emotional distress by "outrageous" conduct. But for reasons heretofore stated this claim cannot, consistently with the First Amendment, form a basis for the award of damages when the conduct in question is the publication of a caricature such as the ad parody involved here.

---

[5] Neither party disputes this conclusion. Respondent is the host of a nationally syndicated television show and was the founder and president of a political organization formerly known as the Moral Majority. He is also the founder of Liberty University in Lynchburg, Virginia, and is the author of several books and publications. Who's Who in America 849 (44th ed. 1986–1987).

BEHIND THE CURTAIN

Justice Antonin Scalia was known for his vibrant exchanges at oral argument. Some might even call him a "wisecracker." An empirical study documenting the funniest Supreme Court Justice counted the number of "laughter" notations in records of Supreme Court transcripts. Justice Scalia was a winner by a large margin. Consider how he riffed with the attorneys in the *Hustler* case:

Oral Argument – December 2, 1987

Justice Antonin Scalia:

Mr. Isaacman, to contradict Vince Lombardi, the First Amendment is not everything. It's a very important value, but it's not the only value in our society, certainly.

You're giving us no help in trying to balance it, it seems to me, against another value, which is that good people should be able to enter public life and public service.

The rule you give us says that if you stand for public office, or become a public figure in any way, you cannot protect yourself, or indeed, your mother, against a parody of your committing incest with your mother in an outhouse.

Now, is that not a value that ought to be protected? Do you think George Washington would have stood for public office if that was the consequence?

And there's no way to protect the values of the First Amendment and yet attract people into public service? Can't you give us some line that would balance the two?

Alan L. Isaacman (*argued the case for the petitioner, Hustler Magazine*):

Well, one of the lines was suggested by a question earlier, and that is in the private figure or public figure area, if the Court really wants to balance.

But somebody who's going into public life, George Washington as an example, there's a cartoon in — I think it's the cartoonists society brief, that has George Washington being led on a donkey and underneath the caption is something about so and so, who is leading the donkey, is leading this ass, or something to that effect.

Justice Antonin Scalia:

I can handle that.

And I think George could handle that. [*Laughter.*] But that's a far cry from committing incest with your mother in an outhouse.

I mean, there's no line between the two? We can't protect that kind of parody and not protect this?

Alan L. Isaacman:

There's no line in terms of the meaning because *Hustler* wasn't saying that he was committing incest with his mother. Nobody could understand it to be saying that as a matter of fact.

And what you're talking about, Justice Scalia, is a matter of taste.

And as Justice Scalia, as you said in *Pope v. Illinois*, just as it's useless to argue about taste, it's useless to litigate it, litigate about it.

And what we're talking about here is, well, is this tasteful or not tasteful. That's really what you're talking about because nobody believed that Jerry Falwell was being accused of committing incest.

The question is, is this in good taste to put him in this, draw this image, paint a picture.

■ ■ ■

Justice Antonin Scalia:

Mr. Grutman, you've given us a lot of words to describe this: outrageous, heinous—

Norman Roy Grutman (*argued the case for respondent, Falwell*):

Repulsive and loathsome.

Justice Antonin Scalia:

—Repulsive and loathsome.

I don't know, maybe you haven't looked at the same political cartoons that I have, but some of them, and a long tradition of this, not just in this country but back into English history, I mean, politicians depicted as horrible looking beasts, and you talk about portraying someone as committing some immoral act.

I would be very surprised if there were not a number of cartoons depicting one or another political figure as at least the piano player in a bordello. [*Laughter.*]

Norman Roy Grutman:

Justice Scalia, we don't shoot the piano player. I understand that.

Justice Antonin Scalia:

Well, but can you give us something that the cartoonist or the political figure can adhere to, other than such general words as heinous and what not.

I mean, does it depend on how ugly the beast is, or what?

Norman Roy Grutman:

No, it's not the amount of hair the beast has or how long his claws may be.

I believe that we have—this is a matter of an evolving social sensibility.

Between the 1700s and today, I would suggest that people have become more acclimatized to the use of the kinds of language or the kinds of things that had they been depicted at an earlier age would have been regarded as socially unacceptable.

And while that evolutionary change is taking place, and it's a salutary thing, there are certain kinds of things. It's difficult to describe them. This Court struggled for years to describe—put a legal definition on obscenity, and Justice Stewart could say no more than, I know what it is when I see it.

Well, this kind of rare aberrational and anomalous behavior, whatever it is, whatever the verbal formulation that the nine of you may come upon, clearly it can be condensed in the form of words that I used, which are not mine—they belong to the oracles of the restatement—who have tried to say that it is for the jury to decide whether or not what is being depicted is done in so offensive, so awful and so horrible a way that it constitutes the kind of behavior that nobody should have to put up with.

QUESTIONS FOR DISCUSSION

7.1   Consider how the *Hustler* Court considered the form of humor known as parody. The Court described parody in favorable terms. It turns out that courts have treated parody well in other legal contexts. What exactly is parody and why would courts treat this form of parody "with kid gloves"?

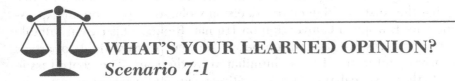

WHAT'S YOUR LEARNED OPINION?
Scenario 7-1

A student at the University of Northern Crackup ("UNC") created a fictional character, "Junius Puke," for the editorial column of his Internet-based journal, *The Howling Pig*. The editorial column displayed altered photographs of Junius Peake, a UNC professor. One photo featured Mr. Peake/Puke wearing dark sunglasses and a Hitler-like mustache, and another was altered to depict him made up as a member of the rock band KISS.

Junius Puke's editorial column addressed subjects on which Mr. Peake would be unlikely to write, in language he would be unlikely to use, asserting views that were diametrically opposed to those of Mr. Peake. For example, the editorial said, "This will be a regular bitch sheet that will speak truth to power, obscenities to clergy, and advice to all the stoners sitting around watching Scooby Doo." It also said, "Dissatisfaction with a cushy do-nothing ornamental position led me to form this subversive little paper."

Mr. Peake was not amused and contacted the police, who started investigating a potential violation of the applicable defamation law. Is Mr. Peake likely to be successful in his defamation claim?

In understanding U.S. constitutional law, much can be learned from comparison with other parts of the world in the handling of humor that is offensive to some. The following case, *Vereinigung Bildender Künstler v. Austria*, 68354/01 Eur. Ct. H.R. (2006), provides a window on that comparison. The case originated in the Austrian court system and found its way to the European Court of Human Rights, which is described as a body that governs many countries—a supranational court—that hears cases involving alleged violations of the European Convention on Human Rights. The court is binding on those nations that have signed onto that convention.

The dispute began when Vereinigung Bildender Künstler (VBK), an association of artists, displayed a painting during its centennial entitled "Apocalypse." The painting was a large mural that depicted exaggerated, cartoonish figures, with heads made from newspaper clippings of prominent members of Austrian society. The figures were engaged in a graphic orgy. One of them was Walter Meischberger, a politician in Austria's far-right Freedom Party, which had a feud with the artist. Meischberger sued VBK for reputational harm and was ultimately awarded money damages and an injunction against further displays of "Apocalypse." VBK petitioned the European Court of Human Rights, arguing that the Austrian high court's decision violated its freedom of expression under the European Convention on Human Rights. This case is notable for its attempt to resolve the tension between the expressive rights of artists and the privacy interests of those humiliated by their art. The central issue here is whether "Apocalypse" was a legitimate artistic expression—worthy of legal protection—or simply puerile obscenity intended to humiliate its subjects.

In reading the case, take note of the respect that the court shows for the human dignity of those who are depicted in the cartoon. This is a stark contrast to the approach to politicians and other public figures in satirical representations in the United States, such as in *Hustler v. Falwell* above. Unlike in the United States, the style of the decision is to have numbered paragraphs.

FROM THE BENCH

VEREINIGUNG BILDENDER KÜNSTLER (VBK) v. AUSTRIA

68354/01 Eur. Ct. H.R. (2006)

(*Case of Vereinigung Bildender Künstler (VBK) v. Austria*, Application no. 68354/01 (European Court of Human Rights 24 January 2009))

The Facts

I. The Circumstances of the Case

■ ■ ■

7. Vereinigung Bildender Künstler Wiener Secession is an association of artists with its seat in the Secession building in Vienna. The Secession, an independent gallery, is devoted entirely to exhibitions of contemporary art. One of the basic objectives of the association is to present current developments in Austrian and international art, and to cultivate an openness to experimentation.

8. Between 3 April and 21 June 1998 the applicant association held an exhibition on its premises. The exhibition, entitled "The century of artistic freedom", was intended as part of the celebrations of the association's 100th anniversary. Among the works to be shown was a painting entitled "Apocalypse", which had been produced for the occasion by the Austrian painter Otto Mühl. The painting, measuring [a little less than 15 feet by 12 feet], showed a collage of various public figures, such as Mother Teresa, the Austrian cardinal Hermann Groer and the former head of the Austrian Freedom Party (FPÖ) Mr Jörg Haider, in sexual positions. While the naked bodies of these figures were painted, the heads and faces were depicted using blown-up photos taken from newspapers. The eyes of some of the persons portrayed were hidden under black bars. Among these persons was Mr Meischberger, a former general secretary of the FPÖ until 1995, who at the time of the events was a member of the [Austrian] National Assembly, a mandate he held until April 1999. Mr Meischberger was shown gripping the ejaculating penis of Mr Haider while at the same time being touched by two other FPÖ politicians and ejaculating on Mother Teresa.

9. The exhibition, for which admission was charged, was open to the public.

10. On 11 June 1998, while the exhibition was in progress, the Austrian newspaper Täglich Alles bristled at the above painting's portrayal of "group sexual situations with Bishop Groer and Mother Teresa".

11. On 12 June 1998 the painting was damaged by a visitor, who covered with red paint the part which showed, among others, Mr Meischberger. As a consequence of this incident the entire painted body of Mr Meischberger and part of his face were covered with red paint.

12. Several Austrian newspapers reported on this event and also published pictures of the painting.

[Mr. Meischberger sued the VBK for money damages and requested an injunction against displaying "Apocalypse" in the future. He argued that the public display of the painting violated his dignity rights under section 78 of the Austrian Copyright Act, and] that the painting, showing him in sexual positions with several persons, debased him and his political activities and made statements as to his allegedly loose sexual life. The black eye-bars did not prevent him from being recognized, because he was shown together with two other FPÖ politicians. He remained recognizable even after the incident of 12 June 1998, which had further increased the publicity given to the painting. Furthermore, there was a danger of recurrence as after the present exhibition the painting was due to be shown at another exhibition in Prague.

[Mr. Meischberger's lawsuit was dismissed by the Vienna Commercial Court, which held that the outlandish, exaggerated depiction in "Apocalypse" could not have debased his private life, because it "obviously did not represent reality." Although the content of the painting was so extreme that it might yet cause him dignitary harm, the court ruled that the artist and gallery's freedom of expression under Article 17a of the Austrian Basic Law outweighed Mr. Meischberger's dignitary interests in this case. This was especially true because (1) the exhibition was of the gallery's artistic spectrum over the past 100 years, and contained much more than this one painting; (2) "Apocalypse" portrayed many other people engaged in similarly humiliating sex acts, including the artist himself and several of his friends and benefactors; (3) Mr. Meischberger's likeness was only a small part of the painting; and (4) he was no longer recognizable after the vandalism.]

[The Vienna Court of Appeal overturned the judgment, finding that Mr. Meischberger's dignitary interests outweighed the gallery's interest in artistic expression. Specifically, the appeals court held that Mr. Meischberger was recognizable despite the vandalism, and t]he limits of artistic freedom were exceeded when the image of a person was substantially deformed by wholly imaginary elements without it being evident that the picture aimed at satire or any other form of exaggeration. The painting in the present case was not intended to be a parable or even an exaggerated criticism conveying a basic message, such as, for example, the statement that Mr Meischberger had disregarded sexual decency and morals. It therefore did not fall within the scope of Article 10 of the [European Convention on Human Rights], but in fact constituted a debasement of Mr Meischberger's public standing. The applicant association could not justify the exhibition of the painting under the artistic freedom protected by Article 17a of the [Austrian] Basic Law. There was, furthermore, nothing to indicate that the applicant association would abstain from exhibiting the painting in the future, so that there was a danger of recurrence.

17. On 18 July 2000 the [Austrian] Supreme Court [affirmed the lower court's award of money damages to Mr. Meischberger and the injunction against showing "Apocalypse" in the future.]

18. That decision was served on the applicant association's counsel on 13 September 2000.

II. Relevant Domestic Law

19. Section 78 of the Copyright Act, in so far as relevant, reads as follows:

"(1) Images of persons shall neither be exhibited publicly, nor in any way made accessible to the public, where injury would be caused to the legitimate interests of the portrayed persons or, in the event that they have died without having authorised or ordered publication, those of a close relative."

20. Artistic freedom is guaranteed by Article 17a of the Basic Law, which provides:

"There shall be freedom of artistic creation and of the publication and teaching of art."

The Law

I. Alleged Violation of Article 10 of the Convention

21. The applicant association complained under Article 10 of the Convention that the Austrian courts' decision forbidding it to exhibit any further the painting at issue had violated its right to freedom of expression.

Article 10, as far as relevant, reads as follows:

"1. Everyone has the right to freedom of expression. This right shall include freedom to hold opinions and to receive and impart information and ideas without interference by public authority and regardless of frontiers. . . .

2. The exercise of these freedoms, since it carries with it duties and responsibilities, may be subject to such formalities, conditions, restrictions or penalties as are prescribed by law and are necessary in a democratic society . . . for the protection of health or morals [or] for the protection of the reputation or rights of others. . . ."

FROM THE BENCH

A. The parties' submissions

22. The Government argued that the Austrian courts' injunction did not constitute an interference with the applicant association's rights within the meaning of Article 10 of the Convention. They submitted in that regard that Article 10 did not protect artistic freedom as such but only provided protection to artists who intended to contribute through their work to a public discussion of political or cultural matters. The present reproduction of public figures in "group sexual situations" could, however, hardly be regarded as a statement of opinion contributing to a cultural or political debate.

23. In the alternative, the Government argued that the interference at issue had been lawful and had served the legitimate aim of protecting morals and the reputation and rights of others. As regards the proportionality of the interference, they argued that since its inauguration, the exhibition at which the painting had been shown had been at the centre of media attention, precisely because of the painting itself. The interest of the media had become even more intense after the painting had been partly damaged, so that after the event in question the part of the painting affected and the fact that it showed Mr Meischberger was known not only to visitors of the exhibition but to the general public. The painting had been displayed in nearly all Austrian newspapers and on television. Accordingly, at least from that date on, Mr Meischberger's personal interests had prevailed over the interests of the applicant association in exhibiting the painting. It was also irrelevant whether Mr Meischberger was a subject of public interest at the time of the events as the painting could by no means be regarded as part of a public discussion of general interest or as relating to Mr Meischberger in his public capacity. Nor could Mr Meischberger be expected to comment in public on the painting since the activities depicted in it could certainly offend the sense of sexual propriety of persons of ordinary sensitivity. The Government lastly pointed out that at the time of the [injunction] the exhibition at issue had already been closed down and that throughout the duration of the exhibition the painting had actually been on display. The applicant association had not intended to exhibit the painting abroad. Furthermore, the prohibition on exhibiting the painting any further concerned only the applicant association as the exhibitor and not the owner of the painting, namely the artist and his manager. Having regard to all these elements, the Government argued that the [injunction] at issue was proportionate within the meaning of paragraph 2 of Article 10 of the Convention.

24. [VBK] argued that the public exhibition of a painting contributed to a debate between the artist, the exhibitor and the public and was therefore protected under Article 10 of the Convention. . . . It submitted that the Government's submissions as regards the protection of morals were irrelevant . . . and that Mr Meischberger could not . . . claim any personal interest worth protecting as the painting obviously did not state or suggest that the way in which he was portrayed corresponded to his actual behaviour. The painting presented the

artist's personal history in an allegorical way and depicted, among several other well-known persons, the painter himself and some of his friends and benefactors. All these persons were depicted engaging in sexual acts, reflecting the painter's conception of the interrelation between power and sexuality. Furthermore, Mr Meischberger and, in any event, the actions he considered libellous were not recognisable after the painting had been partly damaged. In the applicant association's view, the fact that he had instituted proceedings only after the painting had been partly damaged demonstrated that rather than protecting his personal interests he was aiming to discredit the painter's work.

■ ■ ■

B. The Court's assessment

26. The Court reiterates that freedom of expression, as secured in paragraph 1 of Article 10, constitutes one of the essential foundations of a democratic society, indeed one of the basic conditions for its progress and for the self-fulfilment [sic] of the individual. Subject to paragraph 2, it is applicable not only to "information" or "ideas" that are favourably received or regarded as inoffensive or as a matter of indifference, but also to those that offend, shock or disturb the State or any section of the population. Such are the demands of that pluralism, tolerance and broadmindedness without which there is no "democratic society". Those who create, perform, distribute or exhibit works of art contribute to the exchange of ideas and opinions which is essential for a democratic society. Hence the obligation on the State not to encroach unduly on their freedom of expression. Artists and those who promote their work are certainly not immune from the possibility of limitations as provided for in paragraph 2 of Article 10. Whoever exercises his freedom of expression undertakes, in accordance with the express terms of that paragraph, "duties and responsibilities"; their scope will depend on his situation and the means he uses. . . .

27. In the present case, the Austrian courts forbade the applicant association to exhibit any further the painting "Apocalypse" by Otto Mühl. Such decisions interfered with the applicant association's right to freedom of expression. . . .

28. The Court further finds, and this was not disputed before it, that the interference was "prescribed by law," the impugned courts' decisions having been based on section 78 of the Copyright Act.

29. As to the question of the legitimate aim pursued, the Court observes that section 78 of the Austrian Copyright Act provides a remedy against publication of a person's picture where this would violate the legitimate interests of the person concerned or, in the event that he or she has died, those of close relatives. Referring to that legislation, the domestic courts prohibited the applicant association from exhibiting the painting at issue any further as they found that it constituted a debasement of Mr Meischberger's public standing. The Court therefore

FROM THE BENCH

accepts that the impugned measure pursued the legitimate aim of "protection of the rights of others".

[The Court briefly considers and rejects another claim by the Austrian government that the injunction was intended to protect public morals, as permitted by Article 10 of the Convention.]

32. As regards the necessity of the interference, the Court notes at the outset that the painting, in its original state, depicted Mr Meischberger in a somewhat outrageous manner, namely naked and involved in sexual activities. Mr Meischberger, a former general secretary of the Austrian Freedom Party and a member of parliament at the time of the events, was portrayed in interaction with three other prominent members of his party, amongst them Mr Jörg Haider, who at that time was the party's leader and has in the meantime founded another party.

33. However, it must be emphasised that the painting used only photos of the heads of the persons concerned, their eyes being hidden under black bars and their bodies being painted in an unrealistic and exaggerated manner. It was common ground in the understanding of the domestic courts at all levels that the painting obviously did not aim to reflect or even to suggest reality; the Government, in their submissions, have not alleged otherwise. The Court finds that such portrayal amounted to a caricature of the persons concerned using satirical elements. It notes that satire is a form of artistic expression and social commentary and, by its inherent features of exaggeration and distortion of reality, naturally aims to provoke and agitate. Accordingly, any interference with an artist's right to such expression must be examined with particular care.

34. In the present case, the Court considers that the painting could hardly be understood to address details of Mr Meischberger's private life, but rather related to Mr Meischberger's public standing as a politician from the FPÖ. The Court notes that in this capacity Mr Meischberger has to display a wider tolerance in respect of criticism. . . . The Court does not find unreasonable the view taken by the court of first instance that the scene in which Mr Meischberger was portrayed could be understood to constitute some sort of counter-attack against the Austrian Freedom Party, whose members had strongly criticised the painter's work.

36. The Court also observes that, even before Mr Meischberger instituted proceedings, the part of the painting showing him had been damaged so that notably the offensive painting of his body was completely covered by red paint. The Court considers that, at the very latest from this incident onwards, Mr Meischberger's portrayal — even assuming that he was still recognisable, a question that elicited contradictory answers from the different Austrian courts — was certainly diminished, if not totally eclipsed, by the portrayal of all the other, mostly more prominent, persons who were still completely visible on the painting.

37. The Court lastly notes that the Austrian courts' injunction was not limited either in time or in space. It therefore left the applicant association, which directs one of the best-known Austrian galleries specialising in contemporary art, with no possibility of exhibiting the painting irrespective of whether

Mr Meischberger was known, or was still known, at the place and time of a potential exhibition in the future.

38. In sum, having balanced Mr Meischberger's personal interests and taking account of the artistic and satirical nature of his portrayal, as well as the impact of the measure at issue on the applicant association, the Court finds that the Austrian courts' injunction was disproportionate to the aim it pursued and therefore not necessary in a democratic society within the meaning of Article 10 §2 of the Convention.

39. Accordingly, there has been a violation of Article 10 of the Convention.

[The Court proceeded to calculate the money damages owed by the Austrian government to VBK.]

DISSENTING OPINION OF JUDGE LOUCAIDES

I disagree with the opinion of the majority that there has been a violation of Article 10 of the Convention in this case.

The majority found that the images portrayed in the "painting" in question were "artistic and satirical in nature". This assessment had a decisive effect on the judgment. The majority saw the "painting" as a form of criticism by the artist of Mr Meischberger, a politician and one of the persons depicted in it. It was he who brought the proceedings which led to the impugned measure.

The nature, meaning and effect of any image or images in a painting cannot be judged on the basis of what the painter purported to convey. What counts is the effect of the visible image on the observer. Furthermore, the fact that an image has been produced by an artist does not always make the end result "artistic". Likewise, an image will not become "satirical" if the observer does not comprehend or detect any message in the form of a meaningful attack or criticism relating to a particular problem or a person's conduct.

In my view, the picture in question cannot, by any stretch of the imagination, be called satirical or artistic. It showed a number of unrelated personalities (some political, some religious) in a vulgar and grotesque presentation and context of senseless, disgusting images of erect and ejaculating penises and of naked figures adopting repulsive sexual poses, some even involving violence, with coloured and disproportionately large genitals or breasts. The figures included religious personalities such as the Austrian Cardinal Hermann Groer and Mother Teresa, the latter portrayed with protruding bare breasts praying between two men—one of whom was the Cardinal—with erect penises ejaculating on her! Mr Meischberger was shown gripping the ejaculating penis of Mr Haider while at the same time being touched by two other FPÖ politicians and ejaculating on Mother Teresa!

The reader will of course need to look at the "painting" in question in order to be able to form a view of its nature and effect. It is my firm belief that the images depicted in this product of what is, to say the least, a strange imagination, convey no message; the "painting" is just a senseless, disgusting combination of lewd images whose only effect is to debase, insult and ridicule each and every

FROM THE BENCH

person portrayed. Personally, I was unable to find any criticism or satire in this "painting". Why were Mother Teresa and Cardinal Hermann Groer ridiculed? Why were the personalities depicted naked with erect and ejaculating penises? To find that situation comparable with satire or artistic expression is beyond my comprehension. And when we speak about art I do not think that we can include each and every act of artistic expression regardless of its nature and effect. In the same way that we exclude insults from freedom of speech, so we must exclude from the legitimate expression of artists insulting pictures that undermine the reputation or dignity of others, especially if they are devoid of any meaningful message and contain nothing more than senseless, repugnant and disgusting images, as in the present case. . . . Nobody can rely on the fact that he is an artist or that a work is a painting in order to escape liability for insulting others. Like the domestic courts, I find that the "painting" in question undermined the reputation and dignity of Mr Meischberger in a manner for which there can be no legitimate justification and therefore the national authorities were entitled to consider that the impugned measure was necessary in a democratic society for the protection of the reputation or rights of others.

JOINT DISSENTING OPINION OF JUDGES SPIELMANN AND JEBENS

. . .

We voted against finding a violation of Article 10 of the Convention. We are anxious to clarify the reasons for our vote in the following lines.

1. The Court accepted that the prohibition on exhibiting the painting "Apocalypse" was prescribed by law and pursued the legitimate aim of the "protection of the rights of others". However, the majority of the judges found that the interference was disproportionate to the aim pursued and therefore not necessary in a democratic society within the meaning of Article 10 §2 of the Convention. Accordingly, the majority found a breach of Article 10 of the Convention.

2. We do not subscribe to this approach.

3. It should be recalled that the painting was a montage combining painted elements and photographs of people, the overall effect being an unrealistic and exaggerated depiction of public figures in sexually explicit positions. The painting was not intended to portray reality. On the contrary, it is permissible to consider that it sought to convey a message by means of caricature and satire, which, according to the Court, is "a form of artistic expression and social commentary and, by its inherent features of exaggeration and distortion of reality, naturally aims to provoke and agitate" (see paragraph 33 of the judgment).

4. To justify its finding of a violation of Article 10, the Court relied on Mr Meischberger's standing as a politician and the fact that the message conveyed could be construed as a sort of counter-attack against the Austrian Freedom Party, whose members had previously criticised the artist's work (paragraph 34). . . . Having weighed up Mr Meischberger's personal interests and taken account of the artistic and satirical nature of his portrayal and the impact of the

injunction on the applicant association, the Court concluded that the injunction was disproportionate (paragraph 38).

5. We do not agree with this conclusion. Our reason is that where the "protection of the rights of others" is at stake, artistic freedom cannot be unlimited.

6. Admittedly, the Court's case-law consistently reiterates, and rightly so, that freedom of expression "is applicable not only to . . . 'ideas' that are favourably received or regarded as inoffensive or as a matter of indifference, but also to those that offend, shock or disturb the State or any sector of the population. Such are the demands of that pluralism, tolerance and broadmindedness without which there is no 'democratic society'." We also take the view that the State's margin of appreciation should be particularly limited, or indeed practically non-existent, where its interference affects artistic freedom.

7. However, in the present case the painting in question, even if it is an expression of what is known nowadays as "committed" art (art engagé), does not deserve the unlimited protection of Article 10 of the Convention, precisely because it interferes excessively with the rights of others. In other words: "There are . . . limits to excess: one cannot be excessively excessive."

8. The excessive nature of the portrayal results precisely from its attack on the "dignity of others", which in our view is covered by the protection of the "rights of others". On this point, we subscribe to the dissenting opinion of our colleague Judge Loucaides. We would emphasise that the concept of dignity prevails throughout the European Convention on Human Rights, even if it is not expressly mentioned in the text of the Convention. However, the Court has made it clear in its case-law that "[t]he very essence of the Convention is respect for human dignity and human freedom." And as a learned author has put it: "The foundation of human rights cannot be anything other than the 'equal dignity' of all human beings. Dignity and universality are therefore indissociable."

9. In our opinion, it was not the abstract or indeterminate concept of human dignity—a concept which can in itself be dangerous since it may be used as justification for hastily placing unacceptable limitations on fundamental rights—but the concrete concept of "fundamental personal dignity of others" which was central to the debate in the present case, seeing that a photograph of Mr Meischberger was used in a pictorial montage which he felt to be profoundly humiliating and degrading.

10. It should be noted in this connection that in an order of 3 June 1987, in a case about cartoons, the German Federal Constitutional Court relied on the concept of human dignity as expressly enshrined in the Basic Law (Article 1 (1)), in dismissing a complaint by a publisher. The cartoon portrayed a well-known politician as a pig copulating with another pig dressed in judicial robes. The court did not accept the publisher's argument relating to artistic freedom as protected by Article 5 (3) of the Basic Law. It is important to note that the court accepted that the cartoons could be described as a work of art; it was not appropriate to perform a quality control and thus to differentiate between "superior" and "inferior" or "good" and "bad" art. However, it dismissed the complaint,

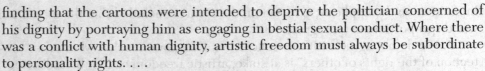

finding that the cartoons were intended to deprive the politician concerned of his dignity by portraying him as engaging in bestial sexual conduct. Where there was a conflict with human dignity, artistic freedom must always be subordinate to personality rights. . . .

13. Returning to the case before us, we therefore consider that the reasons that led the Court to find a violation (see paragraph 4 above) are not relevant. Such considerations must be subordinate to respect for human dignity. . . .

QUESTIONS FOR DISCUSSION

7.2 Compare the decision of the majority in *VBK* (finding a violation of the right to freedom of expression) and the U.S. Supreme Court's opinion in *Hustler v. Falwell*. Do the two decisions treat the status of the plaintiff similarly? What value(s) account for the two decisions coming out similarly? Also compare the opinions of the dissenting justices in *VBK* with the Court in *Hustler*. What value(s) account for the differences among the various groups?

7.3 Although the *VBK* judges seem to agree that artistic expression is a value worth protecting in a democratic society, is the legal system well-equipped to make judgments about what is and is not "art"? How should the courts determine what types of artistic expressions merit protection against individual dignitary interests? How much weight should be given to the artist's subjective intent, versus the objective effect on the observer?

The following opinion is from a recent significant case involving disparaging speech. Disparaging speech impugns the character, integrity, or abilities of a person or entity. As such, one could argue that it is even more constitutionally protected than hate speech, which can include a true threat against an individual.

The case outlined below arose from a challenge to a provision in the Lanham Act, the federal statute that regulates trademarks. The provision prohibited approving a trademark that "may disparage . . . persons, living or dead, institutions, beliefs, or national symbols, or bring them into contempt or disrepute." Simon Tam, the lead singer of the band "The Slants," had appealed the Trademark Office's refusal to register his group's name. Tam had chosen the name to "reclaim" and "take ownership" of stereotypes about people of Asian ethnicity, but the Trademark Office relied on the disparagement clause of the Lanham Act to refuse registration.

Central Hudson Gas & Elec. Corp. v. Public Service Commission of New York (1980) is one relevant prior case in this area. In that case, the Supreme Court held that the First Amendment protects commercial speech from unwarranted governmental regulation. The Court also held that "[i]f the communication is neither misleading nor related to unlawful activity . . . [t]he State must assert a substantial interest to be achieved by restrictions on commercial speech . . . [and] the regulatory technique must be in proportion to that interest." In the Court's opinion in *Lamb's Chapel v. Center Moriches Union Free School Dist.* (1993), it held that "the First Amendment forbids the government to regulate speech in ways that favor some viewpoints or ideas at the expense of others." These cases were among those cited by the Court in its opinion and ultimately influenced its decision to rule in Tam's favor.

FROM THE BENCH

MATAL v. TAM
137 S. Ct. 1744 (2017)

Justice ALITO announced the judgment of the Court and delivered the opinion of the Court with respect to Parts I, II, and III–A, and an opinion with respect to Parts III–B, III–C, and IV, in which The Chief Justice, Justice THOMAS, and Justice BREYER join.

This case concerns a dance-rock band's application for federal trademark registration of the band's name, "The Slants." "Slants" is a derogatory term for persons of Asian descent, and members of the band are Asian-Americans. But the band members believe that by taking that slur as the name of their group, they will help to "reclaim" the term and drain its denigrating force.

The Patent and Trademark Office (PTO) denied the application based on a provision of federal law prohibiting the registration of trademarks that may "disparage . . . or bring . . . into contemp[t] or disrepute" any "persons, living or dead." 15 U.S.C. §1052(a). We now hold that this provision violates the Free Speech Clause of the First Amendment. It offends a bedrock First Amendment principle: Speech may not be banned on the ground that it expresses ideas that offend.

FROM THE BENCH

The Slants, https://rb.gy/5910k. *Reprinted with permission from Simon Tam.*

I

A

"The principle underlying trademark protection is that distinctive marks—words, names, symbols, and the like—can help distinguish a particular artisan's goods from those of others." *B & B Hardware, Inc. v. Hargis Industries, Inc.* (2015). . . . It helps consumers identify goods and services that they wish to purchase, as well as those they want to avoid. . . .

C

The Lanham Act contains provisions that bar certain trademarks from the principal register. . . . At issue in this case is one such provision, which we will call "the disparagement clause." This provision prohibits the registration of a trademark "which may disparage . . . persons, living or dead, institutions, beliefs, or national symbols, or bring them into contempt, or disrepute." . . .

When deciding whether a trademark is disparaging, an examiner at the PTO generally applies a "two-part test." The examiner first considers "the likely meaning of the matter in question, taking into account not only dictionary definitions, but also the relationship of the matter to the other elements in the mark, the nature of the goods or services, and the manner in which the mark is used in the marketplace in connection with the goods or services." "If that meaning is found to refer to identifiable persons, institutions, beliefs or national symbols," the examiner moves to the second step, asking "whether that meaning may be disparaging to a substantial composite of the referenced group." If the examiner finds that a "substantial composite, although not necessarily a majority, of the referenced group would find the proposed mark . . . to be disparaging in the context of contemporary attitudes," a prima facie [initial] case of disparagement is made out, and the burden shifts to the applicant to prove that the trademark is not disparaging. What is more, the PTO has specified that "[t]he fact that an applicant may be a member of that group or has good intentions underlying its use of a term does not obviate the fact that a substantial composite of the referenced group would find the term objectionable."

D

Simon Tam is the lead singer of "The Slants." He chose this moniker in order to "reclaim" and "take ownership" of stereotypes about people of Asian ethnicity. . . . Tam sought federal registration of "THE SLANTS," on the principal register, but an examining attorney at the PTO rejected the request, applying the PTO's two-part framework and finding that "there is . . . a substantial composite of persons who find the term in the applied-for mark offensive." The examining attorney relied in part on the fact that "numerous dictionaries define 'slants' or 'slant-eyes' as a derogatory or offensive term." . . .

III

Because the disparagement clause applies to marks that disparage the members of a racial or ethnic group, we must decide whether the clause violates the Free Speech Clause of the First Amendment. And at the outset, we must consider three arguments that would either eliminate any First Amendment protection or result in highly permissive rational-basis review. Specifically, the Government contends (1) that trademarks are government speech, not private speech, (2) that trademarks are a form of government subsidy, and (3) that the constitutionality of the disparagement clause should be tested under a new "government-program" doctrine. We address each of these arguments below.

A

The First Amendment prohibits Congress and other government entities and actors from "abridging the freedom of speech"; the First Amendment does not say that Congress and other government entities must abridge their own ability to speak freely. And our cases recognize that "[t]he Free Speech Clause . . . does not regulate government speech."

As we have said, "it is not easy to imagine how government could function" if it were subject to the restrictions that the First Amendment imposes on private speech. "'[T]he First Amendment forbids the government to regulate speech in ways that favor some viewpoints or ideas at the expense of others,'" *Lamb's Chapel v. Center Moriches Union Free School Dist.* (1993), but imposing a requirement of viewpoint-neutrality on government speech would be paralyzing. When a government entity embarks on a course of action, it necessarily takes a particular viewpoint and rejects others. The Free Speech Clause does not require government to maintain viewpoint neutrality when its officers and employees speak about that venture.

Here is a simple example. During the Second World War, the Federal Government produced and distributed millions of posters to promote the war effort. There were posters urging enlistment, the purchase of war bonds, and the conservation of scarce resources. These posters expressed a viewpoint, but the First Amendment did not demand that the Government balance the message of these posters by producing and distributing posters encouraging Americans to refrain from engaging in these activities.

But while the government-speech doctrine is important—indeed, essential—it is a doctrine that is susceptible to dangerous misuse. If private speech could be passed off as government speech by simply affixing a government seal of approval, government could silence or muffle the expression of disfavored viewpoints. For this reason, we must exercise great caution before extending our government-speech precedents.

. . . [I]t is far-fetched to suggest that the content of a registered mark is government speech. If the federal registration of a trademark makes the mark government speech, the Federal Government is babbling prodigiously and incoherently. It is saying many unseemly things. It is expressing contradictory views. It is unashamedly endorsing a vast array of commercial products and services. And it is providing Delphic [obscure or ambiguous] advice to the consuming public. For example, if trademarks represent government speech, what does the Government have in mind when it advises Americans to "make.believe" (Sony), "Think different" (Apple), "Just do it" (Nike), or "Have it your way" (Burger King)? . . . Trademarks are private, not government, speech.

C

. . . Our cases use the term "viewpoint" discrimination in a broad sense, and in that sense, the disparagement clause discriminates on the bases of "viewpoint." To be sure, the clause evenhandedly prohibits disparagement of all groups. It applies equally to marks that damn Democrats and Republicans, capitalists and socialists, and those arrayed on both sides of every possible issue. It denies registration to any mark that is offensive to a substantial percentage of the members of any group. But in the sense relevant here, that is viewpoint discrimination: Giving offense is a viewpoint.

We have said time and again that "the public expression of ideas may not be prohibited merely because the ideas are themselves offensive to some of their hearers." For this reason, the disparagement clause cannot be saved by analyzing it as a type of government program in which some content- and speaker-based restrictions are permitted.

IV

[We now] must confront a dispute between the parties on the question whether trademarks are commercial speech and are thus subject to the relaxed scrutiny outlined in *Central Hudson Gas & Elec. Corp. v. Public Serv. Comm'n of N. Y.* (1980). The Government and *amici* supporting its position argue that all trademarks are commercial speech. They note that the central purposes of trademarks are commercial and that federal law regulates trademarks to promote fair and orderly interstate commerce. Tam and his *amici*, on the other hand, contend that many, if not all, trademarks have an expressive component. In other words, these trademarks do not simply identify the source of a product or service but go on to say something more, either about the product or service or some broader issue. The trademark in this case illustrates this point. The name "The Slants" not only identifies the band but expresses a view about social issues.

We need not resolve this debate between the parties because the disparagement clause cannot withstand even *Central Hudson* review. Under *Central Hudson*, a restriction of speech must serve "a substantial interest," and it must be "narrowly drawn." This means, among other things, that "[t]he regulatory technique may extend only as far as the interest it serves." The disparagement clause fails this requirement.

. . . Echoing language in one of the opinions below, the Government asserts an interest in preventing "'underrepresented groups'" from being "'bombarded with demeaning messages in commercial advertising.'" An *amicus* supporting the Government refers to "encouraging racial tolerance and protecting the privacy and welfare of individuals." But no matter how the point is phrased, its unmistakable thrust is this: The Government has an interest in preventing speech expressing ideas that offend. And, as we have explained, that idea strikes at the heart of the First Amendment. Speech that demeans on the basis of race, ethnicity, gender, religion, age, disability, or any other similar ground is hateful; but the proudest boast of our free speech jurisprudence is that we protect the freedom to express "the thought that we hate." *United States v. Schwimmer* (1929) (Holmes, J., dissenting).

The second interest asserted is protecting the orderly flow of commerce. Commerce, we are told, is disrupted by trademarks that "involv[e] disparagement of race, gender, ethnicity, national origin, religion, sexual orientation, and similar demographic classification." Such trademarks are analogized to discriminatory conduct, which has been recognized to have an adverse effect on commerce.

A simple answer to this argument is that the disparagement clause is not "narrowly drawn" to drive out trademarks that support invidious discrimination. The clause reaches any trademark that disparages *any person, group, or institution*. It applies to trademarks like the following: "Down with racists," "Down with sexists," "Down with homophobes." It is not an anti-discrimination clause; it is a happy-talk clause. In this way, it goes much further than is necessary to serve the interest asserted. The clause is far too broad in other ways as well. The clause protects every person living or dead as well as every institution. Is it conceivable that commerce would be disrupted by a trademark saying: "James Buchanan was a disastrous president" or "Slavery is an evil institution"?

There is also a deeper problem with the argument that commercial speech may be cleansed of any expression likely to cause offense. The commercial market is well stocked with merchandise that disparages prominent figures and groups, and the line between commercial and non-commercial speech is not always clear, as this case illustrates. If affixing the commercial label permits the suppression of any speech that may lead to political or social "volatility," free speech would be endangered.

■ ■ ■

For these reasons, we hold that the disparagement clause violates the Free Speech Clause of the First Amendment.

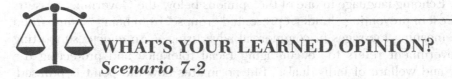

WHAT'S YOUR LEARNED OPINION?
Scenario 7-2

Wandering Dago is a business that operates a food truck and brands itself and the food it sells with language generally viewed as ethnic slurs. The owners of Wandering Dago say that they view their food truck as "the people's truck" and as giving a "nod to [their] Italian heritage" and to their ancestors, who immigrated to the United States as day laborers. Wandering Dago's owners characterize the practice of naming their business and the food they sell with ethnic slurs as "signaling an irreverent, blue collar solidarity with its customers" and "signal[ing] to . . . immigrant groups that this food truck is for them." They also say that using slurs in this way can "weaken the derogatory force" of the slur or "convey affiliation with . . . members of that minority group."

State officials denied Wandering Dago's applications to participate as a food vendor in a city plaza. The officials justified the denial "on the grounds that its name contains an offensive ethnic slur and does not fit with [their] policy of providing family-friendly programming."

Wandering Dago contends that the state officials violated its rights to free speech by denying its applications because of its branding practices. In light of the Supreme Court's decision in *Matal v. Tam*, is Wandering Dago likely to be successful in its claim?

Scenario 7-3

A potential advertiser sought to place an advertisement on the sides of city buses. The ad said: "Fatwa on your head? Is your family or community threatening you? Leaving Islam? Got Questions? Get Answers! Escape IslamNow.com."

The state public transit authority viewed the ad as "political" because "fatwa" referred to sharia law and because the website contained anti-Islamic commentary. The transit authority also found that the ad would likely hold people of the Islamic faith up to scorn or ridicule because it suggested that they might threaten their family members.

The advertiser brought action against the state public transit authority and various transit authority employees, alleging that the transit authority's rejection of its advertisement under the transit authority's bans on "political" advertisements and on advertisements that "scorn or ridicule" violated the First Amendment. What does *Matal v. Tam* suggest about whether the advertiser will be successful in its suit?

BEHIND THE CURTAIN

At the time of *Matal*, a national debate raged in the United States about the use of derogatory names for sports teams. Mirroring this debate, in the *Matal* litigation itself, various Native American organizations filed a joint brief *amici curiae* supporting the trademark office in the U.S. Supreme Court, discussing the harmful effects of disparaging terms and stereotypes on Native American communities and arguing that the government should not need to endorse these terms in the form of trademark protection. Here's a snippet from their brief:

> Amici have a long history of involvement in cultural, economic, educational, health, policy, and social justice issues affecting the Native American nations and tribes, and their citizenry. As a result, they speak authoritatively about the harm caused by racially based "Indian" names and their belief that the "REDSKINS" marks are disparaging to all Native Americans, subjecting them to ridicule, contempt, and disrepute. . . .

On the other hand, the Slants argued to the press and in their brief that the driving motivation for their name was to reappropriate a derogatory term for their own purposes. Supporting the Slants' position, an amicus brief on behalf of the organization Dykes on Bikes made the argument that being able to reclaim disparaging terms from those who would use them against certain groups is an important goal. Dykes on Bikes argued that federal registration is essential for an organization to be able to effectively brand itself, and arbitrary rejections by the Trademark Office have detrimental effects. The Dykes on Bikes brief argued the following:

> Amicus purposefully and intentionally adopted the term "dykes" as part of its trademark in order to highlight and confront the controversial history of that term and dispel the notion that it is disparaging. It uses its trademark to prevent the commercial exploitation of its name or logo, which Dykes on Bikes believes would corrupt and dilute its ability to use its mark to advance its political and social message. . . .

Following *Matal*, the U.S. Supreme Court invalidated yet another provision of the Lanham Act, which prohibited immoral or scandalous trademarks. *Iancu v. Brunetti*, 139 S. Ct. 2294 (2019). The case arose when an artist and entrepreneur, Erik Brunetti, founded a clothing line for which he wanted to use the trademark FUCT. While the name was intended to be pronounced as four letters, many read it as a word sounding like a well-known profanity. The Trademark Office refused to register the mark because it was vulgar.

In striking down this trademark law provision, the *Iancu* Court relied on *Matal* in concluding that because the prohibition on immoral and scandalous trademarks was unconstitutionally viewpoint-based, the prohibition was unconstitutional. Specifically, the Court applied this viewpoint test to the bar against immoral or scandalous trademarks. Pointing to dictionary definitions of *immoral* as "inconsistent with rectitude, purity, or good morals" and *scandalous* as "giv[es] offense to the conscience or moral feelings," the Court reasoned that these and other definitions make clear that the trademark provision "distinguishes between two opposed sets of ideas: those aligned with conventional moral standards and those hostile to them; those inducing societal nods of approval and those provoking offense and condemnation."

In criticizing this discrimination against negative messages, the Court made an intriguing observation that the statute seemed to disfavor negative messages, and to favor positive ones. To illustrate this point, the Court contrasted the type of sayings that might be capable of getting trademark registration with the type that would prompt rejection:

"Love rules"? "Always be good"? Registration follows.

"Hate rules"? "Always be cruel"? Not according to the Lanham Act's "immoral or scandalous" bar.

2. Muzzling the Stand-up Comedian

The opinion below is a landmark decision regarding whether the Federal Communications Commission would violate First Amendment speech rights by imposing sanctions on a radio station for airing a program containing curse words during certain hours. Prior to this dispute, the Court had addressed possible exceptions to the freedom of speech in *Chaplinsky v. New Hampshire* (1942). In that decision, the Court suggested that "the lewd and obscene, [and] the profane" were among the categories of speech that were not protected. The Court confronted the scope of that declaration more directly in *Cohen v. California* (1971), which involved the issue of profane language in the context of political speech. The defendant in that case, Cohen, had been convicted of disturbing the peace for walking through a courthouse while wearing a jacket that had "Fuck the Draft" written on the back. The Court reversed the conviction, holding that it could not "indulge the facile assumption that one can forbid particular words without also running a substantial risk of suppressing ideas in the process. Indeed, governments might soon seize upon the censorship of particular words as a convenient guise for banning the expression of unpopular views."

As the law has developed, the U.S. Supreme Court has drawn a distinction between indecent speech (which encompasses curse words and other expressions) and obscene speech. Indecent speech is considered low-level speech entitled to limited First Amendment protection and obscene speech is outside First Amendment protection. A big challenge, of course, is identifying what falls into each category. To some, neither type of speech is worthy of protection: In their view, neither type of speech is essential to the functioning of a working democracy. In fact, some take the view that sexually explicit speech has nothing to contribute to science or culture, believing that it deeply harms the moral fabric of society and encourages intolerance of women and other groups in society by promoting degrading and dehumanizing visions of other people. Others argue that sexually explicit speech can be an important part of artistic expression and often promotes personal autonomy and tolerance. How do decision makers decide what material is sufficiently unsavory as to merit curtailing whatever individual or collective merits the material might have?

Current legal doctrine makes some things clear. Obscenity and child pornography are unprotected speech. Yet what is obscenity and what is child pornography? Child pornography—which uses or depicts minors—is associated with obscenity because it is sexually oriented, but it remains unprotected even if it does not fall within the definition of obscenity. Profanity and other indecency concern words and expressive conduct that often touch on sexual topics but do not amount to obscenity.

The U.S. Supreme Court attempted again and again—starting in the late 1950s—to provide a useful test for determining what counts as "obscene" speech so as to place it outside First Amendment protection. In 1973, the Court settled on a test that still prevails today, no matter how workable or unworkable it might seem. Announcing the test in *Miller v. California*, 413 U.S. 15 (1973), the Supreme Court set forth the following guidelines for a trier of fact to determine if the sexual content of speech renders it obscene: (a) whether "the average person, applying contemporary community standards" would find that the work, taken as a whole, appeals to the prurient interest; (b) whether the work depicts or describes, in a patently offensive way, sexual conduct specifically defined by the applicable state law; and (c) whether the work, taken as a whole, lacks serious literary, artistic, political, or scientific value.

In reading the following opinion, one point deserves mention: Carlin's monologue was considered indecent, not obscene. Thus, the monologue is eligible for some constitutional protection.

FROM THE BENCH

FEDERAL COMMUNICATIONS COMMISSION v. PACIFICA FOUNDATION
438 U.S. 726 (1978)

Mr. Justice STEVENS delivered the opinion of the Court (Parts I, II, III and IV–C) and an opinion in which The Chief Justice and Mr. Justice REHNQUIST joined (Parts IV–A and IV–B).

[Comedian George Carlin recorded a monologue titled "Filthy Words," during which he listed the words "you definitely wouldn't say, ever" on the public airwaves, repeating them over and over again. On a Tuesday afternoon in 1973, a New York radio station, owned by respondent Pacifica Foundation, broadcast the "Filthy Words" monologue. A man, who stated that he had heard the broadcast while driving with his young son, wrote a letter complaining to the FCC.

Pacifica explained that the monologue had been played during a program about contemporary society's attitude toward language and that, immediately before its broadcast, listeners had been advised that it included "sensitive language which might be regarded as offensive to some." Pacifica stated that "Carlin is not mouthing obscenities, he is merely using words to satirize as harmless and essentially silly our attitudes towards those words." Pacifica stated that it was not aware of any other complaints about the broadcast.

The FCC issued an order granting the complaint and declaring that Pacifica "could have been the subject of administrative sanctions." The Commission did not impose formal sanctions, but it did state that the order would be "associated with the station's license file and in the event that subsequent complaints are received, the Commission will then decide whether it should utilize any of the available sanctions it has been granted by Congress."

The Commission characterized the language used in the Carlin monologue as "patently offensive," though not necessarily obscene. The Commission concluded that certain words depicted sexual and excretory activities in a patently offensive manner and that they "were broadcast at a time when children were undoubtedly in the audience (i.e., in the early afternoon)." In summary, the Commission stated: "We therefore hold that the language as broadcast was indecent and prohibited by 18 U.S.C. [§]1464."]

This case requires that we decide whether the Federal Communications Commission has any power to regulate a radio broadcast that is indecent but not obscene. Having granted the Commission's petition for certiorari, we must decide . . . whether the order violates the First Amendment of the United States Constitution.

IV

Pacifica makes two constitutional attacks on the Commission's order. First, it argues that the Commission's construction of the statutory language broadly encompasses so much constitutionally protected speech that reversal is required even if Pacifica's broadcast of the "Filthy Words" monologue is not itself protected by the First Amendment. Second, Pacifica argues that inasmuch as the recording is not obscene, the Constitution forbids any abridgment of the right to broadcast it on the radio.

A

The first argument fails because our review is limited to the question whether the Commission has the authority to proscribe this particular broadcast. As the Commission itself emphasized, its order was "issued in a specific factual context." That approach is appropriate for courts as well as the Commission when regulation of indecency is at stake, for indecency is largely a function of context—it cannot be adequately judged in the abstract.

The approach is also consistent with *Red Lion Broadcasting Co. v. FCC*. In that case the Court rejected an argument that the Commission's regulations defining the fairness doctrine were so vague that they would inevitably abridge the broadcasters' freedom of speech. The Court of Appeals had invalidated the regulations because their vagueness might lead to self-censorship of controversial program content. This Court reversed. After noting that the Commission had indicated, as it has in this case, that it would not impose sanctions without warning in cases in which the applicability of the law was unclear, the Court stated:

> We need not approve every aspect of the fairness doctrine to decide these cases, and we will not now pass upon the constitutionality of these regulations by envisioning the most extreme applications conceivable, but will deal with those problems if and when they arise.

It is true that the Commission's order may lead some broadcasters to censor themselves. At most, however, the Commission's definition of indecency will deter only the broadcasting of patently offensive references to excretory and sexual organs and activities. While some of these references may be protected, they surely lie at the periphery of First Amendment concern. The danger dismissed so summarily in *Red Lion*, in contrast, was that broadcasters would respond to the vagueness of the regulations by refusing to present programs dealing with important social and political controversies. Invalidating any rule on the basis of its hypothetical application to situations not before the Court is "strong medicine" to be applied "sparingly and only as a last resort." *Broadrick v. Oklahoma*. We decline to administer that medicine to preserve the vigor of patently offensive sexual and excretory speech.

B

When the issue is narrowed to the facts of this case, the question is whether the First Amendment denies government any power to restrict the public broadcast of indecent language in any circumstances. For if the government has any such power, this was an appropriate occasion for its exercise.

The words of the Carlin monologue are unquestionably "speech" within the meaning of the First Amendment. It is equally clear that the Commission's objections to the broadcast were based in part on its content. The order must therefore fall if, as Pacifica argues, the First Amendment prohibits all governmental regulation that depends on the content of speech. Our past cases demonstrate, however, that no such absolute rule is mandated by the Constitution.

The classic exposition of the proposition that both the content and the context of speech are critical elements of First Amendment analysis is Mr. Justice Holmes' statement for the Court in *Schenck v. United States*:

> We admit that in many places and in ordinary times the defendants in saying all that was said in the circular would have been within their constitutional rights. But the character of every act depends upon the circumstances in which it is done. . . . The most stringent protection of free speech would not protect a man in falsely shouting fire in a theatre and causing a panic. . . . The question in every case is whether the words used are used in such circumstances and are of such a nature as to create a clear and present danger that they will bring about the substantive evils that Congress has a right to prevent."

Other distinctions based on content have been approved in the years since *Schenck*. The government may forbid speech calculated to provoke a fight. It may pay heed to the "'commonsense differences' between commercial speech and other varieties." *Bates v. State Bar of Arizona*. It may treat libels against private citizens more severely than libels against public officials. Obscenity may be wholly prohibited. *Miller v. California*. And only two Terms ago we refused to hold that a "statutory classification is unconstitutional because it is based on the content of communication protected by the First Amendment." *Young v. American Mini Theatres, Inc.*

The question in this case is whether a broadcast of patently offensive words dealing with sex and excretion may be regulated because of its content. Obscene materials have been denied the protection of the First Amendment because their content is so offensive to contemporary moral standards. But the fact that society may find speech offensive is not a sufficient reason for suppressing it. Indeed, if it is the speaker's opinion that gives offense, that consequence is a reason for according it constitutional protection. For it is a central tenet of the First Amendment that the government must remain neutral in the marketplace of ideas. If there were any reason to believe that the Commission's characterization of the Carlin monologue as offensive could be traced to its political content—or even to the fact that it satirized contemporary attitudes about four-letter words—First Amendment protection might be required. But that is simply not this case. These words offend for the same reasons that obscenity offends. Their place in the hierarchy of First Amendment values was aptly sketched by Mr. Justice Murphy when he said: "Such utterances are no essential part of any exposition of ideas, and are of such slight social value as a step to truth that any benefit that may be derived from them is clearly outweighed by the social interest in order and morality." *Chaplinsky v. New Hampshire*.

Although these words ordinarily lack literary, political, or scientific value, they are not entirely outside the protection of the First Amendment. Some uses of even the most offensive words are unquestionably protected. Indeed, we may assume, *arguendo*, that this monologue would be protected in other contexts.

FROM THE BENCH

Nonetheless, the constitutional protection accorded to a communication containing such patently offensive sexual and excretory language need not be the same in every context. It is a characteristic of speech such as this that both its capacity to offend and its "social value," to use Mr. Justice Murphy's term, vary with the circumstances. Words that are commonplace in one setting are shocking in another. To paraphrase Mr. Justice Harlan, one occasion's lyric is another's vulgarity.

In this case it is undisputed that the content of Pacifica's broadcast was "vulgar," "offensive," and "shocking." Because content of that character is not entitled to absolute constitutional protection under all circumstances, we must consider its context in order to determine whether the Commission's action was constitutionally permissible.

C

We have long recognized that each medium of expression presents special First Amendment problems. And of all forms of communication, it is broadcasting that has received the most limited First Amendment protection. . . . [A] broadcaster may be deprived of his license and his forum if the Commission decides that such an action would serve "the public interest, convenience, and necessity." . . .

The reasons for these distinctions are complex, but two have relevance to the present case. First, the broadcast media have established a uniquely pervasive presence in the lives of all Americans. Patently offensive, indecent material presented over the airwaves confronts the citizen, not only in public, but also in the privacy of the home, where the individual's right to be left alone plainly outweighs the First Amendment rights of an intruder. Because the broadcast audience is constantly tuning in and out, prior warnings cannot completely protect the listener or viewer from unexpected program content. To say that one may avoid further offense by turning off the radio when he hears indecent language is like saying that the remedy for an assault is to run away after the first blow. One may hang up on an indecent phone call, but that option does not give the caller a constitutional immunity or avoid a harm that has already taken place.

Second, broadcasting is uniquely accessible to children, even those too young to read. . . . Other forms of offensive expression may be withheld from the young without restricting the expression at its source. Bookstores and motion picture theaters, for example, may be prohibited from making indecent material available to children. We held in *Ginsberg v. New York* that the government's interest in the "well-being of its youth" and in supporting "parents' claim to authority in their own household" justified the regulation of otherwise protected expression. The ease with which children may obtain access to broadcast material, coupled with the concerns recognized in *Ginsberg*, amply justify special treatment of indecent broadcasting.

It is appropriate, in conclusion, to emphasize the narrowness of our holding. This case does not involve a two-way radio conversation between a cab driver and a dispatcher, or a telecast of an Elizabethan comedy. We have not decided that an occasional expletive in either setting would justify any sanction or, indeed, that this broadcast would justify a criminal prosecution. The Commission's decision rested entirely on a nuisance rationale under which context is all-important. The concept requires consideration of a host of variables. The time of day was emphasized by the Commission. The content of the program in which the language is used will also affect the composition of the audience, and differences between radio, television, and perhaps closed-circuit transmissions, may also be relevant. As Mr. Justice Sutherland wrote a "nuisance may be merely a right thing in the wrong place,—like a pig in the parlor instead of the barnyard." *Euclid v. Ambler Realty Co.* We simply hold that when the Commission finds that a pig has entered the parlor, the exercise of its regulatory power does not depend on proof that the pig is obscene.

QUESTIONS FOR DISCUSSION

7.4   Can you identify any way that the facts and First Amendment concerns in *Pacifica* connect with *Matal v. Tam*? How can you distinguish the two cases?

7.5   As is the case with many disputes about minors and sexually explicit material, the Court in *Pacifica* and the school speech cases were deferential to officials who were intent on protecting minors from exposure to information about sexual matters. Do you believe the Court's approach is appropriate?

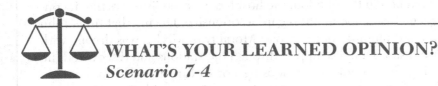

WHAT'S YOUR LEARNED OPINION?
Scenario 7-4

The Minneapolis City Council enacted an ordinance making it unlawful for any person knowingly to display for commercial purposes any material that is "harmful to minors" unless that material is in a sealed wrapper. The ordinance further requires an opaque cover on any material whose "cover, covers, or packaging, standing alone, is harmful to minors."

A subsection of the ordinance defines "harmful to minors" as follows:

"Harmful to minors" means that quality of any description or representation, in whatever form, of nudity, sexual conduct, or sexual excitement, when it:
(1) predominantly appeals to the prurient, shameful, or morbid interest of minors in sex; and
(2) is patently offensive to contemporary standards in the adult community as a whole with respect to what is suitable sexual material for minors; and
(3) taken as a whole, lacks serious literary, artistic, political, or scientific value.

The provisions of the ordinance requiring sealed wrappers and opaque covers do not apply if minors are not allowed to be present or are not able to view the proscribed materials or their covers. A business is considered in compliance with this exception if it physically segregates the proscribed material so that minors cannot be present or cannot view the materials, posts a sign reading "Adults Only — You must be 18 to enter," and enforces these restrictions.

A trade organization of retail merchants and an individual bookseller filed suit against the city seeking to have the ordinance declared unconstitutional on First Amendment grounds. The petitioners argue that the cover and wrapper requirements of the ordinance are overbroad because they impermissibly limit the access of adults to materials that are constitutionally protected as to them. Will the petitioners be successful in their challenge?

BEHIND THE CURTAIN

How did the *Pacifica* case come about? Several months after George Carlin first recorded his routine, an afternoon radio host decided to play the monologue. As explained in the opinion, the host first warned listeners that it contained language that some might regard as offensive. During that time, John Douglas, a board member of the group Morality in Media, was driving with his 15-year-old son. Douglas flipped through the stations and discovered the station playing the monologue. Choosing not to turn the dial to a station he might have found more appropriate for his 15-year-old, Douglas instead stayed tuned in. About a month later, Douglas filed a complaint with the FCC, stating that his "young son" had been with him the day that the station played the Carlin monologue.

Upon receiving the FCC complaint, the station owner, Pacifica Foundation, defended by favorably comparing Carlin to satirists of the stature of Mark Twain and Mort Sahl. In fact, Carlin's routine followed closely the tradition of Lenny Bruce—who also found himself in repeated trouble for his profanity-laced monologues. The lineage between the two is not remote. In 1962, Carlin shared the back seat of a police car with Bruce. Carlin had been arrested for failure to show the age identification needed to enter the club where Bruce was performing. Bruce was arrested on obscenity charges that night, accused of uttering words deemed indecent or obscene.

Like Carlin, Bruce recognized that words were powerful—his means of tearing apart stupidity, hypocrisy, and oppression. Plying his trade many years before Carlin, Lenny Bruce faced even harder times than Carlin: He was blacklisted from performing in U.S. clubs because of his propensity to inflect his routines with indecent references, repeatedly arrested for his comedy, and tried as a criminal.

How wise was the U.S. legal response to avant-garde humor? Did the official response serve its desired ends? The Lenny Bruce and George Carlin examples suggest that the answer is no. Legal prohibitions helped transport these comedians from clowning jokesters into intellectual social critics. Bruce and Carlin have been ultimately regarded as free speech martyrs and cultural heroes. Reminiscing about the *Pacifica* case, Carlin observed, "My name is a footnote in American legal history, which I am perversely kind of proud of." Most constitutional law scholars and pop culture historians would disagree that he is a mere footnote. Carlin's stature increased, not diminished, with the attempted censorship, clearly a result intended by neither the FCC nor the Supreme Court that wrote *Pacifica*. What does that tell you about censorship?

3. Other Ways the Law Regulates Humor

Compare the *Hustler* case with the *Pacifica* case. *Hustler* said that the type of joke at issue in that case should generally be "hands off" for the law. (The same can be said of *Matal v. Tam* and *Vereinigung Bildender Künstler.*) On the other hand, *Pacifica* protected the humor regulation at issue there. These are just a few of many examples where law—whether in the form of a court opinion, a statute, regulation, and the like—makes choices between what type of humor to protect and what type of humor to prohibit or punish. In the city of Philadelphia some years ago, federal prosecutors brought charges against a White hospital employee who hung a noose near the locker of a Black coworker. The White employee said it was "just a joke." The Federal Criminal Code suggested that was not an excuse and federal criminal charges followed. This prohibition is not alone. As is the case for jokes about bombing airplanes, federal criminal law also takes a dim view of quips about killing the U.S. President. Likewise, as the noose case illustrates, the law criminalizes racist jokes that terrorize or violate civil rights. These crime definitions are just one way that government pressures wannabe jokers into silence. A judicial or regulatory order prohibiting someone from telling a particular joke will subject the violator to a contempt-of-court sanction. Because contempt often includes criminal punishment, these orders act as "prior restraints" on joke telling: They effectively prevent the joke from occurring.

These criminal law examples show direct regulation of humor: If you do these things, you will go to jail. More subtle, yet still potent, is the law's indirect regulation of humor. For example, under certain circumstances, a parody of a trademark can be protected from legal regulation under trademark infringement theory. The uniform and emblems surrounding the Girl Scouts are protected by trademark law. See the parody photo below using these symbols—along with the Boy Scouts motto.

The Girl Scouts filed suit and lost. According to the court, this was not a trademark infringement. Rather, it was genuine parody that should not be regulated. In other words, the court protected this parody as legitimate humor contributing to U.S. culture—outside the scope of legal regulation.

Those who are the object of parody often take offense. Accordingly, like Jerry Falwell in the *Hustler* case, that offense is transformed into a lawsuit for a dignitary harm, such as defamation, intentional infliction of emotional distress, and the like. These dignitary harms are theories—known as tort theories—for bringing a lawsuit. If the decision maker (judge or jury) determines that the wrong has been established, a substantial damage award may occur. Thus, one thinking about making an edgy joke or caricature might think twice before making it, for fear they could later be hammered with a monetary penalty.

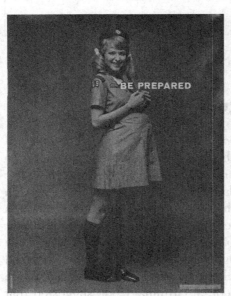

Parody poster subject to trademark infringement lawsuit in *Girl Scouts of the United States of America v. Personality Posters Manufacturing Co.*, 304 F. Supp. 1228 (1969). *Court document.*

Another area of law where humor is the subject of the lawsuit is sexual harassment. Federal and some state statutes create a mechanism for bringing a lawsuit when someone (usually a woman) is subject to such vicious ridicule or joking that her job becomes much more difficult than for others who do the same work. In other words, a barrage of vicious jokes can change the conditions of employment for a person. The result? An employer's tolerance of the joking environment can amount to employment discrimination. Knowing that the penalties flowing from employment discrimination can be significant, employers thus have a strong incentive to suppress the jokes—calling for internal regulation of humor.

Adding to the list of lawsuits that can flow from humor is an unlikely area of regulation: contract law. When you got drunk last night and wrote on a cocktail napkin that you would sell me your car for $125, can I enforce that bargain the next day? Or will you be able to wiggle out of the deal by saying it was "just a joke"? When an advertisement makes extravagant claims about a product and you act on those claims, can you succeed in a breach of contract suit if the claims do not materialize? In those cases, a court considering a contract case must decide whether or not the "just a joke" defense will prevail. The result will be to protect the joker or subject the joker to liability.

Law is everywhere. Humor is everywhere, too. As a consequence, it is no surprise that law gets an opportunity to protect or punish humor in many ways.

B. Free Expression Rights to Express Hate and Other Offense Versus Human Dignity

For those concerned with the harm inflicted by words, hate speech is the concept that comes to mind. Yet to understand where the law stands, one must understand several other concepts as well. Indeed, as is often the case with First Amendment doctrine, rules regulating offensive speech are organized in a jumbled array of overlapping categories: fighting words, hate speech, disparaging speech, and true threats. The amount of protection accorded a particular type of offensive speech depends on which category (or label) one places on the challenged expression. To make matters even more confusing, offensive speech is often similar to speech that incites illegality (such as incitement to riot). The U.S. Supreme Court, however, has scrupulously separated offensive speech doctrines from doctrines that govern incitement of illegality.

The U.S. Supreme Court has defined "fighting words" as those words that "by their very utterance inflict injury or tend to incite an immediate breach of the peace." *Chaplinsky v. State of New Hampshire*, 315 U.S. 568, 572 (1942). The Court emphasizes that the fighting words doctrine generally focuses on the speech recipient's potential reaction. Analytically, true threats are similar to fighting words in that both categories of speech are considered low-value speech (and thus more open to regulation). The true threats doctrine, however, focuses on the intent of the speaker (not the reaction of the recipient): Indeed, true threats cases often turn on whether the speaker intended to inspire fear in the recipient.

Hate speech and disparaging speech are independent of true threats and fighting words. Sometimes hate and disparaging speech can have the same effect on the recipient of speech as fighting words, but that is not always the case. The focus on litigation about hate and disparaging speech is whether government can constitutionally prevent hate speech because it denigrates disadvantaged citizens in ways that damage them psychologically or promote hatred and discrimination against them. Unlike true threats and fighting words, courts treat hate speech as high-value speech and thus are loathe to allow restrictions on it. In other words, under current law, one can generally offend without legal consequence, but one's speech can be regulated when it becomes fighting words or a true threat.

The case that follows analyzes the problem of expression that inflicts harm from the point of view of fighting words. It is an important contribution to the U.S. law in this area.

FROM THE BENCH

R.A.V. v. ST. PAUL
505 U.S. 377 (1992)

Justice SCALIA delivered the opinion of the Court.

In the predawn hours of June 21, 1990, petitioner and several other teenagers allegedly assembled a crudely made cross by taping together broken chair legs. They then allegedly burned the cross inside the fenced yard of a black family that lived across the street from the house where petitioner was staying. Although this conduct could have been punished under any of a number of laws, one of the two provisions under which respondent city of St. Paul chose to charge petitioner (then a juvenile) was the St. Paul Bias-Motivated Crime Ordinance, St. Paul, Minn., Legis. Code 292.02 (1990), which provides:

> Whoever places on public or private property a symbol, object, appellation, characterization or graffiti, including, but not limited to, a burning cross or Nazi swastika, which one knows or has reasonable grounds to know arouses anger, alarm or resentment in others on the basis of race, color, creed, religion or gender commits disorderly conduct and shall be guilty of a misdemeanor.

Petitioner moved to dismiss this count on the ground that the St. Paul ordinance was substantially overbroad and impermissibly content based, and therefore facially invalid under the First Amendment. The trial court granted this motion, but the Minnesota Supreme Court reversed. That court rejected petitioner's overbreadth claim because, as construed in prior Minnesota cases, the modifying phrase "arouses anger, alarm or resentment in others" limited the reach of the ordinance to conduct that amounts to "fighting words," i.e., "conduct that itself inflicts injury or tends to incite immediate violence . . . ," and therefore the ordinance reached only expression "that the first amendment does not protect." The court also concluded that the ordinance was not impermissibly content based because, in its view, "the ordinance is a narrowly tailored means toward accomplishing the compelling governmental interest in protecting the community against bias-motivated threats to public safety and order."

I

In construing the St. Paul ordinance, we are bound by the construction given to it by the Minnesota court. Accordingly, we accept the Minnesota Supreme Court's authoritative statement that the ordinance reaches only those expressions that constitute "fighting words" within the meaning of *Chaplinsky*. Petitioner and his amici urge us to modify the scope of the *Chaplinsky* formulation, thereby invalidating the ordinance as "substantially overbroad." We find it unnecessary to consider this issue. Assuming, arguendo, that all of the expression reached by the ordinance is proscribable under the "fighting words" doctrine, we nonetheless conclude that the ordinance is facially unconstitutional in that it prohibits otherwise permitted speech solely on the basis of the subjects the speech addresses.

The First Amendment generally prevents government from proscribing speech, or even expressive conduct, because of disapproval of the ideas expressed. Content-based regulations are presumptively invalid. From 1791 to the present, however, our society, like other free but civilized societies, has permitted restrictions upon the content of speech in a few limited areas, which are "of such slight social value as a step to truth that any benefit that may be derived from them is clearly outweighed by the social interest in order and morality." We have recognized that "the freedom of speech" referred to by the First Amendment does not include a freedom to disregard these traditional limitations. Our decisions since the 1960's have narrowed the scope of the traditional categorical exceptions for defamation, and for obscenity, but a limited categorical approach has remained an important part of our First Amendment jurisprudence.

We have sometimes said that these categories of expression are "not within the area of constitutionally protected speech;" or that the "protection of the First Amendment does not extend" to them. Such statements must be taken in context, however, and are no more literally true than is the occasionally repeated shorthand characterizing obscenity "as not being speech at all." What they mean is that these areas of speech can, consistently with the First Amendment, be regulated because of their constitutionally proscribable content (obscenity, defamation, etc.) — not that they are categories of speech entirely invisible to the Constitution, so that they may be made the vehicles for content discrimination unrelated to their distinctively proscribable content. Thus, the government may proscribe libel; but it may not make the further content discrimination of proscribing only libel critical of the government.

Our cases surely do not establish the proposition that the First Amendment imposes no obstacle whatsoever to regulation of particular instances of such proscribable expression, so that the government "may regulate [them] freely." That would mean that a city council could enact an ordinance prohibiting only those legally obscene works that contain criticism of the city government or, indeed, that do not include endorsement of the city government. Such a simplistic, all-or-nothing-at-all approach to First Amendment protection is at odds with common sense and with our jurisprudence as well. It is not true that "fighting words" have at most a "de minimis" expressive content, ibid., or that their content is in all respects "worthless and undeserving of constitutional protection;" sometimes they are quite expressive indeed. We have not said that they constitute "no part of the expression of ideas," but only that they constitute "no essential part of any exposition of ideas."

The proposition that a particular instance of speech can be proscribable on the basis of one feature (e.g., obscenity) but not on the basis of another (e.g., opposition to the city government) is commonplace and has found application in many contexts. We have long held, for example, that nonverbal expressive activity can be banned because of the action it entails, but not because of the ideas it expresses—so that burning a flag in violation of an ordinance against outdoor fires could be punishable, whereas burning a flag in violation of an ordinance against dishonoring the flag is not. And just as the power to proscribe particular speech on the basis of a non-content element (e.g., noise) does not entail the power to proscribe the same speech on the basis of a content element, so also the power to proscribe it on the basis of one content element (e.g., obscenity) does not entail the power to proscribe it on the basis of other content elements.

In other words, the exclusion of "fighting words" from the scope of the First Amendment simply means that, for purposes of that Amendment, the unprotected features of the words are, despite their verbal character, essentially a "nonspeech" element of communication. Fighting words are thus analogous to a noisy sound truck: Each is, as Justice Frankfurter recognized, a "mode of speech" . . .; both can be used to convey an idea; but neither has, in and of itself, a claim upon the First Amendment. As with the sound truck, however, so also with fighting words: the government may not regulate use based on hostility—or favoritism—towards the underlying message expressed.

When the basis for the content discrimination consists entirely of the very reason the entire class of speech at issue is proscribable, no significant danger of idea or viewpoint discrimination exists. Such a reason, having been adjudged neutral enough to support exclusion of the entire class of speech from First Amendment protection, is also neutral enough to form the basis of distinction within the class. To illustrate: a State might choose to prohibit only that obscenity which is the most patently offensive in its prurience—i.e., that which involves the most lascivious displays of sexual activity. But it may not prohibit, for example, only that obscenity which includes offensive political messages. And the Federal Government can criminalize only those threats of violence that are directed against the President—since the reasons why threats of violence are outside the First Amendment (protecting individuals from the fear of violence, from the disruption that fear engenders, and from the possibility that the threatened violence will occur) have special force when applied to the person of the President.

Another valid basis for according differential treatment to even a content-defined subclass of proscribable speech is that the subclass happens to be associated with particular "secondary effects" of the speech, so that the regulation is "justified without reference to the content of the . . . speech." A State could, for example, permit all obscene live performances except those involving minors. Moreover, since words can in some circumstances violate laws directed not against speech but against conduct (a law against treason, for example, is violated by telling the enemy the Nation's defense secrets), a particular content-based subcategory of a proscribable class of speech can be swept up incidentally within the reach of a statute directed at conduct, rather than speech. Thus, for example, sexually derogatory "fighting words," among other words, may produce a violation of Title VII's general prohibition against sexual discrimination in employment practices. Where the government does not target conduct on the basis of its expressive content, acts are not shielded from regulation merely because they express a discriminatory idea or philosophy.

These bases for distinction refute the proposition that the selectivity of the restriction is "even arguably 'conditioned upon the sovereign's agreement with what a speaker may intend to say.'" There may be other such bases as well. Indeed, to validate such selectivity (where totally proscribable speech is at issue), it may not even be necessary to identify any particular "neutral" basis, so long as the nature of the content discrimination is such that there is no realistic possibility that official suppression of ideas is afoot. (We cannot think of any First Amendment interest that would stand in the way of a State's prohibiting only those obscene motion pictures with blue-eyed actresses.) Save for that limitation, the regulation of "fighting words," like the regulation of noisy speech, may address some offensive instances and leave other, equally offensive, instances alone.

II

Applying these principles to the St. Paul ordinance, we conclude that, even as narrowly construed by the Minnesota Supreme Court, the ordinance is facially unconstitutional. Although the phrase in the ordinance, "arouses anger, alarm or resentment in others," has been limited by the Minnesota Supreme Court's construction to reach only those symbols or displays that amount to "fighting words," the remaining, unmodified terms make clear that the ordinance applies only to "fighting words" that insult, or provoke violence, "on the basis of race, color, creed, religion or gender." Displays containing abusive invective, no matter how vicious or severe, are permissible unless they are addressed to one of the specified disfavored topics. Those who wish to use "fighting words" in connection with other ideas—to express hostility, for example, on the basis of political affiliation, union membership, or homosexuality—are not covered. The First Amendment does not permit St. Paul to impose special prohibitions on those speakers who express views on disfavored subjects.

In its practical operation, moreover, the ordinance goes even beyond mere content discrimination to actual viewpoint discrimination. Displays containing some words—odious racial epithets, for example—would be prohibited to proponents of all views. But "fighting words" that do not themselves invoke race, color, creed, religion, or gender—aspersions upon a person's mother, for example—would seemingly be usable ad libitum in the placards of those arguing in favor of racial, color, etc., tolerance and equality, but could not be used by those speakers' opponents. One could hold up a sign saying, for example, that all "anti-Catholic bigots" are misbegotten; but not that all "papists" are, for that would insult and provoke violence "on the basis of religion." The content-based discrimination reflected in the St. Paul ordinance comes within neither any of the specific exceptions to the First Amendment prohibition we discussed earlier nor a more general exception for content discrimination that does not threaten censorship of ideas. It assuredly does not fall within the exception for content discrimination based on the very reasons why the particular class of speech at issue (here, fighting words) is proscribable. As explained earlier, the reason why fighting words are categorically excluded from the protection of the First Amendment is not that their content communicates any particular idea, but that their content embodies a particularly intolerable (and socially unnecessary) mode of expressing whatever idea the speaker wishes to convey. . . . [St. Paul] has proscribed fighting words of whatever manner that communicate messages of racial, gender, or religious intolerance. Selectivity of this sort creates the possibility that the city is seeking to handicap the expression of particular ideas. That possibility would alone be enough to render the ordinance presumptively invalid, but St. Paul's comments and concessions in this case elevate the possibility to a certainty.

Finally, St. Paul and its amici defend the conclusion of the Minnesota Supreme Court that, even if the ordinance regulates expression based on hostility towards its protected ideological content, this discrimination is nonetheless justified because it is narrowly tailored to serve compelling state interests. Specifically, they assert that the ordinance helps to ensure the basic human rights of members of groups that have historically been subjected to discrimination, including the right of such group members to live in peace where they wish. We do not doubt that these interests are compelling, and that the ordinance can be said to promote them. But the "danger of censorship" presented by a facially content-based statute, requires that that weapon be employed only where it is "necessary to serve the asserted [compelling] interest." The existence of adequate content-neutral alternatives thus "undercut[s] significantly" any defense of such a statute.

Let there be no mistake about our belief that burning a cross in someone's front yard is reprehensible. But St. Paul has sufficient means at its disposal to prevent such behavior without adding the First Amendment to the fire.

QUESTIONS FOR DISCUSSION

7.6   The Court in *R.A.V.* agreed that fighting words could be punished consistently with the First Amendment. The state court in the case had restricted the prohibition in the case to fighting words, and the U.S. Supreme Court acknowledged that it was bound by that state supreme court interpretation. (Federal courts consider themselves bound by a state supreme court's interpretation of state law.) Given that fighting words are generally not considered protected by the First Amendment, can you articulate why the U.S. Supreme Court found the statute unconstitutional?

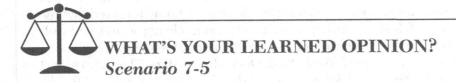

WHAT'S YOUR LEARNED OPINION?
Scenario 7-5

The St. Paul Bias-Motivated Crime Ordinance held to be unconstitutional in *R.A.V. v. St. Paul* read as follows:

> Whoever places on public or private property a symbol, object, appellation, characterization or graffiti, including, but not limited to, a burning cross or Nazi swastika, which one knows or has reason to know arouses anger, alarm or resentment in others on the basis of race, color, creed, religion or gender commits disorderly conduct and shall be guilty of a misdemeanor.

What if the ordinance had simply omitted the phrase "on the basis of race, color, creed, religion or gender"? Do you think the ordinance would then have been upheld? Why or why not?

Scenario 7-6

Suppose that instead the ordinance disallowed burning crosses placed on the property of another without permission. Would such an ordinance implicate the First Amendment? If so, would it be upheld or struck down as unconstitutional?

BEHIND THE CURTAIN

To be sure, the Ku Klux Klan is easily associated with cross burning. But the KKK did not invent the practice. Cross-burning has its origins in fourteenth-century Scotland, where clans would use it as a method of communication. Sir Walter Scott's 1810 poem, "The Lady of the Lake," featured a depiction of this use of burning crosses. The KKK's practice of cross burning was likely inspired by a movie. *Birth of a Nation*, a 1915 silent movie, was the first U.S. blockbuster movie—President Woodrow Wilson even held a private screening at the White House. Originally the movie was titled *The Clansman* after the 1905 novel of the same name by Thomas Dixon. The movie prompted protests across the nation by individuals and organizations such as the NAACP, and also inspired a resurgence of the KKK. The burning cross depicted in both the novel and the movie was first used by the KKK on Thanksgiving of 1915 in Georgia to mark the group's renewal.

As for the *R.A.V.* case itself, the Supreme Court's holding did not end the dispute. At least one newspaper article from the time reported that the Jones family felt that conviction on a trespassing charge would be insufficient relative to the harm done. Ruth Marcus, *A Family's Nightmare: Cross-Burning in St. Paul*, Wash. Post, December 1, 1991. The U.S. District Court for the District of Minnesota and the U.S. Court of Appeals for the Eighth Circuit agreed with the Jones family. *U.S. v. J.H.H.*, 22 F.3d 821, 823 (8th Cir. 1994). J.H.H. and two others were prosecuted for, and convicted of, violating federal statutes regarding civil rights and federal housing rights by force or threat of force. *Id.* The court in that case held that threats are unprotected by the First Amendment and the cross burning in this case was clearly a threat.

Hate speech that targets a person or group of persons based on their race, ethnicity, gender, or sexual orientation has been the subject of several U.S. Supreme Court opinions. Unlike *R.A.V. v. City of St. Paul*, the case below deals with flag burning by treating it as a form of hate speech. Try to evaluate how the Court's approach differs from *R.A.V.*, which overturned the criminal conviction of a minor who crudely constructed a cross and then burned it on the front lawn of a Black family, holding that the act was protected by the First Amendment.

Take note that a technical legal principle is key to understanding the Court's reasoning in *Virginia v. Black*. This is the concept of a prima facie case. The term "prima facie" means accepted as correct unless proven otherwise. A prima facie case refers to a claim that is sufficiently established by the evidence a party (Party A) presents to justify a favorable outcome for Party A, unless Party A's opponent presents evidence that rebuts Party A's evidence.

FROM THE BENCH

VIRGINIA v. BLACK
538 U.S. 343 (2003)

Justice O'CONNOR announced the judgment of the Court and delivered the opinion of the Court with respect to Parts I, II, and III, and an opinion with respect to Parts IV and V, in which The Chief Justice, Justice STEVENS, and Justice BREYER join.

In this case we consider whether the Commonwealth of Virginia's statute banning cross burning with "an intent to intimidate a person or group of persons" violates the First Amendment. We conclude that while a State, consistent with the First Amendment, may ban cross burning carried out with the intent to intimidate, the provision in the Virginia statute treating any cross burning as prima facie evidence of intent to intimidate renders the statute unconstitutional in its current form.

Respondents Barry Black, Richard Elliott, and Jonathan O'Mara were convicted separately of violating Virginia's cross-burning statute. That statute provides:

> It shall be unlawful for any person or persons, with the intent of intimidating any person or group of persons, to burn, or cause to be burned, a cross on the property of another, a highway or other public place. Any person who shall violate any provision of this section shall be guilty of a Class 6 felony. . . . Any such burning of a cross shall be prima facie evidence of an intent to intimidate a person or group of persons.

Klansmen in robes with burning cross in North Carolina, January 1958. *Photographer unknown, courtesy of the State Archives of North Carolina.*

On August 22, 1998, Barry Black led a Ku Klux Klan rally in Carroll County, Virginia. . . . During the rally, Sechrist heard Klan members speak about "what they were" and "what they believed in." The speakers "talked real bad about the blacks and the Mexicans." One speaker told the assembled gathering that "he would love to take a .30/.30 and just randomly shoot the blacks." The speakers also talked about "President Clinton and Hillary Clinton," and about how their tax money "goes to . . . the black people." Sechrist testified that this language made her "very . . . scared."

At the conclusion of the rally, the crowd circled around a 25- to 30-foot cross. . . . According to the sheriff, the cross "then all of a sudden . . . went up in a flame." As the cross burned, the Klan played Amazing Grace over the loudspeakers. Sechrist stated that the cross burning made her feel "awful" and "terrible."

. . . Black was charged with burning a cross with the intent of intimidating a person or group of persons, in violation of §18.2-423. At his trial, the jury was instructed that "intent to intimidate means the motivation to intentionally put a person or a group of persons in fear of bodily harm. Such fear must arise from the willful conduct of the accused rather than from some mere temperamental timidity of the victim." The trial court also instructed the jury that "the burning of a cross by itself is sufficient evidence from which you may infer the required intent." . . .

On May 2, 1998, respondents Richard Elliott and Jonathan O'Mara, as well as a third individual, attempted to burn a cross on the yard of James Jubilee. Jubilee, an African-American, was Elliott's next-door neighbor in Virginia Beach, Virginia. . . . On the night of May 2, respondents drove a truck onto Jubilee's property, planted a cross, and set it on fire. Their apparent motive was to "get back" at Jubilee for complaining about the shooting in the backyard. Respondents were not affiliated with the Klan. The next morning, as Jubilee was pulling his car out of the driveway, he noticed the partially burned cross approximately 20 feet from his house . . . Elliott and O'Mara were charged with attempted cross burning and conspiracy to commit cross burning. O'Mara pleaded guilty to both counts, reserving the right to challenge the constitutionality of the cross-burning statute. . . . The jury found Elliott guilty of attempted cross burning and acquitted him of conspiracy to commit cross burning. . . .

II

. . . Burning a cross in the United States is inextricably intertwined with the history of the Ku Klux Klan. . . . Although the Ku Klux Klan started as a social club, it soon changed into something far different. The Klan fought Reconstruction and the corresponding drive to allow freed blacks to participate in the political process. Soon the Klan imposed "a veritable reign of terror" throughout the South. The Klan employed tactics such as whipping, threatening to burn people at the stake, and murder. The Klan's victims included blacks, southern whites who disagreed with the Klan, and "carpetbagger" northern whites. . . . Throughout the history of the Klan, cross burnings have also remained potent symbols of shared group identity and ideology. The burning cross became a symbol of the Klan itself and a central feature of Klan gatherings. . . . And the Klan has often published its newsletters and magazines under the name The Fiery Cross. . . . In short, a burning cross has remained a symbol of Klan ideology and of Klan unity.

To this day, regardless of whether the message is a political one or whether the message is also meant to intimidate, the burning of a cross is a "symbol of hate." And while cross burning sometimes carries no intimidating message, at other times the intimidating message is the *only* message conveyed. For example, when a cross burning is directed at a particular person not affiliated with the Klan, the burning cross often serves as a message of intimidation, designed to inspire in the victim a fear of bodily harm. Moreover, the history of violence associated with the Klan shows that the possibility of injury or death is not just hypothetical. The person who burns a cross directed at a particular person often is making a serious threat, meant to coerce the victim to comply with the Klan's wishes unless the victim is willing to risk the wrath of the Klan. . . .

III

A

. . . The hallmark of the protection of free speech is to allow "free trade in ideas"—even ideas that the overwhelming majority of people might find distasteful or discomforting. . . . The protections afforded by the First Amendment, however, are not absolute, and we have long recognized that the government may regulate certain categories of expression consistent with the Constitution. The First Amendment permits "restrictions upon the content of speech in a few limited areas, which are 'of such slight social value as a step to truth that any benefit that may be derived from them is clearly outweighed by the social interest in order and morality.'"

Thus, for example, a State may punish those words "which by their very utterance inflict injury or tend to incite an immediate breach of the peace." We have consequently held that fighting words . . . are generally proscribable under the First Amendment. . . . And the First Amendment also permits a State to ban a "true threat."

"True threats" encompass those statements where the speaker means to communicate a serious expression of an intent to commit an act of unlawful violence to a particular individual or group of individuals. The speaker need not actually intend to carry out the threat. Rather, a prohibition on true threats "protects individuals from the fear of violence" and "from the disruption that fear engenders. . . ." Intimidation in the constitutionally proscribable sense of the word is a type of true threat, where a speaker directs a threat to a person or group of persons with the intent of placing the victim in fear of bodily harm or death. Respondents do not contest that some cross burnings fit within this meaning of intimidating speech, and rightly so. . . . [T]he history of cross burning in this country shows that cross burning is often intimidating, intended to create a pervasive fear in victims that they are a target of violence.

IV

. . . The prima facie evidence provision, as interpreted by the jury instruction, renders the statute unconstitutional. . . . As construed by the jury instruction, the prima facie provision strips away the very reason why a State may ban cross burning with the intent to intimidate. The prima facie evidence provision permits a jury to convict in every cross-burning case in which defendants exercise their constitutional right not to put on a defense. And even where a defendant like Black presents a defense, the prima facie evidence provision makes it more likely that the jury will find an intent to intimidate regardless of the particular facts of the case. The provision permits the Commonwealth to arrest, prosecute, and convict a person based solely on the fact of cross burning itself.

It is apparent that the provision as so interpreted "'would create an unacceptable risk of the suppression of ideas.'" The act of burning a cross may mean that a person is engaging in constitutionally proscribable intimidation. But that same act may mean only that the person is engaged in core political speech. The prima facie evidence provision in this statute blurs the line between these two meanings of a burning cross. As interpreted by the jury instruction, the provision chills constitutionally protected political speech because of the possibility that a State will prosecute—and potentially convict—somebody engaging only in lawful political speech at the core of what the First Amendment is designed to protect.

As the history of cross burning indicates, a burning cross is not always intended to intimidate. Rather, sometimes the cross burning is a statement of ideology, a symbol of group solidarity. It is a ritual used at Klan gatherings, and it is used to represent the Klan itself. Thus, "burning a cross at a political rally would almost certainly be protected expression." Indeed, occasionally a person who burns a cross does not intend to express either a statement of ideology or intimidation. Cross burnings have appeared in movies such as Mississippi Burning, and in plays such as the stage adaptation of Sir Walter Scott's The Lady of the Lake.

The prima facie provision makes no effort to distinguish among these different types of cross burnings. It does not distinguish between a cross burning done with the purpose of creating anger or resentment and a cross burning done with the purpose of threatening or intimidating a victim. It does not distinguish between a cross burning at public rally or a cross burning on a neighbor's lawn. It does not treat the cross burning directed at an individual differently from the cross burning directed at a group of like-minded believers. . . . It may be true that a cross burning, even at a political rally, arouses a sense of anger or hatred among the vast majority of citizens who see a burning cross. But this sense of anger or hatred is not sufficient to ban all cross burnings. . . . The prima facie evidence provision in this case ignores all of the contextual factors that are necessary to decide whether a particular cross burning is intended to intimidate. The First Amendment does not permit such a shortcut.

For these reasons, the prima facie evidence provision, as interpreted through the jury instruction and as applied in Barry Black's case, is unconstitutional on its face. . . .

V

With respect to Barry Black, we agree with the Supreme Court of Virginia that his conviction cannot stand, and we affirm the judgment of the Supreme

FROM THE BENCH

Court of Virginia. With respect to Elliott and O'Mara, we vacate the judgment of the Supreme Court of Virginia, and remand the case for further proceedings.

Justice THOMAS, dissenting.

In every culture, certain things acquire meaning well beyond what outsiders can comprehend. That goes for both the sacred, and the profane. I believe that cross burning is the paradigmatic example of the latter. . . . Although I agree with the majority's conclusion that it is constitutionally permissible to "ban . . . cross burning carried out with intent to intimidate," I believe that the majority errs in imputing an expressive component to the activity in question. In my view, whatever expressive value cross burning has, the legislature simply wrote it out by banning only intimidating conduct undertaken by a particular means. A conclusion that the statute prohibiting cross burning with intent to intimidate sweeps beyond a prohibition on certain conduct into the zone of expression overlooks not only the words of the statute but also reality.

A

. . . To me, the majority's brief history of the Ku Klux Klan only reinforces this common understanding of the Klan as a terrorist organization, which, in its endeavor to intimidate, or even eliminate those its dislikes, uses the most brutal of methods. Such methods typically include cross burning—"a tool for the intimidation and harassment of racial minorities, Catholics, Jews, Communists, and any other groups hated by the Klan." For those not easily frightened, cross burning has been followed by more extreme measures, such as beatings and murder. As the Solicitor General points out, the association between acts of intimidating cross burning and violence is well documented in recent American history. . . . In our culture, cross burning has almost invariably meant lawlessness and understandably instills in its victims well-grounded fear of physical violence. . . . Accordingly, this statute prohibits only conduct, not expression. And, just as one cannot burn down someone's house to make a political point and then seek refuge in the First Amendment, those who hate cannot terrorize and intimidate to make their point. In light of my conclusion that the statute here addresses only conduct, there is no need to analyze it under any of our First Amendment tests.

II

Even assuming that the statute implicates the First Amendment, in my view, the fact that the statute permits a jury to draw an inference of intent to intimidate from the cross burning itself presents no constitutional problems. Therein lies my primary disagreement with the plurality. . . . The plurality, however, is troubled by the presumption because this is a First Amendment case. The plurality laments the fate of an innocent cross-burner who burns a cross, but does so without an intent to intimidate. . . . First, it is, at the very least, unclear that the inference comes into play during arrest and initiation of a prosecution, that is, prior to the instructions stage of an actual trial. Second, as I explained above, the inference is rebuttable and, as the jury instructions given in this case demonstrate, Virginia law still requires the jury to find the existence of each element, including intent to intimidate, beyond a reasonable doubt. . . . Because I would uphold the validity of this statute, I respectfully dissent.

QUESTIONS FOR DISCUSSION

7.7   Justice Thomas, in his dissent, examined the history of the Virginia statute, first passed in 1952, and concluded that "[t]he ban on cross burning with intent to intimidate demonstrates that even segregationists understood the difference between intimidating and terroristic conduct and racist expression." *Virginia v. Black*, U.S. 538 U.S. 343, 394 (2003). Justice Thomas maintained that the Virginia statute only criminalized conduct and not expression and therefore did not run afoul of the First Amendment. Do you find this a persuasive argument?

7.8   Note that the *Virginia v. Black* opinion addressed two separate sets of facts. One set concerned the burning of a cross at a KKK rally held on land with the permission of the owner. In that case, Black was the defendant. The other set of facts concerned the burning of a cross on the yard of an African American family without permission. In that case, Elliott and O'Mara were the defendants. The Court treated the two sets of facts differently: remanding the Elliott/O'Mara case for further proceedings (to allow the prosecutors to introduce more evidence) and simply invalidating the Black conviction. Why did the Court treat the two sets of facts differently?

7.9   During oral arguments William H. Hurd, attorney for the petitioner, argued that cross burning was always threatening, precisely because the Klan had designed it to be threatening. Hurd argued that "it rings a little hollow when the Klan comes to court and complains that our law treats that message—treats that burning cross as having exactly the message that they for decades wanted it to have." Transcript of Oral Argument at 17, *Virginia v. Black*, 543 U.S. 343 (2003) (No. 01-1107). Do you think that cross burning can ever be a protected form of expression, not intended to threaten, that should therefore be examined on a case-by-case basis? For example, is a burning cross at a KKK rally political expression or an inherent threat? What about cross burning in a movie or on the news? Wouldn't the prima facie provision in the statute apply to those?

As established in *Virginia v. Black*, the most effective way of regulating anything close to hate speech is successfully characterizing the speech as a true threat. Thus far, the U.S. Supreme Court has not offered much clear guidance as to the First Amendment standards for determining when speech is a true threat. Many questions remain unanswered: Whose perspective is relevant in the consideration of whether speech constitutes a true threat? The speaker? The target of the speech? An average reasonable person? Does it make a difference if the speech is "art"? A "joke"? How do we even know when speech is art or a joke? Again, does the answer change depending on whose perspective we consider?

The case below presented the U.S. Supreme Court with an opportunity to address these lingering questions. It is important to note that the case is not an interpretation of the Constitution, but the interpretation of a statute. When a court is interpreting a statute, the court is trying to divine what Congress wanted words to mean. Congress can disagree with the decision and change the statute. Only the Supreme Court has the final say on the meaning of the U.S. Constitution. If the Constitution allows the government to restrict only true threats, then the Supreme Court's definition of a true threat is final. That said, the Supreme Court's understanding of that term in the context of statutory interpretation provides an important window on how it would come out in the context of constitutional interpretation.

The case below concerns Elonis, a soon-to-be divorced man who made a series of Facebook posts, primarily in the form of rap lyrics, describing acts of violence against his wife, the police, a kindergarten class, an FBI agent, and others. The case discusses the concept of scienter, which refers to a defendant's understanding that an act or conduct is wrong and the intent to engage in the act despite that understanding.

FROM THE BENCH

ELONIS v. UNITED STATES
575 U.S. 723 (2015)

Chief Justice ROBERTS delivered the opinion of the Court.

Federal law [18 U.S.C. §875(c)] makes it a crime to transmit in interstate commerce "any communication containing any threat . . . to injure the person of another." Petitioner was convicted of violating this provision under instructions that required the jury to find that he communicated what a reasonable person would regard as a threat. The question is whether the statute also requires that the defendant be aware of the threatening nature of the communication, and — if not — whether the *First Amendment* requires such a showing.

I

A

Anthony Douglas Elonis was an active user of the social networking Web site Facebook. . . . In May 2010, Elonis's wife of nearly seven years left him, taking with her their two young children. Elonis began "listening to more violent music" and posting self-styled "rap" lyrics inspired by the music. Eventually, Elonis changed the user name on his Facebook page from his actual name to a rap-style [pen name], "Tone Dougie," to distinguish himself from his "on-line persona." The lyrics Elonis posted as "Tone Dougie" included graphically violent language and imagery. This material was often interspersed with disclaimers that the lyrics were "fictitious," with no intentional "resemblance to real persons." Elonis posted an explanation to another Facebook user that "I'm doing this for me. My writing is therapeutic."

■ ■ ■

Elonis's posts frequently included crude, degrading, and violent material about his soon-to-be ex-wife. . . . Elonis posted an adaptation of a satirical sketch that he and his wife had watched together. In the actual sketch, called "It's Illegal to Say . . . ," a comedian [Trevor Moore] explains that it is illegal for a person to say he wishes to kill the President, but not illegal to explain that it is illegal for him to say that. When Elonis posted the script of the sketch, however, he substituted his wife for the President. The posting was part of the basis for Count Two of the indictment, threatening his wife:

"Hi, I'm Tone Elonis.
   Did you know that it's illegal for me to say I want to kill my wife? . . .
   It's one of the only sentences that I'm not allowed to say. . . .
   Now it was okay for me to say it right then because I was just telling you that it's illegal for me to say I want to kill my wife. . . .
   Um, but what's interesting is that it's very illegal to say I really, really think someone out there should kill my wife. . . .
   But not illegal to say with a mortar launcher. Because that's its own sentence. . . . I also found out that it's incredibly illegal, extremely illegal to go on Facebook and say something like the best place to fire a mortar launcher at her house would be from the cornfield behind it because of easy access to a getaway road and you'd have a clear line of sight through the sun room. . . . Yet even more illegal to show an illustrated diagram. [diagram of the house]. . . ."

The details about the home were accurate. At the bottom of the post, Elonis included a link to the video of the original skit, and wrote, "Art is about pushing limits. I'm willing to go to jail for my Constitutional rights. Are you?" After viewing some of Elonis's posts, his wife felt "extremely afraid for [her] life." A state court granted her a three-year protection-from-abuse order against Elonis (essentially, a restraining order). Elonis referred to the order in another post on his "Tone Dougie" page:

Fold up your [protection-from-abuse order] and put it in your pocket
Is it thick enough to stop a bullet?
Try to enforce an Order
that was improperly granted in the first place Me thinks the Judge needs an education
on true threat jurisprudence
And prison time'll add zeros to my settlement . . .
And if worse comes to worse
I've got enough explosives
to take care of the State Police and the Sheriff's Department.

At the bottom of this post was a link to the Wikipedia article on "Freedom of speech." . . .

That same month, interspersed with posts about a movie Elonis liked and observations on a comedian's social commentary, Elonis posted an entry that gave rise to Count Four of his indictment:

"That's it, I've had about enough
I'm checking out and making a name for myself
Enough elementary schools in a ten-mile radius
to initiate the most heinous school shooting ever imagined
And hell hath no fury like a crazy man in a Kindergarten class
The only question is . . . which one?"

Meanwhile, both local police and the Federal Bureau of Investigation [were informed] about Elonis's posts, and FBI Agent Denise Stevens had created a Facebook account to monitor his online activity. After the post about a school shooting, Agent Stevens and her partner visited Elonis at his house. Following their visit, during which Elonis was polite but uncooperative, Elonis posted another entry on his Facebook page, called "Little Agent Lady," which led to Count Five:

"You know your s***'s ridiculous
when you have the FBI knockin' at yo' door
Little Agent lady stood so close
Took all the strength I had not to turn the b**** ghost

Pull my knife, flick my wrist, and slit her throat
Leave her bleedin' from her jugular in the arms of her partner
[laughter]
So the next time you knock, you best be serving a warrant
And bring yo' SWAT and an explosives expert while you're at it
Cause little did y'all know, I was strapped wit' a bomb
Why do you think it took me so long to get dressed with no shoes on?
I was jus' waitin' for y'all to handcuff me and pat me down
Touch the detonator in my pocket and we're all goin'
[BOOM!]
Are all the pieces comin' together?
S***, I'm just a crazy sociopath
that gets off playin' you stupid f***s like a fiddle
And if y'all didn't hear, I'm gonna be famous
Cause I'm just an aspiring rapper who likes the attention
who happens to be under investigation for terrorism
cause y'all think I'm ready to turn the Valley into Fallujah
But I ain't gonna tell you which bridge is gonna fall into which river or road
And if you really believe this s***
I'll have some bridge rubble to sell you tomorrow
[BOOM!][BOOM!][BOOM!]"

B

A grand jury indicted Elonis for making threats to injure [a variety of persons including] his estranged wife, police officers, a kindergarten class, and an FBI agent, all in violation of 18 U.S.C. §875(c). . . .

At trial . . . the jury instructions . . . informed the jury that

> A statement is a true threat when a defendant intentionally makes a statement in a context or under such circumstances wherein a reasonable person would foresee that the statement would be interpreted by those to whom the maker communicates the statement as a serious expression of an intention to inflict bodily injury or take the life of an individual.

The Government's closing argument emphasized that it was irrelevant whether Elonis intended the postings to be threats—"it doesn't matter what he thinks." A jury convicted Elonis on four of the five counts against him. [Elonis challenged the jury instructions in the court of appeals, which held that the intent required by §875(c) is only the intent to communicate words that the defendant understands, and that a reasonable person would view as a threat.]

FROM THE BENCH

II

A

An individual who "transmits in interstate or foreign commerce any communication containing any threat to kidnap any person or any threat to injure the person of another" is guilty of a felony and faces up to five years' imprisonment. This statute requires that a communication be transmitted and that the communication contain a threat. It does not specify that the defendant must have any mental state with respect to these elements. In particular, it does not indicate whether the defendant must intend that his communication contain a threat.

Elonis argues that the word "threat" itself in Section 875(c) imposes such a requirement. According to Elonis, every definition of "threat" or "threaten" conveys the notion of an intent to inflict harm. [The three definitions Elonis considers are from: (1) Oxford English Dictionary—"to declare (usually conditionally) one's intention of inflicting injury upon;" (2) Webster's New International Dictionary—"an expression of an intention to inflict loss or harm on another by illegal means;" and (3) Black's Law Dictionary—"[a] communicated intent to inflict harm or loss on another."]

These definitions, however, speak to what the statement conveys—not to the mental state of the author. For example, an anonymous letter that says "I'm going to kill you" is "an expression of an intention to inflict loss or harm" regardless of the author's intent. A victim who receives that letter in the mail has received a threat, even if the author believes (wrongly) that his message will be taken as a joke.

. . . The most we can conclude from the language of Section 875(c) and its neighboring provisions is that Congress meant to proscribe a broad class of threats in Section 875(c), but did not identify what mental state, if any, a defendant must have to be convicted.

In sum, neither Elonis nor the Government has identified any indication of a particular mental state requirement in the text of Section 875(c).

B

The fact that the statute does not specify any required mental state, however, does not mean that none exists. We have repeatedly held that "mere omission from a criminal enactment of any mention of criminal intent" should not be read "as dispensing with it." This rule of construction reflects the basic principle that "wrongdoing must be conscious to be criminal." [T]his principle is "as universal and persistent in mature systems of law as belief in freedom of the human will and a consequent ability and duty of the normal individual to choose between good and evil." The "central thought" is that a defendant must be "blameworthy in mind" before he can be found guilty, a concept courts have expressed over time through various terms such as *mens rea*, scienter, malice aforethought, guilty knowledge, and the like. Although there are exceptions, the "general rule" is that a guilty mind is "a necessary element in the indictment and proof of every crime. We therefore generally "interpret[ ] criminal statutes to include broadly applicable scienter requirements, even where the statute by its terms does not contain them."

This is not to say that a defendant must know that his conduct is illegal before he may be found guilty. The familiar maxim "ignorance of the law is no excuse" typically holds true. Instead, our cases have explained that a defendant generally must "know the facts that make his conduct fit the definition of the offense," even if he does not know that those facts give rise to a crime. . . .

When interpreting federal criminal statutes that are silent on the required mental state, we read into the statute "only that *mens rea* which is necessary to separate wrongful conduct from 'otherwise innocent conduct.'" . . .

C

Section 875(c) . . . requires proof that a communication was transmitted and that it contained a threat. The "presumption in favor of a scienter requirement should apply to *each* of the statutory elements that criminalize otherwise innocent conduct." The parties agree that a defendant under Section 875(c) must know that he is transmitting a communication. But communicating *something* is not what makes the conduct "wrongful." Here "the crucial element separating legal innocence from wrongful conduct" is the threatening nature of the communication. The mental state requirement must therefore apply to the fact that the communication contains a threat.

Elonis's conviction, however, was premised solely on how his posts would be understood by a reasonable person. Such a "reasonable person" standard is a familiar feature of civil liability in tort law, but is inconsistent with "the conventional requirement for criminal conduct—*awareness* of some wrongdoing."

Having liability turn on whether a "reasonable person" regards the communication as a threat—regardless of what the defendant thinks—"reduces culpability on the all-important element of the crime to negligence," and we "have long been reluctant to infer that a negligence standard was intended in criminal statutes" (defendant could face "liability in a civil action for negligence, but he could only be held criminally for an evil intent actually existing in his mind"). Under these principles, "what [Elonis] thinks" does matter.

■ ■ ■

In light of the foregoing, Elonis's conviction cannot stand. The jury was instructed that the Government need prove only that a reasonable person would regard Elonis's communications as threats, and that was error. Federal criminal liability generally does not turn solely on the results of an act without considering the defendant's mental state. That understanding "took deep and early root in American soil" and Congress left it intact here: Under Section 875(c), "wrongdoing must be conscious to be criminal."

There is no dispute that the mental state requirement in Section 875(c) is satisfied if the defendant transmits a communication for the purpose of issuing a threat, or with knowledge that the communication will be viewed as a threat.

[The Court found it unnecessary to consider any First Amendment issues given their disposition.]

Justice THOMAS, dissenting.

. . . Because §875(c) criminalizes speech, the First Amendment requires that the term "threat" be limited to a narrow class of historically unprotected communications called "true threats." To qualify as a true threat, a communication must be a serious expression of an intention to commit unlawful physical violence, not merely "political hyperbole"; "vehement, caustic, and sometimes unpleasantly sharp attacks"; or "vituperative, abusive, and inexact" statements. It also cannot be determined solely by the reaction of the recipient, but must instead be "determined by the interpretation of a reasonable recipient familiar with the context of the communication," lest historically protected speech be suppressed at the will of an eggshell observer. There is thus no dispute that, at a minimum, §875(c) requires an objective showing: The communication must be one that "a reasonable observer would construe as a true threat to another. And there is no dispute that the posts at issue here meet that objective standard.

The only dispute in this case is about the state of mind necessary to convict Elonis for making those posts. On its face, §875(c) does not demand any particular mental state. As the Court correctly explains, the word "threat" does not itself contain a mens rea requirement. But because we read criminal statutes "in light of the background rules of the common law, in which the requirement of some mens rea for a crime is firmly embedded," we require "some indication of congressional intent, express or implied, . . . to dispense with mens rea as an element of a crime." Absent such indicia, we ordinarily apply the "presumption in favor of scienter" to require only "proof of general intent—that is, that the defendant [must] posses[s] knowledge with respect to the actus reus of the crime."

II

In light of my conclusion that Elonis was properly convicted under the requirements of §875(c), I must address his argument that his threatening posts were nevertheless protected by the First Amendment.

. . . Elonis . . . insists that our precedents require a mental state of intent when it comes to threat prosecutions under §875(c), primarily relying on [*Watts v. United States* (1969) and *Virginia v. Black* (2003)]. Neither of those decisions, however, addresses whether the First Amendment requires a particular mental state for threat prosecutions. True, the Court in *Watts* noted "grave doubts" about Raganksy's construction of "willfully" in the Presidential threats statute. But "grave doubts" do not make a holding, and that stray statement in *Watts* is entitled to no precedential force. If anything, *Watts* continued the long tradition of focusing on objective criteria in evaluating the mental requirement.

The Court's fractured opinion in *Black* likewise says little about whether an intent-to-threaten requirement is constitutionally mandated here. Black concerned a Virginia cross-burning law that expressly required "'an intent to intimidate a person or group of persons,'" and the Court thus had no occasion to decide whether such an element was necessary in threat provisions silent on the matter. Moreover, the focus of the *Black* decision was on the statutory presumption that "any cross burning [w]as prima facie evidence of intent to intimidate." A majority of the Court concluded that this presumption failed to distinguish unprotected threats from protected speech because it might allow convictions "based solely on the fact of cross burning itself," including cross burnings in a play or at a political rally. The objective standard for threats under §875(c) however, helps to avoid this problem by "forc[ing] jurors to examine the circumstances in which a statement is made."

As noted above, the *Elonis* case does not inject certainty into the meaning of a "true threat" for the purpose of the First Amendment. Nonetheless, it is important to note that the government often attempts to regulate true threats through the vehicle of a criminal prosecution. And in *Elonis*, the Court emphasized the historical importance of proving that the defendant knew that his conduct had a quality that places the conduct within the realm of a criminal prohibition. The Court made a subtle distinction, explaining that the defendant must have knowledge that communication was a true threat because that was within the realm of what the criminal statute prohibited. The Court did not hold, however, that the defendant must have knowledge of precisely what the criminal statute provided. Given the government often regulates true threats through the vehicle of criminal law, knowledge that a communication has the quality of a threat will often be an important factor that one would likely see in any First Amendment challenge to the government's attempt to regulate true threats.

Subsequent to *Elonis*, the Supreme Court established the meaning of a "true threat." In particular, the Court clarified the First Amendment restrictions on imposing criminal liability on someone who has made a threat. The Court stated that the standard to use in evaluating whether someone has articulated a true threat is to ask whether the particular defendant acted intentionally or recklessly when making the threat. Individuals act recklessly if they act rashly without regard for the consequence of their actions. Specifically, the Court rules that "the First Amendment . . . demands that the State . . . prove that the defendant was aware . . . of the threatening nature of his communications." *Counterman v. Colorado*, No 22-138 (U.S. Supreme Court June 6, 2023).

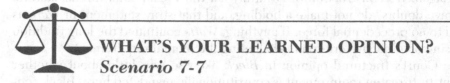

WHAT'S YOUR LEARNED OPINION?
Scenario 7-7

Assume that you live in a state that makes it a crime to make a true threat of violence against another person. And then consider the following post that you made on a social media platform: "This class is so boring, I am totally going to kill [my teacher]." Does this meet the standard of *Elonis*? Would a conviction under this state law withstand First Amendment attack?

In answering these questions, is there any more information that you would like? How should the court proceed if you argue that it is just a joke? Does it matter that the communication was made on social media?

Scenario 7-8

Mike is a college student and an amateur rapper. During the past three years, Mike has recorded songs under the name Money Mike, releasing videos on YouTube about once a month. His videos average about 500 views per month. Mike often shares these videos on his Facebook account under the name Money Mike. Mike's lyrics routinely depict a fictional version of himself as a "gangster." His lyrics often include references to drug dealing and violent crimes that accompany that lifestyle. In reality, Mike has never sold drugs, possessed a gun, or done anything close to what he depicts in his songs.

Until recently, Mike's friend Phil had produced the instrumentals that Mike raps over in his songs under the name Chill Phil. Phil recently told Mike he would no longer produce music for him. Phil was upset over the graphic content of Mike's lyrics and had expressed to Mike that he felt that being associated with Mike "gives people the wrong impression about me." Phil has also never been involved with drug dealing or violent crime.

Mike, feeling betrayed, told Phil, "You may think this is just an act, but I really am a gangster. I would consider that before you betray me." In response, Phil rolled his eyes and said sarcastically, "Sure Mike, you're a real gangster. Everything you rap about is fake." A month later, Mike released a new song called "Kill Chill," which sampled a horn siren from the Quentin Tarantino movie *Kill Bill*. In the song, Mike rapped the lyric, "You made beats for me, now you're gonna get beat by me." Mike rapped several lyrics that describe various ways that he would hurt someone, including by gunshot, samurai sword, and arson. Mike never mentioned Phil by name in the song. Additionally, Mike rapped the lyric "Think I'm just a joke? Watch your back on the corner of Oak. I'll leave your family in a room full of smoke." Phil lives on the corner of Oak Street and Maple Avenue.

Mike released "Kill Chill" on YouTube and uploaded the link to Facebook, as he normally does with new songs. Before the song was uploaded, Mike's new producer, Nick, asked Mike if he thought Phil would be scared. Mike replied, "I hope he will be, but I doubt it. Phil knows most of my lyrics are just exaggerations. Regardless, making this song is helping me get over his betrayal."

Is Mike's song a true threat?

C. The Religion Clauses

Religious values inform the views of many U.S. citizens on prominent social issues such as the rights of LGBTQ+ individuals, contraception, and abortion. For this reason, litigation over these issues often centers on the two clauses of the First Amendment regarding religion: the Free Exercise Clause and the Establishment Clause. The Free Exercise Clause protects individuals' rights to practice their religion without government constraint. The Establishment Clause aims to ensure that religion is separated from the government, thereby preventing it from "establishing" religion. The concerns driving the Establishment Clause are preventing government from preferring one religion over another and prohibiting government from meddling in religious matters.

The two religion clauses are intertwined. Indeed, preventing government from meddling in religious matters protects the exercise of religion. The theory is that separating church and state allows diverse religions to develop and flourish.

Yet this tangled relationship creates tensions between the two clauses, which can arise when state or federal laws are designed to protect against such matters as threats to safety or discrimination on the basis of age or gender. On the one hand, government may be obliged to enforce these legal protections, even though doing so may interfere with the unfettered exercise of religious customs and beliefs. So, for example, a religion might follow the tradition of having only people of a certain age and gender perform certain tasks in connection with religious rituals. If government enforces these antidiscrimination laws against a particular religious institution in these instances, one might argue government is acting consistent with the Establishment Clause by not extending an exemption to the institution because of its religious character. Yet to enforce the discrimination laws against the institution could also interfere with its members' practice of their religion.

Additional situations in which the tension between the clauses arises include questions about government aid to religious schools, tax exemptions for religious organizations, religious group access to public school facilities, and religious symbols on government property. In resolving litigation about each of these areas, the Supreme Court has employed different analyses fine-tuned to the specific circumstances of the case. Complicating matters more, analysis regarding the tension between the two clauses has evolved over time, depending in large part on the Justices' preferences about religion. One matter appears settled, however: In recent times, the Court has resolved tensions between the two clauses using a marked preference for protecting free religious exercise at the expense of enforcing the Constitution's mandate for the separation of church and state. This preference is reflected in the case that follows. In *Kennedy v. Bremerton School District*, a former high school football coach, Joseph Kennedy, sued the Bremerton School District in Washington State after he was placed on administrative leave for refusing to stop praying on the football field after games.

Kennedy had been a part-time coach at the school district for seven years, during which time he prayed on the field after every game—sometimes alone, and sometimes with his team's players and players from the other teams. When the school district learned about Kennedy's behavior, they expressed their disapproval, afraid it violated the First Amendment's Establishment Clause, which prohibits the government from making any law "respecting an establishment of religion." However, Kennedy resumed his midfield prayers, and although the school offered him other options—such as praying after the crowd had left—he continued to pray on the field immediately on completion of the games. The school placed Kennedy on administrative leave and did not renew his contract. Kennedy brought suit against the school, arguing it had violated the First Amendment's Free Exercise Clause.

An important component of the *Kennedy v. Bremerton* case was the Court's treatment of the appropriate "test" for evaluating when a government entity violates the Establishment Clause. Before *Bremerton*, the U.S. Supreme Court struggled with deciding the appropriate test for evaluating Establishment Clause issues. The Court applied a variety of tests in cases, which included evaluation of whether the government endorsed particular religions or whether the government coerced citizens to support or participate in a religion. By far the most consistently used test in the courts, however, was a test named after a case named *Lemon*. The *Lemon* test provides that for a government action to be constitutional, (1) it "must have a secular legislative purpose," (2) "its principal or primary effect must be one that neither advances nor inhibits religion," and (3) it "must not foster an excessive government entanglement with religion." Courts have sometimes mandated that the *Lemon* test requires an inquiry as to whether "a reasonable observer" would consider the government's challenged action an "endorsement" of religion. As becomes clear in the majority opinion, the *Lemon* test had fallen into disfavor in the years before *Bremerton*, particularly among the conservative majority of the Supreme Court.

FROM THE BENCH

KENNEDY v. BREMERTON
597 U.S. ___ (2022)

Justice GORSUCH delivered the opinion of the Court.

Joseph Kennedy lost his job as a high school football coach because he knelt at midfield after games to offer a quiet prayer of thanks. Mr. Kennedy prayed during a period when school employees were free to speak with a friend, call for a reservation at a restaurant, check email, or attend to other personal matters. He offered his prayers quietly while his students were otherwise occupied. Still, the Bremerton School District disciplined him anyway. It did so because it thought anything less could lead a reasonable observer to conclude (mistakenly) that it endorsed Mr. Kennedy's religious beliefs. That reasoning was misguided. Both the Free Exercise and Free Speech Clauses of the First Amendment protect expressions like Mr. Kennedy's. Nor does a proper understanding of the Amendment's Establishment Clause require the government to single out

Photograph of J. Kennedy in prayer circle (Oct. 26, 2015). *From the Dissenting Opinion of Justice Sotomayor,* Kennedy v. Bremerton, *597 U.S. ___ (2022).*

private religious speech for special disfavor. The Constitution and the best of our traditions counsel mutual respect and tolerance, not censorship and suppression, for religious and nonreligious views alike.

I

A

Joseph Kennedy began working as a football coach at Bremerton High School in 2008 after nearly two decades of service in the Marine Corps. Like many other football players and coaches across the country, Mr. Kennedy made it a practice to give "thanks through prayer on the playing field" at the conclusion of each game. In his prayers, Mr. Kennedy sought to express gratitude for "what the players had accomplished and for the opportunity to be part of their lives through the game of football." Mr. Kennedy offered his prayers after the players and coaches had shaken hands, by taking a knee at the 50-yard line and praying "quiet[ly]" for "approximately 30 seconds."

Initially, Mr. Kennedy prayed on his own. But over time, some players asked whether they could pray alongside him. Mr. Kennedy responded by saying, "'This is a free country. You can do what you want.'" The number of players who joined Mr. Kennedy eventually grew to include most of the team, at least after some games. Sometimes team members invited opposing players to join. Other times Mr. Kennedy still prayed alone. Eventually, Mr. Kennedy began incorporating short motivational speeches with his prayer when others were present.

Yet instead of accommodating Mr. Kennedy's request to offer a brief prayer on the field while students were busy with other activities—whether heading to the locker room, boarding the bus, or perhaps singing the school fight song—the District issued an ultimatum. It forbade Mr. Kennedy from engaging in "any overt actions" that could "appea[r] to a reasonable observer to endorse . . . prayer . . . while he is on duty as a District-paid coach." The District did so because it judged that anything less would lead it to violate the Establishment Clause.

[During the controversy,] the District placed Mr. Kennedy on paid administrative leave and prohibited him from "participat[ing], in any capacity, in . . . football program activities." In a letter explaining the reasons for this disciplinary action, the superintendent criticized Mr. Kennedy for engaging in "public and demonstrative religious conduct while still on duty as an assistant coach" by offering a prayer following the games on October 16, 23, and 26.

While Mr. Kennedy received "uniformly positive evaluations" every other year of his coaching career, after the 2015 season ended in November, the District gave him a poor performance evaluation. The evaluation advised against rehiring Mr. Kennedy on the grounds that he "'failed to follow district policy'" regarding religious expression and "'failed to supervise student-athletes after games.'" Mr. Kennedy did not return for the next season.

II

* * *

C

The Ninth Circuit . . . agreed with the District Court that Mr. Kennedy's speech qualified as government rather than private speech because "his expression on the field—a location that he only had access to because of his employment—during a time when he was generally tasked with communicating with students, was speech as a government employee." Like the District Court, the Ninth Circuit further reasoned that, "even if we were to assume . . . that Kennedy spoke as a private citizen," the District had an "adequate justification" for its actions. According to the court, "Kennedy's onfield religious activity," coupled with what the court called "his pugilistic efforts to generate publicity in order to gain approval of those on-field religious activities," were enough to lead an "objective observer" to conclude that the District "endorsed Kennedy's religious activity by not stopping the practice." And that, the court held, would amount to a violation of the Establishment Clause.

III

A

Under this Court's precedents, a plaintiff bears certain burdens to demonstrate an infringement of his rights under the [Free Exercise Clause]. If the plaintiff carries these burdens, the focus then shifts to the defendant to show that its actions were nonetheless justified and tailored consistent with the demands of our case law.

That Mr. Kennedy has discharged his burdens is effectively undisputed. No one questions that he seeks to engage in a sincerely motivated religious exercise. The exercise in question involves, as Mr. Kennedy has put it, giving "thanks through prayer" briefly and by himself "on the playing field" at the conclusion of each game he coaches. Mr. Kennedy has indicated repeatedly that he is willing to "wai[t] until the game is over and the players have left the field" to "wal[k] to mid-field to say [his] short, private, personal prayer." The contested exercise before us does not involve leading prayers with the team or before any other captive audience. Mr. Kennedy's "religious beliefs do not require [him] to lead any prayer . . . involving students." At the District's request, he voluntarily discontinued the school tradition of locker-room prayers and his postgame religious talks to students. The District disciplined him only for his decision to persist in praying quietly without his players after three games in October 2015.

Nor does anyone question that, in forbidding Mr. Kennedy's brief prayer, the District failed to act pursuant to a neutral and generally applicable rule. . . . In this case, the District's challenged policies were neither neutral nor generally applicable. By its own admission, the District sought to restrict Mr. Kennedy's actions at least in part because of their religious character. As it put it in its September 17 letter, the District prohibited "any overt actions on Mr. Kennedy's part, appearing to a reasonable observer to endorse even voluntary, student-initiated prayer." The District further explained that it could not allow "an employee, while still on duty, to engage in *religious* conduct. Prohibiting a religious practice was thus the District's unquestioned "object." The District candidly acknowledged as much below, conceding that its policies were "not neutral" toward religion. . . .

IV

A

[The Court discussed how the District and the lower courts used the long-standing, but much disputed, *Lemon* test for whether any given government action violates the Establishment Clause.]

What the District and the Ninth Circuit overlooked, however, is that the "shortcomings" associated with this "ambitiou[s]," abstract, and ahistorical approach to the Establishment Clause became so "apparent" that this Court long ago abandoned *Lemon* and its endorsement test offshoot. . . . An Establishment Clause violation does not automatically follow whenever a public school or other government entity "fail[s] to censor" private religious speech. Nor does the Clause "compel the government to purge from the public sphere" anything an objective observer could reasonably infer endorses or "partakes of the religious." In fact, just this Term the Court unanimously rejected a city's attempt to censor religious speech based on *Lemon* and the endorsement test.

In place of *Lemon* and the endorsement test, this Court has instructed that the Establishment Clause must be interpreted by " 'reference to historical practices and understandings.' " " '[T]he line' " that courts and governments "must draw between the permissible and the impermissible" has to " 'accor[d] with history and faithfully reflec[t] the understanding of the Founding Fathers.' " An analysis focused on original meaning and history, this Court has stressed, has long represented the rule rather than some " 'exception' " within the "Court's Establishment Clause jurisprudence." The District and the Ninth Circuit erred by failing to heed this guidance.

B

To be sure, this Court has long held that government may not, consistent with a historically sensitive understanding of the Establishment Clause, "make a religious observance compulsory. Government "may not coerce anyone to attend church," nor may it force citizens to engage in "a formal religious exercise," No doubt, too, coercion along these lines was among the foremost hallmarks of religious establishments the framers sought to prohibit when they adopted the First Amendment. Members of this Court have sometimes disagreed on what exactly qualifies as impermissible coercion in light of the original meaning of the Establishment Clause. But in this case Mr. Kennedy's private religious exercise did not come close to crossing any line one might imagine separating protected private expression from impermissible government coercion.

Naturally, Mr. Kennedy's proposal to pray quietly by himself on the field would have meant some people would have seen his religious exercise. Those close at hand might have heard him too. But learning how to tolerate speech or prayer of all kinds is "part of learning how to live in a pluralistic society," a trait of character essential to "a tolerant citizenry." This Court has long recognized as well that "secondary school students are mature enough . . . to understand that a school does not endorse," let alone coerce them to participate in, "speech that it merely permits on a nondiscriminatory basis." Of course, some will take offense to certain forms of speech or prayer they are sure to encounter in a society where those activities enjoy such robust constitutional protection. But "[o]ffense . . . does not equate to coercion."

■ ■ ■

[Our judgment finds] support in this Court's prior cases too. In [*Zorach v. Clauson* 1952], for example, challengers argued that a public school program permitting students to spend time in private religious instruction off campus was impermissibly coercive. The Court rejected that challenge because students were not required to attend religious instruction and there was no evidence that any employee had "us[ed] their office to persuade or force students" to participate in religious activity. What was clear there is even more obvious here — where there is no evidence anyone sought to persuade or force students to participate, and there is no formal school program accommodating the religious activity at issue.

Meanwhile, this case looks very different from those in which this Court has found prayer involving public school students to be problematically coercive. In [*Lee v. Weisman* 1992], this Court held that school officials violated the Establishment Clause by "including [a] clerical membe[r]" who publicly recited prayers "as part of [an] official school graduation ceremony" because the school had "in every practical sense compelled attendance and participation in" a "religious exercise." 505 U.S., at 580, 598. In *Santa Fe Independent School Dist. v. Doe*

FROM THE BENCH

[2000], the Court held that a school district violated the Establishment Clause by broadcasting a prayer "over the public address system" before each football game. The Court observed that, while students generally were not required to attend games, attendance *was* required for "cheerleaders, members of the band, and, of course, the team members themselves." None of that is true here. The prayers for which Mr. Kennedy was disciplined were not publicly broadcast or recited to a captive audience. Students were not required or expected to participate. And, in fact, none of Mr. Kennedy's students did participate in any of the three October 2015 prayers that resulted in Mr. Kennedy's discipline. . . .

[The rule urged by the District] would be a sure sign that our Establishment Clause jurisprudence had gone off the rails. In the name of protecting religious liberty, the District would have us suppress it. Rather than respect the First Amendment's double protection for religious expression, it would have us preference secular activity. . . . We are aware of no historically sound understanding of the Establishment Clause that begins to "mak[e] it necessary for government to be hostile to religion" in this way.

V

Respect for religious expressions is indispensable to life in a free and diverse Republic—whether those expressions take place in a sanctuary or on a field, and whether they manifest through the spoken word or a bowed head. Here, a government entity sought to punish an individual for engaging in a brief, quiet, personal religious observance doubly protected by the Free Exercise and Free Speech Clauses of the First Amendment. And the only meaningful justification the government offered for its reprisal rested on a mistaken view that it had a duty to ferret out and suppress religious observances even as it allows comparable secular speech. The Constitution neither mandates nor tolerates that kind of discrimination. . . . The judgment of the Court of Appeals is Reversed.

Justice SOTOMAYOR, with whom Justice BREYER and Justice KAGAN join, dissenting.

This case is about whether a public school must permit a school official to kneel, bow his head, and say a prayer at the center of a school event. The Constitution does not authorize, let alone require, public schools to embrace this conduct. Since [1962], this Court consistently has recognized that school officials leading prayer is constitutionally impermissible. Official-led prayer strikes at the core of our constitutional protections for the religious liberty of students and their parents, as embodied in both the Establishment Clause and the Free Exercise Clause of the First Amendment.

The Court now charts a different path, yet again paying almost exclusive attention to the Free Exercise Clause's protection for individual religious exercise while giving short shrift to the Establishment Clause's prohibition on state establishment of religion. To the degree the Court portrays petitioner Joseph

Kennedy's prayers as private and quiet, it misconstrues the facts. The record reveals that Kennedy had a longstanding practice of conducting demonstrative prayers on the 50-yard line of the football field. Kennedy consistently invited others to join his prayers and for years led student athletes in prayer at the same time and location. The Court ignores this history.

Today's decision goes beyond merely misreading the record. The Court overrules *Lemon v. Kurtzman*, 403 U.S. 602 (1971), and calls into question decades of subsequent precedents that it deems "offshoot[s]" of that decision. In the process, the Court rejects longstanding concerns surrounding government endorsement of religion and replaces the standard for reviewing such questions with a new "history and tradition" test. In addition, while the Court reaffirms that the Establishment Clause prohibits the government from coercing participation in religious exercise, it applies a nearly toothless version of the coercion analysis, failing to acknowledge the unique pressures faced by students when participating in school-sponsored activities. This decision does a disservice to schools and the young citizens they serve, as well as to our Nation's longstanding commitment to the separation of church and state. I respectfully dissent.

BEHIND THE CURTAIN

Although no longer on the Court when this case was decided, Justice Antonin Scalia was a particularly harsh critic of the *Lemon* test. Check out an example of his colorful prose on this subject in his concurrence in *Lamb's Chapel v. Center Moriches Union Free School District*, 508 U.S. 384, 398 (1993):

> As to the Court's invocation of the *Lemon* test: Like some ghoul in a late-night horror movie that repeatedly sits up in its grave and shuffles abroad, after being repeatedly killed and buried, *Lemon* stalks our Establishment Clause jurisprudence once again, frightening the little children and school attorneys of Center Moriches Union Free School District.

QUESTIONS FOR DISCUSSION

7.10   Are you persuaded that the majority's argument that its upholding of Kennedy's right to pray on the field was consistent with historical practices and understandings?

7.11 The dispute at issue in *Kennedy v. Bremerton* arose in a small coastal city in Washington State. Joseph Kennedy is a practicing Christian and his prayers were of a Christian nature. According to one source, the religious composition of Bremerton citizens is as follows: 26.7 percent of the population is religious, nearly all of which adhere to a Christian faith (26.2 percent of the population).[1] The Justices in the majority of the U.S. Supreme Court who held in favor of Kennedy are all practicing Christians. Discuss whether you believe that these Justices would have handled the matter differently if Kennedy was a practicing Muslim who invited others to join him as he placed his prayer rug and engaged in Islamic prayer on the Bremerton school football field.

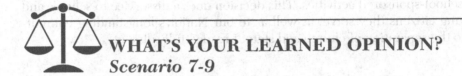

WHAT'S YOUR LEARNED OPINION?
Scenario 7-9

The town of North Galloway has a tradition of opening the town board meeting with prayer by local clergy members. The citizens of North Galloway who adhere to a religious faith are all Christian. All of the local clergy members who participate in the prayers are Christian. Under the Establishment Clause approach in *Bremerton*, is this practice constitutional? Does it matter if the town advertises that the opportunity to pray at the beginning of these meetings is open to citizens of any religion?

Scenario 7-10

The majority in *Kennedy v. Bremerton* emphasizes the importance of Coach Kennedy's right to freely exercise his religion. When can the Free Exercise Clause justify religion-based exemptions to state laws? Consider the practice of the Amish people to discontinue formal education when their children finish the eighth grade. At that point, the Amish provide students with an informal vocational education designed to prepare them for the rural Amish community life. Strong evidence shows that the Amish people believe that their religion prohibits formal education beyond the eighth grade.

State law requires compulsory school attendance beyond the eighth grade. Would a state violate the Establishment Clause if it allowed an exception to this law for Amish children? Would requiring Amish students to attend school beyond eighth grade violate the Free Exercise Clause?

The previous chapter (Chapter 6) pointed out the divergent strands of freedom of communication analysis. For freedom of communication purposes (in the context of humor regulation and hate speech), this chapter continues to illustrate that tendency of freedom of communication cases to generate unique analysis according to the details of the context. Cases reckoning with religion issues are no exception to this jurisprudential tendency to create free-standing, unique strings of legal doctrine. The next chapter also shows this same tendency, albeit in a dramatically different context: gun rights.

QUESTIONS FOR REVIEW

1. *Hustler v. Falwell* seemed to reflect the Supreme Court's strong inclination to extend First Amendment protection for parody. Why was that? What was the holding of the case?
2. The European Court of Human Rights had a different approach to protecting the cartoon in *Vereinigung Bildender Künstler (VBK) v. Austria* than the U.S. Supreme Court followed in *Hustler v. Falwell.* Can you articulate any differences? What were some of the reasons why the European Court decided the way it did?
3. Describe the approach that the U.S. Supreme Court has taken in cases for which the U.S. Trademark Office has refused trademark protection because the Trademark Office concluded the proposed trademarks were disparaging or vulgar.
4. Why did the U.S. Supreme Court uphold the Federal Communication Commission's sanctions based on a radio station's airing of George Carlin's "Filthy Words" monologue?
5. How did the U.S. Supreme Court define "fighting words"? Is it constitutional for a government entity to outlaw fighting words?
6. Why did the U.S. Supreme Court strike down the St. Paul, Minnesota, hate crimes statute in the *R.A.V.* case, even though the Minnesota Supreme Court had interpreted the statute as covering fighting words only?
7. Under the U.S. Supreme Court's decision in *Virginia v. Black*, what must be shown for a state to criminalize an act of cross burning?
8. What is the role of a "true threat" under U.S. Supreme Court precedent? How does the Court define the concept of a "true threat"?
9. What is the *Lemon* test? Describe the test that the *Kennedy v. Bremerton* Court used to replace the *Lemon* test.

ENDNOTE

1. "Religion in Bremerton, Washington," best places, www.bestplaces.net/religion/city/washington/bremerton (accessed July 8, 2023).

The Second Amendment
The Right to Bear Arms

8

Consider carefully the language of the Second Amendment:

> A well regulated Militia, being necessary to the security of a free State, the right of the people to keep and bear Arms, shall not be infringed.

The meaning and scope of the Second Amendment have been a source of intense controversy for many years. Not many Supreme Court cases have addressed this issue, leaving much ambiguity about what the amendment actually grants or restricts. Areas of debate include:

- Does this amendment grant individuals the fundamental right to own and possess arms or should only those individuals participating in the militia have this ability?
- In what way can a person possess a gun inside the home and outside the home?
- What types of gun permit requirements are constitutional for a state to impose on those who wish to possess a gun?
- What types of guns are restricted? Weapons have changed considerably since the Framers wrote these words. Assuming that it is appropriate to extend the word "arms" beyond muskets, how far should it extend to include the plethora of modern firearms and accoutrements?
- Which government should have the ability to regulate gun possession: the state, local, or federal government?

Originally, the Supreme Court decided in *Presser v. Illinois* (1886) that states were able to regulate guns in the context of public mock military activities. In *Presser*, a private all-White militia had been constrained by state law from publicly drilling with their weapons. The Court decided that the Second Amendment constrained only the federal government, thereby

Supervised target practice with a handgun such as those at issue in *District of Columbia v. Heller*. *Wikimedia Commons*.

leaving free rein for the states on matters not regulated by the militia laws of the United States.

In *United States v. Miller* (1939), the Court held that, through its Commerce Clause powers, Congress could ban interstate sale of certain guns. The Court based its rationale on the Second Amendment's language regarding a "well regulated militia," and stated that certain firearms do not promote this agenda (such as a sawed-off shotgun). Importantly, the *Miller* Court reinforced the notions that (1) the Second Amendment was focused on protecting militias (and did not create a right to bear arms by individuals), and (2) Congress could not pass laws that would preclude a state from maintaining an armed militia among its citizens. Then, in *Lewis v. United States* (1980), the Court affirmed the federal government's ability to prohibit convicted felons from owning firearms.

So, at the time the Supreme Court decided the next case, the Court had never held that the Second Amendment protected the gun rights of an individual citizen. As you read the decision below, evaluate whether you agree with the majority's interpretation: The words of the Second Amendment clearly *do* protect the right of an individual to possess a gun for the person's own individual reasons.

FROM THE BENCH

DISTRICT OF COLUMBIA v. HELLER
554 U.S. 570 (2008)

Justice SCALIA delivered the opinion of the Court.

We consider whether a District of Columbia prohibition on the possession of usable handguns in the home violates the Second Amendment to the Constitution.

I

The District of Columbia generally prohibits the possession of handguns. It is a crime to carry an unregistered firearm, and the registration of handguns is prohibited. See D. C. Code §§7-2501.01(12), 7-2502.01(a), 7-2502.02(a)(4) (2001). Wholly apart from that prohibition, no person may carry a handgun without a license, but the chief of police may issue licenses for 1-year periods. See §§22-4504(a), 22-4506. District of Columbia law also requires residents to keep their lawfully owned firearms, such as registered long guns, "unloaded and dissembled or bound by a trigger lock or similar device" unless they are located in a place of business or are being used for lawful recreational activities. See §7-2507.02.[1]

Respondent Dick Heller is a D. C. special police officer authorized to carry a handgun while on duty at the Thurgood Marshall Judiciary Building. He applied for a registration certificate for a handgun that he wished to keep at home, but the District refused. He thereafter filed a lawsuit in the Federal District Court for the District of Columbia seeking, on Second Amendment grounds, to enjoin the city from enforcing the bar on the registration of handguns, the licensing requirement insofar as it prohibits the carrying of a firearm in the home without a license, and the trigger-lock requirement insofar as it prohibits the use of "functional firearms within the home."

II

We turn first to the meaning of the Second Amendment.

---

[1] There are minor exceptions to all of these prohibitions, none of which is relevant here.

A

The Second Amendment provides: "A well regulated Militia, being necessary to the security of a free State, the right of the people to keep and bear Arms, shall not be infringed." In interpreting this text, we are guided by the principle that "[t]he Constitution was written to be understood by the voters; its words and phrases were used in their normal and ordinary as distinguished from technical meaning."

The two sides in this case have set out very different interpretations of the Amendment. Petitioners and today's dissenting Justices believe that it protects only the right to possess and carry a firearm in connection with militia service. Respondent argues that it protects an individual right to possess a firearm unconnected with service in a militia, and to use that arm for traditionally lawful purposes, such as self-defense within the home.

The Second Amendment is naturally divided into two parts: its prefatory clause and its operative clause . . .

1. Operative Clause.

a. "Right of the People." The first salient feature of the operative clause is that it codifies a "right of the people." The unamended Constitution and the Bill of Rights use the phrase "right of the people" two other times, in the First Amendment's Assembly-and-Petition Clause and in the Fourth Amendment's Search-and-Seizure Clause. . . . All three of these instances unambiguously refer to individual rights, not "collective" rights, or rights that may be exercised only through participation in some corporate body. . . . We start therefore with a strong presumption that the Second Amendment right is exercised individually and belongs to all Americans.

b. "Keep and Bear Arms." We move now from the holder of the right — "the people" — to the substance of the right: "to keep and bear Arms."

Before addressing the verbs "keep" and "bear," we interpret their object: "Arms." The 18th-century meaning is no different from the meaning today. The 1773 edition of Samuel Johnson's dictionary defined "arms" as "[w]eapons of offence, or armour of defence." 1 Dictionary of the English Language 107 (4th ed.) (reprinted 1978) (hereinafter Johnson). Timothy Cunningham's important 1771 legal dictionary defined "arms" as "any thing that a man wears for his defence, or takes into his hands, or useth in wrath to cast at or strike another." 1 A New and Complete Law Dictionary (1771).

The term was applied, then as now, to weapons that were not specifically designed for military use and were not employed in a military capacity . . .

We turn to the phrases "keep arms" and "bear arms." Johnson defined "keep" as, most relevantly, "[t]o retain; not to lose," and "[t]o have in custody." [In a dictionary originally published in 1828 and reprinted in 1989,] Webster defined [the phrase] as "[t]o hold; to retain in one's power or possession." No party has apprised us of an idiomatic meaning of "keep Arms." Thus, the most natural reading of "keep Arms" in the Second Amendment is to "have weapons."

From our review of founding-era sources, we conclude that this natural meaning was also the meaning that "bear arms" had in the 18th century. In numerous instances, "bear arms" was unambiguously used to refer to the carrying of weapons outside of an organized militia. The most prominent examples are those most relevant to the Second Amendment: Nine state constitutional provisions written in the 18th century or the first two decades of the 19th, which enshrined a right of citizens to "bear arms in defense of themselves and the state" or "bear arms in defense of himself and the state." It is clear from those formulations that "bear arms" did not refer only to carrying a weapon in an organized military unit . . .

c. Meaning of the Operative Clause. Putting all of these textual elements together, we find that they guarantee the individual right to possess and carry weapons in case of confrontation. This meaning is strongly confirmed by the historical background of the Second Amendment. We look to this because it has always been widely understood that the Second Amendment, like the First and Fourth Amendments, codified a *pre-existing* right. The very text of the Second Amendment implicitly recognizes the pre-existence of the right and declares only that it "shall not be infringed. . . ." There seems to us no doubt, on the basis of both text and history, that the Second Amendment conferred an individual right to keep and bear arms. Of course the right was not unlimited, just as the First Amendment's right of free speech was not. . . .

2. Prefatory Clause.

The prefatory clause reads: "A well regulated Militia, being necessary to the security of a free State. . . ."

a. "Well-Regulated Militia." In *United States v. Miller*, 307 U.S. 174, 179, 59 S. Ct. 816, 83 L. Ed. 1206, 1939-1 C.B. 373 (1939), we explained that "the Militia comprised all males physically capable of acting in concert for the common defense." That definition comports with founding-era sources.

Unlike armies and navies, which Congress is given the power to create ("to raise . . . Armies"; "to provide . . . a Navy," Art. I, §8, cls. 12-13), the militia is assumed by Article I already to be *in existence*. Congress is given the power to "provide for calling forth the Militia," §8, cl. 15; and the power not to create, but to "organiz[e]" it—and not to organize "a" militia, which is what one would expect if the militia were to be a federal creation, but to organize "the" militia, connoting a body already in existence. This is fully consistent with the ordinary definition of the militia as all able-bodied men. . . .

Finally, the adjective "well-regulated" implies nothing more than the imposition of proper discipline and training.

b. "Security of a Free State." The phrase "security of a free State" meant "security of a free polity," not security of each of the several States as the dissent below argued. . . .

3. Relationship Between Prefatory Clause and Operative Clause.

We reach the question, then: Does the preface fit with an operative clause that creates an individual right to keep and bear arms? It fits perfectly, once one knows the history that the founding generation knew and that we have described above. That history showed that the way tyrants had eliminated a militia consisting of all the able-bodied men was not by banning the militia but simply by taking away the people's arms, enabling a select militia or standing army to suppress political opponents. This is what had occurred in England that prompted codification of the right to have arms in the English Bill of Rights.

It is therefore entirely sensible that the Second Amendment's prefatory clause announces the purpose for which the right was codified: to prevent elimination of the militia. The prefatory clause does not suggest that preserving the militia was the only reason Americans valued the ancient right; most undoubtedly thought it even more important for self-defense and hunting. But the threat that the new Federal Government would destroy the citizens' militia by taking away their arms was the reason that right—unlike some other English rights—was codified in a written Constitution. Justice Breyer's assertion that individual self-defense is merely a "subsidiary interest" of the right to keep and bear arms, is profoundly mistaken. He bases that assertion solely upon the prologue—but that can only show that self-defense had little to do with the right's *codification*; it was the *central component* of the right itself.

■ ■ ■

D

We now address how the Second Amendment was interpreted from immediately after its ratification through the end of the 19th century. Three important founding-era legal scholars interpreted the Second Amendment in published writings. All three understood it to protect an individual right unconnected with militia service. We have found only one early-19th century commentator who clearly conditioned the right to keep and bear arms upon service in the militia—and he recognized that the prevailing view was to the contrary.

The 19th-century cases that interpreted the Second Amendment universally support an individual right unconnected to militia service. Many early-19th century state cases indicated that the Second Amendment right to bear arms was an individual right unconnected to militia service, though subject to certain restrictions . . .

Blacks were routinely disarmed by Southern States after the Civil War. Those who opposed these injustices frequently stated that they infringed blacks' constitutional right to keep and bear arms. Needless to say, the claim was not that blacks were being prohibited from carrying arms in an organized state militia. . . .

It was plainly the understanding in the post-Civil War Congress that the Second Amendment protected an individual right to use arms for self-defense. Every late-19th century legal scholar that we have read interpreted the Second Amendment to secure an individual right unconnected with militia service.

■ ■ ■

III

Like most rights, the right secured by the Second Amendment is not unlimited. . . . Although we do not undertake an exhaustive historical analysis today of the full scope of the Second Amendment, nothing in our opinion should be taken to cast doubt on longstanding prohibitions on the possession of firearms by felons and the mentally ill, or laws forbidding the carrying of firearms in sensitive places such as schools and government buildings, or laws imposing conditions and qualifications on the commercial sale of arms.

We also recognize another important limitation on the right to keep and carry arms. *Miller* said, as we have explained, that the sorts of weapons protected were those "in common use at the time." We think that limitation is fairly supported by the historical tradition of prohibiting the carrying of "dangerous and unusual weapons. . . ."

IV

We turn finally to the law at issue here. As we have said, the law totally bans handgun possession in the home. It also requires that any lawful firearm in the home be disassembled or bound by a trigger lock at all times, rendering it inoperable.

As the quotations earlier in this opinion demonstrate, the inherent right of self-defense has been central to the Second Amendment right. The handgun ban amounts to a prohibition of an entire class of "arms" that is overwhelmingly chosen by American society for that lawful purpose. The prohibition extends, moreover, to the home, where the need for defense of self, family, and property is most acute. Under any of the standards of scrutiny that we have applied to enumerated constitutional rights, banning from the home "the most preferred firearm in the nation to 'keep' and use for protection of one's home and family," would fail constitutional muster.

We must also address the District's requirement (as applied to respondent's handgun) that firearms in the home be rendered and kept inoperable at all times. This makes it impossible for citizens to use them for the core lawful purpose of self-defense and is hence unconstitutional . . .

■ ■ ■

We are aware of the problem of handgun violence in this country, and we take seriously the concerns raised by the many *amici* who believe that prohibition of handgun ownership is a solution. The Constitution leaves the District of Columbia a variety of tools for combating that problem, including some measures regulating handguns. But the enshrinement of constitutional rights necessarily takes certain policy choices off the table. These include the absolute prohibition of handguns held and used for self-defense in the home. Undoubtedly some think that the Second Amendment is outmoded in a society where our standing army is the pride of our Nation, where well-trained police forces provide personal security, and where gun violence is a serious problem. That is perhaps debatable, but what is not debatable is that it is not the role of this Court to pronounce the Second Amendment extinct.

Justice STEVENS, with whom Justice SOUTER, Justice GINSBURG, and Justice BREYER join, dissenting.

The question presented by this case is not whether the Second Amendment protects a "collective right" or an "individual right." Surely it protects a right that can be enforced by individuals. But a conclusion that the Second Amendment protects an individual right does not tell us anything about the scope of that right.

Guns are used to hunt, for self-defense, to commit crimes, for sporting activities, and to perform military duties. The Second Amendment plainly does not protect the right to use a gun to rob a bank; it is equally clear that it does encompass the right to use weapons for certain military purposes. Whether it also protects the right to possess and use guns for nonmilitary purposes like hunting and personal self-defense is the question presented by this case. The text of the Amendment, its history, and our decision in *United States v. Miller*, provide a clear answer to that question.

The Second Amendment was adopted to protect the right of the people of each of the several States to maintain a well-regulated militia. It was a response to concerns raised during the ratification of the Constitution that the power of Congress to disarm the state militias and create a national standing army posed an intolerable threat to the sovereignty of the several States. Neither the text of the Amendment nor the arguments advanced by its proponents evidenced the slightest interest in limiting any legislature's authority to regulate private civilian uses of firearms. Specifically, there is no indication that the Framers of the Amendment intended to enshrine the common-law right of self-defense in the Constitution.

In 1934, Congress enacted the National Firearms Act, the first major federal firearms law. Upholding a conviction under the Act, this Court held that, "[i]n the absence of any evidence tending to show that possession or use of a 'shotgun having a barrel of less than eighteen inches in length' at this time has some reasonable relationship to the preservation or efficiency of a well regulated militia, we cannot say that the Second Amendment guarantees the right to keep and bear such an instrument." *United States v. Miller.* The view of the Amendment we took in *Miller*—that it protects the right to keep and bear arms for certain military purposes, but that it does not curtail the Legislature's power to regulate the nonmilitary use and ownership of weapons—is both the most natural reading of the Amendment's text and the interpretation most faithful to the history of its adoption . . .

In this dissent I shall first explain why our decision in *Miller* was faithful to the text of the Second Amendment and the purposes revealed in its drafting history. I shall then comment on the postratification history of the Amendment, which makes abundantly clear that the Amendment should not be interpreted as limiting the authority of Congress to regulate the use or possession of firearms for purely civilian purposes.

I

The text of the Second Amendment is brief. It provides: "A well regulated Militia, being necessary to the security of a free State, the right of the people to keep and bear Arms, shall not be infringed."

"A well regulated Militia, being necessary to the security of a free State"

The preamble to the Second Amendment makes three important points. It identifies the preservation of the militia as the Amendment's purpose; it explains that the militia is necessary to the security of a free State; and it recognizes that the militia must be "well regulated." In all three respects it is comparable to provisions in several State Declarations of Rights that were adopted roughly contemporaneously with the Declaration of Independence. Those state provisions highlight the importance members of the founding generation attached to the maintenance of state militias; they also underscore the profound fear shared by many in that era of the dangers posed by standing armies. . . .

The preamble thus both sets forth the object of the Amendment and informs the meaning of the remainder of its text. . . . The Court today tries to denigrate the importance of this clause of the Amendment by beginning its analysis with the Amendment's operative provision and returning to the preamble merely "to ensure that our reading of the operative clause is consistent with the announced purpose." That is not how this Court ordinarily reads such texts, and it is not how the preamble would have been viewed at the time the Amendment was adopted. . . .

"[T]he right of the people"

The centerpiece of the Court's textual argument is its insistence that the words "the people" as used in the Second Amendment must have the same meaning, and protect the same class of individuals, as when they are used in the First and Fourth Amendments. According to the Court, in all three provisions — as well as the Constitution's preamble — "the term unambiguously refers to all members of the political community, not an unspecified subset." But the Court itself reads the Second Amendment to protect a "subset" significantly narrower than the class of persons protected by the First and Fourth Amendments; when it finally drills down on the substantive meaning of the Second Amendment, the Court limits the protected class to "law-abiding, responsible citizens." But the class of persons protected by the First and Fourth Amendments is not so limited; for even felons (and presumably irresponsible citizens as well) may invoke the protections of those constitutional provisions. The Court offers no way to harmonize its conflicting pronouncements.

"[T]o keep and bear Arms"

Although the Court's discussion of these words treats them as two "phrases" — as if they read "to keep" and "to bear" — they describe a unitary right: to possess arms if needed for military purposes and to use them in conjunction with military activities. . . .

The term "bear arms" is a familiar idiom; when used unadorned by any additional words, its meaning is "to serve as a soldier, do military service, fight." 1 Oxford English Dictionary 634 (2d ed. 1989). It is derived from the Latin arma ferre, which, translated literally, means "to bear [ferre] war equipment [arma]. . . ."

The Amendment's use of the term "keep" in no way contradicts the military meaning conveyed by the phrase "bear arms" and the Amendment's preamble. To the contrary, a number of state militia laws in effect at the time of the Second Amendment's drafting used the term "keep" to describe the requirement that militia members store their arms at their homes, ready to be used for service when necessary . . . "[K]eep and bear arms" thus perfectly describes the responsibilities of a framing-era militia member. . . . When each word in the text is given full effect, the Amendment is most naturally read to secure to the people a right to use and possess arms in conjunction with service in a well-regulated militia. So far as appears, no more than that was contemplated by its drafters or is encompassed within its terms. Even if the meaning of the text were genuinely susceptible to more than one interpretation, the burden would remain on those advocating a departure from the purpose identified in the preamble and from settled law to come forward with persuasive new arguments or evidence. The textual analysis offered by respondent and embraced by the Court falls far short of sustaining that heavy burden. . . .

Indeed, not a word in the constitutional text even arguably supports the Court's overwrought and novel description of the Second Amendment as "elevat[ing] above all other interests the right of law-abiding, responsible citizens to use arms in defense of hearth and home." . . .

V

The Court concludes its opinion by declaring that it is not the proper role of this Court to change the meaning of rights "enshrine[d]" in the Constitution. But the right the Court announces was not "enshrined" in the Second Amendment by the Framers; it is the product of today's law-changing decision. The majority's exegesis has utterly failed to establish that as a matter of text or history, "the right of law-abiding, responsible citizens to use arms in defense of hearth and home" is "elevate[d] above all other interests" by the Second Amendment.

Until today, it has been understood that legislatures may regulate the civilian use and misuse of firearms so long as they do not interfere with the preservation of a well-regulated militia. The Court's announcement of a new constitutional right to own and use firearms for private purposes upsets that settled understanding, but leaves for future cases the formidable task of defining the scope of permissible regulations. Today judicial craftsmen have confidently asserted that a policy choice that denies a "law-abiding, responsible citize[n]" the right to keep and use weapons in the home for self-defense is "off the table." Given the presumption that most citizens are law abiding, and the reality that the need to defend oneself may suddenly arise in a host of locations outside the home, I fear that the District's policy choice may well be just the first of an unknown number of dominoes to be knocked off the table. . . .

. . . The Court would have us believe that over 200 years ago, the Framers made a choice to limit the tools available to elected officials wishing to regulate civilian uses of weapons, and to authorize this Court to use the common-law process of case-by-case judicial lawmaking to define the contours of acceptable gun-control policy. Absent compelling evidence that is nowhere to be found in the Court's opinion, I could not possibly conclude that the Framers made such a choice.

Justice BREYER, with whom Justice STEVENS, Justice SOUTER, and Justice GINSBURG join, dissenting.

We must decide whether a District of Columbia law that prohibits the possession of handguns in the home violates the Second Amendment. The majority, relying upon its view that the Second Amendment seeks to protect a right of personal self-defense, holds that this law violates that Amendment. In my view, it does not.

I

The majority's conclusion is wrong for two independent reasons. The first reason is that set forth by Justice Stevens—namely, that the Second Amendment protects militia-related, not self-defense-related, interests. These two interests are sometimes intertwined . . . But self-defense alone, detached from any militia-related objective, is not the Amendment's concern.

The second independent reason is that the protection the Amendment provides is not absolute. The Amendment permits government to regulate the interests that it serves. Thus, irrespective of what those interests are—whether they do or do not include an independent interest in self-defense—the majority's view cannot be correct unless it can show that the District's regulation is unreasonable or inappropriate in Second Amendment terms. This the majority cannot do.

In respect to the first independent reason, I agree with Justice Stevens, and I join his opinion. In this opinion I shall focus upon the second reason . . .

. . . I here assume that one objective (but, as the majority concedes, not the primary objective) of those who wrote the Second Amendment was to help assure citizens that they would have arms available for purposes of self-defense. Even so, a legislature could reasonably conclude that the law will advance goals of great public importance, namely, saving lives, preventing injury, and reducing crime. The law is tailored to the urban crime problem in that it is local in scope and thus affects only a geographic area both limited in size and entirely urban; the law concerns handguns, which are specially linked to urban gun deaths and injuries, and which are the overwhelmingly favorite weapon of armed criminals; and at the same time, the law imposes a burden upon gun owners that seems proportionately no greater than restrictions in existence at the time the Second Amendment was adopted. In these circumstances, the District's law falls within the zone that the Second Amendment leaves open to regulation by legislatures. . . .

III

I therefore begin by asking a process-based question: How is a court to determine whether a particular firearm regulation (here, the District's restriction on handguns) is consistent with the Second Amendment? What kind of constitutional standard should the court use? How high a protective hurdle does the Amendment erect?

I would simply adopt such an interest-balancing inquiry explicitly. The fact that important interests lie on both sides of the constitutional equation suggests that review of gun-control regulation is not a context in which a court should effectively presume either constitutionality (as in rational-basis review) or unconstitutionality (as in strict scrutiny). Rather, "where a law significantly implicates competing constitutionally protected interests in complex ways," the Court generally asks whether the statute burdens a protected interest in a way or to an extent that is out of proportion to the statute's salutary effects upon other important governmental interests. Any answer would take account both of the statute's effects upon the competing interests and the existence of any clearly superior less restrictive alternative. . . . In applying this kind of standard the Court normally defers to a legislature's empirical judgment in matters where a legislature is likely to have greater expertise and greater institutional factfinding capacity. Nonetheless, a court, not a legislature, must make the ultimate constitutional conclusion, exercising its "independent judicial judgment" in light of the whole record to determine whether a law exceeds constitutional boundaries.

IV

A

No one doubts the constitutional importance of the statute's basic objective, saving lives. But there is considerable debate about whether the District's statute helps to achieve that objective. . . .

First, consider the facts as the legislature saw them when it adopted the District statute. As stated by the local council committee that recommended its adoption . . . "[t]he easy availability of firearms in the United States has been a major factor contributing to the drastic increase in gun-related violence and crime over the past 40 years . . ." [G]uns were "responsible for 69 deaths in this country each day," for a total of "[a]pproximately 25,000 gun-deaths . . . each year," along with an additional 200,000 gun-related injuries. Three thousand of these deaths, the report stated, were accidental. A quarter of the victims in those accidental deaths were children under the age of 14. And according to the committee, "[f]or every intruder stopped by a homeowner with a firearm, there are 4 gun-related accidents within the home."

In respect to local crime, the committee observed that there were 285 murders in the District during 1974—a record number. . . .

The committee report furthermore presented statistics strongly correlating handguns with crime. Of the 285 murders in the District in 1974, 155 were committed with handguns. This did not appear to be an aberration, as the report revealed that "handguns [had been] used in roughly 54% of all murders" (and 87% of murders of law enforcement officers) nationwide over the preceding several years. Nor were handguns only linked to murders, as statistics showed that they were used in roughly 60% of robberies and 26% of assaults. . . ."

From 1993 to 1997, there were 180,533 firearm-related deaths in the United States, an average of over 36,000 per year. . . . Over that same period there were an additional 411,800 nonfatal firearm-related injuries treated in U.S. hospitals, an average of over 82,000 per year. Of these, 62% resulted from assaults, 17% were unintentional, 6% were suicide attempts, 1% were legal interventions, and 13% were of unknown causes.

The statistics are particularly striking in respect to children and adolescents. In over one in every eight firearm-related deaths in 1997, the victim was someone under the age of 20. Firearm-related deaths account for 22.5% of all injury deaths between the ages of 1 and 19. More male teenagers die from firearms than from all natural causes combined. Persons under 25 accounted for 47% of hospital-treated firearm injuries between June 1, 1992, and May 31, 1993. . . .

Statistics further suggest that urban areas, such as the District, have different experiences with gun-related death, injury, and crime than do less densely populated rural areas. A disproportionate amount of violent and property crimes occur in urban areas, and urban criminals are more likely than other offenders to use a firearm during the commission of a violent crime . . . "[S]tudies to date generally support the hypothesis that the greater number of rural gun deaths are from rifles or shotguns, whereas the greater number of urban gun deaths are from handguns. . . ."

For these reasons, I conclude that the District's statute properly seeks to further the sort of life-preserving and public-safety interests that the Court has called "compelling."

B

I next assess the extent to which the District's law burdens the interests that the Second Amendment seeks to protect. . . .

1

The District's statute burdens the Amendment's first and primary objective hardly at all. As previously noted, there is general agreement among the Members of the Court that the principal (if not the only) purpose of the Second Amendment is found in the Amendment's text: the preservation of a "well regulated Militia. . . ."

2

The majority briefly suggests that the "right to keep and bear Arms" might encompass an interest in hunting. But in enacting the present provisions, the District sought to "take nothing away from sportsmen. . . ." For reasons similar to those I discussed in the preceding subsection—that the District's law does not prohibit possession of rifles or shotguns, and the presence of opportunities for sporting activities in nearby States—I reach a similar conclusion, namely, that the District's law burdens any sports-related or hunting-related objectives that the Amendment may protect little, or not at all.

3

The District's law does prevent a resident from keeping a loaded handgun in his home. And it consequently makes it more difficult for the householder to use the handgun for self-defense in the home against intruders, such as burglars.

As the Court of Appeals noted, statistics suggest that handguns are the most popular weapon for self defense. To that extent the law burdens to some degree an interest in self-defense that for present purposes I have assumed the Amendment seeks to further.

C

In weighing needs and burdens, we must take account of the possibility that there are reasonable, but less restrictive, alternatives. Are there *other* potential measures that might similarly promote the same goals while imposing lesser restrictions? Here I see none.

The reason there is no clearly superior, less restrictive alternative to the District's handgun ban is that the ban's very objective is to reduce significantly the number of handguns in the District, say, for example, by allowing a law enforcement officer immediately to assume that *any* handgun he sees is an illegal handgun. And there is no plausible way to achieve that objective other than to ban the guns.

D

. . . I turn now to the final portion of the "permissible regulation" question: Does the District's law disproportionately burden Amendment-protected interests? Several considerations, taken together, convince me that it does not.

First, the District law is tailored to the life-threatening problems it attempts to address. The law concerns one class of weapons, handguns, leaving residents free to possess shotguns and rifles, along with ammunition. The area that falls within its scope is totally urban. That urban area suffers from a serious handgun-fatality problem. The District's law directly aims at that compelling problem. And there is no less restrictive way to achieve the problem-related benefits that it seeks.

Second, the self-defense interest in maintaining loaded handguns in the home to shoot intruders is not the primary interest, but at most a subsidiary interest, that the Second Amendment seeks to serve. The Second Amendment's language, while speaking of a "Militia," says nothing of "self-defense." Further, any self-defense interest at the time of the Framing could not have focused exclusively upon urban-crime-related dangers. Two hundred years ago, most Americans, many living on the frontier, would likely have thought of self-defense primarily in terms of outbreaks of fighting with Indian tribes, rebellions . . . and crime-related dangers to travelers on the roads. . . .

Third, irrespective of what the Framers could have thought, we know what they did think. Samuel Adams, who lived in Boston, advocated a constitutional amendment that would have precluded the Constitution from ever being "'construed'" to "'prevent the people of the United States, who are peaceable citizens, from keeping their own arms.'" And he doubtless knew that Massachusetts law prohibited Bostonians from keeping loaded guns in the house. . . .

Fourth, a contrary view, as embodied in today's decision, will have unfortunate consequences. The decision will encourage legal challenges to gun regulation throughout the Nation. Because it says little about the standards used to evaluate regulatory decisions, it will leave the Nation without clear standards for resolving those challenges. . . .

For these reasons, I conclude that the District's measure is a proportionate, not a disproportionate, response to the compelling concerns that led the District to adopt it.

BEHIND THE CURTAIN

Much academic ink has been spilled on the questions of interpreting and evaluating the impact of the Second Amendment, making it difficult to wade through the different points of view. One way to slice up the controversy is to look at these debates from four diverse angles:

- The United States is one of the only countries in the world (at last count a total of three) to recognize a right to gun ownership. Where in U.S. history and culture did so much of the country's affection for guns arise?
- Did the nation's attitude toward constitutionalizing the citizenry's right to bear arms change in the last half-century?
- Does gun control decrease violence?
- Do all U.S. citizens enjoy the same gun rights?

Here is just a sprinkling of perspectives on these questions:

Origin of U.S. Gun Culture
"Modern American Gun Culture and the American Frontier" by Greg Hickey[1]

Hickey observes that guns were present in the Americas as soon as European settlers began to colonize in the fifteenth century. But it was early U.S. history reflecting unusual focus on guns that renders the United States more "gun-loving" than other nations. Guns played an important role in the colonists' fight for independence from the British. Thereafter, as U.S. residents in the east pushed westward into new territories, guns proved important for hunting (i.e., eating) and protecting newly American settlers from Native Americans (who were not keen on these intruders taking over their—sometimes sacred—land). And for a significant period after that, the Wild West remained as large territories were deemed lawless places. Coping with this state of affairs imbued settlers with a cultural attitude toward the glories of individual self-determination and productivity—attitudes for which gun possession served well.

Change in the Last Half-Century
Michael Waldman, "How the NRA Rewrote the Second Amendment"[2]

Waldman observes that the National Rifle Association (NRA) first began with a focus on marksmanship and safety. He argues that the NRA's current influence on Second Amendment interpretation began in earnest in the 1970s, when the NRA developed considerable influence over election of congressmembers as well as presidents. This in turn influenced the policies of elected officials. In the meantime, the "individual right" reading the Second Amendment started to win in the court of public opinion. Whereas 60 percent of those in the United States favored banning handguns, this dropped to 41 percent in 1975 and 24 percent in 2012. By 2008, Gallop reported that 73 percent of those in the United States believed that the "Second Amendment guaranteed the right of Americans to own guns" outside the militia. Although the NRA's work had a strong influence, Waldman argues that it was a small group of libertarian lawyers who carried the individual gun rights battle flag to the U.S. Supreme Court, acting as the impetus behind the *Heller* case.

Does Gun Control Decrease Violence?
John R. Lott, Jr., *More Guns, Less Crime*[3]

John R. Lott, Jr., is an accomplished economist who has written extensively on the downsides of gun control. Using research, statistical techniques, and modes of theorizing, Lott argues three general points: (1) violent crime is reduced when government issues more concealed handgun permits; (2) individual gun rights serve to equalize power between the sexes; and (3) gun control measures (such as a waiting period and background checks) do not tend to deter gun violence. Although Lott has many detractors who criticize his methodology, his theories remain popular in some corners today.

Do All Citizens Enjoy Gun Rights?
Carol Anderson, *The Second: Race and Guns in a Fatally Unequal America*[4]

Although history scholar Carol Anderson does not state that she is deploying a critical race theory approach to analyzing gun rights in the United States, one finds evidence of that approach in her thinking. Explicitly stating that she is not against gun rights per se, Professor Anderson's analysis shows how the history of the Second Amendment and interpretations of the amendment have systematically kept African Americans—particularly African American men—powerless and vulnerable. Professor Anderson argues that law was designed in such a way that slaves did not have access to firearms. This effort to prevent gun ownership by former slaves continued after the Civil War. Reaching into more current times, Professor Anderson shows how gun control measures disproportionally prevent Black Americans from purchasing, carrying, and using firearms. Think of the experience with law enforcement, she implores, that Black men encounter when simply driving in an automobile.

QUESTIONS FOR DISCUSSION

8.1 The Preamble or Prefatory Clause states, "A well regulated Militia, being necessary to the security of a free State. . . ." The majority and the dissents both agree that this clause is relevant to the purpose of the Second Amendment. Some Justices believe that it shows that the amendment is meant to protect militias only and does not create an individual right to bear arms. Other Justices believe that the clause does not limit the amendment's purpose of enunciating an individual right. Which side has the better part of the argument?

8.2 Do you believe that the increased incidence of mass violence in the United States should be relevant to how the U.S. Supreme Court interprets the Constitution? Or, should the Supreme Court stick to traditional constitutional interpretation, leaving U.S. society to handle the problem in other ways?

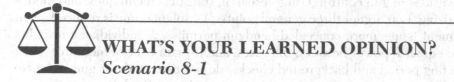

WHAT'S YOUR LEARNED OPINION?
Scenario 8-1

Consider the theories of interpretation described in Chapter 1 of this volume. Focusing on the issue of whether the Second Amendment creates an individual right to bear arms, evaluate how the following theories of interpretation would influence resolution of the issue.

The Approach of an Originalist: the notion that one should interpret the Constitution only by interpreting the text of the language and sources contemporaneous with the drafting of the language.

The Approach of the Living Constitution: the notion that the Framers envisioned that the meaning of the Constitution should grow and change as society evolves.

Critical Race Theory: the notion that racism is more than the result of individual bias and prejudice and, in the context of constitutional interpretation, racism that is imbedded in the history and structure of U.S. institutions and society should be considered.

The *Heller* case concerned a law passed by the government of the District of Columbia (Washington, D.C.). The Constitution dictates that the district is federal, operating under the power of the U.S. Congress. Accordingly, the *Heller* decision concerned the relationship between the federal government and the Second Amendment. As you might have noticed, the Constitution is sensitive to the difference between state and federal power (as well as the relationship between the two). This has been a particularly pointed issue in the Second Amendment context.

For these reasons, the question whether the individual right to bear arms recognized in *Heller* constrained state power remained unsettled following that decision. With dispatch, the Court disposed of that question in *McDonald v. City of Chicago* (2010), establishing that indeed the individual right to bear arms did constrain state and local power, thus restricting gun control measures deemed necessary by state and local governments.

Display of pistols such as those at issue in *New York Rifle & Pistol Association, Inc. v. Bruen*. *Wikimedia Commons.*

Facing an increase in gun violence, state and local governments continued to experiment with different ways to control gun ownership and possession. The next case is an example of that effort and its reception in the Court.

FROM THE BENCH

NEW YORK STATE RIFLE & PISTOL ASSOCIATION, INC. v. BRUEN
597 U.S. ___ (2022)

Justice THOMAS delivered the opinion of the Court.

In *District of Columbia v. Heller*, and *McDonald v. Chicago*, we recognized that the Second and Fourteenth Amendments protect the right of an ordinary, law-abiding citizen to possess a handgun in the home for self-defense. In this case, petitioners and respondents agree that ordinary, law-abiding citizens have a similar right to carry handguns publicly for their self-defense. We too agree, and now hold, consistent with *Heller* and *McDonald*, that the Second and Fourteenth Amendments protect an individual's right to carry a handgun for self-defense outside the home.

The parties nevertheless dispute whether New York's licensing regime respects the constitutional right to carry handguns publicly for self-defense. In 43 States, the government issues licenses to carry based on objective criteria. But in six States, including New York, the government further conditions issuance of a license to carry on a citizen's showing of some additional special need. Because the State of New York issues public-carry licenses only when an applicant demonstrates a special need for self-defense, we conclude that the State's licensing regime violates the Constitution.

I

A

Today's licensing scheme largely tracks that of the early 1900s. It is a crime in New York to possess "any firearm" without a license, whether inside or outside the home, punishable by up to four years in prison or a $5,000 fine for a felony offense, and one year in prison or a $1,000 fine for a misdemeanor. Meanwhile, possessing a loaded firearm outside one's home or place of business without a license is a felony punishable by up to 15 years in prison.

A license applicant who wants to possess a firearm *at home* (or in his place of business) must convince a "licensing officer"—usually a judge or law enforcement officer—that, among other things, he is of good moral character, has no history of crime or mental illness, and that "no good cause exists for the denial of the license." If he wants to carry a firearm *outside* his home or place of business for self-defense, the applicant must obtain an unrestricted license to "have and carry" a concealed "pistol or revolver." To secure that license, the applicant must prove that "proper cause exists" to issue it. If an applicant cannot make that showing, he can receive only a "restricted" license for public carry, which allows him to carry a firearm for a limited purpose, such as hunting, target shooting, or employment.

No New York statute defines "proper cause." But New York courts have held that an applicant shows proper cause only if he can "demonstrate a special need for self-protection distinguishable from that of the general community." This "special need" standard is demanding. For example, living or working in an area "'noted for criminal activity'" does not suffice. Rather, New York courts generally require evidence "of particular threats, attacks or other extraordinary danger to personal safety."

When a licensing officer denies an application, judicial review is limited. New York courts defer to an officer's application of the proper-cause standard unless it is "arbitrary and capricious." In other words, the decision "must be upheld if the record shows a rational basis for it." The rule leaves applicants little recourse if their local licensing officer denies a permit.

B

As set forth in the pleadings below, petitioners Brandon Koch and Robert Nash are law-abiding, adult citizens of Rensselaer County, New York. Koch lives in Troy, while Nash lives in Averill Park. Petitioner New York State Rifle & Pistol Association, Inc., is a public-interest group organized to defend the Second Amendment rights of New Yorkers. Both Koch and Nash are members.

In 2014, Nash applied for an unrestricted license to carry a handgun in public. Nash did not claim any unique danger to his personal safety; he simply wanted to carry a handgun for self-defense. In early 2015, the State denied Nash's application for an unrestricted license but granted him a restricted license for hunting and target shooting only. In late 2016, Nash asked a licensing officer to remove the restrictions, citing a string of recent robberies in his neighborhood. After an informal hearing, the licensing officer denied the request. The officer reiterated that Nash's existing license permitted him "to carry concealed for purposes of off road back country, outdoor activities similar to hunting," such as "fishing, hiking & camping etc." But, at the same time, the officer emphasized that the restrictions were "intended to *prohibit* [Nash] from carrying concealed in ANY LOCATION typically open to and frequented by the general public."

Between 2008 and 2017, Koch was in the same position as Nash: He faced no special dangers, wanted a handgun for general self-defense, and had only a restricted license permitting him to carry a handgun outside the home for hunting and target shooting. In late 2017, Koch applied to a licensing officer to remove the restrictions on his license, citing his extensive experience in safely handling firearms. Like Nash's application, Koch's was denied, except that the officer permitted Koch to "carry to and from work."

[The lower courts rejected Koch and Nash's claims that the New York licensing system violated their Second Amendment rights.]

II

In *Heller* and *McDonald*, we held that the Second and Fourteenth Amendments protect an individual right to keep and bear arms for self-defense. In doing so, we held unconstitutional two laws that prohibited the possession and use of handguns in the home. In the years since, the Courts of Appeals have coalesced around a "two-step" framework for analyzing Second Amendment challenges that combines history with means-end scrutiny.

Today, we decline to adopt that two-part approach. In keeping with *Heller*, we hold that when the Second Amendment's plain text covers an individual's conduct, the Constitution presumptively protects that conduct. To justify its regulation, the government may not simply posit that the regulation promotes an important interest. Rather, the government must demonstrate that the regulation is consistent with this Nation's historical tradition of firearm regulation. Only if a firearm regulation is consistent with this Nation's historical tradition may a court conclude that the individual's conduct falls outside the Second Amendment's "unqualified command."

A

Since *Heller* and *McDonald*, the two-step test that Courts of Appeals have developed to assess Second Amendment claims proceeds as follows. At the first step, the government may justify its regulation by "establish[ing] that the challenged law regulates activity falling outside the scope of the right as originally understood." The Courts of Appeals then ascertain the original scope of the right based on its historical meaning. If the government can prove that the regulated conduct falls beyond the Amendment's original scope, "then the analysis can stop there; the regulated activity is categorically unprotected."

But if the historical evidence at this step is "inconclusive or suggests that the regulated activity is *not* categorically unprotected," the courts generally proceed to step two.

At the second step, courts often analyze "how close the law comes to the core of the Second Amendment right and the severity of the law's burden on that right." The Courts of Appeals generally maintain "that the core Second Amendment right is limited to self-defense *in the home*." If a "core" Second Amendment right is burdened, courts apply "strict scrutiny" and ask whether the Government can prove that the law is "narrowly tailored to achieve a compelling governmental interest." Otherwise, they apply intermediate scrutiny and consider whether the Government can show that the regulation is "substantially related to the achievement of an important governmental interest." Both respondents and the United States largely agree with this consensus, arguing that intermediate scrutiny is appropriate when text and history are unclear in attempting to delineate the scope of the right.

B

Despite the popularity of this two-step approach, it is one step too many. Step one of the predominant framework is broadly consistent with *Heller*, which demands a test rooted in the Second Amendment's text, as informed by history. But *Heller* and *McDonald* do not support applying means-end scrutiny in the Second Amendment context. Instead, the government must affirmatively prove that its firearms regulation is part of the historical tradition that delimits the outer bounds of the right to keep and bear arms.

1

To show why *Heller* does not support applying means-end scrutiny, we first summarize *Heller*'s methodological approach to the Second Amendment.

In *Heller*, we began with a "textual analysis" focused on the " 'normal and ordinary' " meaning of the Second Amendment's language. That analysis suggested that the Amendment's operative clause—"the right of the people to keep and bear Arms shall not be infringed"—"guarantee[s] the individual right to possess and carry weapons in case of confrontation" that does not depend on service in the militia.

From there, we assessed whether our initial conclusion was "confirmed by the historical background of the Second Amendment." We looked to history because "it has always been widely understood that the Second Amendment . . . codified a *pre-existing* right." The Amendment "was not intended to lay down a novel principle but rather codified a right inherited from our English ancestors." After surveying English history dating from the late 1600s, along with

American colonial views leading up to the founding, we found "no doubt, on the basis of both text and history, that the Second Amendment conferred an individual right to keep and bear arms."

We then canvassed the historical record and found yet further confirmation. That history included the "analogous arms-bearing rights in state constitutions that preceded and immediately followed adoption of the Second Amendment," and "how the Second Amendment was interpreted from immediately after its ratification through the end of the 19th century." When the principal dissent charged that the latter category of sources was illegitimate "post[-]enactment legislative history," we clarified that "examination of a variety of legal and other sources to determine *the public understanding* of a legal text in the period after its enactment or ratification" was "a critical tool of constitutional interpretation."

In assessing the post[-]ratification history, we looked to four different types of sources. First, we reviewed "[t]hree important founding-era legal scholars [who] interpreted the Second Amendment in published writings." Second, we looked to "19th-century cases that interpreted the Second Amendment" and found that they "universally support an individual right" to keep and bear arms. Third, we examined the "discussion of the Second Amendment in Congress and in public discourse" after the Civil War, "as people debated whether and how to secure constitutional rights for newly freed slaves." Fourth, we considered how post-Civil War commentators understood the right.

After holding that the Second Amendment protected an individual right to armed self-defense, we also relied on the historical understanding of the Amendment to demark the limits on the exercise of that right. We noted that, "[l]ike most rights, the right secured by the Second Amendment is not unlimited." "From Blackstone through the 19th-century cases, commentators and courts routinely explained that the right was not a right to keep and carry any weapon whatsoever in any manner whatsoever and for whatever purpose." For example, we found it "fairly supported by the historical tradition of prohibiting the carrying of 'dangerous and unusual weapons'" that the Second Amendment protects the possession and use of weapons that are "'in common use at the time.'" That said, we cautioned that we were not "undertak[ing] an exhaustive historical analysis today of the full scope of the Second Amendment" and moved on to considering the constitutionality of the District of Columbia's handgun ban. . . . We assessed the lawfulness of that handgun ban by scrutinizing whether it comported with history and tradition.

C

. . . To be sure, "[h]istorical analysis can be difficult; it sometimes requires resolving threshold questions, and making nuanced judgments about which evidence to consult and how to interpret it." But reliance on history to inform the meaning of constitutional text — especially text meant to codify a *pre-existing* right—is, in our view, more legitimate, and more administrable, than asking judges to "make difficult empirical judgments" about "the costs and benefits of firearms restrictions," especially given their "lack [of] expertise" in the field.

If the last decade of Second Amendment litigation has taught this Court anything, it is that federal courts tasked with making such difficult empirical judgments regarding firearm regulations under the banner of "intermediate scrutiny" often defer to the determinations of legislatures. But while that judicial deference to legislative interest balancing is understandable—and, elsewhere, appropriate—it is not deference that the Constitution demands here. The Second Amendment "is the very *product* of an interest balancing by the people" and it "surely elevates above all other interests the right of law-abiding, responsible citizens to use arms" for self-defense. It is this balance—struck by the traditions of the American people—that demands our unqualified deference.

D

. . . Much like we use history to determine which modern "arms" are protected by the Second Amendment, so too does history guide our consideration of modern regulations that were unimaginable at the founding. When confronting such present-day firearm regulations, this historical inquiry that courts must conduct will often involve reasoning by analogy—a commonplace task for any lawyer or judge. Like all analogical reasoning, determining whether a historical regulation is a proper analogue for a distinctly modern firearm regulation requires a determination of whether the two regulations are "relevantly similar."

. . . Consider, for example, *Heller*'s discussion of "longstanding" "laws forbidding the carrying of firearms in sensitive places such as schools and government buildings." Although the historical record yields relatively few 18th- and 19th-century "sensitive places" where weapons were altogether prohibited—e.g., legislative assemblies, polling places, and courthouses—we are also aware of no disputes regarding the lawfulness of such prohibitions. We therefore can assume it settled that these locations were "sensitive places" where arms carrying could be prohibited consistent with the Second Amendment. And courts can use analogies to those historical regulations of "sensitive places" to determine that modern regulations prohibiting the carry of firearms in *new* and analogous sensitive places are constitutionally permissible.

Although we have no occasion to comprehensively define "sensitive places" in this case, we do think respondents err in their attempt to characterize New York's proper-cause requirement as a "sensitive-place" law. In their view, "sensitive places" where the government may lawfully disarm law-abiding citizens include all "places where people typically congregate and where law-enforcement and other public-safety professionals are presumptively available." It is true that people sometimes congregate in "sensitive places," and it is likewise true that law enforcement professionals are usually presumptively available in those locations.

But expanding the category of "sensitive places" simply to all places of public congregation that are not isolated from law enforcement defines the category of "sensitive places" far too broadly. Respondents' argument would in effect exempt cities from the Second Amendment and would eviscerate the general right to publicly carry arms for self-defense that we discuss in detail below. Put simply, there is no historical basis for New York to effectively declare the island of Manhattan a "sensitive place" simply because it is crowded and protected generally by the New York City Police Department.

III

Having made the constitutional standard endorsed in *Heller* more explicit, we now apply that standard to New York's proper-cause requirement.

A

It is undisputed that petitioners Koch and Nash—two ordinary, law-abiding, adult citizens—are part of "the people" whom the Second Amendment protects. Nor does any party dispute that handguns are weapons "in common use" today for self-defense. We therefore turn to whether the plain text of the Second Amendment protects Koch's and Nash's proposed course of conduct—carrying handguns publicly for self-defense.

We have little difficulty concluding that it does. Respondents do not dispute this. Nor could they. Nothing in the Second Amendment's text draws a home/public distinction with respect to the right to keep and bear arms. As we explained in *Heller*, the "textual elements" of the Second Amendment's operative clause—"the right of the people to keep and bear Arms, shall not be infringed"—"guarantee the individual right to possess and carry weapons in case of confrontation." *Heller* further confirmed that the right to "bear arms" refers to the right to "wear, bear, or carry . . . upon the person or in the clothing or in a pocket, for the purpose . . . of being armed and ready for offensive or defensive action in a case of conflict with another person."

This definition of "bear" naturally encompasses public carry. Most gun owners do not wear a holstered pistol at their hip in their bedroom or while sitting at the dinner table. Although individuals often "keep" firearms in their home, at the ready for self-defense, most do not "bear" (i.e., carry) them in the home beyond moments of actual confrontation. To confine the right to "bear" arms to the home would nullify half of the Second Amendment's operative protections.

Moreover, confining the right to "bear" arms to the home would make little sense given that self-defense is "the *central component* of the [Second Amendment] right itself." After all, the Second Amendment guarantees an "individual right to possess and carry weapons in case of confrontation," and confrontation can surely take place outside the home.

Although we remarked in *Heller* that the need for armed self-defense is perhaps "most acute" in the home, we did not suggest that the need was insignificant elsewhere. Many Americans hazard greater danger outside the home than in it. The text of the Second Amendment reflects that reality.

The Second Amendment's plain text thus presumptively guarantees petitioners Koch and Nash a right to "bear" arms in public for self-defense.

B

Conceding that the Second Amendment guarantees a general right to public carry, respondents instead claim that the Amendment "permits a State to condition handgun carrying in areas 'frequented by the general public' on a showing of a non-speculative need for armed self-defense in those areas." To support that claim, the burden falls on respondents to show that New York's proper-cause requirement is consistent with this Nation's historical tradition of firearm regulation. [We disagree.] [A]ll told, in the century leading up to the Second Amendment and in the first decade after its adoption, there is no historical basis for concluding that the pre-existing right enshrined in the Second Amendment permitted broad prohibitions on all forms of public carry.

Only after the ratification of the Second Amendment in 1791 did public-carry restrictions proliferate. Respondents rely heavily on these restrictions, which generally fell into three categories: common-law offenses, statutory prohibitions, and "surety" statutes. None of these restrictions imposed a substantial burden on public carry analogous to the burden created by New York's restrictive licensing regime.

Common-Law Offenses. . . . As during the colonial and founding periods, the common-law offenses of "affray" or going armed "to the terror of the people" continued to impose some limits on firearm carry in the antebellum period. But as with the earlier periods, there is no evidence indicating that these common-law limitations impaired the right of the general population to peaceable public carry.

Statutory Prohibitions. In the early to mid-19th century, some States began enacting laws that proscribed the concealed carry of pistols and other small weapons. As we recognized in *Heller*, "the majority of the 19th-century courts to consider the question held that [these] prohibitions on carrying concealed weapons were lawful under the Second Amendment or state analogues." . . . All told, these antebellum state-court decisions evince a consensus view that States could not altogether prohibit the public carry of "arms" protected by the Second Amendment or state analogues.

Surety Statutes. In the mid-19th century, many jurisdictions began adopting surety statutes that required certain individuals to post bond before carrying weapons in public. Although respondents seize on these laws to justify the proper-cause restriction, their reliance on them is misplaced. These laws were not *bans* on public carry, and they typically targeted only those threatening to do harm. . . . It is unlikely that these surety statutes constituted a "severe" restraint on public carry, let alone a restriction tantamount to a ban, when they were supplemented by direct criminal prohibitions on specific weapons and methods of carry.

To summarize: The historical evidence from antebellum America does demonstrate that *the manner* of public carry was subject to reasonable regulation. Under the common law, individuals could not carry deadly weapons in a manner likely to terrorize others. Similarly, although surety statutes did not directly restrict public carry, they did provide financial incentives for responsible arms carrying. Finally, States could lawfully eliminate one kind of public carry—concealed carry—so long as they left open the option to carry openly.

None of these historical limitations on the right to bear arms approach New York's proper-cause requirement because none operated to prevent law-abiding citizens with ordinary self-defense needs from carrying arms in public for that purpose.

[Turning to a later era of U.S. history,] we think a short review of the public discourse surrounding Reconstruction is useful in demonstrating how public carry for self-defense remained a central component of the protection that the Fourteenth Amendment secured for all citizens.

A short prologue is in order. Even before the Civil War commenced in 1861, this Court indirectly affirmed the importance of the right to keep and bear arms in public. Writing for the Court in *Dred Scott v. Sandford*, Chief Justice Taney offered what he thought was a parade of horribles that would result from recognizing that free blacks were citizens of the United States. If blacks were citizens, Taney fretted, they would be entitled to the privileges and immunities of citizens, including the right "to keep and carry arms *wherever they went*." Thus, even Chief Justice Taney recognized (albeit unenthusiastically in the case of blacks) that public carry was a component of the right to keep and bear arms—a right free blacks were often denied in antebellum America.

After the Civil War, of course, the exercise of this fundamental right by freed slaves was systematically thwarted. This Court has already recounted some of the Southern abuses violating blacks' right to keep and bear arms.

In the years before the 39th Congress proposed the Fourteenth Amendment, the Freedmen's Bureau regularly kept it abreast of the dangers to blacks and Union men in the postbellum South. The reports described how blacks used publicly carried weapons to defend themselves and their communities. For example, the Bureau reported that a teacher from a Freedmen's school in Maryland had written to say that, because of attacks on the school, "[b]oth the mayor and sheriff have warned the colored people to go armed to school, (which they do,)" and that the "[t]he superintendent of schools came down and brought [the teacher] a revolver" for his protection.

Witnesses before the Joint Committee on Reconstruction also described the depredations visited on Southern blacks, and the efforts they made to defend themselves. One Virginia music professor related that when "[t]wo Union men were attacked . . . they drew their revolvers and held their assailants at bay." An assistant commissioner to the Bureau from Alabama similarly reported that men were "robbing and disarming negroes upon the highway," indicating that blacks indeed carried arms publicly for their self-protection, even if not always with success.

Blacks had "procured great numbers of old army muskets and revolvers, particularly in Texas," and "employed them to protect themselves" with "vigor and audacity." Seeing that government was inadequately protecting them, "there [was] the strongest desire on the part of the freedmen to secure arms, revolvers particularly."

On July 6, 1868, Congress extended the 1866 Freedmen's Bureau Act, and reaffirmed that freedmen were entitled to the "full and equal benefit of all laws and proceedings concerning personal liberty [and] personal security . . . *including the constitutional right to keep and bear arms.*" That same day, a Bureau official reported that freedmen in Kentucky and Tennessee were still constantly under threat: "No Union man or negro who attempts to take any active part in politics, or the improvement of his race, is safe a single day; and nearly all sleep upon their arms at night, and carry concealed weapons during the day."

Of course, even during Reconstruction the right to keep and bear arms had limits. But those limits were consistent with a right of the public to peaceably carry handguns for self-defense. For instance, when General D. E. Sickles issued a decree in 1866 pre-empting South Carolina's Black Codes—which prohibited firearm possession by blacks—he stated: "The constitutional rights of all loyal and well-disposed inhabitants to bear arms will not be infringed; nevertheless this shall not be construed to sanction the unlawful practice of carrying concealed weapons. . . . And no disorderly person, vagrant, or disturber of the peace, shall be allowed to bear arms." Around the same time, the editors of The Loyal Georgian, a prominent black-owned newspaper, were asked by "A Colored Citizen" whether "colored persons [have] a right to own and carry fire arms." The editors responded that blacks had "the *same* right to own and carry fire arms that *other* citizens have." And, borrowing language from a Freedmen's Bureau circular, the editors maintained that "[a]ny person, white or black, may be disarmed if convicted of making an improper or dangerous use of weapons," even though "no military or civil officer has the right or authority to disarm any class of people, thereby placing them at the mercy of others."

. . . Finally, respondents point to the slight uptick in gun regulation during the late-19th century—principally in the Western Territories. As we suggested in *Heller*, however, late-19th-century evidence cannot provide much insight into the meaning of the Second Amendment when it contradicts earlier evidence. Here, moreover, respondents' reliance on late-19th-century laws has several serious flaws even beyond their temporal distance from the founding.

The vast majority of the statutes that respondents invoke come from the Western Territories. Two Territories prohibited the carry of pistols in towns, cities, and villages, but seemingly permitted the carry of rifles and other long guns everywhere. . . . These territorial restrictions fail to justify New York's proper-cause requirement for several reasons. First, the bare existence of these localized restrictions cannot overcome the overwhelming evidence of an otherwise enduring American tradition permitting public carry. . . . The exceptional nature of these western restrictions is all the more apparent when one considers the miniscule territorial populations who would have lived under them. Put simply, these western restrictions were irrelevant to more than 99% of the American population. . . . Second, because these territorial laws were rarely subject to judicial scrutiny, we do not know the basis of their perceived legality. . . . Finally, these territorial restrictions deserve little weight because they were—consistent with the transitory nature of territorial government—short lived.

■ ■ ■

At the end of this long journey through the Anglo-American history of public carry, we conclude that respondents have not met their burden to identify an American tradition justifying the State's proper-cause requirement. The Second Amendment guaranteed to "all Americans" the right to bear commonly used arms in public subject to certain reasonable, well-defined restrictions. Those restrictions, for example, limited the intent for which one could carry arms, the manner by which one carried arms, or the exceptional circumstances under which one could not carry arms, such as before justices of the peace and other government officials. Apart from a few late-19th-century outlier jurisdictions, American governments simply have not broadly prohibited the public carry of commonly used firearms for personal defense. Nor, subject to a few late-in-time outliers, have American governments required law-abiding, responsible citizens to "demonstrate a special need for self-protection distinguishable from that of the general community" in order to carry arms in public.

IV

The constitutional right to bear arms in public for self-defense is not "a second-class right, subject to an entirely different body of rules than the other Bill of Rights guarantees." We know of no other constitutional right that an individual may exercise only after demonstrating to government officers some special need. That is not how the First Amendment works when it comes to unpopular speech or the free exercise of religion. It is not how the Sixth Amendment works when it comes to a defendant's right to confront the witnesses against him. And it is not how the Second Amendment works when it comes to public carry for self-defense.

New York's proper-cause requirement violates the Fourteenth Amendment in that it prevents law-abiding citizens with ordinary self-defense needs from exercising their right to keep and bear arms. We therefore reverse the judgment of the Court of Appeals and remand the case for further proceedings consistent with this opinion.

Justice BREYER, with whom Justice SOTOMAYOR and Justice KAGAN join, dissenting.

In 2020, 45,222 Americans were killed by firearms. Since the start of this year (2022), there have been 277 reported mass shootings—an average of more than one per day. Gun violence has now surpassed motor vehicle crashes as the leading cause of death among children and adolescents.

Many States have tried to address some of the dangers of gun violence just described by passing laws that limit, in various ways, who may purchase, carry, or use firearms of different kinds. The Court today severely burdens States' efforts to do so. It invokes the Second Amendment to strike down a New York law regulating the public carriage of concealed handguns. In my view, that decision rests upon several serious mistakes.

First, the Court decides this case on the basis of the pleadings, without the benefit of discovery or an evidentiary record. As a result, it may well rest its decision on a mistaken understanding of how New York's law operates in practice. Second, the Court wrongly limits its analysis to focus nearly exclusively on history. It refuses to consider the government interests that justify a challenged gun regulation, regardless of how compelling those interests may be. The Constitution contains no such limitation, and neither do our precedents. Third, the Court itself demonstrates the practical problems with its history-only approach. In applying that approach to New York's law, the Court fails to correctly identify and analyze the relevant historical facts. Only by ignoring an abundance of historical evidence supporting regulations restricting the public carriage of firearms can the Court conclude that New York's law is not "consistent with the Nation's historical tradition of firearm regulation."

In my view, when courts interpret the Second Amendment, it is constitutionally proper, indeed often necessary, for them to consider the serious dangers and consequences of gun violence that lead States to regulate firearms. The Second Circuit has done so and has held that New York's law does not violate the Second Amendment. I would affirm that holding.

QUESTIONS FOR DISCUSSION

8.3 In the *Heller* case, the majority made clear that its holding did not foreclose gun regulation, although the Court did little to clarify what regulation would be constitutional. Critics pointed out that this uncertainty would give rise to a cat-and-mouse game, with state legislatures creating new gun regulations in attempt to outmaneuver the U.S. Supreme Court's edicts and the legislation ultimately being swatted down by the Supreme Court. Does the legislation at issue in this case help to prove that point?

8.4 In his majority opinion, Justice Thomas stated that "reliance on history to inform the meaning of constitutional text—especially text meant to codify a *pre-existing* right—is, in our view, more legitimate, and more administrable, than asking judges to 'make difficult empirical judgments' about 'the costs and benefits of firearms restrictions.'" Why did he conclude that making historical rather than empirical judgments is more appropriate for judges?

8.5 Are you convinced that the majority's recitation of the history regarding gun rights following the Civil War supports the Court's bottom line that the historical tradition embodied gun-carry rights? Explain your answer.

8.6 The *Bruen* Court adopted an approach that instructed that one must look to tradition throughout the history of the United States to discern the proper interpretation of the Second Amendment. Is the following statement in the majority opinion consistent with that approach: "As we suggested in *Heller*, however, late-19th-century evidence cannot provide much insight into the meaning of the Second Amendment when it contradicts earlier evidence"? Support your answer.

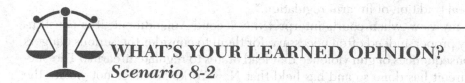

WHAT'S YOUR LEARNED OPINION?
Scenario 8-2

In both *Heller* and *Bruen*, the Court endorsed the notion that an exception to free-reigning Second Amendment freedom could properly exist in "sensitive spaces." Although the Court balked at the notion that spaces could be deemed "sensitive" simply because they were crowded with people, the Court did list places that were indisputably sensitive: schools, government buildings, legislative assemblies, polling places, and courthouses. The Court added that a space is not a "sensitive space" simply because many people typically congregate there and law enforcement is readily available.

A large city where transportation on the subway is essential to the population would like to designate subways as a "sensitive space." In addition, because the city is a cultural center that attracts visitors from throughout the country, the city would also like to designate the following venues as "sensitive spaces": theaters, museums, and other places where performances and concerts are held. Would you advise the city that these fora are "sensitive spaces" in which the city may prohibit individuals from personally carrying guns? (You can assume that the sensitive spaces exemption does not apply to law enforcement, security guards, and the like.)

Scenario 8-3

Consider the definition of a sensitive space described in Scenario 8-2. Do you see a basis for challenging the notion that an airplane is a sensitive space for which gun possession may be prohibited?

From the material that you have read in this chapter, you can see that the meaning and scope of the Second Amendment presents a highly controversial and politicized question. Other parts of the Bill of Rights share this quality. On the other hand, as you will see in the remainder of the chapters in this volume covering other parts of the Bill of Rights, the Second Amendment is unusual given the debate about whether it actually even grants an individual right. No question exists on whether other Bill of Rights provisions refer to liberties possessed by individual citizens, but controversy remains as to the meaning and scope of these liberties.

QUESTIONS FOR REVIEW

1. Explain the arguments for why the Second Amendment should not be read to provide for an individual right to bear arms.
2. Explain the arguments for why the Second Amendment could be read to provide for an individual right.
3. Under the interpretation in the *Heller* case, is the right to bear arms unlimited? If limits are allowed under *Heller*, describe the type of limits that *Heller* allows.
4. Describe how gun culture developed early in the history of the United States.
5. Describe the gun control law at issue in *Bruen*. Did the *Bruen* Court uphold that law?
6. *Bruen* set forth what a government must prove to establish that a gun control law is constitutional. Explain what *Bruen* requires a government to prove to justify a gun control law.

ENDNOTES

1. History Is Now Magazine (posted 2022), available at http://www.historyisnowmagazine.com/blog/2022/4/6/modern-american-gun-culture-and-the-american-frontier#.Y_5543bMI2w (last accessed July 8, 2023).
2. The Brennan Center for Justice (2014), available at https://www.brennancenter.org/our-work/research-reports/how-nra-rewrote-second-amendment (last accessed July 8, 2023).
3. 1998.
4. 2021.

Introduction to the Fourteenth Amendment

9

A. Background and Components of the Amendment

Focusing on establishing a strong union, the Constitutional Convention delegates of 1787 centered attention on buttressing the power of the federal government and steered away from controlling state power. Perhaps most notably, the delegates chose not to wrestle the question of slavery, and, as explained in Chapter 1 of this volume, even compromised by including several pro-slavery components in the Constitution's text. As reflected throughout this volume, constitutional history up to the present day shows a struggle between the power of states and the power of the federal government.

The give and take between state and federal power created an uneasy equipoise at the beginning of U.S. constitutional history. In other words, the system of federalism appeared to work—albeit with flashes of friction. This is reflected, for example, in the treatment of slave status issues among the states. A system developed between "free states" in the North and "slave states" in the South whereby the status of slaves and free persons would be honored when a Black person—enslaved or free—traveled through and stayed briefly in a territory in which persons in that territory held a different status than in the person's home. Under this so-called traveled and sojourned rule, if a slave owner from Alabama traveled with a slave to spend the hottest summer months in New York, the northern authorities would respect the status of the slave as a slave, so long as the New York stay was relatively short. Ultimately, however, the northern states stopped honoring this rule, and the system broke down.

Together with divergences of economic interests, the issue of slavery precipitated a breakdown of relations among the states. Fueled by clashing allegiances and anger, the United States of America effectively broke. A bloody Civil War followed. Toward the end of the war, through a process of wheeling and dealing among politicians, compromises were reached. The war ended and a period of reconciliation—trying to glue the country back together—followed, but wounds on both sides of the controversy did not heal quickly or easily. Indeed, we see today (more than 150 years later) continuing stress and controversy over such issues as confederate statutes, teaching Black American history, and the like.

Nonetheless, a giant step toward putting the country back together occurred with the ratification of the Fourteenth Amendment in 1848. This amendment was introduced in Congress, with language primarily addressed to undoing the consequences of chattel slavery. Congressional debate raged over the proposed amendment and its effect on states' rights. Eventually, the Fourteenth Amendment was ratified with five sections. The first section details the rights of U.S. citizens within their respective states. This chapter and the rest of this volume focus on that section—section 1—which provides:

> All persons born or naturalized in the United States and subject to the jurisdiction thereof, are citizens of the United States and of the State wherein they reside. No State shall make or enforce any law which shall abridge the privileges or immunities of citizens of the United States; nor shall any State deprive any person of life, liberty, or property, without due process of law; nor deny to any person within its jurisdiction the equal protection of the laws.

For the purposes of this chapter, the main components of this section of the Fourteenth Amendment are:

- Abridge the privileges or immunities of citizens of the United States
- Nor shall any State deprive any person of life, liberty, or property, without due process of law
- Nor deny to any person within its jurisdiction the equal protection of the laws

The consolidated cases discussed below, *The Slaughterhouse Cases*, were the first authoritative interpretation of this language. Although much of the interpretation of the amendment in the cases is no longer good law, some interpretations do survive, and the consolidated cases provide a vivid look at the federal–state power struggles that have continued well after the Civil War.

1. The Slaughterhouse Cases

In 1869, the Louisiana State Legislature passed a law giving the Crescent City Livestock Landing & Slaughterhouse Company exclusive operating rights in New Orleans. Although this created a monopoly for the Crescent City Company, it was required to comply with stipulations the legislature set forth, including allowing independent butchers to work on the company's grounds at a set rate.

The state also had requirements for the quality of the facilities, the volume of the output, and the price of the products. A group of independent butchers came together to sue Louisiana, arguing that the law violated the Fourteenth Amendment's (1) Due Process Clause by taking their property without due process of law; (2) Equal Protection Clause; and (3) Privileges and Immunities Clause by depriving them of the privilege to earn a living. The U.S. Supreme Court denied each of these claims. A salient fact: The butchers claiming these violations of their rights were all White men.

In denying the Equal Protection Clause claim, the *Slaughterhouse* Court emphasized that the Fourteenth Amendment was ratified solely to protect former slaves, ruling that the law was constitutional for equal protection purposes. As for the due process claim, the Court declared that the clause did not embody a right to practice one's trade and was fashioned to outlaw unfair procedures only, thus giving no credence to the plaintiffs' due process claim. Both of these holdings have been overruled—with the Equal Protection Clause having been extended well beyond former slaves and the Due Process Clause having been interpreted to provide a basis for recognizing substantive rights (and not just fair procedures).

But the Court's narrow Privileges and Immunities Clause interpretation has never been overruled. Interpreting that clause, the Court stated it was never meant to protect U.S. citizens from state actions or to empower courts applying federal law to invalidate state laws. Instead, the Court opined that the clause guaranteed those federal rights belonging to U.S. citizens alone, not those rights belonging to state citizens. In other words, the Court focused on the rights of *federal* citizenship only. And what are those rights? The Court gave a few examples:

> The right of the citizen . . . to come to the seat of the government to assert any claim he may have upon that government, to transact any business he may have with it, to seek its protections, to share its offices, to engage in administering its functions . . . to free access to its seaports . . . and courts of justice in the several States [and] to demand the care and protection of the Federal government . . . when on the high seas or within the jurisdiction of a foreign government.

The limited interpretation of the Privileges and Immunities Clause of the Fourteenth Amendment is curious—perhaps even suspicious—because citizens already had the federal rights listed above *before* the clause became part of the Constitution. Thus, in the words of dissenting Justice Field in *The Slaughterhouse Cases*, the majority's interpretation rendered the Privileges and Immunities Clause "a vain and idle enactment, which accomplished nothing, and most unnecessarily excited Congress and the people on its passage." The debates surrounding the Privileges and Immunities Clause suggest that Justice Field was onto something. The history of the Fourteenth Amendment debates reveals that many representatives and senators argued that the clause was intended as a protection of basic civil liberties from state interference.

Some hope emerged in 1999 that the Fourteenth Amendment's Privileges and Immunities Clause might be invigorated to protect against state interference. In *Saenz v. Roe*, 526 U.S. 489 (1999), the Court struck down a California law that limited welfare benefits to new residents of the state. Observing that the right to interstate travel was a right of national citizenship, the Court found that the California law violated the Fourteenth Amendment's Privileges and Immunities Clause. In the decades since the Court handed down *Saenz*, however, the Court has not struck down another state statute under the clause. In fact, in a 2010 Second Amendment decision, the Court explicitly declined to disturb the *Slaughterhouse* interpretation of the Privileges and Immunities Clause.

BEHIND THE CURTAIN

Why would Louisiana blatantly favor a single slaughterhouse company by granting it a monopoly? Well, the legislature maintained that this was necessary to protect against the health and safety concerns surrounding the slaughterhouses in the city. At the time of the legislation, the New Orleans area boasted 150 slaughterhouses, but no public sewers. Each year hundreds of thousands of animals were slaughtered and the waste, blood, and offal ran into the surrounding water and the streets. "When the river is low, it is not uncommon to see intestines and portions of putrefied animal matter lodged immediately around the pipes. . . . Vessels arriving here with cattle . . . invariably throw the dead cattle—of which they often have many—into the river at the stock landing. . . . It is not unusual, during the sultry heat of months, to see these floating objects about the shipping, no doubt causing disease among the sailors on board."[1]

Contradicting the health and safety justification for the law, critics claimed that the law was clearly an attempt to curry political favor. In 1875, during Louisiana litigation, Judge William Cooley said that he believed that the legislators had been bribed into the monopoly with gifts of stock in the company.

Also of historical note, the butchers were represented before the U.S. Supreme Court by a former U.S. Supreme Court Justice, John Archibald Campbell. Campbell was vehemently pro-slavery and pro-states' rights. At the outset of the Civil War he resigned from the Court and became an official in the Confederacy. After the conclusion of the Civil War, he was suspected to have been involved in Lincoln's assassination and was imprisoned. However, he was never charged and eventually returned to practicing law and argued many cases in front of the Supreme Court.

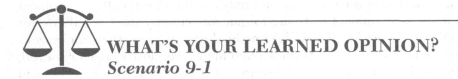

Depiction of a pork slaughterhouse by an unidentified illustrator. *Courtesy of The Historic New Orleans Collection.*

WHAT'S YOUR LEARNED OPINION?
Scenario 9-1

Protesters camped out in front of a courthouse to protest what they believed was an unfair and illegal election. The protesters had peacefully occupied the area for several weeks. However, one night, a group of armed and organized men attacked the protesters. The men were charged under a federal law that allows prosecution of offenders for participating in intimidation of voters or for conspiring to prevent citizens from exercising their constitutional rights. The attackers were charged with violating the protesters' federal right to lawfully assemble to protest government action. The federal trial court hearing the charges ruled that the protesters' actions are not covered by the Privileges and Immunities Clause of the Fourteenth Amendment and that the clause did not justify the legality of the charges. Is the court correct?

Scenario 9-2

One state has a statute that requires a $20 tax to be collected from each person who attempts to leave the state by vehicle. One man, who owns a taxicab, refuses to pay the tax as he travels out of state with several passengers. He claims that the law violates the U.S. Constitution. He has sued the state. Will he succeed?

B. The State Action Requirement

On and off throughout this book, you have read mention that the Constitution's civil rights protections for individuals exist only where a government threatens those protections. For example, individuals have no First Amendment protection when a private organization imposes a rule that individuals on the organization's premises may not criticize a particular politician. When the Bill of Rights became part of the Constitution, the Framers and the ratifying states understood that the Bill of Rights' protections constrained only how the federal government interacted with citizens—but did not constrain the states. It was not until the Fourteenth Amendment was ratified that those protections bound state and local governments. Not only was the Fourteenth Amendment an important development in trying to glue the country back together after the bloody Civil War, but it has also provided crucial protections for citizens from government overreach. As the United States has always been organized, state and local governments are the source of frontline, necessary services in the lives of citizens: services such as schools, police protection, garbage collection, fire protection, and the like. Accordingly, state and local governments are in the best position to fill citizens' needs or to jeopardize citizens' individual rights. For this reason, it was crucially important that the Bill of Rights protections be extended to protect citizens against improper action by state and local governments.

For all the Fourteenth Amendment accomplished, it did not change the basic fact about the reach of civil rights protections—these protections do not generally control private conduct. In other words, the Bill of Rights provisions now extend to protect against the actions of federal, state, and local governments only. Although this concept is known as the "state action" requirement, it is slightly misleading because the Bill of Rights protections bind all government officials, not just officials of a state of the United States. The protections bind the federal government as well as local governments (municipal, county, township, etc.). The word "state" is used in a generic sense in this context to refer to any governmental action and to distinguish actions taken by private entities.

This general rule requiring state action notwithstanding, a particularly explicit exception exists for the state action doctrine: the Thirteenth Amendment. This amendment prohibits slavery or involuntary servitude, protecting against those who might impose a state of labor captivity on others. For obvious reasons, this amendment had to apply to private individuals who held others in servitude to eliminate slavery from our nation's society and economy.

Less straightforward are other conceptual wrinkles to the state action doctrine. The conservative Supreme Court in the last decade or more has not been inclined to extend most of the civil rights protections any farther than the status quo and has in fact cut back on earlier extensions. For that reason, the Court has not shown itself to be keen on expansively reading the wrinkles in the state action requirements. The wrinkles nonetheless remain on the books and call for an understanding of how they operate.

First is the issue of when an entity that appears to operate as a private organization is created by federal law to promote governmental purposes. Examples include utility companies (electricity, gas, cable, Internet service providers, and a broad range of television outlets) and private port authorities that regulate activities along waterways that separate two states (e.g., the Port Authority of New York and New Jersey). The factors to consider in deciding whether the organization should be treated as a private organization include:

- Did Congress create and charter the entity?
- Does the entity receive government funding?
- How are the officers and directors appointed?
- Does the entity provide a service that directly serves a governmental objective?

The Court has never been clear about how many of these factors are necessary to transform an apparently private organization into a state actor.

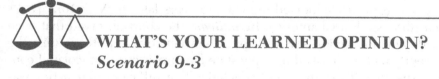

WHAT'S YOUR LEARNED OPINION?
Scenario 9-3

Congress chartered a corporation to provide train service throughout the United States. The corporation was created by federal law, its board is appointed by the U.S. President, and it receives substantial federal funding. Advertisements appeared on various locations throughout the trains, but the corporation refused to accept a request from Joe Liberal to allow an advertisement on the premise that it was "too political in nature." Joe Liberal had complied with all other requirements necessary to have an advertisement displayed on the train and sued the corporation for a violation of his First Amendment rights. Is the corporation a state actor for the purpose of this lawsuit?

The Court has also created other wrinkles in the state action doctrine, which might be characterized as exceptions. Two prominent exceptions deserve special mention: the public functions exception and the entanglement exception.

The public functions exception provides that state actions can exist when a private entity exercises powers usually "reserved exclusively to the government." To apply this test, one must get an understanding of what types of powers are usually "reserved exclusively to the government." Over the years, the Supreme Court has held the following tasks fall into that category: running a private utility providing service to citizens, managing open space in a company town, controlling elections, and running or regulating schools.

The entanglement exception is even more expansive (and perhaps even more vague) than the public functions exception. This exception applies if the government provides a mechanism for facilitating, implementing, or authorizing private conduct that allegedly violates the Constitution. Making the exception hard to pin down, however, the Court has applied it inconsistently to activities that cover a wide range of government tasks: judicial proceedings, law enforcement, government subsidies, government licensing, and voter initiatives.

Perhaps the most important example of entanglement occurred in *Shelley v. Kramer*, 334 U.S. 1 (1948). The suit in this case concerned whether courts could enforce a private contractual agreement under which the neighbors agreed not to sell their property to Black people. Confronting the question whether a court could enforce a private contract with a provision that is discriminatory and unconstitutional, the Court reasoned that without the strong arm of the court action the discriminatory provision may not be enforced. For that reason, that Court reasoned that when state courts enforce such a provision, state action exists. Accordingly, the Court concluded that state action was present and courts in the United States may not enforce racially discriminatory agreements.

Shelley is regarded as a controversial opinion. This question arises: Where are its limits? Does something become state action any time the government is involved in some kind of enforcement? The answer remains unclear. That said, the Court explicitly endorsed the case 15 years later in *New York Times v. Sullivan* (discussed in Chapter 6). In *Sullivan*, the court observed that even though a defamation action was a dispute between two private parties, the Alabama courts had been asked to apply state law provisions that violated constitutional principles. Thus, the Court concluded that sufficient state action was present to insist that trial courts enforce First Amendment restrictions on how a defamation action may proceed.

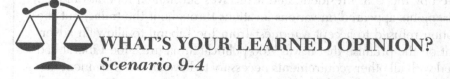

WHAT'S YOUR LEARNED OPINION?
Scenario 9-4

State A operated a parking complex. State A leased a part of the complex to a private restaurant and granted the restaurant a license to operate. As part of the lease and license, State A was responsible for the cleaning, maintenance, and upkeep of the building. The customers at the restaurant parked their cars in the complex.

The restaurant decided not to serve certain groups of people based on their race. A group of individuals who had been denied service sued the restaurant owners and the state for violating their constitutional rights to be free from racial discrimination. Is there sufficient state action to hold both the state and the private restaurant responsible for a constitutional violation?

The Fourteenth Amendment ushered in dramatic changes to the constitutional governance of our federalist system. To this day, the amendment enables stark changes in the trajectory of civil rights protections. In evaluating the scope of these protections, the restrictions in this chapter on the Fourteenth Amendment's reach should be kept in mind: *The Slaughterhouse Cases'* lingering, restricted interpretations of the Fourteenth Amendment Privileges and Immunities Clause and the state action requirement stand as important obstacles to the full use of the Fourteenth Amendment. In the several chapters that follow, look for additional rationales (devices?) for restricting or expanding the reach of the Fourteenth Amendment.

REVIEW QUESTIONS

1. Name the three main components of the first section of the Fourteenth Amendment. Explain what those three items are intended to do to protect citizens.
2. The Court in *The Slaughterhouse Cases* reviewed several different claims under the guarantees in the Fourteenth Amendment. The Court's holding and discussion on only one of the guarantees has survived subsequent interpretations of the Fourteenth Amendment. Name the surviving guarantee and describe why the restriction on its reach might have contemporary relevance.
3. The Fourteenth Amendment has a Privileges and Immunities Clause. What constitutes a "privilege and immunity" within the meaning of that Fourteenth Amendment clause?
4. How does the state action doctrine generally restrict the types of activity covered by the civil rights protections of the Fourteenth Amendment?
5. Sometimes the federal government creates a private entity to promote government purposes. What are three factors that bear on whether that private entity is considered the government for the purposes of the state action doctrine?

6. One exception to the state action doctrine is the public functions exception. That exception may apply when a private entity provides a function "reserved exclusively to the government." List three examples of such functions and explain why they might be considered government functions.

7. Describe circumstances in which one might appropriately apply the entanglement exception to the state action doctrine.

ENDNOTE

1. John Snow, UCLA Department of Epidemiology, "Ode to the Communication of Cholera," available at https://www.ph.ucla.edu/epi/snow/snowbook.html (last accessed June 16, 2023).

Racial Discrimination

10

Race intersects with the Constitution in myriad ways. To begin, you might remember from Chapter 1 that the original Constitution itself contains many provisions—such as the Fugitive Slave Clause—that directly or indirectly supported slavery. As society moved away from that position, the so-called original sin of holding Black Americans as slaves became a lineage to erase rather than support. Ultimately, provisions of the Constitution began to be used as instruments for eliminating the vestiges of slavery. This led to litigation—much of which made its way to the U.S. Supreme Court—touching many facets of life. Recall from Chapter 3's discussion of presidential authority that the Court announced in the context of the federal government's internment of Japanese American citizens, in *Korematsu v. United States*, that courts in the United States should apply the strictest scrutiny when evaluating the constitutionality of discrimination on the basis of race. This chapter covers four more highly specific areas dealing with racial discrimination: (1) the status of slaves or former slaves as citizens, (2) separation of the races, (3) affirmative action, and (4) voting rights.

A. The Status of Slaves or Former Slaves as Citizens

The case that follows, *Dred Scott v. Sanford*, is perhaps the most reviled decision in all of constitutional law. In fact, the case is sometimes described as the most overruled case in U.S. history—a statement that beckons the vision of Lady Macbeth walking in her sleep, obsessively washing her hands, and declaring "Out damn spot." In a metaphoric effort to erase the blood of a king in whose murder she is implicated, Lady Macbeth cries, "Here's yet a spot. . . . Here's the smell of blood still."

Dred Scott: Not capable of being a citizen.
Courtesy of the Missouri Historical Society via Wikimedia Commons.

The case involved Dred and Harriet Scott, two African Americans who had been born into slavery and filed lawsuits in 1846 petitioning for their freedom in Missouri. Under the ownership of Dr. John Emerson, Dred Scott had resided in free territory, including Illinois and Fort Snelling (in what was later Minnesota), which he argued made him a free man on his return to Missouri, a slave state. As such, he brought suit against his current owner, John Sandford, who had gained possession of the family once Dr. Emerson passed away and left his estate to his wife Irene Emerson. Irene Emerson had in turn sold the Scotts to her brother, John Sandford (whose name is misspelled "Sanford" in this case's official records).

Following years of precedent in similar slave suits seeking freedom, the Missouri state court initially granted Scott his freedom in 1850. Nonetheless, the Missouri Supreme Court reversed, noting changing public attitudes around slavery and declaring, "Times are not now as they were when the former decisions . . . were made."

Scott then brought suit against Sandford in federal court, invoking the Constitution's grant of power to federal courts to decide disputes between citizens of two different states. The Supreme Court in *Dred Scott v. Sanford*, however, held that the federal courts had no power to decide the case because as a slave, Dred Scott was not a citizen of the United States, and had "no rights which the white man was bound to respect," including no right to bring a suit. Neither slaves nor free Black people were or could be U.S. citizens, wrote Chief Justice Taney in the opinion of the Court, because the Framers had never intended for them to be included in the Constitution's guarantee of rights.

More than just holding that African Americans were not citizens, the Court also overturned the Missouri Compromise of 1820, which had established Missouri as a slave state in exchange for the promise that all states within the Louisiana Purchase above the 36° 30' parallel would be free states. Taney's opinion held that this Act unconstitutionally interfered with slaveowners' property rights and was therefore overturned as a "void and inoperative" exercise of congressional power. Significantly, *Dred Scott* represents the first time the U.S. Supreme Court declared an act of Congress unconstitutional since the 1803 decision in *Marbury v. Madison* (presented in Chapter 3 of this volume).

FROM THE BENCH

DRED SCOTT v. SANFORD
60 U.S. 393 (1857)

Chief Justice TANEY delivered the opinion of the Court.

This is certainly a very serious question, and one that now for the first time has been brought for decision before this court. But it is brought here by those who have a right to bring it, and it is our duty to meet it and decide it.

The question is simply this: Can a negro, whose ancestors were imported into this country, and sold as slaves, become a member of the political community formed and brought into existence by the Constitution of the United States, and as such become entitled to all the rights, and privileges, and immunities, guarantied by that instrument to the citizen? One of which rights is the privilege of suing in a court of the United States in the cases specified in the Constitution.

The words 'people of the United States' and 'citizens' are synonymous terms, and mean the same thing. They both describe the political body who, according to our republican institutions, form the sovereignty, and who hold the power and conduct the Government through their representatives. They are what we familiarly call the 'sovereign people,' and every citizen is one of this people, and a constituent member of this sovereignty. The question before us is, whether the class of persons described in the plea in abatement compose a portion of this people, and are constituent members of this sovereignty? We think they are not, and that they are not included, and were not intended to be included, under the word 'citizens' in the Constitution, and can therefore claim none of the rights and privileges which that instrument provides for and secures to citizens of the United States. On the contrary, they were at that time considered as a subordinate and inferior class of beings, who had been subjugated by the dominant race, and, whether emancipated or not, yet remained subject to their authority, and had no rights or privileges but such as those who held the power and the Government might choose to grant them.

It is not the province of the court to decide upon the justice or injustice, the policy or impolicy, of these laws. The decision of that question belonged to the political or law-making power; to those who formed the sovereignty and framed the Constitution. The duty of the court is, to interpret the instrument they have framed, with the best lights we can obtain on the subject, and to administer it as we find it, according to its true intent and meaning when it was adopted.

FROM THE BENCH

The Constitution has conferred on Congress the right to establish a uniform rule of naturalization, and this right is evidently exclusive, and has always been held by this court to be so. Consequently, no State, since the adoption of the Constitution, can by naturalizing an alien invest him with the rights and privileges secured to a citizen of a State under the Federal Government, although, so far as the State alone was concerned, he would undoubtedly be entitled to the rights of a citizen, and clothed with all the rights and immunities which the Constitution and laws of the State attached to that character.

It is very clear, therefore, that no State can, by any act or law of its own, passed since the adoption of the Constitution, introduce a new member into the political community created by the Constitution of the United States. It cannot make him a member of this community by making him a member of its own. And for the same reason it cannot introduce any person, or description of persons, who were not intended to be embraced in this new political family, which the Constitution brought into existence, but were intended to be excluded from it.

It becomes necessary, therefore, to determine who were citizens of the several States when the Constitution was adopted. And in order to do this, we must recur to the Governments and institutions of the thirteen colonies, when they separated from Great Britain and formed new sovereignties, and took their places in the family of independent nations. We must inquire who, at that time, were recognized as the people or citizens of a State, whose rights and liberties had been outraged by the English Government; and who declared their independence, and assumed the powers of Government to defend their rights by force of arms.

In the opinion of the court, the legislation and histories of the times, and the language used in the Declaration of Independence shows, that neither the class of persons who had been imported as slaves, nor their descendants, whether they had become free or not, were then acknowledged as a part of the people, nor intended to be included in the general words used in that memorable instrument.

The language of the Declaration of Independence is equally conclusive:

It begins by declaring that, 'when in the course of human events it becomes necessary for one people to dissolve the political bands which have connected them with another, and to assume among the powers of the earth the separate and equal station to which the laws of nature and nature's God entitle them, a decent respect for the opinions of mankind requires that they should declare the causes which impel them to the separation.'

It then proceeds to say: 'We hold these truths to be self-evident: that all men are created equal; that they are endowed by their Creator with certain unalienable rights; that among them is life, liberty, and the pursuit of happiness; that to secure these rights, Governments are instituted, deriving their just powers from the consent of the governed.'

The general words above quoted would seem to embrace the whole human family, and if they were used in a similar instrument at this day would be so understood. But it is too clear for dispute, that the enslaved African race were not intended to be included, and formed no part of the people who framed and adopted this declaration; for if the language, as understood in that day, would embrace them, the conduct of the distinguished men who framed the Declaration of Independence would have been utterly and flagrantly inconsistent with the principles they asserted; and instead of the sympathy of mankind, to which they so confidently appealed, they would have deserved and received universal rebuke and reprobation.

This state of public opinion had undergone no change when the Constitution was adopted, as is equally evident from its provisions and language.

No one of that race had ever migrated to the United States voluntarily; all of them had been brought here as articles of merchandise. The number that had been emancipated at that time were but few in comparison with those held in slavery; and they were identified in the public mind with the race to which they belonged, and regarded as a part of the slave population rather than the free. It is obvious that they were not even in the minds of the framers of the Constitution when they were conferring special rights and privileges upon the citizens of a State in every other part of the Union.

Indeed, when we look to the condition of this race in the several States at the time, it is impossible to believe that these rights and privileges were intended to be extended to them.

And upon a full and careful consideration of the subject, the court is of opinion, that, upon the facts stated in the plea in abatement, Dred Scott was not a citizen of Missouri within the meaning of the Constitution of the United States, and not entitled as such to sue in its courts; and, consequently, that the Circuit Court had no jurisdiction of the case, and that the judgment on the plea in abatement is erroneous.

The act of Congress, upon which the plaintiff relies, declares that slavery and involuntary servitude, except as a punishment for crime, shall be forever prohibited in all that part of the territory ceded by France, under the name of Louisiana, which lies north of thirty-six degrees thirty minutes north latitude, and not included within the limits of Missouri. And the difficulty which meets us at the threshold of this part of the inquiry is, whether Congress was authorized to pass this law under any of the powers granted to it by the Constitution; for if the authority is not given by that instrument, it is the duty of this court to declare it void and inoperative, and incapable of conferring freedom upon any one who is held as a slave under the laws of any one of the States.

Now, as we have already said in an earlier part of this opinion, upon a different point, the right of property in a slave is distinctly and expressly affirmed in the Constitution. The right to traffic in it, like an ordinary article of merchandise and property, was guaranteed to the citizens of the United States, in every State that might desire it, for twenty years. And the Government in express terms is pledged to protect it in all future time, if the slave escapes from his owner. This is done in plain words — too plain to be misunderstood. And no word can be found in the Constitution which gives Congress a greater power over slave property, or which entitles property of that kind to less protection that property of any other description. The only power conferred is the power coupled with the duty of guarding and protecting the owner in his rights.

Upon these considerations, it is the opinion of the court that the act of Congress which prohibited a citizen from holding and owning property of this kind in the territory of the United States north of the line therein mentioned, is not warranted by the Constitution, and is therefore void; and that neither Dred Scott himself, nor any of his family, were made free by being carried into this territory; even if they had been carried there by the owner, with the intention of becoming a permanent resident.

BEHIND THE CURTAIN

The question of whether the decision in *Dred Scott v. Sanford* was the spark that started the Civil War is often debated, but scholars agree that despite Chief Justice Taney's intentions to resolve the debate about slavery once and for all, his opinion only heightened tensions between the North and the South on the issue. Abolitionist groups rejected Taney's opinion as the final answer to the issue of slavery, following the guidance of leaders like Frederick Douglass, who mocked Taney's certainty that the issue of slavery was settled in *Dred Scott* by saying, "The more the question has been settled, the more it has needed settling."

The Court's decision was also a major factor in the famous debates between Illinois Senate candidates Abraham Lincoln and Stephen Douglas. In his speeches there, Lincoln expressed his concern that *Dred Scott* would be extended to constitutionalize slavery even in free states. Lincoln expressed this fear in one of his most famous speeches by referring to "a House Divided," which he believed was put at further risk of division by the Court's decision in *Dred Scott*. Although Douglas won the nomination for the Illinois Senate in 1859, within only four years of the decision in *Dred Scott*, Abraham Lincoln took the oath of office as the nation's first Republican President after winning the election of 1860.

Once the Civil War ended, the Republican Congress explicitly rejected the decision, first by the Civil Rights Act of 1866, and then by the language of the Fourteenth Amendment. Through the Civil Rights Act of 1866, Congress overrode a presidential veto from Andrew Johnson in a rare feat to define citizens as "all persons born in the United States." Later that year, Congress constitutionalized birthright citizenship for all races in section 1 of the Fourteenth Amendment, which states: "All persons born or naturalized in the United States and subject to the jurisdiction thereof, are citizens of the United States. . . ."

QUESTIONS FOR DISCUSSION

10.1 Chief Justice Taney mentioned that the Declaration of Independence declared that "All men are created equal." Discuss whether you are persuaded by his explanations for why these words were not meant to apply to African Americans. If you are not persuaded, what is missing from his reasoning that could have convinced you otherwise?

10.2 A large part of the holding of the *Dred Scott* decision concerned whether Dred Scott could be considered a citizen of the United States. What does it mean to be a citizen of the United States? What does it mean to be a citizen of any governmental unit?

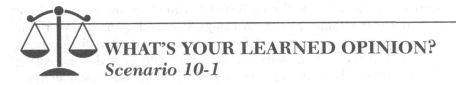 **WHAT'S YOUR LEARNED OPINION?**
Scenario 10-1

Taney's opinion inspired two dissents in *Dred Scott*, both written by Justices from the North: one from Justice Benjamin Curtis and one by Justice John McLean. In his opinion, Justice McLean argued that slaves are not "mere chattel," or property, but are people deserving of liberty as human beings. Justice Curtis took a different methodological approach in his opinion, instead providing evidence against Taney's assertion that the Framers could never have intended to include slaves or freed African Americans in the rights guaranteed in the Constitution. To do so, Curtis showed that before the adoption of the Constitution, five states had recognized free Black people as citizens and had even granted them the right to vote. Abolitionists hailed these opinions and used them to bolster their arguments against slavery across the country. Which of these dissents' mode of reasoning is more compelling to you, and why? What might the dissents in *Dred Scott* demonstrate about the various roles of dissenting opinions in general?

Scenario 10-2

Can you imagine any ways in which abolitionists could have used the pro-slavery decision in *Dred Scott* to their advantage? In 1859, two free Black men, John Copeland and Shields Green, joined abolitionist John Brown at his raid on Harpers Ferry. When the insurrection failed, Copeland and Green, along with Brown, were prosecuted for murder and treason in Virginia. At trial, their abolitionist attorney George Sennott used the decision in *Dred Scott* as a defense to the treason charge, arguing that as noncitizens under *Dred Scott*, Copeland and Green could not be guilty of treason. Why might this defense have succeeded in the Virginia court? Why might it have failed? Does the defense of lack of citizenship seem likely to be successful against a charge of treason, the crime of betraying one's own country? Could it be a defense to a murder charge?

B. Separation of the Races

The Reconstruction era followed the Civil War. During that time, the southern states operated under military rule, with Congress enacting many civil rights laws designed to protect the rights of former slaves. Once the Reconstruction era was over in the 1880s, southern states enacted laws discriminating against Black citizens and private violence increased, including many lynchings of Black citizens. Southern states enacted statutes that required separation of the races, known as Jim Crow laws. These laws touched most facets of public life, with schools, transportation, and public accommodation being prime examples.

The following case arose from a Louisiana law requiring railroads to provide separate but equal accommodations for White and Black people on railroads. This mandated that railway companies provide separate coaches divided by a partition. Louisiana prosecuted Homer Adolph Plessy, who was seven-eighths Caucasian, for refusing to leave the "White" railroad car.

Cover of the Louisiana Separate Car Act, 1890. *The Making of the Modern U.S.*

FROM THE BENCH

PLESSY v. FERGUSON
163 U.S. 537 (1896)

Justice BROWN, delivered the opinion of the court.

This case turns upon the constitutionality of an act of the General Assembly of the State of Louisiana, passed in 1890, providing for separate railway carriages for the white and colored races. The first section of the statute enacts "that all railway companies carrying passengers in their coaches in this State shall provide equal but separate accommodations for the white and colored races by providing two or more passenger coaches for each passenger train, or by dividing the passenger coaches by a partition so as to secure separate accommodations: *Provided*, That this section shall not be construed to apply to street railroads. No person or persons, shall be admitted to occupy seats in coaches other than the ones assigned to them on account of the race they belong to."

. . . The petition for the writ of prohibition averred that petitioner was seven-eighths Caucasian and one eighth African blood; that the mixture of colored blood was not discernible in him, and that he was entitled to every right, privilege and immunity secured to citizens of the United States of the white race; and that, upon such theory, he took possession of a vacant seat in a coach where passengers of the white race were accommodated, and was ordered by the conductor to vacate.

The constitutionality of this act is attacked upon the ground that it conflicts both with the Thirteenth Amendment of the Constitution, abolishing slavery, and the Fourteenth Amendment, which prohibits certain restrictive legislation on the part of the States.

That it does not conflict with the Thirteenth Amendment, which abolished slavery and involuntary servitude, except as a punishment for crime, is too clear for argument. Slavery implies involuntary servitude—a state of bondage; the ownership of mankind as a chattel, or at least the control of the labor and services of one man for the benefit of another, and the absence of a legal right to the disposal of his own person, property and services. . . .

A statute which implies merely a legal distinction between the white and colored races—a distinction which is founded in the color of the two races and which must always exist so long as white men are distinguished from the other race by color—has no tendency to destroy the legal equality of the two races, or reestablish a state of involuntary servitude. Indeed, we do not understand that the Thirteenth Amendment is strenuously relied upon by the plaintiff in error in this connection.

So far, then, as a conflict with the Fourteenth Amendment is concerned, the case reduces itself to the question whether the statute of Louisiana is a reasonable regulation, and, with respect to this, there must necessarily be a large discretion on the part of the legislature. In determining the question of reasonableness, it is at liberty to act with reference to the established usages, customs, and traditions of the people, and with a view to the promotion of their comfort and the preservation of the public peace and good order. Gauged by this standard, we cannot say that a law which authorizes or even requires the separation of the two races in public conveyances is unreasonable, or more obnoxious to the Fourteenth Amendment than the acts of Congress requiring separate schools for colored children in the District of Columbia, the constitutionality of which does not seem to have been questioned, or the corresponding acts of state legislatures.

We consider the underlying fallacy of the plaintiff's argument to consist in the assumption that the enforced separation of the two races stamps the colored race with a badge of inferiority. If this be so, it is not by reason of anything found in the act, but solely because the colored race chooses to put that construction upon it. The argument necessarily assumes that if, as has been more than once the case and is not unlikely to be so again, the colored race should become the dominant power in the state legislature, and should enact a law in precisely similar terms, it would thereby relegate the white race to an inferior position. We imagine that the white race, at least, would not acquiesce in this assumption. The argument also assumes that social prejudices may be overcome by legislation, and that equal rights cannot be secured to the negro except by an enforced commingling of the two races. We cannot accept this proposition.

If the two races are to meet upon terms of social equality, it must be the result of natural affinities, a mutual appreciation of each other's merits, and a voluntary consent of individuals. . . . Legislation is powerless to eradicate racial instincts or to abolish distinctions based upon physical differences, and the attempt to do so can only result in accentuating the difficulties of the present situation. If the civil and political rights of both races be equal, one cannot be inferior to the other civilly or politically. If one race be inferior to the other socially, the Constitution of the United States cannot put them upon the same plane.

Justice HARLAN, dissenting.

. . . [I]f this statute of Louisiana is consistent with the personal liberty of citizens, why may not the State require the separation in railroad coaches of native and naturalized citizens of the United States, or of Protestants and Roman Catholics?

The white race deems itself to be the dominant race in this country. And so it is in prestige, in achievements, in education, in wealth and in power. So, I doubt not, it will continue to be for all time if it remains true to its great heritage and holds fast to the principles of constitutional liberty. But in view of the Constitution, in the eye of the law, there is in this country no superior, dominant, ruling class of citizens. There is no caste here. Our Constitution is color-blind, and neither knows nor tolerates classes among citizens. In respect of civil rights, all citizens are equal before the law. The humblest is the peer of the most powerful. The law regards man as man, and takes no account of his surroundings or of his color when his civil rights as guaranteed by the supreme law of the land are involved. It is therefore to be regretted that this high tribunal, the final expositor of the fundamental law of the land, has reached the conclusion that it is competent for a State to regulate the enjoyment by citizens of their civil rights solely upon the basis of race.

In my opinion, the judgment this day rendered will, in time, prove to be quite as pernicious as the decision made by this tribunal in the *Dred Scott Case*. [I]t seems that we have yet, in some of the States, a dominant race—a superior class of citizens, which assumes to regulate the enjoyment of civil rights, common to all citizens, upon the basis of race. The present decision, it may well be apprehended, will not only stimulate aggressions, more or less brutal and irritating, upon the admitted rights of colored citizens, but will encourage the belief that it is possible, by means of state enactments, to defeat the beneficent purposes which the people of the United States had in view when they adopted the recent amendments of the Constitution, by one of which the blacks of this country were made citizens of the United States and of the States in which they respectively reside, and whose privileges and immunities, as citizens, the States are forbidden to abridge. Sixty million of whites are in no danger from the presence here of eight million of blacks. The destinies of the two races in this country are indissolubly linked together, and the interests of both require that the common government of all shall not permit the seeds of race hate to be planted under the sanction of law. What can more certainly arouse race hate, what more certainly create and perpetuate a feeling of distrust between these races, than state enactments which, in fact, proceed on the ground that colored citizens are so inferior and degraded that they cannot be allowed to sit in public coaches occupied by white citizens. That, as all will admit, is the real meaning of such legislation as was enacted in Louisiana. . . . There is a race so different from our own that we do not permit those belonging to it to become citizens of the United States. Persons belonging to it are, with few exceptions, absolutely excluded from our country. I allude to the Chinese race. But, by the statute in question, a Chinaman can ride in the same passenger coach with white citizens of the United States, while citizens of the black race in Louisiana, many of whom, perhaps, risked their lives for the preservation of the Union, who are entitled, by law, to participate in the political control of the state and nation, who are not excluded, by law or by reason of their race, from public stations of any kind, and who have all the legal rights that belong to white citizens, are yet declared to be criminals, liable to imprisonment, if they ride in a public coach occupied by citizens of the white race. It is scarcely just to say that a colored citizen should not object to occupying a public coach assigned to his own race. He does not object, nor, perhaps, would he object to separate coaches for his race if his rights under the law were recognized. But he does object, and he ought never to cease objecting, that citizens of the white and black races can be adjudged criminals because they sit, or claim the right to sit, in the same public coach on a public highway.

I am of opinion that the statute of Louisiana is inconsistent with the personal liberty of citizens, white and black, in that State, and hostile to both the spirit and letter of the Constitution of the United States.

BEHIND THE CURTAIN

Scholars debate the historical preconditions that lead to the *Plessy* majority's support for segregation. For example, some scholars maintain that the forced integration during Reconstruction created strong conditions for a backlash. Under this view, state legislators moved to impose segregation as a means to legitimize and maintain a racial caste system that continued oppressing the Black population. Other scholars emphasize that even without state-sponsored separation of the races, segregation existed in both northern and southern states largely by force of social custom.

Segregation in transportation—including steamboats and railroads— was particularly strict. The arrangements offered to Black riders were far from equal and were particularly problematic for Black women and children who were forced to ride in smoke-filled, filthy cars where coarse behavior was common. From the point of view of White riders, gender also had a role to play. Segregation was seen as a way to protect pristine White womanhood and maintain the sacred status of White women as a symbol of White supremacy. Although the *Plessy* majority spoke in terms of "separate can be equal," the decision is largely viewed as a visible, daily confirmation of the status of the Black population as second-class citizens.[1]

QUESTIONS FOR DISCUSSION

10.3 Much of our constitutional history depends on the definition of race. How do you describe the definition of a race?

10.4   In his dissent, Justice Harlan declared:

> Our Constitution is color-blind, and neither knows nor tolerates classes among citizens. In respect of civil rights, all citizens are equal before the law. The humblest is the peer of the most powerful. The law regards man as man, and takes no account of his surroundings or of his color when his civil rights as guaranteed by the supreme law of the land are involved.

What does this message mean for the current day's racial politics issues?

10.5   Consider another statement by Justice Harlan:

> There is a race so different from our own that we do not permit those belonging to it to become citizens of the United States. Persons belonging to it are, with few exceptions, absolutely excluded from our country. I allude to the Chinese race. But, by the statute in question, a Chinaman can ride in the same passenger coach with white citizens of the United States, while citizens of the black race in Louisiana, many of whom, perhaps, risked their lives for the preservation of the Union, who are entitled, by law, to participate in the political control of the state and nation, who are not excluded, by law or by reason of their race, from public stations of any kind, and who have all the legal rights that belong to white citizens, are yet declared to be criminals, liable to imprisonment, if they ride in a public coach occupied by citizens of the white race.

What do you think of this statement? Does it help Justice Harlan's goal of eliminating segregation of Black and White people?

10.6   The *Plessy* majority found preposterous the proposition that "the enforced separation of the two races stamps the colored race with a badge of inferiority." In explaining its conclusion, the majority reasoned that, if the tables were turned and a state legislature was dominated by Black legislators who enforced segregation, White citizens would not project an inferiority inference on the forced segregation. Are you persuaded by that reasoning?

After *Plessy v. Ferguson* held that official segregation was permissible under the state's police powers if the accommodations provided for each race were equal, the nation entered the twentieth century when this attitude started to wane. For example, in the 1938 decision in *United States v. Carolene Products Co.*, 304 U.S. 144 (1938), the Court began to demonstrate its willingness to address structural disadvantages placed on minority groups who were excluded from the political processes. In 1944, the *Korematsu* case regarding Japanese relocation to internment camps demonstrated that the Court was ready to hold

Future U.S. Supreme Court Justice Thurgood Marshall in 1957, then an attorney for the NAACP. *Thomas J. O'Halloran*, U.S. News & World Report Magazine. *Library of Congress.*

racial classification to a higher standard to be deemed constitutional. Six years later, in *Sweatt v. Painter*, 39 U.S. 629 (1950), the Court began tackling segregation in education by ordering the desegregation of the University of Texas School of Law based on the notion that segregated legal education would always be unequal. The same year, in *McLaurin v. Oklahoma State Regents for Higher Education*, 339 U.S. 637 (1950), the Supreme Court held that restrictions on an African American's education once admitted to a previously all-White law school, such as cafeteria seating options, were unconstitutional.

Efforts to fight segregated schools continued, with the National Association for the Advancement of Colored People (NAACP) Legal Defense Fund taking the lead. Charles Hamilton Houston and his protege, Thurgood Marshall, concluded that the laws enforcing segregation (Jim Crow laws) had a weak point: education. They therefore embarked on a decades-long legal campaign, recruiting historians, lawyers, and scientists to their cause. After the successes in *Sweatt* and *McLaurin*, the NAACP Legal Defense Fund began focusing on primary and secondary public education.

The decision below is remarkable for its brevity. While reading, consider the Court's approach and motivations. Is the opinion a stroke of diplomatic genius? Does it seem like anything is missing from the opinion?

FROM THE BENCH

BROWN v. BOARD OF EDUCATION
347 U.S. 483 (1954)

Mr. Chief Justice WARREN delivered the opinion of the Court.

These cases come to us from the States of Kansas, South Carolina, Virginia, and Delaware. They are premised on different facts and different local conditions, but a common legal question justifies their consideration together in this consolidated opinion. In each of the cases, minors of the Negro race, through their legal representatives, seek the aid of the courts in obtaining admission to the public schools of their community on a nonsegregated basis. In each instance, they had been denied admission to schools attended by white children under laws requiring or permitting segregation according to race. This segregation was alleged to deprive the plaintiffs of the equal protection of the laws under the Fourteenth Amendment.

The plaintiffs contend that segregated public schools are not "equal" and cannot be made "equal," and that hence they are deprived of the equal protection of the laws. Argument was heard in the 1952 Term, and reargument was heard this Term on certain questions propounded by the Court.

Reargument was largely devoted to the circumstances surrounding the adoption of the Fourteenth Amendment in 1868. It covered exhaustively consideration of the Amendment in Congress, ratification by the states, then-existing practices in racial segregation, and the views of proponents and opponents of the Amendment. This discussion and our own investigation convince us that, although these sources cast some light, it is not enough to resolve the problem with which we are faced. At best, they are inconclusive. The most avid proponents of the post-War Amendments undoubtedly intended them to remove all legal distinctions among "all persons born or naturalized in the United States." Their opponents, just as certainly, were antagonistic to both the letter and the spirit of the Amendments and wished them to have the most limited effect. What others in Congress and the state legislatures had in mind cannot be determined with any degree of certainty.

An additional reason for the inconclusive nature of the Amendment's history with respect to segregated schools is the status of public education at that time. In the South, the movement toward free common schools, supported by general taxation, had not yet taken hold. Education of white children was largely in the hands of private groups. Education of Negroes was almost nonexistent, and practically all of the race were illiterate. In fact, any education of Negroes was forbidden by law in some states. Today, in contrast, many Negroes have achieved outstanding success in the arts and sciences, as well as in the business and professional world. It is true that public school education at the time of the Amendment had advanced further in the North, but the effect of the Amendment on Northern States was generally ignored in the congressional debates. Even in the North, the conditions of public education did not approximate those existing today. The curriculum was usually rudimentary; ungraded schools were common in rural areas; the school term was but three months a year in many states, and compulsory school attendance was virtually unknown. As a consequence, it is not surprising that there should be so little in the history of the Fourteenth Amendment relating to its intended effect on public education.

In the first cases in this Court construing the Fourteenth Amendment, decided shortly after its adoption, the Court interpreted it as proscribing all state-imposed discriminations against the Negro race. The doctrine of "separate but equal" did not make its appearance in this Court until 1896 in the case of *Plessy v. Ferguson, supra,* involving not education but transportation. In more recent cases, all on the graduate school level, inequality was found in that specific benefits enjoyed by white students were denied to Negro students of the same educational qualifications. And in *Sweatt v. Painter, supra*, the Court expressly reserved decision on the question whether *Plessy v. Ferguson* should be held inapplicable to public education.

In the instant cases, that question is directly presented. Here, unlike *Sweatt v. Painter*, there are findings below that the Negro and white schools involved have been equalized, or are being equalized, with respect to buildings, curricula, qualifications and salaries of teachers, and other "tangible" factors. Our decision, therefore, cannot turn on merely a comparison of these tangible factors in the Negro and white schools involved in each of the cases. We must look instead to the effect of segregation itself on public education.

In approaching this problem, we cannot turn the clock back to 1868, when the Amendment was adopted, or even to 1896, when *Plessy v. Ferguson* was written. We must consider public education in the light of its full development and its present place in American life throughout the Nation. Only in this way can it be determined if segregation in public schools deprives these plaintiffs of the equal protection of the laws.

Today, education is perhaps the most important function of state and local governments. Compulsory school attendance laws and the great expenditures for education both demonstrate our recognition of the importance of education to our democratic society. It is required in the performance of our most basic public responsibilities, even service in the armed forces. It is the very foundation of good citizenship. Today it is a principal instrument in awakening the child to cultural values, in preparing him for later professional training, and in helping him to adjust normally to his environment. In these days, it is doubtful that any child may reasonably be expected to succeed in life if he is denied the opportunity of an education. Such an opportunity, where the state has undertaken to provide it, is a right which must be made available to all on equal terms.

We come then to the question presented: does segregation of children in public schools solely on the basis of race, even though the physical facilities and other "tangible" factors may be equal, deprive the children of the minority group of equal educational opportunities? We believe that it does.

To separate [children] from others of similar age and qualifications solely because of their race generates a feeling of inferiority as to their status in the community that may affect their hearts and minds in a way unlikely ever to be undone. The effect of this separation on their educational opportunities was well stated by a finding in the Kansas case by a court which nevertheless felt compelled to rule against the Negro plaintiffs:

"Segregation of white and colored children in public schools has a detrimental effect upon the colored children. The impact is greater when it has the sanction of the law, for the policy of separating the races is usually interpreted as denoting the inferiority of the negro group. A sense of inferiority affects the motivation of a child to learn. Segregation with the sanction of law, therefore,

Headlines all over the country featured the Supreme Court's decision in *Brown v. Board of Education*. The Topeka State Journal/*Kansas Historical Society.*

has a tendency to [retard] the educational and mental development of negro children and to deprive them of some of the benefits they would receive in a racial[ly] integrated school system."

Whatever may have been the extent of psychological knowledge at the time of *Plessy v. Ferguson*, this finding is amply supported by modern authority.[11] Any language in *Plessy v. Ferguson* contrary to this finding is rejected.

We conclude that, in the field of public education, the doctrine of "separate but equal" has no place. Separate educational facilities are inherently unequal. Therefore, we hold that the plaintiffs and others similarly situated for whom the actions have been brought are, by reason of the segregation complained of, deprived of the equal protection of the laws guaranteed by the Fourteenth Amendment.

It is so ordered.

---

11. K.B. Clark, Effect of Prejudice and Discrimination on Personality Development (Mid-century White House Conference on Children and Youth, 1950); Witmer and Kotinsky, Personality in the Making (1952), c. VI; Deutscher and Chein, The Psychological Effects of Enforced Segregation A Survey of Social Science Opinion, 26 J.Psychol. 259 (1948); Chein, What are the Psychological Effects of Segregation Under Conditions of Equal Facilities?, 3 Int. J. Opinion and Attitude Res. 229 (1949); Brameld, Educational Costs, in Discrimination and National Welfare (MacIver, ed., 1949), 44-48; Frazier, The Negro in the United States (1949), 674-681. *And see generally* Myrdal, An American Dilemma (1944).

BEHIND THE CURTAIN

Brown v. Board of Education is a dichotomous phenomenon. On one hand, it is one of the most significant opinions in constitutional law. The opinion is plainly written, without much legalese and without insinuating that anyone was acting in a racist fashion. The opinion was designed to be short enough to appear on the front page of the newspaper. This strategy succeeded in many towns and cities around the United States. As such, the opinion educated the public in an important way on the scope and impact of the Constitution and proved an important spark for the civil rights movement.

Further evidence of *Brown*'s impact can be seen in how conservative constitutional thinkers treat the opinion. For conservatives who embrace originalism or textualism, the opinion should represent a problematic reading of the Fourteenth Amendment because that amendment was drafted at a time when public education did not even exist, much less operate in an integrated manner. In responding to this fact and his support of *Brown*, Justice Antonin Scalia quipped: "I'm an Originalist; I'm a Textualist; I'm not a Nut." Although Scalia used his nimble intellect to develop an analytical justification for his apparently contradictory position, at bottom the real explanation of why the opinion is held in such regard for a wide spectrum of thinkers is that it is a sacred cow—embodying an idea that is above criticism.

On the other hand, there is the unpleasant truth that *Brown* did not work. Judged by the state of public schools in U.S. cities today, *Brown* failed miserably. As of 2017, Black children were five times as likely as White children to attend schools that are highly segregated by race and ethnicity. Additionally, Black children are more than twice as likely as White children to attend high-poverty schools. The opinion set forth above was followed the next term by what is known as *Brown II*, which addressed what public schools must do to bring home the promise of *Brown I*. *Brown II* took a relatively light touch in approaching the topic—not mandating that states take specific action other than "to effectuate a transition to a racially nondiscriminatory school system." The Court's broad message to the states was to move with "all deliberate speed" to remove the effects of state-required segregation.

"Speed" does not describe the states' initiatives to eliminate segregation and its effects. Ultimately federal courts oversaw various attempts to integrate the schools, including redrawing school district boundaries, busing, and creation of magnet schools. Although true integration never occurred, the Supreme Court ultimately said it was time to give up. Citing the intractable issues of White flight as well demographic and private residential living patterns, the Court declared that all states and local communities need do is all that is "practicable" to eliminate the vestiges of state-sponsored segregation.

QUESTIONS FOR DISCUSSION

10.7 The NAACP Legal Defense Fund was made up of a highly talented and skilled group of lawyers dedicated to racial justice. Because segregation occurred in all aspects of life in the early- to mid-twentieth century, they had a number of issues toward which to focus their advocacy. Identify and discuss the pros and cons of focusing legal advocacy on primary and secondary school education.

10.8 In the United States, the litigation system is generally regarded as an institution designed to provide individual remedies to individuals who have been harmed. *Brown v. Board of Education* represents a different view of the function of lawsuits: *Brown* is a shining example of using the litigation system as an instrument of social change. Public interest lawyers committed to social issue litigation are focused in substantial part on changing unjust conditions in society—that is, using a lawsuit to make general principles of law that will benefit a large swath of people. Yet, to pursue the litigation, the public interest lawyers need to identify specific individuals who have been harmed by a particular injustice in society to serve as a complaining party to the lawsuit. What are some sensitive ethical issues that the lawyers confront in pursuing this litigation strategy?

10.9 After the *Brown v. Board of Education* decision was handed down, some states responded by closing down public schools altogether, a tactic that did not last too long. Another less drastic technique was for school districts to implement freedom of choice plans. Under this system, the government no longer required segregation. Instead, districts were to follow the policy that students could choose which school they wanted to attend: White students could attend historically Black schools and Black students could attend historically White schools. These plans failed to improve integration in the schools. How do you explain why that approach failed?

A *Rewrite of the* Brown *Opinion*

Recent legal scholarship features an interesting technique for highlighting the qualities of a Supreme Court opinion, demonstrating how the opinion is a product of the times in which it was written, and for commenting on its strengths and weaknesses. Not surprisingly, much of this work focuses on civil rights. Later in this volume, you will have the opportunity to read a rewrite of a women's rights opinion.

For the *Brown* opinion, a whole book of rewrites exists, *What "Brown v. Board of Education" Should Have Said*.[2] The rewritten opinions run the gamut, from opinions that have little critique of the original opinion to those that dissent from its approach. The rewrite below falls into the latter category. It is written by Derrick Bell, a legal scholar largely credited (or blamed, depending on your point of view) for founding critical race theory (often known as CRT). From Bell's point of view, this approach to analyzing the law should neither be threatening nor reflect nefarious goals. According to Bell, the theory is not designed to disparage White people or to cast them all as incorrigible racists; it is merely focused on highlighting how entrenched societal norms, customs, and institutions perpetuate a racist societal attitude and culture. Those who disapprove of critical race theory worry that it can be misused to suggest to White people that they are deeply racist and that they have built and reinforced a society based on White supremacy. Critics are therefore concerned that the theory exacerbates race relations, rather than working to heal past wounds, and could therefore stand in the way of favorable societal change. As you read the selection below, consider this dispute about the merits and demerits of critical race theory.

What "Brown v. Board of Education" Should Have Said[3]

BELL, J., dissenting.

I dissent today from the majority's decision in these cases because the detestable segregation in the public schools that the majority finds unconstitutional is a manifestation of the evil of racism the depths and pervasiveness of which this Court fails even to acknowledge, much less address and attempt to correct.

For reasons that I will explain in some detail, I cannot join in a decision that, while serving well the nation's foreign policy and domestic concerns, provides petitioners with no more than a semblance of the racial equality that they and theirs have sought for so long. The Court's long-overdue findings that Negroes are harmed by racial segregation is, regrettably, unaccompanied by an understanding of the economic, political, and psychological advantages whites gain because of that harm.

With some difficulty, the Court finds that *Plessy v. Ferguson*, 163 U.S. 537 (1896), cannot now serve as constitutional justification for segregated schools. *Plessy*, though, is only fortuitously a legal precedent. In actuality, it is a judicial affirmation of an unwritten but no less clearly understood social compact that, older than the Constitution, was incorporated into that document, and has been continually affirmed. Chief Justice Roger Taney's observation in *Dred Scott v. Sandford*, 60 U.S. (19 How.) 393, 407 (1857), that Negroes "had no rights that the white man was bound to respect" was excessive even for its time. The essence of the racial compact, however, is that whites, whatever their status, can view themselves as entitled to privileges and priorities over blacks. Indeed, beyond an appropriate pride in ethnic heritage, this racial compact provides the definitive definition of what it means to be white in America.

Without recognizing and attempting to dismantle this racial compact and in particular the indirect promises made to whites and the surrender of opportunities whites made to gain these racial privileges, today's decision, while viewed as a triumph by Negro petitioners and the class they represent, will be condemned by many whites as a breach of the compact. Their predictable outraged resistance will undermine and eventually negate judicial enforcement efforts, while political support for the Court's decision, like virtually every other racial rights measure adopted basically to serve white interests once those interests have been served, will become irrelevant.

I regret that the Court fails to see in these cases the opportunity to lay bare the simplistic hypocrisy of the "separate but equal" standard, not by overturning *Plessy*, but by ordering its strict enforcement. The "separate" in the "separate but equal" standard has been rigorously enforced. The "equal" has served as a total refutation of equality. Counsel for the Negro children have gone to great lengths to prove what must be obvious to every person who gives the matter even cursory attention: with some notable exceptions, schools provided for Negroes in segregated systems are unequal in facilities—often obscenely so. And yet, until today, this Court has averted its gaze and has rejected challenges to state-run schools that were both segregated and ruinously unequal.

Responding to a series of challenges in recent years, this Court has acknowledged the flouting of the "separate but equal" standard at the graduate school level. Today, it extends those holdings to encompass segregation in literally thousands of school districts. In doing so, the Court speaks eloquently of the damage segregation does to Negro children's hearts and minds, but the equating of constitutional and educational harm without cognizance of the sources of that harm will worsen the plight of black children for decades to come. By its silent assumption that segregation is an obsolete artifact of a bygone age, the Court sets the stage not for compliance, but for levels of defiance that will prove the antithesis of the equal educational opportunity the petitioners seek.

In their determination to strike down state-mandated segregation, the petitioners ignore the admonishment of W. E. B. DuBois, one of the nation's finest thinkers. "Negro children need neither segregated schools nor mixed schools. What they need is education." The three phases of relief that I will describe below focus attention on what is needed now by the children of both races. It is the only way to avoid a generation or more of strife over an ideal that, while worthwhile, will not achieve the educationally effective education that petitioners' children need and that existing constitutional standards, stripped of their racist understandings, should provide.

The Court has failed to consider three major components of racial segregation that must be addressed in order to provide meaningful relief. They are:

1. Racial segregation furthers societal stability by subordinating Negro Americans, which makes it easier for rich white Americans to dominate poor white Americans.
2. Negro rights are recognized and protected for only so long as they advance the nation's interests.
3. Realistic rather than symbolic relief for segregated schools will require a specific, judicially monitored plan designed primarily to promote educational equity.

I will discuss each of these components in turn:

Racial segregation furthers societal stability by subordinating Negro Americans, which makes it easier for rich white Americans to dominate poor white Americans.

Segregation grew out of a series of unofficial racial compromises between white elites and poorer whites who demanded laws segregating public facilities to insure official recognition of their superior status over Negroes, with whom, save for color, they shared a similar economic plight. Yale historian C. Vann Woodward reports that after at first resisting these demands, southern leaders in the post-Reconstruction era enacted segregation laws mainly at the insistence of poor whites, who, given their precarious social and economic status, demanded these barriers to retain a sense of racial superiority over blacks. Why would whites conflate Jim Crow laws with real economic well-being? The full answer is likely to be complex, but whites' confusion of race and self-interest is not a recent phenomenon. It dates back to early colonial times. Slaveholders appealed to working-class whites by urging that their shared whiteness compelled the two groups to unite against the threat of slave revolts or escapes. The strategy worked. In their poverty, whites vented their frustrations by hating the slaves rather than their masters, who held both black slave and free white in economic bondage. When slavery ended, the economic disjuncture, camouflaged by racial division, continued unabated.

We must not forget that in a country that views property ownership as a measure of worth, there are a great many whites with relatively little property of a traditional kind—money, securities, land—who come to view their whiteness as a property right. In ways so closely tied to an individual's sense of self that it may not be apparent, the set of assumptions, privileges, and benefits that accompany the status of being white can become a valuable asset that whites seek to protect. Segregation in virtually every aspect of public life became a physical manifestation of this property right, one the law enforced.

For Negroes, the withdrawal of Union troops from the South presaged the destruction through intimidation and terror of economic and political gains some blacks had made during the Reconstruction years. Jim Crow laws that eventually segregated Negroes in every aspect of public life also rendered them vulnerable to physical violence, including literally thousands of lynchings by white mobs whose hate likely had its roots in an unconscious realization that their property right in whiteness had real meaning only as they terrorized and murdered defenseless Negroes.

A much-neglected history requires the admission that *Plessy v. Ferguson* provided legal confirmation to more than a century of political compromises that diminished the citizenship rights of blacks to the point of invisibility to resolve conflicts among differing groups of whites or further interests deemed important to the nation. Three examples will illustrate the perhaps unconscious but no less pernicious policy.

1. In drafting the Constitution, the framers confronted the already well-established patterns of slavery. While insuring that the foundation of our basic law would recognize rights to life and liberty for every citizen, they knew that America had systematically denied those rights to those of African descent. For the better part of two centuries, the colonies and then the United States developed the country on the labor of literally millions of human beings kidnapped by force from their native Africa and transported under inhuman conditions. The survivors and their progeny were held in a particularly vicious form of human slavery. The war for independence was financed in substantial part out of the profits of slavery.

Among the framers were some who abhorred the "peculiar institution," and many others who viewed slaves as their most important property. In at least ten provisions, the framers turned aside the many petitions from slaves and abolitionists of both races urging them to abolish slavery. Instead, they agreed to language that both gave legitimacy to slavery and provided for its protection. For the first but sadly far from the last time, the rights of black people were sacrificed to facilitate compromises between whites with conflicting views.

2. Over time, the friction between free and slave states grew, sparked by scores of lawsuits seeking to utilize the judicial forums of free states to win freedom for slaves who were brought or escaped from slave states. In *Dred Scott v. Sandford*, Chief Justice Roger Taney, as reviled as the framers are revered, attempted to do what they had done. By again refusing to recognize rights for Negroes—whether slave or free—the Court could settle the increasingly divisive slavery issue. The *Dred Scott* decision had the opposite effect, and according to many historians helped precipitate the Civil War.

3. When, hardly a decade after enactment of the Civil War Amendments, it appeared that renewed hostilities might break out following the close and bitterly disputed presidential election of 1876, a congressional commission appointed to resolve the dispute did so through what became known as the Hayes-Tilden compromise. For their part of the bargain, southern Democrats received a number of concessions including the promise—devastating to those so recently freed—to withdraw federal troops and leave their fate to the far from tender mercies of those who deemed Negroes fit only for slavery and subjugation.

These illustrations provide a foundation for understanding how the state-mandated racial segregation that is the subject of this litigation did not suddenly appear like a bad weed in an otherwise beautiful racial garden, a weed the majority seeks to eradicate with a single swing of its judicial hoe. It illustrates as well how segregation provided whites with a sense of belonging based on neither economic nor political well-being, but simply on an identification based on race with the ruling class and a state-supported belief that, as whites, they were superior to blacks.

American racism, though, is not simply a "taint" or "bias." It is the dominant interpretive framework for rendering bodies intelligible. That is to say, racism organizes the American garden's very configuration. Jim Crow was not merely an oppressive legal regime; it consolidated the imaginative lens through which Americans would view race going forward in the future. Jim Crow reaffirmed the binary system through which we (Americans) tend to think of race—i.e., "black" and "white." When racism is positioned as a thinking problem (rather than just a "bad weed"), the Court majority's pronouncement can be seen as more a racial provocation than a remedy.

Rather than a now obsolete obstacle to racial equality in the public schools, *Plessy* functioned as a confirmation of myriad racist compromises. By again confirming the historic status of Negroes as the hated and despised "other," *Plessy* marked a transformation in the politics of otherness: the genesis of a new imperative to rigidly fix black people as black. This renewed politics of otherness not only allowed entire categories of poor whites to develop a powerful sense of racial belonging, but allowed entire categories of erstwhile nonwhite immigrants (the Irish are the most prominent example) to become white. The vociferous articulation of rigidly expansive notions of blackness created an entire range of racial opportunities for "would-be" whites.

Consider that during the latter half of the nineteenth century, a shared feeling of superiority to Negroes was one of the few things that united a nation of immigrants from Europe, themselves horribly exploited by the mine and factory owners for whom they toiled long hours under brutal conditions for subsistence wages. These immigrants were far more recent arrivals than the Negroes they mocked. The black-faced and racially derogatory minstrel shows of that period helped immigrants acculturate and assimilate by inculcating a nationalism whose common theme was the disparagement and disadvantaging of blacks. Thus, policies of racial segregation simultaneously subordinated Negroes while providing whites with a comforting sense of their position in society. Racism's stabilizing force was not limited to poorer whites. Even for wealthier whites, their identities were unstable because intrinsically dependent upon an "other." White racist antipathy belied the extent to which white people desperately needed and—as I fear the majority's decision will show—still need Negroes in a subordinate status in order to sustain the myriad fictions of white racial integrity.

Ideologically, then, the statement "I am not black" has functioned as a kind of border, a psychic demarcation that allows "American" to be quickly (perhaps even thoughtlessly) distinguished from "not American." America has been able to define itself as a white country by marking blacks as that which does not constitute it. The law has served to rationalize racial boundaries with fictions that, in fact, conceal exploitation and marginalization of individuals on both sides of the color line.

Consider how legal fictions adopted by this Court in *Plessy v. Ferguson* in 1896 and *Lochner v. New York* in 1905 served to disadvantage both whites and blacks. In *Lochner*, the fiction was that both employer and worker were each equally free to bargain on an employment contract. In *Plessy*, the fiction was that separate but equal actually provided equality of treatment. Both decisions protected existing property arrangements at the expense of powerless groups—exploited workers in *Lochner* and degraded blacks in *Plessy*. Wage and race oppression were mutually reinforcing. Whites applauded—even insisted on the subordination of blacks as a self-distracting mechanism for a system that transformed them into wage slaves.

The Court categorically equates "equality" with "integration," where integration entails securing some sort of proximal relationship to white bodies in the same school or class. This integration ethic centralizes whiteness. White bodies are represented as somehow exuding an intrinsic value that percolates into the "hearts and minds" of black children. The Brown majority subtly braids proximal situatedness with becoming a good citizen—i.e., a good American. The Court very deliberately seems to avoid staging any sort of elaborate substantive due process analysis. This seems significant because under the rubric of substantive due process the Court might have more easily engaged the question of equalization without hinging black people's rights upon being proximally situated to white people.

Petitioners, viewing integration with whites as the only means of overthrowing "separate but equal," urge an end to state-mandated racial segregation. Whites, of course, resist any change in the "separate but equal" standard they view as a vested property right. Resistance under these circumstances is a manifestation of white victimization, willing, it is true, but victimization nevertheless. The question for this Court then is not the obvious one of whether racially segregated schools violate the Equal Protection Clause of the Fourteenth Amendment, but how can this Court grant racial relief desired by Negroes, resisted by whites, and needed by both? As important, how can the relief granted break out of the reform-retrenchment mold that has doomed earlier racial reforms?

II.

Negro rights are recognized and protected for only so long as they advance the nation's interests.

This Court's decision will replicate a familiar pattern of relief for racial injustices. A semblance of justice for Negroes serves as the vehicle for furthering interests of the nation. Examining the history of civil rights policies, we find that even the most serious injustices suffered by Negroes, including slavery, segregation, and patterns of murderous violence, are not sufficient to gain real relief from any branch of government. Rather, relief from racial discrimination, when it comes, requires that policy makers perceive that the relief will provide a clear benefit for the nation. While it is nowhere mentioned in the majority's opinion, it is quite clear that a major motivation for the Court to outlaw racial segregation now when it declined to do so in the past is the major boost this decision will provide in our competition with communist governments abroad and our fight to uproot subversive elements at home.

A few examples are illustrative:

The Emancipation Proclamation. Even though he was reluctant to arbitrarily deprive even the rebellious Southerners of their property without due process or compensation, President Lincoln finally issued the document, because it would disrupt the labor force in the South and open the way for the enlistment of thousands of former slaves who had left their plantations and were following the union armies. By its terms, of course, the executive order actually freed no slaves for it excluded all slave-owning territories on the Union side and had no legal effect on slavery within the Confederacy.

The Civil War Amendments. The Republicans recognized that unless some action was taken to legitimate the freedmen's status, Southerners would utilize violence to force blacks into slavery, thereby renewing the economic dispute that had led to the Civil War. To avoid this "win the war but lose the peace" result, the Fourteenth and Fifteenth Amendments and Civil Rights Acts of 1870–75 were enacted. The Fourteenth Amendment, unpassable as a specific protection for black rights, was enacted finally as a general guarantee of life, liberty, and property of all "persons." Corporations, following a period of ambivalence, were deemed persons under the Fourteenth Amendment, and for several generations received far more protection from the Courts than did Negroes, much of it under a doctrine of "substantive due process" not clearly contained in the amendment's language.

Indeed, Negroes became victims of judicial interpretations of the Fourteenth and Fifteenth Amendments and legislation based on them so narrow as to render the promised protection meaningless in virtually all situations. We may regret the pattern in which self-interest is the apparent major *motivant* in racial remediation policies that are then abandoned when the nation's interest has been served, but we should not ignore this self-interest phenomenon, particularly as it is functioning in the cases now before us. In petitioners' briefs and more particularly in the amicus briefs filed by the Justice Department, the "separate but equal" precedent of *Plessy* is challenged as not only unjust to blacks, but also bad for the country's image, a barrier to development in the South, and harmful to its foreign policy. To make the latter point, the government's brief quoted at some length Secretary of State Dean Acheson, who reported:

"[R]acial discrimination in the United States remains a source of constant embarrassment to this government in the day-to-day conduct of its foreign relations; and it jeopardizes the effective maintenance of our moral leadership of the free and democratic nations of the world."

In addition, this Court is not unaware of the nation's need to protect its national security against those who would exploit our internal difficulties for the benefit of external forces. Justice Frankfurter, while concurring in *Dennis v. United States*, wrote that the Court "may take judicial notice that the communist doctrines which these defendants have conspired to advocate are in the ascendency in powerful nations who cannot be acquitted of unfriendliness to the institutions of this country."

It is likely that not since the Civil War has the need to remedy racial injustice been so firmly aligned with the country's vital interests at home and abroad. The majority's ringing statement will provide a symbolic victory to petitioners and the class of Negroes they represent while, in fact, giving a new, improved face to the nation's foreign policy and responding to charges of blatant racial bias at home, thus furnishing a fresh example of the historic attraction to granting recognition and promising reform of racial injustice when such action converges with the nation's interests.

I do not ignore the potential value of this Court's simply recognizing the evil of segregation, an evil Negroes have experienced first-hand for too long. There is, I also agree, a place for symbols in law for a people abandoned by law for much of the nation's history. I recognize and hail the impressive manner in which Negroes have made symbolic gains and given them meaning by the sheer force of their belief. Is it not precisely because of their unstinting faith in this country's ideals that they deserve better than an expression of benign paternalism, no matter how well intended? It will serve as a sad substitute for the needed empathy of action called for when a history of racial subordination is to be undone.

The racial reform-retrenchment pattern so evident here indicates that when the tides of white resentment rise and again swamp the expectations of Negroes in a flood of racial hostility, this Court and likely the country will vacillate. Then, as with the Emancipation Proclamation and the Civil War Amendments, it will rationalize its inability and—let us be honest—its unwillingness to give real meaning to the rights we declare so readily and so willingly sacrifice when our interests turn to new issues, more pressing concerns.

III.

Realistic rather than symbolic relief for segregated schools will require a specific, judicially monitored plan designed primarily to promote educational equity.

While declaring racial segregation harmful to black children, the majority treats these policies as though they descended unwanted from the skies and can now be mopped up like a heavy rainfall and flushed away. The fact is that, as my brief review of the nation's racial history makes clear, a great many white as well as Negro children have been harmed by segregation. Segregation requires school systems to operate duplicate sets of schools that are as educationally inefficient as their gross incompliance with the "separate but equal" *Plessy* mandate makes them constitutionally deficient.

As a primary step toward the disestablishment of the dual school system, I would order relief that must be provided all children in racially segregated districts in three phases:

Phase 1: Equalization. (1) Effective immediately on receipt of this Court's mandate, school officials of the respondent school districts must ascertain through appropriate measures the academic standing of each school district as compared with nationwide norms for school systems of comparable size and financial resources. This data will be published and made available to all patrons of the district. (2) All schools within the district must be fully equalized in physical facilities, teacher training, experience, and salary with the goal that each district as a whole will measure up to national norms within three years.

Phase 2. Representation. The battle cry of those who fought and died to bring this country into existence was "Taxation without representation is tyranny." Effective relief in segregated school districts requires no less than the immediate restructuring of school boards and other policy-making bodies to insure that those formally excluded from representation have persons selected by them in accordance with the percentage of their children in the school system.

Phase 3. Judicial oversight. To implement these orders efficiently, federal district judges should be instructed to set up three-person monitoring committees, with the Negro and white communities each selecting a monitor and those two agreeing on a third. The monitoring committees will work with school officials to prepare the necessary plans and procedures enabling the school districts to comply with phases 1 and 2. The district courts will oversee compliance and will address firmly any actions intended to subvert or hinder the compliance program.

In my view, the petitioners' goal—the disestablishment of the dual school system—will be more effectively achieved for students, parents, teachers, administrators, and other individuals connected directly or indirectly with the school system by these means than by the majority's ringing order, which I fear will not be effectively enforced and will be vigorously resisted.

In conclusion, I recognize that this dissent comports neither with the hopes of petitioners that we order immediate desegregation nor the pleas of respondent boards that we retain the racial status quo. Our goal, though, should not be to determine winners and losers. It is rather our obligation to unravel the nation's greatest contradiction. Perhaps unwittingly, Justice Harlan, dissenting in *Plessy*, articulated it in definitive fashion when he observed:

> The white race deems itself to be the dominant race in this country. And so it is, in prestige, in achievements, in education, in wealth and in power. So, I doubt not, it will continue to be for all time, if it remains true to its great heritage and holds fast to the principles of constitutional liberty. But in view of the Constitution, in the eye of the law, there is in this country no superior, dominant, ruling class of citizens. There is no caste here. Our Constitution is color-blind, and neither knows nor tolerates classes among citizens.

The majority's decision to overturn *Plessy* is inadequate because it systematically glosses over the extent to which *Plessy*'s stark formalism participated in the consolidation of American racism. Rather than critically engaging American racism's complexities, the Court substitutes one mantra for another: where "separate" was once equal, "separate" is now categorically unequal. Rewiring the rhetoric of equality (rather than laying bare *Plessy*'s racist underpinnings and consequences) constructs American racism as an eminently fixable aberration. First, by doing nothing more than rewiring the rhetoric of equality, the Court's majority forecloses the possibility of recognizing racism as a broadly shared cultural condition. Imagining racism as a fixable aberration obfuscates the way in which racism functions as an ideological lens through which Americans perceive themselves, their nation, and their nation's Other. Second, the *Brown* majority's vision of racism as an unhappy accident of history immunizes "the law" (as a logical system) from antiracist critique. That is to say, the majority positions the law as that which fixes racism rather than as that which participates in its consolidation. By dismissing *Plessy* without dismantling it, the Court seems to predict if not underwrite eventual failure. Negroes, who despite all are perhaps the nation's most faithful citizens, deserve better.

QUESTIONS FOR DISCUSSION

10.10 Bell drafted this rewrite of *Brown* with the benefit of hindsight. That is, he drafted the opinion after it became clear that the opinion had not succeeded in what it set out to do (integrate public schools in the United States). Comment on whether this timing discredits Bell's argument in any way, or, alternatively, whether it makes his argument more valid.

10.11 Bell recommends three "phases" as steps toward educational equality: equalization, representation, and judicial oversight. Discuss whether you agree that these three initiatives are appropriate. In particular, evaluate whether the judicial oversight he recommends is the type of task that the judiciary is well equipped to pursue. Discuss any other initiatives that you would add to the list.

10.12 At the end of Bell's narrative, he sets forth a thesis for what *Brown* did wrong: (1) the opinion failed to recognize that racism is a "broadly shared cultural condition," and (2) the opinion operated on the incorrect assumption that law could fix racism, rather than recognizing that law cooperates with the "consolidation" of racism. Explain what you think he means by these statements and discuss whether you agree with them.

C. Affirmative Action

Affirmative action covers a broad range of initiatives that attempt to remedy the entrenched consequences of past discrimination. These initiatives are generally seen where preferences are given on the basis of race, gender, or national origin in education, contracting, or employment. Invariably, the determination of whether any affirmative action is constitutional is linked to whether a majority of the Court believe that preferences based on race, gender, or national origin are an unequivocal violation of the Constitution's promise that everyone is entitled to equal protection of the laws.

Those who tend to support affirmative action initiatives point to the entrenched consequences of past discrimination and continued prejudice in contemporary society. The notion here is that it is not simply enough for government to outlaw discrimination. Instead, active, affirmative steps are required to eliminate the effects of past discrimination. They might contrast the limited opportunities generally available to minority citizens with the opportunities that majority citizens have, as they have been boosted, networked, and otherwise advantaged throughout their lives to position them to enjoy the best education, the best jobs, and the like.

Those who tend to oppose affirmative action initiatives argue that our Constitution is designed to treat individuals equally regardless of their demographic affiliation and that affirmative action initiatives do precisely the opposite by endorsing preferences. Arguments are also made that such initiatives are condescending and insulting. Finally, opponents observe that affirmative action programs could inaccurately and unfairly cast a pall on minority individuals because they might be viewed as holding their positions as a result of their demographics and not their intrinsic worth, accomplishments, or credentials.

The affirmative action area received an unexpected change with the decision in *Students for Fair Admissions (SFFA), Inc. v. Harvard College*, 600 U.S. ___ (2023). The change was dramatic. Contrary to previous precedent, *SFFA. v. Harvard* affirmatively disaffirmed the use of race as a separate factor in college admissions. Interpreting the Equal Protection Clause as "colorblind," the Court has now deemed the consideration of race unconstitutional due to the stereotypes that invariably arise and the accompanying negative consequences. According to the Court, benefitting one race detriments another. According to the Court's decision, prospective students may discuss how race has contributed to their lived experience, but applicants' personal qualities, rather than the color of their skin, may enter the decision-making process. Although our Constitution might have been intended to be race-neutral or "colorblind," dissenters argue that inequality is inherent in today's society and affirmative action is necessary to even the odds. According to proponents of affirmative action, the Fourteenth Amendment started progress, but future (affirmative) initiatives are required.

The backlash against the *SFFA* decision was remarkable. Acceptance to a prestigious institution of higher education can benefit from many factors: Two prominent examples include having family who attended the institution (legacy admissions) and athletic prowess. This case focused on only one preference: race.

QUESTIONS FOR DISCUSSION

10.13 Describe the benefits and detriments of admissions policies that embody preferences. In answering this question, think only of the pros and cons of giving a boost for admission, regardless of the reason for that boost.

10.14 Leave aside the problems with providing any type of preference for admission to a higher education institution. If one is to attack a particular preference, would racial preferences be your first choice? Is there anything about the spirit of the Fourteenth Amendment that justifies the singling out of race as a particularly repugnant preference, as reflected in the *SFFA* case?

D. Voting Rights

Each of the post–Civil War amendments—the Thirteenth, Fourteenth, and Fifteenth Amendments—contains an enforcement clause, authorizing Congress to make appropriate legislation in an attempt to secure the promises of the amendments. As the United States is devoted to ensuring that its citizens participate meaningfully in democratic elections, those who drafted the post–Civil War amendments found it essential to make clear that race or color could not disqualify citizens from voting. Indeed, section 1 of the Fifteenth Amendment states:

> The right of citizens of the United States to vote shall not be denied or abridged by the United States or by any State on account of race, color, or previous condition of servitude.

Exercising its enforcement power in 1965, Congress passed the Voting Rights Act (VRA) to protect minority voters from the racial discrimination that they often encountered. Section 4 of the Act was focused on ensuring that states did not make changes to matters affecting voting in a discriminatory way. Other sections allowed states to "bail out" of the preclearance requirement if the state could demonstrate that they had not used a test or device to discriminate against voters in the past five years.

After its initial passage in 1965, the VRA was reauthorized in 1970 for five years and again in 1975. The Act was also later reauthorized in 1982 and 2006, each time for 25 years, with no changes to the coverage formula in section 4(b). In 1965, in *South Carolina v. Katzenbach*, the Supreme Court upheld the VRA, including the coverage formula. In that case, the Court reasoned that because voting discrimination was so pervasive, Congress's enforcement of the Fifteenth Amendment through the VRA and its coverage formula was "rational in both practice and theory" and was therefore constitutional.

In the following case, the Court ruled that section 4 was illegal because it was no longer needed. As you read the decision, evaluate whether you agree that voter discrimination has diminished in the United States to the point where the VRA's preclearance process is no longer needed.

FROM THE BENCH

SHELBY COUNTY, ALABAMA v. HOLDER
570 U.S. 529 (2013)

Chief Justice ROBERTS delivered the opinion of the Court.

The Voting Rights Act of 1965 employed extraordinary measures to address an extraordinary problem. Section 5 of the Act required States to obtain federal permission before enacting any law related to voting—a drastic departure from basic principles of federalism. And §4 of the Act applied that requirement only to some States—an equally dramatic departure from the principle that all States enjoy equal sovereignty. This was strong medicine, but Congress determined it was needed to address entrenched racial discrimination in voting, "an insidious and pervasive evil which had been perpetuated in certain parts of our country through unremitting and ingenious defiance of the Constitution." As we explained in upholding the law [in *South Carolina v. Katzenbach*], "exceptional conditions can justify legislative measures not otherwise appropriate." Reflecting the unprecedented nature of these measures, they were scheduled to expire after five years.

Nearly 50 years later, they are still in effect; indeed, they have been made more stringent, and are now scheduled to last until 2031. There is no denying, however, that the conditions that originally justified these measures no longer characterize voting in the covered jurisdictions. By 2009, "the racial gap in voter registration and turnout [was] lower in the States originally covered by §5 than it [was] nationwide." Since that time, Census Bureau data indicate that African-American voter turnout has come to exceed white voter turnout in five of the six States originally covered by §5, with a gap in the sixth State of less than one half of one percent.

At the same time, voting discrimination still exists; no one doubts that. The question is whether the Act's extraordinary measures, including its disparate treatment of the States, continue to satisfy constitutional requirements. As we put it a short time ago, "the Act imposes current burdens and must be justified by current needs."

I.

A.

The Fifteenth Amendment was ratified in 1870, in the wake of the Civil War. It provides that "[t]he right of citizens of the United States to vote shall not be denied or abridged by the United States or by any State on account of race, color, or previous condition of servitude," and it gives Congress the "power to enforce this article by appropriate legislation."

"The first century of congressional enforcement of the Amendment, however, can only be regarded as a failure." In the 1890s, Alabama, Georgia, Louisiana, Mississippi, North Carolina, South Carolina, and Virginia began to enact literacy tests for voter registration and to employ other methods designed to prevent African-Americans from voting. Congress passed statutes outlawing some of these practices and facilitating litigation against them, but litigation remained slow and expensive, and the States came up with new ways to discriminate as soon as existing ones were struck down. Voter registration of African-Americans barely improved.

Inspired to action by the civil rights movement, Congress responded in 1965 with the Voting Rights Act. Section 2 was enacted to forbid, in all 50 States, any "standard, practice, or procedure . . . imposed or applied . . . to deny or abridge the right of any citizen of the United States to vote on account of race or color." The current version forbids any "standard, practice, or procedure" that "results in a denial or abridgement of the right of any citizen of the United States to vote on account of race or color." Both the Federal Government and individuals have sued to enforce §2, and injunctive relief is available in appropriate cases to block voting laws from going into effect. Section 2 is permanent, applies nationwide, and is not at issue in this case.

Other sections targeted only some parts of the country. At the time of the Act's passage, these "covered" jurisdictions were those States or political sub-divisions that had maintained a test or device as a prerequisite to voting as of November 1, 1964, and had less than 50 percent voter registration or turnout in the 1964 Presidential election. Such tests or devices included literacy and knowl-edge tests, good moral character requirements, the need for vouchers from reg-istered voters, and the like. A covered jurisdiction could "bail out" of coverage if it had not used a test or device in the preceding five years "for the purpose or with the effect of denying or abridging the right to vote on account of race or color." In 1965, the covered States included Alabama, Georgia, Louisiana, Mississippi, South Carolina, and Virginia. The additional covered subdivisions included 39 counties in North Carolina and one in Arizona.

In those jurisdictions, §4 of the Act banned all such tests or devices. Section 5 provided that no change in voting procedures could take effect until it was approved by federal authorities in Washington, D.C. — either the Attorney General or a court of three judges. A jurisdiction could obtain such "preclearance" only by proving that the change had neither "the purpose [nor] the effect of denying or abridging the right to vote on account of race or color."

Sections 4 and 5 were intended to be temporary; they were set to expire after five years. In 1970, Congress reauthorized the Act for another five years, and extended the coverage formula in §4(b) to jurisdictions that had a voting test and less than 50 percent voter registration or turnout as of 1968. That swept in several counties in California, New Hampshire, and New York. Congress also extended the ban in §4(a) on tests and devices nationwide.

[Congress reauthorized the Act again in 1975 and extended coverage to jurisdictions using tests or devices that discriminate against non-English-speaking voters.]

In 1982, Congress reauthorized the Act for 25 years, but did not alter its coverage formula. Congress did, however, amend the bailout provisions, allowing political subdivisions of covered jurisdictions to bail out. Among other prerequisites for bailout, jurisdictions and their subdivisions must not have used a forbidden test or device, failed to receive preclearance, or lost a §2 suit, in the ten years prior to seeking bailout.

We upheld each of these reauthorizations against constitutional challenge.

In 2006, Congress again reauthorized the Voting Rights Act for 25 years, again without change to its coverage formula. Congress also amended §5 to prohibit more conduct than before. Section 5 now forbids voting changes with "any discriminatory purpose" as well as voting changes that diminish the ability of citizens, on account of race, color, or language minority status, "to elect their preferred candidates of choice."

B.

Shelby County is located in Alabama, a covered jurisdiction. It has not sought bailout, as the Attorney General has recently objected to voting changes proposed from within the county. Instead, in 2010, the county sued the Attorney General in Federal District Court in Washington, D.C., seeking a declaratory judgment that sections 4(b) and 5 of the Voting Rights Act are facially unconstitutional, as well as a permanent injunction against their enforcement.

[The Court of Appeals for the D.C. Circuit affirmed that sections 4(b) and 5 were constitutional.]

II.

A.

The Constitution and laws of the United States are "the supreme Law of the Land." State legislation may not contravene federal law. The Federal Government does not, however, have a general right to review and veto state enactments before they go into effect. A proposal to grant such authority to "negative" state laws was considered at the Constitutional Convention, but rejected in favor of allowing state laws to take effect, subject to later challenge under the Supremacy Clause.

Outside the strictures of the Supremacy Clause, States retain broad autonomy in structuring their governments and pursuing legislative objectives. Indeed, the Constitution provides that all powers not specifically granted to the Federal Government are reserved to the States or citizens. Amdt. 10. This "allocation of powers in our federal system preserves the integrity, dignity, and residual sovereignty of the States." But the federal balance "is not just an end in itself: Rather, federalism secures to citizens the liberties that derive from the diffusion of sovereign power."

More specifically, "the Framers of the Constitution intended the States to keep for themselves, as provided in the Tenth Amendment, the power to regulate elections." Of course, the Federal Government retains significant control over federal elections . . . But States have "broad powers to determine the conditions under which the right of suffrage may be exercised." And "[e]ach State has the power to prescribe the qualifications of its officers and the manner in which they shall be chosen." Drawing lines for congressional districts is likewise "primarily the duty and responsibility of the State."

Not only do States retain sovereignty under the Constitution, there is also a "fundamental principle of *equal* sovereignty" among the States. Over a hundred years ago, this Court explained that our Nation "was and is a union of States, equal in power, dignity and authority." Indeed, "the constitutional equality of the States is essential to the harmonious operation of the scheme upon which the Republic was organized."

The Voting Rights Act sharply departs from these basic principles. It suspends "*all* changes to state election law—however innocuous—until they have been precleared by federal authorities in Washington, D.C." States must beseech the Federal Government for permission to implement laws that they would otherwise have the right to enact and execute on their own, subject of course to any injunction in a §2 action. The Attorney General has 60 days to object to a preclearance request, longer if he requests more information. If a State seeks preclearance from a three-judge court, the process can take years.

And despite the tradition of equal sovereignty, the Act applies to only nine States (and several additional counties). While one State waits months or years and expends funds to implement a validly enacted law, its neighbor can typically put the same law into effect immediately, through the normal legislative process.

All this explains why, when we first upheld the Act in 1966, we described it as "stringent" and "potent." We recognized that it "may have been an uncommon exercise of congressional power," but concluded that "legislative measures not otherwise appropriate" could be justified by "exceptional conditions." We have since noted that the Act "authorizes federal intrusion into sensitive areas of state and local policymaking," and represents an "extraordinary departure from the traditional course of relations between the States and the Federal Government." As we reiterated in *Northwest Austin*, the Act constitutes "extraordinary legislation otherwise unfamiliar to our federal system."

B.

In 1966, we found these departures from the basic features of our system of government justified. The "blight of racial discrimination in voting" had "infected the electoral process in parts of our country for nearly a century." Several States had enacted a variety of requirements and tests "specifically designed to prevent" African-Americans from voting. Case-by-case litigation had proved inadequate to prevent such racial discrimination in voting, in part because States "merely switched to discriminatory devices not covered by the federal decrees," "enacted difficult new tests," or simply "defied and evaded court orders." Shortly before enactment of the Voting Rights Act, only 19.4 percent of African-Americans of voting age were registered to vote in Alabama, only 31.8 percent in Louisiana, and only 6.4 percent in Mississippi. Those figures were roughly 50 percentage points or more below the figures for whites.

In short, we concluded that "[u]nder the compulsion of these unique circumstances, Congress responded in a permissibly decisive manner." We also noted then and have emphasized since that this extraordinary legislation was intended to be temporary, set to expire after five years.

At the time, the coverage formula—the means of linking the exercise of the unprecedented authority with the problem that warranted it—made sense. We found that "Congress chose to limit its attention to the geographic areas where immediate action seemed necessary." The formula ensured that the "stringent remedies [were] aimed at areas where voting discrimination ha[d] been most flagrant."

C.

Nearly 50 years later, things have changed dramatically. Shelby County contends that the preclearance requirement, even without regard to its disparate coverage, is now unconstitutional. Its arguments have a good deal of force. In the covered jurisdictions, "[v]oter turnout and registration rates now approach parity.

Blatantly discriminatory evasions of federal decrees are rare. And minority candidates hold office at unprecedented levels." The tests and devices that blocked access to the ballot have been forbidden nationwide for over 40 years.

Those conclusions are not ours alone. Congress said the same when it reauthorized the Act in 2006, writing that "[s]ignificant progress has been made in eliminating first generation barriers experienced by minority voters, including increased numbers of registered minority voters, minority voter turnout, and minority representation in Congress, State legislatures, and local elected offices."

Yet the Act has not eased the restrictions in §5 or narrowed the scope of the coverage formula in §4(b) along the way. Those extraordinary and unprecedented features were reauthorized—as if nothing had changed. In fact, the Act's unusual remedies have grown even stronger. When Congress reauthorized the Act in 2006, it did so for another 25 years on top of the previous 40—a far cry from the initial five-year period. Congress also expanded the prohibitions in §5.

The provisions of §5 apply only to those jurisdictions singled out by §4. We now consider whether that coverage formula is constitutional in light of current conditions.

III.

A.

When upholding the constitutionality of the coverage formula in 1966, we concluded that it was "rational in both practice and theory."

By 2009, however, we concluded that the "coverage formula raise[d] serious constitutional questions." As we explained, a statute's "current burdens" must be justified by "current needs," and any "disparate geographic coverage" must be "sufficiently related to the problem that it targets." The coverage formula met that test in 1965, but no longer does so.

Coverage today is based on decades-old data and eradicated practices. The formula captures States by reference to literacy tests and low voter registration and turnout in the 1960s and early 1970s. But such tests have been banned nationwide for over 40 years. And voter registration and turnout numbers in the covered States have risen dramatically in the years since. Racial disparity in those numbers was compelling evidence justifying the preclearance remedy and the coverage formula. There is no longer such a disparity.

B.

The Government falls back to the argument that because the formula was relevant in 1965, its continued use is permissible so long as any discrimination remains in the States Congress identified back then—regardless of how that discrimination compares to discrimination in States unburdened by coverage.

But history did not end in 1965. By the time the Act was reauthorized in 2006, there had been 40 more years of it. In assessing the "current need [ ]" for a preclearance system that treats States differently from one another today, that history cannot be ignored. During that time, largely because of the Voting Rights Act, voting tests were abolished, disparities in voter registration and turnout due to race were erased, and African-Americans attained political office in record numbers. And yet the coverage formula that Congress reauthorized in 2006 ignores these developments, keeping the focus on decades-old data relevant to decades-old problems, rather than current data reflecting current needs.

The Fifteenth Amendment commands that the right to vote shall not be denied or abridged on account of race or color, and it gives Congress the power to enforce that command. The Amendment is not designed to punish for the past; its purpose is to ensure a better future. To serve that purpose, Congress—if it is to divide the States—must identify those jurisdictions to be singled out on a basis that makes sense in light of current conditions. It cannot rely simply on the past.

C.

In defending the coverage formula, the Government, the intervenors, and the dissent also rely heavily on data from the record that they claim justify disparate coverage. Congress compiled thousands of pages of evidence before reauthorizing the Voting Rights Act.

But a more fundamental problem remains: Congress did not use the record it compiled to shape a coverage formula grounded in current conditions. It instead reenacted a formula based on 40-year-old facts having no logical relation to the present day. The dissent relies on "second-generation barriers," which are not impediments to the casting of ballots, but rather electoral arrangements that affect the weight of minority votes. That does not cure the problem. Viewing the preclearance requirements as targeting such efforts simply highlights the irrationality of continued reliance on the §4 coverage formula, which is based on voting tests and access to the ballot, not vote dilution. We cannot pretend that we are reviewing an updated statute, or try our hand at updating the statute ourselves, based on the new record compiled by Congress. Contrary to the dissent's contention, we are not ignoring the record; we are simply recognizing that it played no role in shaping the statutory formula before us today.

D.

There is no valid reason to insulate the coverage formula from review merely because it was previously enacted 40 years ago. If Congress had started from scratch in 2006, it plainly could not have enacted the present coverage formula. It would have been irrational for Congress to distinguish between States in such a fundamental way based on 40-year-old data, when today's statistics tell an entirely different story. And it would have been irrational to base coverage on the use of voting tests 40 years ago, when such tests have been illegal since that time. But that is exactly what Congress has done.

■ ■ ■

Our decision in no way affects the permanent, nationwide ban on racial discrimination in voting found in §2. We issue no holding on §5 itself, only on the coverage formula. Congress may draft another formula based on current conditions. Such a formula is an initial prerequisite to a determination that exceptional conditions still exist justifying such an "extraordinary departure from the traditional course of relations between the States and the Federal Government." Our country has changed, and while any racial discrimination in voting is too much, Congress must ensure that the legislation it passes to remedy that problem speaks to current conditions.

Justice GINSBURG, with whom Justice BREYER, Justice SOTOMAYOR, and Justice KAGAN join, dissenting.

In the Court's view, the very success of §5 of the Voting Rights Act demands its dormancy. Congress was of another mind. Recognizing that large progress has been made, Congress determined, based on a voluminous record, that the scourge of discrimination was not yet extirpated. The question this case presents is who decides whether, as currently operative, §5 remains justifiable, this Court, or a Congress charged with the obligation to enforce the post-Civil War Amendments "by appropriate legislation." With overwhelming support in both Houses, Congress concluded that, for two prime reasons, §5 should continue in force, unabated. First, continuance would facilitate completion of the impressive gains thus far made; and second, continuance would guard against backsliding. Those assessments were well within Congress' province to make and should elicit this Court's unstinting approbation.

I.

"[V]oting discrimination still exists; no one doubts that." But the Court today terminates the remedy that proved to be best suited to block that discrimination. The Voting Rights Act of 1965 (VRA) has worked to combat voting discrimination where other remedies had been tried and failed. Particularly effective is the VRA's requirement of federal preclearance for all changes to voting laws in the regions of the country with the most aggravated records of rank discrimination against minority voting rights.

A century after the Fourteenth and Fifteenth Amendments guaranteed citizens the right to vote free of discrimination on the basis of race, the "blight of racial discrimination in voting" continued to "infec[t] the electoral process in parts of our country." Early attempts to cope with this vile infection resembled battling the Hydra. Whenever one form of voting discrimination was identified and prohibited, others sprang up in its place.

After a century's failure to fulfill the promise of the Fourteenth and Fifteenth Amendments, passage of the VRA finally led to signal improvement on this front. "The Justice Department estimated that in the five years after [the VRA's] passage, almost as many blacks registered [to vote] in Alabama, Mississippi, Georgia, Louisiana, North Carolina, and South Carolina as in the entire century before 1965." And in assessing the overall effects of the VRA in 2006, Congress found that "[s]ignificant progress has been made in eliminating first generation barriers experienced by minority voters, including increased numbers of registered minority voters, minority voter turnout, and minority representation in Congress, State legislatures, and local elected offices. This progress is the direct result of the Voting Rights Act of 1965."

Although the VRA wrought dramatic changes in the realization of minority voting rights, the Act, to date, surely has not eliminated all vestiges of discrimination against the exercise of the franchise by minority citizens. Jurisdictions covered by the preclearance requirement continued to submit, in large numbers, proposed changes to voting laws that the Attorney General declined to approve, auguring that barriers to minority voting would quickly resurface were the preclearance remedy eliminated. Congress also found that as "registration and voting of minority citizens increas[ed], other measures may be resorted to which would dilute increasing minority voting strength." Efforts to reduce the impact of minority votes, in contrast to direct attempts to block access to the ballot, are aptly described as "second-generation barriers" to minority voting.

Second-generation barriers come in various forms. One of the blockages is racial gerrymandering, the redrawing of legislative districts in an "effort to segregate the races for purposes of voting." Another is adoption of a system of at-large voting in lieu of district-by-district voting in a city with a sizable black minority. By switching to at-large voting, the overall majority could control the election of each city council member, effectively eliminating the potency of the minority's votes. A similar effect could be achieved if the city engaged in discriminatory annexation by incorporating majority-white areas into city limits, thereby decreasing the effect of VRA-occasioned increases in black voting. Whatever the device employed, this Court has long recognized that vote dilution, when adopted with a discriminatory purpose, cuts down the right to vote as certainly as denial of access to the ballot.

In response to evidence of these substituted barriers, Congress reauthorized the VRA for five years in 1970, for seven years in 1975, and for 25 years in 1982. Each time, this Court upheld the reauthorization as a valid exercise of congressional power. As the 1982 reauthorization approached its 2007 expiration date, Congress again considered whether the VRA's preclearance mechanism remained an appropriate response to the problem of voting discrimination in covered jurisdictions.

In the long course of the legislative process, Congress "amassed a sizable record." The House and Senate Judiciary Committees held 21 hearings, heard from scores of witnesses, received a number of investigative reports and other written documentation of continuing discrimination in covered jurisdictions. In all, the legislative record Congress compiled filled more than 15,000 pages. The compilation presents countless "examples of flagrant racial discrimination" since the last reauthorization; Congress also brought to light systematic evidence that "intentional racial discrimination in voting remains so serious and widespread in covered jurisdictions that section 5 preclearance is still needed."

After considering the full legislative record, Congress made the following findings: The VRA has directly caused significant progress in eliminating first-generation barriers to ballot access, leading to a marked increase in minority voter registration and turnout and the number of minority elected officials. But despite this progress, "second generation barriers constructed to prevent minority voters from fully participating in the electoral process" continued to exist, as well as racially polarized voting in the covered jurisdictions, which increased the political vulnerability of racial and language minorities in those jurisdictions. Extensive "[e]vidence of continued discrimination," Congress concluded, "clearly show[ed] the continued need for Federal oversight" in covered jurisdictions. The overall record demonstrated to the federal lawmakers that, "without the continuation of the Voting Rights Act of 1965 protections, racial and language minority citizens will be deprived of the opportunity to exercise their right to vote, or will have their votes diluted, undermining the significant gains made by minorities in the last 40 years."

II.

[In this section, Justice Ginsburg argues that a low form of scrutiny, the rational basis test, applies to this act, a test which only requires that Congress use any rational means appropriate to a legitimate end for the Court to find its exercise of power constitutional.]

In answering this question, the Court does not write on a clean slate. It is well established that Congress' judgment regarding exercise of its power to enforce the Fourteenth and Fifteenth Amendments warrants substantial deference. The VRA addresses the combination of race discrimination and the right to vote, which is "preservative of all rights." When confronting the most constitutionally invidious form of discrimination, and the most fundamental right in our democratic system, Congress' power to act is at its height.

The basis for this deference is firmly rooted in both constitutional text and precedent. The Fifteenth Amendment, which targets precisely and only racial discrimination in voting rights, states that, in this domain, "Congress shall have power to enforce this article by appropriate legislation." In choosing this language, the Amendment's framers invoked Chief Justice Marshall's formulation of the scope of Congress' powers under the Necessary and Proper Clause: "Let the end be legitimate, let it be within the scope of the constitution, and *all means which are appropriate, which are plainly adapted to that end*, which are not prohibited, but consist with the letter and spirit of the constitution, are constitutional."

It cannot tenably be maintained that the VRA, an Act of Congress adopted to shield the right to vote from racial discrimination, is inconsistent with the letter or spirit of the Fifteenth Amendment, or any provision of the Constitution read in light of the Civil War Amendments.

This is not to suggest that congressional power in this area is limitless. It is this Court's responsibility to ensure that Congress has used appropriate means. The question meet for judicial review is whether the chosen means are "adapted to carry out the objects the amendments have in view." The Court's role, then, is not to substitute its judgment for that of Congress, but to determine whether the legislative record sufficed to show that "Congress could rationally have determined that [its chosen] provisions were appropriate methods."

In summary, the Constitution vests broad power in Congress to protect the right to vote, and in particular to combat racial discrimination in voting. This Court has repeatedly reaffirmed Congress' prerogative to use any rational means in exercise of its power in this area. And both precedent and logic dictate that the rational-means test should be easier to satisfy, and the burden on the statute's challenger should be higher, when what is at issue is the reauthorization of a remedy that the Court has previously affirmed, and that Congress found, from contemporary evidence, to be working to advance the legislature's legitimate objective.

III.

The 2006 reauthorization of the Voting Rights Act fully satisfies the standard stated in *McCulloch*: Congress may choose any means "appropriate" and "plainly adapted to" a legitimate constitutional end. As we shall see, it is implausible to suggest otherwise.

A.

I begin with the evidence on which Congress based its decision to continue the preclearance remedy. The surest way to evaluate whether that remedy remains in order is to see if preclearance is still effectively preventing discriminatory changes to voting laws. On that score, the record before Congress was huge. In fact, Congress found there were *more* DOJ objections between 1982 and 2004 (626) than there were between 1965 and the 1982 reauthorization (490).

All told, between 1982 and 2006, DOJ objections blocked over 700 voting changes based on a determination that the changes were discriminatory.

The number of discriminatory changes blocked or deterred by the preclearance requirement suggests that the state of voting rights in the covered jurisdictions would have been significantly different absent this remedy.

True, conditions in the South have impressively improved since passage of the Voting Rights Act. Congress noted this improvement and found that the VRA was the driving force behind it. But Congress also found that voting discrimination had evolved into subtler second-generation barriers, and that eliminating preclearance would risk loss of the gains that had been made. Concerns of this order, the Court previously found, gave Congress adequate cause to reauthorize the VRA.

B.

There is no question, moreover, that the covered jurisdictions have a unique history of problems with racial discrimination in voting. Consideration of this long history, still in living memory, was altogether appropriate. The Court criticizes Congress for failing to recognize that "history did not end in 1965." But the Court ignores that "what's past is prologue." W. Shakespeare, The Tempest, act 2, sc. 1. And "[t]hose who cannot remember the past are condemned to repeat it." 1 G. Santayana, The Life of Reason 284 (1905). Congress was especially mindful of the need to reinforce the gains already made and to prevent backsliding.

Of particular importance, even after 40 years and thousands of discriminatory changes blocked by preclearance, conditions in the covered jurisdictions demonstrated that the formula was still justified by "current needs."

The case for retaining a coverage formula that met needs on the ground was therefore solid. Congress might have been charged with rigidity had it afforded covered jurisdictions no way out or ignored jurisdictions that needed superintendence. Congress, however, responded to this concern. Critical components of the congressional design are the statutory provisions allowing jurisdictions to "bail out" of preclearance, and for court-ordered "bail ins." The VRA permits a jurisdiction to bail out by showing that it has complied with the Act for ten years, and has engaged in efforts to eliminate intimidation and harassment of voters. It also authorizes a court to subject a noncovered jurisdiction to federal preclearance upon finding that violations of the Fourteenth and Fifteenth Amendments have occurred there.

Congress was satisfied that the VRA's bailout mechanism provided an effective means of adjusting the VRA's coverage over time. Nearly 200 jurisdictions have successfully bailed out of the preclearance requirement, and DOJ has consented to every bailout application filed by an eligible jurisdiction since the current bailout procedure became effective in 1984.

IV.

Congress approached the 2006 reauthorization of the VRA with great care and seriousness. The same cannot be said of the Court's opinion today. The Court makes no genuine attempt to engage with the massive legislative record that Congress assembled. Instead, it relies on increases in voter registration and turnout as if that were the whole story. Without even identifying a standard of review, the Court dismissively brushes off arguments based on "data from the record," and declines to enter the "debat[e about] what [the] record shows." One would expect more from an opinion striking at the heart of the Nation's signal piece of civil-rights legislation.

C.

Instead, the Court strikes §4(b)'s coverage provision because, in its view, the provision is not based on "current conditions." It discounts, however, that one such condition was the preclearance remedy in place in the covered jurisdictions, a remedy Congress designed both to catch discrimination before it causes harm, and to guard against return to old ways. Volumes of evidence supported Congress' determination that the prospect of retrogression was real. Throwing out preclearance when it has worked and is continuing to work to stop discriminatory changes is like throwing away your umbrella in a rainstorm because you are not getting wet.

Beyond question, the VRA is no ordinary legislation. It is extraordinary because Congress embarked on a mission long delayed and of extraordinary importance: to realize the purpose and promise of the Fifteenth Amendment. For a half century, a concerted effort has been made to end racial discrimination in voting. Thanks to the Voting Rights Act, progress once the subject of a dream has been achieved and continues to be made.

The record supporting the 2006 reauthorization of the VRA is also extraordinary. It was described by the Chairman of the House Judiciary Committee as "one of the most extensive considerations of any piece of legislation that the United States Congress has dealt with in the 27 [and a half] years" he had served in the House. After exhaustive evidence-gathering and deliberative process, Congress reauthorized the VRA, including the coverage provision, with overwhelming bipartisan support. It was the judgment of Congress that "40 years has not been a sufficient amount of time to eliminate the vestiges of discrimination following nearly 100 years of disregard for the dictates of the 15th amendment and to ensure that the right of all citizens to vote is protected as guaranteed by the Constitution." That determination of the body empowered to enforce the Civil War Amendments "by appropriate legislation" merits this Court's utmost respect. In my judgment, the Court errs egregiously by overriding Congress' decision.

BEHIND THE CURTAIN

After the decision in *Shelby County, Alabama v. Holder*, many states that had previously been covered under the formula in section 4(b) quickly changed their election laws, including by enacting voter ID laws, some of which had been previously struck down. Beyond the immediate aftermath of the decision, voter suppression increased. Here are some examples:

- Between 2014 and 2018, 13 states closed 1,173 polling locations—with the most being closed in Texas, Arizona, and Georgia. In just the year after the ruling in *Shelby County*, Texas "erased 363,000 more voters from the rolls" than it had erased during the previous election cycle. The reasons for this purging go far beyond the death of a voter or a move out of state.
- In 2021, Florida enacted a law limiting the availability and accessibility of mail ballot drop boxes and required voters to put their state ID number or Social Security number on the mail-in ballot application without providing an alternative for voters who lack this information. The law also limited who can assist voters with returning their ballots.
- Georgia enacted a statute making it a crime to distribute water and snacks to voters waiting in line to vote.
- Iowa passed a law referring county election officials for criminal prosecution if they do not implement the law's new voter-roll purge provisions.
- Montana eliminated its long-standing Election Day registration option.

QUESTIONS FOR DISCUSSION

10.15 Justice Ginsburg's dissent features colorful figurative language, but perhaps no example is more famous than her umbrella analogy. "[T]hrowing out preclearance when it has worked and is continuing to work to stop discriminatory changes," she wrote, "is like throwing away your umbrella in a rainstorm because you are not getting wet." Justice Ginsburg's dissent distinguishes between first-generation and second-generation barriers to voting, arguing that second-generation barriers persist despite the VRA's success. Which characterization of current barriers to voting do you think is most accurate—the majority's, or Justice Ginsburg's? Which kind of barriers do you think the VRA was intended to address at its inception? Which kind do you think the VRA should address now, if any?

10.16 Much of constitutional law focuses on the balance of power between the branches of government. What does the majority's decision in *Shelby County v. Holder* say about the relationship between Congress and the Court? How much weight do you think the Supreme Court should give to the 15,000-page congressional record in support of the VRA's reauthorization, or to the fact that Congress voted to reauthorize the Act unanimously? Which branch of the federal government is in the best possible position to evaluate the country's current needs on the voting issue? What does the majority's decision say about the relationship between the federal government and the state governments?

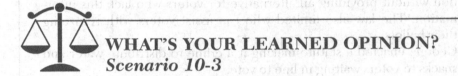

WHAT'S YOUR LEARNED OPINION?
Scenario 10-3

The state legislature of Arizona has enacted a restriction on who may collect early ballots for mail-in voting. You are an Arizona voter, and you give your completed mail-in ballot to your neighbor to drop off alongside theirs at your local voting center because you cannot make it to the center on your own. The Arizona law, however, makes it a crime for anyone other than an election official, household member, or a mail carrier to "knowingly collect" someone's mail-in ballot. Assume Arizona was covered by the formula in section 4(b) of the VRA before the decision in *Shelby County, Alabama v. Holder*. Now, after the decision, could you use Arizona's failure to get federal preclearance, because it had been a covered state, to challenge this state law? As of the decision in *Shelby County*, is section 2 of the VRA available as an alternative way to challenge the Arizona law?

Scenario 10-4

Under the principle of the "equal sovereignty of the states" relied on by the majority in *Shelby County*, can the federal government *ever* treat states differently? Imagine that the state of Maine wants to drop Medicaid coverage for 19- and 20-year-olds in the state to balance its state budget.

The federal Department of Health and Human Services then denies this attempted change under the federal Patient Protection and Affordable Care Act ("ACA"), which requires that states maintain, or "freeze," their eligibility standards for Medicaid for children (including 18- to 20-year-olds) until a certain date, or else the state will no longer receive federal Medicaid funding. Can the federal government deny Maine its ability to change its own Medicaid eligibility standards under the principle of equal sovereignty? In what ways, if any, can the federal government treat states differently without violating their equal sovereignty?

Race is a question that will remain in the forefront of our thought about the function of our Constitution. The cases and legal changes immediately after the Civil War are understandable in light of the historical and cultural context in which they occurred. Yet, the slavery of Black citizens continues to haunt the United States. Controversies remain to the present day in myriad contexts, with education and voting rights being the most prominent contemporary issues. As you read through the remaining material in this book, consider the treatment of other marginalized groups in the United States and ask yourself whether race continues to be a unique and particularly prominent issue in U.S. law and society.

QUESTIONS FOR REVIEW

1. What did *Korematsu v. United States* contribute to constitutional standards governing racial discrimination?
2. *Dred Scott v. Sanford* had two important holdings. Describe each of these two holdings and explain their importance.
3. What is the relationship between *Dred Scott v. Sanford* and the U.S. Civil War?
4. What were Jim Crow laws? How did they affect daily life in the states that had enacted them?
5. What were the reasons for the majority in *Plessy v. Ferguson* to reject the proposition that the separation of the races on railroad cars was a denial of the equal rights of Black citizens?
6. What reasons did Justice Harlan give for his dissent in *Plessy v. Ferguson*?
7. Why might the NAACP Legal Defense Fund lawyers have chosen primary and secondary public education as the first focus of the organization's initiatives to integrate various aspects of life in the United States?
8. Describe the initiatives that were implemented to integrate the public schools after *Brown v. Board of Education*. Did they work?
9. What are the arguments for and against affirmative action?

10. *Shelby County v. Holder* struck down §4 of the Voting Rights Act as unconstitutional. What did that section provide? Why did the Court believe it was appropriate to strike down that section?
11. Explain the concept of "equal sovereignty of the states."
12. What types of initiatives pertaining to voting rights did states institute after the *Shelby County v. Holder* decision?

ENDNOTES

1. Cheryl I. Harris, The Story of *Plessy v. Ferguson*, 187-229 in *Constitutional Law Stories* (M. C. Dorf, ed. 2004).
2. *What "Brown v. Board of Education" Should Have Said: The Nation's Top Legal Experts Rewrite America's Landmark Civil Rights Decision* (J. Balkin, ed. 2002).
3. *Id.* at 185-200.

Women's Equality Rights

11

This chapter does not present as much case law as earlier chapters and instead provides a narrative history of women's rights in the context of social mores of different times in the United States. The reason for this is straightforward: Few women's rights cases exist. The steady and low status of women in society for long periods in U.S. history accounts in large part for the dearth of case law. Perhaps equally telling is the continued scarcity of constitutional case law pertaining to women's rights in contemporary society. Several civil rights statutes protecting against gender discrimination in employment, ensuring family leave, and the like partially explain this in contemporary times. Yet you will also see hostility to these statutes in U.S. Supreme Court case law, such as that interpreting the Violence Against Women Act discussed in Chapter 4. As you read through this chapter, ask yourself why—in this age when women are sitting as Justices on the U.S. Supreme Court—the Court still continues to render few significant constitutional decisions concerning the rights of women.

A. Development of Recognition of Women's Rights

1. Early Years

In 1873, the time the case below was decided, two significant forces were at work in the United States. On one hand, a nascent feminism movement was gaining steam, as evidenced by the woman's suffrage movement. At the same time, efforts were underway to develop an expansive interpretation of the Thirteenth, Fourteenth, and Fifteenth Amendments—the post–Civil War amendments. The U.S. Supreme Court reacted as though the restructuring contemplated

Portrait of Myra Bradwell by an unknown artist.

by these three amendments might cause a destabilizing shift in power from the states to the federal government. Between 1870 and 1873, the Court avoided endorsing exertions of federal power by invalidating acts of Congress and refusing to restrict discriminatory state actions.

The plaintiff in the case that follows, Myra Bradwell, founded and ran a weekly legal newspaper, the *Chicago Legal News*. For the publication, she wrote regular columns advocating for women's rights and other social and legal advancements. When she took and passed the Illinois bar exam in 1869, few female attorneys practiced law. The Illinois Supreme Court initially denied Bradwell's admission because she suffered from a "disability imposed by [her] married condition." The reasoning relied upon the law of coverture, which provided that a married woman's legal status existed only by virtue of her husband and thus impaired her right to enter into legal agreements and her ability to practice law. She applied again, but the Illinois Supreme Court rejected her application, concluding that it could not act contrary to the intent of the Illinois legislature. This latter decision appeared to expand Bradwell's "disability" for law practice from her status as a married woman to her status as a woman.

Bradwell took her case to the U.S. Supreme Court, and through her lawyer, argued that denying her application to the state bar violated her right to "to carry on a trade," as protected by the Privileges and Immunities Clause. Her lawyer argued to the Supreme Court that the Fourteenth Amendment's Privileges and Immunities Clause protected the fundamental civil rights of all people.

Interestingly, Bradwell's case came before the U.S. Supreme Court at the same time as *The Slaughterhouse Cases*, discussed in Chapter 8 of this book. You may recall that *The Slaughterhouse Cases* challenged a Louisiana law that granted a monopoly to a butcher organization in New Orleans in exchange for compliance with economic, health, and safety regulations. These were the first cases in which the Court interpreted and applied the Fourteenth Amendment's Privileges and Immunities Clause. Ultimately, the *Slaughterhouse* Court decided that the Privileges and Immunities Clause of the Fourteenth Amendment applies only to rights that derive from U.S. citizenship and not rights stemming from the citizenship of a particular state.

Although Bradwell's lawyer argued for an expansive interpretation of the Fourteenth Amendment in her case, he simultaneously argued for a narrow interpretation in *The Slaughterhouse Cases*, for which he had been hired to present the contrary argument! As illustrated below, the lawyer won *The Slaughterhouse Cases*, but not Bradwell's. *Bradwell* and *The Slaughterhouse Cases* took approximately three years to decide in the U.S. Supreme Court. This was an unusually long time for a case to linger in the Court, even for that period in history. The *Slaughterhouse* decision was announced first and the *Bradwell* decision was announced the next day, presumably because they both dealt with a Fourteenth Amendment interpretation and had been argued by the same lawyer.

FROM THE BENCH

BRADWELL v. PEOPLE OF THE STATE OF ILLINOIS
83 U.S. (16. Wall) 130 (1873)

Mr. Justice MILLER delivered the opinion of the court.

The record in this case is not very perfect, but it may be fairly taken that the plaintiff asserted her right to a license on the grounds, among others, that she was a citizen of the United States, and that having been a citizen of Vermont at one time, she was, in the State of Illinois, entitled to any right granted to citizens of the latter State.

■ ■ ■

As regards the provision of the Constitution that citizens of each State shall be entitled to all the privileges and immunities of citizens in the several States, the plaintiff in her affidavit has stated very clearly a case to which it is inapplicable.

The protection designed by that clause, as has been repeatedly held, has no application to a citizen of the State whose laws are complained of. If the plaintiff was a citizen of the State of Illinois, that provision of the Constitution gave her no protection against its courts or its legislation.

The plaintiff seems to have seen this difficulty, and attempts to avoid it by stating that she was born in Vermont. [And thus, Bradwell's reasoning is that the Illinois Supreme Court's holding interferes with her rights as a U.S. citizen and citizen of Vermont—not merely her rights as an Illinois resident. Such interstate discrimination would likely be covered by the Fourteenth Amendment and would have provided a strong argument in her favor.]

While she remained in Vermont that circumstance made her a citizen of that State. But she states, at the same time, that she is a citizen of the United States, and that she is now, and has been for many years past, a resident of Chicago, in the State of Illinois.

The Fourteenth Amendment declares that citizens of the United States are citizens of the State within which they reside; therefore the plaintiff was, at the time of making her application, a citizen of the United States and a citizen of the State of Illinois. . . .

In regard to that amendment counsel for the plaintiff in this court truly says that there are certain privileges and immunities which belong to a citizen of the United States as such; otherwise it would be nonsense for the Fourteenth Amendment to prohibit a State from abridging them, and he proceeds to argue that admission to the bar of a State of a person who possesses the requisite learning and character is one of those which a State may not deny.

In this latter proposition we are not able to concur with counsel. We agree with him that there are privileges and immunities belonging to citizens of the United States, in that relation and character, and that it is these and these alone which a State is forbidden to abridge. But the right to admission to practice in the courts of a State is not one of them. This right in no sense depends on citizenship of the United States. It has not, as far as we know, ever been made in any State, or in any case, to depend on citizenship at all. Certainly many prominent and distinguished lawyers have been admitted to practice, both in the State and Federal courts, who were not citizens of the United States or of any State. But, on whatever basis this right may be placed, so far as it can have any relation to citizenship at all, it would seem that, as to the courts of a State, it would relate to citizenship of the State, and as to Federal courts, it would relate to citizenship of the United States.

The opinion just delivered in the *Slaughter-House Case* renders elaborate argument in the present case unnecessary; for, unless we are wholly and radically mistaken in the principles on which those cases are decided, the right to control and regulate the granting of license to practice law in the courts of a State is one of those powers which are not transferred for its protection to the Federal government, and its exercise is in no manner governed or controlled by citizenship of the United States in the party seeking such license.

It is unnecessary to repeat the argument on which the judgment in those cases is founded. It is sufficient to say they are conclusive of the present case.

Concurrence Mr. Justice BRADLEY:

I concur in the judgment of the court in this case, by which the judgment of the Supreme Court of Illinois is affirmed, but not for the reasons specified in the opinion just read. . . .

The claim that, under the Fourteenth Amendment of the Constitution, which declares that no State shall make or enforce any law which shall abridge the privileges and immunities of citizens of the United States, the statute law of Illinois, or the common law prevailing in that State, can no longer be set up as a barrier against the right of females to pursue any lawful employment for a livelihood (the practice of law included), assumes that it is one of the privileges and immunities of women as citizens to engage in any and every profession, occupation, or employment in civil life.

It certainly cannot be affirmed, as an historical fact, that this has ever been established as one of the fundamental privileges and immunities of the sex. On the contrary, the civil law, as well as nature herself, has always recognized a wide difference in the respective spheres and destinies of man and woman. Man is, or should be, woman's protector and defender. The natural and proper timidity and delicacy which belongs to the female sex evidently unfits it for many of the occupations of civil life.

■ ■ ■

It is true that many women are unmarried and not affected by any of the duties, complications, and incapacities arising out of the married state, but these are exceptions to the general rule. The paramount destiny and mission of woman are to fulfil the noble and benign offices of wife and mother. This is the law of the Creator. And the rules of civil society must be adapted to the general constitution of things, and cannot be based upon exceptional cases.

The humane movements of modern society, which have for their object the multiplication of avenues for woman's advancement, and of occupations adapted to her condition and sex, have my heartiest concurrence. But I am not prepared to say that it is one of her fundamental rights and privileges to be admitted into every office and position, including those which require highly special qualifications and demanding special responsibilities. In the nature of things it is not every citizen of every age, sex, and condition that is qualified for every calling and position. It is the prerogative of the legislator to prescribe regulations founded on nature, reason, and experience for the due admission of qualified persons to professions and callings demanding special skill and confidence. This fairly belongs to the police power of the State; and . . . it is within the province of the legislature to ordain what offices, positions, and callings shall be filled and discharged by men. . . .

For these reasons I think that the laws of Illinois now complained of are not obnoxious to the charge of abridging any of the privileges and immunities of citizens of the United States.

Mr. Justice SWAYNE and Mr. Justice FIELD concurred in the foregoing opinion of Mr. Justice BRADLEY. The Chief Justice dissented from the judgment of the court, and from all the opinions.

BEHIND THE CURTAIN

While awaiting the outcome, Bradwell helped pass an Illinois statute that allowed all persons, regardless of sex, the freedom to select their occupation, profession, or employment. Bradwell, however, did not try again to obtain her license. Nonetheless, the Illinois Supreme Court acted on its own motion and admitted Bradwell to the Illinois bar in 1890. She was then admitted to practice before the U.S. Supreme Court in 1892, but died of cancer immediately before she was admitted.

QUESTIONS FOR DISCUSSION

11.1 Justice Miller begins his majority opinion in this case with the unflattering statement, "The record in this case is not very perfect." The record in a case is made up of hearing transcripts, briefs, and other documents submitted to the lower courts as well as court orders and opinions. The quality of the record coming to the U.S. Supreme Court depends in large part on whether the lawyer(s) in the case adequately presented and preserved the facts and law in the lower courts such that the U.S. Supreme Court can render a fully informed opinion. Where is Justice Miller's criticism directed? Explain whether you think he is criticizing Bradwell's lawyering in the lower courts, providing a protective statement in case he got something wrong about the record, has another reason for the statement, or is motivated by some combination of these factors.

11.2 Do you have a reaction to Bradwell's lawyer arguing an opposing position on the Privileges and Immunities Clause before the Supreme Court in *The Slaughterhouse Cases* during the same time that he represented her? Does that sound ethical?

11.3 In *The Slaughterhouse Cases*, Justices Field, Swayne, and Bradley dissented, complaining that citizens in a "free government" must have the right to pursue happiness or exercise their liberty to participate in the profession of their choice. Are these Justices' decisions to join the majority in *Bradwell* consistent with their *Slaughterhouse Cases* votes?

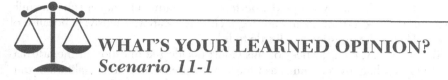

WHAT'S YOUR LEARNED OPINION?
Scenario 11-1

Assume Illinois passed a law requiring all state contracts for servicing state-owned vehicles go to female mechanics or woman-owned mechanic shops. Under the reasoning of *Bradwell*, could male mechanics living and working in Illinois successfully claim that the state law violates the Privileges and Immunities Clause of the Fourteenth Amendment? Would it matter if the male mechanics lived in neighboring states but worked in Illinois?

A *Rewrite of the* Bradwell *Opinion*

As mentioned in Chapter 10, recent legal scholarship has followed the strategy of rewriting Supreme Court opinions with the goal of demonstrating how the opinion is the product of the times in which it was written, and for commenting on its strengths and weaknesses. A group of feminist scholars have pursued that enterprise in a number of contexts. In the book *Feminist Judgments: Rewritten Opinions of the United States Supreme Court*,[1] scholars and lawyers reimagined Supreme Court opinions written using feminist reasoning and perspectives. The volume features 25 cases related to gender. Some of the reimagined opinions agree with the original outcome of the case, but provide different reasoning; others are cast as dissenting opinions. Here is a fictional dissent from the majority's opinion in *Bradwell*.

Bradwell v. Illinois[2]

Justice Phyllis GOLDFARB, dissenting.

    This term marks the Court's first occasion to give meaning to America's new national structure, as enshrined in three constitutional amendments adopted in 1868 in the aftermath of our terrible and protracted Civil War. Designed to alter the political dynamics of our union, these Amendments establish fundamental freedoms protected by federal power.

    The Fourteenth Amendment, a bright new star in this constitutional firmament, speaks expansively. It is a deep honor and a profound responsibility to announce initial interpretations of its high-minded words. The importance of exercising our constitutional responsibility to interpret the Fourteenth Amendment scrupulously cannot be overstated, as our first words on its application will reverberate for generations to come on what it means to be a citizen of America.

. . . Under the newly adopted Fourteenth Amendment, may a state lawfully prevent a qualified person from entering a chosen vocation exclusively because of her sex? That is the question we decide today.

To my dismay, eight justices of this Court decide the question in the affirmative. . . . Grounding my reasoning, as I must, in the democratic and egalitarian principles of the constitutional structure of our postwar union, and having endeavored to comport my legal judgments with the letter and spirit of our reconstructed constitutional design, I respectfully dissent.

The text of Amendment XIV, Section One, of the United States Constitution

Bradwell asks us to overturn the Illinois Supreme Court's decision upholding the denial of her license to practice law. Her argument is based on the not-yet-five-year-old text of Section One of the Fourteenth Amendment. . . . Section One is broad and unqualified. Its language requires equality before the law, allowing no class-based distinctions such as those of race or sex. According to Section One, all former slaves born in the United States are citizens. So too is Petitioner Bradwell.

What is the meaning of United States citizenship? The second sentence of Section One bears at least part of the answer: citizens have privileges—freedom to do things—and immunities—freedom from state restrictions in exercising their privileges. In short, the Privileges and Immunities Clause tells us that citizens like Bradwell have rights that all states—while showing regard for equal protection and due process of law—must protect. In sum, through the operation of the Fourteenth Amendment, the Constitution now restricts state governments, not just the federal government, from impeding civil rights and individual liberties.

. . . We have read [the Article IV, section 2 Privileges and Immunities] clause to mean that states cannot discriminate in their laws against persons from other states. But the language of the Fourteenth Amendment is different, indicating that by virtue of their *federal* citizenship, all Americans have rights, and that both state and federal governments must respect these rights of citizenship. . . .

The privileges and immunities of citizenship encompass the fundamental civil rights found in common law. In his well-known opinion in *Corfield v. Coryell*, Justice Washington asserts that protected privileges and immunities are those "which are, in their nature, fundamental; which belong of right, to the citizens of all free governments." These include "protection by the government; the enjoyment of life and liberty, with the right to acquire and possess property . . . and to pursue and obtain happiness and safety; subject nevertheless to such restraints as the government may justly prescribe for the general good of the whole."

Congress knew Justice Washington's words well, echoing them in the Civil Rights Act of 1866, which guaranteed racial equality with respect to the common law rights. . . . Through [its] language, the Civil Rights Act of 1866 evinces an awareness that a central injustice of slavery was its denial of the fundamental right of all people, regardless of race, to own their own labor, to contract for gainful employment, and to reap the fruits of their labors. . . .

While race discrimination was—and remains—a critical concern of the moment, Congress rejected the race-specific draft in favor of a more general one. Providing a constitutional basis for racial equality as well as the equality of other classes of persons, the Fourteenth Amendment protects members of subordinated groups from law's disfavor. The provision, extending across the ages a principle of equality writ large, authorizes federal power to invalidate discriminatory laws and practices, including those enacted by states, that treat classes of people as less than full citizens. Because the Amendment does not recognize degrees or tiers of citizenship, and all citizens have fundamental rights, post-Civil War America can no longer have second-class citizens under law.

Whether Bradwell will be granted an attorney's license depends on this Court's determination of whether she is a citizen in possession of rights that the Fourteenth Amendment directs all states to honor and honor equally. As I have described above, in my view, the remarkable breadth of the hard-won language of Section One of the Fourteenth Amendment, its inclusive grant of citizenship, its focus on citizens' individual rights, its concern with equality, its grounding in ownership of one's labor, and its reallocation of power and responsibility between the states and the federal government require this Court to overturn the Illinois court's refusal to issue the license to practice law that Bradwell so richly deserves. Unfortunately, the majority's miserly reading of the Fourteenth Amendment in the *Slaughter-House Cases* now poses an obstacle to this outcome.

The Slaughter-House Cases

Having read the *Slaughter-House* opinions in draft, I find myself in sharp disagreement with the five justices whose majority opinion offers a cramped reading of the Fourteenth Amendment. Now the Court has compounded the error—dispensing with Bradwell's petition in short order and with nary a mention of the rights of women—by relying on the faulty reasoning of the majority in *Slaughter-House*. . . .

Given the current state of interpretive development of this new constitutional provision, I believe—contrary to the *Slaughter-House* majority—that Bradwell's strongest case sounds in the Privileges and Immunities Clause. . . .

The privileges and immunities clause

. . . The privileges and immunities guaranteed to the citizens of a state have long been understood to be their fundamental civil rights at common law. Bradwell's right to pursue a livelihood for which she is well qualified would certainly fall within those common law privileges and immunities that the Fourteenth Amendment empowered federal courts to protect from the sort of state interference that Illinois has presented.

Moreover, the Supremacy Clause of Article Six, Section Two, already prohibits states from abridging their citizens' federal rights. If the Fourteenth Amendment now protects only those privileges and immunities that were already protected from state violations, then, as Justice Field wrote in his *Slaughter-House* dissent, "it was a vain and idle enactment which accomplished nothing, and most unnecessarily excited Congress and the people on its passage."

Because Congress surely would not have bothered to craft, with great fanfare, a meaningless and redundant Amendment, I can only conclude that Justice Miller, and the four justices who join his *Slaughter-House* opinion, are mistaken in asserting that the Fourteenth Amendment's Privileges and Immunities Clause means nothing new. Nonetheless, their erroneous reading, smothering the Clause just as it was taking its first breath, now disrupts Bradwell's claim for its protection of her right to pursue the occupation she has chosen.

Beyond oppression by a centralized power, such as the British monarch that America had overthrown, the circumstances that led to the Civil War taught us about decentralized oppression by states as well. Because recent experience has shown that federal power can serve as a check on state tyranny, the Fourteenth Amendment deliberately recalibrates the relationship between the federal government and the states. Apparently, Justice Miller objects to the new federal–state balance. . . . He expresses discomfort with "so great a departure from the structure and spirit of our institutions; when the effect is to fetter and degrade the State governments by subjecting them to the control of Congress . . . when in fact it radically changes the whole theory of the relations of the State and Federal governments to each other and of both these governments to the people."

I concede that these are bold new federal powers. But the results Justice Miller complains of, that lead him to be "convinced that no such results were intended," are precisely those that Congress sought to achieve. They are the Fourteenth Amendment's *raison d'etre*. Unlike Justice Miller, I trust that Congress meant what it said when it undertook to grant federal constitutional protection of individual rights from trespass by the states. In the aftermath of the Civil War, the turbulent circumstances in our nation warrant this important constitutional innovation.

We cannot shrink from the responsibilities that Congress has bestowed upon us. States retain complete discretion to exercise their police power and regulatory authority as they choose, so long as they do not infringe upon Fourteenth Amendment freedoms, such as the privileges and immunities of citizenship, "which of right belong to the citizens of all free governments." Where states infringe these rights, as I believe Louisiana has done in the *Slaughter-House Cases* and Illinois has done in the *Bradwell* case, federal courts are required to identify these violations and to secure the rights of American citizenship.

Under . . . the Fourteenth Amendment, one of the primary rights of citizenship is the right to pursue vocation. . . .

The ideology of separate spheres

The view that women should remain at home and men should have a near-exclusive monopoly on the activities of civic life is one of long vintage. Under the doctrine of coverture, British common law and custom rendered married women subjects of their husband's rule. . . . She had no economic rights and, without her husband's consent, could not make contracts or hold property in her own name. Through the operation of these legal norms, women were excluded from the public sphere.

At the same time, our law has admitted of many exceptions to the strict rules of coverture, and the boundaries of the separate spheres have been much traversed. Slave women, pioneer women, women who settled the frontiers of this vast nation, women who managed lands and businesses while men were fighting the Civil War, all have demonstrated their skills as laborers. Single women, widowed women, women separated from their husbands have, by necessity, become wage-earners and business people, showing their aptitude for self-support. In various circumstances before the courts, judges have recognized these realities and granted women, single and married, an independent civic status, modifying common law proscriptions to enable women to sue and be sued, to contract, to earn wages, to inherit, to own property. Married Women's Property Acts—passed in many states, including Illinois—have endorsed these changes. Indeed, in operating her publishing business, Bradwell has been empowered by the Illinois legislature to make all manner of contracts, to retain her own earnings, and to hold her own property. The legislature has recognized the quality of her work, and by extension her talent in the sphere of civic and professional life, by authorizing all Illinois courts to admit into evidence the contents of her weekly legal publication.

In light of these liberalizations, it is not entirely fair to say, as Justice Bradley does, that experience points only in the direction of women's separate domestic sphere. There are too many counter-examples, including that of this Petitioner, to support his general assertion that "the natural and proper timidity and delicacy which belongs to the female sex evidently unfits it for many of the occupations of civil life." In fact, the language of the concurring justices, dissenters all in *Slaughter-House*, shows less concern for principled doctrinal consistency than for the imagined specter of gender equality. Their expressed belief in a hierarchical social order in which men and women should forever and always operate in separate spheres appears to cloud their Fourteenth Amendment vision, so elegantly expressed in other contexts. When their separate spheres ideology allies itself, as here, with those who misread the Fourteenth Amendment to allow states to infringe the fundamental rights of citizens, women become less than the full citizens that the Constitution entitles them to be.

In his concurring opinion in *Bradwell*, Justice Bradley declares that "the sterner sex," should be "woman's protector and defender." He wishes to shelter women from the harsh demands of public life, such as those entailed in the practice of law. This kind of paternalism represents a peculiar form of protection, for it imprisons women in men's purported high esteem for them. Man becomes a defender only of woman's dependency, and she is relegated to the status of his inferior. Barred from public pursuits, with no authority, no economic power, and no enforceable rights, she is at the mercy of his beneficence (which is not forthcoming in all instances). Such a system is a description not of family harmony but of gender hegemony.

The concurring justices in *Bradwell* appeal to powers even more authoritative than the United States Constitution to support the separate spheres philosophy by which they would adjudicate Bradwell's case. They appeal to "the general constitution of things" as dictated by "nature," which "has always recognized a wide difference in the respective spheres and destinies of man and woman." They invoke "the divine ordinance," which "indicates the domestic sphere as that which properly belongs to the domain and functions of womanhood." These irrebuttable forces are "repugnant to the idea of a woman adopting a distinct and independent career from that of her husband." They comprise "the law of the Creator."

Men, not God, are the creators of these laws. Men who make laws in the legislature, men who enforce laws, and men who adjudicate them on this and all other courts are also the principal beneficiaries. They guarantee freedom to themselves, and compel women to support men in the exercise of freedoms that women are denied. While I certainly understand why men may be reluctant to relinquish these arrangements that establish for themselves a position of social dominance — just as many broke from and fought the Union before relinquishing their slaves — I see no basis for assuming that the Creator, with a capital "C," shares that reluctance.

The hierarchies of gender reside less in nature and more in the hearts of men. Lawmakers and judges produce what they call the natural order by enforcing separate spheres, and erasing from their minds any awareness of their role in creating it. Women's "natural" fitness for the home is undoubtedly shaped by laws that have long confined them there. And if separate spheres are the natural order of things, why are laws required to enforce them? Why have women organized to draft a Declaration of Sentiments to advance their rights? Why does Myra Bradwell, with her husband's blessing, operate a thriving business in legal publishing and seek a license to practice law? The natural order will take its course only when oppressive laws are removed and all people can exercise equally their fundamental liberties, including the liberty to choose their callings. . . .

Conclusion

Just as it will take an extended span of years to shake off the ideologies of white supremacy that for centuries supported American slavery — understood as a form of domestic relations — so too will it take an extended span of years to break the yoke of gender ideology that underlies the domestic relations of men and women and blocks both our nation's promise and its progress. But the Fourteenth Amendment beckons us toward greater freedom. Egalitarian democracy — of the sort that our best selves and our best rhetoric espouse — lies over the horizon, if only we can summon the strength to hold true to the humane course that our new Constitution charts.

For now, however, this Court places the imprimatur of law on woman's confinement to the private sphere, no matter her desires or talents. To advance in this way inequality under law is to invert the meaning and purpose of the new constitutional design that it is our duty to respect. I trust that the clarity of the Fourteenth Amendment's purpose, and its vision of equality for all before the law, will ultimately prevail. Given the importance and urgency of the issue to our democratic future, I hope the day is not too far distant when all our laws and institutions recognize the fundamental rights and equality of women, and all other classes who are treated as subordinate citizens. Until then, I respectfully dissent.

QUESTION FOR DISCUSSION

11.4   The feminist rewriting of *Bradwell* calls out the Supreme Court's approach to the case as reinforcing the view that women are best suited to homemaking and subordinate to their husbands. Do you think that the Court's view of women's role in society still lingers among the members of U.S. society today?

2. The Nineteenth Amendment

The period following the *Bradwell* decision did not change patriarchal attitudes about women. For example, during a period in constitutional law when the Supreme Court was aggressively protecting contract rights and striking down legislation designed to protect the conditions for workers, the Court was willing to uphold laws if women were the workers whom legislators sought to protect. Consider the case of *Muller v. Oregon*, 208 U.S. 412 (1908), upholding laws placing a cap on the number of hours women could be forced to work in factories. In that opinion, the Court stated:

> That woman's physical structure and the performance of maternal functions place her at a disadvantage in the struggle for subsistence is obvious. This is especially true when the burdens of motherhood are upon her. Even when they are not, by abundant testimony of the medical fraternity continuance for a long time on her feet at work, repeating this from day to day, tends to injurious effects upon the body, and, as healthy mothers are essential to vigorous offspring, the physical well-being of woman becomes an object of public interest and care in order to preserve the strength and vigor of the race . . .
>
> The two sexes differ in structure of body, in the functions to be performed by each, in the amount of physical strength, in the capacity for long continued labor, particularly when done standing, the influence of vigorous health upon the future well-being of the race, the self-reliance which enables one to assert full rights, and in the capacity to maintain the struggle for subsistence. This difference justifies a difference in legislation, and upholds that which is designed to compensate for some of the burdens which rest upon her.

Despite this prevailing attitude, women began to organize for greater rights as citizens, as evidenced particularly by the suffragette movement seeking to secure the right of women to vote.

Suffragette stories often begin with Abigail Adams's entreaty to her husband, John Adams: "[I]n the new Code of Laws which I suppose it will be necessary for you to make I desire you would Remember the Ladies, and be more generous and favourable to them than your ancestors." What is often omitted from her letter is the following threat: "If [particular] care and attention is not paid to the [Ladies] we are determined to foment a [Rebellion], and will not hold ourselves bound by any Laws in which we have no voice, or Representation." Despite her entreaties and her threats, the Constitution was written without mention of the rights of women. Over a hundred years later, Abigail's threat became reality. Women rebelled and finally had a voice in their government, just as Abigail hoped.

The U.S. women's suffrage movement was a generational journey filled with incremental progress, quiet failures, and grand displays. In 1848, Elizabeth Cady Stanton and Lucretia Mott organized the country's first convention supporting women's rights. Held in Seneca Falls, New York, the conference was a turning point in the fight for women's suffrage. The attendees discussed women's rights through the lens of a document written by Stanton, the Declaration of Sentiments. Many of the resolutions in the Declaration were passed with ease, but one sparked a heated debate: "It is the duty of the women of this country to secure themselves their sacred right to the elective franchise." Eventually, the resolution was passed.

The American Equal Rights Association (AERA) was an organization that campaigned for universal suffrage on the state level. Membership included activists like Susan B. Anthony, Elizabeth Cady Stanton, Fredrick Douglass, Lucretia Mott, and Sojourner Truth. When the proposed Fifteenth Amendment granted Black men the right to vote with no acknowledgment of sex, the AERA began to fissure. Despite the shared goals of suffragists and abolitionists, Anthony and Stanton vehemently opposed the association. Many other members supported the Fifteenth Amendment. Douglass particularly emphasized its urgency: "with us, the question, is a matter of life and death. . . ." Truth, on the other hand, worried about the exclusion of Black women: "if colored men get their rights, and not colored women get theirs, there will be a bad time about it." On the other hand, Anthony's objection to the amendment was tainted by racism, stating, "If you will not give the whole loaf of suffrage to the entire people, give it to the most intelligent first." Soon after the ratification of the Fifteenth Amendment, the AERA fell apart. The tensions that led to its demise persisted throughout the fight for universal suffrage.

In 1912, young suffrage leaders Alice Paul and Lucy Burns became chairs of the National American Woman Suffrage Association (NAWSA). The organization struggled with dissention, but they found an effective tactic in 1917, holding a persistent White House picket line. Every day, 12 women, dubbed "Silent Sentinels," stood at the White House gate, acting as a constant thorn in the President's side. Even as the United States entered World War I and pleas for national unity became more urgent, the women did not cease their protest. The government branded the suffragists as pro-German agitators, but the demonstrators were unwavering. They endured three days of violence before six women were arrested and sentenced to 60 days at Occoquan Workhouse. The conditions in the workhouse were abysmal.

In October 1917, Alice Paul was arrested and sentenced to a seven-month prison term. Shortly after her imprisonment, she and fellow suffragist Rose Winslow began a hunger strike. Their rebellion was met with brutal resistance. Three times a day, Paul and Winslow were held down while a tube was forced up their nostrils to pump liquid food, typically milk and raw eggs, into their stomachs. These force-feeding sessions were painful, often leading to vomiting, stomach ulcers, and internal bruising.

Struggles continued and further imprisonment at the Occoquan Workhouse occurred. As the 31 prisoners were transferred to the workhouse, they once again demanded to be treated as political prisoners. Their request was denied. Intent on teaching them a lesson, the superintendent watched as the guards dragged the women to cells in the men's section of the workhouse. The male

guards shackled the prisoners and beat many unconscious. The guards did everything they could to stop the prisoners from engaging in political action through
brutal force-feeding sessions, violent beatings, and outright lies about the status
of their cases.

The suffragists reasoned, however, that the biases that worked against them
could also be employed in their favor. Women, especially middle-class White
women, were viewed as objects to be protected against the harsh ways of the
world. So when the women chose to go on a hunger strike, they were inspiring
the country's desire to protect them. Leadership publicized photographs of the
suffragists leaving jail, emaciated and unsteady on their feet. The transformation
of the brutalized prisoners into martyrs inspired support all around the country
and turned the tide of the movement.

The public pressure grew and grew until, on January 10, 1918, the U.S. House
of Representatives passed the measure for a federal woman suffrage amendment
by a vote of 274 yeas to 136 nays. Closer to victory than ever, the women's movement began to lobby the U.S. Senate. Leadership went on speaking tours around
the country, while members were dispatched to pressure individual senators into
supporting the amendment. Nonetheless, on October 1, 1918, the U.S. Senate
defeated the amendment.

The women's movement continued its protests. Another unsuccessful
Senate vote occurred. Finally, though, the suffragists were victorious. The House
passed the amendment again. Just a few weeks later on June 4, 1919, the Senate also passed the amendment, initiating the statewide ratification campaign.
The suffragists campaigned for ratification after ratification, and, in August 1920,
Tennessee became the 36th state to ratify. At that point, the Nineteenth Amendment became part of the Constitution:

> *The right of citizens of the United States to vote shall not be denied or abridged by*
> *the United States or by any State on account of sex.*
> *Congress shall have power to enforce this article by appropriate legislation.*

Women flocked to the polls for the November 1920 election. Nonetheless, a
Maryland judge filed a lawsuit challenging the Nineteenth Amendment, claiming that the amendment was not of the required character to have the power of a
constitutional amendment. He claimed that as the amendment was ratified without his state's consent, it inherently destroyed the state's "autonomy as a political
body." The Supreme Court rejected that argument, holding that the amendment
was valid, just as the Fifteenth Amendment was before it.

Winning the vote was merely a first step in the long fight for gender equality.
The wording of the Nineteenth Amendment left it vulnerable to loopholes. The
text forbids states from denying women the vote because of their gender but
does not guarantee women the right to vote. Laws that prevented individuals
from voting based on their age, citizenship, and mental competence kept many
women from voting in the 1920 election. Black women in particular were subject to the same disenfranchisement tactics already experienced by Black men.

The Fifteenth Amendment, worded similarly to the Nineteenth Amendment, allowed for similar loopholes. Black voters were threatened with violence, subjected to poll taxes, and forced to take literacy tests in an effort to keep them from voting.

Even today, true universal suffrage has not been achieved in the United States, nor has complete gender equality. Voters are still being disenfranchised through the implementation of voter ID laws, lack of access to polling places, and housing segregation. In addition, a gender-based wage gap remains and reproductive freedom is under attack. The women's suffrage movement was just the start of a long journey to freedom. As one woman said after the passage of the Nineteenth Amendment, "[W]omen, if I know them, are saying, 'Now at last we can begin.' . . . Now [we] can say what they are really after; and what they are after, in common with all the rest of the struggling world, is freedom. Freedom is a large word."

BEHIND THE CURTAIN

The suffragette movement carefully chose its rhetoric and symbols. For example, the term "suffragette" was initially used to disparage and belittle the women who fought for the right to vote. In Great Britain, where the term originated, activists adopted the moniker as a badge of pride — reappropriating the insult in service of their own goals. Many U.S. activists, however, found the name offensive, and used the term "suffragist" to describe any person who supported the movement, no matter their gender.

The suffragists in the United States used a number of tactics to bring the movement into the national consciousness including parades, pickets, and speaking tours. Music was a strong tool for organization and gaining public attention. (Perhaps you are familiar with the song "Sister Suffragette" from the movie *Mary Poppins.*) The suffragists carefully curated their image for the public, seeking to present themselves in a way that evoked sympathy and garnered support. For example, the women often wore white at public events to emphasize their femininity and to combat the antisuffrage idea that they were masculine or ugly. One group draped their members with satin sashes of purple, white, and gold to express the ideals of their organization: constancy, quality of purpose, and guidance. They also presented the women who had been imprisoned with pins shaped like a jail cell door to wear with pride like a military medal.

Animals would be used as symbols for the movement. Cats were used in antisuffrage propaganda to promote women's passivity and connection to the home. However, the cat as a symbol was soon reclaimed by the suffragists. Two women in the United States embarked on a cross-country campaign

"Silent Sentinels" picketing at the White House gate in January 1917. *Records of the National Woman's Party, Library of Congress.*

where they spoke to citizens about women's suffrage. At some point on the trip, they were given a small, black cat they named Saxon, which became a mascot for the movement.

Moving through history chronologically, the United States continued a more welcoming approach to women's rights in a 1937 Supreme Court decision upholding a law guaranteeing a minimum wage for women. That said, even after the influx of women into the labor force during World War II, the U.S. Supreme Court continued to uphold gender discrimination laws. For example, in 1948, the Supreme Court upheld a state law that prevented a woman from being licensed as a bartender unless she was the wife or daughter of a male owner of the bar where she worked. Moving on to 1961, the Court confronted a state law that automatically exempted women from jury service unless they waived the exemption. Applying a rational basis test, the Court accepted the rationale for the exemption that women are still "the center of the home and family life" and upheld the law because it left to women their own judgment as to whether they could serve on a jury, but still fulfill their "own special responsibilities."

Times began to change, however, in 1971, when the Court, applying rational basis scrutiny, invalidated a gender classification concerning the inheritance process under state law. In the meantime, Ruth Bader Ginsburg had entered the scene as a civil rights advocate. She argued her first discrimination case before

Ruth Bader Ginsburg at her confirmation hearing in 1993. *R. Michael Jenkins/Library of Congress.*

the Court in *Frontiero v. Richardson*, 411 U.S. 677 (1973), challenging a federal law that allowed a man to automatically claim his wife as a dependent for the purpose of housing and medical benefits, but allowed a woman to claim her husband as a dependent only upon the showing of proof of his dependence. Ruth Bader Ginsburg claimed that this distinction amounted to unconstitutional gender discrimination and won the case. In fact, four Justices in the case ruled that gender discrimination should be evaluated with strict scrutiny. Nonetheless, because a majority of the Court did not join this position, the proper level of scrutiny for gender classifications remained unsettled.

Ruth Bader Ginsburg argued six cases before the Supreme Court, most of them touching on gender equality. She later became an Associate Justice of the U.S. Supreme Court.

B. Intermediate Scrutiny

The U.S. Supreme Court settled its view of the appropriate level of scrutiny for gender discrimination in *Craig v. Boren*, 419 U.S. 522 (1975). Specifically, the Court created an intermediate level of evaluating the constitutionality of gender discrimination, stating that "[t]o withstand constitutional challenge, previous cases establish that classifications by gender must serve important governmental objectives and must be substantially related to those objectives." Interestingly, this standard emerged in a case in which males were (arguably) the gender suffering the discrimination. The law at issue allowed women to buy low-level alcohol (3.2 percent beer) at age 18, but men could not buy such beer until age 21. Although traffic safety was an important state interest, the court concluded that the gender discrimination was not substantially related to that objective. The Court compared the statistics for drunk driving arrests: 0.18 percent of females versus 2.00 percent of males between the ages of 19 and 21. Declaring that this "disparity is not trivial in a statistical sense," the Court added, "but it hardly can form the basis employment of a gender line as a classifying device."

The Court affirmed this intermediate scrutiny standard several times after the *Craig v. Boren* decision. Consider, though, how the Court may have "juiced up" the standard in the following case, *United States v. Virginia*.

United States v. Virginia concerned the Virginia Military Institute (VMI), a publicly funded male-only university. An unidentified woman filed a complaint with the Attorney General of the United States, stating that the male-only admission policy violated the Equal Protection Clause of the Fourteenth Amendment.

The Attorney General brought suit on behalf of the woman and others similarly situated. The respondent, the Commonwealth of Virginia, argued that women were unsuitable for VMI's adversarial and severe form of military instruction and that a newly minted institution, the Virginia Women's Institute for Leadership, would provide women with analogous training and opportunities. The Court disagreed. Justice Ruth Bader Ginsburg authored the majority opinion of the Court.

FROM THE BENCH

UNITED STATES v. VIRGINIA
518 U.S. 515 (1996)

Justice GINSBURG delivered the opinion of the Court.

Virginia's public institutions of higher learning include an incomparable military college, Virginia Military Institute (VMI). The United States maintains that the Constitution's equal protection guarantee precludes Virginia from reserving exclusively to men the unique educational opportunities VMI affords. We agree.

I

Founded in 1839, VMI is today the sole single-sex school among Virginia's 15 public institutions of higher learning. VMI's distinctive mission is to produce "citizen-soldiers," men prepared for leadership in civilian life and in military service. VMI pursues this mission through pervasive training of a kind not available anywhere else in Virginia. Assigning prime place to character development, VMI uses an "adversative method" modeled on English public schools and once characteristic of military instruction. VMI constantly endeavors to instill physical and mental discipline in its cadets and impart to them a strong moral code. The school's graduates leave VMI with heightened comprehension of their capacity to deal with duress and stress, and a large sense of accomplishment for completing the hazardous course.

VMI has notably succeeded in its mission to produce leaders; among its alumni are military generals, Members of Congress, and business executives. The school's alumni overwhelmingly perceive that their VMI training helped them to realize their personal goals. VMI's endowment reflects the loyalty of its graduates; VMI has the largest per-student endowment of all public undergraduate institutions in the Nation.

Neither the goal of producing citizen-soldiers nor VMI's implementing methodology is inherently unsuitable to women. And the school's impressive record in producing leaders has made admission desirable to some women. Nevertheless, Virginia has elected to preserve exclusively for men the advantages and opportunities a VMI education affords.

II

C

In response to the Fourth Circuit's ruling, Virginia proposed a parallel program for women: Virginia Women's Institute for Leadership (VWIL). The 4-year, state-sponsored undergraduate program would be located at Mary Baldwin College, a private liberal arts school for women, and would be open, initially, to about 25 to 30 students. Although VWIL would share VMI's mission—to produce "citizen-soldiers"—the VWIL program would differ, as does Mary Baldwin College, from VMI in academic offerings, methods of education, and financial resources.

The average combined SAT score of entrants at Mary Baldwin is about 100 points lower than the score for VMI freshmen. Mary Baldwin's faculty holds "significantly fewer Ph. D.'s than the faculty at VMI," and receives significantly lower salaries. While VMI offers degrees in liberal arts, the sciences, and engineering, Mary Baldwin, at the time of trial, offered only bachelor of arts degrees. A VWIL student seeking to earn an engineering degree could gain one, without public support, by attending Washington University in St. Louis, Missouri, for two years, paying the required private tuition. . . .

III

The cross-petitions in this case present two ultimate issues. First, does Virginia's exclusion of women from the educational opportunities provided by VMI—extraordinary opportunities for military training and civilian leadership development—deny to women "capable of all of the individual activities required of VMI cadets," the equal protection of the laws guaranteed by the Fourteenth Amendment? Second, if VMI's "unique" situation—as Virginia's sole single-sex public institution of higher education—offends the Constitution's equal protection principle, what is the remedial requirement?

IV

We note, once again, the core instruction of this Court's pathmarking decisions . . . : Parties who seek to defend gender-based government action must demonstrate an "exceedingly persuasive justification" for that action.

Today's skeptical scrutiny of official action denying rights or opportunities based on sex responds to volumes of history. As a plurality of this Court acknowledged a generation ago, "our Nation has had a long and unfortunate history of sex discrimination." *Frontiero v. Richardson* (1973). Through a century plus three decades and more of that history, women did not count among voters composing "We the People"; not until 1920 did women gain a constitutional right to the franchise. And for a half century thereafter, it remained the prevailing doctrine that government, both federal and state, could withhold from women opportunities accorded men so long as any "basis in reason" could be conceived for the discrimination. . . .

The heightened review standard our precedent establishes does not make sex a proscribed classification. Supposed "inherent differences" are no longer accepted as a ground for race or national origin classifications. Physical differences between men and women, however, are enduring . . .

"Inherent differences" between men and women, we have come to appreciate, remain cause for celebration, but not for denigration of the members of either sex or for artificial constraints on an individual's opportunity. Sex classifications may be used to compensate women "for particular economic disabilities [they have] suffered," *Califano v. Webster* (1977) (*per curiam*), to "promote equal employment opportunity," to advance full development of the talent and capacities of our Nation's people. But such classifications may not be used, as they once were, to create or perpetuate the legal, social, and economic inferiority of women.

Measuring the record in this case against the review standard just described, we conclude that Virginia has shown no "exceedingly persuasive justification" for excluding all women from the citizen-soldier training afforded by VMI. We therefore affirm the Fourth Circuit's initial judgment, which held that Virginia had violated the Fourteenth Amendment's Equal Protection Clause. Because the remedy proffered by Virginia—the Mary Baldwin VWIL program—does not cure the constitutional violation, *i.e.*, it does not provide equal opportunity, we reverse the Fourth Circuit's final judgment in this case.

V

. . . Virginia challenges that "liability" ruling and asserts two justifications in defense of VMI's exclusion of women. First, the Commonwealth contends, "single-sex education provides important educational benefits," and the option of single-sex education contributes to "diversity in educational approaches."

FROM THE BENCH

Second, the Commonwealth argues, "the unique VMI method of character development and leadership training," the school's adversative approach, would have to be modified were VMI to admit women. We consider these two justifications in turn.

A

Single-sex education affords pedagogical benefits to at least some students, Virginia emphasizes, and that reality is uncontested in this litigation. Similarly, it is not disputed that diversity among public educational institutions can serve the public good. But Virginia has not shown that VMI was established, or has been maintained, with a view to diversifying, by its categorical exclusion of women, educational opportunities within the Commonwealth. In cases of this genre, our precedent instructs that "benign" justifications proffered in defense of categorical exclusions will not be accepted automatically; a tenable justification must describe actual state purposes, not rationalizations for actions in fact differently grounded. . . .

B

Virginia next argues that VMI's adversative method of training provides educational benefits that cannot be made available, unmodified, to women. Alterations to accommodate women would necessarily be "radical," so "drastic," Virginia asserts, as to transform, indeed "destroy," VMI's program. Neither sex would be favored by the transformation, Virginia maintains: Men would be deprived of the unique opportunity currently available to them; women would not gain that opportunity because their participation would "eliminate the very aspects of [the] program that distinguish [VMI] from . . . other institutions of higher education in Virginia. . . ."

The notion that admission of women would downgrade VMI's stature, destroy the adversative system and, with it, even the school, is a judgment hardly proved, a prediction hardly different from other "self-fulfilling prophec[ies]," once routinely used to deny rights or opportunities. . . .

The Commonwealth's misunderstanding and, in turn, the District Court's, is apparent from VMI's mission: to produce "citizen-soldiers," individuals

> imbued with love of learning, confident in the functions and attitudes of leadership, possessing a high sense of public service, advocates of the American democracy and free enterprise system, and ready . . . to defend their country in time of national peril.

Surely that goal is great enough to accommodate women, who today count as citizens in our American democracy equal in stature to men. Just as surely, the

Commonwealth's great goal is not substantially advanced by women's categorical exclusion, in total disregard of their individual merit, from the Commonwealth's premier "citizen-soldier" corps. Virginia, in sum, "has fallen far short of establishing the 'exceedingly persuasive justification,'" that must be the solid base for any gender-defined classification.

VI

In the second phase of the litigation, Virginia presented its remedial plan—maintain VMI as a male-only college and create VWIL as a separate program for women. The plan met District Court approval. . . .

A

A remedial decree, this Court has said, must closely fit the constitutional violation; it must be shaped to place persons unconstitutionally denied an opportunity or advantage in "the position they would have occupied in the absence of [discrimination]." The constitutional violation in this case is the categorical exclusion of women from an extraordinary educational opportunity afforded men. A proper remedy for an unconstitutional exclusion, we have explained, aims to "eliminate [so far as possible] the discriminatory effects of the past" and to "bar like discrimination in the future."

Virginia chose not to eliminate, but to leave untouched, VMI's exclusionary policy. . . .

. . . The Task Force charged with developing the leadership program for women, drawn from the staff and faculty at Mary Baldwin College, "determined that a military model and, especially VMI's adversative method, would be wholly inappropriate for educating and training *most women*." . . .

As earlier stated, generalizations about "the way women are," estimates of what is appropriate for *most women*, no longer justify denying opportunity to women whose talent and capacity place them outside the average description. Notably, Virginia never asserted that VMI's method of education suits *most men*. It is also revealing that Virginia accounted for its failure to make the VWIL experience "the entirely militaristic experience of VMI" on the ground that VWIL "is planned for women who do not necessarily expect to pursue military careers." By that reasoning, VMI's "entirely militaristic" program would be inappropriate for men in general or *as a group*, for "only about 15% of VMI cadets enter career military service."

In contrast to the generalizations about women on which Virginia rests, we note again these dispositive realities: VMI's "implementing methodology" is not "inherently unsuitable to women," "some women . . . do well under [the] adversative model," "some women, at least, would want to attend [VMI] if they had the opportunity," "some women are capable of all of the individual activities required of VMI cadets," and "can meet the physical standards [VMI] now impose[s] on men." It is on behalf of these women that the United States has instituted this suit, and it is for them that a remedy must be crafted, a remedy that will end their exclusion from a state-supplied educational opportunity for which they are fit, a decree that will "bar like discrimination in the future." . . .

Justice SCALIA, dissenting.

Today the Court shuts down an institution that has served the people of the Commonwealth of Virginia with pride and distinction for over a century and a half. To achieve that desired result, it rejects (contrary to our established practice) the factual findings of two courts below, sweeps aside the precedents of this Court, and ignores the history of our people. As to facts: It explicitly rejects the finding that there exist "gender-based developmental differences" supporting Virginia's restriction of the "adversative" method to only a men's institution, and the finding that the all-male composition of the Virginia Military Institute (VMI) is essential to that institution's character. As to precedent: It drastically revises our established standards for reviewing sex-based classifications. And as to history: It counts for nothing the long tradition, enduring down to the present, of men's military colleges supported by both States and the Federal Government.

Much of the Court's opinion is devoted to deprecating the closed-mindedness of our forebears with regard to women's education, and even with regard to the treatment of women in areas that have nothing to do with education. Closed minded they were—as every age is, including our own, with regard to matters it cannot guess, because it simply does not consider them debatable. The virtue of a democratic system with a First Amendment is that it readily enables the people, over time, to be persuaded that what they took for granted is not so, and to change their laws accordingly. That system is destroyed if the smug assurances of each age are removed from the democratic process and written into the Constitution. So to counterbalance the Court's criticism of our ancestors, let me say a word in their praise: They left us free to change. The same cannot be said of this most illiberal Court, which has embarked on a course of inscribing one after another of the current preferences of the society (and in some cases only the counter majoritarian preferences of the society's law-trained elite) into our Basic Law. Today it enshrines the notion that no substantial educational value is to be served by an all-men's military academy—so that the decision by the people of Virginia to maintain such an institution denies equal protection to women who cannot attend that institution but can attend others. Since it is entirely clear that the Constitution of the United States—the old one—takes no sides in this educational debate, I dissent. . . .

Cadets in training at Virginia Military Institute. *Lockwood McLaughlin/Virginia Military Institute.*

After this decision, the Virginia Military Institute did ponder ways to avoid the decision's mandate. Ultimately, however, VMI did admit women.

QUESTIONS FOR DISCUSSION

11.5 Justice Scalia states in his dissent that the majority's standard for evaluating the constitutionality of VMI's exclusion of women "drastically revises our established standards for reviewing sex-based classifications." Do you agree?

11.6 Do you see any validity in VMI's argument that single-sex education has an important role to play in society, particularly in the context of military-oriented education?

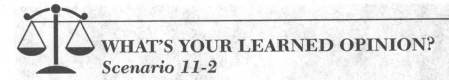

WHAT'S YOUR LEARNED OPINION?
Scenario 11-2

A state-supported nursing school, Women's Nursing College (WNC), allows only women to earn nursing degrees, but allows men to audit classes. Other than only admitting women, WNC's nursing program is unremarkable: It is similar to the other state nursing colleges. Chad, a man who lives near WNC, wishes to attend and earn a nursing degree. There are other nursing colleges he could attend but they are located farther away. WNC says its female-only admission policy is meant to make up for the lack of educational opportunities available to women in the past. Chad applies for admission to obtain a nursing degree, and he is denied because of his gender. He sues, alleging WNC violated the Equal Protection Clause of the Fourteenth Amendment. If you were Chad's lawyer, how would you use the holding in *United States v. Virginia* to argue your client's case? If you were WNC's lawyer, what would you argue?

Scenario 11-3

California has an Alternative Custody Program (ACP) for female prisoners in the state. There is no ACP for male prisoners. The ACP allows enrolled inmates to serve 24 months of their sentence in the community. The State makes this program available to women because:

(1) A large body of research and literature shows that female offenders are a low risk to public safety with complex needs that are better met in the community;

(2) Incarcerated women are more likely than incarcerated men to report extensive histories of trauma, including emotional, physical, and sexual abuse as children, adolescents, and adults;

(3) Although a male inmate can have all these problems, he is less likely to, and these problems tend to have a differential impact on women;

(4) Women are less likely to be employed before or after incarceration, and are more likely to have primary caregiver responsibilities compared to men in all states;

(5) Reuniting with children has been shown to reduce the risk of recidivism for women, but not for men.

California says that it created the ACP with the objective of reducing recidivism for female offenders and ameliorating the disproportionate burdens they face in prison, particularly by treating the lasting effects of separation from their children, trauma, abuse, and addiction, and the program's availability to only women provides gender-responsive programming tailored to female offenders' needs.

Before an inmate can enroll in the ACP, she will have an individual hearing to determine her need and her suitability for the program. Male inmates in California brought a lawsuit alleging that California's decision to make the program available to female inmates but not male inmates violated the Equal Protection Clause of the Fourteenth Amendment.

How would the Court rule if applying the holding and reasoning in *United States v. Virginia*?

C. The Equal Rights Amendment

Could the Equal Rights Amendment already be the law of the land? It is possible. Check out this long tale.

First introduced to Congress in 1923 and ratified by the final required state in 2020, the proposed Equal Rights Amendment (ERA) provides, in pertinent part, as follows:

> Resolved by the Senate and House of Representatives of the United States of America in Congress assembled (two-thirds of each House concurring therein), that the following article is proposed as an amendment to the Constitution of the United States, which shall be valid to all intents and purposes as part of the Constitution when ratified by the legislatures of three-fourths of the several States within seven years from the dates of its submission by the Congress:
> SECTION 1. Equality of rights under the law shall not be denied or abridged by the United States or by any State on account of sex.

Note that the proposed amendment was submitted to Congress in 1923, and the initial version of the amendment quoted above stated that the requisite number of states needed to ratify the amendment in seven years — that is, by 1930. This did not happen. Congress tinkered with the amendment thereafter, but the last expiration date that Congress set — June 20, 1982 — has long since passed. Thus, the lingering question of the lapse of time between when the amendment was initially introduced and the ratification by the requisite number of states in 2020 render the amendment a nullity. Some points in constitutional history suggest that that the ERA, however, is still alive and is only pending publication to take its place as the Twenty-Eighth Amendment to the U.S. Constitution.

Most, but not all, agree that the ERA has retained its relevancy since it was first proposed. This is important because the Supreme Court has held that ratification of constitutional amendments must take place "within some reasonable time after the proposal." The Court subsequently gave vague guidance on factors to consider in determining whether the ratification procedures were reasonable but held that Congress held "the final determination" on that score.[3]

Important precedent concerning whether the ERA can now become part of the U.S. Constitution occurred in 1992 when Congress wielded its authority to promulgate what had been called the Madison Amendment and is now the Twenty-Seventh Amendment. That amendment provides, "No law, varying the compensation for the services of the Senators and Representatives, shall take effect, until an election of representatives shall have intervened." This amendment has generally been viewed as a clever way to get Congress to think twice before giving itself a pay raise—with the fear that members of Congress might get voted out of office if they get too greedy about their pay. The Madison Amendment had originally been proposed in 1789, 203 years before it became part of the Constitution. Notably, after the requisite number of states had ratified the amendment, the Archivist of the United States determined that the amendment was valid and should be included in the constitutional document.

The message of the Twenty-Seventh Amendment story is that the passage of a substantial period of time between congressional approval and ultimate ratification by the requisite number of states might not be a problem. Although 100 years have passed since the ERA was introduced, that is less than half the time that stood between the Twenty-Seventh Amendment's proposal and its ratification.

Many believe that the ERA is as sorely needed now as it ever was. Alice Paul, who drafted and introduced the ERA, is credited with predicting: "We shall not be safe until the principle of equal rights is written into the framework of our government." The Equal Protection Clause of the Fourteenth Amendment is often applied to gender rights, but that interpretation could change as the Supreme Court and the federal legislature change. Consider, for example, the U.S. Supreme Court's change in direction on the constitutionality of early trimester abortion—flipping what was once constitutionally protected to something outside the ambit of the Constitution. In addition, the ERA would provide more clarity to judicial standards in gender discrimination cases, which would, in turn, lead to greater protections for women's rights, as well as potentially protecting the rights of transgendered individuals and others whose sense of personal identity does not conform to their birth sex. The potential impact of the ERA remains huge, spanning from discriminatory laws still on the books, to health care and family law issues, to workplace inequities such as the pay gap and sexual harassment laws.

One distinction between the ERA and the Madison Amendment is the presence of a long-past expiration date that Congress placed on the ERA. This, however, might not present a problem. Although the Constitution, specifically Article V, is silent on the issue, Congress has the power to set a deadline for the ratification of an amendment. Scholars disagree on whether this is an irredeemable obstacle. Many argue that even though the law prohibits ignoring the deadline in the proposing clause, it is, at the very least, possible for Congress to extend the time limit. After all, Congress did extend the original deadline and could do so again.

The portion of the Constitution pertaining to amendments, Article V, is silent on whether a state may rescind its ratification of an amendment. This is relevant because five states—Idaho, Kentucky, Nebraska, South Dakota, and Tennessee—have voted to rescind their ratifications of the ERA. The Supreme Court has relatively recently held that the issue whether this deratification is effective is a nonjusticiable political question reserved for Congress. History, however, suggests that a state's ratification, once given, must stand.

The statutes of the United States, known as the United States Code, provide the only guidance on the procedural alchemy that turns a proposed amendment into an adopted amendment, and the Code does not require that Congress promulgate (i.e., give its blessing to) an amendment. The Department of Justice has stated that "there is no requirement of congressional approval," and, in fact, the only two amendments that Congress promulgated after being ratified were the Fourteenth and Twenty-Seventh Amendments. This suggests the possibility that all that remains to make the ERA law is for the states that have ratified the ERA to officially notify the National Archives and Records Administration, if they have not already done so, and for the Archivist to affix their certificate and publish the amendment.

The Constitution has enormous norm-setting power. Officially making the ERA part of the Constitution sends the unequivocal message that people of all genders are equal citizens and discrimination on the basis of sex will not be tolerated. Without the ERA, equal rights for any gender can hinge on a single vote in Congress or the decision of a majority of five in the Supreme Court. As we have seen, the preferences of the U.S. Supreme Court Justices can swing dramatically in a short period of time, particularly if one President is in the position of appointing more than one Justice during the President's term. An amendment to the Constitution can be a powerful check to that kind of dramatic ideological turn in the Court's decision making and thereby help to maintain stability in the law.

QUESTIONS FOR REVIEW

1. What part of the U.S. Constitution did Myra Bradwell rely on when she argued that she should be entitled to become a member of the Illinois bar? Did she win her constitutional argument in the U.S. Supreme Court? Why or why not?
2. What was the view of women's role in society expressed by Justice Bradley in his concurrence in *Bradwell v. People of the State of Illinois*?
3. What year did the women of the United States win the right to suffrage? Describe some of the obstacles and official resistance that the suffragists encountered as part of their struggle for that right.
4. Did the Nineteenth Amendment put to rest all obstacles to the right of women to vote in democratic elections? If not, what obstacles remained?

5. What is the current level of scrutiny appropriate to evaluate whether a law that discriminates on the basis of gender is constitutional? In addition to the name of the level of scrutiny, describe what questions that level of scrutiny requires a court to ask to evaluate the constitutionality of a law's distinctions based on gender.

6. What was the gender discrimination problem at issue in *United States v. Virginia*? The Supreme Court ruled that the discrimination was unconstitutional. What were the Court's reasons for that decision?

7. What would be the possible function of the Equal Rights Amendment today?

8. What are the arguments for why the Equal Rights Amendment is currently poised to become part of the Constitution? What are the arguments for why the Equal Rights Amendment could not be included in the Constitution now?

ENDNOTES

1. Kathryn M. Stanchi, Linda L. Berger & Bridget J. Crawford, *Feminist Judgments: Rewritten Opinions of the United States Supreme Court* (2016).
2. *Id.* at 60-77.
3. *Coleman v. Miller*, 307 U.S. 433, 456 (1939). As for the factors a court should consider, the *Coleman* Court said:

> When a proposed amendment springs from a conception of economic needs, it would be necessary, in determining whether a reasonable time had elapsed since its submission, to consider the economic conditions prevailing in the country, whether these had so far changed since the submission as to make the proposal no longer responsive to the conception which inspired it or whether conditions were such as to intensify the feeling of need and the appropriateness of the proposed remedial action. In short, the question of a reasonable time in many cases would involve, as in this case it does involve, an appraisal of a great variety of relevant conditions, political, social and economic.

Id. at 453.

Introduction to Chapters 12, 13, and 14

The final three chapters in this part—12, 13, and 14—concern reproductive rights, sexual freedoms, and marriage. Each of these rights has its roots in the Due Process Clause of the Fourteenth Amendment (as well as the Due Process Clause of the Fifth Amendment if the federal government is involved). Although all are guarantees of individual rights akin to those discussed earlier in this part, they have a unique lineage. All three are associated with a branch of Due Process Clauses jurisprudence known as substantive due process.

As interpreted by the U.S. Supreme Court, the Due Process Clauses have two components relating to the "due process" phrase. The first is the focus on how government handles your rights. For this concern, one asks this: Are the procedures provided sufficient to provide adequate notice of governmental action and an opportunity for citizens to be heard on their side of a controversy? This is called procedural due process; that is, focusing on how government treats you in processing grievances and the like. Inquiries under this view of the Due Process Clauses focus on the fairness of procedures for resolving differences. For example, the question of whether government can take away your driver's license without giving you an opportunity to defend yourself in writing or a hearing is a procedural due process question.

The second is a more controversial component of the Due Process Clauses. This component focuses on what government does to you. If the government prohibits you from accessing birth control, a substantive due process question is presented. The question is whether you are entitled to access a method of birth control as a matter of constitutional guarantee protecting against government interference with your right to liberty. Proponents of substantive due process point to its utility as a concept to ensure that the Constitution remains viable by accommodating the realities of the contemporary age. Confronting claims to trash the concept now, proponents also point to an entrenched legacy of substantive due process, long relied on by citizens as part of the essence of the civil society in which they have lived. Critics of substantive due process argue that substantive due process theories reach far beyond the procedural fairness concerns undergirding the impetus for the Due Process Clauses. Under this critical view, procedural fairness is the essence and the limit of the reach of due process concerns. Substantive due process, the criticism proceeds, is merely a theory that invites individual judicial preference into constitutional decision making. Proponents of substantive due process, however, argue that the Constitution is concerned with liberty, dignity, and the pursuit of happiness for citizens—all values embodied in the spirit of the Due Process Clauses of the Constitution's Fifth and Fourteenth Amendments. (Interestingly, you will rarely actually see the term "substantive due process" in opinions essentially relying on its premises. Instead the term appears most frequently in scholarly writing and often comes with a negative connotation.)

As you read through the chapters that follow, consider whether you agree or disagree with the proposition that the Constitution protects unstated (known as unenumerated) rights through the Due Process Clauses or other portions. Or, alternatively, consider whether the U.S. Supreme Court indulged personal (liberal) preferences of a majority of Justices when using the theory of substantive due process to embrace rights they believe are important to modern life, concluded that these rights are logical outgrowths of constitutional values, or both. Finally, consider whether the more recent trend among a majority of Justices to reject earlier substantive due process decisions stems from disapproval of the jurisprudential foundations of substantive due process in the Constitution, an opportunity to indulge conservative social preferences, or both.

Reproductive Rights

12

As in many areas about individual constitutional rights, reproductive freedoms developed incrementally. More than for other individual rights issues, however, the Justices have experimented with and debated where recognition of reproductive freedoms should be found within the constitutional text.

The path toward reproductive rights recognition in the U.S. Supreme Court began with the issue of whether married couples were entitled to be free from government interference with their desire to obtain contraception. The majority opinion mentioned that prior decisions recognized that "specific guarantees in the Bill of Rights have penumbras, formed by emanations from those guarantees that help give them life and substance." The Court identified a number of Bill of Rights amendments as containing guarantees for protecting "zones of privacy." From this premise, the Court observed that the marital relationship is among the most intimate of these zones. From this promise, the Court held that a state statute disapproving birth control unconstitutionally infringed "directly on an intimate relation of husband and wife and their physician's role in one aspect of that relation."

Where did the Court get this so-called right to privacy? First, the Court frequently cited the 1925 decision in *Pierce v. Society of Sisters*, which found that "the right to educate one's children as one chooses is made applicable to the States by the force of the First and Fourteenth Amendments." The Court also several times referenced the 1923 decision in *Meyer v. State of Nebraska*, in which the Court declared unconstitutional a state statute prohibiting teaching school children foreign languages, finding that regulating "the right to study any particular subject or any foreign language" violated the Due Process Clause of the Fourteenth Amendment. As the Court also stated in *Meyer*: "While this Court has not attempted to define with exactness the liberty thus guaranteed [by the Fourteenth Amendment] . . . without doubt, it denotes not merely freedom from bodily restraint but also [for example,] the right to marry, establish a home and bring up children." Consider whether these two cases, *Pierce* and *Meyer*, provided a firm footing for the Court's decision below in *Griswold*.

FROM THE BENCH

GRISWOLD v. CONNECTICUT
381 U.S. 479 (1965)

Mr. Justice DOUGLAS delivered the opinion of the Court.

Appellant Griswold is Executive Director of the Planned Parenthood League of Connecticut. Appellant Buxton is a licensed physician and a professor at the Yale Medical School. . . . They gave information, instruction, and medical advice to *married persons* as to the means of preventing conception. They examined the wife and prescribed the best contraceptive device or material for her use. Fees were usually charged, although some couples were serviced free.

The statute[] whose constitutionality is involved in this appeal . . . provides:

"Any person who uses any drug, medicinal article or instrument for the purpose of preventing conception shall be fined not less than fifty dollars or imprisoned not less than sixty days nor more than one year or be both fined and imprisoned." . . .

The appellants were found guilty as accessories and fined $100 each, against the claim that the accessory statute as so applied violated the Fourteenth Amendment.

[In considering this case], we are met with a wide range of questions that implicate the Due Process Clause of the Fourteenth Amendment. . . . This law . . . operates directly on an intimate relation of husband and wife and their physician's role in one aspect of that relation. . . . The association of people is not mentioned in the Constitution nor in the Bill of Rights. The right to educate a child in a school of the parents' choice—whether public or private or parochial—is also not mentioned. Nor is the right to study any particular subject or any foreign language. Yet the First Amendment has been construed to include certain of those rights. By *Pierce v. Society of Sisters*, [we recognized] the right to educate one's children as one chooses is made applicable to the States by the force of the First and Fourteenth Amendments. [And by] *Meyer v. State of Nebraska*, the same dignity is given the right to study the German language in a private school. In other words, the State may not, consistently with the spirit of the First Amendment, contract the spectrum of available knowledge. . . .

Without those peripheral rights the specific rights would be less secure. And so we reaffirm the principle of the *Pierce* and the *Meyer* cases.

In *NAACP v. State of Alabama*, we protected the "freedom to associate and privacy in one's associations," noting that freedom of association was a peripheral First Amendment right. Disclosure of membership lists of a constitutionally valid association, we held, was invalid "as entailing the likelihood of a substantial restraint upon the exercise by petitioner's members of their right to freedom of association." In other words, the First Amendment has a penumbra where privacy is protected from governmental intrusion. In like context, we have protected forms of "association" that are not political in the customary sense but pertain to the social, legal, and economic benefit of the members. [For example, we have held] . . . it not permissible to bar a lawyer from practice, because he had once been a member of the Communist Party. The man's "association with that Party" was not shown to be "anything more than a political faith in a political party" and was not action of a kind proving bad moral character.

Those cases involved more than the "right of assembly"—a right that extends to all irrespective of their race or ideology. The right of "association," like the right of belief, is more than the right to attend a meeting; it includes the right to express one's attitudes or philosophies by membership in a group or by affiliation with it or by other lawful means. Association in that context is a form of expression of opinion; and while it is not expressly included in the First Amendment its existence is necessary in making the express guarantees fully meaningful.

The foregoing cases suggest that specific guarantees in the Bill of Rights have penumbras, formed by emanations from those guarantees that help give them life and substance. Various guarantees create zones of privacy. The right of association contained in the penumbra of the First Amendment is one, as we have seen. The Third Amendment in its prohibition against the quartering of soldiers "in any house" in time of peace without the consent of the owner is another facet of that privacy. The Fourth Amendment explicitly affirms the "right of the people to be secure in their persons, houses, papers, and effects, against unreasonable searches and seizures." The Fifth Amendment in its Self-Incrimination Clause enables the citizen to create a zone of privacy which government may not force him to surrender to his detriment. The Ninth Amendment provides: "The enumeration in the Constitution, of certain rights, shall not be construed to deny or disparage others retained by the people." . . .

The present case, then, concerns a relationship lying within the zone of privacy created by several fundamental constitutional guarantees. And it concerns a law which, in forbidding the use of contraceptives rather than regulating their manufacture or sale, seeks to achieve its goals by means having a maximum destructive impact upon that relationship. Such a law cannot stand in light of the familiar principle, so often applied by this Court, that a "governmental purpose to control or prevent activities constitutionally subject to state regulation may not be achieved by means which sweep unnecessarily broadly and thereby invade the area of protected freedoms." Would we allow the police to search the sacred precincts of marital bedrooms for telltale signs of the use of contraceptives? The very idea is repulsive to the notions of privacy surrounding the marriage relationship.

We deal with a right of privacy older than the Bill of Rights—older than our political parties, older than our school system. Marriage is a coming together for better or for worse, hopefully enduring, and intimate to the degree of being sacred. It is an association that promotes a way of life, not causes; a harmony in living, not political faiths; a bilateral loyalty, not commercial or social projects. Yet it is an association for as noble a purpose as any involved in our prior decisions.

Reversed.

Mr. Justice GOLDBERG, whom The Chief Justice and Mr. Justice BRENNAN join, concurring.

I agree with the Court that Connecticut's birth-control law unconstitutionally intrudes upon the right of marital privacy, and I join in its opinion and judgment. Although I have not accepted the view that "due process" as used in the Fourteenth Amendment includes all of the first eight Amendments, I do agree that the concept of liberty protects those personal rights that are fundamental, and is not confined to the specific terms of the Bill of Rights. My conclusion that the concept of liberty is not so restricted and that it embraces the right of marital privacy though that right is not mentioned explicitly in the Constitution is supported both by numerous decisions of this Court, referred to in the Court's opinion, and by the language and history of the Ninth Amendment. In reaching the conclusion that the right of marital privacy is protected, as being within the protected penumbra of specific guarantees of the Bill of Rights, the Court refers to the Ninth Amendment. I add these words to emphasize the relevance of that Amendment to the Court's holding.

The Court stated many years ago that the Due Process Clause protects those liberties that are "so rooted in the traditions and conscience of our people as to be ranked as fundamental." . . .

And, in *Meyer v. State of Nebraska*, the Court, referring to the Fourteenth Amendment, stated:

> "While this court has not attempted to define with exactness the liberty thus guaranteed, the term has received much consideration and some of the included things have been definitely stated. Without doubt, it denotes not merely freedom from bodily restraint but also (for example,) the right . . . to marry, establish a home and bring up children. . . ."

This Court, in a series of decisions, has held that the Fourteenth Amendment absorbs and applies to the States those specifics of the first eight amendments which express fundamental personal rights. The language and history of the Ninth Amendment reveal that the Framers of the Constitution believed that there are additional fundamental rights, protected from governmental infringe-ment, which exist alongside those fundamental rights specifically mentioned in the first eight constitutional amendments.

The Ninth Amendment reads, "The enumeration in the Constitution, of cer-tain rights, shall not be construed to deny or disparage others retained by the people." . . . It was proffered to quiet expressed fears that a bill of specifically enumerated rights could not be sufficiently broad to cover all essential rights and that the specific mention of certain rights would be interpreted as a denial that others were protected. . . .

While this Court has had little occasion to interpret the Ninth Amendment, "(i)t cannot be presumed that any clause in the constitution is intended to be without effect." *Marbury v. Madison*. In interpreting the Constitution, "real effect should be given to all the words it uses." *Myers v. United States*. The Ninth Amendment to the Constitution may be regarded by some as a recent discovery and may be forgotten by others, but since 1791 it has been a basic part of the Constitution which we are sworn to uphold. To hold that a right so basic and fundamental and so deep rooted in our society as the right of privacy in marriage may be infringed because that right is not guaranteed in so many words by the first eight amendments to the Constitution is to ignore the Ninth Amendment and to give it no effect whatsoever. Moreover, a judicial construction that this fundamental right is not protected by the Constitution because it is not men-tioned in explicit terms by one of the first eight amendments or elsewhere in the Constitution would violate the Ninth Amendment, which specifically states that "(t)he enumeration in the Constitution, of certain rights shall not be construed to deny or disparage others retained by the people." . . .

. . . [T]he Ninth Amendment shows a belief of the Constitution's authors that fundamental rights exist that are not expressly enumerated in the first eight amendments and an intent that the list of rights included there not be deemed exhaustive. As any student of this Court's opinions knows, this Court has held, often unanimously, that the Fifth and Fourteenth Amendments protect certain fundamental personal liberties from abridgment by the Federal Government or the States. The Ninth Amendment simply shows the intent of the Constitution's authors that other fundamental personal rights should not be denied such pro-tection or disparaged in any other way simply because they are not specifically listed in the first eight constitutional amendments. I do not see how this broad-ens the authority of the Court; rather it serves to support what this Court has been doing in protecting fundamental rights.

Nor am I turning somersaults with history in arguing that the Ninth Amendment is relevant in a case dealing with a State's infringement of a fun-damental right. While the Ninth Amendment—and indeed the entire Bill of Rights—originally concerned restrictions upon federal power, the subsequently enacted Fourteenth Amendment prohibits the States as well from abridging fundamental personal liberties. And, the Ninth Amendment, in indicating that not all such liberties are specifically mentioned in the first eight amendments, is surely relevant in showing the existence of other fundamental personal rights, now protected from state, as well as federal, infringement. In sum, the Ninth Amendment simply lends strong support to the view that the "liberty" protected by the Fifth and Fourteenth Amendments from infringement by the Federal Government or the States is not restricted to rights specifically mentioned in the first eight amendments.

In determining which rights are fundamental, judges are not left at large to decide cases in light of their personal and private notions. Rather, they must look to the "traditions and (collective) conscience of our people" to determine whether a principle is "so rooted (there) . . . as to be ranked as fundamental." The inquiry is whether a right involved "is of such a character that it cannot be denied without violating those 'fundamental principles of liberty and justice which lie at the base of all our civil and political institutions.'" "Liberty" also "gains content from the emanations of . . . specific (constitutional) guarantees" and "from experience with the requirements of a free society."

I agree fully with the Court that, applying these tests, the right of privacy is a fundamental personal right, emanating "from the totality of the constitutional scheme under which we live." Mr. Justice Brandeis, dissenting in *Olmstead v. United States*, comprehensively summarized the principles underlying the Constitution's guarantees of privacy:

> The protection guaranteed by the (Fourth and Fifth) amendments is much broader in scope. The makers of our Constitution undertook to secure conditions favorable to the pursuit of happiness. They recognized the significance of man's spiritual nature, of his feelings and of his intellect. They knew that only a part of the pain, pleasure and satisfactions of life are to be found in material things. They sought to protect Americans in their beliefs, their thoughts, their emotions and their sensations. They conferred, as against the government, the right to be let alone—the most comprehensive of rights and the right most valued by civilized men.

The Connecticut statutes here involved deal with a particularly important and sensitive area of privacy—that of the marital relation and the marital home. This Court recognized in *Meyer v. Nebraska* that the right "to marry, establish a home and bring up children" was an essential part of the liberty guaranteed by the Fourteenth Amendment. . . .

I agree with Mr. Justice Harlan's statement in his dissenting opinion in *Poe v. Ullman*: "Certainly the safeguarding of the home does not follow merely from the sanctity of property rights. The home derives its pre-eminence as the seat of family life. And the integrity of that life is something so fundamental that it has been found to draw to its protection the principles of more than one explicitly granted Constitutional right. . . . Of this whole 'private realm of family life' it is difficult to imagine what is more private or more intimate than a husband and wife's marital relations."

The entire fabric of the Constitution and the purposes that clearly underlie its specific guarantees demonstrate that the rights to marital privacy and to marry and raise a family are of similar order and magnitude as the fundamental rights specifically protected. . . . While it may shock some of my Brethren that the Court today holds that the Constitution protects the right of marital privacy, in my view it is far more shocking to believe that the personal liberty guaranteed by the Constitution does not include protection against such totalitarian limitation of family size, which is at complete variance with our constitutional concepts. Yet, if upon a showing of a slender basis of rationality, a law outlawing voluntary birth control by married persons is valid, then, by the same reasoning, a law requiring compulsory birth control also would seem to be valid. In my view, however, both types of law would unjustifiably intrude upon rights of marital privacy which are constitutionally protected.

. . . Although the Connecticut birth-control law obviously encroaches upon a fundamental personal liberty, the State does not show that the law serves any "subordinating (state) interest which is compelling" or that it is "necessary . . . to the accomplishment of a permissible state policy." The State, at most, argues that there is some rational relation between this statute and what is admittedly a legitimate subject of state concern—the discouraging of extra-marital relations. It says that preventing the use of birth-control devices by married persons helps prevent the indulgence by some in such extra-marital relations. The rationality of this justification is dubious, particularly in light of the admitted widespread availability to all persons in the State of Connecticut, unmarried as well as married, of birth-control devices for the prevention of disease, as distinguished from the prevention of conception. But, in any event, it is clear that the state interest in safeguarding marital fidelity can be served by a more discriminately tailored statute, which does not, like the present one, sweep unnecessarily broadly, reaching far beyond the evil sought to be dealt with and intruding upon the privacy of all married couples. Here, as elsewhere, "(p)recision of regulation must be the touchstone in an area so closely touching our most precious freedoms." The State of Connecticut does have statutes, the constitutionality of which is beyond doubt, which prohibit adultery and fornication. These statutes demonstrate that means for achieving the same basic purpose of protecting marital fidelity are available to Connecticut without the need to "invade the area of protected freedoms." . . .

In sum, I believe that the right of privacy in the marital relation is fundamental and basic—a personal right "retained by the people" within the meaning of the Ninth Amendment. Connecticut cannot constitutionally abridge this fundamental right, which is protected by the Fourteenth Amendment from infringement by the States. I agree with the Court that petitioners' convictions must therefore be reversed.

FROM THE BENCH

Mr. Justice BLACK, with whom Mr. Justice STEWART joins, dissenting.

I agree with my Brother Stewart's dissenting opinion. And like him I do not to any extent whatever base my view that this Connecticut law is constitutional on a belief that the law is wise or that its policy is a good one. In order that there may be no room at all to doubt why I vote as I do, I feel constrained to add that the law is every bit as offensive to me as it is my Brethren of the majority and my Brothers Harlan, White and Goldberg who, reciting reasons why it is offensive to them, hold it unconstitutional. There is no single one of the graphic and eloquent strictures and criticisms fired at the policy of this Connecticut law either by the Court's opinion or by those of my concurring Brethren to which I cannot subscribe—except their conclusion that the evil qualities they see in the law make it unconstitutional. . . .

The Court talks about a constitutional "right of privacy" as though there is some constitutional provision or provisions forbidding any law ever to be passed which might abridge the "privacy" of individuals. But there is not. There are, of course, guarantees in certain specific constitutional provisions which are designed in part to protect privacy at certain times and places with respect to certain activities. Such, for example, is the Fourth Amendment's guarantee against "unreasonable searches and seizures." But I think it belittles that Amendment to talk about it as though it protects nothing but "privacy." To treat it that way is to give it a niggardly interpretation, not the kind of liberal reading I think any Bill of Rights provision should be given. The average man would very likely not have his feelings soothed any more by having his property seized openly than by having it seized privately and by stealth. He simply wants his property left alone. And a person can be just as much, if not more, irritated, annoyed and injured by an unceremonious public arrest by a policeman as he is by a seizure in the privacy of his office or home.

One of the most effective ways of diluting or expanding a constitutionally guaranteed right is to substitute for the crucial word or words of a constitutional guarantee another word or words, more or less flexible and more or less restricted in meaning. This fact is well illustrated by the use of the term "right of privacy" as a comprehensive substitute for the Fourth Amendment's guarantee against "unreasonable searches and seizures." "Privacy" is a broad, abstract and ambiguous concept which can easily be shrunken in meaning but which can also, on the other hand, easily be interpreted as a constitutional ban against many things other than searches and seizures. I have expressed the view many times that First Amendment freedoms, for example, have suffered from a failure of the courts to stick to the simple language of the First Amendment in construing it, instead of invoking multitudes of words substituted for those the Framers used. For these reasons I get nowhere in this case by talk about a constitutional "right of privacy" as an emanation from one or more constitutional provisions. I like my privacy as well as the next one, but I am nevertheless compelled to admit that government has a right to invade it unless prohibited by some specific constitutional provision. For these reasons I cannot agree with the Court's judgment and the reasons it gives for holding this Connecticut law unconstitutional.

This brings me to the arguments made by my Brothers Harlan, White and Goldberg for invalidating the Connecticut law. Brothers Harlan and White would invalidate it by reliance on the Due Process Clause of the Fourteenth Amendment, but Brother Goldberg, while agreeing with Brother Harlan, relies also on the Ninth Amendment. I have no doubt that the Connecticut law could be applied in such a way as to abridge freedom of speech and press and therefore violate the First and Fourteenth Amendments. My disagreement with the Court's opinion holding that there is such a violation here is a narrow one, relating to the application of the First Amendment to the facts and circumstances of this particular case. But my disagreement with Brothers Harlan, White and Goldberg is more basic. I think that if properly construed neither the Due Process Clause nor the Ninth Amendment, nor both together, could under any circumstances be a proper basis for invalidating the Connecticut law. I discuss the due process and Ninth Amendment arguments together because on analysis they turn out to be the same thing—merely using different words to claim for this Court and the federal judiciary power to invalidate any legislative act which the judges find irrational, unreasonable or offensive.

The due process argument which my Brothers Harlan and White adopt here is based, as their opinions indicate, on the premise that this Court is vested with power to invalidate all state laws that it consider to be arbitrary, capricious, unreasonable, or oppressive, or this Court's belief that a particular state law under scrutiny has no "rational or justifying" purpose, or is offensive to a "sense of fairness and justice." If these formulas based on "natural justice," or others which mean the same thing, are to prevail, they require judges to determine what is or is not constitutional on the basis of their own appraisal of what laws are unwise or unnecessary. The power to make such decisions is of course that of a legislative body. Surely it has to be admitted that no provision of the Constitution specifically gives such blanket power to courts to exercise such a supervisory veto over the wisdom and value of legislative policies and to hold unconstitutional those laws which they believe unwise or dangerous. I readily admit that no legislative body, state or national, should pass laws that can justly be given any of the invidious labels invoked as constitutional excuses to strike down state laws. But perhaps it is not too much to say that no legislative body ever does pass laws without believing that they will accomplish a sane, rational, wise and justifiable purpose. While I completely subscribe to the holding of *Marbury v. Madison*, and subsequent cases, that our Court has constitutional power to strike down statutes, state or federal, that violate commands of the Federal Constitution, I do not believe that we are granted power by the Due Process Clause or any other constitutional provision or provisions to measure constitutionality by our belief that legislation is arbitrary, capricious or unreasonable, or accomplishes no justifiable purpose, or is offensive to our own notions of "civilized standards of conduct." Such an appraisal of the wisdom of legislation is an attribute of the power to make laws, not of the power to interpret them. The use by federal courts of such a formula or doctrine or what not to veto federal or state laws simply takes away from Congress and States the power to make laws based on their own judgment of fairness and wisdom and transfers that power to this Court for ultimate determination—a power which was specifically denied to federal courts by the convention that framed the Constitution. . . .

My Brother Goldberg has adopted the recent discovery that the Ninth Amendment as well as the Due Process Clause can be used by this Court as authority to strike down all state legislation which this Court thinks violates "fundamental principles of liberty and justice," or is contrary to the "traditions and (collective) conscience of our people." He also states, without proof satisfactory to me, that in making decisions on this basis judges will not consider "their personal and private notions." One may ask how they can avoid considering them. Our Court certainly has no machinery with which to take a Gallup Poll. And the scientific miracles of this age have not yet produced a gadget which the Court can use to determine what traditions are rooted in the "(collective) conscience of our people." Moreover, one would certainly have to look far beyond the language of the Ninth Amendment to find that the Framers vested in this Court any such awesome veto powers over lawmaking, either by the States or by the Congress. Nor does anything in the history of the Amendment offer any support for such a shocking doctrine. The whole history of the adoption of the Constitution and Bill of Rights points the other way, and the very material quoted by my Brother Goldberg shows that the Ninth Amendment was intended to protect against the idea that "by enumerating particular exceptions to the grant of power" to the Federal Government, "those rights which were not singled out, were intended to be assigned into the hands of the General Government (the United States), and were consequently insecure." That Amendment was passed, not to broaden the powers of this Court or any other department of "the General Government," but, as every student of history knows, to assure the people that the Constitution in all its provisions was intended to limit the Federal Government to the powers granted expressly or by necessary implication. If any broad, unlimited power to hold laws unconstitutional because they offend what this Court conceives to be the "(collective) conscience of our people" is vested in this Court by the Ninth Amendment, the Fourteenth Amendment, or any other provision of the Constitution, it was not given by the Framers, but rather has been bestowed on the Court by the Court. This fact is perhaps responsible for the peculiar phenomenon that for a period of a century and a half no serious suggestion was ever made that the Ninth Amendment, enacted to protect state powers against federal invasion, could be used as a weapon of federal power to prevent state legislatures from passing laws they consider appropriate to govern local affairs. Use of any such broad, unbounded judicial authority would make of this Court's members a day-to-day constitutional convention.

I repeat so as not to be misunderstood that this Court does have power, which it should exercise, to hold laws unconstitutional where they are forbidden by the Federal Constitution. My point is that there is no provision of the Constitution which either expressly or impliedly vests power in this Court to sit as a supervisory agency over acts of duly constituted legislative bodies and set aside their laws because of the Court's belief that the legislative policies adopted are unreasonable, unwise, arbitrary, capricious or irrational. The adoption of such a loose, flexible, uncontrolled standard for holding laws unconstitutional, if ever it is finally achieved, will amount to a great unconstitutional shift of power to the courts which I believe and am constrained to say will be bad for the courts and worse for the country. Subjecting federal and state laws to such an unrestrained and unrestrainable judicial control as to the wisdom of legislative enactments would, I fear, jeopardize the separation of governmental powers that the Framers set up and at the same time threaten to take away much of the power of States to govern themselves which the Constitution plainly intended them to have. . . .

Mr. Justice STEWART, whom Mr. Justice BLACK joins, dissenting.

Since 1879 Connecticut has had on its books a law which forbids the use of contraceptives by anyone. I think this is an uncommonly silly law. As a practical matter, the law is obviously unenforceable, except in the oblique context of the present case. As a philosophical matter, I believe the use of contraceptives in the relationship of marriage should be left to personal and private choice, based upon each individual's moral, ethical, and religious beliefs. As a matter of social policy, I think professional counsel about methods of birth control should be available to all, so that each individual's choice can be meaningfully made. But we are not asked in this case to say whether we think this law is unwise, or even asinine. We are asked to hold that it violates the United States Constitution. And that I cannot do.

In the course of its opinion the Court refers to no less than six Amendments to the Constitution: the First, the Third, the Fourth, the Fifth, the Ninth, and the Fourteenth. But the Court does not say which of these Amendments, if any, it thinks is infringed by this Connecticut law.

We are told that the Due Process Clause of the Fourteenth Amendment is not, as such, the "guide" in this case. With that much I agree. There is no claim that this law, duly enacted by the Connecticut Legislature, is unconstitutionally vague. There is no claim that the appellants were denied any of the elements of procedural due process at their trial, so as to make their convictions constitutionally invalid. And, as the Court says, the day has long passed since the Due Process Clause was regarded as a proper instrument for determining "the wisdom, need, and propriety" of state laws. My Brothers Harlan and White to the contrary, "(w)e have returned to the original constitutional proposition that courts do not substitute their social and economic beliefs for the judgment of legislative bodies, who are elected to pass laws." *Ferguson v. Skrupa.*

FROM THE BENCH

As to the First, Third, Fourth, and Fifth Amendments, I can find nothing in any of them to invalidate this Connecticut law, even assuming that all those Amendments are fully applicable against the States. It has not even been argued that this is a law "respecting an establishment of religion, or prohibiting the free exercise thereof." And surely, unless the solemn process of constitutional adjudication is to descend to the level of a play on words, there is not involved here any abridgment of "the freedom of speech, or of the press; or the right of the people peaceably to assemble, and to petition the Government for a redress of grievances." No soldier has been quartered in any house. There has been no search, and no seizure. Nobody has been compelled to be a witness against himself.

The Court also quotes the Ninth Amendment, and my Brother Goldberg's concurring opinion relies heavily upon it. But to say that the Ninth Amendment has anything to do with this case is to turn somersaults with history. The Ninth Amendment, like its companion the Tenth, which this Court held "states but a truism that all is retained which has not been surrendered," *United States v. Darby*, was framed by James Madison and adopted by the States simply to make clear that the adoption of the Bill of Rights did not alter the plan that the Federal Government was to be a government of express and limited powers, and that all rights and powers not delegated to it were retained by the people and the individual States. Until today no member of this Court has ever suggested that the Ninth Amendment meant anything else, and the idea that a federal court could ever use the Ninth Amendment to annul a law passed by the elected representatives of the people of the State of Connecticut would have caused James Madison no little wonder.

What provision of the Constitution, then, does make this state law invalid? The Court says it is the right of privacy "created by several fundamental constitutional guarantees." With all deference, I can find no such general right of privacy in the Bill of Rights, in any other part of the Constitution, or in any case ever before decided by this Court.

At the oral argument in this case we were told that the Connecticut law does not "conform to current community standards." But it is not the function of this Court to decide cases on the basis of community standards. We are here to decide cases "agreeably to the Constitution and laws of the United States." It is the essence of judicial duty to subordinate our own personal views, our own ideas of what legislation is wise and what is not. If, as I should surely hope, the law before us does not reflect the standards of the people of Connecticut, the people of Connecticut can freely exercise their true Ninth and Tenth Amendment rights to persuade their elected representatives to repeal it. That is the constitutional way to take this law off the books.

QUESTIONS FOR DISCUSSION

12.1   You will note that the various opinions in this case supporting the right of married couples to make private decisions about birth control, each focused on different parts and different readings of the supporting constitutional provisions. For example, the opinion of the Court written by Justice Douglas described a "penumbra" emanating from the various specific liberties mentioned in the Constitution. Literal definitions of a penumbra vary, but most agree that a classic example of a penumbra occurs during an eclipse when a partial shadow appears between the regions of full shadow and full illumination.

The earth's penumbra appears during a lunar eclipse. *Sumruay Rattanataipob/Shutterstock.*

Do you think the reference to a penumbra giving rise to a right to privacy is a useful analogy? Are you convinced that the various emanations from parts of the Bill of Rights establish a free-standing right to privacy?

12.2   As explored further in the "Behind the Curtain" sidebar to this case below, Justice Goldberg relied on the Ninth Amendment to support his decision striking down the contraception prohibition law. How does that compare with Justice Douglas's penumbra theory? Which is more persuasive to you, Justice Goldberg's or Justice Douglas's approach to finding a foundation in the Constitution for a right to privacy? Explain your reasoning.

12.3   At the time the *Griswold* decision was handed down, every Justice on the Supreme Court was male. Is that significant? Do you perceive the absence of a female voice in any of the opinions? Explain your answer.

12.4   For some lawmakers at the time, the prohibition against birth control was deemed important to promoting marital fidelity. Is the value of marital fidelity an appropriate justification for evaluating whether a legal prohibition on birth control is constitutional? How so? How not?

12.5   As discussed at the end of Chapter 6, the Constitution includes a prohibition against government establishment of religion. More colloquially, this is known as the Constitution's wall of separation between church and state. Various religions practiced by U.S. citizens either prohibit artificial contraception altogether or promote restrictions on its use. To what extent does constitutional recognition of a married couple's privacy right about whether or not to use birth control implicate these beliefs? Does the *Griswold* decision override these religious edicts or does the case simply stand as a protection for those who do not abide by these religious edicts?

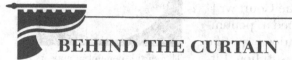

BEHIND THE CURTAIN

To the constitutional theorist, Justice Goldberg's use of the Ninth Amendment is one of the most important aspects of the *Griswold* case. The Ninth Amendment's mandate is simple: The enumeration of certain rights in the Constitution should not be construed to mean that the Constitution does not protect rights that are not listed. Constitutional historians agree that the Framers included the Ninth Amendment in the Bill of Rights to address fears that expressly protecting certain rights might be misinterpreted implicitly to sanction the infringement of others not mentioned.

Prior to *Griswold*, the Supreme Court rarely grappled with the meaning of the Ninth Amendment and consistently rejected constitutional challenges based on the amendment. For that reason, the reference in *Griswold* sparked particular interest.

The Supreme Court, however, has not followed through on its interest in the Ninth Amendment as a free-standing guarantee of individual freedoms. Instead, the Court has reverted to its original understanding of the amendment as an interpretative rule of construction, making clear the enunciation of specific rights in the Constitution does not negate the existence of rights that the Constitution does not list expressly.

The Ninth Amendment is intimately connected to the history of the Bill of Rights. You may remember from earlier in this book that the original Constitution did not include a Bill of Rights. Federalists—represented by such individuals as Alexander Hamilton—had successfully argued that no need existed for a Bill of Rights because the federal government possessed extremely limited powers. The Federalists also argued that the enumeration of specific rights might imply that those individual rights not identified were not protected. James Madison acceded to this concern, but argued that the concern would be satisfied by language that ultimately became the text of the Ninth Amendment once the Bill of Rights was proposed and ratified, soon after the Constitution itself was ratified.

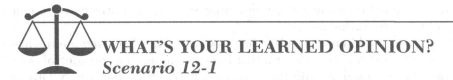

WHAT'S YOUR LEARNED OPINION?
Scenario 12-1

Lloyd Mallan was arrested in the parking lot of a restaurant after police officers, attracted by the odor of burning marijuana, found a partially burnt marijuana cigarette in Mallan's automobile. Mallan was charged with promoting a detrimental drug, in violation of a state statute. Mallan argues that he was pursuing his sense of happiness and that he thought he could enjoy that happiness in privacy because no one was around. Mallan argues that the right to smoke marijuana is protected by the right to privacy. Does *Griswold v. Connecticut* add any support for Mallan's claim?

In *Eisenstadt v. Baird* (1972), the Court extended *Griswold's* holding, the right to possess contraception, to unmarried persons. As Justice Brennan stated in the majority's opinion in *Eisenstadt*, "If the right of privacy means anything, it is the right of the individual, married or single, to be free from unwarranted governmental intrusion into matters so fundamentally affecting a person as the decision whether to bear or beget a child."

Griswold and *Eisenstadt* set a trajectory for the Court to recognize further restrictions on government intrusion into individual reproductive choices and set the stage for the next well-known and much anticipated abortion case, *Roe v. Wade.* Although the question of providing more protections for a right to abortion was well within public debate, the state-law landscape in place at the time that the Court decided *Roe* was generally quite hostile to such a right. Indeed, when *Roe* was handed down, many states in the United States had sweeping prohibitions on abortion procedures. In fact, the particular statutory form at issue in *Roe* was not unusual: an outright prohibition of all abortions except those necessary "for the purpose of saving the life of the mother."

In evaluating what the Court decided in *Roe*, consider some of the many possible approaches the Court could have embraced in disposing of the constitutionality of the Texas prohibition. Here are a few choices:[1]

- The Court could have decided that the decision when life begins is not settled, and that even a decision not to act to make possible the joinder of egg and sperm is a decision that deprives life from developing. For this reason, the government has no appropriate role to play in deciding whether a pregnancy may be terminated.
- The Court could have decided that the joinder of egg and sperm—resulting in conception—creates a person within the meaning of the Fourteenth Amendment, hence shrouding such a "person" with protection from

deprivation of their life without due process or from deprivation of equal protection of the laws.

■ The Court could have decided that a person who is carrying a fetus has complete bodily autonomy and that the government has no control over what the person does with the fetus until it is outside the womb. Otherwise, government would be forcing childbearing individuals to serve as incubators. The government may act to protect the fetus only once it is outside the womb.

■ The Court could have emphasized that given the disparity among state laws regulating abortion as well as the disparity among the laws of other countries, wealthier childbearing individuals can access abortion more readily than poorer childbearing individuals. Similar disparities exist among different racial groups. This inequality could potentially amount to a denial of equal protection of the laws—particularly when viewed in light of the impact of childbearing and childrearing between individuals with childbearing capacity and those lacking that capacity.

■ The Court could have decided that government has no business interfering with the decision of whether a childbearing individual may terminate a pregnancy so long as the termination procedure is performed safely under the circumstances and the fetus is unable to live outside the womb, even with the assistance of medical technology.

As you read the Court's opinion, evaluate which approach the Court chose and whether the approach chosen best comports with the most important, clear constitutional guarantees implicated.

FROM THE BENCH

ROE v. WADE
410 U.S. 113 (1973)

Mr. Justice BLACKMUN delivered the opinion of the Court.

This Texas federal appeal and its Georgia companion, *Doe v. Bolton*, present constitutional challenges to state criminal abortion legislation. The Texas statutes under attack here are typical of those that have been in effect in many States for approximately a century. The Georgia statutes, in contrast, have a modern cast and are a legislative product that, to an extent at least, obviously reflects the influences of recent attitudinal change, of advancing medical knowledge and techniques, and of new thinking about an old issue.

We forthwith acknowledge our awareness of the sensitive and emotional nature of the abortion controversy, of the vigorous opposing views, even among physicians, and of the deep and seemingly absolute convictions that the subject inspires. One's philosophy, one's experiences, one's exposure to the raw edges of human existence, one's religious training, one's attitudes toward life and family and their values, and the moral standards one establishes and seeks to observe, are all likely to influence and to color one's thinking and conclusions about abortion.

In addition, population growth, pollution, poverty, and racial overtones tend to complicate and not to simplify the problem.

Our task, of course, is to resolve the issue by constitutional measurement, free of emotion and of predilection. We seek earnestly to do this, and, because we do, we have inquired into, and in this opinion place some emphasis upon, medical and medical-legal history and what that history reveals about man's attitudes toward the abortion procedure over the centuries. . . .

I

The Texas statutes that concern us here . . . make it a crime to "procure an abortion," as therein defined, or to attempt one, except with respect to "an abortion procured or attempted by medical advice for the purpose of saving the life of the mother." Similar statutes are in existence in a majority of the States. . . .

II

Jane Roe, a single woman who was residing in Dallas County, Texas, instituted this federal action . . . Roe alleged that she was unmarried and pregnant; that she wished to terminate her pregnancy by an abortion "performed by a competent, licensed physician, under safe, clinical conditions"; that she was unable to get a "legal" abortion in Texas because her life did not appear to be threatened by the continuation of her pregnancy; and that she could not afford to travel to another jurisdiction in order to secure a legal abortion under safe conditions. She claimed that the Texas statutes were unconstitutionally vague and that they abridged her right of personal privacy, protected by the First, Fourth, Fifth, Ninth, and Fourteenth Amendments. By an amendment to her complaint Roe purported to sue "on behalf of herself and all other women" similarly situated. . . .

FROM THE BENCH

VI

It perhaps is not generally appreciated that the restrictive criminal abortion laws in effect in a majority of States today are of relatively recent vintage. Those laws, generally proscribing abortion or its attempt at any time during pregnancy except when necessary to preserve the pregnant woman's life, are not of ancient or even of common-law origin. Instead, they derive from statutory changes effected, for the most part, in the latter half of the 19th century. . . .

. . . In this country, the law in effect in all but a few States until mid-19th century was the pre-existing English common law. Connecticut, the first State to enact abortion legislation, adopted in 1821 that part of Lord Ellenborough's Act that related to a woman "quick with child." . . . By 1840, when Texas had received the common law, only eight American States had statutes dealing with abortion. It was not until after the War Between the States that legislation began generally to replace the common law. Most of these initial statutes dealt severely with abortion after quickening but were lenient with it before quickening. . . .

Gradually, in the middle and late 19th century the quickening distinction disappeared from the statutory law of most States and the degree of the offense and the penalties were increased. By the end of the 1950's a large majority of the jurisdictions banned abortion, however and whenever performed, unless done to save or preserve the life of the mother. The exceptions, Alabama and the District of Columbia, permitted abortion to preserve the mother's health. . . . In the past several years, however, a trend toward liberalization of abortion statutes has resulted in adoption, by about one-third of the States, of less stringent laws . . .

It is thus apparent that at common law, at the time of the adoption of our Constitution, and throughout the major portion of the 19th century, abortion was viewed with less disfavor than under most American statutes currently in effect. Phrasing it another way, a woman enjoyed a substantially broader right to terminate a pregnancy than she does in most States today. . . .

VII

Three reasons have been advanced to explain historically the enactment of criminal abortion laws in the 19th century and to justify their continued existence.

It has been argued occasionally that these laws were the product of a Victorian social concern to discourage illicit sexual conduct. Texas, however, does not advance this justification in the present case, and it appears that no court or commentator has taken the argument seriously. . . .

A second reason is concerned with abortion as a medical procedure. When most criminal abortion laws were first enacted, the procedure was a hazardous one for the woman. . . . Abortion mortality was high. . . . Thus, it has been argued that a State's real concern in enacting a criminal abortion law was to protect the pregnant woman, that is, to restrain her from submitting to a procedure that placed her life in serious jeopardy.

Modern medical techniques have altered this situation. Appellants and various amici refer to medical data indicating that abortion in early pregnancy, that is, prior to the end of the first trimester, although not without its risk, is now relatively safe. Mortality rates for women undergoing early abortions, where the procedure is legal, appear to be as low as or lower than the rates for normal childbirth. Consequently, any interest of the State in protecting the woman from an inherently hazardous procedure, except when it would be equally dangerous for her to forgo it, has largely disappeared. Of course, important state interests in the areas of health and medical standards do remain. The State has a legitimate interest in seeing to it that abortion, like any other medical procedure, is performed under circumstances that insure maximum safety for the patient. This interest obviously extends at least to the performing physician and his staff, to the facilities involved, to the availability of after-care, and to adequate provision for any complication or emergency that might arise. . . . Moreover, the risk to the woman increases as her pregnancy continues. Thus, the State retains a definite interest in protecting the woman's own health and safety when an abortion is proposed at a late stage of pregnancy,

The third reason is the State's interest — some phrase it in terms of duty — in protecting prenatal life. Some of the argument for this justification rests on the theory that a new human life is present from the moment of conception. The State's interest and general obligation to protect life then extends, it is argued, to prenatal life. Only when the life of the pregnant mother herself is at stake, balanced against the life she carries within her, should the interest of the embryo or fetus not prevail. Logically, of course, a legitimate state interest in this area need not stand or fall on acceptance of the belief that life begins at conception or at some other point prior to life birth. In assessing the State's interest, recognition may be given to the less rigid claim that as long as at least potential life is involved, the State may assert interests beyond the protection of the pregnant woman alone. . . .

It is with these interests, and the weight to be attached to them, that this case is concerned.

VIII

The Constitution does not explicitly mention any right of privacy. In a line of decisions, however, going back perhaps as far as *Union Pacific R. Co. v. Botsford* (1891), the Court has recognized that a right of personal privacy, or a guarantee of certain areas or zones of privacy, does exist under the Constitution. . . . These decisions make it clear that only personal rights that can be deemed "fundamental" or "implicit in the concept of ordered liberty," *Palko v. Connecticut* (1937), are included in this guarantee of personal privacy. . . .

This right of privacy, whether it be founded in the Fourteenth Amendment's concept of personal liberty and restrictions upon state action, as we feel it is, or, as the District Court determined, in the Ninth Amendment's reservation of rights to the people, is broad enough to encompass a woman's decision whether or not to terminate her pregnancy. The detriment that the State would impose upon the pregnant woman by denying this choice altogether is apparent. Specific and direct harm medically diagnosable even in early pregnancy may be involved. Maternity, or additional offspring, may force upon the woman a distressful life and future. Psychological harm may be imminent. Mental and physical health may be taxed by child care. There is also the distress, for all concerned, associated with the unwanted child, and there is the problem of bringing a child into a family already unable, psychologically and otherwise, to care for it. In other cases, as in this one, the additional difficulties and continuing stigma of unwed motherhood may be involved. All these are factors the woman and her responsible physician necessarily will consider in consultation.

On the basis of elements such as these, appellant and some amici argue that the woman's right is absolute and that she is entitled to terminate her pregnancy at whatever time, in whatever way, and for whatever reason she alone chooses. With this we do not agree. Appellant's arguments that Texas either has no valid interest at all in regulating the abortion decision, or no interest strong enough to support any limitation upon the woman's sole determination, are unpersuasive. The Court's decisions recognizing a right of privacy also acknowledge that some state regulation in areas protected by that right is appropriate. As noted above, a State may properly assert important interests in safeguarding health, in maintaining medical standards, and in protecting potential life. At some point in pregnancy, these respective interests become sufficiently compelling to sustain regulation of the factors that govern the abortion decision. The privacy right involved, therefore, cannot be said to be absolute. In fact, it is not clear to us that the claim asserted by some amici that one has an unlimited right to do with one's body as one pleases bears a close relationship to the right of privacy previously articulated in the Court's decisions. The Court has refused to recognize an unlimited right of this kind in the past.

We, therefore, conclude that the right of personal privacy includes the abortion decision, but that this right is not unqualified and must be considered against important state interests in regulation. . . .

Where certain "fundamental rights" are involved, the Court has held that regulation limiting these rights may be justified only by a "compelling state interest," and that legislative enactments must be narrowly drawn to express only the legitimate state interests at stake. . . .

IX

A. The appellee and certain amici argue that the fetus is a "person" within the language and meaning of the Fourteenth Amendment. In support of this, they outline at length and in detail the well-known facts of fetal development. If this suggestion of personhood is established, the appellant's case, of course, collapses, for the fetus' right to life would then be guaranteed specifically by the Amendment. . . . The Constitution does not define "person" in so many words. . . . [T]he word "person," as used in the Fourteenth Amendment, does not include the unborn. This is in accord with the results reached in those few cases where the issue has been squarely presented. . . .

This conclusion, however, does not of itself fully answer the contentions raised by Texas, and we pass on to other considerations.

B. The pregnant woman cannot be isolated in her privacy. She carries an embryo and, later, a fetus, if one accepts the medical definitions of the developing young in the human uterus. The situation therefore is inherently different from marital intimacy, or bedroom possession of obscene material, or marriage, or procreation, or education[.] . . . As we have intimated above, it is reasonable and appropriate for a State to decide that at some point in time another interest, that of health of the mother or that of potential human life, becomes significantly involved. The woman's privacy is no longer sole and any right of privacy she possesses must be measured accordingly.

Texas urges that, apart from the Fourteenth Amendment, life begins at conception and is present throughout pregnancy, and that, therefore, the State has a compelling interest in protecting that life from and after conception. We need not resolve the difficult question of when life begins. When those trained in the respective disciplines of medicine, philosophy, and theology are unable to arrive at any consensus, the judiciary, at this point in the development of man's knowledge, is not in a position to speculate as to the answer. . . .

X

In view of all this, we do not agree that, by adopting one theory of life, Texas may override the rights of the pregnant woman that are at stake. We repeat, however, that the State does have an important and legitimate interest in preserving and protecting the health of the pregnant woman, whether she be a resident of the State or a non-resident who seeks medical consultation and treatment there, and that it has still another important and legitimate interest in protecting the potentiality of human life. These interests are separate and distinct. Each grows in substantiality as the woman approaches term and, at a point during pregnancy, each becomes "compelling."

With respect to the State's important and legitimate interest in the health of the mother, the "compelling" point, in the light of present medical knowledge,

FROM THE BENCH

is at approximately the end of the first trimester. This is so because of the now-established medical fact . . . that until the end of the first trimester mortality in abortion may be less than mortality in normal childbirth. It follows that, from and after this point, a State may regulate the abortion procedure to the extent that the regulation reasonably relates to the preservation and protection of maternal health. Examples of permissible state regulation in this area are requirements as to the qualifications of the person who is to perform the abortion; as to the licensure of that person; as to the facility in which the procedure is to be performed, that is, whether it must be a hospital or may be a clinic or some other place of less-than-hospital status; as to the licensing of the facility; and the like.

This means, on the other hand, that, for the period of pregnancy prior to this "compelling" point, the attending physician, in consultation with his patient, is free to determine, without regulation by the State, that, in his medical judgment, the patient's pregnancy should be terminated. If that decision is reached, the judgment may be effectuated by an abortion free of interference by the State.

With respect to the State's important and legitimate interest in potential life, the "compelling" point is at viability. This is so because the fetus then presumably has the capability of meaningful life outside the mother's womb. . . . If the State is interested in protecting fetal life after viability, it may go so far as to proscribe abortion during that period, except when it is necessary to preserve the life or health of the mother.

Measured against these standards, Art. 1196 of the Texas Penal Code, in restricting legal abortions to those "procured or attempted by medical advice for the purpose of saving the life of the mother," sweeps too broadly. The statute makes no distinction between abortions performed early in pregnancy and those performed later, and it limits to a single reason, "saving" the mother's life, the legal justification for the procedure. The statute, therefore, cannot survive the constitutional attack made upon it here. . . .

XI

To summarize and to repeat:

1. A state criminal abortion statute of the current Texas type, that excepts from criminality only a life-saving procedure on behalf of the mother, without regard to pregnancy stage and without recognition of the other interests involved, is violative of the Due Process Clause of the Fourteenth Amendment.

(a) For the stage prior to approximately the end of the first trimester, the abortion decision and its effectuation must be left to the medical judgment of the pregnant woman's attending physician.

(b) For the stage subsequent to approximately the end of the first trimester, the State, in promoting its interest in the health of the mother, may, if it chooses, regulate the abortion procedure in ways that are reasonably related to maternal health.

(c) For the stage subsequent to viability, the State in promoting its interest in the potentiality of human life may, if it chooses, regulate, and even proscribe, abortion except where it is necessary, in appropriate medical judgment, for the preservation of the life or health of the mother. . . .

This holding, we feel, is consistent with the relative weights of the respective interests involved, with the lessons and examples of medical and legal history, with the lenity of the common law, and with the demands of the profound problems of the present day. The decision leaves the State free to place increasing restrictions on abortion as the period of pregnancy lengthens, so long as those restrictions are tailored to the recognized state interests. The decision vindicates the right of the physician to administer medical treatment according to his professional judgment up to the points where important state interests provide compelling justifications for intervention. Up to those points, the abortion decision in all its aspects is inherently, and primarily, a medical decision, and basic responsibility for it must rest with the physician. If an individual practitioner abuses the privilege of exercising proper medical judgment, the usual remedies, judicial and intra-professional, are available.

Mr. Justice REHNQUIST, dissenting.

The Court's opinion brings to the decision of this troubling question both extensive historical fact and a wealth of legal scholarship. While the opinion thus commands my respect, I find myself nonetheless in fundamental disagreement with those parts of it that invalidate the Texas statute in question, and therefore dissent.

. . . I have difficulty in concluding, as the Court does, that the right of "privacy" is involved in this case. Texas, by the statute here challenged, bars the performance of a medical abortion by a licensed physician on a plaintiff such as Roe. A transaction resulting in an operation such as this is not "private" in the ordinary usage of that word. Nor is the "privacy" that the Court finds here even a distant relative of the freedom from searches and seizures protected by the Fourth Amendment to the Constitution, which the Court has referred to as embodying a right to privacy.

. . . If the Court means by the term "privacy" no more than that the claim of a person to be free from unwanted state regulation of consensual transactions may be a form of "liberty" protected by the Fourteenth Amendment, there is no doubt that similar claims have been upheld in our earlier decisions on the basis of that liberty. . . . But that liberty is not guaranteed absolutely against deprivation, only against deprivation without due process of law. The test traditionally applied in the area of social and economic legislation is whether or not a law such as that challenged has a rational relation to a valid state objective. The Due Process Clause of the Fourteenth Amendment undoubtedly does place a limit, albeit a broad one, on legislative power to enact laws such as this. If the Texas statute were to prohibit an abortion even where the mother's life is in jeopardy,

FROM THE BENCH

I have little doubt that such a statute would lack a rational relation to a valid state objective. . . . But the Court's sweeping invalidation of any restrictions on abortion during the first trimester is impossible to justify under that standard, and the conscious weighing of competing factors that the Court's opinion apparently substitutes for the established test is far more appropriate to a legislative judgment than to a judicial one. . . . The fact that a majority of the States reflecting, after all the majority sentiment in those States, have had restrictions on abortions for at least a century is a strong indication, it seems to me, that the asserted right to an abortion is not "so rooted in the traditions and conscience of our people as to be ranked as fundamental[.]" Even today, when society's views on abortion are changing, the very existence of the debate is evidence that the "right" to an abortion is not so universally accepted as the appellant would have us believe.

. . . For all of the foregoing reasons, I respectfully dissent.

QUESTIONS FOR DISCUSSION

12.6 What is the relevance of the fact that most states had significant abortion prohibitions in their state statutes at the time the Court handed down *Roe*? Does that fact render the *Roe* decision more legitimate or less legitimate? What does that state legislative landscape at the time suggest about the role of the Supreme Court in governing the citizens of the United States and ensuring that they fully enjoy their civil liberties? Does it suggest that the Court's role as the interpreter of the Constitution is particularly crucial as a check against "the tyranny of the majority" reflected in state legislation? Or does it suggest that the Court was overly activist—injecting its own personal views into a controversial issue?

12.7 Did the majority opinion in *Roe* provide clear guidance to state legislatures about restrictions on abortion during the various stages of pregnancy? The Court's "bottom line" is that some abortion access is constitutionally protected. Assuming the validity of this bottom line, was the Court's guidance well-constructed?

12.8 Why did then-Justice Rehnquist assert that the level of scrutiny for evaluating the Texas statute should be the most deferential: rational basis. In so arguing, he concluded that a person's desire to have an abortion should not be considered a right. Do you agree with that reasoning? Does the observation that pregnancy and childrearing tend to impact women more than others call for a more rigorous analysis of an abortion restriction?

12.9 The Court stated that it did not resolve the age-old question of when life begins to decide the case. Some commentators argue that, despite this statement, the Court effectively did decide when life begins. Do you agree?

12.10 As mentioned in the introduction to this section, the Justices have disagreed on where (if anywhere) in the Constitution rights concerning reproduction are grounded. Are you satisfied with how Justice Blackmun handled that question?

12.11 When defending the Texas abortion restriction at oral argument before the U.S. Supreme Court, the lawyer arguing on behalf of the state of Texas began by referencing the two young female civil rights attorneys on the other side (who argued the restriction was unconstitutional): "It's an old joke, but when a man argues against two beautiful ladies like this, they are going to have the last word." If one listens to the transcript of the argument, one hears nothing but silence—dead silence—following that introductory joke. In other words, the joke was a flop. Is it ever appropriate for an attorney to make a joke in a court proceeding?

WHAT'S YOUR LEARNED OPINION?
Scenario 12-2

On March 21, 1974, the Minnesota abortion law, passed in response to the decision of the Supreme Court in *Roe v. Wade*, was signed into law. The law incorporates the concept of "potential viability" into the definition of viability. The law states: "'Viable' means able to live outside the womb even though artificial aid may be required. During the second half of its gestation period a fetus shall be considered potentially viable."

The law also states that:

It shall be unlawful to perform an abortion when the fetus is potentially viable unless:

> (1) the abortion is performed in a hospital;
> (2) the attending physician certifies in writing that in his best medical judgment the abortion is necessary to preserve the life or health of the pregnant woman; and
> (3) to the extent consistent with sound medical practice the abortion is performed under circumstances which will reasonably assure the live birth and survival of the fetus.

In light of the Court's decision in *Roe v. Wade*, is the law constitutional?

BEHIND THE CURTAIN

Much ink has been spilled on the history of abortion in the United States. Most historians agree, however, that before the 1860s abortion was practiced widely—practiced as a private matter between a pregnant woman and a midwife. Even the Catholic Church did not oppose abortion before quickening, the time when a pregnant person feels fetal movement. Physician groups (including the American Medical Association) supported safely performed abortions as a necessary option to preserve a woman's physical and mental health. Thereafter, opposition to abortion increased—not necessarily out of concern with preserving potential human life—but rather out of concern with chastity and sexual licentiousness.

Various social forces thereafter increased criminalization efforts focused on abortion. Negative medical reactions to so-called back-alley abortions increased the prohibition efforts. Nonetheless, with the liberalization of sexual attitudes and the economic realities of the Great Depression beginning with the stock market crash of 1929, more physicians were willing to perform illegal abortions. The pendulum swung again after World War II and the retreat of women from the labor market. The rise of general social conservatism on gender roles strengthened the legislative condemnation of abortion.

Yet the pendulum started to reverse direction in the late 1950s and early 1960s. Interestingly, an elite legal organization known as the American Law Institute drafted model laws endorsing liberalization of abortion laws. At the end of the 1960s, legislative reform activity increased, with reform bills being introduced into more than half of the U.S. state legislatures. Several states, including Arkansas, Delaware, Georgia, Kansas, Maryland, and Oregon, passed liberalized laws. Controversy flourished, with the women's liberation movement urging legalization of abortion on one hand, and groups such as the Catholic Church clashing with these groups on the other. Meanwhile, court battles over prohibitions against abortions burgeoned—many of which proved unsuccessful. Ultimately, however, two young female lawyers, Sarah Weddington and Linda Coffee, convinced the U.S. Supreme Court to take on the issue in a case they filed on behalf of a pregnant woman, Norma McGarvey, under the name of "Jane Roe."[2]

Following *Roe*, a cat-and-mouse game began between courts (mostly federal) and state legislatures. States could be creative in requiring preconditions and obstacles before a woman could obtain an abortion. Some requirements focused on the consent required: Spouses or parents of minors had to be notified of a person's desire to have an abortion. Other requirements focused on information to be shared with a person seeking an abortion: details on the bodily characteristics of the fetus to be aborted, graphic photographs, and the like. Waiting periods after abortion care were initially sought—a requirement that often increased the cost of abortions—as another restriction. Later restrictions focused on abortion providers themselves: Examples included requiring abortions only in expensive medical facilities, hospital admitting privileges for doctors, and detailed specifications on how the abortion procedure must be followed (without regard to the effect of the procedure used on the health of the mother).

For a time, the U.S. Supreme Court handled each of these restrictions individually. Ultimately, however, the Court reaffirmed, but modified, *Roe's* teachings in *Planned Parenthood v. Casey*, 505 U.S. 833 (1992). To begin with, the Court maintained the focus on viability as the appropriate point at which a state could prohibit abortion altogether but rejected *Roe's* adherence to a trimester approach to regulating abortion, noting that ever-advancing technology moved the point of viability and improved safety issues.

In an unusual opinion jointly written by three Justices, the Court also announced a new standard for evaluating the constitutionality of restrictions on abortion. Specifically, the Court eliminated the strict scrutiny standard for evaluating restrictions, replacing it with an "undue burden" test. According to the *Casey* decision, a court evaluating the constitutionality of a restriction was to ask whether a regulation of abortion before viability placed an undue burden on a person's right to terminate an early pregnancy. The decision explained that a burden should be deemed "undue" if the government acted with the purpose or effect of discouraging abortion before viability.

Fights over abortion restrictions continued after the *Casey* case, and highly charged rhetoric flourished. For example, state and federal statutes referred to a "partial birth abortions," and the Court conjectured on the negative effect of abortions on a person's psychological well-being following their visit to gynecologists, referred to by the Court as "abortion doctors."[3]

Such was the state of affairs when a turn of fate and political wrangling enabled President Donald Trump to appoint three Justices to the U.S. Supreme Court who were known for their opposition to abortion. This change in the Court's composition created a super-majority of justices prepared to overrule *Roe* and *Casey's* recognition of previability abortion as a fundamental constitutional guarantee. Some state legislatures swiftly responded with statutes that appeared to violate the dictates of *Roe* and *Casey*. Challenges to these statutes began to wend their way through the lower courts, and it was the following case, *Dobbs v. Jackson Women's Health Organization*, that ultimately served as the vehicle for overruling *Roe* and *Casey*.

FROM THE BENCH

DOBBS v. JACKSON WOMEN'S HEALTH ORGANIZATION
142 S. Ct. 2228 (2022)

Justice ALITO delivered the opinion of the Court.

The State of Mississippi asks us to uphold the constitutionality of a law that generally prohibits an abortion after the 15th week of pregnancy—several weeks before the point at which a fetus is now regarded as "viable" outside the womb. In defending this law, the State's primary argument is that we should reconsider and overrule *Roe* and *Casey* and once again allow each State to regulate abortion as its citizens wish.

We hold that *Roe* and *Casey* must be overruled. The Constitution makes no reference to abortion, and no such right is implicitly protected by any constitutional provision, including the one on which the defenders of *Roe* and *Casey* now chiefly rely—the Due Process Clause of the Fourteenth Amendment.

It is time to heed the Constitution and return the issue of abortion to the people's elected representatives. "The permissibility of abortion, and the limitations, upon it, are to be resolved like most important questions in our democracy: by citizens trying to persuade one another and then voting." That is what the Constitution and the rule of law demand.

The law at issue in this case, Mississippi's Gestational Age Act, contains this central provision: "Except in a medical emergency or in the case of a severe fetal abnormality, a person shall not intentionally or knowingly perform . . . or induce an abortion of an unborn human being if the probable gestational age of the unborn human being has been determined to be greater than fifteen (15) weeks."

We begin by considering the critical question whether the Constitution, properly understood, confers a right to obtain an abortion. First, we explain the standard that our cases have used in determining whether the Fourteenth Amendment's reference to "liberty" protects a particular right. Second, we examine whether the right at issue in this case is rooted in our Nation's history and tradition and whether it is an essential component of what we have described as "ordered liberty." Finally, we consider whether a right to obtain an abortion is part of a broader entrenched right that is supported by other precedents.

Constitutional analysis must begin with "the language of the instrument," which offers a "fixed standard" for ascertaining what our founding document means. The Constitution makes no express reference to a right to obtain an abortion, and therefore those who claim that it protects such a right must show that the right is somehow implicit in the constitutional text.

Roe, however, was remarkably loose in its treatment of the constitutional text. It held that the abortion right, which is not mentioned in the Constitution, is part of a right to privacy, which is also not mentioned. The underlying theory on which this argument rests — that the Fourteenth Amendment's Due Process Clause provides substantive, as well as procedural, protection for "liberty" — has long been controversial. But our decisions have held that the Due Process Clause protects two categories of substantive rights.

The first consists of rights guaranteed by the first eight Amendments. Those Amendments originally applied only to the Federal Government, but this Court has held that the Due Process Clause of the Fourteenth Amendment "incorporates" the great majority of those rights and thus makes them equally applicable to the States. The second category — which is the one in question here — comprises a select list of fundamental rights that are not mentioned anywhere in the Constitution.

Not only was there no support for such a constitutional right until shortly before *Roe*, but abortion had long been a *crime* in every single State. At common law, abortion was criminal in at least some stages of pregnancy and was regarded as unlawful and could have very serious consequences at all stages. American law followed the common law until a wave of statutory restrictions in the 1800s expanded criminal liability for abortions. By the time of the adoption of the Fourteenth Amendment, three-quarters of the States had made abortion a crime at any stage of pregnancy, and the remaining States would soon follow. *Roe* either ignored or misstated this history, and *Casey* declined to reconsider *Roe*'s faulty historical analysis. It is therefore important to set the record straight.

We begin with the common law, under which abortion was a crime at least after "quickening" — *i.e.*, the first felt movement of the fetus in the womb, which usually occurs between the 16th and 18th week of pregnancy. The "eminent common-law authorities (Blackstone, Coke, Hale, and the like)," *all* describe abortion after quickening as criminal. Henry de Bracton's 13th-century treatise explained that if a person has "struck a pregnant woman, or has given her poison, whereby he has caused abortion, if the foetus be already formed and animated, and particularly if it be animated, he commits homicide."

Sir Edward Coke's 17th-century treatise likewise asserted that abortion of a quick child was "murder" if the "childe be born alive" and a "great misprision" if the "childe dieth in her body." Two treatises by Sir Matthew Hale likewise described abortion of a quick child who died in the womb as a "great crime" and a "great misprision." And writing near the time of the adoption of our Constitution, William Blackstone explained that abortion of a "quick" child was "by the ancient law homicide or manslaughter," and at least a very "heinous misdemeanor." English cases dating all the way back to the 13th century corroborate the treatises' statements that abortion was a crime. In sum, although common-law authorities differed on the severity of punishment for abortions committed at different points in pregnancy, none endorsed the practice. Moreover, we are aware of no common-law case or authority, and the parties have not pointed to any, that remotely suggests a positive *right* to procure an abortion at any stage of pregnancy.

In this country during the 19th century, the vast majority of the States enacted statutes criminalizing abortion at all stages of pregnancy. By 1868, the year when the Fourteenth Amendment was ratified, three-quarters of the States, 28 out of 37, had enacted statutes making abortion a crime even if it was performed before quickening. Of the nine States that had not yet criminalized abortion at all stages, all but one did so by 1910.

This overwhelming consensus endured until the day *Roe* was decided. At that time, also by the *Roe* Court's own count, a substantial majority—30 States—still prohibited abortion at all stages except to save the life of the mother. And though *Roe* discerned a "trend toward liberalization" in about "one-third of the States," those States still criminalized some abortions and regulated them more stringently than *Roe* would allow. In short, the "Court's opinion in *Roe* itself convincingly refutes the notion that the abortion liberty is deeply rooted in the history or tradition of our people."

The inescapable conclusion is that a right to abortion is not deeply rooted in the Nation's history and traditions. On the contrary, an unbroken tradition of prohibiting abortion on pain of criminal punishment persisted from the earliest days of the common law until 1973.

The Solicitor General suggests that history supports an abortion right because the common law's failure to criminalize abortion before quickening means that "at the Founding and for decades thereafter, women generally could terminate a pregnancy, at least in its early stages." But the insistence on quickening was not universal, and regardless, the fact that many States in the late 18th and early 19th century did not criminalize pre-quickening abortions does not mean that anyone thought the States lacked the authority to do so.

Instead of seriously pressing the argument that the abortion right itself has deep roots, supporters of *Roe* and *Casey* contend that the abortion right is an integral part of a broader entrenched right. *Roe* termed this a right to privacy, and *Casey* described it as the freedom to make "intimate and personal choices" that are "central to personal dignity and autonomy." *Casey* elaborated: "At the heart of liberty is the right to define one's own concept of existence, of meaning, of the universe, and of the mystery of human life."

The Court did not claim that this broadly framed right is absolute, and no such claim would be plausible. While individuals are certainly free *to think* and *to say* what they wish about "existence," "meaning," the "universe," and "the mystery of human life," they are not always free *to act* in accordance with those thoughts. License to act on the basis of such beliefs may correspond to one of the many understandings of "liberty," but it is certainly not "ordered liberty."

These attempts to justify abortion through appeals to a broader right to autonomy and to define one's "concept of existence" prove too much. Those criteria, at a high level of generality, could license fundamental rights to illicit drug use, prostitution, and the like. None of these rights has any claim to being deeply rooted in history.

What sharply distinguishes the abortion right from the rights recognized in the cases on which *Roe* and *Casey* rely is something that both those decisions acknowledged: Abortion destroys what those decisions call "potential life" and what the law at issue in this case regards as the life of an "unborn human being." None of the other decisions cited by *Roe* and *Casey* involved the critical moral question posed by abortion. They are therefore inapposite. They do not support the right to obtain an abortion, and by the same token, our conclusion that the Constitution does not confer such a right does not undermine them in any way.

Defenders of *Roe* and *Casey* do not claim that any new scientific learning calls for a different answer to the underlying moral question, but they do contend that changes in society require the recognition of a constitutional right to obtain an abortion. Without the availability of abortion, they maintain, people will be inhibited from exercising their freedom to choose the types of relationships they desire, and women will be unable to compete with men in the workplace and in other endeavors.

Americans who believe that abortion should be restricted press countervailing arguments about modern developments. They note that attitudes about the pregnancy of unmarried women have changed drastically; that federal and state laws ban discrimination on the basis of pregnancy; that leave for pregnancy and childbirth are now guaranteed by law in many cases; that the costs of medical care associated with pregnancy are covered by insurance or government assistance; that States have increasingly adopted "safe haven" laws, which generally allow women to drop off babies anonymously; and that a woman who puts her newborn up for adoption today has little reason to fear that the baby will not find a suitable home. They also claim that many people now have a new appreciation of fetal life and that when prospective parents who want to have a child view a sonogram, they typically have no doubt that what they see is their daughter or son.

Both sides make important policy arguments, but supporters of *Roe* and *Casey* must show that this Court has the authority to weigh those arguments and decide how abortion may be regulated in the States. They have failed to make that showing, and we thus return the power to weigh those arguments to the people and their elected representatives.

We next consider whether the doctrine of *stare decisis* counsels continued acceptance of *Roe* and *Casey*. *Stare decisis* plays an important role in our case law, and we have explained that it serves many valuable ends. It protects the interests of those who have taken action in reliance on a past decision. It "reduces incentives for challenging settled precedents, saving parties and courts the expense of endless relitigation." It fosters "evenhanded" decision making by requiring that like cases be decided in a like manner. It "contributes to the actual and perceived integrity of the judicial process." And it restrains judicial hubris and reminds us to respect the judgment of those who have grappled with important questions in the past. "Precedent is a way of accumulating and passing down the learning of past generations, a font of established wisdom richer than what can be found in any single judge or panel of judges."

We have long recognized, however, that *stare decisis* is "not an inexorable command." It has been said that it is sometimes more important that an issue "'be settled than that it be settled right.'" But when it comes to the interpretation of the Constitution—the "great charter of our liberties," which was meant "to endure through a long lapse of ages,"—we place a high value on having the matter "settled right." In addition, when one of our constitutional decisions goes astray, the country is usually stuck with the bad decision unless we correct our own mistake. An erroneous constitutional decision can be fixed by amending the Constitution, but our Constitution is notoriously hard to amend. Therefore, in appropriate circumstances we must be willing to reconsider and, if necessary, overrule constitutional decisions.

No Justice of this Court has ever argued that the Court should *never* overrule a constitutional decision, but overruling a precedent is a serious matter. It is not a step that should be taken lightly. Our cases have attempted to provide a framework for deciding when a precedent should be overruled, and they have identified factors that should be considered in making such a decision.

In this case, five factors weigh strongly in favor of overruling *Roe* and *Casey*: the nature of their error, the quality of their reasoning, the "workability" of the rules they imposed on the country, their disruptive effect on other areas of the law, and the absence of concrete reliance.

The nature of the Court's error. An erroneous interpretation of the Constitution is always important, but some are more damaging than others.

Roe was on a collision course with the Constitution from the day it was decided, *Casey* perpetuated its errors, and those errors do not concern some arcane corner of the law of little importance to the American people. Rather, wielding nothing but "raw judicial power," the Court usurped the power to address a question of profound moral and social importance that the Constitution unequivocally leaves for the people. *Casey* described itself as calling both sides of the national controversy to resolve their debate, but in doing so, *Casey* necessarily declared a winning side. Those on the losing side—those who sought to advance the State's interest in fetal life—could no longer seek to persuade their elected representatives to adopt policies consistent with their views. The Court short-circuited the democratic process by closing it to the large number of Americans who dissented in any respect from *Roe*. "*Roe* fanned into life an issue that has inflamed our national politics in general, and has obscured with its smoke the selection of Justices to this Court in particular, ever since." Together, *Roe* and *Casey* represent an error that cannot be allowed to stand.

The quality of the reasoning. Under our precedents, the quality of the reasoning in a prior case has an important bearing on whether it should be reconsidered.

Roe found that the Constitution implicitly conferred a right to obtain an abortion, but it failed to ground its decision in text, history, or precedent. It relied on an erroneous historical narrative; it devoted great attention to and presumably relied on matters that have no bearing on the meaning of the Constitution; it disregarded the fundamental difference between the precedents on which it relied and the question before the Court; it concocted an elaborate set of rules, with different restrictions for each trimester of pregnancy, but it did not explain how this veritable code could be teased out of anything in the Constitution, the history of abortion laws, prior precedent, or any other cited source; and its most important rule (that States cannot protect fetal life prior to "viability") was never raised by any party and has never been plausibly explained. *Roe*'s reasoning quickly drew scathing scholarly criticism, even from supporters of broad access to abortion.

The *Casey* plurality, while reaffirming *Roe*'s central holding, pointedly refrained from endorsing most of its reasoning. It revised the textual basis for the abortion right, silently abandoned *Roe*'s erroneous historical narrative, and jettisoned the trimester framework. But it replaced that scheme with an arbitrary "undue burden" test and relied on an exceptional version of *stare decisis* that, as explained below, this Court had never before applied and has never invoked since.

An even more glaring deficiency was *Roe*'s failure to justify the critical distinction it drew between pre- and post-viability abortions. Here is the Court's entire explanation:

"With respect to the State's important and legitimate interest in potential life, the 'compelling' point is at viability. This is so because the fetus then presumably has the capability of meaningful life outside the womb."

Casey either refused to reaffirm or rejected important aspects of *Roe*'s analysis, failed to remedy glaring deficiencies in *Roe*'s reasoning, endorsed what it termed *Roe*'s central holding while suggesting that a majority might not have thought it was correct, provided no new support for the abortion right other than *Roe*'s status as precedent, and imposed a new and problematic test with no firm grounding in constitutional text, history, or precedent.

Workability. Our precedents counsel that another important consideration in deciding whether a precedent should be overruled is whether the rule it imposes is workable—that is, whether it can be understood and applied in a consistent and predictable manner. *Casey*'s "undue burden" test has scored poorly on the workability scale.

Problems begin with the very concept of an "undue burden." As Justice Scalia noted in his *Casey* partial dissent, determining whether a burden is "due" or "undue" is "inherently standardless."

FROM THE BENCH

Casey has generated a long list of Circuit conflicts. Most recently, the Courts of Appeals have disagreed about whether the balancing test from *Whole Woman's Health* correctly states the undue-burden framework. They have disagreed on the legality of parental notification rules. They have disagreed about bans on certain dilation and evacuation procedures. They have disagreed about when an increase in the time needed to reach a clinic constitutes an undue burden. And they have disagreed on whether a State may regulate abortions performed because of the fetus's race, sex, or disability.

Effect on other areas of law. *Roe* and *Casey* have led to the distortion of many important but unrelated legal doctrines, and that effect provides further support for overruling those decisions.

The Court's abortion cases have diluted the strict standard for facial constitutional challenges. They have ignored the Court's third-party standing doctrine. They have disregarded standard *res judicata* principles. They have flouted the ordinary rules on the severability of unconstitutional provisions, as well as the rule that statutes should be read where possible to avoid unconstitutionality. And they have distorted First Amendment doctrines. When vindicating a doctrinal innovation requires courts to engineer exceptions to longstanding background rules, the doctrine "has failed to deliver the 'principled and intelligible' development of the law that *stare decisis* purports to secure."

Reliance interests. We last consider whether overruling *Roe* and *Casey* will upend substantial reliance interests.

Traditional reliance interests arise "where advance planning of great precision is most obviously a necessity." In *Casey*, the controlling opinion conceded that those traditional reliance interests were not implicated because getting an abortion is generally "unplanned activity," and "reproductive planning could take virtually immediate account of any sudden restoration of state authority to ban abortions." For these reasons, we agree with the *Casey* plurality that conventional, concrete reliance interests are not present here.

When a concrete reliance interest is asserted, courts are equipped to evaluate the claim, but assessing the novel and intangible form of reliance endorsed by the *Casey* plurality is another matter. That form of reliance depends on an empirical question that is hard for anyone — and in particular, for a court — to assess, namely, the effect of the abortion right on society and in particular on the lives of women. The contending sides in this case make impassioned and conflicting arguments about the effects of the abortion right on the lives of women. The contending sides also make conflicting arguments about the status of the fetus. This Court has neither the authority nor the expertise to adjudicate those disputes, and the *Casey* plurality's speculations and weighing of the relative importance of the fetus and mother represent a departure from the "original constitutional proposition" that "courts do not substitute their social and economic beliefs for the judgment of legislative bodies."

Our decision returns the issue of abortion to those legislative bodies, and it allows women on both sides of the abortion issue to seek to affect the legislative process by influencing public opinion, lobbying legislators, voting, and running for office. Women are not without electoral or political power. It is noteworthy that the percentage of women who register to vote and cast ballots is consistently higher than the percentage of men who do so. In the last election in November 2020, women, who make up around 51.5 percent of the population of Mississippi, constituted 55.5 percent of the voters who cast ballots.

Having shown that traditional *stare decisis* factors do not weigh in favor of retaining *Roe* or *Casey*, we must address one final argument that featured prominently in the *Casey* plurality opinion.

The argument was cast in different terms, but stated simply, it was essentially as follows. The American people's belief in the rule of law would be shaken if they lost respect for this Court as an institution that decides important cases based on principle, not "social and political pressures." There is a special danger that the public will perceive a decision as having been made for unprincipled reasons when the Court overrules a controversial "watershed" decision, such as *Roe*. A decision overruling *Roe* would be perceived as having been made "under fire" and as a "surrender to political pressure," and therefore the preservation of public approval of the Court weighs heavily in favor of retaining *Roe*.

We do not pretend to know how our political system or society will respond to today's decision overruling *Roe* and *Casey*. And even if we could foresee what will happen, we would have no authority to let that knowledge influence our decision. We can only do our job, which is to interpret the law, apply longstanding principles of *stare decisis*, and decide this case accordingly.

We therefore hold that the Constitution does not confer a right to abortion. *Roe* and *Casey* must be overruled, and the authority to regulate abortion must be returned to the people and their elected representatives.

Finally, the dissent suggests that our decision calls into question *Griswold, Eisenstadt, Lawrence,* and *Obergefell*. But we have stated unequivocally that "[n]othing in this opinion should be understood to cast doubt on precedents that do not concern abortion." We have also explained why that is so: rights regarding contraception and same-sex relationships are inherently different from the right to abortion because the latter (as we have stressed) uniquely involves what *Roe* and *Casey* termed "potential life." Therefore, a right to abortion cannot be justified by a purported analogy to the rights recognized in those other cases or by "appeals to a broader right to autonomy." It is hard to see how we could be clearer. Moreover, even putting aside that these cases are distinguishable, there is a further point that the dissent ignores: Each precedent is subject to its own *stare decisis* analysis, and the factors that our doctrine instructs us to consider like reliance and workability are different for these cases than for our abortion jurisprudence.

The concurrence would "leave for another day whether to reject any right to an abortion at all," but "another day" would not be long in coming. Some States have set deadlines for obtaining an abortion that are shorter than Mississippi's. If we held only that Mississippi's 15-week rule is constitutional, we would soon be called upon to pass on the constitutionality of a panoply of laws with shorter deadlines or no deadline at all. The "measured course" charted by the concurrence would be fraught with turmoil until the Court answered the question that the concurrence seeks to defer.

Under our precedents, rational-basis review is the appropriate standard for such challenges. As we have explained, procuring an abortion is not a fundamental constitutional right because such a right has no basis in the Constitution's text or in our Nation's history. It follows that the States may regulate abortion for legitimate reasons, and when such regulations are challenged under the Constitution, courts cannot "substitute their social and economic beliefs for the judgment of legislative bodies." That respect for a legislature's judgment applies even when the laws at issue concern matters of great social significance and moral substance.

A law regulating abortion, like other health and welfare laws, is entitled to a "strong presumption of validity." It must be sustained if there is a rational basis on which the legislature could have thought that it would serve legitimate state interests. These legitimate interests include respect for and preservation of prenatal life at all stages of development; the protection of maternal health and safety; the elimination of particularly gruesome or barbaric medical procedures; the preservation of the integrity of the medical profession; the mitigation of fetal pain; and the prevention of discrimination on the basis of race, sex, or disability.

These legitimate interests justify Mississippi's Gestational Age Act. Except "in a medical emergency or in the case of a severe fetal abnormality," the statute prohibits abortion "if the probable gestational age of the unborn human being has been determined to be greater than fifteen (15) weeks." The Mississippi Legislature's findings recount the stages of "human prenatal development" and assert the State's interest in "protecting the life of the unborn." The legislature also found that abortions performed after 15 weeks typically use the dilation and evacuation procedure, and the legislature found the use of this procedure "for nontherapeutic or elective reasons [to be] a barbaric practice, dangerous for the maternal patient, and demeaning to the medical profession." These legitimate interests provide a rational basis for the Gestational Age Act, and it follows that respondents' constitutional challenge must fail.

We end this opinion where we began. Abortion presents a profound moral question. The Constitution does not prohibit the citizens of each State from regulating or prohibiting abortion. *Roe* and *Casey* arrogated that authority. We now overrule those decisions and return that authority to the people and their elected representatives.

Justice THOMAS, concurring.

I write separately to emphasize a second, more fundamental reason why there is no abortion guarantee lurking in the Due Process Clause. Considerable historical evidence indicates that "due process of law" merely required executive and judicial actors to comply with legislative enactments and the common law when depriving a person of life, liberty, or property. Other sources, by contrast, suggest that "due process of law" prohibited legislatures "from authorizing the deprivation of a person's life, liberty, or property without providing him the customary procedures to which freemen were entitled by the old law of England." Either way, the Due Process Clause at most guarantees *process*. It does not, as the Court's substantive due process cases suppose, "forbi[d] the government to infringe certain 'fundamental' liberty interests *at all*, no matter what process is provided."

As I have previously explained, "substantive due process" is an oxymoron that "lack[s] any basis in the Constitution." "The notion that a constitutional provision that guarantees only 'process' before a person is deprived of life, liberty, or property could define the substance of those rights strains credulity for even the most casual user of words." The resolution of this case is thus straightforward. Because the Due Process Clause does not secure *any* substantive rights, it does not secure a right to abortion.

For that reason, in future cases, we should reconsider all of this Court's substantive due process precedents, including *Griswold*, *Lawrence*, and *Obergefell*. Because any substantive due process decision is "demonstrably erroneous," we have a duty to "correct the error" established in those precedents. After overruling these demonstrably erroneous decisions, the question would remain whether other constitutional provisions guarantee the myriad rights that our substantive due process cases have generated. For example, we could consider whether any of the rights announced in this Court's substantive due process cases are "privileges or immunities of citizens of the United States" protected by the Fourteenth Amendment. To answer that question, we would need to decide important antecedent questions, including whether the Privileges or Immunities Clause protects *any* rights that are not enumerated in the Constitution and, if so, how to identify those rights. That said, even if the Clause does protect unenumerated rights, the Court conclusively demonstrates that abortion is not one of them under any plausible interpretive approach.

Chief Justice ROBERTS, concurring in the judgment.

We granted certiorari to decide one question: "Whether all pre-viability prohibitions on elective abortions are unconstitutional." That question is directly implicated here: Mississippi's Gestational Age Act generally prohibits abortion after the fifteenth week of pregnancy—several weeks before a fetus is regarded as "viable" outside the womb. In urging our review, Mississippi stated that its case was "an ideal vehicle" to "reconsider the bright-line viability rule," and that a judgment in its favor would "not require the Court to overturn" *Roe v. Wade*, and *Planned Parenthood of Southeastern Pa. v. Casey*.

Today, the Court nonetheless rules for Mississippi by doing just that. I would take a more measured course. I agree with the Court that the viability line established by *Roe* and *Casey* should be discarded under a straightforward *stare decisis* analysis. That line never made any sense. Our abortion precedents describe the right at issue as a woman's right to choose to terminate her pregnancy. That right should therefore extend far enough to ensure a reasonable opportunity to choose, but need not extend any further—certainly not all the way to viability. Mississippi's law allows a woman three months to obtain an abortion, well beyond the point at which it is considered "late" to discover a pregnancy. I see no sound basis for questioning the adequacy of that opportunity.

But that is all I would say, out of adherence to a simple yet fundamental principle of judicial restraint: If it is not necessary to decide more to dispose of a case, then it is necessary *not* to decide more. The Court's opinion is thoughtful and thorough, but those virtues cannot compensate for the fact that its dramatic and consequential ruling is unnecessary to decide the case before us. The Court's decision to overrule *Roe* and *Casey* is a serious jolt to the legal system—regardless of how you view those cases. A narrower decision rejecting the misguided viability line would be markedly less unsettling, and nothing more is needed to decide this case.

Both the Court's opinion and the dissent display a relentless freedom from doubt on the legal issue that I cannot share. I therefore concur only in the judgment.

Justice BREYER, Justice SOTOMAYOR, and Justice KAGAN, dissenting.

Roe and *Casey* well understood the difficulty and divisiveness of the abortion issue. The Court knew that Americans hold profoundly different views about the "moral[ity]" of "terminating a pregnancy, even in its earliest stage." And the Court recognized that "the State has legitimate interests from the outset of the pregnancy in protecting" the "life of the fetus that may become a child." So the Court struck a balance, as it often does when values and goals compete.

Today, the Court discards that balance. It says that from the very moment of fertilization, a woman has no rights to speak of. A State can force her to bring a pregnancy to term, even at the steepest personal and familial costs. An abortion restriction, the majority holds, is permissible whenever rational, the lowest level of scrutiny known to the law. And because, as the Court has often stated, protecting fetal life is rational, States will feel free to enact all manner of restrictions.

Enforcement of all these draconian restrictions will also be left largely to the States' devices. A State can of course impose criminal penalties on abortion providers, including lengthy prison sentences. But some States will not stop there. Perhaps, in the wake of today's decision, a state law will criminalize the woman's conduct too, incarcerating or fining her for daring to seek or obtain an abortion. And as Texas has recently shown, a State can turn neighbor against neighbor, enlisting fellow citizens in the effort to root out anyone who tries to get an abortion, or to assist another in doing so.

Whatever the exact scope of the coming laws, one result of today's decision is certain: the curtailment of women's rights, and of their status as free and equal citizens. And no one should be confident that this majority is done with its work. The right *Roe* and *Casey* recognized does not stand alone. To the contrary, the Court has linked it for decades to other settled freedoms involving bodily integrity, familial relationships, and procreation. Most obviously, the right to terminate a pregnancy arose straight out of the right to purchase and use contraception. In turn, those rights led, more recently, to rights of same-sex intimacy and marriage. They are all part of the same constitutional fabric, protecting autonomous decision making over the most personal of life decisions. The majority (or to be more accurate, most of it) is eager to tell us today that nothing it does "cast[s] doubt on precedents that do not concern abortion." But how could that be? The lone rationale for what the majority does today is that the right to elect an abortion is not "deeply rooted in history": Not until *Roe*, the majority argues, did people think abortion fell within the Constitution's guarantee of liberty. The same could be said, though, of most of the rights the majority claims it is not tampering with.

One piece of evidence on that score seems especially salient: The majority's cavalier approach to overturning this Court's precedents. *Stare decisis* is the Latin phrase for a foundation stone of the rule of law: that things decided should stay decided unless there is a very good reason for change. It is a doctrine of judicial modesty and humility. Those qualities are not evident in today's opinion. The majority has no good reason for the upheaval in law and society it sets off. *Roe* and *Casey* have been the law of the land for decades, shaping women's expectations of their choices when an unplanned pregnancy occurs. Women have relied on the availability of abortion both in structuring their relationships and in planning their lives. The legal framework *Roe* and *Casey* developed to balance the competing interests in this sphere has proved workable in courts across the country. No recent developments, in either law or fact, have eroded or cast doubt on those precedents. Nothing, in short, has changed. Indeed, the Court in *Casey* already found all of that to be true. *Casey* is a precedent about precedent. It reviewed the same arguments made here in support of overruling *Roe*, and it found that doing so was not warranted. The Court reverses course today for one reason and one reason only: because the composition of this Court has changed. *Stare decisis*, this Court has often said, "contributes to the actual and perceived integrity of the judicial process" by ensuring that decisions are "founded in the law rather than in the proclivities of individuals." Today, the proclivities of individuals rule. The Court departs from its obligation to faithfully and impartially apply the law. We dissent.

The majority makes this change based on a single question: Did the reproductive right recognized in *Roe* and *Casey* exist in "1868, the year when the Fourteenth Amendment was ratified"? The majority says (and with this much we agree) that the answer to this question is no: In 1868, there was no nationwide right to end a pregnancy, and no thought that the Fourteenth Amendment provided one.

Of course, the majority opinion refers as well to some later and earlier history. On the one side of 1868, it goes back as far as the 13th (the 13th!) century.

But that turns out to be wheel-spinning. First, it is not clear what relevance such early history should have, even to the majority. If the early history obviously supported abortion rights, the majority would no doubt say that only the views of the Fourteenth Amendment's ratifiers are germane. Second—and embarrassingly for the majority—early law in fact does provide some support for abortion rights. Common-law authorities did not treat abortion as a crime before "quickening"—the point when the fetus moved in the womb. And early American law followed the common-law rule. So the criminal law of that early time might be taken as roughly consonant with *Roe*'s and *Casey*'s different treatment of early and late abortions. Better, then, to move forward in time. On the other side of 1868, the majority occasionally notes that many States barred abortion up to the time of *Roe*. That is convenient for the majority, but it is window dressing. As the same majority (plus one) just informed us, "post-ratification adoption or acceptance of laws that are *inconsistent* with the original meaning of the constitutional text obviously cannot overcome or alter that text."

The majority's core legal postulate, then, is that we in the 21st century must read the Fourteenth Amendment just as its ratifiers did. And that is indeed what the majority emphasizes over and over again. If the ratifiers did not understand something as central to freedom, then neither can we. Or said more particularly: If those people did not understand reproductive rights as part of the guarantee of liberty conferred in the Fourteenth Amendment, then those rights do not exist.

As an initial matter, note a mistake in the just preceding sentence. We referred there to the "people" who ratified the Fourteenth Amendment: What rights did those "people" have in their heads at the time? But, of course, "people" did not ratify the Fourteenth Amendment. Men did. So it is perhaps not so surprising that the ratifiers were not perfectly attuned to the importance of reproductive rights for women's liberty, or for their capacity to participate as equal members of our Nation. Indeed, the ratifiers—both in 1868 and when the original Constitution was approved in 1788—did not understand women as full members of the community embraced by the phrase "We the People." When the majority says that we must read our foundational charter as viewed at the time of ratification (except that we may also check it against the Dark Ages), it consigns women to second-class citizenship.

Casey explicitly rejected the present majority's method. "[T]he specific practices of States at the time of the adoption of the Fourteenth Amendment," *Casey* stated, do not "mark[ ] the outer limits of the substantive sphere of liberty which the Fourteenth Amendment protects." To hold otherwise—as the majority does today—"would be inconsistent with our law." Why? Because the Court has "vindicated [the] principle" over and over that (no matter the sentiment in 1868) "there is a realm of personal liberty which the government may not enter"—especially relating to "bodily integrity" and "family life."

And that conclusion still held good, until the Court's intervention here. It was settled at the time of *Roe*, settled at the time of *Casey*, and settled yesterday that the Constitution places limits on a State's power to assert control over an individual's body and most personal decision making. A multitude of decisions supporting that principle led to *Roe*'s recognition and *Casey*'s reaffirmation of the right to choose; and *Roe* and *Casey* in turn supported additional protections for intimate and familial relations. The majority has embarrassingly little to say about those precedents. It (literally) rattles them off in a single paragraph; and it implies that they have nothing to do with each other, or with the right to terminate an early pregnancy. But that is flat wrong. The Court's precedents about bodily autonomy, sexual and familial relations, and procreation are all interwoven—all part of the fabric of our constitutional law, and because that is so, of our lives. Especially women's lives, where they safeguard a right to self-determination.

Today's decision, the majority first says, "does not undermine" the decisions cited by *Roe* and *Casey*—the ones involving "marriage, procreation, contraception, [and] family relationships"—"in any way." Note that this first assurance does not extend to rights recognized after *Roe* and *Casey*, and partly based on them—in particular, rights to same-sex intimacy and marriage. On its later tries, though, the majority includes those too: "Nothing in this opinion should be understood to cast doubt on precedents that do not concern abortion." That right is unique, the majority asserts, "because [abortion] terminates life or potential life."

The first problem with the majority's account comes from Justice Thomas's concurrence—which makes clear he is not with the program. In saying that nothing in today's opinion casts doubt on non-abortion precedents, Justice Thomas explains, he means only that they are not at issue in this very case. But he lets us know what he wants to do when they are. "[I]n future cases," he says, "we should reconsider all of this Court's substantive due process precedents, including *Griswold*, *Lawrence*, and *Obergefell*." And when we reconsider them? Then "we have a duty" to "overrul[e] these demonstrably erroneous decisions."

Consider, as our last word on this issue, contraception. The Constitution, of course, does not mention that word. And there is no historical right to contraception, of the kind the majority insists on. To the contrary, the American legal landscape in the decades after the Civil War was littered with bans on the sale of contraceptive devices. So again, there seem to be two choices. If the majority is serious about its historical approach, then *Griswold* and its progeny are in the line of fire too. Or if it is not serious, then . . . what *is* the basis of today's decision?

As a matter of constitutional substance, the majority's opinion has all the flaws its method would suggest. Because laws in 1868 deprived women of any control over their bodies, the majority approves States doing so today. Because those laws prevented women from charting the course of their own lives, the majority says States can do the same again. Because in 1868, the government could tell a pregnant woman—even in the first days of her pregnancy—that she could do nothing but bear a child, it can once more impose that command. Today's decision strips women of agency over what even the majority agrees is a contested and contestable moral issue. It forces her to carry out the State's will, whatever the circumstances and whatever the harm it will wreak on her and her family. In the Fourteenth Amendment's terms, it takes away her liberty. Even before we get to *stare decisis*, we dissent.

By overruling *Roe*, *Casey*, and more than 20 cases reaffirming or applying the constitutional right to abortion, the majority abandons *stare decisis*, a principle central to the rule of law. "*Stare decisis*" means "to stand by things decided." Blackstone called it the "established rule to abide by former precedents." *Stare decisis* "promotes the evenhanded, predictable, and consistent development of legal principles." It maintains a stability that allows people to order their lives under the law.

Nothing—and in particular, no significant legal or factual change—supports overturning a half-century of settled law giving women control over their reproductive lives. First, for all the reasons we have given, *Roe* and *Casey* were correct. In holding that a State could not "resolve" the debate about abortion "in such a definitive way that a woman lacks all choice in the matter," the Court protected women's liberty and women's equality in a way comporting with our Fourteenth Amendment precedents. Contrary to the majority's view, the legal status of abortion in the 19th century does not weaken those decisions. And the majority's repeated refrain about "usurp[ing]" state legislatures' "power to address" a publicly contested question does not help it on the key issue here. To repeat: The point of a right is to shield individual actions and decisions "from the vicissitudes of political controversy, to place them beyond the reach of majorities and officials and to establish them as legal principles to be applied by the courts." However divisive, a right is not at the people's mercy.

In any event "[w]hether or not we . . . agree" with a prior precedent is the beginning, not the end, of our analysis—and the remaining "principles of *stare decisis* weigh heavily against overruling" *Roe* and *Casey*. *Casey* itself applied those principles, in one of this Court's most important precedents about precedent. After assessing the traditional *stare decisis* factors, *Casey* reached the only conclusion possible—that *stare decisis* operates powerfully here. It still does. The standards *Roe* and *Casey* set out are perfectly workable. No changes in either law or fact have eroded the two decisions. And tens of millions of American women have relied, and continue to rely, on the right to choose. So under traditional *stare decisis* principles, the majority has no special justification for the harm it causes.

And indeed, the majority comes close to conceding that point. The majority barely mentions any legal or factual changes that have occurred since *Roe* and *Casey*. It suggests that the two decisions are hard for courts to implement, but cannot prove its case. In the end, the majority says, all it must say to override *stare decisis* is one thing: that it believes *Roe* and *Casey* "egregiously wrong." That rule could equally spell the end of any precedent with which a bare majority of the present Court disagrees. So how does that approach prevent the "scale of justice" from "waver[ing] with every new judge's opinion"? It does not. It makes radical change too easy and too fast, based on nothing more than the new views of new judges. The majority has overruled *Roe* and *Casey* for one and only one reason: because it has always despised them, and now it has the votes to discard them. The majority thereby substitutes a rule by judges for the rule of law.

Contrary to the majority's view, there is nothing unworkable about *Casey's* "undue burden" standard. Its primary focus on whether a State has placed a "substantial obstacle" on a woman seeking an abortion is "the sort of inquiry familiar to judges across a variety of contexts." And it has given rise to no more conflict in application than many standards this Court and others unhesitatingly apply every day. Of course, it has provoked some disagreement among judges. *Casey* knew it would: That much "is to be expected in the application of any legal standard which must accommodate life's complexity." Which is to say: That much is to be expected in the application of any legal standard. But the majority vastly overstates the divisions among judges applying the standard.

Anyone concerned about workability should consider the majority's substitute standard. The majority says a law regulating or banning abortion "must be sustained if there is a rational basis on which the legislature could have thought that it would serve legitimate state interests." And the majority lists interests like "respect for and preservation of prenatal life," "protection of maternal health," elimination of certain "medical procedures," "mitigation of fetal pain," and others. This Court will surely face critical questions about how that test applies. Must a state law allow abortions when necessary to protect a woman's life and health? And if so, exactly when? How much risk to a woman's life can a State force her to incur, before the Fourteenth Amendment's protection of life kicks in? Suppose a patient with pulmonary hypertension has a 30-to-50 percent risk of dying with ongoing pregnancy; is that enough? And short of death, how much illness or injury can the State require her to accept, consistent with the Amendment's protection of liberty and equality? Further, the Court may face questions about the application of abortion regulations to medical care most people view as quite different from abortion. What about the morning-after pill? IUDs? In vitro fertilization? And how about the use of dilation and evacuation or medication for miscarriage management?

Finally, the majority's ruling today invites a host of questions about interstate conflicts. Can a State bar women from traveling to another State to obtain an abortion? Can a State prohibit advertising out-of-state abortions or helping women get to out-of-state providers? Can a State interfere with the mailing of drugs used for medication abortions? The Constitution protects travel and speech and interstate commerce, so today's ruling will give rise to a host of new constitutional questions. Far from removing the Court from the abortion issue, the majority puts the Court at the center of the coming "interjurisdictional abortion wars."

FROM THE BENCH

FROM THE BENCH

When overruling constitutional precedent, the Court has almost always pointed to major legal or factual changes undermining a decision's original basis. The majority briefly invokes the current controversy over abortion. But it has to acknowledge that the same dispute has existed for decades: Conflict over abortion is not a change but a constant. In the end, the majority throws longstanding precedent to the winds without showing that anything significant has changed to justify its radical reshaping of the law.

[N]o subsequent factual developments have undermined *Roe* and *Casey*. Women continue to experience unplanned pregnancies and unexpected developments in pregnancies. Pregnancies continue to have enormous physical, social, and economic consequences. Even an uncomplicated pregnancy imposes significant strain on the body, unavoidably involving significant physiological change and excruciating pain. For some women, pregnancy and childbirth can mean life-altering physical ailments or even death. Today, as noted earlier, the risks of carrying a pregnancy to term dwarf those of having an abortion. Experts estimate that a ban on abortions increases maternal mortality by 21 percent, with white women facing a 13 percent increase in maternal mortality while black women face a 33 percent increase. Pregnancy and childbirth may also impose large-scale financial costs.

Mississippi's own record illustrates how little facts on the ground have changed since *Roe* and *Casey*, notwithstanding the majority's supposed "modern developments." Sixty-two percent of pregnancies in Mississippi are unplanned, yet Mississippi does not require insurance to cover contraceptives and prohibits educators from demonstrating proper contraceptive use. The State neither bans pregnancy discrimination nor requires provision of paid parental leave. It has strict eligibility requirements for Medicaid and nutrition assistance, leaving many women and families without basic medical care or enough food. Although 86 percent of pregnancy-related deaths in the State are due to postpartum complications, Mississippi rejected federal funding to provide a year's worth of Medicaid coverage to women after giving birth. Perhaps unsurprisingly, health outcomes in Mississippi are abysmal for both women and children. Mississippi has the highest infant mortality rate in the country, and some of the highest rates for preterm birth, low birthweight, cesarean section, and maternal death. It is approximately 75 times more dangerous for a woman in the State to carry a pregnancy to term than to have an abortion. We do not say that every State is Mississippi, and we are sure some have made gains since *Roe* and *Casey* in providing support for women and children. But a state-by-state analysis by public health professionals shows that States with the most restrictive abortion policies also continue to invest the least in women's and children's health.

The reasons for retaining *Roe* and *Casey* gain further strength from the overwhelming reliance interests those decisions have created. The Court adheres to precedent not just for institutional reasons, but because it recognizes that stability in the law is "an essential thread in the mantle of protection that the law affords the individual." So when overruling precedent "would dislodge [individuals'] settled rights and expectations," *stare decisis* has "added force." *Casey* understood that to deny individuals' reliance on *Roe* was to "refuse to face the fact[s]." Today the majority refuses to face the facts. "The most strik-ing feature of the [majority] is the absence of any serious discussion" of how its ruling will affect women. By characterizing *Casey*'s reliance arguments as "gen-eralized assertions about the national psyche," it reveals how little it knows or cares about women's lives or about the suffering its decision will cause.

In *Casey*, the Court observed that for two decades individuals "have orga-nized intimate relationships and made" significant life choices "in reliance on the availability of abortion in the event that contraception should fail." Over another 30 years, that reliance has solidified. For half a century now, in *Casey*'s words, "[t]he ability of women to participate equally in the economic and social life of the Nation has been facilitated by their ability to control their reproductive lives." Indeed, all women now of childbearing age have grown up expecting that they would be able to avail themselves of *Roe*'s and *Casey*'s protections.

[T]he expectation of reproductive control is integral to many women's iden-tity and their place in the Nation. That expectation helps define a woman as an "equal citizen[ ]," with all the rights, privileges, and obligations that status entails. It reflects that she is an autonomous person, and that society and the law recog-nize her as such. Like many constitutional rights, the right to choose situates a woman in relationship to others and to the government. It helps define a sphere of freedom, in which a person has the capacity to make choices free of govern-ment control. As *Casey* recognized, the right "order[s]" her "thinking" as well as her "living." Beyond any individual choice about residence, or education, or career, her whole life reflects the control and authority that the right grants.

Withdrawing a woman's right to choose whether to continue a pregnancy does not mean that no choice is being made. It means that a majority of today's Court has wrenched this choice from women and given it to the States. To allow a State to exert control over one of "the most intimate and personal choices" a woman may make is not only to affect the course of her life, monumental as those effects might be. It is to alter her "views of [herself]" and her understanding of her "place[ ] in society" as someone with the recognized dignity and authority to make these choices. Women have relied on *Roe* and *Casey* in this way for 50 years. Many have never known anything else. When *Roe* and *Casey* disappear, the loss of power, control, and dignity will be immense.

"The promise of constancy, once given" in so charged an environment, *Casey* explained, "binds its maker for as long as" the "understanding of the issue has not changed so fundamentally as to render the commitment obsolete." A breach of that promise is "nothing less than a breach of faith." "[A]nd no Court that broke its faith with the people could sensibly expect credit for principle." No Court breaking its faith in that way would *deserve* credit for principle. As one of *Casey*'s authors wrote in another case, "Our legitimacy requires, above all, that we adhere to *stare decisis*" in "sensitive political contexts" where "partisan controversy abounds."

Justice Jackson once called a decision he dissented from a "loaded weapon," ready to hand for improper uses. We fear that today's decision, departing from *stare decisis* for no legitimate reason, is its own loaded weapon. Weakening *stare decisis* threatens to upend bedrock legal doctrines, far beyond any single decision. Weakening *stare decisis* creates profound legal instability. And as *Casey* recognized, weakening *stare decisis* in a hotly contested case like this one calls into question this Court's commitment to legal principle. It makes the Court appear not restrained but aggressive, not modest but grasping. In all those ways, today's decision takes aim, we fear, at the rule of law.

With sorrow—for this Court, but more, for the many millions of American women who have today lost a fundamental constitutional protection—we dissent.

QUESTIONS FOR DISCUSSION

12.12 In his opinion for the Court, Justice Alito mentions that "*Roe* was on a collision course from the day it was decided" as a reason why the decision should be overruled. Since the time *Dobbs* was decided, disputes have erupted among the states concerning a number of proposed and actual state laws. Examples in the immediate aftermath of the ruling have included laws that make an individual criminally culpable if they assist another individual in getting an abortion, laws that attempt to prohibit the mailing of abortion-inducing pharmaceuticals across state lines, and rulings announcing that abortion-inducing pharmaceuticals were not properly approved by the U.S. Food and Drug Administration. In addition, some anti-abortion laws have proven so expansive that physicians have been reluctant to perform medical procedures deemed necessary for the health of the mother for fear of prosecution—a state of affairs that has sometimes resulted in permanent damage to the pregnant person's reproductive capacity and other health effects. Making matters more unpredictable, these abortion laws have tended not to include scientific language, making interpretation by doctors difficult and providing an incentive for doctors to proceed with extreme caution. This state of affairs has caused a dramatic backlash from some members of the public.

What do these developments suggest about *Roe*'s "collision course" that Justice Alito mentioned? What do they suggest about the controversial nature of the abortion issue?

12.13 A repeated criticism of the *Dobbs* result focuses on the profound effect of an unwanted pregnancy on a person's life and the extensive period of time in which constitutional law has provided some protection for the right to abortion. According to this thinking, the overruling of *Roe* and *Casey* is particularly improper because of the years of reliance on the existence of the abortion right and the effect of the overruling on the perception of autonomy and self-determination on those capable of bearing a child. Explain whether you think this criticism is justified or not.

12.14 As mentioned in the introduction of this chapter, many cases that discuss rights that emanate from the substantive component of the Due Process Clause do not use the words "substantive due process." In his concurrence, Justice Thomas put the words front and center, stating, "[I]n future cases, we should reconsider all of this Court's substantive due process precedents, including *Griswold*, *Lawrence*, and *Obergefell* . . . we have a duty . . . to overrul[e] these demonstrably erroneous decisions." *Griswold* is the birth control case that we read at the beginning of this chapter. The next chapter, concerning sexual freedoms, covers *Lawrence*, which provided constitutional protection against criminalizing sexual conduct between individuals of the same sex. The final case Thomas mentions, *Obergefell*, guaranteed the fundamental right to marry for same-sex couples.

Critics of Justice Thomas pointed out that he omitted from his list of "must overrule" cases another case that implicated substantive due process: *Loving v. Virginia*. That case guaranteed the fundamental right to marry for individuals of different races. In part, *Loving v. Virginia* was premised on the notion of substantive due process. Some argued that his omission of *Loving v. Virginia* from the "must overrule" list was hypocritical because Thomas (a Black man) is married to a White woman. Note that *Loving v. Virginia* concerns a question of race. Does that fact render the case constitutionally different from the other cases on Thomas's "must overrule" list?

12.15 In thinking about Justice Thomas's concurrence noted in Question 12.14 immediately above, note that the majority opinion (joined by Justice Thomas) stated twice: "Nothing in this opinion should be understood to cast doubt on precedents that do not concern abortion." Having joined the majority opinion, was it appropriate for Justice Thomas to suggest that *Dobbs* provided a "set up" for overruling other substantive due process decisions that did not concern abortion?

12.16 Although precise poll numbers vary, nearly all, if not all, polls document that a majority of U.S. citizens believe that abortion should be allowed in many instances. Should this fact be relevant to evaluating the legitimacy of the *Dobbs* decision?

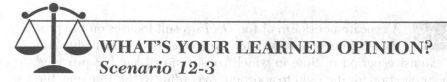

WHAT'S YOUR LEARNED OPINION?
Scenario 12-3

Assume that State A passed a law prohibiting all abortions. Assume further that State A also passed a law prohibiting a person from crossing state lines for the purpose of obtaining an abortion in a state where abortion is legal. Lucy lives in State A and becomes pregnant. She wants to terminate the pregnancy and travels to State B, where abortion is legal. Upon reentering State A, Lucy is arrested and prosecuted for crossing into State B to obtain the abortion. Does Lucy have any defenses to the prosecution based on the U.S. Constitution?

Scenario 12-4

The American Medical Association (AMA) criticized the *Dobbs* decision as follows:

> In alignment with our long-held position that the early termination of a pregnancy is a medical matter between the patient and physician, subject only to the physician's clinical judgment and the patient's informed consent, the AMA condemns the high court's interpretation in this case.

The *Dobbs* majority made clear that viability is not the deciding issue for deciding whether the decision to obtain an abortion is constitutionally protected. Accepting the validity of the AMA's position that the decision to have an abortion is a medical matter to be determined by physician and patient, could *Dobbs* pave the way for decriminalizing abortions at all stages of pregnancy?

BEHIND THE CURTAIN

The period leading up to the Court handing down the *Dobbs* decision as well as the decision itself sent shock waves through U.S. society and likely touched much of the rest of the world. One particularly unusual and jarring event leading up to the official announcement of the decision in the case was the leak of the draft majority opinion in May 2022.

The practice of closed deliberations at the Supreme Court began with Chief Justice John Marshall at the beginning of the nineteenth century.

To: The Chief Justice
       Justice Thomas
       Justice Breyer
       Justice Sotomayor
       Justice Kagan
       Justice Gorsuch
       Justice Kavanaugh
       Justice Barrett

From:

Justice Alito

Circulated: February 10, 2022 _____

Recirculated: _____

1st Draft

NOTICE: This opinion is subject to formal revision before publication in the preliminary print of the United States Reports. Readers are requested to notify the Reporter of Decisions, Supreme Court of the United States, Washington, D. C. 20543, of any typographical or other formal errors, in order that corrections may be made before the preliminary print goes to press.

SUPREME COURT OF THE UNITED STATES

No. 19–1392

THOMAS E. DOBBS, STATE HEALTH OFFICER OF THE MISSISSIPPI DEPARTMENT OF HEALTH, ET AL., PETITIONERS *v.* JACKSON WOMEN'S HEALTH ORGANIZATION, ET AL.

ON WRIT OF CERTIORARI TO THE UNITED STATES COURT OF APPEALS FOR THE FIFTH CIRCUIT

[February ___, 2022]

JUSTICE ALITO delivered the opinion of the Court.

Abortion presents a profound moral issue on which Americans hold sharply conflicting views. Some believe fervently that a human person comes into being at conception and that abortion ends an innocent life. Others feel just as strongly that any regulation of abortion invades a woman's right to control her own body and prevents women from achieving full equality. Still others in a third group think that abortion should be allowed under some but not all circumstances, and those within this group hold a variety of views about the particular restrictions that should be imposed.

For the first 185 years after the adoption of the Constitution, each State was permitted to address this issue in accordance with the views of its citizens. Then, in 1973, this Court decided *Roe* v. *Wade*, 410 U. S. 113. Even though the Constitution makes no mention of abortion, the Court held that it confers a broad right to obtain one. It did not claim that American law or the common law had ever recognized

First page of the leaked draft of the majority opinion in *Dobbs v. Jackson Women's Health Organization.*

Marshall used secrecy strategically to fortify the Court and protect it from political attacks. Thomas Jefferson criticized Marshall's "practice of making up opinions in secret and delivering them as the orders of the court" and accused Marshall of "smothering evidence." The Court has extended this

Protesters in Foley Square, New York City, defending the right to abortion following the leak of a draft Supreme Court opinion that would overturn *Roe v. Wade. Legoktm/Wikimedia Commons.*

culture of confidentiality to the Justices' law clerks. Indeed, confidentiality of the Court's deliberations has been labeled an "honored tradition."[4]

Although not the first glimpse into the inner workings of the Court, the leak of the draft opinion caused an uproar among both the Justices and the public. Chief Justice Roberts issued a press release announcing the launch of an investigation into the source of the leak, calling it a "betrayal of Court confidence." (As of this writing, the "leaker" has not been identified.)

The *Dobbs* leak might have felt like a betrayal to the Justices, but it sounded the alarm and alerted the public that an established constitutional right was about to be taken away. The practice of confidentiality that once protected the Court arguably highlighted damage to its professionalism and legitimacy.

Arguments for and against maintaining the judicial deliberation privilege center around public opinion — public opinion on the issues, as well as public opinion of the Court and its Justices. Proponents argue that secrecy during deliberations fosters judicial impartiality by allowing judges to work free of public opinion pressures. Proponents of privacy also warn that careful consideration and open discussion and exchanges of ideas will be curtailed if that confidentiality is removed. Individual justices might avoid sharing preliminary lines of reasoning that might not be fully formed, but could ultimately yield important insights into resolving difficult legal questions. Most of the issues the Supreme Court confronts are intellectually challenging: Brainstorming about different results and alternative theories assists in identifying an optimum resolution. Finally, some warn that "[t]he judicial process necessarily . . . involves compromises among judges . . . [P]ublic confidence in the judicial system could be eroded by the exposure of these compromises and uncertainties."[5]

Opponents of judicial deliberation confidentiality argue that allowing public scrutiny of the Court's deliberations can instruct on the reasons for decisions and thereby guide future holdings by revealing "how the attitudes and views of the justices affect their decisions."[6] As you have read opinions in this book, you likely found some opinions unclear, perhaps even baffling. A decision's meaning can be especially unclear when multiple concurrences and dissents are included. Shining a bright light on the give-and-take among the Justices in creating an end product can assist in sorting through the confusing array of arguments in the dissents and concurrences. Given that the Supreme Court has great control over what U.S. citizens can say or do, this type of clarity—the argument goes—is particularly important.

Public approval of the Supreme Court was already at an all-time low before the *Dobbs* leak and continues to tumble. Is secrecy a problem, or a solution to this crisis of esteem? This is hard to gauge, given that the public's low view of the Court results from a number of factors. The following is a partial list:

- The failure of the Court to abide by an explicit code of ethics.
- Great economic advantages received by the Justices or their spouses from matters that benefit from the Court's decision making.
- The failure of some Justices to recuse themselves from deciding a case when circumstances suggest that they should.
- Questions that arise about the mental competence of elderly Justices who refuse to resign.
- The increased use of the so-called shadow docket, by which the Court affects the outcome of a case without any public proceeding and sometimes even without an explanatory opinion.

The *Dobbs* leak exacerbated the perception that the once august institution is in tatters.

The U.S. Supreme Court not only governs, but it educates the public about the contours of constitutional law. Repeated defaults in the Court's procedures undermine this important function as well. Citizens might think this: What could I learn from a dysfunctional and possibly corrupt institution? More generally, the practices that the Court once adopted to protect itself from outside attacks are now threatening the Court's authority and legitimacy from within. After all, the rule of law in a democracy not only depends on a knowledgeable citizenry, but a citizenry that respects the institutions of government.

Contraception and abortion embody issues charged with emotion, morality, religion, and economic status. We see in the cases presented in this chapter that access to abortion has spawned greater discord in society than access to contraception. That said, most now agree that both contraceptive and abortion rights derive their constitutional power from substantive due process. As substantive due process has come under fire from some powerful legal thinkers, the question arises whether the recognized constitutional right to contraception might also be eliminated. The next two chapters concern recognized constitutional rights that also implicate substantive due process: protection of sexual freedoms and the right to marry as one chooses. As you read through the chapters, consider how the rights at issue there differ from abortion and contraception.

QUESTIONS FOR REVIEW

1. What is the difference between procedural due process and substantive due process? Describe each concept and give an example of each.
2. Describe the different ways of explaining how the "right to privacy" is grounded in the Constitution. Which specifically enumerated individual rights can best provide a basis for the right to privacy?
3. What did the criminal statute challenged in *Griswold v. Connecticut* prohibit?
4. In his concurrence in *Griswold v. Connecticut*, Justice Goldberg relied on a specific provision in the Bill of Rights that had rarely been used before. What was the provision and how did Justice Goldberg interpret it?
5. The Court extended the holding of *Griswold* in a subsequent case, *Eisenstadt v. Baird.* In what way did *Eisenstadt* extend *Griswold*? What language did the Court use in *Eisenstadt* that suggested how it might rule in *Roe v. Wade?*
6. Which amendment to the Constitution did Justice Blackmun say that the Court believed was the most likely foundation for the right to secure an abortion under safe conditions in *Roe v. Wade*? What was his reasoning?
7. At what point in pregnancy did the *Roe* Court decide that a state had a sufficiently compelling interest to prohibit abortion altogether? How did it arrive at that point?
8. List three or more requirements that some states imposed on persons seeking abortions after the *Roe* decision.
9. Describe the precise holding of *Dobbs v. Jackson Women's Health Organization.*
10. In his concurrence in *Dobbs*, what issues other than abortion rights did Justice Thomas say should be reconsidered? Why did he believe they needed to be reconsidered?
11. Discuss the pros and cons of the U.S. Supreme Court's practice of keeping deliberations and opinion drafts secret.

ENDNOTES

1. Most of these options are derived from ideas set forth in the Teaching Manual to Erwin Chemerinsky's *Constitutional Law* (2020).
2. For more detail on these changing attitudes toward abortion, *see* Lucinda M. Finley, The Story of *Roe v. Wade*, in *Constitutional Law Stories* 333-382 (Michael C. Dorf ed. 2009).
3. *Gonzales v. Carhart*, 550 U.S. 124 (2007).
4. *The Law Clerk's Duty of Confidentiality*, 129 U. Pa. L. Rev. 1230, 1230 (May 1981) (citing Wright, *Observations of an Appellate Judge: The Use of Law Clerks*, 26 Vand. L. Rev. 1179, 1189 n.38 (1973)).
5. Charles W. Sorenson, Jr., *Adopting the Judicial Deliberations Privilege: Making Explicit What Has Been Implicit*, 95 Mass. L. Rev. 243, 249 (Mar. 2014).
6. Erwin Chemerinsky, *Opening Closed Chambers*, 108 Yale L.J. 1087, 1089 & 1104 (March 1999).

Sexual Freedoms

13

Although the beginning of rights struggles for LGBTQIA+ individuals is hard to pinpoint, some of the earliest organizations were founded in the 1950s. The first public protests became visible in the mid-1960s. The mantra of these protests tended toward the following message: "We're not sick, we're not sinful, we're just as good and moral as anyone else and we demand our rights."[1] An important early inflection point in these struggles occurred during the morning hours of June 28, 1969, with a police raid of the Stonewall Bar in New York City. Many historians report that those present at the bar that night were gay men, lesbians, drag queens, and transgender individuals. These individuals resisted the police and a riot ensued. Activists captured the event as a catalyst for an ever more vibrant rights movement, and groups such as the Gay Liberation Front and the Gay Activists' Alliance emerged.

Throughout the period from 1950 into the 1990s, U.S. government and society exhibited mixed messages on LGBTQIA+ rights. From 1952 to 1974, the American Psychological Association listed "homosexuality" as a sociopathic personality disturbance, essentially characterizing its status as an illness. In 1953, President Eisenhower signed an executive order banning homosexuals from working for the federal government or any of its contractors. In 1958, however, the U.S. Supreme Court found First Amendment protection for the publication *One: The Homosexual Magazine*, which the U.S. Postal Service and FBI had declared obscene. In 1962, Illinois became the first U.S. state to decriminalize homosexuality. A series of developments favorable to the movement occurred in the next two decades, including the election of LGBTQIA+ persons to political office, large demonstrations in Washington, D.C., and the decision by the state of Washington to outlaw discrimination based on sexual orientation. Nonetheless, hostility to LGBTQIA+ rights continued strong in many parts of U.S. society. The case that follows is an example of that sentiment.

[Author note: A note about language: In the cases that follow, the Court speaks of "homosexual rights" and occasionally "gays and lesbians." To ensure understanding of the scope (and limitations) of the Court's rulings, discussion of the cases will be limited to the words that the Court used. To expand the Court's holdings to include reference to the rights of all LGBTQIA+ individuals could lead to a misrepresentation of what the Court decided.]

The following case, *Bowers v. Hardwick*, arose out of a police officer's visit to the home of Michael Hardwick with a warrant for failure to appear at his court date for an arrest for public drinking. As it turned out, the warrant had been issued in error because the matter had been resolved. When the officer knocked on Hardwick's door, his roommate answered the door, said that Hardwick was in the bedroom, and invited the officer to look for himself. In the bedroom, the officer found Hardwick engaged in consensual sex with another man. Hardwick and his partner were charged under a Georgia statute prohibiting sodomy—defined in the statute as anything other than genital to genital contact (without regard to the gender of the parties involved). Although the statute did not make relevant the gender of the parties involved in the conduct, the U.S. Supreme Court's majority opinion focused only on homosexual intimacy.

FROM THE BENCH

BOWERS v. HARDWICK
478 U.S. 186 (1986)

[After Michael Hardwick was charged with violating the Georgia statute criminalizing sodomy, the district attorney chose not to prosecute the charges because of the invalid warrant and the belief that the statute should not be enforced in instances of consensual sexual activity. With representation from the ACLU, Hardwick brought a civil rights suit in federal court against the Attorney General for the State of Georgia, Michael Bowers, seeking declarative relief that the statute was invalid because it violated his right to privacy under the Ninth Amendment and the Due Process Clause of the Fourteenth Amendment. The federal trial court granted Bowers's motion to dismiss for failure to state a claim, then the Court of Appeals reversed and remanded, holding that the statute violated Hardwick's fundamental rights. Bowers appealed to the U.S. Supreme Court, which upheld the statute in the decision below, ruling that the Constitution does not offer a right to engage in sodomy.]

Mr. Justice WHITE delivered the opinion of the Court.

This case does not require a judgment on whether laws against sodomy between consenting adults in general, or between homosexuals in particular, are wise or desirable. It raises no question about the right or propriety of state legislative decisions to repeal their laws that criminalize homosexual sodomy, or of state-court decisions invalidating those laws on state constitutional grounds. The issue presented is whether the Federal Constitution confers a fundamental right upon homosexuals to engage in sodomy and hence invalidates the laws of the many States that still make such conduct illegal and have done so for a very long time. The case also calls for some judgment about the limits of the Court's role in carrying out its constitutional mandate. . . .

[Mr. Hardwick] would have us announce, as the Court of Appeals did, a fundamental right to engage in homosexual sodomy. This we are quite unwilling to do. It is true that despite the language of the Due Process Clauses of the Fifth and Fourteenth Amendments, which appears to focus only on the processes by which life, liberty, or property is taken, . . . those Clauses have been interpreted to have substantive content, subsuming rights that to a great extent are immune from federal or state regulation or proscription. Among such cases are those recognizing rights that have little or no textual support in the constitutional language. . . . Striving to assure itself and the public that announcing rights not readily identifiable in the Constitution's text involves much more than the imposition of the Justices' own choice of values on the States and the Federal Government, the Court has sought to identify the nature of the rights qualifying for heightened judicial protection. . . .

[No formulation] would extend a fundamental right to homosexuals to engage in acts of consensual sodomy. Proscriptions against that conduct have ancient roots. . . . Sodomy was a criminal offense at common law and was forbidden by the laws of the original thirteen States when they ratified the Bill of Rights. In 1868, when the Fourteenth Amendment was ratified, all but 5 of the 37 States in the Union had criminal sodomy laws. In fact, until 1961, all 50 States outlawed sodomy, and today, 24 States and the District of Columbia continue to provide criminal penalties for sodomy performed in private and between consenting adults. . . . Against this background, to claim that a right to engage in such conduct is "deeply rooted in this Nation's history and tradition" or "implicit in the concept of ordered liberty" is, at best, facetious.

Nor are we inclined to take a more expansive view of our authority to discover new fundamental rights imbedded in the Due Process Clause. The Court is most vulnerable and comes nearest to illegitimacy when it deals with judge-made constitutional law having little or no cognizable roots in the language or design of the Constitution. . . . There should be, therefore, great resistance to expand the substantive reach of those Clauses, particularly if it requires redefining the category of rights deemed to be fundamental. Otherwise, the Judiciary necessarily takes to itself further authority to govern the country without express constitutional authority. The claimed right pressed on us today falls far short of overcoming this resistance.

Respondent, however, asserts that the result should be different where the homosexual conduct occurs in the privacy of the home. He relies on *Stanley v. Georgia*. . . . *Stanley* did protect conduct that would not have been protected outside the home, and it partially prevented the enforcement of state obscenity laws; but the decision was firmly grounded in the First Amendment. The right pressed upon us here has no similar support in the text of the Constitution, and it does not qualify for recognition under the prevailing principles for construing the Fourteenth Amendment. Its limits are also difficult to discern. Plainly enough, otherwise illegal conduct is not always immunized whenever it occurs in the home. . . . And if respondent's submission is limited to the voluntary sexual conduct between consenting adults, it would be difficult, except by fiat, to limit the claimed right to homosexual conduct while leaving exposed to prosecution adultery, incest, and other sexual crimes even though they are committed in the home. We are unwilling to start down that road.

Even if the conduct at issue here is not a fundamental right, respondent asserts that there must be a rational basis for the law and that there is none in this case other than the presumed belief of a majority of the electorate in Georgia that homosexual sodomy is immoral and unacceptable. This is said to be an inadequate rationale to support the law. The law, however, is constantly based on notions of morality, and if all laws representing essentially moral choices are to be invalidated under the Due Process Clause, the courts will be very busy indeed. Even respondent makes no such claim, but insists that majority sentiments about the morality of homosexuality should be declared inadequate. We do not agree, and are unpersuaded that the sodomy laws of some 25 States should be invalidated on this basis.

Accordingly, the judgment of the Court of Appeals is *Reversed*.

QUESTIONS FOR DISCUSSION

13.1 Justice White relied on the history of proscriptions against homosexuality in place at the time of the ratification of the Constitution and the Bill of Rights. Compare that approach to history to the approach of *Griswold v. Connecticut* in recognizing a constitutional right for married couples to use birth control and the approach of *Roe v. Wade* in recognizing a constitutional right to abortion. Both of those cases were written against a backdrop of at least some historical disapproval of conduct to which the Court was extending constitutional recognition. Which approach to history do you believe is more valid? Do you wonder whether the Justices sometimes rely on history when the history is consistent with the position they have previously decided that they would like to take?

13.2 In claiming that the criminal prohibition of his conduct could not even be upheld under the rational basis standard, Hardwick effectively argued that the reason for the prohibition was illegitimate. Justice White dismissed this claim with one swipe, observing that the prohibition—like many laws—was based on morality. Implicit in this observation is Justice White's conclusion that a moral judgment is a legitimate purpose, proving a rational basis for a law. Do you agree with that proposition? Can you think of any moral judgments that are not legitimate in your view? Does it make a difference that the moral judgment behind the Georgia prohibition might be characterized as animus toward a particular group of people?

BEHIND THE CURTAIN

Bowers is one of many cases that boiled down to questions about the appropriate intersection between constitutional law and morality. As mentioned in Question for Discussion 13.2, you will note that, in rejecting the claim that the criminal prohibition was unconstitutional, even under a rational basis standard, the Court stated, "The law, however, is constantly based on notions of morality, and if all laws representing essentially moral choices are to be invalidated under the Due Process Clause, the courts will be very busy indeed." This connection between the Constitution and morality is also well illustrated in the exchange during oral argument between Justice John Paul Stevens and the attorney for the Attorney General, seeking to persuade the Court that arguing that the Georgia prohibition against sexual conduct between two individuals of the same sex was constitutional. Justice Stevens found it significant that even the District Attorney in Georgia had decided not to prosecute the case:

> Justice John Paul Stevens: Does the state really have an interest in stopping this kind of conduct? If not, why wouldn't they enforce the statute? . . . It would

have been very easy in this case, in this instance. . . . It seems to me there is some tension between the obvious ability to convict this gentleman and the supposed interest in general enforcement.

Michael E. Hobbs (Attorney for Bowers): I would agree, Your Honor . . . The Respondent, as I was saying, and some amici have urged that the relationship of the family should be redefined and this is one of the interests that the State of Georgia is most concerned about.

We are very concerned that there is a potential, should the Eleventh Circuit's decision be upheld, for a reshuffling of our society, for a reordering of our society.

. . . There must be limits and it is submitted that in finding these limits we must be wary of creating a regime in the name of a constitutional right which is little more than one of self-gratification and indulgence.

The Constitution must remain a charter of tolerance for individual liberty. We have no quarrel with that. But, it must not become an instrument for a change in the social order.

The Respondents have made a crack-in-the-door argument that if the Eleventh Circuit's decision is affirmed in this case it will not go beyond consensual private homosexual sodomy; that it is submitted that this crack-in-the-door argument is truly a Pandora's box for I believe that if the Eleventh Circuit's decision is affirmed that this Court will quite soon be confronted with questions concerning the legitimacy of statutes which prohibit polygamy, homosexual, same-sex marriage, consensual incest, prostitution, fornication, adultery, and possibly even personal possession in private of illegal drugs.

Moral issues and social issues, it is submitted to the Court, should be decided by the people of this nation. Laws which are written concerning those issues are rescinded concerning those issues should be by the representatives of those people. Otherwise, the natural order of the public debate and the formulation of consensus concerning these issues, it is submitted, would be interrupted and misshapen.

It is the right of the nation and of the states to maintain a decent society, representing the collective moral aspirations of the people. . . .

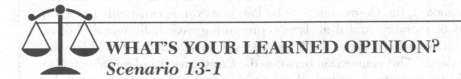

WHAT'S YOUR LEARNED OPINION?
Scenario 13-1

Cruz was enlisted in the U.S. Army. At the time of her enlistment, the Army had a policy that required that all individuals who are not binary heterosexuals be administratively discharged. After some people in her unit spotted her on a date with another woman, an investigation was launched that discovered that Cruz was a lesbian. She was discharged. Cruz sued claiming that the policy violated her right to equal protection of the laws. How would the Court resolve this case if *Bowers v. Hardwick* is the governing precedent?

The American Civil Liberties Union used Hardwick's case as a test case to challenge anti-sodomy laws. Even though Hardwick lost the case, the ACLU's strategy might have had an intended effect: Some states repealed anti-sodomy laws in the wake of the case. Even Georgia repealed the anti-sodomy law in *Powell v. State* (1998). After the Stonewall uprising, movements across the United States worked to secure civil rights for the LGBTIA+ community.

In the 1970s and 1980s, activist groups successfully lobbied for protections against discrimination based on sexual orientation throughout Colorado. By the early 1990s, however, Colorado demographics and political power had shifted. Conservative Christian groups wielded significant political power. Through petitions, conservative groups in the state secured a referendum on making a change to the state's constitution. This proposed law—Amendment 2—would prohibit state officials from making laws that prevented discrimination against gay, lesbian, and bisexual people. Amendment 2 was passed by Colorado voters by a narrow margin. Richard Evans, a civil servant in Denver, sued Roy Romer, the Governor of Colorado, alleging that Amendment 2 violated the Equal Protection Clause of the Fourteenth Amendment. The Supreme Court ruled in Evans's favor striking down Amendment 2. The ruling in *Romer v. Evans* was a milestone in the LGBTQIA+ rights movement that ultimately provided impetus for overruling *Bowers v. Hardwick*.

FROM THE BENCH

ROMER ET AL. v. EVANS ET AL.
517 U.S. 620 (1996)

[Richard G. Evans, along with three other people and three municipalities, sued to declare Amendment 2 invalid and enjoin its enforcement. The trial court's preliminary injunction was sustained by the Colorado Supreme Court, which held that Amendment 2 infringed the fundamental right of gays and lesbians to participate in the political process. On remand, the trial court found that the Amendment failed to satisfy strict scrutiny. The court enjoined Amendment 2's enforcement, and the State Supreme Court affirmed. The State filed for appeal with the U.S. Supreme Court.]

Justice KENNEDY delivered the opinion of the Court.

One century ago, the first Justice Harlan admonished this Court that the Constitution "neither knows nor tolerates classes among citizens." *Plessy v.*

Ferguson. . . . Unheeded then, those words now are understood to state a commitment to the law's neutrality where the rights of persons are at stake. The Equal Protection Clause enforces this principle and today requires us to hold invalid a provision of Colorado's Constitution. . . .

Amendment 2, in explicit terms, . . . prohibits all legislative, executive or judicial action at any level of state or local government designed to protect the named class, a class we shall refer to as homosexual persons or gays and lesbians. The amendment reads:

> "No Protected Status Based on Homosexual, Lesbian, or Bisexual Orientation. Neither the State of Colorado, through any of its branches or departments, nor any of its agencies, political subdivisions, municipalities or school districts, shall enact, adopt or enforce any statute, regulation, ordinance or policy whereby homosexual, lesbian or bisexual orientation, conduct, practices or relationships shall constitute or otherwise be the basis of or entitle any person or class of persons to have or claim any minority status, quota preferences, protected status or claim of discrimination. This Section of the Constitution shall be in all respects self-executing."

The State's principal argument in defense of Amendment 2 is that it puts gays and lesbians in the same position as all other persons. So, the State says, the measure does no more than deny homosexuals special rights. This reading of the amendment's language is implausible. We rely not upon our own interpretation of the amendment but upon the authoritative construction of Colorado's Supreme Court. The state court, deeming it unnecessary to determine the full extent of the amendment's reach, found it invalid even on a modest reading of its implications. . . .

Sweeping and comprehensive is the change in legal status effected by this law. So much is evident from the ordinances that the Colorado Supreme Court declared would be void by operation of Amendment 2. Homosexuals, by state decree, are put in a solitary class with respect to transactions and relations in both the private and governmental spheres. The amendment withdraws from homosexuals, but no others, specific legal protection from the injuries caused by discrimination, and it forbids reinstatement of these laws and policies.

The change that Amendment 2 works in the legal status of gays and lesbians in the private sphere is far-reaching, both on its own terms and when considered in light of the structure and operation of modern anti-discrimination laws. That structure is well illustrated by contemporary statutes and ordinances prohibiting discrimination by providers of public accommodations. . . . Colorado's state and municipal laws typify this emerging tradition of statutory protection and follow a consistent pattern. The laws first enumerate the persons or entities subject to a duty not to discriminate. The list goes well beyond the entities covered by the common law. The Boulder ordinance, for example, has a comprehensive definition of entities deemed places of "public accommodation." They include "any place of business engaged in any sales to the general public and any place that offers services, facilities, privileges, or advantages to the general public or that receives financial support through solicitation of the general public or through governmental subsidy of any kind." Boulder Rev. Code Section(s) 12-1-1(j) (1987). . . .

These statutes and ordinances also depart from the common law by enumerating the groups or persons within their ambit of protection. Enumeration is the essential device used to make the duty not to discriminate concrete and to provide guidance for those who must comply. In following this approach, Colorado's state and local governments have not limited anti-discrimination laws to groups that have so far been given the protection of heightened equal protection scrutiny under our cases. . . . Rather, they set forth an extensive catalogue of traits which cannot be the basis for discrimination, including age, military status, marital status, pregnancy, parenthood, custody of a minor child, political affiliation, physical or mental disability of an individual or of his or her associates—and, in recent times, sexual orientation. . . . Amendment 2 bars homosexuals from securing protection against the injuries that these public-accommodations laws address. That in itself is a severe consequence, but there is more. Amendment 2, in addition, nullifies specific legal protections for this targeted class in all transactions in housing, sale of real estate, insurance, health and welfare services, private education, and employment. . . .

Not confined to the private sphere, Amendment 2 also operates to repeal and forbid all laws or policies providing specific protection for gays or lesbians from discrimination by every level of Colorado government. . . . The repeal of these measures and the prohibition against their future reenactment demonstrates that Amendment 2 has the same force and effect in Colorado's governmental sector as it does elsewhere and that it applies to policies as well as ordinary legislation.

Amendment 2's reach may not be limited to specific laws passed for the benefit of gays and lesbians. It is a fair, if not necessary, inference from the broad language of the amendment that it deprives gays and lesbians even of the protection of general laws and policies that prohibit arbitrary discrimination in governmental and private settings. . . . At some point in the systematic administration of these laws, an official must determine whether homosexuality is an arbitrary and thus forbidden basis for decision. Yet a decision to that effect would itself amount to a policy prohibiting discrimination on the basis of homosexuality, and so would appear to be no more valid under Amendment 2 than the specific prohibitions against discrimination the state court held invalid.

If this consequence follows from Amendment 2, as its broad language suggests, it would compound the constitutional difficulties the law creates. . . . In any event, even if, as we doubt, homosexuals could find some safe harbor in laws of general application, we cannot accept the view that Amendment 2's prohibition on specific legal protections does no more than deprive homosexuals of special rights. To the contrary, the amendment imposes a special disability upon those persons alone. Homosexuals are forbidden the safeguards that others enjoy or may seek without constraint. They can obtain specific protection against discrimination only by enlisting the citizenry of Colorado to amend the state constitution or perhaps, on the State's view, by trying to pass helpful laws of general applicability. This is so no matter how local or discrete the harm, no matter how public and widespread the injury. We find nothing special in the protections Amendment 2 withholds. These are protections taken for granted by most people either because they already have them or do not need them; these are protections against exclusion from an almost limitless number of transactions and endeavors that constitute ordinary civic life in a free society.

III

The Fourteenth Amendment's promise that no person shall be denied the equal protection of the laws must co-exist with the practical necessity that most legislation classifies for one purpose or another, with resulting disadvantage to various groups or persons. . . . We have attempted to reconcile the principle with the reality by stating that, if a law neither burdens a fundamental right nor targets a suspect class, we will uphold the legislative classification so long as it bears a rational relation to some legitimate end. Amendment 2 fails, indeed defies, even this conventional inquiry. First, the amendment has the peculiar property of imposing a broad and undifferentiated disability on a single named group, an exceptional and, as we shall explain, invalid form of legislation. Second, its sheer breadth is so discontinuous with the reasons offered for it that the amendment seems inexplicable by anything but animus toward the class that it affects; it lacks a rational relationship to legitimate state interests.

Taking the first point, even in the ordinary equal protection case calling for the most deferential of standards, we insist on knowing the relation between the classification adopted and the object to be attained. The search for the link between classification and objective gives substance to the Equal Protection Clause; it provides guidance and discipline for the legislature, which is entitled to know what sorts of laws it can pass; and it marks the limits of our own authority. In the ordinary case, a law will be sustained if it can be said to advance a legitimate government interest, even if the law seems unwise or works to the disadvantage of a particular group, or if the rationale for it seems tenuous. . . . By requiring that the classification bear a rational relationship to an independent and legitimate legislative end, we ensure that classifications are not drawn for the purpose of disadvantaging the group burdened by the law. . . .

Amendment 2 confounds this normal process of judicial review. It is at once too narrow and too broad. It identifies persons by a single trait and then denies them protection across the board. The resulting disqualification of a class of persons from the right to seek specific protection from the law is unprecedented in our jurisprudence. The absence of precedent for Amendment 2 is itself instructive. . . .

It is not within our constitutional tradition to enact laws of this sort. Central both to the idea of the rule of law and to our own Constitution's guarantee of equal protection is the principle that government and each of its parts remain open on impartial terms to all who seek its assistance. . . . Respect for this principle explains why laws singling out a certain class of citizens for disfavored legal status or general hardships are rare. A law declaring that in general it shall be more difficult for one group of citizens than for all others to seek aid from the government is itself a denial of equal protection of the laws in the most literal sense. . . .

A second and related point is that laws of the kind now before us raise the inevitable inference that the disadvantage imposed is born of animosity toward the class of persons affected. "[I]f the constitutional conception of 'equal protection of the laws' means anything, it must at the very least mean that a bare . . . desire to harm a politically unpopular group cannot constitute a legitimate governmental interest." Even laws enacted for broad and ambitious purposes often can be explained by reference to legitimate public policies which justify the incidental disadvantages they impose on certain persons. Amendment 2, however, in making a general announcement that gays and lesbians shall not have any particular protections from the law, inflicts on them immediate, continuing, and real injuries that outrun and belie any legitimate justifications that may be claimed for it. We conclude that, in addition to the far-reaching deficiencies of Amendment 2 that we have noted, the principles it offends, in another sense, are conventional and venerable; a law must bear a rational relationship to a legitimate governmental purpose . . . and Amendment 2 does not.

The primary rationale the State offers for Amendment 2 is respect for other citizens' freedom of association, and in particular the liberties of landlords or employers who have personal or religious objections to homosexuality. Colorado also cites its interest in conserving resources to fight discrimination against other groups. The breadth of the Amendment is so far removed from these particular justifications that we find it impossible to credit them. We cannot say that Amendment 2 is directed to any identifiable legitimate purpose or discrete objective. It is a status-based enactment divorced from any factual context from which we could discern a relationship to legitimate state interests; it is a classification of persons undertaken for its own sake, something the Equal Protection Clause does not permit. . . .

We must conclude that Amendment 2 classifies homosexuals not to further a proper legislative end but to make them unequal to everyone else. This Colorado cannot do. A State cannot so deem a class of persons a stranger to its laws. Amendment 2 violates the Equal Protection Clause, and the judgment of the Supreme Court of Colorado is affirmed.

QUESTIONS FOR DISCUSSION

13.3 In many parts of equal protection law, a distinction based on a quality or distinctive characteristic of an individual in a group often triggers great suspicion and thus a strict scrutiny standard of review. Why do you think the majority did not use strict scrutiny in evaluating Amendment 2, but relied on rational basis review instead?

13.4 What is your explanation for the reason that the majority in *Bowers v. Hardwick* rejected the suggestion that criminalizing homosexual intimate conduct failed rational basis review, whereas the majority in *Romer v. Evans* easily concluded that Amendment 2 violated rational basis review?

13.5 In March 2022, the state of Florida passed the Parental Rights in Education law, which opponents referred to as the "Don't Say Gay bill." The text of the statute stated, "[c]lassroom instruction by school personnel or third parties on sexual orientation or gender identity may not occur in kindergarten through grade 3 or in a manner that is not age-appropriate or developmentally appropriate for students in accordance with state standards." In promoting the bill, the governor of Florida stated that the process of learning about sexual orientation and gender identity should be removed entirely from schools, and parents deserve the right to choose if their children should or should not be educated on sexual orientation or gender identity. If you were asked to frame a constitutional challenge to this law, how might you use *Romer v. Evans*?

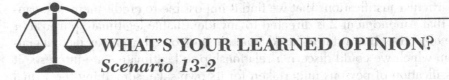

WHAT'S YOUR LEARNED OPINION?
Scenario 13-2

A state law prohibits adoption by same-sex couples. The state's goal is to provide children adopted in the state with a stable, nurturing relationship as provided by heterosexual marriage and, given that many children in the state will develop heterosexual preferences after puberty and into adulthood, to provide children with parents who can advise concerning relationships with the opposite sex. The state does allow single, heterosexual people to adopt children in the state. In addition, the state does permit same-sex couples to be foster parents. Steven and Roger had been foster parents to a young girl for several years. When reunification between the girl and her birth parents became impossible, Steven and Roger filed papers seeking to adopt the daughter they had been raising. Their application to adopt was denied pursuant to the statute prohibiting same-sex couples from adopting. The couple challenges the constitutionality of the law arguing that it violates their Fourteenth Amendment equal protection rights. What would the Court's analysis of the adoption statute be if it applies the holding in *Romer v. Evans*?

Scenario 13-3

A state statute criminalizes sexual relations between relatives of the opposite sex and the same sex. The statute defines "relatives" broadly and prohibits sex between those related genetically and those related by affinity—that is, by adoption or by marriage. The state statute provides that the purpose of this statute is to protect public health through the prevention of in-breeding. A man was arrested after police found him having intercourse with his consenting adult stepson. The man has no genetic relationship with the stepson. The stepson is not capable of bearing children. The man defends his criminal prosecution by arguing that the statute unfairly discriminates against the relationship that he has with his stepson. As this man's lawyer, what argument would you make on his behalf using the precedent set in *Romer*?

Whereas *Romer v. Evans* relied on rational basis review under the Equal Protection Clause, the following case considered the constitutionality of an anti-sodomy law and took a different tack to considering the challenge. The case arose when John-Geddes Lawrence, Jr. and Tyron Garner were arrested after police entered Lawrence's apartment and found the men having sex. The police were responding to a false report of a weapons disturbance called in by Garner's ex-boyfriend. The men were charged under a Texas anti-sodomy law, which specifically prohibited only homosexual intimate sexual behavior. They pled no contest. A civil rights organization, Lambda Legal, defended their case and challenged the constitutionality of the anti-sodomy law. The U.S. Supreme Court ruled that anti-sodomy laws violated the individuals' right to privacy and overturned their holding in *Bowers*. The ruling of *Lawrence v. Texas* provided a legal foundation for several civil rights cases for the LGBTQIA+ community, including the recognition of same-sex marriage (covered in the next chapter).

FROM THE BENCH

LAWRENCE ET AL. v. TEXAS
539 U.S. 558 (2003)

[In 1998, Houston police responded to a reported weapons disturbance at the residence of John Lawrence. Entering the apartment, they discovered Lawrence having intercourse with Tyron Garner. It was Garner's ex-boyfriend who made the call to report a weapons disturbance. Both men were arrested and charged with misdemeanor deviant sexual intercourse; they pled no contest and received a fine. Lawrence made several appeals and ultimately the case made its way to the U.S. Supreme Court.]

Justice KENNEDY delivered the opinion of the Court.

Liberty protects the person from unwarranted government intrusions into a dwelling or other private places. In our tradition the State is not omnipresent in the home. And there are other spheres of our lives and existence, outside the home, where the State should not be a dominant presence. Freedom extends beyond spatial bounds. Liberty presumes an autonomy of self that includes freedom of thought, belief, expression, and certain intimate conduct. The instant case involves liberty of the person both in its spatial and more transcendent dimensions.

I

The question before the Court is the validity of a Texas statute making it a crime for two persons of the same sex to engage in certain intimate sexual conduct. . . . We conclude the case should be resolved by determining whether the petitioners were free as adults to engage in the private conduct in the exercise of their liberty under the Due Process Clause of the Fourteenth Amendment to the Constitution. For this inquiry we deem it necessary to reconsider the Court's holding in *Bowers*.

[The Court next reevaluates its precedential assessment in *Bowers*. The opinion traces "the right to make certain decisions regarding sexual conduct," including cases covered earlier in this book such as *Griswold v. Connecticut* (1965), *Eisenstadt v. Baird* (1972), and *Roe v. Wade* (1973). After reviewing these precedents, the Court decides it must reassess *Bowers* via this history of expanding Due Process rights.]

[*Bowers* formulated the issue presented as follows:] "[W]hether the Federal Constitution confers a fundamental right upon homosexuals to engage in sodomy and hence invalidates the laws of the many States that still make such conduct illegal and have done so for a very long time." . . . That statement, we now conclude, discloses the Court's own failure to appreciate the extent of the liberty at stake. To say that the issue in *Bowers* was simply the right to engage in certain sexual conduct demeans the claim the individual put forward, just as it would demean a married couple were it to be said marriage is simply about the right to have sexual intercourse. The laws involved in *Bowers* and here . . . [touch] upon the most private human conduct, sexual behavior, and in the most private of places, the home. The statutes do seek to control a personal relationship that, whether or not entitled to formal recognition in the law, is within the liberty of persons to choose without being punished as criminals.

This, as a general rule, should counsel against attempts by the State, or a court, to define the meaning of the relationship or to set its boundaries absent injury to a person or abuse of an institution the law protects. It suffices for us to acknowledge that adults may choose to enter upon this relationship in the confines of their homes and their own private lives and still retain their dignity as free persons. When sexuality finds overt expression in intimate conduct with another person, the conduct can be but one element in a personal bond that is more enduring. The liberty protected by the Constitution allows homosexual persons the right to make this choice.

[Turning to the claim that proscriptions against sodomy "have ancient roots," the *Lawrence* Court concluded that three key observations undermines *Bowers*' "definitive conclusions." First, sodomy in the American legal tradition criminalized nonprocreative sex acts irrespective of participants' gender or sexuality. Second, laws preventing sodomy were not enforced against consenting adults acting in private. Third, there was scant evidence of legal concern: few cases were tried and legal writings rarely discuss them. Rather, "American laws targeting same-sex couples did not develop until the last third of the 20th century" and "it was not until the 1970s that any State singled out same-sex relations for criminal prosecution."]

It must be acknowledged, of course, that the Court in *Bowers* was making the broader point that for centuries there have been powerful voices to condemn homosexual conduct as immoral. The condemnation has been shaped by religious beliefs, conceptions of right and acceptable behavior, and respect for the traditional family. For many persons these are not trivial concerns but profound and deep convictions accepted as ethical and moral principles to which they aspire and which thus determine the course of their lives. These considerations do not answer the question before us, however. The issue is whether the majority may use the power of the State to enforce these views on the whole society through operation of the criminal law. . . . The sweeping references [in *Bowers*] to the history of Western civilization and to Judeo-Christian moral and ethical standards did not take account of other authorities pointing in an opposite direction. A committee advising the British Parliament recommended in 1957 repeal of laws punishing homosexual conduct. The Wolfenden Report: Report of the Committee on Homosexual Offenses and Prostitution (1963). Parliament enacted the substance of those recommendations 10 years later. Sexual Offences Act 1967, §1.

Of even more importance, almost five years before *Bowers* was decided the European Court of Human Rights considered a case with parallels to *Bowers* and to today's case. An adult male resident in Northern Ireland alleged he was a practicing homosexual who desired to engage in consensual homosexual conduct. The laws of Northern Ireland forbade him that right. He alleged that he had been questioned, his home had been searched, and he feared criminal prosecution. The court held that the laws proscribing the conduct were invalid under the European Convention on Human Rights. *Dudgeon v. United Kingdom*, 45 Eur. Ct. H.R. (1981) ¶ 52. Authoritative in all countries that are members of the Council of Europe (21 nations then, 45 nations now), the decision is at odds with the premise in *Bowers* that the claim put forward was insubstantial in our Western civilization. [The Court also noted U.S. changes post-*Bowers*: a decrease in the number of states proscribing sodomy and a "pattern of nonenforcement with respect to consenting adults acting in private."]

Two principal cases decided after *Bowers* cast its holding into even more doubt. In *Planned Parenthood of Southeastern Pa. v. Casey*, the Court reaffirmed the substantive force of the liberty protected by the Due Process Clause. The *Casey* decision again confirmed that our laws and tradition afford constitutional protection to personal decisions relating to marriage, procreation, contraception, family relationships, child rearing, and education. In explaining the respect that the Constitution demands for the autonomy of the person in making these choices, we stated as follows:

"These matters, involving the most intimate and personal choices a person may make in a lifetime, choices central to personal dignity and autonomy, are central to the liberty protected by the Fourteenth Amendment. At the heart of liberty is the right to define one's own concept of existence, of meaning, of the universe, and of the mystery of human life. Beliefs about these matters could not define the attributes of personhood were they formed under compulsion of the State."

Persons in a homosexual relationship may seek autonomy for these purposes, just as heterosexual persons do. The decision in *Bowers* would deny them this right.

The second post-*Bowers* case of principal relevance is *Romer v. Evans*. There the Court struck down class-based legislation directed at homosexuals as a violation of the Equal Protection Clause. *Romer* invalidated an amendment to Colorado's constitution which named as a solitary class of persons who were homosexuals, lesbians, or bisexual either by "orientation, conduct, practices or relationships," and deprived them of protection under state antidiscrimination laws. We concluded that the provision was "born of animosity toward the class of persons affected" and further that it had no rational relation to a legitimate governmental purpose.

As an alternative argument in this case, counsel for the petitioners and some *amici* contend that *Romer* provides the basis for declaring the Texas statute invalid under the Equal Protection Clause. That is a tenable argument, but we conclude the instant case requires us to address whether *Bowers* itself has continuing validity. Were we to hold the statute invalid under the Equal Protection Clause some might question whether a prohibition would be valid if drawn differently, say, to prohibit the conduct both between same-sex and different-sex participants.

Equality of treatment and the due process right to demand respect for conduct protected by the substantive guarantee of liberty are linked in important respects, and a decision on the latter point advances both interests. If protected conduct is made criminal and the law which does so remains unexamined for its substantive validity, its stigma might remain even if it were not enforceable as drawn for equal protection reasons. When homosexual conduct is made criminal by the law of the State, that declaration in and of itself is an invitation to subject homosexual persons to discrimination both in the public and in the private spheres. The central holding of *Bowers* has been brought in question by this case, and it should be addressed. Its continuance as precedent demeans the lives of homosexual persons.

The stigma this criminal statute imposes, moreover, is not trivial. The offense, to be sure, is but a class C misdemeanor, a minor offense in the Texas legal system. Still, it remains a criminal offense with all that imports for the dignity of the persons charged. The petitioners will bear on their record the history of their criminal convictions. Just this Term we rejected various challenges to state laws requiring the registration of sex offenders. . . . We are advised that if Texas convicted an adult for private, consensual homosexual conduct under the statute here in question the convicted person would come within the registration laws of at least four States were he or she to be subject to their jurisdiction. . . . This underscores the consequential nature of the punishment and the state-sponsored condemnation attendant to the criminal prohibition. Furthermore, the Texas criminal conviction carries with it the other collateral consequences always following a conviction, such as notations on job application forms, to mention but one example.

The foundations of *Bowers* have sustained serious erosion from our recent decisions in *Casey* and *Romer*. When our precedent has been thus weakened, criticism from other sources is of greater significance. In the United States criticism of *Bowers* has been substantial and continuing, disapproving of its reasoning in all respects, not just as to its historical assumptions.

To the extent *Bowers* relied on values we share with a wider civilization, it should be noted that the reasoning and holding in *Bowers* have been rejected elsewhere. The European Court of Human Rights has followed not *Bowers* but its own decision in *Dudgeon v. United Kingdom*. Other nations, too, have taken action consistent with an affirmation of the protected right of homosexual adults to engage in intimate, consensual conduct. . . . The right the petitioners seek in this case has been accepted as an integral part of human freedom in many other countries. There has been no showing that in this country the governmental interest in circumscribing personal choice is somehow more legitimate or urgent.

The doctrine of *stare decisis* is essential to the respect accorded to the judgments of the Court and to the stability of the law. It is not, however, an inexorable command. . . . In *Casey* we noted that when a Court is asked to overrule a precedent recognizing a constitutional liberty interest, individual or societal reliance on the existence of that liberty cautions with particular strength against reversing course. . . . The holding in *Bowers*, however, has not induced detrimental reliance comparable to some instances where recognized individual rights are involved. Indeed, there has been no individual or societal reliance on *Bowers* of the sort that could counsel against overturning its holding once there are compelling reasons to do so. *Bowers* itself causes uncertainty, for the precedents before and after its issuance contradict its central holding. . . .

Bowers was not correct when it was decided, and it is not correct today. It ought not to remain binding precedent. *Bowers v. Hardwick* should be and now is overruled.

The present case does not involve minors. It does not involve persons who might be injured or coerced or who are situated in relationships where consent might not easily be refused. It does not involve public conduct or prostitution. It does not involve whether the government must give formal recognition to any relationship that homosexual persons seek to enter. The case does involve

Tyron Garner and John Geddes Lawrence in 2003. *Michael Stravato/Associated Press.*

two adults who, with full and mutual consent from each other, engaged in sexual practices common to a homosexual lifestyle. The petitioners are entitled to respect for their private lives. The State cannot demean their existence or control their destiny by making their private sexual conduct a crime. Their right to liberty under the Due Process Clause gives them the full right to engage in their conduct without intervention of the government. "It is a promise of the Constitution that there is a realm of personal liberty which the government may not enter." *Casey, supra,* at 847. The Texas statute furthers no legitimate state interest which can justify its intrusion into the personal and private life of the individual.

Had those who drew and ratified the Due Process Clauses of the Fifth Amendment or the Fourteenth Amendment known the components of liberty in its manifold possibilities, they might have been more specific. They did not presume to have this insight. They knew times can blind us to certain truths and later generations can see that laws once thought necessary and proper in fact serve only to oppress. As the Constitution endures, persons in every generation can invoke its principles in their own search for greater freedom.

The judgment of the Court of Appeals for the Texas Fourteenth District is reversed, and the case is remanded for further proceedings not inconsistent with this opinion.

BEHIND THE CURTAIN

As is often the case with cases such as *Lawrence v. Texas*, interchanges during oral argument turned to the question of whether states have unfettered power to legislate moral principles and distaste for certain citizens. Consider the following interchange between Justice Breyer and the attorney for the State of Texas:

Justice Stephen G. Breyer:

Now from what you recently said, I don't see what it has to do with marriage, since, in fact, marriage has nothing to do with the conduct that either this or other statutes do or don't forbid. I don't see what it has to do with children, since, in fact, the gay people can certainly adopt children and they do. And I don't see what it has to do with procreation, because that's the same as the children . . . so what is the justification for this statute, other than, you know, it's not what they say on the other side, is this is simply, I do not like thee, Doctor Fell, the reason why I cannot tell. . . .

Mr. Rosenthal:

I think what . . . what I'm saying is . . . Texas has the right to set moral standards and can set bright line moral standards for its people. And in the setting of those moral standards, I believe that they can say that certain kinds of activity can exist and certain kinds of activity cannot exist.

Justice Breyer:

Could they say, for example, it is against the law at the dinner table to tell really serious lies to your family?

Mr. Rosenthal:

   Yes, they can make that a law, but there would be no rational basis for the law.

Justice Breyer:

   Oh, really. It's very immoral. . . .

QUESTIONS FOR DISCUSSION

13.6   In the *Dobbs* opinion (discussed in Chapter 12), the Court cited the following four factors that it considered in overruling *Roe v. Wade* and *Casey v. Planned Parenthood*: (1) nature of the Court's initial error, (2) quality of the reasoning, (3) workability of the decision, and (4) reliance interests. How does this four-factor approach compare with the Court's reasoning in *Lawrence v. Texas* as to why it overruled *Bowers v. Hardwick*?

13.7   Note that in his majority opinion, Justice Kennedy relied on transnational law. Transnational law is the internal law of other parts of the world, such as case law from the European Court of Human Rights and parliamentary edicts from England. Is relying on the internal laws of other jurisdictions an appropriate technique for interpreting the U.S. Constitution? What are the pros and cons of relying on the laws and perceptions of other countries? Does it make a difference that the prerogative to engage in private consensual sexual conduct is regarded in many parts of the world as a universal human right?

13.8   The Court in *Lawrence v. Texas* stopped short of declaring that the right to engage in homosexual conduct was a fundamental right, requiring strict scrutiny when the right is infringed. How does the Court's treatment of the right compare with the Court's reasoning in *Romer v. Evans*, in which the Court invoked rational basis review? Does it make a difference that *Lawrence v. Texas* was a due process case, whereas *Romer v. Evans* was an equal protection case?

13.9   One explanation for why the Court ruled differently in *Lawrence v. Texas* than it did in *Bowers v. Hardwick* is a change in the membership of the Court. After *Bowers* but before *Lawrence*, four conservative Justices who had voted with the majority in *Bowers* retired or died (Justices White, Powell, O'Connor, and Rehnquist) and were replaced with Justices on the more liberal end of the ideological spectrum. Is it troubling that the change in Court membership heavily changes case outcomes? This connection between case outcome and Court membership is a consequence of our Constitution's design, which gives democratically elected Presidents and Senators enormous power in selecting the candidates for justice and grants life tenure to those who are confirmed. Are these qualities in the constitutional design ill-conceived? Should the Constitution be amended to reduce the effect of these qualities?

13.10 You may recall that in the *Dobbs* decision overruling *Roe v. Wade* and *Planned Parenthood v. Casey* (Chapter 12 of this volume) that Justice Alito in the majority opinion stated that the result of *Dobbs* does not mean that *Lawrence v. Texas* will be or should be overruled. Justice Thomas wrote a concurring opinion suggesting that the rejection of the substantive due process theory in *Dobbs* cast doubt on the validity of cases such as *Lawrence*. Now that you have read *Lawrence*, do you have a view about whether Alito or Thomas is correct?

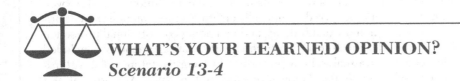

WHAT'S YOUR LEARNED OPINION?
Scenario 13-4

Ms. Romano was arrested for violating Hawaii state law prohibiting prostitution when she initiated an exchange with an undercover police officer in a hotel room. Ms. Romano claimed that the state's anti-prostitution statute violated her fundamental liberty, a right to privacy under the Due Process Clause of the Fourteenth Amendment, because she attempted to engage with a fully consenting adult in the privacy of a hotel room. Should the anti-prostitution law be upheld or struck down as unconstitutional if *Lawrence v. Texas* is the controlling precedent?

Scenario 13-5

Below are excerpts of the briefs from *Bowers v. Hardwick* and *Lawrence v. Texas*. Consider the following questions as you review the excerpts:

1. What was the strategy of the party who wrote the brief? Why did the party decide to pursue the strategy? Did the strategy work?
2. Note that ethical rules hold lawyers to a strong duty of candor and honesty in communicating with the Court. With this in mind, consider whether the strategy pursued was appropriate. Was any of the language misleading? Did it appear ethical and fair?
3. Did the party make good use of existing case law to support its position?

In evaluating these questions, consider which party lost in the court below. For *Bowers v. Hardwick*, the losing party below was the State of Texas. For *Lawrence v. Texas*, the losing party below was the man who was arrested. The U.S. Supreme Court tends to take cases in which at least four Justices believe that the lower court ruled incorrectly. Although it is not assured that the Supreme Court will reverse the lower court in the cases it decides to review, the Court's decision to take the case suggests that the "winner" in the lower court may have a tougher time than the lower court loser in making arguments that ensure its victory in the Supreme Court.

Bowers v. Hardwick
Portion of the brief of the Petitioner, the Texas Attorney General:

> The Court of Appeals for the Eleventh Circuit has failed to follow binding precedent. . . . [The court] below erroneously concluded that there had been [recent] doctrinal developments which would release lower federal courts from the binding effects of *Doe* [an earlier U.S. Supreme Court decision], permitting the lower courts to reach their own conclusions as to whether a fundamental right to engage in homosexual sodomy exists under the constitution. . . . Moreover, the court below seriously erred in judicially creating a fundamental right of privacy to engage in homosexual sodomy, and by finding constitutional protection for this perceived right. Furthermore, the court below erroneously concluded that the act of homosexual sodomy proscribed by Georgia statute violates Hardwick's right of intimate association protected by the Ninth Amendment and perceptions of fundamental fairness embodied in the Due Process Clause of the Fourteenth Amendment. These erroneous conclusions are unsupported by any previous decisions of this Court, the textual content of the Constitution itself, or any adherence to the concept that such rights that can be deemed fundamental must be rooted in traditional values and encompass only those rights "implicit in the concept of ordered liberty."

Portion of the brief of the Respondent Hardwick:

> The State of Georgia would extend its criminal law into the very bedrooms of its citizens, to break up even wholly consensual, noncommercial sexual relations between willing adults. And the State contends before this Court that it may freely do so without giving any good reason. All that Respondent [Hardwick] argues is that a Georgia citizen is entitled by the Constitution to demand not only a warrant of the Georgia police officer who would enter his bedroom, but also a substantial justification of the Georgia legislature when it declares criminal the consensual intimacies he chooses to engage in there.
>
> No less justification is acceptable in a society whose constitutional traditions have always placed the highest value upon the sanctity of the home against governmental intrusion or control. Nor is the mere invocation of contestable moral views sufficient to defend a law that so thoroughly invades individuals' most intimate affairs.

Thus the law challenged here must be subjected to heightened scrutiny, and it may be upheld upon remand only if the State of Georgia offers a far more powerful justification than the one it has offered here: namely, the tautology that the State has criminalized the private acts at issue because a majority of Georgia's legislators disapprove of them.

Lawrence v. Texas
Portion of the Brief of Petitioner Lawrence:

As the experience of Lawrence and Garner vividly illustrates, Section 21.06 puts the State of Texas inside its citizens' homes, policing the details of their most intimate and private physical behavior and dictating with whom they may share a profound part of adulthood. Texas has enacted and enforced a criminal law that takes away—from same-sex couples only—the freedom to make their own decisions, based upon their own values and relationships, about the forms of private, consensual sexual intimacy they will engage in or refrain from. The State defends this law only by saying the majority wants it so. Texas asserts a power of the majority to free itself from state dictates about private, consensual sexual choices, while using the criminal law to condemn and limit the choices of a minority.

This law and its application to Petitioners violate both the guarantee of equal protection and fundamental liberties safeguarded by the Fourteenth Amendment. Petitioners explain below why the equality claim and the liberty claim are each well rooted in the Constitution. The Court, however, need not rule on both constitutional violations if it chooses to focus on one infirmity rather than the other. Petitioners discuss the fundamental liberty claim under the Due Process Clause first, because even if the Court were not to reach that issue, a full appreciation of the personal interests affected by Section 21.06 also illuminates and informs the equal protection analysis that follows.

Fundamental liberty and privacy interests in adults' private, consensual sexual choices are essential to the ordered liberty our Constitution protects. The State may not, without overriding need, regiment and limit this personal and important part of its citizens' lives. More so than in 1986, when *Bowers v. Hardwick* was decided, it is clear today that such a fundamental right is supported by our basic constitutional structure, by multiple lines of precedent, and by a decisive historical turn in the vast majority of the States to repudiate this type of government invasion into private life. The well-established fundamental interests in intimate relationships, bodily integrity, and the sanctity of the home all converge in the right asserted here. That right belongs to all Americans, including gay men and lesbians, and should be shielded from Section 21.06's unjustified invasion. Much more is needed to outweigh fundamental individual interests than the majority's preferences. Indeed, the Fourteenth Amendment's protection of liberty exists to guard against the very impulse Texas acted on here. Principles of stare decisis do not, in these circumstances, justify adherence to *Bowers*.

Texas also has violated the Fourteenth Amendment's guarantee of equal protection of the laws. The Homosexual Conduct Law creates classes of persons, treating the same acts of consensual sexual behavior differently depending on who the participants are. By this law, Texas imposes a discriminatory prohibition on all gay and lesbian couples, requiring them to limit their expressions of affection in ways that heterosexual couples, whether married or unmarried, need not. The law's discriminatory focus sends the message that gay people are second-class citizens and lawbreakers, leading to ripples of discrimination throughout society. Such a discriminatory law cannot satisfy even the minimal requirement that a legislative classification must be rationally related to a legitimate State purpose. The bare negative attitudes of the majority, whether viewed as an expression of morality, discomfort, or blatant bias, cannot take away the equality of a smaller group.

Portion of the Brief of Respondent Texas:

The record is inadequate to serve as a basis for recognition of a limited constitutional right to engage in extramarital sexual conduct, because the absence of information concerning the petitioners and the circumstances of their offense precludes a determination of whether they would actually benefit from the Court's recognition of the limited right which they assert. The record is also inadequate to establish that the petitioners belong to the class for which they seek equal protection relief.

The States of the Union have historically prohibited a wide variety of extramarital sexual conduct, a legal tradition which is utterly inconsistent with any recognition, at this point in time, of a constitutionally protected liberty interest in engaging in any form of sexual conduct with whomever one chooses. Nothing in this Court's "substantive due process" jurisprudence supports recognition of a constitutional right to engage in sexual misconduct outside the venerable institution of marriage. This Court should adhere to its previous holding on this issue in *Bowers v. Hardwick* and it should reaffirm that the personal liberties protected by the Due Process Clause of the Fourteenth Amendment from State regulation are limited to those "so rooted in the traditions and conscience of our people as to be ranked as fundamental."

Since enforcement of the homosexual conduct statute does not interfere with the exercise of a fundamental right, and the statute is not based upon a suspect classification, it must only be rationally related to a permissible state goal in order to withstand equal protection challenge. This legislative proscription of one form of extramarital sexual misconduct is in keeping with longstanding national tradition, and bears a rational relationship to the worthy governmental goals of implementation of public morality and promotion of family values.

. . . The petitioners initially advocate the recognition of a broadly drawn constitutional right to choose to engage in any "private consensual sexual intimacy with another adult, including one of the same sex." However, the petitioners later clarify that their challenge does not extend to the validity of statutes prohibiting prostitution, incest or adultery, which they describe as implicating additional "state concerns" not present in this case. In short, the petitioners are asking the Court to recognize a fundamental right of an adult to engage in private, non-commercial, consensual sex with an unrelated, unmarried adult. The slim record reveals only that the petitioners are adult males and that they engaged in anal intercourse in an apartment that petitioner Lawrence identified as his residence. It does not answer any of the following questions concerning the factual basis of their constitutional claims:

- Whether the petitioners' sexual conduct was non-commercial. (The lack of profit motivation cannot be inferred from the lack of prosecution for the more serious offense of prostitution, see Tex. Penal Code 43.02 (Vernon Supp. 2003), because the police could not possibly determine whether prostitution was occurring if both participants in the sexual conduct declined to discuss that issue.)
- Whether the petitioners' sexual conduct was mutually consensual. (While neither of the petitioners was charged with any variant of sexual assault, prosecution for such an offense would require an acknowledgement from at least one of the parties that the sexual activity was non-consensual. Because there are any number of reasons why a person might choose not to cooperate with authorities in the investigation and prosecution of a sexual offense, mutual consent cannot necessarily be inferred from the parties' silence.)
- Whether the petitioners' conduct was "private." (While the record reflects that the sexual conduct occurred in Lawrence's apartment, the record does not indicate whether anyone else was present in that apartment at the time. Lower courts have held that any right of privacy that protects marital sex from governmental interference is waived when an onlooker is welcomed into the marital bedchamber.)
- Whether the petitioners are related to one another.
- Whether either of the petitioners is married.
- Whether either (or both) of the petitioners is exclusively homosexual. (The sexual orientation of the petitioners appears to be irrelevant to the disposition of their substantive due process argument, because they assert a constitutional right to engage in sodomy with persons of either gender, but it may be significant in determining whether the petitioners are members of any specific class in addressing their arguments premised upon the Equal Protection Clause.)

The three cases covered in this chapter have many messages on the process of Supreme Court decision making. These messages have many angles, including the relationship between law and morality, the effect of a change in the membership of the U.S. Supreme Court, changes in societal attitudes toward LGBTQIA+ individuals, and changes in the legal landscape. The three cases covered, *Bowers v. Hardwick, Romer v. Evans*, and *Lawrence v. Texas*, reflected each of these angles. The opinions and the results of each case raise important questions about the legitimacy of constitutional decision making in this contemporary era. The material covered in the next chapter concerning marriage reflects the same angles on constitutional decision making and similarly raises legitimacy questions.

QUESTIONS FOR REVIEW

1. Describe the cultural and historical context in which *Bowers v. Hardwick* was decided.
2. Which part(s) of the Constitution did the *Bowers* Court rely on in disposing of the case?
3. How did the majority in *Bowers* handle issues related to the connection between constitutional decision making and morality?
4. What was the law challenged in *Romer v. Evans*?
5. Which part(s) of the Constitution did the *Romer v. Evans* Court rely on in striking down the law at issue in the case? What standard of scrutiny did the Court use?
6. Discuss the reasons that the *Lawrence v. Texas* Court gave for why it overruled *Bowers v. Hardwick*.
7. Which part(s) of the Constitution did the *Lawrence v. Texas* Court rely on in striking down the law at issue there? Did the Court specify the standard of scrutiny that it used? If so, what was that standard of scrutiny?
8. Discuss the possible future of *Lawrence v. Texas*. What are the reasons why its continued validity is subject to question?

ENDNOTES

1. Eric Marcus, Stonewall: Key Turning Point—Not Starting Point—in LGBTQ Rights Movement, Arcus Foundation Blog, available at https://www.arcusfoundation.org/blog/social-justice-lgbt/stonewall-key-turning-point-not-starting-point-in-lgbtq-rights-movement (last accessed June 6, 2023).

Marriage

14

Throughout the final part of this volume, we have seen a blend of rights implicating racial relations, reproductive freedom, intimacy, and sex. You will recall the Court's holding in *Korematsu v. United States* that any racial classifications should be scrutinized very closely. *Korematsu* announced the strict scrutiny standard of review, which requires that a state demonstrate an objective independent of racial discrimination to justify a racial classification. The objective must be compelling and the means used must be narrowly tailored to the objective. Only after a showing of this narrowly tailored, compelling, and nonracially motivated reason for the classification should a Court uphold the classification as constitutional.

The right to reproductive freedom grew from the right to use birth control for married couples in *Griswold v. Connecticut*. This led to *Roe v. Wade*'s finding of a fundamental right to abortion before viability, a holding ultimately overruled by the *Dobbs* opinion. In the last chapter we saw a recognition of constitutional protection for intimate sexual activity between individuals of the same sex.

This chapter—dealing with the constitutional right to marriage—touches on each of those rights, thereby providing a fitting ending to this part (and this book). Yet marriage is a unique construct that differs from other individual rights. Leaving aside religious considerations, marriage can be defined as a status obtained when the government issues a license recognizing an individual's status as a spouse. In other words, a request to marry can be seen as a request for government imprimatur, formally recognizing a relationship with all of the rights and privileges attached to that government-recognized relationship.

When it comes to the question of who or what can be married, some matters are uncontroversial: You cannot marry your cat; you cannot marry a bright, starry evening; and you cannot marry your parent. Other matters have been settled in constitutional decisions such as *Reynolds v. United States*, 98 U.S. 145 (1879), which upheld a prohibition against plural marriage against constitutional attack. *Reynolds* held that a federal statute prohibiting one man from marrying several wives was consistent with the First Amendment freedom of religion principles. Subsequent cases pertaining to marriage largely relied on the Tenth Amendment of the U.S. Constitution in highlighting that marriage is a matter that should be left exclusively to state regulation.

The following case addresses anti-miscegenation laws, laws prohibiting marriage between individuals of different races. One of the earliest cases on interracial relations dates back to 1883, when the Supreme Court held in *Pace v. Alabama* that the criminal conviction of an Alabama couple for participating in interracial sex did not violate the Fourteenth Amendment to the U.S. Constitution. In the following opinion, however, the Court took a more tolerant stance, emphasizing the right to privacy in family and marriage free from government interference. This case is thought to have set the stage for the U.S. Supreme Court to recognize a constitutional right to marry someone of the same sex. As you read through the decision immediately below, look for language that might have been helpful for the same-sex marriage decision.

FROM THE BENCH

LOVING v. VIRGINIA
388 U.S. 1 (1967)

Mr. Chief Justice WARREN delivered the opinion of the Court.

This case presents a constitutional question never addressed by this Court: whether a statutory scheme adopted by the State of Virginia to prevent marriages between persons solely on the basis of racial classifications violates the Equal Protection and Due Process Clauses of the Fourteenth Amendment. For reasons which seem to us to reflect the central meaning of those constitutional commands, we conclude that these statutes cannot stand consistently with the Fourteenth Amendment.

In June 1958, two residents of Virginia, Mildred Jeter, a Negro woman, and Richard Loving, a white man, were married in the District of Columbia pursuant to its laws. Shortly after their marriage, the Lovings returned to Virginia and established their marital abode in Caroline County. At the October Term, 1958, of the Circuit Court of Caroline County, a grand jury issued an indictment charging the Lovings with violating Virginia's ban on interracial marriages. On January 6, 1959, the Lovings pleaded guilty to the charge and were sentenced to one year in jail; however, the trial judge suspended the sentence for a period of 25 years on the condition that the Lovings leave the State and not return to Virginia together for 25 years. He stated in an opinion that:

> "Almighty God created the races white, black, yellow, malay and red, and he placed them on separate continents. And but for the interference with his arrangement there would be no cause for such marriages. The fact that he separated the races shows that he did not intend for the races to mix."

After their convictions, the Lovings took up residence in the District of Columbia. On November 6, 1963, they filed a motion in the state trial court to vacate the judgment and set aside the sentence on the ground that the statutes which they had violated were repugnant to the Fourteenth Amendment. The motion not having been decided by October 28, 1964, the Lovings instituted a class action in the United States District Court for the Eastern District of Virginia requesting that a three-judge court be convened to declare the Virginia anti-miscegenation statutes unconstitutional and to enjoin state officials from enforcing their convictions. On January 22, 1965, the state trial judge denied the motion to vacate the sentences, and the Lovings perfected an appeal to the Supreme Court of Appeals of Virginia. On February 11, 1965, the three-judge District Court continued the case to allow the Lovings to present their constitutional claims to the highest state court.

The Supreme Court of Appeals upheld the constitutionality of the anti-miscegenation statutes and, after modifying the sentence, affirmed the convictions. The Lovings appealed this decision, and we noted probable jurisdiction on December 12, 1966, 385 U.S. 986.

The two statutes under which appellants were convicted and sentenced are part of a comprehensive statutory scheme aimed at prohibiting and punishing interracial marriages. The Lovings were convicted of violating §20-58 of the Virginia Code:

> "*Leaving State to evade law.* — If any white person and colored person shall go out of this State, for the purpose of being married, and with the intention of returning, and be married out of it, and afterwards return to and reside in it, cohabiting as man and wife, they shall be punished as provided in §20-59, and the marriage shall be governed by the same law as if it had been solemnized in this State. The fact of their cohabitation here as man and wife shall be evidence of their marriage."

Section 20-59, which defines the penalty for miscegenation, provides:

> "*Punishment for marriage.* — If any white person intermarry with a colored person, or any colored person intermarry with a white person, he shall be guilty of a felony and shall be punished by confinement in the penitentiary for not less than one nor more than five years."

■ ■ ■

Virginia is now one of 16 States which prohibit and punish marriages on the basis of racial classifications. Penalties for miscegenation arose as an incident to slavery and have been common in Virginia since the colonial period. The present statutory scheme dates from the adoption of the Racial Integrity Act of 1924, passed during the period of extreme nativism which followed the end of the First World War. The central features of this Act, and current Virginia law, are the absolute prohibition of a "white person" marrying other than another "white person," a prohibition against issuing marriage licenses until the issuing official is satisfied that the applicants' statements as to their race are correct, certificates of "racial composition" to be kept by both local and state registrars, and the carrying forward of earlier prohibitions against racial intermarriage.

I

In upholding the constitutionality of these provisions in the decision below, the Supreme Court of Appeals of Virginia referred to its 1955 decision in *Naim v. Naim*, as stating the reasons supporting the validity of these laws. In *Naim*, the state court concluded that the State's legitimate purposes were "to preserve the racial integrity of its citizens," and to prevent "the corruption of blood," "a mongrel breed of citizens," and "the obliteration of racial pride," obviously an endorsement of the doctrine of White Supremacy. The court also reasoned that marriage has traditionally been subject to state regulation without federal intervention, and, consequently, the regulation of marriage should be left to exclusive state control by the Tenth Amendment.

While the state court is no doubt correct in asserting that marriage is a social relation subject to the State's police power, *Maynard v. Hill*, the State does not contend in its argument before this Court that its powers to regulate marriage are unlimited notwithstanding the commands of the Fourteenth Amendment. Nor could it do so in light of *Meyer v. Nebraska*, and *Skinner v. Oklahoma*. Instead, the State argues that the meaning of the Equal Protection Clause, as illuminated by the statements of the Framers, is only that state penal laws containing an interracial element as part of the definition of the offense must apply equally to whites and Negroes in the sense that members of each race are punished to the same degree. Thus, the State contends that, because its miscegenation statutes punish equally both the white and the Negro participants in an interracial marriage, these statutes, despite their reliance on racial classifications, do not constitute an invidious discrimination based upon race. The second argument advanced by the State assumes the validity of its equal application theory. The argument is that, if the Equal Protection Clause does not outlaw miscegenation statutes because of their reliance on racial classifications, the question of constitutionality would thus become whether there was any rational basis for a State to treat interracial marriages differently from other marriages. On this question, the State argues, the scientific evidence is substantially in doubt and, consequently, this Court should defer to the wisdom of the state legislature in adopting its policy of discouraging interracial marriages.

Because we reject the notion that the mere "equal application" of a statute containing racial classifications is enough to remove the classifications from the Fourteenth Amendment's proscription of all invidious racial discriminations, we do not accept the State's contention that these statutes should be upheld if there is any possible basis for concluding that they serve a rational purpose. The mere fact of equal application does not mean that our analysis of these statutes should follow the approach we have taken in cases involving no racial discrimination where the Equal Protection Clause has been arrayed against a statute discriminating between the kinds of advertising which may be displayed on trucks in New York City, *Railway Express Agency, Inc. v. New York*, or an exemption in Ohio's ad valorem tax for merchandise owned by a nonresident in a storage warehouse, *Allied Stores of Ohio, Inc. v. Bowers*. In these cases, involving distinctions not drawn according to race, the Court has merely asked whether there is any rational foundation for the discriminations, and has deferred to the wisdom of the state legislatures.

In the case at bar, however, we deal with statutes containing racial classifications, and the fact of equal application does not immunize the statute from the very heavy burden of justification which the Fourteenth Amendment has traditionally required of state statutes drawn according to race. The State argues that statements in the Thirty-ninth Congress about the time of the passage of the Fourteenth Amendment indicate that the Framers did not intend the Amendment to make unconstitutional state miscegenation laws. Many of the statements alluded to by the State concern the debates over the Freedmen's Bureau Bill, which President Johnson vetoed, and the Civil Rights Act of 1866, 14 Stat. 27, enacted over his veto. While these statements have some relevance to the intention of Congress in submitting the Fourteenth Amendment, it must be understood that they pertained to the passage of specific statutes and not to the broader, organic purpose of a constitutional amendment. As for the various statements directly concerning the Fourteenth Amendment, we have said in connection with a related problem, that although these historical sources "cast some light" they are not sufficient to resolve the problem; "[at] best, they are inconclusive. The most avid proponents of the post-War Amendments undoubtedly intended them to remove all legal distinctions among 'all persons born or naturalized in the United States.' Their opponents, just as certainly, were antagonistic to both the letter and the spirit of the Amendments and wished them to have the most limited effect." *Brown v. Board of Education*. We have rejected the proposition that the debates in the Thirty-ninth Congress or in the state legislatures which ratified the Fourteenth Amendment supported the theory advanced

FROM THE BENCH

by the State, that the requirement of equal protection of the laws is satisfied by penal laws defining offenses based on racial classifications so long as white and Negro participants in the offense were similarly punished. *McLaughlin v. Florida*, 379 U.S. 184 (1964).

The State finds support for its "equal application" theory in the decision of the Court in *Pace v. Alabama*. In that case, the Court upheld a conviction under an Alabama statute forbidding adultery or fornication between a white person and a Negro which imposed a greater penalty than that of a statute proscribing similar conduct by members of the same race. The Court reasoned that the statute could not be said to discriminate against Negroes because the punishment for each participant in the offense was the same. However, as recently as the 1964 Term, in rejecting the reasoning of that case, we stated "*Pace* represents a limited view of the Equal Protection Clause which has not withstood analysis in the subsequent decisions of this Court." *McLaughlin v. Florida*. As we there demonstrated, the Equal Protection Clause requires the consideration of whether the classifications drawn by any statute constitute an arbitrary and invidious discrimination. The clear and central purpose of the Fourteenth Amendment was to eliminate all official state sources of invidious racial discrimination in the States.

There can be no question but that Virginia's miscegenation statutes rest solely upon distinctions drawn according to race. The statutes proscribe generally accepted conduct if engaged in by members of different races. Over the years, this Court has consistently repudiated "distinctions between citizens solely because of their ancestry" as being "odious to a free people whose institutions are founded upon the doctrine of equality." *Hirabayashi v. United States*. At the very least, the Equal Protection Clause demands that racial classifications, especially suspect in criminal statutes, be subjected to the "most rigid scrutiny," and, if they are ever to be upheld, they must be shown to be necessary to the accomplishment of some permissible state objective, independent of the racial discrimination which it was the object of the Fourteenth Amendment to eliminate. Indeed, two members of this Court have already stated that they "cannot conceive of a valid legislative purpose . . . which makes the color of a person's skin the test of whether his conduct is a criminal offense." *McLaughlin v. Florida*. There is patently no legitimate overriding purpose independent of invidious racial discrimination which justifies this classification. The fact that Virginia prohibits only interracial marriages involving white persons demonstrates that the racial classifications must stand on their own justification, as measures designed to maintain White Supremacy. We have consistently denied the constitutionality of measures which restrict the rights of citizens on account of race. There can be no doubt that restricting the freedom to marry solely because of racial classifications violates the central meaning of the Equal Protection Clause.

II

These statutes also deprive the Lovings of liberty without due process of law in violation of the Due Process Clause of the Fourteenth Amendment. The freedom to marry has long been recognized as one of the vital personal rights essential to the orderly pursuit of happiness by free men. Marriage is one of the "basic civil rights of man," fundamental to our very existence and survival. To deny this fundamental freedom on so unsupportable a basis as the racial classifications embodied in these statutes, classifications so directly subversive of the principle of equality at the heart of the Fourteenth Amendment, is surely to deprive all the State's citizens of liberty without due process of law. The Fourteenth Amendment requires that the freedom of choice to marry not be restricted by invidious racial discriminations. Under our Constitution, the freedom to marry, or not marry, a person of another race resides with the individual and cannot be infringed by the State.

These convictions must be reversed.

In arguing their case before the U.S. Supreme Court, attorneys for the Lovings presented two arguments: First, the Virginia anti-miscegenation laws, criminalizing interracial marriage, violated the Equal Protection Clause of the Fourteenth Amendment; second, marriage is a fundamental right protected by the Due Process Clause. Both arguments—classifications based on race and the implication of a fundamental right—generally trigger strict scrutiny, meaning the laws can only be upheld if they are narrowly tailored to meet a compelling state interest.

The Court found that Virginia's miscegenation statute violated both clauses, although it could have stopped at the Equal Protection analysis. In relying on both clauses, the Lovings were concerned about the Court providing a narrow holding that would give the state room to work around it. As reflected in the opinion, the Court found the law violated both clauses.

Note that when it wrote of the Due Process Clause, the Court stated that "[t]he freedom to marry has long been recognized as one of the vital personal rights essential to the orderly pursuit of happiness by free men. Marriage is one of the 'basic civil rights of man,' fundamental to our very existence and survival." This statement is relevant to much of the Court's substantive due process jurisprudence because a fundamental right automatically triggers strict scrutiny when abridged. To determine whether a right is fundamental, the Court looks to whether it is "deeply rooted in our Nation's history and tradition." The Court's determination that marriage that is a fundamental right proved significant in deciding the next case.

BEHIND THE CURTAIN

The law at issue in *Loving* was titled the Racial Integrity Act of 1924. Among the state's professed purposes for the law was to prevent "the corruption of blood" and "a mongrel breed of citizens." The same day the Racial Integrity Act of 1924 was signed into law, Virginia also passed an act allowing forced sterilization of people living with certain disabilities. That statute was upheld by the Supreme Court as constitutional in 1927, when it explained, "[i]t is better for all the world, if instead of waiting to execute

Richard and Mildred Loving on their wedding anniversary in 1965. *Associated Press.*

degenerate offspring for crime, or to let them starve for their imbecility, society can prevent those who are manifestly unfit from continuing their kind." *Buck v. Bell*, 274 U.S. 200, 207 (1927).

These laws reflect an embrace of eugenics, which is generally defined as the pursuit of improving a population's genetics through selective breeding and sterilization. Although not supported by science, eugenics was a popular doctrine in the early twentieth century. It has taken different forms throughout history: from laws criminalizing interracial intimacy and forced sterilization of criminals to Hitler's campaign for creating a master Aryan race. Although the Court headed by Chief Justice Warren openly rejected marriage laws designed to further White supremacy, the Court has not overruled the disability opinion, *Buck v. Bell*. Even today, Justice Thomas has expressed concerns about the relationship between America's history of embracing eugenics and abortion. Justice Alito also included a reference to the threat of eugenics in the majority *Dobbs* opinion, which refused to recognize constitutional protection for abortion rights. Alito's mention of eugenics has been read as a "tip of the hat" to Justice Thomas's concerns.

QUESTIONS FOR DISCUSSION

14.1 In striking down the Virginia law, the Supreme Court used the force of federal constitutional law. In other words, the Court insisted that federal law should determine whether individuals of different races should be allowed to marry. One often hears that domestic relations questions, such as those pertaining to marriage, should be left to state law. Part of the thinking on this is that domestic relations implicate moral questions and different parts of the country reflect different moral attitudes on those questions. If state law should govern, the laws pertaining to marriage might vary from state to state. Is it a good idea to have different laws regarding the validity of marriage in different states of the United States?

14.2 At the time that the *Loving* case was decided, 16 states had anti-miscegenation laws. Thus, all those laws were rendered unconstitutional under the *Loving* decision. Does that fact make it more legitimate or less legitimate that the Court decided *Loving* the way that it did?

14.3 *Loving* was decided in 1967, a time when the civil rights movement had been underway for over a decade. Viewed in light of this history and the existing jurisprudence of the Court, did the fact that the *Loving* case implicated a question of race render the decision easier or harder for the Court to decide the way that it did?

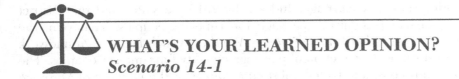

WHAT'S YOUR LEARNED OPINION?
Scenario 14-1

A state statute prohibits any noncustodial parent from marrying without proving they are up-to-date on all child support payments and that their child will never require welfare benefits. Roy is a resident of the state where he fathered a child as a high school student. The child lives with her mother. He was unemployed for several years and unable to make his child support payments. When he met a new partner and was expecting another child, he applied for a marriage license. He was denied the license because of his outstanding child support and because his first child had been receiving welfare benefits for her entire life.

Roy sued, alleging the state statute violated the Equal Protection and Due Process Clauses of the Fourteenth Amendment. The state claimed the law was designed to encourage parents to fulfill their financial obligations and to discourage them from incurring more. More specifically, are these interests sufficient to justify infringing Roy's right to marry?

Scenario 14-2

An interracial couple married. The woman was White and had two children from an earlier marriage to a White man. Her new Black husband, Mark, is a member of the Armed Forces and sought to adopt the children. Evaluating the circumstances, the adoption court found the children to be "proper subjects of adoption" and the home to be a suitable place for the minor children to live. Nonetheless, the adoption would be invalid under a state statute prohibiting adoption of a White child by an African American person. The state's proffered reason for this prohibition was to ensure the welfare of the children. As a result of the prohibition, the court was forced to deny the adoption. Mark filed suit claiming the racial ban on adoption violated the Equal Protection Clause of the Fourteenth Amendment. What would the outcome be under *Loving v. Virginia*?

As noted above, the Court's language in *Loving* proved important in the disposition of the following case, particularly given the *Loving* Court's determination that marriage is a fundamental right. As you read through the opinion in *Obergefell v. Hodges*, 133 S. Ct. 2584 (2015), evaluate how important that determination proved to be. Did the Court rely on other factors and reasoning in coming to its conclusion that the Constitution protected the right to same-sex marriage?

The legal landscape leading up to *Obergefell* showed a strong trend in favor of accepting same-sex marriage. Indeed, by 2013, 12 states and the District of Columbia had recognized marriage for same-sex couples. That year, the Supreme Court decided *United States v. Windsor*, which laid the groundwork for the constitutional protection of marriage equality for same-sex couples. The *Windsor* Court considered a federal statute, known as the Defense of Marriage Act (DOMA). *Windsor* declared unconstitutional under the Equal Protection Clause of the Fourteenth Amendment a provision in DOMA that defined marriage for the purpose of federal tax exemptions and benefits. Specifically, DOMA declared that marriage would be recognized under federal law only when the partners to the marriage were a man and a woman. Writing for the *Windsor* majority, Justice Kennedy wrote that marriage is traditionally regulated by the states. By denying benefits to couples in same-sex marriages that states had recognized, he reasoned that the federal government was treating the couples as second-class citizens. The Court ruled that the statute violated the Fifth Amendment, "for no legitimate purpose overcomes the purpose and effect to disparage and to injure those whom the State, by its marriage laws, sought to protect in personhood and dignity." In addition to this specific case law on the same-sex marriage issue, at least two other U.S. Supreme Court decisions — *Romer v. Evans* (1996) and *Lawrence v. Texas* (2003) — established constitutional recognition for homosexual rights before the *Obergefell* case reached the Court.

After *Windsor*, the momentum in states toward accepting same-sex marriage accelerated. By the time the Supreme Court agreed to review state laws limiting marriage to opposite-sex couples, 37 states and the District of Columbia had passed laws recognizing same-sex marriage. Although the marriage equality movement had encountered significant success, the political terrain at the time of oral arguments in the case that follows was still fractured, with strong opinions both for and against same-sex marriage.

A note on language: As was the case with the homosexual rights case—*Lawrence v. Texas*—the Supreme Court did not use expansive references to nonheterosexual binary individuals or their marital rights, such as reference to LGBTQIA+ marriages. The Court spoke only of same sex-marriage rights. For that reason, a cautious reading of the Court's holding is confined to constitutional protection for "same-sex marriage," which by necessity is the terminology used to discuss *Obergefell* in this volume.

FROM THE BENCH

OBERGEFELL v. HODGES
576 U.S. 644 (2015)

Justice **KENNEDY** delivered the opinion of the Court.

The Constitution promises liberty to all within its reach, a liberty that includes certain specific rights that allow persons, within a lawful realm, to define and express their identity. The petitioners in these cases seek to find that liberty by marrying someone of the same sex and having their marriages deemed lawful on the same terms and conditions as marriages between persons of the opposite sex.

I

These cases come from . . . States that define marriage as a union between one man and one woman. The petitioners are 14 same-sex couples and two men whose same-sex partners are deceased. The respondents are state officials responsible for enforcing the laws in question. The petitioners claim the respondents violate the Fourteenth Amendment by denying them the right to marry or to have their marriages, lawfully performed in another State, given full recognition.

II

A

From their beginning to their most recent page, the annals of human history reveal the transcendent importance of marriage. The lifelong union of a man and a woman always has promised nobility and dignity to all persons, without

Richard Hodges, former Director of the Ohio Health Department. *Courtesy of Richard Hodges.*

regard to their station in life. Marriage is sacred to those who live by their religions and offers unique fulfillment to those who find meaning in the secular realm. Its dynamic allows two people to find a life that could not be found alone, for a marriage becomes greater than just the two persons. Rising from the most basic human needs, marriage is essential to our most profound hopes and aspirations.

The centrality of marriage to the human condition makes it unsurprising that the institution has existed for millennia and across civilizations. Since the dawn of history, marriage has transformed strangers into relatives, binding families and societies together. Confucius taught that marriage lies at the foundation of government. This wisdom was echoed centuries later and half a world away by Cicero, who wrote, "The first bond of society is marriage; next, children; and then the family." There are untold references to the beauty of marriage in religious and philosophical texts spanning time, cultures, and faiths, as well as in art and literature in all their forms. It is fair and necessary to say these references were based on the understanding that marriage is a union between two persons of the opposite sex.

That history is the beginning of these cases. The respondents say it should be the end as well. To them, it would demean a timeless institution if the concept and lawful status of marriage were extended to two persons of the same sex. Marriage, in their view, is by its nature a gender-differentiated union of man and woman. This view long has been held—and continues to be held—in good faith by reasonable and sincere people here and throughout the world.

The petitioners acknowledge this history but contend that these cases cannot end there. . . . [I]t is the enduring importance of marriage that underlies the petitioners' contentions. This, they say, is their whole point. Far from seeking to devalue marriage, the petitioners seek it for themselves because of their respect—and need—for its privileges and responsibilities. And their immutable nature dictates that same-sex marriage is their only real path to this profound commitment.

Recounting the circumstances of three of these cases illustrates the urgency of the petitioners' cause from their perspective. Petitioner James Obergefell, a plaintiff in the Ohio case, met John Arthur over two decades ago. They fell in love and started a life together, establishing a lasting, committed relation. In 2011, however, Arthur was diagnosed with amyotrophic lateral sclerosis, or ALS. This debilitating disease is progressive, with no known cure. Two years ago, Obergefell and Arthur decided to commit to one another, resolving to marry before Arthur died. To fulfill their mutual promise, they traveled from Ohio to

Maryland, where same-sex marriage was legal. It was difficult for Arthur to move, and so the couple were wed inside a medical transport plane as it remained on the tarmac in Baltimore. Three months later, Arthur died. Ohio law does not permit Obergefell to be listed as the surviving spouse on Arthur's death certificate. By statute, they must remain strangers even in death, a state-imposed separation Obergefell deems "hurtful for the rest of time." He brought suit to be shown as the surviving spouse on Arthur's death certificate.

April DeBoer and Jayne Rowse are co-plaintiffs in the case from Michigan. They celebrated a commitment ceremony to honor their permanent relation in 2007. . . . In 2009, DeBoer and Rowse fostered and then adopted a baby boy. Later that same year, they welcomed another son into their family. The new baby, born prematurely and abandoned by his biological mother, required around-the-clock care. The next year, a baby girl with special needs joined their family. Michigan, however, permits only opposite-sex married couples or single individuals to adopt, so each child can have only one woman as his or her legal parent. If an emergency were to arise, schools and hospitals may treat the three children as if they had only one parent. And, were tragedy to befall either DeBoer or Rowse, the other would have no legal rights over the children she had not been permitted to adopt. This couple seeks relief from the continuing uncertainty their unmarried status creates in their lives.

Army Reserve Sergeant First Class Ijpe DeKoe and his partner Thomas Kostura, co-plaintiffs in the Tennessee case, fell in love. In 2011, DeKoe received orders to deploy to Afghanistan. Before leaving, he and Kostura married in New York. A week later, DeKoe began his deployment, which lasted for almost a year. When he returned, the two settled in Tennessee, where DeKoe works full-time for the Army Reserve. Their lawful marriage is stripped from them whenever they reside in Tennessee, returning and disappearing as they travel across state lines. DeKoe, who served this Nation to preserve the freedom the Constitution protects, must endure a substantial burden.

The cases now before the Court involve other petitioners as well, each with their own experiences. Their stories reveal that they seek not to denigrate marriage but rather to live their lives, or honor their spouses' memory, joined by its bond.

B

The ancient origins of marriage confirm its centrality, but it has not stood in isolation from developments in law and society. The history of marriage is one of both continuity and change. That institution—even as confined to opposite-sex relations—has evolved over time. These new insights have strengthened, not weakened, the institution of marriage. Indeed, changed understandings of marriage are characteristic of a Nation where new dimensions of freedom become apparent to new generations, often through perspectives that begin in pleas or protests and then are considered in the political sphere and the judicial process.

This dynamic can be seen in the Nation's experiences with the rights of gays and lesbians. Until the mid-20th century, same-sex intimacy long had been condemned as immoral by the state itself in most Western nations, a belief often embodied in the criminal law. For this reason, among others, many persons did not deem homosexuals to have dignity in their own distinct identity. A truthful declaration by same-sex couples of what was in their hearts had to remain unspoken. . . . Same-sex intimacy remained a crime in many States. Gays and lesbians were prohibited from most government employment, barred from military service, excluded under immigration laws, targeted by police, and burdened in their rights to associate.

For much of the 20th century, moreover, homosexuality was treated as an illness. . . . Only in more recent years have psychiatrists and others recognized that sexual orientation is both a normal expression of human sexuality and immutable.

In the late 20th century, following substantial cultural and political developments, same-sex couples began to lead more open and public lives and to establish families. This development was followed by a quite extensive discussion of the issue in both governmental and private sectors and by a shift in public attitudes toward greater tolerance. As a result, questions about the rights of gays and lesbians soon reached the courts, where the issue could be discussed in the formal discourse of the law. . . .

III

Under the Due Process Clause of the Fourteenth Amendment, no State shall "deprive any person of life, liberty, or property, without due process of law." The fundamental liberties protected by this Clause include most of the rights enumerated in the Bill of Rights. In addition these liberties extend to certain personal choices central to individual dignity and autonomy, including intimate choices that define personal identity and beliefs.

The identification and protection of fundamental rights is an enduring part of the judicial duty to interpret the Constitution. That responsibility, however, "has not been reduced to any formula." Rather, it requires courts to exercise reasoned judgment in identifying interests of the person so fundamental that the State must accord them its respect. . . . History and tradition guide and discipline this inquiry but do not set its outer boundaries. That method respects our history and learns from it without allowing the past alone to rule the present.

The nature of injustice is that we may not always see it in our own times. The generations that wrote and ratified the Bill of Rights and the Fourteenth Amendment did not presume to know the extent of freedom in all of its dimensions, and so they entrusted to future generations a charter protecting the right of all persons to enjoy liberty as we learn its meaning. . . .

Applying these established tenets, the Court has long held the right to marry is protected by the Constitution. In *Loving v. Virginia*, which invalidated bans on interracial unions, a unanimous Court held marriage is "one of the vital personal rights essential to the orderly pursuit of happiness by free men." Over time and in other contexts, the Court has reiterated that the right to marry is fundamental under the Due Process Clause.

It cannot be denied that this Court's cases describing the right to marry presumed a relationship involving opposite-sex partners. The Court, like many institutions, has made assumptions defined by the world and time of which it is a part. . . .

Still, there are other, more instructive precedents. . . . In defining the right to marry these cases have identified essential attributes of that right based in history, tradition, and other constitutional liberties inherent in this intimate bond. And in assessing whether the force and rationale of its cases apply to same-sex couples, the Court must respect the basic reasons why the right to marry has been long protected.

This analysis compels the conclusion that same-sex couples may exercise the right to marry. The four principles and traditions to be discussed demonstrate that the reasons marriage is fundamental under the Constitution apply with equal force to same-sex couples.

A first premise of the Court's relevant precedents is that the right to personal choice regarding marriage is inherent in the concept of individual autonomy. This abiding connection between marriage and liberty is why *Loving* invalidated interracial marriage bans under the Due Process Clause. Like choices concerning contraception, family relationships, procreation, and childrearing, all of which are protected by the Constitution, decisions concerning marriage are among the most intimate that an individual can make. Indeed, the Court has noted it would be contradictory "to recognize a right of privacy with respect to other matters of family life and not with respect to the decision to enter the relationship that is the foundation of the family in our society."

Choices about marriage shape an individual's destiny. . . . The nature of marriage is that, through its enduring bond, two persons together can find other freedoms, such as expression, intimacy, and spirituality. This is true for all persons, whatever their sexual orientation. There is dignity in the bond between two men or two women who seek to marry and in their autonomy to make such profound choices.

A second principle in this Court's jurisprudence is that the right to marry is fundamental because it supports a two-person union unlike any other in its importance to the committed individuals. This point was central to *Griswold v. Connecticut*, which held the Constitution protects the right of married couples to use contraception.

The right to marry thus dignifies couples who "wish to define themselves by their commitment to each other." Marriage responds to the universal fear that a lonely person might call out only to find no one there. It offers the hope of companionship and understanding and assurance that while both still live there will be someone to care for the other.

A third basis for protecting the right to marry is that it safeguards children and families and thus draws meaning from related rights of childrearing, procreation, and education. . . . By giving recognition and legal structure to their parents' relationship, marriage . . . affords the permanency and stability important to children's best interests.

As all parties agree, many same-sex couples provide loving and nurturing homes to their children, whether biological or adopted. And hundreds of thousands of children are presently being raised by such couples. Most States have allowed gays and lesbians to adopt, either as individuals or as couples, and many adopted and foster children have same-sex parents. This provides powerful confirmation from the law itself that gays and lesbians can create loving, supportive families.

Excluding same-sex couples from marriage thus conflicts with a central premise of the right to marry. Without the recognition, stability, and predictability marriage offers, their children suffer the stigma of knowing their families are somehow lesser. They also suffer the significant material costs of being raised by unmarried parents, relegated through no fault of their own to a more difficult and uncertain family life. The marriage laws at issue here thus harm and humiliate the children of same-sex couples.

That is not to say the right to marry is less meaningful for those who do not or cannot have children. An ability, desire, or promise to procreate is not and has not been a prerequisite for a valid marriage in any State. In light of precedent protecting the right of a married couple not to procreate, it cannot be said the Court or the States have conditioned the right to marry on the capacity or commitment to procreate. The constitutional marriage right has many aspects, of which childbearing is only one.

Fourth and finally, this Court's cases and the Nation's traditions make clear that marriage is a keystone of our social order. . . .

For that reason, just as a couple vows to support each other, so does society pledge to support the couple, offering symbolic recognition and material benefits to protect and nourish the union. Indeed, while the States are in general free to vary the benefits they confer on all married couples, they have throughout our history made marriage the basis for an expanding list of governmental rights, benefits, and responsibilities.

There is no difference between same- and opposite-sex couples with respect to this principle. Yet by virtue of their exclusion from that institution, same-sex couples are denied the constellation of benefits that the States have linked to marriage. This harm results in more than just material burdens. . . . As the State itself makes marriage all the more precious by the significance it attaches to it, exclusion from that status has the effect of teaching that gays and lesbians are unequal in important respects. It demeans gays and lesbians for the State to lock them out of a central institution of the Nation's society. Same-sex couples, too, may aspire to the transcendent purposes of marriage and seek fulfillment in its highest meaning.

The limitation of marriage to opposite-sex couples may long have seemed natural and just, but its inconsistency with the central meaning of the fundamental right to marry is now manifest. With that knowledge must come the recognition that laws excluding same-sex couples from the marriage right impose stigma and injury of the kind prohibited by our basic charter.

Objecting that this does not reflect an appropriate framing of the issue, the respondents . . . assert the petitioners do not seek to exercise the right to marry but rather a new and nonexistent "right to same-sex marriage." . . . *Loving* did not ask about a "right to interracial marriage"; *Turner* did not ask about a "right of inmates to marry"; and *Zablocki* did not ask about a "right of fathers with unpaid child support duties to marry." Rather, each case inquired about the right to marry in its comprehensive sense, asking if there was a sufficient justification for excluding the relevant class from the right.

That principle applies here. If rights were defined by who exercised them in the past, then received practices could serve as their own continued justification and new groups could not invoke rights once denied. This Court has rejected that approach, both with respect to the right to marry and the rights of gays and lesbians.

The right to marry is fundamental as a matter of history and tradition, but rights come not from ancient sources alone. They rise, too, from a better informed understanding of how constitutional imperatives define a liberty that remains urgent in our own era. Many who deem same-sex marriage to be wrong reach that conclusion based on decent and honorable religious or philosophical premises, and neither they nor their beliefs are disparaged here. But when that sincere, personal opposition becomes enacted law and public policy, the necessary consequence is to put the imprimatur of the State itself on an exclusion that soon demeans or stigmatizes those whose own liberty is then denied. Under the Constitution, same-sex couples seek in marriage the same legal treatment as opposite-sex couples, and it would disparage their choices and diminish their personhood to deny them this right.

The right of same-sex couples to marry that is part of the liberty promised by the Fourteenth Amendment is derived, too, from that Amendment's guarantee of the equal protection of the laws. The Due Process Clause and the Equal Protection Clause are connected in a profound way, though they set forth independent principles. Rights implicit in liberty and rights secured by equal protection may rest on different precepts and are not always co-extensive, yet in some instances each may be instructive as to the meaning and reach of the other. . . . This interrelation of the two principles furthers our understanding of what freedom is and must become.

Indeed, in interpreting the Equal Protection Clause, the Court has recognized that new insights and societal understandings can reveal unjustified inequality within our most fundamental institutions that once passed unnoticed and unchallenged.

FROM THE BENCH

This dynamic also applies to same-sex marriage. It is now clear that the challenged laws burden the liberty of same-sex couples, and it must be further acknowledged that they abridge central precepts of equality. Here the marriage laws enforced by the respondents are in essence unequal: same-sex couples are denied all the benefits afforded to opposite-sex couples and are barred from exercising a fundamental right. Especially against a long history of disapproval of their relationships, this denial to same-sex couples of the right to marry works a grave and continuing harm. The imposition of this disability on gays and lesbians serves to disrespect and subordinate them. And the Equal Protection Clause, like the Due Process Clause, prohibits this unjustified infringement of the fundamental right to marry.

These considerations lead to the conclusion that the right to marry is a fundamental right inherent in the liberty of the person, and under the Due Process and Equal Protection Clauses of the Fourteenth Amendment couples of the same-sex may not be deprived of that right and that liberty. The Court now holds that same-sex couples may exercise the fundamental right to marry. No longer may this liberty be denied to them. . . .

IV

There may be an initial inclination in these cases to proceed with caution—to await further legislation, litigation, and debate. . . . Yet there has been far more deliberation than this argument acknowledges. There have been referenda, legislative debates, and grassroots campaigns, as well as countless studies, papers, books, and other popular and scholarly writings. There has been extensive litigation in state and federal courts. . . .

Of course, the Constitution contemplates that democracy is the appropriate process for change, so long as that process does not abridge fundamental rights. . . . Indeed, it is most often through democracy that liberty is preserved and protected in our lives. But . . . , when the rights of persons are violated, "the Constitution requires redress by the courts," notwithstanding the more general value of democratic decisionmaking. This holds true even when protecting individual rights affects issues of the utmost importance and sensitivity.

The dynamic of our constitutional system is that individuals need not await legislative action before asserting a fundamental right. The Nation's courts are open to injured individuals who come to them to vindicate their own direct, personal stake in our basic charter. An individual can invoke a right to constitutional protection when he or she is harmed, even if the broader public disagrees and even if the legislature refuses to act. . . . It is of no moment whether advocates of same-sex marriage now enjoy or lack momentum in the democratic process. The issue before the Court here is the legal question whether the Constitution protects the right of same-sex couples to marry.

. . . Finally, it must be emphasized that religions, and those who adhere to religious doctrines, may continue to advocate with utmost, sincere conviction that, by divine precepts, same-sex marriage should not be condoned. The First Amendment ensures that religious organizations and persons are given proper protection as they seek to teach the principles that are so fulfilling and so central to their lives and faiths, and to their own deep aspirations to continue the family structure they have long revered. The same is true of those who oppose same-sex marriage for other reasons. In turn, those who believe allowing same-sex marriage is proper or indeed essential, whether as a matter of religious conviction or secular belief, may engage those who disagree with their view in an open and searching debate. The Constitution, however, does not permit the State to bar same-sex couples from marriage on the same terms as accorded to couples of the opposite sex.

■ ■ ■

No union is more profound than marriage, for it embodies the highest ideals of love, fidelity, devotion, sacrifice, and family. In forming a marital union, two people become something greater than once they were. As some of the petitioners in these cases demonstrate, marriage embodies a love that may endure even past death. It would misunderstand these men and women to say they disrespect the idea of marriage. Their plea is that they do respect it, respect it so deeply that they seek to find its fulfillment for themselves. Their hope is not to be condemned to live in loneliness, excluded from one of civilization's oldest institutions. They ask for equal dignity in the eyes of the law. The Constitution grants them that right.

Chief Justice ROBERTS, with whom Justice SCALIA and Justice THOMAS join, dissenting.

Petitioners make strong arguments rooted in social policy and considerations of fairness. They contend that same-sex couples should be allowed to affirm their love and commitment through marriage, just like opposite-sex couples. That position has undeniable appeal; over the past six years, voters and legislators in eleven States and the District of Columbia have revised their laws to allow marriage between two people of the same sex.

But this Court is not a legislature. Whether same-sex marriage is a good idea should be of no concern to us. Under the Constitution, judges have power to say what the law is, not what it should be.

Although the policy arguments for extending marriage to same-sex couples may be compelling, the legal arguments for requiring such an extension are not. The fundamental right to marry does not include a right to make a State change its definition of marriage. And a State's decision to maintain the meaning of marriage that has persisted in every culture throughout human history can hardly be called irrational. In short, our Constitution does not enact any one theory of

FROM THE BENCH

James Obergefell and attorney Al Gerhardstein at Marriage Equality Decision Day Rally 2015. *Elvert Barnes/Wikimedia Commons.*

marriage. The people of a State are free to expand marriage to include same-sex couples, or to retain the historic definition.

Today, however, the Court takes the extraordinary step of ordering every State to license and recognize same-sex marriage. Many people will rejoice at this decision, and I begrudge none their celebration. But for those who believe in a government of laws, not of men, the majority's approach is deeply disheartening. Supporters of same-sex marriage have achieved considerable success persuading their fellow citizens—through the democratic process—to adopt their view. That ends today. Five lawyers have closed the debate and enacted their own vision of marriage as a matter of constitutional law. Stealing this issue from the people will for many cast a cloud over same-sex marriage, making a dramatic social change that much more difficult to accept.

The majority's decision is an act of will, not legal judgment. The right it announces has no basis in the Constitution or this Court's precedent. The majority expressly disclaims judicial "caution" and omits even a pretense of humility, openly relying on its desire to remake society according to its own "new insight" into the "nature of injustice." As a result, the Court invalidates the marriage laws of more than half the States and orders the transformation of a social institution that has formed the basis of human society for millennia, for the Kalahari Bushmen and the Han Chinese, the Carthaginians and the Aztecs. Just who do we think we are?

. . . Those who founded our country would not recognize the majority's conception of the judicial role. They after all risked their lives and fortunes for the precious right to govern themselves. They would never have imagined yielding that right on a question of social policy to unaccountable and unelected judges. . . . As a plurality of this Court explained just last year, "It is demeaning to the democratic process to presume that voters are not capable of deciding an issue of this sensitivity on decent and rational grounds."

When decisions are reached through democratic means, some people will inevitably be disappointed with the results. But those whose views do not prevail at least know that they have had their say, and accordingly are—in the tradition of our political culture—reconciled to the result of a fair and honest debate. In addition, they can gear up to raise the issue later, hoping to persuade enough on the winning side to think again. "That is exactly how our system of government is supposed to work."

But today the Court puts a stop to all that. By deciding this question under the Constitution, the Court removes it from the realm of democratic decision. There will be consequences to shutting down the political process on an issue of such profound public significance. Closing debate tends to close minds. People denied a voice are less likely to accept the ruling of a court on an issue that does not seem to be the sort of thing courts usually decide. . . . Indeed, however heartened the proponents of same-sex marriage might be on this day, it is worth acknowledging what they have lost, and lost forever: the opportunity to win the true acceptance that comes from persuading their fellow citizens of the justice of their cause. And they lose this just when the winds of change were freshening at their backs.

Federal courts are blunt instruments when it comes to creating rights. Today's decision, for example, creates serious questions about religious liberty. Many good and decent people oppose same-sex marriage as a tenet of faith, and their freedom to exercise religion is—unlike the right imagined by the majority—actually spelled out in the Constitution.

■ ■ ■

If you are among the many Americans—of whatever sexual orientation—who favor expanding same-sex marriage, by all means celebrate today's decision. Celebrate the achievement of a desired goal. Celebrate the opportunity for a new expression of commitment to a partner. Celebrate the availability of new benefits. But do not celebrate the Constitution. It had nothing to do with it.

I respectfully dissent.

Justice SCALIA, with whom Justice THOMAS joins, dissenting.

I join The Chief Justice's opinion in full. I write separately to call attention to this Court's threat to American democracy.

FROM THE BENCH

FROM THE BENCH

The substance of today's decree is not of immense personal importance to me. The law can recognize as marriage whatever sexual attachments and living arrangements it wishes. . . . It is of overwhelming importance, however, who it is that rules me. Today's decree says that my Ruler, and the Ruler of 320 million Americans coast-to-coast, is a majority of the nine lawyers on the Supreme Court. . . . This practice of constitutional revision by an unelected committee of nine, always accompanied (as it is today) by extravagant praise of liberty, robs the People of the most important liberty they asserted in the Declaration of Independence and won in the Revolution of 1776: the freedom to govern themselves.

. . . But what really astounds is the hubris reflected in today's judicial Putsch. The five Justices who compose today's majority are entirely comfortable concluding that every State violated the Constitution for all of the 135 years between the Fourteenth Amendment's ratification and Massachusetts' permitting of same-sex marriages in 2003. They have discovered in the Fourteenth Amendment a "fundamental right" overlooked by every person alive at the time of ratification, and almost everyone else in the time since. They see what lesser legal minds—minds like Thomas Cooley, John Marshall Harlan, Oliver Wendell Holmes, Jr., Learned Hand, Louis Brandeis, William Howard Taft, Benjamin Cardozo, Hugo Black, Felix Frankfurter, Robert Jackson, and Henry Friendly—could not. . . . These Justices *know* that limiting marriage to one man and one woman is contrary to reason; they *know* that an institution as old as government itself, and accepted by every nation in history until 15 years ago, cannot possibly be supported by anything other than ignorance or bigotry. And they are willing to say that any citizen who does not agree with that, who adheres to what was, until 15 years ago, the unanimous judgment of all generations and all societies, stands against the Constitution.

Justice THOMAS, with whom Justice SCALIA joins, dissenting.

The Court's decision today is at odds not only with the Constitution, but with the principles upon which our Nation was built. Since well before 1787, liberty has been understood as freedom from government action, not entitlement to government benefits. The Framers created our Constitution to preserve that understanding of liberty. Yet the majority invokes our Constitution in the name of a "liberty" that the Framers would not have recognized, to the detriment of the liberty they sought to protect. Along the way, it rejects the idea—captured in our Declaration of Independence—that human dignity is innate and suggests instead that it comes from the Government. This distortion of our Constitution not only ignores the text, it inverts the relationship between the individual and the state in our Republic. I cannot agree with it.

. . . Had the majority allowed the definition of marriage to be left to the political process—as the Constitution requires—the People could have considered the religious liberty implications of deviating from the traditional definition as part of their deliberative process. Instead, the majority's decision short-circuits that process, with potentially ruinous consequences for religious liberty.

IV

Perhaps recognizing that these cases do not actually involve liberty as it has been understood, the majority goes to great lengths to assert that its decision will advance the "dignity" of same-sex couples. The flaw in that reasoning, of course, is that the Constitution contains no "dignity" Clause, and even if it did, the government would be incapable of bestowing dignity . . .

Justice ALITO, with whom Justice SCALIA and Justice THOMAS join, dissenting.

Until the federal courts intervened, the American people were engaged in a debate about whether their States should recognize same-sex marriage. The question in these cases, however, is not what States *should* do about same-sex marriage but whether the Constitution answers that question for them. It does not. The Constitution leaves that question to be decided by the people of each State.

I

The Constitution says nothing about a right to same-sex marriage, but the Court holds that the term "liberty" in the Due Process Clause of the Fourteenth Amendment encompasses this right. Our Nation was founded upon the principle that every person has the unalienable right to liberty, but liberty is a term of many meanings. . . .

To prevent five unelected Justices from imposing their personal vision of liberty upon the American people, the Court has held that "liberty" under the Due Process Clause should be understood to protect only those rights that are "'deeply rooted in this Nation's history and tradition.'" And it is beyond dispute that the right to same-sex marriage is not among those rights.

For today's majority, it does not matter that the right to same-sex marriage lacks deep roots or even that it is contrary to long-established tradition. The Justices in the majority claim the authority to confer constitutional protection upon that right simply because they believe that it is fundamental.

. . . This understanding of marriage, which focuses almost entirely on the happiness of persons who choose to marry, is shared by many people today, but it is not the traditional one. For millennia, marriage was inextricably linked to the one thing that only an opposite-sex couple can do: procreate. . . .

III

Today's decision usurps the constitutional right of the people to decide whether to keep or alter the traditional understanding of marriage. The decision will also have other important consequences.

FROM THE BENCH

It will be used to vilify Americans who are unwilling to assent to the new orthodoxy. . . . Perhaps recognizing how its reasoning may be used, the majority attempts, toward the end of its opinion, to reassure those who oppose same-sex marriage that their rights of conscience will be protected. We will soon see whether this proves to be true. I assume that those who cling to old beliefs will be able to whisper their thoughts in the recesses of their homes, but if they repeat those views in public, they will risk being labeled as bigots and treated as such by governments, employers, and schools.

. . . The system of federalism established by our Constitution provides a way for people with different beliefs to live together in a single nation. If the issue of same-sex marriage had been left to the people of the States, it is likely that some States would recognize same-sex marriage and others would not. . . . The majority today makes that impossible. By imposing its own views on the entire country, the majority facilitates the marginalization of the many Americans who have traditional ideas. . . .

Today's decision will also have a fundamental effect on this Court and its ability to uphold the rule of law. If a bare majority of Justices can invent a new right and impose that right on the rest of the country, the only real limit on what future majorities will be able to do is their own sense of what those with political power and cultural influence are willing to tolerate. Even enthusiastic supporters of same-sex marriage should worry about the scope of the power that today's majority claims.

BEHIND THE CURTAIN

The various opinions in *Obergefell* debated many significant jurisprudential questions pertaining to constitutional interpretation. One dominant debate concerned differing views of the U.S. system of federalism. The dissents emphasized the power of state democracies to decide important moral and legal questions, a power that counseled federal courts to use a light touch in evaluating the constitutionality of state law. The majority opinion, however, emphasized the importance of federal constitutional guarantees and the legitimacy of allowing the values expressed in the Constitution to override state laws.

Another jurisprudential debate concerned the source of values that should guide constitutional decision making. Articulating a "reasoned judgment" approach to decision making, the *Obergefell* majority's opinion identified four principles and traditions that outline the reasons marriage is a fundamental right protected by the Constitution: (1) the ability to choose who one wants to marry "is inherent in the concept of individual autonomy"; (2) marriage's ability to dignify couples who choose to commit to each other and provide security in that commitment; (3) marriage's role in "safeguard[ing] children and families and thus draw[ing] meaning from the related rights of childrearing, procreation, and education"; and (4) marriage's status as "a keystone of our social order" through which married couples gain societal support and benefits. The Court found that with regard to those four principles, same-sex couples do not vary from opposite-sex couples. This "reasoned judgment" approach is very distinct from the precedent requiring rights to be narrowly defined and "deeply rooted" in history, an approach espoused in the dissenting opinions.

Another remarkable component of the case was the Justices' varying views on the role of human dignity in constitutional decision making. Justice Kennedy mentioned the concept of dignity several times in the majority opinion. Where does this concept of "dignity" come from? Merriam-Webster defines it as "the quality or state of being worthy, honored, or esteemed." Justice Thomas argued that dignity is intrinsic in people, something that we are born with, that cannot be bestowed or taken away by any government. (This would lead to the conclusion that the government has no obligation to protect the dignity of individuals, even as a part of the "liberty" interests shielded by the Fifth and Fourteenth Amendments.)

Justice Thomas emphasized that the word "dignity" is mentioned nowhere in the United States Constitution. Justice Thomas is correct in that observation; the U.S. Constitution differs in this respect from the constitutions of many other democracies. Indeed, over 150 countries explicitly recognize human dignity at least once in their constitutions. Many of these countries use "dignity" to limit and protect certain rights, including freedom of speech, either through their constitutions or through judicial decisions. The concept also appears in the United Nations Charter and in an entire section of the Charter of Fundamental Rights of the European Union. In the wake of *Obergefell*, commentators observed that Justice Kennedy's opinion may be heralding a new role for the concept of human dignity in U.S. constitutional jurisprudence. One scholar, Professor Larry Tribe, heralded the Kennedy opinion as creating a "double helix of Due Process and Equal Protection" that produced a concept of equal dignity. With Justice Kennedy now gone from the Supreme Court and the Court's sharp turn to conservative social values, this role of equal dignity in U.S. constitutional decision making seems to have faded (at least for the present time).

One final point about the jurisprudential foundations of *Obergefell*: As was the case in the Court's decision protecting freedom to engage in homosexual activity, *Lawrence v. Texas*, the *Obergefell* decision did not identify the appropriate level of judicial scrutiny a court should use in evaluating restrictions on same-sex marriage, be it strict or intermediate scrutiny or rational basis. This leaves an uncertainty for deciding the constitutionality of future restrictions on same-sex marriage that are less absolute than the outright refusal of a state to recognize a same-sex marriage, such as at issue in *Obergefell*.

QUESTIONS FOR DISCUSSION

14.4 Justice Kennedy departed from the previous fundamental rights cases in that he adopted a very broad description of the asserted right and found the tradition and history of marriage to be only the beginning of the analysis. He explained, "History and tradition guide and discipline this inquiry but do not set its outer boundaries." The dissents expressed great concerns about the majority's disregard of earlier history and case precedent, claiming this decision amounted to judicial overreach that grabbed a contentious question from the political process prematurely. Do you agree with Justice Kennedy that we should be guided by history, but not confined to it? Or, do you agree with Justices Roberts, Scalia, Thomas, and Alito that the majority's approach allows for too much judicial discretion?

14.5 One wonders what the *Dobbs* Court's abortion decision overruling *Roe v. Wade* means for the future of *Obergefell*'s constitutional protection of same-sex marriage. Recall that Justice Alito stated in the *Dobbs* majority opinion that the opinion did not hold ramifications for other decisions such as *Obergefell*. Justice Thomas, however, said the opposite in his concurrence. Considering the views expressed by both Thomas and Alito in their *Obergefell* dissents, which Justice do you believe regarding the future effect of *Dobbs*?

14.6 You may recall that at the time *Roe v. Wade* recognized a constitutional right to abortion before viability, most states had significant abortion prohibitions in place. The situation for *Obergefell* was much different, given the burgeoning acceptance of same-sex marriage among the states at the time of decision. Does the fact that same-sex marriage had gained political favor in 37 states at the time the Court handed down *Obergefell* render the decision less vulnerable to overruling than *Roe*? In addition, note that *Obergefell* relied on both substantive due process principles and equal protection guarantees, whereas *Roe* focused on the concept of liberty. Could that difference ensure that *Obergefell* is less vulnerable to overruling than *Roe*?

14.7 One might describe the majority opinion in *Obergefell* as a "love letter" for the institution of marriage. Do you agree with the Court's description of the importance of marriage to human happiness and a properly functioning society? Consider the Court's statement that same-sex couples are seeking official recognition of their relationship because "[t]heir hope is not to be condemned to live in loneliness, excluded from one of civilization's oldest institutions." Does this description show sufficient understanding of societal contributions and the full lives led by single (unmarried) individuals?

14.8 The *Obergefell* decision was celebrated across the country by supporters of marriage equality. However, many citizens opposed the decision. For many, the decision conflicted with firmly held religious beliefs. In fact, Chief Justice Roberts expressed concerns about the conflict between marriage equality and religious liberty in his dissent. Did the majority adequately address that concern?

14.9 Is the *Obergefell* decision consistent with the Supreme Court's 1879 decision in *Reynolds v. United States*, which upheld against constitutional attack a prohibition against plural marriage? Can you distinguish constitutional protection for same-sex marriage from constitutional protection from polygamy?

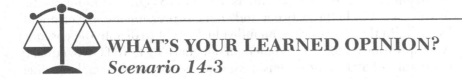

WHAT'S YOUR LEARNED OPINION?
Scenario 14-3

A state statute requires children's birth certificates to list the name of the mother and her husband if she is married at the time of conception or birth. This includes children conceived by artificial insemination with the sperm of a donor. A married same-sex couple gave birth to a child and listed both spouses as parents. The state, however, only listed the mother who gave birth to the child on the birth certificate. Is this statute consistent with *Obergefell*?

The two cases presented in this chapter illustrate various angles on an issue that directly implicates morality, domesticity, religious beliefs, human sexuality, and love. Not all U.S. Supreme Court cases can boast such implications! The *Loving* case, recognizing constitutional protection for interracial marriage, was much less contentious than the same-sex marriage protection at issue in *Obergefell*. This contention arose even in the face of significant movement toward legalizing same-sex marriage among the states in the period leading up to the decision. A look at the *Obergefell* dissents shows that the same-sex marriage issue struck a nerve with the dissenting Justices on various issues: federalism, the propriety of the judicial role, jurisprudential theories on how to interpret the constitution, and religious beliefs.

Obergefell is part of a larger trend begun in a case discussed in Chapter 13, *Romer v. Evans*. From *Romer* to *Lawrence v. Texas* and onto *Obergefell*, the U.S. Supreme Court embarked on a trend of recognizing the freedom and equality rights of the LGBTQIA+ community. Although this has been reason to celebrate for many, members of conservative groups opposed this trend. In service of LGBTQIA+ rights, many states (such as Colorado) have public accommodation laws that prohibit public-facing businesses from discriminating based on sexual orientation of others. In a dispute culminating in *303 Creative LLC v. Elenis*, 600 U.S. ____ (2023), a conservative website designer, looking to enter the wedding industry, sought to enjoin the state of Colorado from forcing her to promote messages contrary to her religious beliefs that marriage should occur only between a man and a woman. In June 2023, the U.S. Supreme Court decided *303 Creative*, holding that the First Amendment prohibited the state from compelling the website designer to create expressive messages inimical to the designer's views. While the Court recognized that a state has a compelling interest in preventing discrimination in public places, it clarified that public accommodation laws must defer to the First Amendment's individual liberties protections. Rather than considering how limiting the reach of public accommodation laws might negatively affect members of the LGBTQIA+ community, the Court saw this case as a battle between individual expression and government-imposed speech. In the Court's view, an individual's right to dictate the contours of their own expression is more important than safeguarding LGBTQIA+ equality rights. In the wake of *303 Creative*, businesses, whose expression can be characterized as "pure speech," may ignore anti-discrimination public accommodation laws by invoking the First Amendment's protection. The *303 Creative* case continues a trend started by the Supreme Court around 2020—a trend that appears destined to reverse the types of recognition reflected in *Romer*, *Lawrence*, and *Obergefell*.

This apparent trend reversal highlights an important issue in constitutional jurisprudence: Should individual rights depend on the composition of the U.S. Supreme Court?

QUESTIONS FOR REVIEW

1. Describe the U.S. Supreme Court's stance on the constitutionality of prohibitions against plural marriage.
2. Explain the justification offered for Virginia's prohibition of interracial marriages at issue in *Loving v. Virginia*.

3. What clause or clauses of the Constitution did the U.S. Supreme Court rely on in striking down the Virginia statute in *Loving v. Virginia?*
4. Describe the majority's jurisprudential approach to constitutional interpretation in *Obergefell.*
5. What were the four principles that the majority in *Obergefell* cited as providing a reasoned basis for recognizing constitutional protection for same-sex marriage? How were those principles applied?
6. How does the majority's reliance on the concept of human dignity compare to other U.S. constitutional decisions, and how does it compare to treatment of the concept in other democracies?
7. Describe why the U.S. Supreme Court's overruling of the *Roe v. Wade* abortion decision in the *Dobbs* case suggests that *Obergefell* also may be overruled.

Epilogue

I hope you have enjoyed this tour through some of the mysteries of constitutional law. In particular, I hope you gained an appreciation for the importance of the structure of government. If nothing else, the Framers had a clear vision of how the machinery of democracy should be assembled to maintain the rule of law, to ensure that the diverse states cooperated as part of one union, and to protect individual freedoms. We saw this vision played out in the well-established precedent regarding the powers of the judicial (*Marbury v. Madison*), legislative (*McCullogh v. Maryland*), and executive (*Youngstown Sheet & Tube Co. v. Sawyer*) branches of the federal government. The relative stability of this precedent provided a foundation for the individual rights that framers later enumerated in the Constitution and the U.S. Supreme Court later recognized. That said, we saw that it took some tinkering for the Court to work out precisely how the three governmental branches should interact with each other and with state governments. For both governmental structure and individual rights, the Framers created a document that was specific enough to lay a fixed architecture to ensure the government could work effectively, but left matters general enough to be able to grow as society changed. The flexibility has been made possible in large part by the general, sometimes vague, language of the Constitution.

Prime examples of this general language that allow for flexibility are the words "due process of law" in the Fifth and Fourteenth Amendments. Indeed, perhaps you saw how the law evolved most clearly in the individual rights section of this book, much of which referred to the due process language. (As an archetypal model of drastic changes in the law over time, I would select the evolution of the laws governing the rights of women.) Of course, these changes concerning individual rights do not necessarily move in a clear trajectory toward expansion of rights. The law of affirmative action based on race, abortion rights, and First Amendment protections for corporate campaign contributions are examples of when an earlier interpretation of a right faced a backlash.

As you read about the changes in rights recognition, perhaps you wondered whether the current Court's decisions result from a need to reign in the excesses of the past, an impulse to indulge personal whims, or a combination of both. When the Court makes a 180-degree change in answering a constitutional question—particularly a question touching on individual rights—is that inexcusable lawlessness? Or does that change simply disclose the unavoidable connection between moral judgments and constitutional law? If you disagree with a case result, should you charge that the Court is acting illegitimately? Or should you simply understand that you disagree with the moral judgment reflected in the decision and argue why that judgment is wrong?

If you feel that you have left your study of constitutional law in this book with more questions than you brought to the material, do not find fault. That's the magic of constitutional law. Consider some of the many comments about the power of questioning offered by human history's greatest minds:

Judge a man by his questions rather than his answers.

—*Voltaire*

The scientist is not a person who gives the right answers, he's one who asks the right questions.

—*Claude Lévi-Strauss*

The art and science of asking questions is the source of all knowledge.

—*Thomas Berger*

When we engage people across ideological divides, asking questions helps us map the disconnect between our differing points of view.

—*Megan Phelps-Roper*

Questions, it turns out, are part of the joy of constitutional law: to be celebrated, not despaired.

The Text of the U.S. Constitution

We the People of the United States, in Order to form a more perfect Union, establish Justice, insure domestic Tranquility, provide for the common defence, promote the general Welfare, and secure the Blessings of Liberty to ourselves and our Posterity, do ordain and establish this Constitution for the United States of America.

Article. I

SECTION. 1

All legislative Powers herein granted shall be vested in a Congress of the United States, which shall consist of a Senate and House of Representatives.

SECTION. 2

The House of Representatives shall be composed of Members chosen every second Year by the People of the several States, and the Electors in each State shall have the Qualifications requisite for Electors of the most numerous Branch of the State Legislature.

No Person shall be a Representative who shall not have attained to the Age of twenty five Years, and been seven Years a Citizen of the United States, and who shall not, when elected, be an Inhabitant of that State in which he shall be chosen.

[Representatives and direct Taxes shall be apportioned among the several States which may be included within this Union, according to their respective Numbers, which shall be determined by adding to the whole Number of free Persons, including those bound to Service for a Term of Years, and excluding Indians not taxed, three fifths of all other Persons.]° The actual Enumeration shall be made within three Years after the first Meeting of the Congress of the United States, and within every subsequent Term of ten Years, in such Manner as they shall by Law direct. The Number of Representatives shall not exceed one for every thirty Thousand, but each State shall have at Least one Representative; and until such enumeration shall be made, the State of New Hampshire shall be entitled to chuse three, Massachusetts eight, Rhode-Island and Providence Plantations one, Connecticut five, New-York six, New Jersey four, Pennsylvania eight, Delaware one, Maryland six, Virginia ten, North Carolina five, South Carolina five, and Georgia three.

When vacancies happen in the Representation from any State, the Executive Authority thereof shall issue Writs of Election to fill such Vacancies.

The House of Representatives shall chuse their Speaker and other Officers; and shall have the sole Power of Impeachment.

SECTION. 3

The Senate of the United States shall be composed of two Senators from each State, [chosen by the Legislature thereof,] for six Years; and each Senator shall have one Vote.

Immediately after they shall be assembled in Consequence of the first Election, they shall be divided as equally as may be into three Classes. The Seats of the Senators of the first Class shall

---

° Language in brackets throughout this document has been changed or superseded by amendment.

be vacated at the Expiration of the second Year, of the second Class at the Expiration of the fourth Year, and of the third Class at the Expiration of the sixth Year, so that one third may be chosen every second Year; [and if Vacancies happen by Resignation, or otherwise, during the Recess of the Legislature of any State, the Executive thereof may make temporary Appointments until the next Meeting of the Legislature, which shall then fill such Vacancies.]

No Person shall be a Senator who shall not have attained to the Age of thirty Years, and been nine Years a Citizen of the United States, and who shall not, when elected, be an Inhabitant of that State for which he shall be chosen

The Vice President of the United States shall be President of the Senate, but shall have no Vote, unless they be equally divided.

The Senate shall chuse their other Officers, and also a President pro tempore, in the Absence of the Vice President, or when he shall exercise the Office of President of the United States

The Senate shall have the sole Power to try all Impeachments. When sitting for that Purpose, they shall be on Oath or Affirmation. When the President of the United States is tried, the Chief Justice shall preside: And no Person shall be convicted without the Concurrence of two thirds of the Members present.

Judgment in Cases of Impeachment shall not extend further than to removal from Office, and disqualification to hold and enjoy any Office of honor, Trust or Profit under the United States: but the Party convicted shall nevertheless be liable and subject to Indictment, Trial, Judgment and Punishment, according to Law.

SECTION. 4

The Times, Places and Manner of holding Elections for Senators and Representatives, shall be prescribed in each State by the Legislature thereof; but the Congress may at any time by Law make or alter such Regulations, except as to the Places of chusing Senators.

The Congress shall assemble at least once in every Year, and such Meeting shall be [on the first Monday in December,] unless they shall by Law appoint a different Day.

SECTION. 5

Each House shall be the Judge of the Elections, Returns and Qualifications of its own Members, and a Majority of each shall constitute a Quorum to do Business; but a smaller Number may adjourn from day to day, and may be authorized to compel the Attendance of absent Members, in such Manner, and under such Penalties as each House may provide.

Each House may determine the Rules of its Proceedings, punish its Members for disorderly Behaviour, and, with the Concurrence of two thirds, expel a Member.

Each House shall keep a Journal of its Proceedings, and from time to time publish the same, excepting such Parts as may in their Judgment require Secrecy; and the Yeas and Nays of the Members of either House on any question shall, at the Desire of one fifth of those Present, be entered on the Journal.

Neither House, during the Session of Congress, shall, without the Consent of the other, adjourn for more than three days, nor to any other Place than that in which the two Houses shall be sitting.

SECTION. 6

The Senators and Representatives shall receive a Compensation for their Services, to be ascertained by Law, and paid out of the Treasury of the United States. They shall in all Cases, except Treason, Felony and Breach of the Peace, be privileged from Arrest during their Attendance at the Session of their respective Houses, and in going to and returning from the same; and for any Speech or Debate in either House, they shall not be questioned in any other Place.

No Senator or Representative shall, during the Time for which he was elected, be appointed to any civil Office under the Authority of the United States, which shall have been created, or the Emoluments whereof shall have been encreased during such time; and no Person holding any Office under the United States, shall be a Member of either House during his Continuance in Office.

SECTION. 7

All Bills for raising Revenue shall originate in the House of Representatives; but the Senate may propose or concur with Amendments as on other Bills.

Every Bill which shall have passed the House of Representatives and the Senate, shall, before it become a Law, be presented to the President of the United States; If he approve he shall sign it, but if not he shall return it, with his Objections to that House in which it shall have originated, who shall enter the Objections at large on their Journal, and proceed to reconsider it. If after such Reconsideration two thirds of that House shall agree to pass the Bill, it shall be sent, together with the Objections, to the other House, by which it shall likewise be reconsidered, and if approved by two thirds of that House, it shall become a Law. But in all such Cases the Votes of both Houses shall be determined by Yeas and Nays, and the Names of the Persons voting for and against the Bill shall be entered on the Journal of each House respectively, If any Bill shall not be returned by the President within ten Days (Sundays excepted) after it shall have been presented to him, the Same shall be a Law, in like Manner as if he had signed it, unless the Congress by their Adjournment prevent its Return, in which Case it shall not be a Law.

Every Order, Resolution, or Vote to which the Concurrence of the Senate and House of Representatives may be necessary (except on a question of Adjournment) shall be presented to the President of the United States; and before the Same shall take Effect, shall be approved by him, or being disapproved by him, shall be repassed by two thirds of the Senate and House of Representatives, according to the Rules and Limitations prescribed in the Case of a Bill.

SECTION. 8

The Congress shall have Power To lay and collect Taxes, Duties, Imposts and Excises, to pay the Debts and provide for the common Defence and general Welfare of the United States; but all Duties, Imposts and Excises shall be uniform throughout the United States;

To borrow Money on the credit of the United States;

To regulate Commerce with foreign Nations, and among the several States, and with the Indian Tribes;

To establish an uniform Rule of Naturalization, and uniform Laws on the subject of Bankruptcies throughout the United States;

To coin Money, regulate the Value thereof, and of foreign Coin, and fix the Standard of Weights and Measures;

To provide for the Punishment of counterfeiting the Securities and current Coin of the United States;

To establish Post Offices and post Roads;

To promote the Progress of Science and useful Arts, by securing for limited Times to Authors and Inventors the exclusive Right to their respective Writings and Discoveries;

To constitute Tribunals inferior to the supreme Court;

To define and punish Piracies and Felonies committed on the high Seas, and Offenses against the Law of Nations;

To declare War, grant Letters of Marque and Reprisal, and make Rules concerning Captures on Land and Water;

To raise and support Armies, but no Appropriation of Money to that Use shall be for a longer Term than two Years;

To provide and maintain a Navy;

To make Rules for the Government and Regulation of the land and naval Forces;

To provide for calling forth the Militia to execute the Laws of the Union, suppress Insurrections and repel Invasions;

To provide for organizing, arming, and disciplining, the Militia, and for governing such Part of them as may be employed in the Service of the United States, reserving to the States respectively, the Appointment of the Officers, and the Authority of training the Militia according to the discipline prescribed by Congress;

To exercise exclusive Legislation in all Cases whatsoever, over such District (not exceeding ten Miles square) as may, by Cession of particular States, and the Acceptance of Congress, become the Seat of the Government of the United States, and to exercise like Authority over all Places purchased by the Consent of the Legislature of the State in which the Same shall be, for the Erection of Forts, Magazines, Arsenals, dock-Yards and other needful Buildings;

—And

To make all Laws which shall be necessary and proper for carrying into Execution the foregoing Powers, and all other Powers vested by this Constitution in the Government of the United States, or in any Department or Officer thereof.

SECTION. 9

The Migration or Importation of such Persons as any of the States now existing shall think proper to admit, shall not be prohibited by the Congress prior to the Year one thousand eight hundred and eight, but a Tax or duty may be imposed on such Importation, not exceeding ten dollars for each Person.

The Privilege of the Writ of Habeas Corpus shall not be suspended, unless when in Cases of Rebellion or Invasion the public Safety may require it.

No Bill of Attainder or ex post facto Law shall be passed.

[No Capitation, or other direct, Tax shall be laid, unless in Proportion to the Census or Enumeration herein before directed to be taken.]

No Tax or Duty shall be laid on Articles exported from any State.

No Preference shall be given by any Regulation of Commerce or Revenue to the Ports of one State over those of another: nor shall Vessels bound to, or from, one State, be obliged to enter, clear, or pay Duties in another.

No Money shall be drawn from the Treasury, but in Consequence of Appropriations made by Law; and a regular Statement and Account of the Receipts and Expenditures of all public Money shall be published from time to time.

No Title of Nobility shall be granted by the United States: And no Person holding any Office of Profit or Trust under them, shall, without the Consent of the Congress, accept of any present, Emolument, Office, or Title, of any kind whatever, from any King, Prince, or foreign State.

SECTION. 10

No State shall enter into any Treaty, Alliance, or Confederation; grant Letters of Marque and Reprisal; coin Money; emit Bills of Credit; make any Thing but gold and silver Coin a Tender in Payment of Debts; pass any Bill of Attainder, ex post facto Law, or Law impairing the Obligation of Contracts, or grant any Title of Nobility.

No State shall, without the Consent of the Congress, lay any Imposts or Duties on Imports or Exports, except what may be absolutely necessary for executing it's inspection Laws: and the net Produce of all Duties and Imposts, laid by any State on Imports or Exports, shall be for the Use of the Treasury of the United States; and all such Laws shall be subject to the Revision and Controul of the Congress.

No State shall, without the Consent of Congress, lay any Duty of Tonnage, keep Troops, or Ships of War in time of Peace, enter into any Agreement or Compact with another State, or with a foreign Power, or engage in War, unless actually invaded, or in such imminent Danger as will not admit of delay.

Article. II

SECTION. 1

The executive Power shall be vested in a President of the United States of America. He shall hold his Office during the Term of four Years, and, together with the Vice President, chosen for the same Term, be elected, as follows:

Each State shall appoint, in such Manner as the Legislature thereof may direct, a Number of Electors, equal to the whole Number of Senators and Representatives to which the State may be entitled in the Congress: but no Senator or Representative, or Person holding an Office of Trust or Profit under the United States, shall be appointed an Elector.

[The Electors shall meet in their respective States, and vote by Ballot for two Persons, of whom one at least shall not be an Inhabitant of the same State with themselves. And they shall make a List of all the Persons voted for, and of the Number of Votes for each; which List they shall sign and certify, and transmit sealed to the Seat of the Government of the United States, directed to the President of the Senate. The President of the Senate shall, in the Presence of the Senate and House of Representatives, open all the Certificates, and the Votes shall then be counted. The Person having the greatest Number of Votes shall be the President, if such Number be a Majority of the whole Number of Electors appointed; and if there be more than one who have such Majority, and have an equal Number of Votes, then the House of Representatives shall immediately chuse by Ballot one of them for President; and if no Person have a Majority, then from the five highest on the List the said House shall in like Manner chuse the President. But in chusing the President, the Votes shall be taken by States, the Representation from each State having one Vote; A quorum for this Purpose shall consist of a Member or Members from two thirds of the States, and a Majority of all the States shall be necessary to a Choice. In every Case, after the Choice of the President, the Person having the greatest Number of Votes of the Electors shall be the Vice President. But if there should remain two or more who have equal Votes, the Senate shall chuse from them by Ballot the Vice President.]

The Congress may determine the Time of chusing the Electors, and the Day on which they shall give their Votes; which Day shall be the same throughout the United States.

No Person except a natural born Citizen, or a Citizen of the United States, at the time of the Adoption of this Constitution, shall be eligible to the Office of President; neither shall any person be eligible to that Office who shall not have attained to the Age of thirty five Years, and been fourteen Years a Resident within the United States.

In Case of the Removal of the President from Office, or of his Death, Resignation, or Inability to discharge the Powers and Duties of the said Office, the Same shall devolve on the Vice President, and the Congress may by Law provide for the Case of Removal, Death, Resignation or Inability, both of the President and Vice President, declaring what Officer shall then act as President, and such Officer shall act accordingly, until the Disability be removed, or a President shall be elected.

The President shall, at stated Times, receive for his Services, a Compensation, which shall neither be increased nor diminished during the Period for which he shall have been elected, and he shall not receive within that Period any other Emolument from the United States, or any of them.

Before he enter on the Execution of his Office, he shall take the following Oath or Affirmation: "I do solemnly swear (or affirm) that I will faithfully execute the Office of President of the United States, and will to the best of my Ability, preserve, protect and defend the Constitution of the United States."

SECTION. 2

The President shall be Commander in Chief of the Army and Navy of the United States, and of the Militia of the several States, when called into the actual Service of the United States; he may require the Opinion, in writing, of the principal Officer in each of the executive Departments, upon any Subject relating to the Duties of their respective Offices, and he shall have Power to grant Reprieves and Pardons for Offenses against the United States, except in Cases of Impeachment.

He shall have Power, by and with the Advice and Consent of the Senate, to make Treaties, provided two thirds of the Senators present concur; and he shall nominate, and by and with the Advice and Consent of the Senate, shall appoint Ambassadors, other public Ministers and Consuls, Judges of the supreme Court, and all other Officers of the United States, whose Appointments are not herein otherwise provided for, and which shall be established by Law: but the Congress may by Law vest the Appointment of such inferior Officers, as they think proper, in the President alone, in the Courts of Law, or in the Heads of Departments.

The President shall have Power to fill up all Vacancies that may happen during the Recess of the Senate, by granting Commissions which shall expire at the End of their next Session.

SECTION. 3

He shall from time to time give to the Congress Information of the State of the Union, and recommend to their Consideration such Measures as he shall judge necessary and expedient; he may, on extraordinary Occasions, convene both Houses, or either of them, and in Case of Disagreement between them, with Respect to the Time of Adjournment, he may adjourn them to such Time as he shall think proper; he shall receive Ambassadors and other public Ministers; he shall take Care that the Laws be faithfully executed, and shall Commission all the Officers of the United States.

SECTION. 4

The President, Vice President and all civil Officers of the United States, shall be removed from Office on Impeachment for, and Conviction of, Treason, Bribery, or other high Crimes and Misdemeanors.

Article. III

SECTION. 1

The judicial Power of the United States, shall be vested in one supreme Court, and in such inferior Courts as the Congress may from time to time ordain and establish. The Judges, both of the supreme and inferior Courts, shall hold their Offices during good Behaviour, and shall at stated Times, receive for their Services, a Compensation, which shall not be diminished during their Continuance in Office.

SECTION. 2

The judicial Power shall extend to all Cases, in Law and Equity, arising under this Constitution, the Laws of the United States, and Treaties made, or which shall be made, under their Authority;—to all Cases affecting Ambassadors, other public Ministers and Consuls;—to all Cases of admiralty and maritime Jurisdiction;—to Controversies to which the United States shall be a Party;—to Controversies between two or more States;—[between a State and Citizens of another State;—] between Citizens of different States,—between Citizens of the same State claiming Lands under Grants of different States, [and between a State, or the Citizens thereof;—and foreign States, Citizens or Subjects.]

In all Cases affecting Ambassadors, other public Ministers and Consuls, and those in which a State shall be Party, the supreme Court shall have original Jurisdiction. In all the other Cases before mentioned, the supreme Court shall have appellate Jurisdiction, both as to Law and Fact, with such Exceptions, and under such Regulations as the Congress shall make.

The Trial of all Crimes, except in Cases of Impeachment; shall be by Jury; and such Trial shall be held in the State where the said Crimes shall have been committed; but when not committed within any State, the Trial shall be at such Place or Places as the Congress may by Law have directed.

SECTION. 3

Treason against the United States, shall consist only in levying War against them, or in adhering to their Enemies, giving them Aid and Comfort. No Person shall be convicted of Treason unless on the Testimony of two Witnesses to the same overt Act, or on Confession in open Court.

The Congress shall have Power to declare the Punishment of Treason, but no Attainder of Treason shall work Corruption of Blood, or Forfeiture except during the Life of the Person attainted.

Article. IV

SECTION. 1

Full Faith and Credit shall be given in each State to the public Acts, Records, and judicial Proceedings of every other State. And the Congress may by general Laws prescribe the Manner in which such Acts, Records and Proceedings shall be proved, and the Effect thereof.

SECTION. 2

The Citizens of each State shall be entitled to all Privileges and Immunities of Citizens in the several States.

A Person charged in any State with Treason, Felony, or other Crime, who shall flee from Justice, and be found in another State, shall on Demand of the executive Authority of the State from which he fled, be delivered up, to be removed to the State having Jurisdiction of the Crime.

No Person held to Service or Labour in one State, under the Laws thereof, escaping into another, shall, in Consequence of any Law or Regulation therein, be discharged from such Service or Labour, but shall be delivered up on Claim of the Party to whom such Service or Labour may be due.

SECTION. 3

New States may be admitted by the Congress into this Union; but no new State shall be formed or erected within the Jurisdiction of any other State; nor any State be formed by the Junction of two or more States, or Parts of States, without the Consent of the Legislatures of the States concerned as well as of the Cogress.

The Congress shall have Power to dispose of and make all needful Rules and Regulations respecting the Territory or other Property belonging to the United States; and nothing in this Constitution shall be so construed as to Prejudice any Claims of the United States, or of any particular State.

SECTION. 4

The United States shall guarantee to every State in this Union a Republican Form of Government, and shall protect each of them against Invasion; and on Application of the Legislature, or of the Executive (when the Legislature cannot be convened) against domestic Violence.

Article. V

The Congress, whenever two thirds of both Houses shall deem it necessary, shall propose Amendments to this Constitution, or, on the Application of the Legislatures of two thirds of the several States, shall call a Convention for proposing Amendments, which in either Case, shall be valid to all Intents and Purposes, as Part of this

Constitution, when ratified by the Legislatures of three-fourths of the several States, or by Conventions in three fourths thereof, as the one or the other Mode of Ratification may be proposed by the Congress; Provided that no Amendment which may be made prior to the Year One thousand eight hundred and eight shall in any Manner affect the first and fourth Clauses in the Ninth Section of the first Article; and that no State, without its Consent, shall be deprived of its equal Suffrage in the Senate.

Article. VI

All Debts contracted and Engagements entered into, before the Adoption of this Constitution, shall be as valid against the United States under this Constitution, as under the Confederation.

This Constitution, and the Laws of the United States which shall be made in Pursuance thereof; and all Treaties made, or which shall be made, under the Authority of the United States, shall be the supreme Law of the Land; and the Judges in every State shall be bound thereby, any Thing in the Constitution or Laws of any State to the Contrary notwithstanding.

The Senators and Representatives before mentioned, and the Members of the several State Legislatures, and all executive and judicial Officers, both of the United States and of the several States, shall be bound by Oath or Affirmation, to support this Constitution; but no religious Test shall ever be required as a Qualification to any Office or public Trust under the United States.

Article. VII

The Ratification of the Conventions of nine States, shall be sufficient for the Establishment of this Constitution between the States so ratifying the Same.

Done in Convention by the Unanimous Consent of the States present the Seventeenth Day of September in the Year of our Lord one thousand seven hundred and Eighty seven and of the Independence of the United States of America the Twelfth In Witness whereof We have hereunto subscribed our Names,

Go. Washington—Presidt:
and deputy from Virginia
NEW HAMPSHIRE
John Langdon
Nicholas Gilman
MASSACHUSETTS
Nathaniel Gorham
Rufus King
CONNECTICUT
Wm. Saml. Johnson
Roger Sherman
NEW YORK
Alexander Hamilton
NEW JERSEY
Wil: Livingston
David Brearley
Wm. Paterson
Jona: Dayton
PENNSYLVANIA
B Franklin
Thomas Mifflin
Robt Morris
Geo. Clymer
Thos. FitzSimons
Jared Ingersoll
James Wilson
Gouv Morris
DELAWARE
Geo: Read
Gunning Bedford jun
John Dickinson
Richard Bassett
Jaco: Broom
MARYLAND
James McHenry
Dan of St. Thos. Jenifer
Danl Carroll

VIRGINIA
John Blair-
James Madison Jr.
NORTH CAROLINA
Wm. Blount
Richd. Dobbs Spaight
Hu Williamson
SOUTH CAROLINA
J. Rutledge
Charles Cotesworth Pinckney
Charles Pinckney
Pierce Butler
GEORGIA
William Few
Abr Baldwin
Attest William Jackson Secretary

In Convention Monday September 17th, 1787. Present

The States of

New Hampshire, Massachusetts, Connecticut, Mr. Hamilton from New York, New Jersey, Pennsylvania, Delaware, Maryland, Virginia, North Carolina, South Carolina and Georgia.

Resolved,

That the preceeding Constitution be laid before the United States in Congress assembled, and that it is the Opinion of this Convention, that it should afterwards be submitted to a Convention of Delegates, chosen in each State by the People thereof, under the Recommendation of its Legislature, for their Assent and Ratification; and that each Convention assenting to, and ratifying the Same, should give Notice thereof to the United States in Congress assembled. Resolved, That it is the Opinion of this Convention, that as soon as the Conventions of nine States shall have ratified this Constitution, the United States in Congress assembled should fix a Day on which Electors should be appointed by the States which shall have ratified the same, and a Day on which the Electors should assemble to vote for the President, and the Time and Place for commencing Proceedings under this Constitution.

That after such Publication the Electors should be appointed, and the Senators and Representatives elected: That the Electors should meet on the Day fixed for the Election of the President, and should transmit their Votes certified, signed, sealed and directed, as the Constitution requires, to the Secretary of the United States in Congress assembled, that the Senators and Representatives should convene at the Time and Place assigned; that the Senators should appoint a President of the Senate, for the sole Purpose of receiving, opening and counting the Votes for President; and, that after he shall be chosen, the Congress, together with the President, should, without Delay, proceed to execute this Constitution

By the unanimous Order of the Convention
Go. Washington-Presidt:
W. JACKSON Secretary.

THE AMENDMENTS TO THE CONSTITUTION OF THE UNITED STATES AS RATIFIED BY THE STATES

Preamble to the Bill of Rights Congress of the United States begun and held at the City of New-York, on Wednesday the fourth of March.

THE Conventions of a number of the States, having at the time of their adopting the Constitution, expressed a desire, in order to prevent misconstruction or abuse of its powers, that further declaratory and restrictive clauses should be added: And as extending the ground of public confidence in the Government, will best ensure the beneficent ends of its institution.

RESOLVED by the Senate and House of Representatives of the United States of America, in Congress assembled, two thirds of both Houses concurring, that the following Articles be proposed to the Legislatures of the several States, as amendments to the Constitution of the United States, all, or any of which Articles, when ratified by three fourths of the said Legislatures, to be valid to all intents and purposes, as part of the said Constitution; viz.

ARTICLES in addition to, and Amendment of the Constitution of the United States of America, proposed by Congress, and ratified by the Legislatures of the several States, pursuant to the fifth Article of the original Constitution.

(Note: The first 10 amendments to the Constitution were ratified December 15, 1791, and form what is known as the "Bill of Rights.")

Amendment I

Congress shall make no law respecting an establishment of religion, or prohibiting the free exercise thereof; or abridging the freedom of speech, or of the press, or the right of the people peaceably to assemble, and to petition the Government for a redress of grievances.

Amendment II

A well regulated Militia, being necessary to the security of a free State, the right of the people to keep and bear Arms, shall not be infringed.

Amendment III

No Soldier shall, in time of peace be quartered in any house, without the consent of the Owner, nor in time of war, but in a manner to be prescribed by law.

Amendment IV

The right of the people to be secure in their persons, houses, papers, and effects, against unreasonable searches and seizures, shall not be violated, and no Warrants shall issue, but upon probable cause, supported by Oath or affirmation, and particularly describing the place to be searched, and the persons or things to be seized.

Amendment V

No person shall be held to answer for a capital, or otherwise infamous crime, unless on a presentment or indictment of a Grand Jury, except in cases arising in the land or naval forces, or in the Militia, when in actual service in time of War or public danger; nor shall any person be subject for the same offence to be twice put in jeopardy of life or limb; nor shall be compelled in any criminal case to be a witness against himself, nor be deprived of life, liberty, or property, without due process of law; nor shall private property be taken for public use, without just compensation.

Amendment VI

In all criminal prosecutions, the accused shall enjoy the right to a speedy and public trial, by an impartial jury of the State and district wherein the crime shall have been committed, which district shall have been previously ascertained by law, and to be informed of the nature and cause of the accusation; to be confronted with the witnesses against him; to have compulsory process for obtaining witnesses in his favor, and to have the Assistance of Counsel for his defence.

Amendment VII

In suits at common law, where the value in controversy shall exceed twenty dollars, the right of trial by jury shall be preserved, and no fact tried by a jury shall be otherwise reexamined in any Court of the United States, than according to the rules of the common law.

Amendment VIII

Excessive bail shall not be required, nor excessive fines imposed, nor cruel and unusual punishments inflicted.

Amendment IX

The enumeration in the Constitution, of certain rights, shall not be construed to deny or disparage others retained by the people.

Amendment X

The powers not delegated to the United States by the Constitution, nor prohibited by it to the States, are reserved to the States respectively, or to the people.

Amendment XI

Passed by Congress March 4, 1794. Ratified February 7, 1795.

(Note: A portion of Article III, Section 2 of the Constitution was modified by the Eleventh Amendment.)

The Judicial power of the United States shall not be construed to extend to any suit in law or equity, commenced or prosecuted against one of the United States by Citizens of another State, or by Citizens or Subjects of any Foreign State.

Amendment XII

Passed by Congress December 9, 1803. Ratified June 15, 1804.

(Note: A portion of Article II, Section 1 of the Constitution was changed by the Twelfth Amendment.)

The Electors shall meet in their respective states, and vote by ballot for President and Vice-President, one of whom, at least, shall not be an inhabitant of the same state with themselves; they shall name in their ballots the person voted for as President, and in distinct ballots the person voted for as Vice-President, and they shall make distinct lists of all persons voted for as President, and of all persons voted for as Vice-President, and of the number of votes for each, which lists they shall sign and certify, and transmit sealed to the seat of the government of the United States, directed to the President of the Senate;—the President of the Senate shall, in the presence of the Senate and House of Representatives, open all the certificates and the votes shall then be counted;—The person having the greatest number of votes for President, shall be the President, if such number be a majority of the whole number of Electors appointed; and if no person have such majority, then from the persons having the highest numbers not exceeding three on the list of those voted for as President, the House of Representatives shall choose immediately, by ballot, the President. But in choosing the President, the votes shall be taken by states, the representation from each state having one vote; a quorum for this purpose shall consist of a member or members from two-thirds of the states, and a majority of all the states shall be necessary to a choice. [And if the House of Representatives shall not choose a President whenever the right of choice shall devolve upon them, before the fourth day of March next following, then the Vice-President shall act as President, as in case of the death or other constitutional disability of the President.—]° The person having the greatest number of votes as Vice-President, shall be the Vice-President, if such number be a majority of the whole number of Electors appointed, and if no person have a majority, then from the two highest numbers on the list, the Senate shall choose the Vice-President; a quorum for the purpose shall consist of two-thirds of the whole number of Senators, and a majority

---

° Superseded by Section 3 of the 20th Amendment.

of the whole number shall be necessary to a choice. But no person constitutionally ineligible to the office of President shall be eligible to that of Vice-President of the United States.

Amendment XIII

Passed by Congress January 31, 1865. Ratified December 6, 1865.

(Note: A portion of Article IV, Section 2 of the Constitution was changed by the Thirteenth Amendment.)

SECTION 1

Neither slavery nor involuntary servitude, except as a punishment for crime whereof the party shall have been duly convicted, shall exist within the United States, or any place subject to their jurisdiction.

SECTION 2

Congress shall have power to enforce this article by appropriate legislation.

Amendment XIV

Passed by Congress June 13, 1866. Ratified July 9, 1868.

(Note: Article I, Section 2 of the Constitution was modified by Section 2 of the Fourteenth Amendment.)

SECTION 1

All persons born or naturalized in the United States and subject to the jurisdiction thereof, are citizens of the United States and of the State wherein they reside. No State shall make or enforce any law which shall abridge the privileges or immunities of citizens of the United States; nor shall any State deprive any person of life, liberty, or property, without due process of law; nor deny to any person within its jurisdiction the equal protection of the laws.

SECTION 2

Representatives shall be apportioned among the several States according to their respective numbers, counting the whole number of persons in each State, excluding Indians not taxed. But when the right to vote at any election for the choice of electors for President and Vice President of the United States, Representatives in Congress, the Executive and Judicial officers of a State, or the members of the Legislature thereof, is denied to any of the male inhabitants of such State, [being twenty-one years of age,]° and citizens of the United States, or in any way abridged, except for participation in rebellion, or other crime, the basis of representation therein shall be reduced in the proportion which the number of such male citizens shall bear to the whole number of male citizens twenty-one years of age in such State.

SECTION 3

No person shall be a Senator or Representative in Congress, or elector of President and Vice President, or hold any office, civil or military, under the United States, or under any State, who, having previously taken an oath, as a member of Congress, or as an officer of the United States, or as a member of any State legislature, or as an executive or judicial officer of any State, to support the Constitution of the United States, shall have engaged in insurrection or rebellion against the same, or given aid or comfort to the enemies thereof. But Congress may by a vote of two-thirds of each House, remove such disability.

° Changed by Section 1 of the 26th Amendment.

SECTION 4

The validity of the public debt of the United States, authorized by law, including debts incurred for payment of pensions and bounties for services in suppressing insurrection or rebellion, shall not be questioned. But neither the United States nor any State shall assume or pay any debt or obligation incurred in aid of insurrection or rebellion against the United States, or any claim for the loss or emancipation of any slave; but all such debts, obligations and claims shall be held illegal and void.

SECTION 5

The Congress shall have the power to enforce, by appropriate legislation, the provisions of this article.

Amendment XV

Passed by Congress February 26, 1869. Ratified February 3, 1870.

SECTION 1

The right of citizens of the United States to vote shall not be denied or abridged by the United States or by any State on account of race, color, or previous condition of servitude.

SECTION 2

The Congress shall have the power to enforce this article by appropriate legislation.

Amendment XVI

Passed by Congress July 2, 1909. Ratified February 3, 1913.

(Note: Article I, Section 9 of the Constitution was modified by the Sixteenth Amendment.)

The Congress shall have power to lay and collect taxes on incomes, from whatever source derived, without apportionment among the several States, and without regard to any census or enumeration.

Amendment XVII

Passed by Congress May 13, 1912. Ratified April 8, 1913.

(Note: Article I, Section 3 of the Constitution was modified by the Seventeenth Amendment.)

The Senate of the United States shall be composed of two Senators from each State, elected by the people thereof, for six years; and each Senator shall have one vote. The electors in each State shall have the qualifications requisite for electors of the most numerous branch of the State legislatures.

When vacancies happen in the representation of any State in the Senate, the executive authority of such State shall issue writs of election to fill such vacancies: Provided, That the legislature of any State may empower the executive thereof to make temporary appointments until the people fill the vacancies by election as the legislature may direct.

This amendment shall not be so construed as to affect the election or term of any Senator chosen before it becomes valid as part of the Constitution.

Amendment XVIII

Passed by Congress December 18, 1917. Ratified January 16, 1919. Repealed by the Twenty-First Amendment, December 5, 1933.

SECTION 1

After one year from the ratification of this article the manufacture, sale, or transportation of intoxicating liquors within, the importation thereof into, or the exportation thereof from the United States and all territory subject to the jurisdiction thereof for beverage purposes is hereby prohibited.

SECTION 2

The Congress and the several States shall have concurrent power to enforce this article by appropriate legislation.

SECTION 3

This article shall be inoperative unless it shall have been ratified as an amendment to the Constitution by the legislatures of the several States, as provided in the Constitution, within seven years from the date of the submission hereof to the States by the Congress.

Amendment XIX

Passed by Congress June 4, 1919. Ratified August 18, 1920.

The right of citizens of the United States to vote shall not be denied or abridged by the United States or by any State on account of sex.

Congress shall have power to enforce this article by appropriate legislation.

Amendment XX

Passed by Congress March 2, 1932. Ratified January 23, 1933.

(Note: Article I, Section 4 of the Constitution was modified by Section 2 of this Amendment. In addition, a portion of the Twelfth Amendment was superseded by Section 3.)

SECTION 1

The terms of the President and the Vice President shall end at noon on the 20th day of January, and the terms of Senators and Representatives at noon on the 3d day of January, of the years in which such terms would have ended if this article had not been ratified; and the terms of their successors shall then begin.

SECTION 2

The Congress shall assemble at least once in every year, and such meeting shall begin at noon on the 3d day of January, unless they shall by law appoint a different day.

SECTION 3

If, at the time fixed for the beginning of the term of the President, the President elect shall have died, the Vice President elect shall become President. If a President shall not have been chosen before the time fixed for the beginning of his term, or if the President elect shall have failed to qualify, then the Vice President elect shall act as President until a President shall have qualified; and the Congress may by law provide for the case wherein neither a President elect nor a Vice President shall have qualified, declaring who shall then act as President, or the manner in which one who is to act shall be selected, and such person shall act accordingly until a President or Vice President shall have qualified.

SECTION 4

The Congress may by law provide for the case of the death of any of the persons from whom the House of Representatives may choose a President whenever the right of choice shall have devolved upon them, and for the case of the death of any of the persons from whom the Senate may choose a Vice President whenever the right of choice shall have devolved upon them.

SECTION 5

Sections 1 and 2 shall take effect on the 15th day of October following the ratification of this article.

SECTION 6

This article shall be inoperative unless it shall have been ratified as an amendment to the Constitution by the legislatures of three-fourths of the several States within seven years from the date of its submission.

Amendment XXI

Passed by Congress February 20, 1933. Ratified December 5, 1933.

SECTION 1

The eighteenth article of amendment to the Constitution of the United States is hereby repealed.

SECTION 2

The transportation or importation into any State, Territory, or possession of the United States for delivery or use therein of intoxicating liquors, in violation of the laws thereof, is hereby prohibited.

SECTION 3

This article shall be inoperative unless it shall have been ratified as an amendment to the Constitution by conventions in the several States, as provided in the Constitution, within seven years from the date of the submission hereof to the States by the Congress.

Amendment XXII

Passed by Congress March 21, 1947. Ratified February 27, 1951.

SECTION 1

No person shall be elected to the office of the President more than twice, and no person who has held the office of President, or acted as President, for more than two years of a term to which some other person was elected President shall be elected to the office of President more than once. But this Article shall not apply to any person holding the office of President when this Article was proposed by Congress, and shall not prevent any person who may be holding the office of President, or acting as President, during the term within which this Article becomes operative from holding the office of President or acting as President during the remainder of such term.

SECTION 2

This article shall be inoperative unless it shall have been ratified as an amendment to the Constitution by the legislatures of three-fourths of the several States within seven years from the date of its submission to the States by the Congress.

Amendment XXIII

Passed by Congress June 16, 1960. Ratified March 29, 1961.

SECTION 1

The District constituting the seat of Government of the United States shall appoint in such manner as Congress may direct:

A number of electors of President and Vice President equal to the whole number of Senators and Representatives in Congress to which the District would be entitled if it were a State, but in no event more than the least populous State; they shall be in addition to those appointed by the States, but they shall be considered, for the purposes of the election of President and Vice President, to be electors appointed by a State; and they shall meet in the District and perform such duties as provided by the twelfth article of amendment.

SECTION 2

The Congress shall have power to enforce this article by appropriate legislation.

Amendment XXIV

Passed by Congress August 27, 1962. Ratified January 23, 1964.

SECTION 1

The right of citizens of the United States to vote in any primary or other election for President or Vice President, for electors for President or Vice President, or for Senator or Representative in Congress, shall not be denied or abridged by the United States or any State by reason of failure to pay poll tax or other tax.

SECTION 2

The Congress shall have power to enforce this article by appropriate legislation.

Amendment XXV

Passed by Congress July 6, 1965. Ratified February 10, 1967.

(Note: Article II, Section 1 of the Constitution was modified by the Twenty-Fifth Amendment.)

SECTION 1

In case of the removal of the President from office or of his death or resignation, the Vice President shall become President.

SECTION 2

Whenever there is a vacancy in the office of the Vice President, the President shall nominate a Vice President who shall take office upon confirmation by a majority vote of both Houses of Congress.

SECTION 3

Whenever the President transmits to the President pro tempore of the Senate and the Speaker of the House of Representatives his written declaration that he is unable to discharge the powers and duties of his office, and until he transmits to them a written declaration to the contrary, such powers and duties shall be discharged by the Vice President as Acting President.

SECTION 4

Whenever the Vice President and a majority of either the principal officers of the executive departments or of such other body as Congress may by law provide, transmit to the President pro tempore of the Senate and the Speaker of the House of Representatives their written declaration that the President is unable to discharge the powers and duties of his office, the Vice President shall immediately assume the powers and duties of the office as Acting President.

Thereafter, when the President transmits to the President pro tempore of the Senate and the Speaker of the House of Representatives his written declaration that no inability exists, he shall resume the powers and duties of his office unless the Vice President and a majority of either the principal officers of the executive department or of such other body as Congress may by law provide, transmit within four days to the President pro tempore of the Senate and the Speaker of the House of Representatives their written declaration that the President is unable to discharge the powers and duties of his office. Thereupon Congress shall decide the issue, assembling within forty-eight hours for that purpose if not in session. If the Congress, within twenty-one days after receipt of the latter written declaration, or, if Congress is not in session, within twenty-one days after Congress is required to assemble, determines by two-thirds vote of both Houses that the President is unable to discharge the powers and duties of his office, the Vice President shall continue to discharge the same as Acting President; otherwise, the President shall resume the powers and duties of his office.

Amendment XXVI

Passed by Congress March 23, 1971. Ratified July 1, 1971.

(Note: Amendment 14, Section 2 of the Constitution was modified by Section 1 of the Twenty-Sixth Amendment.)

SECTION 1

The right of citizens of the United States, who are eighteen years of age or older, to vote shall not be denied or abridged by the United States or by any State on account of age.

SECTION 2

The Congress shall have power to enforce this article by appropriate legislation.

Amendment XXVII

Originally proposed Sept. 25, 1789. Ratified May 7, 1992.

No law, varying the compensation for the services of the Senators and Representatives, shall take effect, until an election of representatives shall have intervened.

Chronological Tables of U.S. Supreme Court Justices

CHIEF JUSTICES

	Appointing President	Date of Service
Jay, John	Washington	1789-1795
Rutledge, John	Washington	1795
Ellsworth, Oliver	Washington	1796-1800
Marshall, John	Adams, J.	1801-1835
Taney, Roger Brooke	Jackson	1836-1864
Chase, Salmon Portland	Lincoln	1864-1873
Waite, Morrison Remick	Grant	1874-1888
Fuller, Melville Weston	Cleveland	1888-1910
White, Edward Douglas	Taft	1910-1921
Taft, William Howard	Harding	1921-1930
Hughes, Charles Evans	Hoover	1930-1941
Stone, Harlan Fiske	Roosevelt, F.	1941-1946
Vinson, Frederick Moore	Truman	1946-1953
Warren, Earl	Eisenhower	1953-1969
Burger, Warren Earl	Nixon	1969-1986
Rehnquist, William Hubbs	Reagan	1986-2005
Roberts, John G., Jr.	Bush, G. W.	2005-

ASSOCIATE JUSTICES

	Appointing President	Date of Service
Rutledge, John	Washington	1790-1791
Cushing, William	Washington	1790-1810
Wilson, James	Washington	1789-1798
Blair, John, Jr.	Washington	1790-1796
Iredell, James	Washington	1790-1799
Johnson, Thomas	Washington	1792-1793

	Appointing President	Date of Service
Paterson, William	Washington	1793-1806
Chase, Samuel	Washington	1796-1811
Washington, Bushrod	Adams, J.	1799-1829
Moore, Alfred	Adams, J.	1800-1804
Johnson, William	Jefferson	1804-1834
Livingston, Henry Brockholst	Jefferson	1807-1823
Todd, Thomas	Jefferson	1807-1826
Duvall, Gabriel	Madison	1811-1835
Story, Joseph	Madison	1812-1845
Thompson, Smith	Monroe	1823-1843
Trimble, Robert	Adams, J. Q.	1826-1828
McLean, John	Jackson	1830-1861
Baldwin, Henry	Jackson	1830-1844
Wayne, James Moore	Jackson	1835-1867
Barbour, Philip Pendleton	Jackson	1836-1841
Catron, John	Jackson	1837-1865
McKinley, John	Van Buren	1838-1852
Daniel, Peter Vivian	Van Buren	1842-1860
Nelson, Samuel	Tyler	1845-1872
Woodbury, Levi	Polk	1845-1851
Grier, Robert Cooper	Polk	1846-1870
Curtis, Benjamin Robbins	Fillmore	1851-1857
Campbell, John Archibald	Pierce	1853-1861
Clifford, Nathan	Buchanan	1858-1881
Swayne, Noah Haynes	Lincoln	1862-1881
Miller, Samuel Freeman	Lincoln	1862-1890
Davis, David	Lincoln	1862-1877
Field, Stephen Johnson	Lincoln	1863-1897
Strong, William	Grant	1870-1880
Bradley, Joseph P.	Grant	1870-1892
Hunt, Ward	Grant	1873-1882
Harlan, John Marshall	Hayes	1877-1911
Woods, William Burnham	Hayes	1881-1887
Matthews, Stanley	Garfield	1881-1889
Gray, Horace	Arthur	1882-1902

	Appointing President	Date of Service
Blatchford, Samuel	Arthur	1882-1893
Lamar, Lucius Quintus C.	Cleveland	1888-1893
Brewer, David Josiah	Harrison	1890-1910
Brown, Henry Billings	Harrison	1891-1906
Shiras, George, Jr.	Harrison	1892-1903
Jackson, Howell Edmunds	Harrison	1893-1895
White, Edward Douglas	Cleveland	1894-1910
Peckham, Rufus Wheeler	Cleveland	1896-1909
McKenna, Joseph	McKinley	1898-1925
Holmes, Oliver Wendell	Roosevelt, T.	1902-1932
Day, William Rufus	Roosevelt, T.	1903-1922
Moody, William Henry	Roosevelt, T.	1906-1910
Lurton, Horace Harmon	Taft	1910-1914
Hughes, Charles Evans	Taft	1910-1916
Van Devanter, Willis	Taft	1911-1937
Lamar, Joseph Rucker	Taft	1911-1916
Pitney, Mahlon	Taft	1912-1922
McReynolds, James Clark	Taft	1914-1941
Brandeis, Louis Dembitz	Wilson	1916-1939
Clarke, John Hessin	Wilson	1916-1922
Sutherland, George	Harding	1921-1938
Butler, Pierce	Harding	1923-1939
Sanford, Edward Terry	Harding	1923-1930
Stone, Harlan Fiske	Coolidge	1925-1941
Roberts, Owen Josephus	Hoover	1930-1945
Cardozo, Benjamin Nathan	Hoover	1932-1938
Black, Hugo Lafayette	Roosevelt, F.	1937-1971
Reed, Stanley Forman	Roosevelt, F.	1938-1957
Frankfurter, Felix	Roosevelt, F.	1939-1962
Douglas, William Orville	Roosevelt, F.	1939-1975
Murphy, Frank	Roosevelt, F.	1940-1949
Byrnes, James Francis	Roosevelt, F.	1941-1942
Jackson, Robert Houghwout	Roosevelt, F.	1941-1954
Rutledge, Wiley Blount	Roosevelt, F.	1943-1949
Burton, Harold Hitz	Truman	1945-1958

	Appointing President	Date of Service
Clark, Thomas Campbell	Truman	1949-1967
Minton, Sherman	Truman	1949-1956
Harlan, John Marshall (II)	Eisenhower	1955-1971
Brennan, William Joseph, Jr.	Eisenhower	1956-1990
Whittaker, Charles Evans	Eisenhower	1957-1962
Stewart, Potter	Eisenhower	1958-1981
White, Byron Raymond	Kennedy	1962-1993
Goldberg, Arthur Joseph	Kennedy	1962-1965
Fortas, Abe	Johnson, L.	1965-1969
Marshall, Thurgood	Johnson, L.	1967-1991
Blackmun, Harry A.	Nixon	1970-1994
Powell, Lewis Franklin, Jr.	Nixon	1972-1987
Rehnquist, William Hubbs	Nixon	1972-1986
Stevens, John Paul	Ford	1975-2010
O'Connor, Sandra Day	Reagan	1981-2006
Scalia, Antonin	Reagan	1986-2016
Kennedy, Anthony	Reagan	1988-2018
Souter, David H.	Bush, G. H. W.	1990-2009
Thomas, Clarence	Bush, G. H. W.	1991-
Ginsburg, Ruth Bader	Clinton	1993-2020
Breyer, Stephen G.	Clinton	1994-2022
Alito, Samuel, Jr.	Bush, G. W.	2006-
Sotomayor, Sonia	Obama	2009-
Kagan, Elena	Obama	2010-
Gorsuch, Neil	Trump	2017-
Kavanaugh, Brett	Trump	2018-
Barrett, Amy Coney	Trump	2020-
Jackson, Ketanji Brown	Biden	2022-

Brief Biographies of Selected U.S. Supreme Court Justices

Alito, Samuel, Jr.

Samuel Alito grew up in New Jersey as the child of an Italian immigrant and an Italian American teacher. Alito worked for the Justice Department during the Reagan administration and as the U.S. Attorney for the District of New Jersey before serving as a judge for the Third Circuit Court of Appeals for 15 years. As a reliable conservative throughout his career, Justice Alito's nomination to replace the moderate Sandra Day O'Connor on the Court was highly controversial. Some of his most significant majority opinions on the bench have been in *Burwell v. Hobby Lobby* and most recently, *Dobbs v. Jackson Women's Health Organization*.

Barrett, Amy Coney

A conservative Catholic, Amy Coney Barrett was a professor of law at Notre Dame and a judge for the Seventh Circuit Court of Appeals before she joined the Supreme Court. President Donald Trump nominated Barrett to the Court only a week after Justice Ruth Bader Ginsburg's death on September 18, 2020. After the Republican majority in the Senate had opposed President Barack Obama's nomination of Merrick Garland to the Court in 2016 because it was an election year, many were critical of the Republican-led Senate's confirmation of Barrett only months before the 2020 election. Barrett's replacement of the liberal Ginsburg also changed the ideological composition of the Court, adding a consistent conservative vote to replace Ginsburg's liberal one. Barrett follows an originalist approach to constitutional interpretation inspired by Justice Antonin Scalia, for whom she had been a clerk.

Blackmun, Harry A.

Justice Harry A. Blackmun was the first resident counsel for the Mayo Clinic, a major medical center, before joining the Court as President Richard Nixon's third attempt to fill the seat left by Justice Abe Fortas. Blackmun was the lifelong friend of another Nixon appointee, Chief Justice Warren Burger, and the two were referred to as the "Minnesota twins." However, Blackmun often diverged from his "twin" by voting with the liberal Justices of the Court, instead of as a conservative, as Nixon and others had expected him to, especially in cases involving individual rights. For example, Blackmun voted with the liberal majority and wrote the majority opinion in *Roe v. Wade*. Justice Blackmun retired in 1994 and passed away on March 4, 1999.

Brennan, William Joseph, Jr.

Justice William Brennan was one of the Court's longest serving justices and was known for his talent at building coalitions to reach a majority vote. Brennan came from a family of Irish immigrants and studied under Justice Frankfurter while at Harvard Law, with whom he would eventually serve on the Court. After school, he worked for a firm in New Jersey and then joined the Army during World War II. Despite their partisan differences, Republican President Dwight D. Eisenhower appointed Brennan to the Supreme Court after he had gained the President's attention as a judge on the New Jersey Supreme Court. Throughout his 33-year career on the Court, Brennan was the author of many landmark progressive opinions involving individual rights, such as *Baker v. Carr*, *Texas v. Johnson*, and *Frontiero v. Richardson*. Justice Brennan retired from the Court in 1990 and passed away on July 27, 1997.

Breyer, Stephen G.

Justice Stephen G. Breyer grew up as the child of Jewish parents in San Francisco. Before he was on the Court, Breyer held several positions related to Congress, such as an assistant special prosecutor in the Watergate investigation. After the investigation, he continued to work for the Senate Judiciary Committee, including on the deregulation of airlines in the late 1970s. President Jimmy Carter appointed Breyer to serve on the U.S. Court of Appeals for the First Circuit, which he did for 14 years. Breyer was next appointed by President Bill Clinton to replace Justice Blackmun on the Supreme Court. Known for his pragmatic approach to the law, Breyer served as a consistent member of the Court's liberal wing until his retirement in 2022.

Burger, Warren

Chief Justice Warren Burger grew up the youngest of seven children in a working-class family in Minnesota. Before he was on the Court, he worked for a Minnesota law firm and was active in Minnesota Republican politics, including work to support Dwight D. Eisenhower's campaign for the presidency. In return, once elected, Eisenhower appointed Burger to the U.S. Court of Appeals for the District of Columbia. As a circuit court judge, Burger gained a reputation for protecting "law-and-order" policies when dealing with the rights of the accused, which led President Nixon to appoint him as the new Chief Justice to replace Earl Warren. On the Court, Burger aimed to improve the efficiency of the federal judicial system in the face of its rapidly increasing caseload. The Burger Court dealt with a wide range of issues from abortion to capital punishment to obscenity. Burger retired from the Court in 1986 after serving for 17 years as the Chief Justice.

Douglas, William Orville

Justice William Orville Douglas was the longest-tenured Justice in the history of the Supreme Court, serving for more than 35 years. Douglas grew up in poverty and contracted polio at age three. He survived and retained a lifelong love of the outdoors because of the hiking program he undertook to recover. After law school, Douglas worked on the New Deal under the Franklin D. Roosevelt administration, and then as the chairman of the newly established Securities and Exchange Commission, until Roosevelt appointed him to the Court. On the Court, Douglas continued to support New Deal legislation and was known as the "Great Dissenter" for the number of dissents he wrote arguing against the decisions of the Burger Court. Douglas is remembered both for his divisive personality and deep ideological commitments. He was known as a strident environmentalist and an outspoken civil libertarian—as well as for his historic opinions that limited government intrusion on the rights of individuals, such as *Griswold v. Connecticut*.

Fortas, Abe

Justice Abraham "Abe" Fortas held a variety of government jobs during the New Deal era—assistant director of the Securities and Exchange Commission under William O. Douglas, general counsel to the Public Works Administration, and undersecretary for the Department of the Interior—before moving into private practice. There, he successfully advocated for the right of the accused to counsel in criminal trials in front of the Supreme Court in *Gideon v. Wainwright*. In 1965, Fortas was appointed to the Court by President Lyndon B. Johnson. Later, when Johnson tried to elevate Fortas to replace Earl Warren as Chief Justice, the Senate filibustered his nomination until President Johnson withdrew it. Fortas was the first Supreme Court Justice to resign from the Court under threat of impeachment, which he did when *Life* magazine revealed that he had had a transaction in the past with a financier who had been indicted for securities violations.

Frankfurter, Felix

Born in Austria, Felix Frankfurter and his family immigrated to the United States in the late 1800s. There, he graduated first in his class at Harvard Law, where he would later teach. Frankfurter worked for a variety of presidential administrations: for the Secretary of War in the Taft administration, and as the Chairman of the War Labor Policies Board during World War I, working alongside Franklin D. Roosevelt. In 1920, Frankfurter became one of the founding members of the American Civil Liberties Union (ACLU). Frankfurter next returned to Washington, D.C., to help his friend Roosevelt in drafting the New Deal before being appointed to the Court. Much of Frankfurter's work on the Court embodied the philosophy of judicial restraint—the idea that judges should limit themselves through precedent and should defer to the expertise of the other branches of government. Frankfurter resigned from the Court in 1962 after suffering from a stroke and passed away in 1965.

Ginsburg, Ruth Bader

Born and raised in Brooklyn, New York, Ruth Bader Ginsburg, "the Notorious R.B.G.," was one of the Court's most iconic recent Justices, known for her lifelong fight for women's equality. Before she was on the Court, Ginsburg was a law professor and the director of the Women's Rights Project at the ACLU. In that position, she successfully argued several important sex discrimination cases in front of the Supreme Court, including *Frontiero v. Richardson*. Ginsburg next served as a federal judge on the D.C. Circuit Court for 13 years before being appointed to the Supreme Court by President Clinton. Ginsburg was well known for her zealous dissents against decisions from the Court's conservative majority, such as in *Bush v. Gore* and *Shelby County v. Holder*. Never retiring from the Court despite numerous health struggles, Ginsburg passed away while on the bench in September 2020.

Goldberg, Arthur Joseph

Before he was on the Court, Justice Arthur Goldberg had a long career as a labor lawyer: He served as general counsel for the CIO, advised the AFL-CIO merger, and served as the Secretary of Labor under President John F. Kennedy. Kennedy later appointed Goldberg to the Court to replace Justice Felix Frankfurter. Goldberg only served three terms on the Court, but voted consistently with the liberal bloc under Chief Justice Warren in major individual rights cases and prioritized defending the nation's workers. Goldberg was asked to leave the Court to become the U.S. Ambassador to the United Nations under President Lyndon B. Johnson, but he resigned from that position during Johnson's escalation of the Vietnam War and returned to private practice. Goldberg passed away in 1990.

Gorsuch, Neil

The first of President Donald Trump's three appointees to the Supreme Court, Justice Neil Gorsuch is best known as a proponent of an originalist and textualist approach to interpreting the Constitution. After clerking for Justices Byron White and Anthony Kennedy, Gorsuch worked for a Washington, D.C. firm and for the Department of Justice under George W. Bush. He also served on the U.S. Court of Appeals for the Tenth Circuit for more than ten years. Gorsuch's nomination to replace Justice Antonin Scalia, who had passed away in February 2016, was controversial because Senate Republicans had refused to hold a vote on Merrick Garland, President Barack Obama's appointment to the position, due to the coming presidential election eight months in the future. By joining the Court alongside Justice Kennedy, Gorsuch became the first Justice to serve at the same time as someone for whom he had clerked.

Harlan, John Marshall (II)

Justice John Marshall Harlan II came from a wealthy family of many lawyers, including his grandfather, who had served as an Associate Justice on the Court before him. On a Rhodes Scholarship, Harlan attended Oxford and returned to attend law school in the United States at New York Law School. After that,

Harlan served as an assistant U.S. Attorney, where he worked on Prohibition cases. During World War II, he volunteered for service in the Air Force. Harlan returned to the United States and rejoined private practice, most notably handling antitrust litigation, and was appointed to the U.S. Court of Appeals for the Second Circuit by President Dwight D. Eisenhower in 1954. The next year, Eisenhower nominated Harlan to replace Justice Jackson on the Supreme Court, where he frequently advocated for judicial restraint during the Warren Court. Harlan retired from the Court in 1971 and passed away later that year.

Jackson, Ketanji Brown

During his 2020 campaign, President Joseph Biden repeatedly promised to appoint the first Black woman to the Court if elected. Biden fulfilled his promise by appointing Justice Ketanji Brown Jackson, who, in addition to being the first Black woman to serve on the Court, is also the first former public defender to become a Supreme Court Justice. Before she was a Washington, D.C. public defender, Justice Brown worked in private practice and then for the United States Sentencing Commission. Later, she was appointed by President Barack Obama to serve on the U.S. District Court in Washington, D.C. and was sworn in by Justice Stephen Breyer, for whom she had clerked earlier in her career. In 2021, President Biden appointed her to the Court of Appeals for the D.C. Circuit, where she served for a year before her nomination to the Supreme Court in 2022.

Jackson, Robert Houghwout

Born in 1892, Justice Robert H. Jackson had no formal education after high school except for one year at Albany Law School. After being admitted to the bar at age 21, Jackson became an adviser to President Franklin D. Roosevelt through his work in various positions in Washington: General Counsel to the Bureau of Internal Revenue, assistant U.S. Attorney General, Solicitor General, and ultimately, U.S. Attorney General. Once appointed to the Court by Roosevelt, Jackson's opinions generally expanded the power of the federal government, and one of his best known writings is his concurrence in *Youngstown Sheet & Tube Co. v. Sawyer*, in which he laid out a framework for categories of executive power. In addition to his domestic work, Jackson took a break from the Court to serve as a prosecutor in the Nuremberg war trials after World War II. Jackson passed away of a heart attack in 1954.

Kagan, Elena

Elena Kagan's career before her time on the Court varied between academic and government work. Kagan taught at the University of Chicago Law School before she held various positions in the Clinton administration, such as Deputy Director of the Domestic Policy Council. However, when the Senate failed to confirm her nomination to the D.C. Court of Appeals, Kagan returned to teaching, this time at Harvard Law School, where she became the first female dean in 2003. She returned to government work once again in 2008 as the first female Solicitor General and was soon appointed by President Barack Obama to fill Justice John Paul Stevens's spot on the Supreme Court. As one of the Court's youngest Justices when appointed to the Court, Kagan has been known for her sense of humor and for using references to popular culture in her writings on the Court, such as in *Kimble v. Marvel Entertainment* or her dissent in *Yates v. United States*, which includes a citation to Dr. Suess's *One Fish Two Fish Red Fish Blue Fish*.

Kavanaugh, Brett

Before he was on the Court, Justice Brett Kavanaugh worked under Solicitor General Kenneth Starr, including the investigation of President Bill Clinton that led to his impeachment. Along with Chief Justice John Roberts and Justice Amy Coney Barrett, Kavanaugh also worked for President George W. Bush's legal team in *Bush v. Gore*, concerning the highly contested presidential election of 2000. President Bush appointed Kavanaugh to the D.C. Circuit Court a second time after his first attempted nomination failed. Kavanaugh's subsequent nomination to the Supreme Court resulted in one of the most controversial confirmation hearings the country has ever seen. Within the context of the #MeToo movement, the Senate Judiciary Committee added an additional day of hearings to Kavanaugh's nomination to address a claim from Professor Christine Blasey Ford that Kavanaugh had sexually assaulted her when they were both in high school. These supplemental hearings were contentious and emotional for all parties who testified. After the vote was initially delayed for a week-long FBI investigation into the claim, Kavanaugh's nomination passed by a vote of 50-48, and he joined the Supreme Court in 2018.

Kennedy, Anthony

Justice Anthony Kennedy came from a family of lawyers and worked in private practice and as a law professor before joining the Court. During his time in private practice, Kennedy lobbied for the Republican Party and advised the Governor of California Ronald Reagan. Kennedy was next appointed as a judge to the Court of Appeals for the Ninth Circuit, where he was the youngest federal appellate judge in the country at the time. After President Reagan's attempt to nominate Robert Bork to the Court failed, Reagan nominated Kennedy, who successfully joined the bench in 1988. On the Court, Kennedy was known for being a critical swing vote, writing for the majority in major cases such as *Citizens United v. FEC* and *Obergefell v. Hodges*. Kennedy retired from the Court in 2018 and was replaced by Justice Brett Kavanaugh, one of his former law clerks.

Marshall, Thurgood

Justice Thurgood Marshall was the first African American justice on the U.S. Supreme Court and a passionate advocate for civil rights throughout his career.

Before his time as a judge, as an attorney for the NAACP, Marshall successfully argued against segregation in front of the Court in *Brown v. Board of Education*. In fact, Marshall won 29 out of the 32 cases he argued in front of the Supreme Court throughout his career as an attorney. President John F. Kennedy appointed Marshall to the Second Circuit Court of Appeals and Kennedy's successor, Lyndon B. Johnson, appointed Marshall as the Solicitor General. After only two years as the Solicitor General, however, Johnson appointed Marshall to the Supreme Court, where he was a proponent of progressive judicial activism, and he continued his support for civil rights. Marshall retired in 1991 and was replaced by Justice Clarence Thomas.

O'Connor, Sandra Day

Appointed in 1981, Justice Sandra Day O'Connor was the first female justice on the Supreme Court. She had a lengthy career in Arizona politics, first as the assistant Attorney General of Arizona, and then in the Arizona State Senate. (Not many of the Justices in the modern era have been politicians and her credentials were lauded as important to a Justice's role in evaluating the work of a legislature.) She also served on the Arizona Supreme Court of Appeals before being nominated by President Ronald Reagan to serve on the U.S. Supreme Court. Her time working in state government informed her understanding of state and federal relations once on the Court, and she was also known as a swing vote in cases involving controversial issues such as affirmative action, the death penalty, and abortion. O'Connor retired from the Court in 2006 to care for her husband, who suffered from Alzheimer's disease.

Powell, Lewis Franklin, Jr.

Justice Lewis F. Powell began his career as a trial lawyer but enlisted in the Army in World War II, working for the Military Intelligence Service decoding German radio messages. Upon his return, he became member and then president of the Virginia State Board of Education in the aftermath of *Brown v. Board of Education* and the beginnings of desegregation. At this time, Powell also became one of the best known attorneys in the country as the president of the American Bar Association, a reputation that led President Richard Nixon to nominate him as an Associate Justice in 1971. During his 16 years on the Court, Powell took a centrist approach to controversial issues, such as affirmative action in *Regents of the University of California v. Bakke*. Powell retired from the Court in 1987 and passed away in 1998.

Rehnquist, William Hubbs

Chief Justice William Rehnquist's early education at Kenyon College was interrupted by three years of service in the Army Air Corps, but he ultimately graduated at the top of his class at Stanford Law School after his return to the United States. After graduating, as a law clerk to Justice Robert Jackson, Rehnquist wrote an infamous memo urging the justice to affirm *Plessy v. Ferguson* when deliberating *Brown v. Board of Education*. After clerking, Rehnquist worked in private practice and then in government as a member of President Richard Nixon's Justice Department. Nixon then appointed Rehnquist to the Court in 1972. Sometimes referred to as the "Lone Ranger" in his early years on the bench, Rehnquist authored a number of solitary dissents in cases such as *Roe v. Wade*. After Warren Burger retired from the Court, President Reagan elevated Rehnquist to replace him as Chief Justice, and in this position, Rehnquist led a new conservative majority, with an emphasis on pragmatism and federalism. Rehnquist remained on the Court until he died of cancer in 2005.

Roberts, John G., Jr.

Chief Justice John Roberts attended Harvard Law School, and after graduating, worked as a clerk for Justice William Rehnquist. Before his time on the Court, Roberts rotated between working in private practice—where he argued 39 cases before the Court—and working for both the Ronald Reagan and George H.W. Bush administrations. President George W. Bush nominated Roberts to serve on the Court of Appeals for the District of Columbia Circuit in 2003. Later, in 2005, Roberts was originally nominated to replace the retiring Sandra Day O'Connor, but when Chief Justice Rehnquist died, Bush instead appointed Roberts as Chief Justice of the Supreme Court. At his confirmation hearings, Roberts famously summarized his judicial approach through the image of baseball: "Judges are like umpires. Umpires don't make the rules, they apply them. . . . It's my job to call balls and strikes, and not to pitch or bat." Accordingly, as Chief Justice, Roberts has been concerned with preserving the legitimacy of the Court as an institution.

Scalia, Antonin Reagan

Justice Antonin Scalia is best known for his professed originalist approach to the Constitution—the judicial method of interpretation that finds constitutional meaning in the Framers' intent—which he has described at length in his often-cited book *A Matter of Interpretation*. Scalia worked at a private firm for several years after graduating law school and then became a professor at the University of Virginia. He next moved to government work by serving in several positions in the executive branch, such as general counsel for the Office of Telecommunications Policy. Scalia returned to teaching after the Watergate scandal, until he was appointed by President Ronald Reagan to the federal judiciary: first to the Court of Appeals for the District of Columbia Circuit, and then to the Supreme Court in 1986. On the Court, Scalia authored what was then the greatest number of concurring opinions of any Justice to ever sit on the Court, and a significant number of dissenting opinions. He passed away in February 2016 and was replaced by Justice Neil Gorsuch.

Sotomayor, Sonia

Justice Sonia Sotomayor knew once she watched an episode of *Perry Mason* at age ten that she would be an attorney, and not just an attorney. Sotomayor became the first Hispanic American and only the third woman to serve on the U.S. Supreme Court. After graduating from Yale Law School, Sotomayor worked as an assistant district attorney in Manhattan. In addition to her time as a prosecutor, Sotomayor also worked in private practice in business and corporate law, until she was appointed by George H.W. Bush to serve on the District Court for the Southern District of New York. Next, she was appointed by President Bill Clinton to serve on the Court of Appeals for the Second Circuit, which she did for a decade before being nominated by President Barack Obama to the Supreme Court. On the Court, Sotomayor is known for being active during oral arguments and for voting often with the Court's liberal wing.

Souter, David H.

Known as a "stealth nominee," Justice David Souter defied expectations during his time on the Court by voting reliably with liberal justices despite his nomination by the conservative President George H.W. Bush. Before he was on the Court, Souter was a Rhodes scholar who had studied at Harvard and Oxford before starting his career as an attorney in private practice. Dissatisfied with private practice, Souter left to work in the New Hampshire Attorney General's Office, where he eventually became the New Hampshire Attorney General himself in 1976. From there, Souter was appointed as a justice on the New Hampshire Superior Court, then to the Supreme Court of New Hampshire. He was next successfully appointed to the U.S. Supreme Court in light of this long-standing record of service as a state court judge. While on the Court, he often voted with the liberal majority; for example, he coauthored the plurality opinion in *Planned Parenthood v. Casey* with Justices O'Connor and Kennedy. In 2009, Souter retired from the Court and currently resides in New Hampshire.

Stevens, John Paul

Justice John Paul Stevens was born in 1920 and came of age during the Great Depression, an experience that likely contributed to his long career in antitrust law. Early in his life, Stevens served as a codebreaker in the Navy during World War II. Afterward, he attended law school at Northwestern Law School through the G.I. Bill, graduating with a record-breaking GPA. After graduation, Stevens went into private practice, where he became renowned for his expertise in antitrust litigation. Stevens taught the subject at law schools in Chicago and advised various legislative and executive branch projects, for example, as counsel to a U.S. House of Representatives subcommittee on monopolies. Stevens next served on the U.S. Court of Appeals for the Seventh Circuit before being appointed by President Gerald Ford to the Supreme Court in 1975. There, he was the third longest serving Justice in Supreme Court history. Justice Stevens retired from the Court in 2010 and passed away from a stroke in July 2019.

Stewart, Potter

Justice Potter Stewart was best known for being a pragmatic swing vote during an era of fierce division on the Court. Stewart worked for a corporate firm after graduating from Yale Law School but quickly left to serve in the U.S. Navy during World War II. After, he returned to his hometown of Cincinnati—where his family had been involved in state politics for decades—and became involved in local politics himself, serving on the city council and as vice mayor. Stewart was next appointed by President Dwight D. Eisenhower as a judge for the U.S. Court of Appeals for the Sixth Circuit, and then to the Supreme Court. Perhaps his best known quote from his time on the Court is the definition of "hard-core" pornography he offered in *Jacobellis v. Ohio*: "I know it when I see it." Stewart retired from the Court in 1981 and passed away from a stroke in 1985.

Thomas, Clarence

Rather than a Supreme Court Justice, Clarence Thomas originally planned on becoming a Catholic priest—he even entered a seminary before changing his mind, and attending law school at Yale instead. After graduating, Thomas worked for the Missouri Attorney General and then as the Assistant Secretary for Civil Rights in the U.S. Department of Education under President Ronald Reagan. After that, Thomas served as the Chairman of the U.S. Equal Employment Opportunity Commission before his appointment to the U.S. Court of Appeals for the District of Columbia and to the Supreme Court. During Justice Thomas's Supreme Court confirmation hearings, Professor Anita Hill came forward and publicly alleged that he had sexually harassed her when she had been working as his aide. Thomas's nomination was ultimately confirmed by the Senate, but he described the hearings as a "high-tech lynching" as the Senate investigated Professor Hill's claim. On the Court, Justice Thomas was known for only rarely participating in oral arguments, for his professed originalism, and for his opposition to programs such as affirmative action.

Warren, Earl

Chief Justice Earl Warren is known for leading one of the most progressive Courts in the institution's history, leading the country on civil rights issues with cases such as *Brown v. Board of Education*. Warren grew up in California during the end of the nineteenth century and began working at the age of only nine. After attending law school and working in private practice for a few years, he later became the District Attorney of Alameda County, California, a role he would retain for 13 years. Warren was next elected as attorney general of California, and then as governor of the state in 1942, both times running on non-partisan themes. In 1953, President Dwight D. Eisenhower chose Warren as the new Chief Justice of the Supreme Court. In this role, Warren guided the Court through questions involving racial segregation and voting rights, and toward a vision of "living Constitutionalism"—the idea that constitutional interpretation need not be limited to the text of the document exactly as it meant to the Framers. Warren retired from the Court in 1969 and died from cardiac arrest in 1974.

White, Byron Raymond

Before he was on the Supreme Court, Justice Byron White was a nationally recognized college football player, and played briefly for both the Pittsburgh Pirates (now Steelers) and the Detroit Lions in the NFL. At the same time, White was a distinguished student and studied at Oxford on a Rhodes Scholarship before attending Yale Law School. After he worked on John F. Kennedy's presidential campaign, White was appointed by Robert Kennedy as assistant Attorney General in the Kennedy administration. In 1962, President Kennedy appointed White to the Supreme Court. As a member of the Court, Justice White typically voted with the liberal justices in cases concerning voting rights, but dissented on other expansions of individual rights, in cases such as *Roe v. Wade* and *Miranda v. Arizona*. White retired from the Court in 1993, and passed away from pneumonia in 2002.

Glossary

Acquittal A court decision that a person charged with a crime is not guilty. An acquittal is not necessarily a decision that the person is innocent.

Advisory opinion A judicial interpretation of a legal question generally requested by a legislature or an executive. The request usually comes before an actual case or controversy has arisen. Advisory opinions are largely disfavored by both state and federal courts.

Advice and consent Constitutional term for the Senate's role in deciding whether to accept presidential nominations to the judiciary and other posts.

Affidavit A written statement of facts voluntarily made under oath or affirmation.

Affirm To uphold a decision of a lower court.

Aggravating circumstances Conditions that increase the seriousness of a crime but are not a part of the crime's legal definition.

Amicus curiae "Friend of the court." A person (or group), not a party to a case, who submits views (usually in the form of written briefs) on how the case should be decided.

Appeal The procedure by which a case is taken to a superior court for a review of the lower court's decision.

Appellant The party dissatisfied with a lower court ruling who appeals the case to a superior court for review.

Appellate jurisdiction The legal authority of a superior court to review and render judgment on a decision by a lower court.

Appellee The party usually satisfied with a lower court ruling against whom an appeal is filed.

Arguendo "In the course of argument." A term that is often used for the purpose of assuming facts or law during the process of reasoning or explaining a conclusion.

Arraignment A formal stage of the criminal process in which defendants are brought before a judge and are confronted with the charges against them. The defendants then enter a plea (such as "not guilty") to those charges.

Arrest   The act of physically taking into custody or otherwise depriving of freedom a person suspected of violating the law.

Articles of Confederation   The government for the 13 states that preceded the U.S. Constitution. Ratified in 1781, the Articles remained in effect until 1789.

Bona fide   "Good faith." A term often used to describe facts or circumstances as genuine or real.

Brief   A written argument of law and fact submitted to the court. Although parties can personally file briefs, briefs are usually filed by an attorney representing a party having an interest in a lawsuit.

Case   A legal dispute or controversy brought to a court for resolution.

Case law   Law that has evolved from past court decisions, as opposed to law created by legislative or executive action or by administrative regulations.

Case or controversy rule   The constitutional requirement the courts may hear only real disputes brought by adverse parties.

Cases and controversies   Language used in Article III that courts have interpreted to describe genuine disputes. Courts have interpreted the phrase to avoid giving advisory opinions in cases where there are not litigants with concrete interests at stake.

Certification   A procedure under which a lower court requests that a superior court rule on specified legal questions so that the lower court may correctly apply the law to a case pending before the lower court.

Certiorari, Writ of   *See* Writ of certiorari.

Checks and balances   A system of government in which various branches and levels of government are designed to prevent abuse of powers by the others.

Chief Justice of the United States   The Justice designated by the U.S. Constitution to preside over the U.S. Supreme Court. The Chief Justice is often described as the first among equals, with little more power than the other Justices (known as Associate Justices). Unlike Associate Justices, the Chief Justice has the power to assign the writing of opinions where he or she is in the majority, to preside over trials of presidential impeachments, and to act as the administrative head of the federal judiciary.

Civil case   A lawsuit, usually between private parties, in which the party bringing the case is seeking a remedy other than criminal punishment, such as damages or an injunction.

Civil law   (1) The law that governs a civil case (as opposed to the criminal law), or (2) law applied in systems that is set forth in statutes rather than case law (which is court-made law that is applied in common law systems).

Class action   A lawsuit brought by one or more persons who are representatives of their own interests and others similarly situated.

Comity   Respect of one government system for the preferences and law of another government system. Comity is based on deference rather than legal compulsion.

Common law   Law that has evolved from precedent, usage, and custom as reflected in the decisions of courts.

Compensatory damages   A monetary award, equivalent to the loss sustained, to be paid to an injured party by the party at fault.

Concurrent power   Power that is shared by more than one component of government. In U.S. constitutional law, concurrent power usually refers to power shared between state and federal governments.

Concurring opinion   A separate opinion written by a judge who agrees with the opinion of the court but expresses additional views, or a separate opinion written by a judge who agrees with the court's disposition of a case but either wishes to supplement the court's opinion or disagrees with the rationale used by the majority to reach the case disposition.

Content neutrality   A term used to describe a government's determination that an attempt to regulate speech does not discriminate according to the content, subject matter, or viewpoint expressed in the speech.

Courts of appeals (federal)   The intermediate-level appellate courts in the federal system, each of which has a jurisdiction over a particular region known as a circuit.

Criminal law   Law governing the relationship between individuals and society. Criminal law enforces the laws governing, and the punishment for, those who, by breaking laws, commit crimes.

De facto   "Actual," based on an observation of discernable facts.

De jure   "By law," according to a right or entitlement established by a law or official government action.

De minimis   Small or unimportant. A de minimis issue is an issue considered too trivial for a court to consider.

De novo   "New, from the beginning." Often used to refer to a judge's review of a prior ruling that takes a fresh approach and does not rely on results of a prior ruling.

Declaratory judgment   A judgment of law (not to be confused with advisory opinions) that stems from an actual dispute. A declaratory judgment is binding on the parties, but provides only an explanation of how the law applies to the parties' disputes.

Defendant A party at the trial level being sued in a civil case or charged with a crime in a criminal case.

Dicta (or Obiter dicta) Those portions of a judge's opinion that are not essential to deciding the case.

Discovery A pretrial procedure whereby one party to a lawsuit gains access to information or evidence held by the opposing party.

Dissenting opinion An opinion in which a judge disagrees with the majority opinion and explains the judge's reasoning in hopes of persuading others that the opinion is wrong.

District courts (federal) The trial courts of general jurisdiction in the federal system.

Docket The list of cases to be heard by a court.

Due process The notion that government procedures should follow principles of essential fairness.

During good behavior The constitutional provision that grants that judges and Justices will serve until they die, retire, or are impeached, convicted, and removed from office.

En banc A meeting of all members of a court, typically a U.S. court of appeals, whose members more typically serve on three-judge panels.

Enjoin An order from a court requiring a party to do or refrain from doing certain acts.

Equity Law based on principles of fairness rather than strictly applied statutes or fixed legal rules.

Ex parte "By or for one party." An ex parte hearing is in which only one party to a dispute is present.

Exclusionary rules A principle of law that illegally gathered evidence may not be admitted in court.

Federal question A legal issue based on the U.S. Constitution, laws, or treaties.

Federal system A government system that divides authority among different components, each possessing some sovereign power. In the United States, the federal system divides power between the federal and state governments.

Federalists Individuals who supported ratification of the U.S. Constitution. They designated their opponents as Anti-Federalists. One of the first two political parties in the United States subsequently took this as its name. In contemporary parlance, a federalist is often regarded as a legal thinker who emphasizes the importance of a limited federal government and strong state governments.

Felony   A serious criminal offense, usually punishable by incarceration of one year or more.

Frisk   To pat the outer portion of an individual's clothing (generally to check for weapons).

Gerrymander   To construct political boundaries for the purpose of giving advantage to a particular political party or interest.

Grand jury   A panel of 12 to 23 citizens who review prosecutorial evidence to determine if there are sufficient grounds to issue an indictment binding an individual over for trial on criminal charges.

Guilty verdict   A determination that a person accused of a criminal offense is legally responsible as charged.

Habeas corpus   "Produce the body." A writ of habeas corpus is issued to determine if a person held in custody is being unlawfully detained or imprisoned.

Immutable characteristic   A concept used in equal protection law that describes a quality of an individual that is not easily changeable. A person's race, sex, and eye color are considered qualities that cannot be easily changed.

Impeachment   A constitutional mechanism through which the House of Representatives may charge the president, judges, and other civil officers with "Treason, Bribery, or other High Crimes and Misdemeanors." Impeachment leads to a trial in the U.S. Senate, where it takes a two-thirds vote to convict and remove from office.

In forma pauperis   "In the form of a pauper." A special status granted to indigents that allows them to proceed without payment of court fees and to be exempt from certain procedural requirements.

In re   "In the matter of." The designation used in a judicial proceeding in which there are no formal adversaries.

Incorporation   The process whereby provisions of the Bill of Rights are declared to be included in the due process guarantee of the Fourteenth Amendment and made applicable to state and local governments.

Indictment   A document issued by a grand jury officially charging an individual with criminal violations and binding the accused over for trial.

Information   A finding reflected in a document that confirms that there is sufficient evidence to support criminal charges to justify putting the defendant on trial. An information often takes the place of a grand jury indictment, which is required in the federal system.

Injunction   A writ prohibiting the person to whom it is directed from committing certain specified acts.

Judgment of the court   The final ruling of a court, independent of the legal reasoning supporting it.

Judicial activism   Decision making by judges that integrates a judge's personal point of view, engages in social engineering, gives little deference to prior case law, and/or shows little deference to the decisions of a legislature or an executive.

Judicial notice   The recognition by a court of the truth of certain facts without requiring one of the parties to put proof of them into evidence.

Judicial restraint   Decision making by a judge that withholds the judge's personal point of view and generally defers to the decisions of a legislature or an executive.

Judicial review   The authority of a court to determine the constitutionality of acts promulgated or committed by the legislative and executive branches and to strike down acts judged to be in violation of the Constitution.

Jurisdiction   The authority of a court to hear and decide legal disputes and to enforce its rulings.

Justiciable   Capable of being heard and decided by a court.

Justiciability   Before a court will deliver an opinion, the parties before must show that the controversy that brings them before the court or the remedy that they seek is one that is appropriate for judges to decide.

Libel   A written and published communication that is false and causes injury. Libel is the written form of defamation and slander is the oral form of defamation.

Litigant   A party to a lawsuit.

Magistrate   A low-level judge with limited authority.

Magna Carta   A document signed by King John with his noblemen in England in 1215 generally regarded as the origin of the British Parliament, and subsequent representative institutions, and of the idea of written constitutionalism.

Majority opinion   An opinion that reflects a Supreme Court majority that has the effect of operative law.

Mandamus   "We command." A writ issued by a court commanding a public official to carry out a particular act or duty.

Misdemeanor   A less serious criminal act, usually punishable by less than one year of incarceration.

Mistrial   A trial that is prematurely ended by a judge because of procedural irregularities.

Moot   A question presented in a lawsuit that cannot be answered by a court either because the issue has resolved itself or because conditions have so changed that the court is unable to grant the requested relief. A moot case no longer presents an active case or controversy.

Mootness doctrine   A justiciability doctrine that prevents a federal court from hearing a case where an event has occurred that effectively removes the active dispute at the core of the case, such as the repeal of an objectionable statute, the death of a party, or an agreement between the parties that settles their dispute.

Motion   A request made to a court for a certain ruling or action.

Opinion of the court   An opinion announcing the judgment and reasoning of a court endorsed by a majority of the judges participating.

Order   A written command issued by a judge.

Original intent (also known as original understanding)   The motivation or idea of the U.S. Constitution's Framers behind particular provisions in the Constitution. The concept uses historical methods to ascertain their motivation and provides the basis for the "originalist" method of interpreting the Constitution. Originalism rejects the view that contemporary understanding of terms and concepts should inform constitutional interpretation.

Original jurisdiction   The power of a court to hear a case that is filed in that court before being heard by another court. The U.S. Supreme Court exercises original jurisdiction in very few instances, but rather uses most of its power to review cases that lower courts have decided.

Per curiam   "By the court." An unsigned or collectively written opinion issued by a court that does not bear the name of the judge or justice who wrote the opinion.

Plaintiff   The party who brings a legal action to court for resolution or remedy.

Plurality opinion   An opinion announcing the judgment of a court with supporting reasoning that is not endorsed by a majority of the justices participating.

Police powers   The power of the state to regulate for the health, safety, morals, and general welfare of its citizens.

Political question doctrine   A justiciability doctrine that prevents a federal court from hearing cases when they conclude that the question(s) in the case are best decided by a democratically accountable branch of government: the legislature or the executive.

Precedent   A previously decided case that serves as a guide for deciding a current case.

Prima facie   "At first sight." A party's argument or evidence that is sufficient to prevail unless effectively countered by the opposing side.

Privacy tort   Claims that someone is entitled to damage for intrusion on their private affairs, disclosure of their private information, publication that casts them in a false light, or uses their name or visage for personal gain. Privacy torts fall under the category of dignitary harms, which also include claims based on defamation and intentional infliction of emotional distress.

Pro se   "For himself or herself." A person who appears in court without an attorney, because either the person cannot afford an attorney or simply prefers to represent themselves.

Punitive damages   A monetary award (separate from compensatory damages) imposed by a court for punishment purposes to be paid by the party at fault to the injured party.

Recusal   The action taken by a judge who decides not to participate in a case because of a conflict of interest or another disqualifying condition.

Remand   To send a case back to an inferior court for further action.

Reverse   An action by an appellate court setting aside or changing a decision of a lower court.

Ripeness doctrine   A justiciability doctrine that prevents a federal court from hearing a case that has not yet evolved into a concrete controversy such that the court may properly resolve the issues in the case.

Selective incorporation   The policy of the Supreme Court to decide incorporation issues regarding individual rights on a case-by-case, right-by-right basis.

Separation of powers   A concept that each branch of government should enjoy unique powers and that each branch should have a mechanism to ensure that another branch does not abuse its power. In the United States, government powers are divided among the judiciary, the executive, and the two branches of the legislature.

Solicitor general   The Justice Department official whose office represents the federal government in all litigation before the U.S. Supreme Court.

Standard of review   The amount of deference that one court gives to another court when reviewing the latter court's determination. A rigorous standard of review allows the reviewing court more latitude to disagree with the lower court's decision. A deferential standard of review allows the reviewing court to make changes to the lower court's decision only upon showing of obvious error. Courts use a variety of standards of review, depending on the circumstances. In constitutional law, courts generally use one of three standards in evaluating the constitutionality of actions taken by a legislature, another court, or an executive official. The most deferential is rational basis scrutiny (or reasonableness) and the most rigorous is strict scrutiny (which requires a government to have a compelling reason for taking certain action.) In between the two is intermediate scrutiny, which requires that a government have an important reason for taking certain actions.

Standing doctrine   A justiciability doctrine that prevents a federal court from hearing a case when the party who brought the case is not directly affected by the legal issue that is raised. In some instances, a court determines that a party lacks standing to bring a case because the party's lack of legally recognizable injury deprives the court of power. In other instances, a court concludes that the case has qualities that render it imprudent for the court to hear the case.

Stare decisis   "Let the decision stand." The doctrine that a settled legal issue should be followed as precedent in future cases presenting the same question.

State action   An action taken by an agency or official of a state or local government or federal agency.

Stay   To stop or suspend. When a court issues a stay of the judgment in a case, the judgment cannot take effect until the stay is lifted.

Summary judgment   A decision by a court made without a full hearing.

Supremacy Clause   A provision in Article VI of the U.S. Constitution that mandates that federal law supersedes conflicting state law.

Temporary restraining order   A judicial order prohibiting certain challenged actions from being taken prior to a full hearing on the question.

Trier of fact   U.S. law separates decisions on the meaning of law and decisions on what facts underlie a dispute. The trier of fact is the entity who decides which facts occurred that gave rise to the suit. Sometimes the trier of fact is a jury and sometimes the judge.

U.S. Court of Appeals (also known as U.S. Circuit Courts)   Courts that possess interim power, sitting midway between the federal district courts and the U.S. Supreme Court. The U.S. Court of Appeals has the power to change the judgment of a district court, but the U.S. Supreme Court has the power to review and change Court of Appeals decisions. There are currently 11 numbered circuits (organized according to geographic proximity), a District of Columbia Circuit, and a specialized circuit.

U.S. District Courts   Federal trial courts that generally act as the court in which a case is originally filed.

U.S. Supreme Court   The highest court in the United States with power over both state and federal courts. Housed in Washington, D.C.

Vacate   To void or rescind. Generally applied to the judgment of another court.

Vel non   "Or not."

Writ   A written order of a court commanding the recipient to perform or not to perform certain specified acts.

Writ of certiorari   An order of an appellate court to an inferior court to send up the records of a case that the appellate court has elected to review. The primary method by which the U.S. Supreme Court exercises its discretionary jurisdiction to accept cases for a full hearing is through petitions for a writ of certiorari, generally filed by the loser in the lower court.

Writ of mandamus   *See* Mandamus.

Table of Cases

303 Creative LLC v. Elenis, 544

Abrams v. United States, 189
Allied Stores of Ohio, Inc. v. Bowers, 521
Ark. Educ. Comm'n v. Forbes, 332

B & B Hardware, Inc. v. Hargis Industries, Inc., 260
Baker v. Carr, 76, 572
Bates v. State Bar of Arizona, 271
Bethel School District v. Fraser, 219
Bond v. United States, 40-50, 89
Bowers v. Hardwick, 492-497, 502-516
Brandenburg v. Ohio, 190-194, 202
Broadrick v. Oklahoma, 270
Brown v. Board of Education, 16-17, 24-26, 54, 371-377, 381, 385, 403, 521, 577-578, 580
Buck v. Bell, 524

Calder v. Bull, 55
Califano v. Webster, 425
Central Hudson Gas & Elec. Corp. v. Public Service Commission of New York, 259, 263
Chaplinsky v. New Hampshire, 244, 267, 271, 277, 279
Christian Legal Soc'y Chapter of the Univ. of Cal. v. Martinez, 230-231
Cohen v. California, 267
Coleman v. Miller, 434
Corfield v. Coryell, 412
Counterman v. Colorado, 300
Craig v. Boren, 422

Dennis v. United States, 190, 192, 383
District of Columbia v. Heller, 314-345
Dobbs v. Jackson Women's Health Organization, 463-488, 510-511, 517, 524, 542, 545, 571
Doe v. Bolton, 451
Dred Scott v. Sanford, 64, 340, 357-364, 368, 377, 380, 403
Dudgeon v. United Kingdom, 506-507

Eisenstadt v. Baird, 451, 471, 488, 504
Elk Grove Unified School District v. Newdow, 68-72, 88
Elonis v. United States, 292-300
Euclid v. Ambler Realty Co., 268-275

Federal Communications Commission v. Pacifica Foundation, 268-275
Friends of the Earth, Inc. v. Laidlaw Envtl. Servs., Inc., 75
Frohwerk v. United States, 189
Frontiero v. Richardson, 422, 425, 572, 574

Gertz v. Robert Welch, Inc., 240
Gibbons v. Ogden, 63, 91-92, 96
Gideon v. Wainwright, 9, 573
Ginsberg v. New York, 272
Gitlow v. New York, 189-190
Goldwater v. Carter, 152
Gonzales v. Raich, 50, 121
Griswold v. Connecticut, 438-451, 471, 473, 477, 483, 488, 494, 504, 517, 531, 573

Hamdi v. Rumsfeld, 162-177
Hazelwood School District v. Kuhlmeier, 219-220
Hirabayashi v. United States, 154, 156, 522
Hustler Magazine v. Falwell, 215, 241-248, 258, 275-276, 311

Iancu v. Brunetti, 266
International Society for Krishna Consciousness v. Lee, 232

Kennedy v. Bremerton, 302-311
Korematsu v. United States, 154-162, 171, 176-177, 357, 370, 403, 517

Lamb's Chapel v. Center Moriches Union Free School Dist., 259, 262, 309
Lawrence et al. v. Texas, 471, 473, 477, 483, 503-516, 526-527, 541, 544

Lee v. Weisman, 307
Lemon v. Kurtzman, 302, 306, 309, 311
Lewis v. United States, 314
Lopez v. United States, 98-99, 100-113, 115-121, 128
Loving v. Virginia, 483, 518-526, 530-531, 533, 543-545

Mahanoy Area School District v. B. L., 224, 229-232
Marbury v. Madison, 55-64, 83, 103, 130, 358, 441, 445, 547
Matal v. Tam, 259-266, 273, 275
Mathews v. Eldridge, 168, 170
Maynard v. Hill, 520
McCulloch v. Maryland, 63, 89-91, 130, 398
McDonald v. City of Chicago, 331-332, 334-335
McLaughlin v. Florida, 522
Meyer v. State of Nebraska, 437-440, 442, 520
Miller v. California, 268, 271
Miranda v. Arizona, 9, 581
Morse v. Frederic, 220-223
Muller v. Oregon, 417
Myers v. United States, 135, 441
Myra Bradwell v. State of Illinois, 406-417, 433

NAACP v. State of Alabama, 439
Naim v. Naim, 520
National Federation of Independent Business v. Sebelius, 127
New York State Rifle & Pistol Association, Inc. v. Bruen, 331-345
New York Times Co. v. Sullivan, 208-215, 237, 240, 242-244, 354
Noto v. United States, 192

Obergefell v. Hodges, 471, 473, 477, 483, 526-545, 576
Olmstead v. United States, 442

Pace v. Alabama, 518, 522
Palko v. Connecticut, 456
Perry Educ. Ass'n v. Perry Local Educators' Ass'n, 231, 579
Pierce v. Society of Sisters, 437-439
Planned Parenthood of Southeastern Pa. v. Casey, 463, 473, 506, 510-511, 579
Plessy v. Ferguson, 364-370, 372-374, 377-385, 403-404, 497, 578
Poe v. Ullman, 442
Powell v. State, 497
Presser v. Illinois, 313

R.A.V. v. St. Paul, 278-285, 311
Railway Express Agency, Inc. v. New York, 521

Red Lion Broadcasting Co. v. FCC, 270
Reed v. Town of Gilbert, 186-187
Roe v. Wade, 17-18, 75, 97, 350, 451-483, 486, 488-489, 495, 504, 510-511, 517, 542, 545, 571, 578, 581
Romer v. Evans, 497-503, 506-507, 510, 515-516, 544
Rucho v. Common Cause, 78-88

Saenz v. Roe, 350
Santa Fe Independent School Dist. v. Doe, 307
Schenck v. United States, 189, 271
Skinner v. Oklahoma, 520
Slaughterhouse Cases, 348-351, 355, 406-407, 410
South Dakota v. Dole, 122-125
Spence v. Washington, 200
Stanley v. Georgia, 494

Texas v. Johnson, 200-207, 236
Tinker v. Des Moines Independent Community School District, 216-220, 222-225, 227
Trump v. Hawaii, 161

Union Pacific R. Co. v. Botsford, 455
United States v. Bass, 102
United States v. J.H.H., 284
United States v. Jones, 9
United States v. Lopez, 98-113, 115-117, 119-121, 128
United States v. Miller, 314, 317, 319-321
United States v. Morrison, 113-121, 127
United States v. O'Brien, 196-199, 202, 236
United States v. Schwimmer, 263
United States v. Virginia, 422-431, 434
United States v. Windsor, 526

Vereinigung Bildender Künstler v. Austria, 248-258, 275, 311
Virginia v. Black, 285-292, 299, 311

Watts v. United States, 298-299
West Coast v. Parrish, 92
Whitney v. California, 190, 192
Whole Woman's Health, 470
Wickard v. Filburn, 93-101, 112, 115, 118, 120, 128

Young v. American Mini Theatres, Inc., 271
Youngstown Sheet & Tube v. Sawyer, 130-143, 145, 149-150, 153, 172-173, 176, 547, 575

Zablocki, 533
Zivotofsky v. Kerry, 77, 144-153, 176
Zorach v. Clauson, 307

Index

Abortion, 17-18, 54, 75, 97, 432, 451, 452-489, 495, 517, 524, 542. *See also* Reproductive Freedom
Advisory Opinions, *see* Article III
Affirmative Action, 357, 385-386, 547
Affordable Care Act, 127, 403
Agricultural Adjustment Act, 94, 118
Ambassadors, 59, 77, 129, 144, 147-151, 554
Anti-Federalist, 88
Appellate Jurisdiction, 59
Armed Forces, *see* Military
Article III
    Advisory Opinions, 149, 583, 584, 585. *See also* Case or Controversy Requirement
    Federal Judicial Power, Defined in Article III, 53-56
    Judiciary Act of 1789, 53
    Judiciary Act of 2021, 95
Articles of Confederation, 2, 33, 36, 584
Authorization for the Use of Military Force (AUMF), 187

Bank of the United States, 90
Bar Admission, 406-411
Bill of Rights, 4, 64, 127, 179-182, 211, 316, 318, 342, 345, 352, 347, 438-441, 444, 446, 448-450, 493-494, 557-558, 587
Birth Control, 23, 54, 435, 436, 437, 443, 447-450, 483, 495, 517

Campaign Finance or Campaign Contributions, 547
Carolene Products, 370
Case or Controversy Requirement, 53, 65, 182, 583, 584, 589. *See also* Article III, Advisory Opinions
Certiorari, Writ of, 10-15, 592
Commander-in-Chief, 1, 129, 131-137, 554

Commerce Clause or Commerce Power
    Generally, 54-121
    Interaction with Tenth Amendment, 127-128
Commercial Speech, 181, 259, 263-265
Critical Race Theory, 25-26, 329, 377
Cross Burning, 165, 278-291, 292

Defamation, 208-215, 240-241, 248, 276, 279, 354, 588, 590, 592
Discrimination
    Against Women, 125, 405-436, 467, 480
    Employment Discrimination, 276, 278, 281, 405
    On the Basis of Age, 301
    On the Basis of Content of Speech, 230-235, 262, 263, 279-282
    On the Basis of Race, 82, 158-159, 180, 264, 355, 357-403, 517-523
    On the Basis of Religion, 301, 308
    On the Basis of Sexual Orientation, 491-516, 544
Dormant Commerce Clause, 111
Draft, Military, 195, 196-199, 267
Due Process
    Liberty Rights, 437, 504-508, 513, 523, 530, 533, 539
    Procedural Due Process
        Generally, 158-159, 162-163
        Matthews v. Eldridge test, 168-170
    Scope, 24, 348-349, 412, 435-436, 439, 445, 447, 531, 534, 586
    Substantive Due Process, 381-382, 436, 438, 452, 458-459, 464-465, 472-473, 477, 483, 488, 492-494, 511, 514, 523, 530, 542

Equal Protection, 24, 80, 86, 158, 181, 349, 372-374, 386, 410, 422-432, 492, 496-506, 510, 513-515, 518-525, 533, 534, 541-542, 560, 587
Establishment Clause, *see* Separation of Church and State

Federalism, 31-32, 33-50, 105, 113, 115, 118-119, 347, 388, 391, 340, 344,
Federalist Papers, 23
Feminist Jurisprudence, 26
First Amendment, 181-312, 558. *See also* Freedom of Speech
Foreign Affairs
    Generally, 52, 77, 138, 143-152, 175
    Jerusalem, 143-152
    Post–9-11, 175
Freedom of Speech
    Content-Based and Content-Neutral Regulation, 185-188
    Cross Burning, 284-291, 299, 311
    Hate Speech, 277-301
    Humor Regulation, 239-277
    Incitement of Violence, 188-194
    Public Forums, Designated Public Forums, Limited Public Forums, 230-236
    School Regulation, 216-230
    Symbolic Speech, 194-207
    Viewpoint Discrimination, 186, 217, 222-223, 234-235, 259, 262-263, 266, 280, 292, 585
Freedom of the Press, 208-215. *See also* First Amendment; Freedom of Speech; Press Rights

Gerrymandering, 77-88, 396
Gender Discrimination, *see* Discrimination, Against Women; Women
Gun-Free School Zones Act, 98

Habeas Corpus, 166
Hate Speech, 277-301. *See also*
    Freedom of Speech
Homosexual Rights
    Sexual Activity, 491-516
    Marriage, 526-543
Humor Regulation, 239-277

Implied Powers, 89-90, 127-128, 129
Intermediate Scrutiny, 187, 335, 337,
    422-428, 541
Interpretation Theories, 22-29, 329,
    330, 337
Israel, *see* Foreign Affairs

Judicial Review, 50, 54-64
Justiciability, 64-88, 588, 589, 590,
    591

Legitimate State Interests, 455, 456,
    472, 479, 500, 501, 508
LGBTQIA+ Individuals, *see*
    Homosexual Rights
Life Tenure, 7, 54, 511
Living Constitution, 25, 27, 330, 581
Lochner, significance of, 381

Marriage
    Interracial Marriage, 483, 518-526,
    530-533, 543-545
    Same Sex Marriage, 496, 503, 518,
    526-545
Military, 40, 114, 137-139, 154-177,
    196-197, 313, 316-317,
    320-322, 341, 422-429
Mootness, 66, 74-75, 88, 589

Necessary and Proper Clause, 22-23,
    39-40, 43, 49-50, 52, 89-90,
    127-129, 198, 398, 509, 552
Ninth Amendment, 179, 439-450,
    456, 492, 512, 559

Obscenity, 181, 247-248, 268,
    271-275, 279-281, 294
Originalism, 23-27, 375, 589
Original Jurisdiction, 59

Political Question Doctrine, 66,
    76-77, 86, 88, 152, 589
Popular Constitution Theory, 25

Preemption of State Law by Federal
    Law, *see* Supremacy Clause
Press Rights, 208-215
Prior Restraint, 208
Privileges and Immunities Clause of
    Article IV, 555
Privileges and Immunities Clause
    of the Fourteenth
    Amendment, 349-351, 359,
    369, 406-414, 560
Procedural Due Process. *See also*
    Due Process
    Generally, 158-159, 162-163
    Matthews v. Eldridge test, 168-170
Public Forums, Limited Public
    Forums, Designated Public
    Forums, 230-237
Public Officials
    Defined for the Purpose of the
    New York Times Co. v.
    Sullivan Standard, 214-215,
    240
Punitive Damages, 115, 241, 590

Racial Discrimination, 357-404
    Affirmative Action, 385-387
    Segregation and Integration, 26,
    156, 208, 364-385
    Slavery, 357-364
    Voting, 4, 86, 387-404
Rational Basis Test, 109-111, 118,
    121, 333, 397, 421, 460, 472,
    479, 494-495, 502-503, 510,
    512, 542, 591
Religious Freedom, 68-72, 108, 182,
    301-311
Reproductive Rights, 437-489
    Abortion, 452-487
    Birth Control, 438-452
Ripeness, 65, 74, 590

Same-Sex Marriage, 496, 503, 518,
    526-545
Second Amendment, 313-345,
    350, 558
Separation of Church and State, 181,
    182, 301, 302-310, 448, 449,
    548
Separation of Powers, 2-3, 7, 11, 23,
    28, 31, 40, 50, 135, 141, 167,
    170, 590

Slavery, 2-3, 264, 329-330, 336-340,
    347-353, 357-366, 379-382,
    403, 412, 414, 416, 520,
    560, 561
Spending Power, 54, 121-128
Standing Doctrine, 65, 67-69, 591
State Action Doctrine, 179-180,
    352-356, 591
Steel Mills, Seizure of, 130-140
Strict Scrutiny, 154, 162, 186-187,
    189, 230, 231, 233, 324, 355,
    422, 463, 497, 502, 510, 517,
    523, 591
Substantive Due Process, 381-382,
    436, 438, 452, 458-459,
    464-465, 472-473, 477, 483,
    488, 492-494, 511, 514, 523,
    530, 542
Supremacy Clause, 33, 34, 36, 39, 50,
    97, 369, 391, 413, 591
Symbolic Speech, 181, 194-206, 236

Taxing and Spending Power, *see*
    Spending Power
Tenth Amendment, 36, 43, 98,
    122-124, 127, 143, 391, 448,
    518, 520, 559
Thirteenth Amendment, 352, 366-367,
    387, 405
Travel, Right to, 350, 479
Treaty-Making Power, 41, 48-49, 144,
    146-147, 152, 554

Undue Burden Test, 463, 469-470,
    479. *See also* Abortion

Viewpoint Discrimination, 186, 217,
    222-223, 234-235, 259,
    262-263, 266, 280, 292,
    585. *See also* Freedom
    of Speech

Women
    Equal Protection Test or
    Intermediate Scrutiny,
    422-423, 425
    Equal Rights Amendment,
    431-433
    Right to Practice Law, 405-416
    Virginia Military Academy,
    423-429